Studies in the
Harley Manuscript

A scribe at work, MS Harley 273, fol. 70r (detail), a miniature pen drawing illustrating Richard de Fournival's *Bestiare d'amour*. Harley 273 is one of three surviving books that contain the hand of the Harley scribe. By permission of The British Library.

Studies in the
Harley Manuscript

The Scribes, Contents, and Social Contexts

of British Library MS Harley 2253

Edited by
Susanna Fein

Published for TEAMS
(The Consortium for the Teaching of the Middle Ages)
in Association with the University of Rochester

by

Medieval Institute Publications

WESTERN MICHIGAN UNIVERSITY

Kalamazoo, Michigan — 2000

Library of Congress Cataloging-in-Publication Data

Studies in the Harley manuscript : the scribes, contents, and social contexts of British
Library MS Harley 2253 / edited by Susanna Fein.

    p. cm.

  "Published for TEAMS (The Consortium for the Teaching of the Middle Ages) in
association with the University of Rochester."

  Includes bibliographical references (p.) and indexes.

  ISBN 1-58044-060-6 (casebound : alk. paper) -- ISBN 1-58044-061-4 (paperbound :
alk. paper)

  1. English literature--Middle English, 1100-1500--Criticism, Textual. 2. Latin
literature, Medieval and modern--England--Criticism, Textual. 3. Literature and
society--England--History--To 1500. 4. British Library. Manuscript. Harley 2253. 5.
Anglo-Norman literature--Criticism, Textual. 6. Manuscripts,
Medieval--England--London. 7. Scriptoria--England. 8. Transmission of texts. I. Fein,
Susanna Greer. II. Consortium for the Teaching of the Middle Ages.

PR275.T45 S78 2000
809'.02--dc21

99-462126

ISBN 1-58044-060-6 (casebound)
   1-58044-061-4 (paperbound)

Printed in the United States of America

Cover design by Linda K. Judy

Dedicated to
the memory of
Rossell Hope Robbins

Contents

Acknowledgments

The existence of this book owes much to the knowledge and labor of three important scholars whose work flourished only a few decades ago: N. R. Ker, G. L. Brook, and R. H. Robbins. By distinguishing Harley 2253 as a manuscript of singular import to English medievalists, they cleared the way for those who follow. To them I owe my first debt of gratitude. The dedication of this volume to Rossell Hope Robbins commemorates, in particular, his desire and effort, some twenty years ago, to produce a volume of scholarly essays on Harley, one much like this one. Although that book was never completed, Robbins's enthusiasm lives on among the scholars who wrote this volume.

I am also very grateful to the fourteen contributors — Marilyn Corrie, Mary Dove, David L. Jeffrey, Michael P. Kuczynski, Frances McSparran, Richard Newhauser, Barbara Nolan, Helen Phillips, Karl Reichl, Carter Revard, John Scattergood, Elizabeth Solopova, Theo Stemmler, John J. Thompson — who generously donated their deep learning and time to the accomplishment of this book. Their zeal for the project gave it energy and momentum, and their readiness fueled my own conviction that a concerted study of Harley was long overdue. I admire their willingness to undertake new research in a spirit of collaborative discovery and to offer their results in a form that welcomes both experienced scholars and novice students. It is my hope and theirs that these essays will initiate a more comprehensive phase of research on the remarkable features of the book now known as MS Harley 2253.

For kindling, sharing, or supporting my interest in Harley MS, I thank many other colleagues and friends: Larry Benson, Carolyn Collette, Ian Doyle, Tony Edwards, Alan Gaylord, Al Hartung, Tony Hunt, Jeanne Krochalis, Rebecca Leeper, Michael Nagy, Jason O'Rourke, Malcolm Parkes, Derek Pearsall, David Raybin, Peter Robinson, Tom Shippey, Judith Tschann, Thorlac Turville-Petre, and Jan Ziolkowski. One who is also a contributor to this volume is exceptionally well acquainted with the Harley scribe: thus I am uniquely indebted to Carter Revard for sharing numerous insights, and especially for the elation experienced one day last fall when, upon opening a packet of photos from Carter, I instantly recognized the scribe's familiar hand in forty-one Ludlow-area charters and deeds.

I also acknowledge the ever-dynamic and creative guidance offered by editor Russell Peck. Russell's first criteria are that the work be accurate, important, and offered in ways that advance knowledge. The sphere of modern medieval English studies is indeed much

Acknowledgments

the richer for Russell's impressive Middle English Texts Series. This volume is linked to the METS edition of the Harley codex. Its lineal descent from the work of R. H. Robbins makes its emergence from the University of Rochester and the TEAMS staff centered at the Robbins Library seem particularly right.

For the labor of setting up the text, I thank Mara Amster of the University of Rochester, whose fine eye caught errors, tightened stylistic matters, and delicately laid out complicated charts and tables. I am grateful to others affiliated with The Consortium for the Teaching of the Middle Ages (TEAMS) who saw and reviewed the book through its stages of production: in Rochester — Alan Lupack — and in Kalamazoo — Tom Seiler and Richard S. Burfoot. Elizabeth Fein provided valuable assistance in indexing. The authors and I are indebted to The British Library, the Bodleian Library, the South Shropshire District Council, the Ludlow Town Council, and Lord Plymouth for permission to reproduce documents in their care. I also wish to acknowledge financial support from the National Endowment for the Humanities, which awarded me a summer stipend used to transcribe Harley 2253; and from the Kent State University Research Council, whose funds enabled me to examine the manuscript in London and to have time to prepare the greater part of this book.

Abbreviations

AN	Anglo-Norman
ANLL	*Anglo-Norman Language and Literature* (Vising)
ANTS	Anglo-Norman Text Society
BL	British Library, London
BN	Bibliothèque Nationale, Paris
CCR	*Calendar of Close Rolls*
CFR	*Calendar of Fine Rolls*
CIMC	*Calendar of Inquisitions Miscellaneous (Chancery)*
CIPM	*Calendar of Inquisitions Post Mortem*
CPR	*Calendar of Patent Rolls*
CUL	Cambridge University Library
EETS	Early English Text Society
EMEVP	*Early Middle English Verse and Prose* (Bennett and Smithers)
FFW	*Fouke le Fitz Waryn*
IMEV	*Index of Middle English Verse* (Brown and Robbins)
LALME	*A Linguistic Atlas of Late Mediaeval English* (McIntosh et al.)
ME	Middle English
MED	*Middle English Dictionary*
MS(S)	manuscript(s)
NRCF	*Nouveau Recueil complet des fabliaux* (Noomen and van den Boogaard)
OBMLV	*The Oxford Book of Medieval Latin Verse* (Raby)
OE	Old English
PL	*Patrologia Latina* (Migne)
PRO	Public Record Office, London
SRR	Shropshire Records and Research Centre, Shrewsbury
TCC	Trinity College, Cambridge

Notes on Contributors

Marilyn Corrie is Lecturer of English at University College London

Mary Dove is Lecturer of English and American Studies at the University of Sussex

Susanna Fein is Professor of English at Kent State University

David L. Jeffrey is Distinguished Professor of Literature and Humanities at Baylor University

Michael P. Kuczynski is Professor of English and Chair of the Medieval Studies Program at Tulane University

Frances McSparran is Professor of English and Chief Editor of the *Middle English Compendium* at the University of Michigan

Richard Newhauser is Professor of English and Chair of the Medieval and Renaissance Studies Committee at Trinity University, San Antonio

Barbara Nolan is Vice Provost and Robert C. Taylor Professor of English at the University of Virginia

Helen Phillips is Professor of English Studies at the University of Glamorgan

Karl Reichl is Professor of English at the University of Bonn

Carter Revard is Emeritus Professor of English at Washington University, St. Louis

John Scattergood is Dean of the Faculty of Arts (Letters) and Professor of Medieval and Renaissance English at Trinity College Dublin

Elizabeth Solopova is Postdoctoral Scholar in English at the University of Kentucky

Theo Stemmler is Professor of English at the University of Mannheim

John J. Thompson is Senior Lecturer in English at Queen's University Belfast

Note on the Presentation of Text from MS Harley 2253

Orthography. Quotations of works from MS Harley 2253 are taken directly from the manuscript facsimile, regardless of printed editions that may be cited. Difficult readings have been verified by reference to the manuscript itself at the British Library, London. Archaic letter forms (yogh, thorn, *i* for *j*, *u/v*) are not modernized, but yogh written for *z* in French texts and to pluralize nouns in English texts has been rendered *z*. Brackets are used whenever a manuscript reading has been emended. First lines of verse are capitalized. Elsewhere, capitalization is added or removed according to the conventions for English, French, or Latin. Word breaks are modern.

Abbreviations. Abbreviated words have been expanded silently: & to *ant*; *ihu* to *Iesu*; final *k* (often with a looped flourish) to *k* not *ke*. (On these expansions, compare the comments of Brook, ed., *Harley Lyrics*, p. 29, and Ker, *Facsimile*, p. xix.)

Punctuation. The authors have added modern punctuation, either their own or that of cited editors.

Foliation. Material from the manuscript is cited by folio number, recto or verso ("r" or "v"), and, where appropriate, column ("a," "b," or "c").

Line numbers. Verse texts are cited by line number. Stanza layouts follow the cited edition unless otherwise noted.

Titles and item numbers. The titles of works from MS Harley 2253 agree, in general, with those given by Ker. Item numbers derive from Ker's list of contents (*Facsimile*, pp. ix–xvi).

List of Plates, Tables, Figures, and Appendices

List of Plates, Tables, Figures, and Appendices

Introduction

British Library MS Harley 2253:
The Lyrics, the Facsimile, and the Book

Susanna Fein

Sir Robert Harley's interest in purchasing the books of the late Dr. John Batteley first appears in the diary of his librarian Humfrey Wanley on July 18, 1718. A fellow of Trinity College, Cambridge, Dr. Batteley (1647–1708) had held the offices of archdeacon of Canterbury and prebendary for twenty years. He had written a treatise upon the ancient Isle of Thanet (published 1711), and he left behind a substantial library of old books.[1] Negotiations for its sale were handled by Dr. Batteley's nephew John Batteley, and they proceeded steadily for years, with the bookseller Jonah Bowyer (at the Rose in Ludgate Street) serving as intermediary. On May 21, 1720, Wanley had opportunity to inspect the library himself, finding the books "in Confusion & most of the MSS. in very ill Condition." He records the offer that Bowyer made: buy the lot, obtain "the Old MSS. & Charters at 20 Guineas," and have the pick of the printed books "before they come to Auction."[2]

The sale and transfer of manuscripts took place on November 5, 1723. Seventy-one volumes in the Harley collection bear this date, and they apparently represent the full extent of that transaction (which did not exhaust the holdings of the Batteley library).[3] Within this parcel was the trilingual miscellany now known by its modern shelfmark Harley 2253. The business notes Wanley kept in his diary betray no hint of an unusual interest in this one unusual manuscript. Nonetheless, Harley 2253 (catalogued as "99.A.7.") was the first Batteley item Wanley included in his *Catalogus Brevior*, an on-going project to itemize the full contents of Harley's large library. His handwritten entry on 99.A.7. was made after September 30, 1724, but well before July 6, 1726 (the day of his death), in the seventh volume of the catalogue, which was later finished by David

---

[1] Humfrey Wanley, *The Diary of Humfrey Wanley 1715–1726*, ed. C. E. Wright and Ruth C. Wright, 2 vols. (London, 1966), 1.15, and for the career of Archdeacon Batteley, 2.440.

[2] Wanley, *Diary*, 1.48, and for John Batteley and Jonah Bowyer, 2.440, 441.

[3] Wanley, *Diary*, 2.263, 476. The seventy-one items are listed 2.263n1.

Casley and others. Sir Robert Harley had died previously, on May 21, 1724. Of the Batteley purchase Wanley described only eight volumes before his own death.[4] Surely it is significant that he selected Harley 2253 first among these, and not until he had described some 120 more items did he select another Batteley book.

The sixteen-page description made by Wanley was published virtually unchanged in the posthumous completion of his catalogue, *A Catalogue of the Harleian Collection of Manuscripts in Two Volumes* (1759), which was later reprinted by the British Museum in four volumes (1808–12).[5] Wanley's detailed itemization of the contents does not betray his feelings about his discovery other than those suggested when an erudite bibliographer pauses to give exceptionally close attention and unusually lengthy excerpts of material he has never encountered before. There can be no doubt that Wanley knew the rarity of the manuscript's contents, especially of its English contents, but there is no evidence that he shared this knowledge outside the privacy of his own study. Harley 2253 was not discovered by the world until after Wanley's description was published in 1759.

The first popularizer of things antiquarian to find Harley of peculiar interest was Bishop Thomas Percy, who printed the political poem *A Song of Lewes* (Wanley's no. 23) as the lead piece in his second volume of *Reliques of Ancient English Poetry* (1765). He lambasted the poem as an "antique libel" that demonstrates "the liberty, assumed by the good people of this realm, of abusing their kings and princes at pleasure," and, for good measure, the piece was flourished with a propagandistic engraving designed to illustrate the ill effects of such libel.[6] Bishop Percy followed *A Song of Lewes* with one more item

---

[4] The other Batteley books catalogued by Wanley himself are MSS Harley 2374, 2375, 2381, 2386, 2388, 2400, and 2407. Wanley's seven-volume *Catalogus Brevior* is now British Library MSS Addit. 45701–45707; each volume is dated. For the description of Harley 2253, see Addit. 45707, pp. 81–96.

[5] H. Wanley, D. Casley, et al., *A Catalogue of the Harleian Manuscripts in the British Museum* (1759; rev. and repr. 4 vols. London, 1808–12). For Harley 2253, see 2.585–91. The published catalogue faithfully transcribes Wanley's text but loses Wanley's careful reproduction of the layouts of stanzas and of verse texts written as prose. Wanley also made some errors in numbering that were corrected in the printed editions; two of his errors are still evident in the duplication of numbers 113 and 114 for what should be 115 and 116.

[6] Thomas Percy, ed., *Reliques of Ancient English Poetry*, 3 vols. (London, 1765), 2.1–3. The two Harley poems appear at 2.3–10. Percy describes the engraving as follows:

> On the one side a Satyr, (emblem of Petulance and Ridicule) is trampling on the ensigns of Royalty; on the other Faction under the masque of Liberty is exciting Ignorance and Popular Rage to deface the Royal Image; which stands on a pedestal inscribed MAGNA CARTA, to denote that the rights of the king, as well as those of the people, are founded on the laws; and that to attack one, is in effect to demolish the other.

from Harley, *The Death of Edward I* (Wanley's no. 47). Percy's *Reliques* was part of a swelling nationalistic and aesthetic movement to recover and explore the origins of English verse. Another leader in this effort, poet laureate Thomas Warton, came to the manuscript by way of Wanley and Percy, calling it, in 1774, "this curious Harleian volume, to which we are so largely indebted."[7] Warton's capacity to understand the manuscript was, however, limited; rarely do his excerpts from it exceed those found in Wanley's fourteen long, dense columns, and in a few instances he confuses items gotten right by Wanley.[8]

Nonetheless, the earliest historians of writings in English were much intrigued by what they excavated from the Harley MS by means of their own digging. J. Strutt printed *When þe Nyhtegale Singes* in 1776, praising the poet as "very modest" and "entirely within the bounds of reason."[9] Meanwhile, Joseph Ritson had begun his career of launching scathing attacks upon what he saw to be acts of irresponsible scholarship on the part of Warton and (especially) Percy, which he set about to rectify in his landmark *Ancient Songs* (printed 1786–87, but probably not issued until 1792). Here he gave to the world the first select sampling of the now-famous lyrics in complete form — *Alysoun*; *Spring*; *Blow, Northerne Wynd*; *A Winter Song*; *When þe Nyhtegale Singes*; and *The Man in the Moon* — and also two new political songs, *The Execution of Sir Simon Fraser* and *The Flemish Insurrection*.[10]

---

[7] Thomas Warton, *The History of English Poetry from the Eleventh to the Seventeenth Century*, 4 vols. (London, 1774–81), 1.33. In the more generally accessible second edition (1824; repr. New York, 1968), the discussion of items from Harley 2253 occurs on pp. 24–30, the quote on p. 28.

[8] Warton confuses, for example, pairs of poems in identical stanzas: *Spring* and *Advice to Women* (p. 26); *De Clerico et Puella* and *When þe Nyhtegale Singes* (p. 27).

[9] J. Strutt, *Horda Angel-Cynnan* (London, 1776), 3.151.

[10] Joseph Ritson, ed., *Ancient Songs, from the Reign of King Henry the Second to the Revolution* (London, 1790), pp. 5–38. On the date of publication, see Bertrand H. Bronson, *Joseph Ritson, Scholar-at-Arms*, 2 vols. (Berkeley, 1938), 1.176. In the second edition Ritson published four more Harley items: *Advice to Women*, *A Song of Lewes*, and the French *Lament for Simon de Montfort* (with a translation by George Ellis) and *Trailbaston*; see *Ancient Songs and Ballads, from the Reign of King Henry the Second to the Revolution,* 2 vols. (London, 1829), 1.12–39, 51–70. On Ritson's contention with Percy and Warton, see Ritson, *Ancient Songs* (1790), p. 37 (an attack omitted from later editions); Joseph Ritson (but published anonymously), *Observations on the Three First Volumes of the History of English Poetry, in a Familiar Letter to the Author* (London, 1782), pp. 4–6; and Harris Nicolas, "A Memoir of the Author," in *The Letters of Joseph Ritson*, ed. Joseph Frank (London, 1833), pp. xvii–xlv.

The next notice of Harley 2253 appears to have been that of George Ellis, ed., *Specimens of the Early English Poets*, 2nd ed., 3 vols. (London, 1801), pp. 84–89. Ellis did not include Harley items

Thus did the modern world begin to recover the literary remnants to be found in MS Harley 2253. The chance preservation of this one volume allows us a strange and privileged glimpse into what is indeed (to us) a "curious" world of a once trilingual England, one quite rich for the making of vernacular poetry and where such verse did in fact flourish — somewhat to our astonishment — well before the Ricardian era. Ever since the days of Percy and Ritson, the assorted lyrics in Harley 2253 have dominated our reasons for looking at this old book. The rare secular songs vie for attention beside the equally rare array of political verses, with their blunt grumblings about national events and local injustices.[11] The "curious Harleian volume" is therefore of supreme value to literary scholars of medieval England. Because it gathers poems "whose loss would wipe out our knowledge of whole areas of English poetry . . . in a critical time of change," it may well be "the most important single MS of Middle English poetry."[12] Harley preserves more poems about love and politics than any other manuscript from the era, and for almost all of these items, preservation depends entirely on the book's own fortuitous survival.

The better comprehension of this extraordinary codex is the basic investigative goal of each writer whose essay is printed in this volume. Ever since the inquisitive early notices highlighted above, studies touching upon the Harley MS have typically dwelt on favorite English songs or political diatribes and given little attention to other items or to the distinctive qualities of the full book. Two influential publications may be seen as emblematic of this problem, even as they are the landmarks of present-day Harley studies; indeed, it is by their presence that the field and its boundaries are presently set. One is G.

---

in his first edition of 1790, but since he does not correct for Ritson's work until the 1802 edition, the 1801 text probably reflects work contemporaneous with Ritson's. Ellis prints only two Harley lyrics, *Alysoun* and *A Winter Song*. Other early notices appear in Edwin Guest, *A History of English Rhythms* (London, 1838), pp. 578–83, 590–91, 600–03, 628–29, and Thomas Wright and James Orchard Halliwell, eds., *Reliquiae Antiquae*, 2 vols. (London, 1841, 1843), 1.102, 2.216.

The earliest publication of substantial portions of Harley 2253 (most of the English and French lyrics) was Thomas Wright's *Specimens of Lyric Poetry, Composed in the Reign of Edward the First*, Percy Society 4 (1842; repr. New York, 1965). The fullest early printing of the political poems was Thomas Wright's *Political Songs of England, from the Reign of John to That of Edward II* (London, 1839), recently reprinted with an introduction by Peter Coss (Cambridge, 1996).

[11] One early legal historian, influenced by Percy's *Reliques*, went so far as to suggest that *A Song of Lewes* led directly to the passing of a statute outlawing the slander of royalty. See Daines Barrington, *Observations on the More Ancient Statutes from Magna Charta to the Twenty-First of James I. Cap. XXVII* (London, 1767), pp. 94–95, cited and rejected by John Kirby Hedges, *The History of Wallingford*, 2 vols. (London, 1881), 1.329.

[12] Derek Pearsall, *Old English and Middle English Poetry* (London, 1977), p. 120. Pearsall ranks Harley beside Cotton Nero A.x. as our most precious preserver of fragile vernacular verse.

Introduction

L. Brook's standard edition of *The Harley Lyrics*, first published in 1948 and then revised and reissued in 1956, 1964, and 1968 (the fourth edition).[13] Brook's anthology contains thirty-two poems, some of which, like *Alysoun* ("Bytuene Mersh ant Aueril") and *Spring* ("Lenten ys come wiþ loue to toune"), number among the best lyrics written in the language. Brook's tidy edition has become something of a classic among anthologies of medieval verse. The second definitive work is the facsimile published by the Early English Text Society in 1965 with an important introduction by N. R. Ker.[14] This volume was one of the earliest in a series of facsimiled early books produced by the Society, whose prompt selection of Harley 2253 testified to the volume's preeminence among medieval codices containing English texts.

Taken together, Brook's edition and Ker's facsimile give scholars and students far more evidence than did the eighteenth-century writers of the early notices, but it is still not nearly enough. What we have are just tantalizing glimmers and shadows. Each limited in its purpose, the edition and the facsimile can be seen to illustrate how Harley scholarship continues to be compartmentalized. Consider first the anthology: the English lyrics codified there constitute a mere fraction of the book's poetry. In practical terms, Brook's *Harley Lyrics* is a modern collection.[15] In manuscript the English poems are *not* gathered in one place: they appear intermittently across seventy pages, and mixed in with them are forty-odd items. By making obscure the original arrangement of texts, the Brook edition omits what that arrangement might tell us about the Harley compiler's aims and achievement.

The facsimile, too, is limited in its present usefulness. Its very existence tends to make accessibility more perceived than real. The handiness of a reproduced Harley MS does not in fact deliver the items to a modern readership if pieces stay unprinted or unexplored, which is the case with many of Harley's contents. For texts that do have critical editions, such as *King Horn*, the Harley redaction may not draw much notice

---

[13] G. L. Brook, ed., *The Harley Lyrics: The Middle English Lyrics of MS. Harley 2253*, 4th ed. (Manchester, 1968).

[14] N. R. Ker, intro., *Facsimile of British Museum MS. Harley 2253*, EETS o.s. 255 (London, 1965). For Ker's corrigenda to the facsimile, see Appendix (pp. 18–19).

[15] Brook's title gives the impression that the group forms a manuscript collection, as with the Vernon Lyrics, when what we have is a modern selection of verse pulled from various locations. For the Vernon Lyrics, see Carleton Brown, ed., *Religious Lyrics of the XIVth Century*, 2nd ed. rev. G. V. Smithers (Oxford, 1957), pp. 125–208, and A. I. Doyle, intro., *The Vernon Manuscript: A Facsimile of Bodleian Library, Oxford, MS. Eng. Poet. a.1.* (Cambridge, 1987), fols. 407r–412r. To be fair to Brook, one may note that Brown's and Robbins' anthologies (see nn. 16–17) do virtually the same thing, though their broader offerings more clearly display the ways editors select and compile.

because there is an acknowledged better text, as there is for *Horn* in Cambridge University Library MS Gg. iv.27 (2). Consequently, the existence of the facsimile seems to contribute little to discussions of such works. At the same time, there is also the problem of what the facsimile excludes from view: it reproduces only the folios written by the man now called the "Harley scribe" (fols. 49–140), but it omits fols. 1–48, more than one-third of the book. In this way, it — like the Brook edition — distorts the codex, and with it, the recoverable intent of the Harley scribe as he shaped a new volume out of an older beginning.

If the nature of the whole book is not well known, the cause may reside in how our modern academic disciplines are themselves divided by genre and language. These divisions, in turn, influence the making of editions (and facsimiles), and editorial selections and arrangements affect to a large degree how subsequent readers perceive and use books from the past, as these judgments determine which texts readers are most likely to know and value. In the case of the English Harley lyrics, the standard editorial method has long been to extract and to categorize. Such presentation has varied little since 1878, when Karl Böddeker printed most of the English verse texts. Following Böddeker's German edition, the Harley poems became more readily available to English readers through several authoritative, well-disseminated anthologies published from 1924 to 1959. The first were Carleton Brown's *Religious Lyrics of the XIVth Century* (1924) and *English Lyrics of the XIIIth Century* (1932), in which twenty-six lyrics, including two political ones, appeared.[16] In 1948 Brook's edition established a corpus of thirty-two secular and religious lyrics, with the political songs excluded. Then R. H. Robbins, in his *Historical Poems of the XIVth and XVth Centuries* (1959), printed seven more political pieces as a group.[17] By virtue of these anthologies, the canon has attained its present shape: thirty-two "Harley Lyrics" (Brook's edition) and nine more political poems or social satires (two printed by Brown, seven more by Robbins).[18]

---

[16] Carleton Brown, ed., *Religious Lyrics of the XIVth Century* (Oxford, 1924), pp. 3–14, and *English Lyrics of the XIIIth Century* (Oxford, 1932), pp. 131–63. The political poems printed by Brown are *A Song of Lewes* (no. 23) and *On the Follies of Fashion* (no. 25a). See also Karl Böddeker, ed., *Altenglische Dichtungen des MS. Harl. 2253* (1878; repr. Amsterdam, 1969).

[17] Rossell Hope Robbins, ed., *Historical Poems of the XIVth and XVth Centuries* (New York, 1959), pp. 7–29.

[18] See Table on pp. 16–17. By this brief overview of modern reception, I do not mean to suggest that the poems were not in print before 1924. The standard lyrics were all printed by Thomas Wright in 1839 and 1842 (see n. 10). I have prepared a detailed bibliography of the Harley Lyrics (Brook's selection), which will appear in *A Manual of the Writings in Middle English 1050–1500*, ed. Albert E. Hartung, Vol. 11.

Introduction

Böddeker's edition began the practice of filing the lyrics under category-names: "politische," "weltliche," or "geistliche" (Böddeker); "thirteenth century" or "fourteenth-century religious" (Brown); "historical" (Robbins); or simply "Harley," which meant either secular or religious but not political (Brook).[19] An ingrained habit of modern reception by these nineteenth- and twentieth-century markers and distinctions has tended to make obscure what might be recovered about the contemporary reception of the verses by means of the book preserving them. Only a brief look at the Harley MS itself is needed to perceive that the scribe did not observe our categories. A political song may turn up in the midst of love lyrics. Religious poems do not cluster in one place, as the interspersing of them with secular songs in Brook's edition illustrates.[20] Prose texts reside next to verse texts; verse texts are not exclusively "lyric"; and, most importantly for our renewed understanding of the book, many texts in French or Latin exist beside English texts and vie for their own kind of authority. The editors' categories have thus affected how we see the manuscript — or how we have failed to see it. What is wanted at this point in the study of the lyrics is not more anthologized groupings but rather a letting-go of the categorical terms by which we have laid canonical claim to them. With the Harley poems so widely praised, it seems odd indeed that few readers understand the nature of the parchment artifact containing them.

Viewed overall, Harley is best characterized as a miscellany of texts in three languages.[21] Wanley's 240-year-old description captures well the even-handedness of its distinctive variety:

---

[19] Brook states that the term "Harley Lyrics" was already current before his edition came into existence (p. 1), and in his adoption of most of the titles found in the two Brown anthologies it appears that he regarded the collection as fairly established. Nevertheless, he chose to augment the canon by adding eight more works: *The Fair Maid of Ribblesdale* (no. 34), *The Meeting in the Wood* (no. 35), *A Wayle Whyt ase Whalles Bon* (no. 36), *A Spring Song on the Passion* (no. 53), *Dum ludis floribus* (no. 55), *Stond Wel, Moder, vnder Rode* (no. 60), *I Syke When Y Singe* (no. 62), and *Blessed Be Þou, Leuedy* (no. 66).

[20] Brook prints the lyrics in their manuscript order. For Brook's tenuous criteria for selecting "lyrics," see his preface, p. 2.

[21] The term "miscellany" is here used in the broadest sense (a collection of texts miscellaneous in genre, style, and languages, and not selected for a single discernible purpose). Its use is not meant to deny the sequenced grouping of items that is often apparent in the book. On the complexity — and rather unsatisfactory nature — of the term "miscellany," see the collection of essays edited by Stephen G. Nichols and Siegfried Wenzel, *The Whole Book: Cultural Perspectives on the Medieval Miscellany* (Ann Arbor, 1996). See too, in this volume, Theo Stemmler's and Marilyn Corrie's essays.

. . . written by several hands, upon several Subjects; partly in old French, partly in Latin, and partly in old English; partly in Verse & partly in Prose. . . .[22]

Anthologizing tendencies are evident in it. The contents in some places seem to be grouped by section, topic, genre, language, meter, or medium (verse or prose). Less well known than the surviving lyrics, for example, is Harley's preservation of the largest collection of fabliaux in Anglo-Norman, and although these texts are also not specifically grouped together, the scribe has clustered them in one area of the book. The person referred to in this collection of essays as the "Harley scribe" was a professional who worked in Ludlow and its environs from at least 1314 until at least 1346. He copied the bulk of the book, folios 49–140, around the year 1340. More than twenty years of assiduous research by Carter Revard has unearthed forty-one Latin deeds and charters also written by this scribe, and there are two other surviving manuscripts that contain his work, preserving clues as to his training, reading, and collecting habits.[23] This very interesting scribe is also usually credited with being the agent behind the way the texts are compiled; it is thought that he is responsible for the selection and probably the order of items drawn from various exemplars in Latin, Anglo-Norman, and various dialects of English. Much of what he copied into Harley (and the two prior manuscripts) may be presumed, then, to betray somewhat his own tastes, training, and temperament — most likely tailored, as well, to the needs and desires of a patron. If the range of contents may be taken to represent his (or a patron's) diverse interests, one may see how provocatively they resemble the assemblage of styles and topics found in Chaucer's work some fifty years later. In a single volume we find romances and dialogues; tracts on pilgrimage and dream theory; profane fabliaux; pious saints' legends; an aesthetic concern with poetry, with genre mixing, and with literary uses of the vernacular; and humor in handling the volatile subjects of women, gender, and marriage.

The Harley scribe as compiler appears to embed certain literate purposes in the ways that he selected and arranged texts, that is, in what texts he put next to each other and,

---

[22] Wanley et al., *Catalogue*, 2.585.

[23] The other MSS are London, BL MSS Royal 12.C.xii and Harley 273. For Revard's research, see his essay in this volume (pp. 21–109). Reports of his findings at earlier stages appear in the following essays: "The Lecher, the Legal Eagle, and the Papelard Priest: Middle English Confessional Satires in MS. Harley 2253 and Elsewhere," in *His Firm Estate: Essays for F. J. Eikenberry*, ed. D. E. Hayden (Tulsa, Okla., 1967), pp. 54–71; "Richard Hurd and MS. Harley 2253," *Notes and Queries*, n.s. 26 (1979): 199–202; "Three More Holographs in the Hand of the Scribe of MS. Harley 2253 in Shrewsbury," *Notes and Queries*, n.s. 28 (1981): 199–200; "The Scribe of MS Harley 2253," *Notes and Queries*, n.s. 29 (1982): 62–63; and "*Gilote et Johane*: An Interlude in B. L. MS. Harley 2253," *Studies in Philology* 79 (1982): 122–46.

sometimes, in how he laid texts out on the page. Working fluently in three languages, the scribe's output exemplifies early fourteenth-century understandings of what kind of matter was deemed appropriate to each linguistic medium: devotional topics in Latin; religious, political, and bawdy subjects in French; and, mixed in with these, an important collection of early English texts. On the 140 folios of MS Harley 2253 appear no fewer than 121 items.[24] The first forty-eight folios were written by an earlier scribe in a textura hand, and the religious texts copied by this English scribe are exclusively in French. The Harley scribe copied the items found on fols. 49–140, and, according to Ker, he was probably responsible for the linkage of his work to the preceding folios.

Among English works in Harley one finds two venerable works that popularize religious doctrine (*The Harrowing of Hell* and *Debate between Body and Soul*), a romance of rich native appeal (*King Horn*), as well as the apparently innovative lyrics that blend continental trope and English idiom. Beyond these there are several arresting odds and ends: *Marina*, a tale of a cross-dressed female saint; a verse translation of *Dulcis Iesu memoria*; *Maximian*, an old man's lyric lament; the moralizing *Sayings of St. Bernard*; the proverb-packed *Hending*; and *A Bok of Sweuenyng*, a verse treatise on the origin of dreams. Mixed liberally in are many Anglo-Norman texts, for example, saints' legends and passions in prose and verse; the *Gospel of Nicodemus*; many religious, secular, or political verses, including an ABC for women and poems taking a pro or con stance in the debate on women; a tract on pilgrimage sites; four or five irreverent fabliaux; and *Gilote et Johane*, an unusual work of much originality, a "debate cum interlude cum fabliau."[25] The Latin prose texts include prayers; a list of the biblical books; occasions for certain psalms; Anselm's prescribed questions to the dying; and the lives of Saints Ethelbert, Etfrid, and Wistan, the latter saint martyred at Wistanstow, which is ten miles northwest of Ludlow, the seat of the scribe's activity.

Convenient copies of all textual items appear, of course, in the facsimile, where they are accompanied by Ker's authoritative list of contents.[26] Ker has also supplied important summaries of codicological details and the clues that may help to localize Harley. But the potential research value of a facsimile is only as good as its accompanying resources. Few

---

[24] For this count, see Ker's listing of items, pp. ix–xvi, where, however, the numbering is somewhat confusing because it follows that of Wanley's catalogue (while listing item no. 42 as "Vacant") and adds six new items (nos. 24a, 24b, 25a, 75a, 108a, 109a). In addition, one probably ought to count as a separate item the tale of Thaïs, which is appended to no. 1 (the French verse *Vitas patrum*), bringing the actual number of items to 122.

[25] The term is Mary Dove's, quoted by Revard, "*Gilote et Johane*," p. 122n3

[26] The item numbers appearing throughout this volume derive from Ker's list in the *Facsimile*, pp. ix–xvi.

people of our time have the training or even desire to laboriously read texts in three medieval languages written in a fourteenth-century anglicana hand. Thus, while the facsimile is essential to Harley studies, until there is an edition of the contents and more follow-up descriptions and investigations, our knowledge of what the curious Harleian volume contains will remain piecemeal at best. A big obstacle continues to be the accessing of texts. The Harley texts of three Latin saints' lives, for example, have never been printed. A collaborative edition in the Middle English Texts Series will include texts of all the contents of Harley 2253, with translations given for non-English works.

Meanwhile, as we search for critical ground more than two centuries after Wanley's catalogue listing and half a century after Brook's slim, definitive edition, it is clearly of timely import that we usher in a new phase in Harley studies, one that is attuned to finer nuances of historical influence and to interdisciplinary methods. That there have not been, up to now, any studies of the Harley volume's general character and features to follow upon Ker's facsimile is indeed startling. Such a study was initiated in the late 1970s, under the editorship of R. H. Robbins, but it remained unfinished at the time of his death and was never published.[27] Instead, there exists only a handful of narrow studies, with one recent preliminary study showing what the potential of such investigations may be.[28]

The essays in this volume are offered in the hope, then, that they will lead to many more like them — and that they will reopen and begin to resolve, perhaps, several of the still unsettled points about this book, its contents, and its milieu. With the exception of one essay (a revised reprint of an article by Theo Stemmler), the work gathered here represents new research. The authors are unified by a desire to see the manuscript whole, that is, in ways not restricted to single forms or separate linguistic fields. The goal has been to identify what evidence at hand may reveal to us about the individuals and cultures that produced this codex, and what avenues are most promising for future study. As scholars grow more able to embrace the Harley MS in all its complexity, it will become better situated in its own particular time, place, and literate values, and we will begin to recognize and piece out the process of how one anonymous but fairly well-documented man of scribal skill, working in South West England for an unknown patron, patrons, or just himself, affixed his trilingual reading in religious and profane texts to that of an earlier scribe whose interests leaned toward pious tales, saints' legends, and biblical narratives.

The lead-off essay begins the discussion with crucial new evidence on the identity of the Harley scribe. The fruits of Carter Revard's long research in scores of public record

---

[27] Citation to it as "forthcoming" has occurred occasionally in the critical literature, as in Revard, "*Gilote et Johane*," p. 122n3, and in Stemmler's 1991 article reprinted in this volume.

[28] See Thorlac Turville-Petre, *England the Nation: Language, Literature, and National Identity, 1290–1340* (Oxford, 1996), pp. 192–217.

offices and libraries are displayed in photographic reproductions of forty-one newly recovered deeds and charters written by this man. Because these documents are precisely dated, they provide a chronological record of changes in the scribe's handwriting over time and therefore a means for exact dating of his three manuscripts and the texts therein. Revard's remarkable achievement provides an intimate look at the scribe's professional life, setting him among named associates in legal and business contexts that are far more intricate and particularized than were before understood.

Following Revard's study is Theo Stemmler's article, "Miscellany or Anthology?," a piece first published in 1991 in the German journal *Zeitschrift für Anglistik und Amerikanistik*. It is here reprinted with authorial revisions. Stemmler shows how critics have tended to apply the terms "miscellany" and "anthology" rather loosely, even interchangeably, and by applying these words' definitions more strictly, he assesses the features and different sections of Harley accordingly. He determines that although MS Harley 2253 exhibits "no traces of a sustained organizing principle," it does have several groups of texts "discernibly arranged" and thus betrays the anthologizing impulse of its compiler.

Stemmler's piece having thus set up one of the larger debates about the nature of the Harley MS, the next two essays provide comprehensive reevaluations of two broad categories of contents in the book: religion and politics. Michael P. Kuczynski describes the array of religious material present in three languages and in prose and verse, that is, everything from the French and English lyrics, to the Latin saints' legends, to admonitory pieces, to the biblical narratives and instructions on reading the psalms. His illustrative essay — which is closely attentive to the few bits of gloss and marginalia provided by the scribe — reminds us that the lyrics do not exist as isolated moments of devotion, but as part of a larger culture of piety shared by the scribe and his audience.

Covering the political verse of Harley 2253, John Scattergood shows how it is steeped in a regional form of nationalism, one deeply loyal to the concept of nation but suspicious of centralized authority. Several works address national events; others are more personal. Attitudes on the decline of the times sometimes tend to surface as grumblings about the repressiveness of officialdom by individuals caught on the wrong side of the system, whether that system is represented by the articles of trailbaston, oppressive tax collectors, or an allegedly unfair judicial process. Satires against forms of bastard feudalism and against the clerical orders are similarly rooted in an "atavistic conservatism" suspicious of and resistant to a new culture of change.

Richard Newhauser's essay upon "historicity and complaint" in the metrically intricate *Song of the Husbandman* uses a critical analysis of that poem to dismantle the view that its complaint stems from a particularized historical moment. Instead, Newhauser finds in it allusions to an eternal "theodicy" wherein through God's justice "the presence of evil is seen to contain within itself the promise of its ultimate punishment." The poem is, in

11

this reading, a moral complaint on how the abstractions Will, Falsehood, Woe, and Misery walk the land. The analysis exposes a theoretical issue lurking throughout the essays, the issue of reception then and now. What we have long read as political may in fact have been cast as religious for fourteenth-century readers. Our own distinctions need to remain open and fluid.

The two essays that come after Newhauser's follow this thread into more detailed examinations of popular genres and motifs that obviously appealed to the Harley scribe: debates and dreams. They draw our attention to the prevalence of forms in the Harley MS that are not generally recognized as part of its make-up. Karl Reichl considers the presence of key debate poems in the volume, and, in particular, he highlights those deriving from long-standing European traditions: the French dispute between Winter and Spring (the second piece copied by the Harley scribe) and the English one between Body and Soul. There are also debates of a more comic turn — including one drawing upon the "question of women," the bawdy *Gilote et Johane*, and another with a jongleur cleverly inverting the social pretensions of a king — and pastourelle-like arguments between potential lovers, as found in two English lyrics.

Helen Phillips's study of dream lore in the Harley MS points to a more subtle interest displayed by the compiler. One of the least-known of the English works in Harley is *A Bok of Sweuenyng*, a treatise on the myriad variety of dreams and the predicted outcomes of precise dream topics. Phillips explains the Latin context behind this work and shows how the Harley piece derives from two Middle English versions of the *Somnia Danielis* "run together." Elsewhere in Harley, in *King Horn*, dream imagery plays an important symbolic role that forwards a romance narrative, while the dream tradition found in the body-soul debate poem *In a Þestri Stude* is entirely visionary and admonitory.

The varied contents of Harley viewed in relation to codicological categories of evidence — specifically, scribe/anthologist and author — are the concerns of the next two scholars. David L. Jeffrey determines who are some of the identifiable authors of Harley material, and he examines which items are shared by other manuscripts. In so doing, he situates Harley among comparable early English anthologies, many of which are suffused with Franciscan spirituality. The influence of fraternal theology is also to be found, he demonstrates, in some lyrics and meditations of Harley 2253. Because authorship in Harley is an elusive issue, Jeffrey's list of authors is useful and illuminating: Anselm of Canterbury, Jacques de Vitry, John of Wales, Nicholas Bozon (or Bohun, of the well-known Hereford patronage family), and anonymous translators of works by Jacopone da Todi, Bernard of Clairvaux, and pseudo-Bonaventure.

John J. Thompson's essay on the biblical texts of Harley 2253 offers another perspective on scribal activity, authorship, and topic in Harley 2253. Thompson reminds us to consider that more than one scribe is involved in the overall product that Harley represents and that each of the two main ones executes a sizeable redaction of biblical narrative.[29] Scribe A (of fols. 1–48) created a "mini-anthology" of "diverse French vernacular biblical material" including the *Vitas patrum* and an extract of Herman of Valenciennes's *Bible*. Scribe B (the Harley scribe) copied the lengthy Old Testament Bible stories at the end of the ninth quire. Thompson's study supports the intriguing theory, first proposed by A. D. Wilshere, that the Harley scribe himself made this biblical translation in Anglo-Norman prose, and that he likewise is author of the dialectally similar *Fouke le Fitz Waryn* of MS Royal 12.C.xii. The level of active reflection and authority embedded in the Harley scribe's redactive output is thus a continuing question that conjoins with issues of how thoroughly Harley 2253 is a planned book and how deliberately it follows an agenda set by its scribal maker.

Like Thompson, the next writer is concerned with some French contents, but of a different sort. Texts written in Anglo-Norman occupy more manuscript space than all the Latin and English texts combined. The items examined now are, however, very distant in manner from the implicit piety of Bible stories. Barbara Nolan looks at the clustering of five fabliaux in the Harley MS's sixth independent block (comprised of Quires 12–14), and she notes how the material interspersed with them tends to reinforce a sense that what is going on here is a discussion of women and their duplicity, meant to entertain, warn, and instruct young men, as fabliaux and texts on women's nature coexist amidst the more overt didacticism of courtesy books. Of keen interest is Nolan's detection of unique prologues and epilogues in several of the Harley fabliaux, two of which appear to borrow phrasings from Chrétien de Troyes or Marie de France, and which may be the Harley scribe's own creations.

Mary Dove's work is closely related to Nolan's as she examines many of those other texts about women. Dove's emphasis is mostly on the French, but also some English, verse that draws on a traditional discourse about the "characteristics of women," producing texts either of accusation or praise. An associated tradition offers pro or con arguments upon the wisdom of marrying, and the range of such texts extends even to the Latin extract of John of Wales's *Communeloquium*. In comparing the formal relationships within this literary type, Dove suggests that questions of "priority and influence" need to yield to newer questions of "mediation and negotiation." Furthermore, she asks that this literature be contextualized within an audience of both women and men so that the "intimacy of shared vernacular texts" may be perceived as being in play in their enactment between genders.

---

[29] Wanley distinguishes the "round Text Hand" of fols. 1–48 from the "English Law hand" of fols. 49–140 (*Catalogue*, 2.585). A third hand adds recipes in English on fol. 52va–b (the end of the fifth quire). See also Ker, *Facsimile*, pp. xviii–xx.

Can one discern, therefore, in the sheer arrangement of texts, reasonably obvious indicators of meaning for a medieval reader, and, if so, can one plausibly ascribe these constructed arguments to the Harley scribe? My essay on *Marina* and the English love lyrics addresses this issue as it continues the focus upon secular texts, again in the context of manuscript making and specific codicological features. Many of the most revered English lyrics — for example, *Annot and John*, *Alysoun*, *The Fair Maid of Ribblesdale* — appear in the seventh quire of Harley 2253. Mixed with these lyrics are several other categories of discourse: a political poem, a saint's tale, a quasi-religious poem, a pastourelle, a bawdy French interlude. By examining the neglected saint's legend *Marina*, a fascinating English tale of penitence, sexuality, and cross-gendering, I suggest that the quire achieves an amusing unity of purpose in the motif of women's parts hidden under clothes, a favored convention of love poets, which is here submitted to many permutations in a textual sequence composed by someone (possibly this scribe-compiler) and filling up this quire.

Allied to my suggestion that we more closely analyze the manuscript according to its makeup by quires and blocks, Elizabeth Solopova and Frances McSparran point to other physical means by which we ought to renew our study of Harley 2253. Solopova offers an analysis of the Harley scribe's habits in copying English verse: how he observes a systematic practice in regards to layout, punctuation, and stress patterns. Comparison to analogous manuscripts, particularly to the Oxford manuscripts Digby 86 and Jesus College 29, reveals a method in use by pre-1350 scribes of English verse texts whereby lines were by scribal understanding recorded with end rhymes, so that where alternate rhymes occurred, they were copied as belonging to internally rhyming caesural lines. As with Revard's paleographical study, Solopova's essay causes us to regard anew the scribe's sense of his craft.

Frances McSparran looks at the Harley scribe's orthographical practices and attempts to determine the degree to which he (1) reproduced the forms he found in his exemplars, (2) translated to his own dialect, or (3) created forms "in between these two poles of replication and translation." McSparran's study carefully reexamines the English dialects in Harley 2253 in light of the data now available in *A Linguistic Atlas of Late Mediaeval English*.[30] She is able to determine much of the scribe's active and passive repertoires of spelling, and by dialectal evidence, to detect the orthographic patterns of some exemplars that he used for certain texts. In these "suggestive networks of connection" within groups of texts we may begin to glimpse, on occasion, those exemplars that gave the scribe more than one text.

---

[30] Angus McIntosh, M. L. Samuels, Michael Benskin, with the assistance of Margaret Laing and Keith Williamson, *A Linguistic Atlas of Late Mediaeval English*, 4 vols. (Aberdeen, 1986).

Introduction

The final essayist in this collection, Marilyn Corrie, asks us to view Harley 2253 in relation to other English books of its time, and particularly to Digby 86, which has recently appeared in another facsimile edition published by the Early English Text Society. Comparison of the two codices indicates the rich variety of native and continental French literature circulating in England ca. 1270–1340. Corrie shows, specifically, that the corpus of available texts in Anglo-Norman was "rather less consistently bleak, and less unremittingly improving" than the standard surveys would lead us to believe. Indeed, our knowledge of the literary landscape of the period is woefully incomplete because of monolingual biases among scholars and the often selective aims of modern anthologists and editors. Corrie also reminds us how different were the medieval compilers' criteria of selection ("a lack of self-consciousness" and a concern for the "potential usefulness" of texts) compared to those of modern editors.

In essence, Marilyn Corrie's essay brings us full circle to the problem of recovery. These documents — Harley 2253, Digby 86, and others — have survived through more than six centuries. They are now well protected and preserved in university or national libraries. They are, moreover, facsimiled for everyone to view. But amidst this recognition of their treasured value and their unique status as artifacts from a certain time and place in British history, it is quite remarkable that they have not yet been scrutinized as thoroughly as they might for what they may yield about the reading lives of those in the fairly particularized society that created them. The essays in this volume demonstrate not so much what we know about these books as what we still need to investigate and find out from them. Paleography, codicology, dialectology, metrics, physical layout — these are some of the sciences that help us to learn more. Literary-historical studies in religion, politics, and day-to-day culture — with the many intersections and interdependencies of these forces — will produce yet more results. And, most of all, our reading the books in the ways that they were composed — that is, whole and in awareness of each of the alternating languages used by scribes — will clearly give us a fuller grasp of the textual interrelations as they were received and understood by the medieval people for whom they were made.

TABLE. *The canon of English lyric verse from MS Harley 2253 by category*

Item numbers derive from Ker, except where otherwise noted. For a comparative listing of all English works in Harley and their modern editions, see the appendix to Frances McSparran's essay (pp. 421–26).

POLITICAL VERSE (Brown nos. 72, 74; Robbins nos. 2–8)

23 *A Song of Lewes*
25 *The Execution of Sir Simon Fraser*
25a *On the Follies of Fashion*
31 *Song of the Husbandman*
40 *Satire on the Consistory Courts*
47 *The Death of Edward I*
48 *The Flemish Insurrection*
88 *Satire on the Retinues of the Great*
90 *The Prophecy of Thomas of Ercledoune*

RELIGIOUS VERSE (Brook nos. 1–2, 10, 13, 15–18, 20–23, 26–29, 31)

24b *Earth upon Earth*
27 *The Three Foes of Man*
41 *The Labourers in the Vineyard*
45 *An Old Man's Prayer*
50 *Suete Iesu, King of Blysse*
51 *Iesu Crist, Heouene Kyng*
52 *A Winter Song*
53 *A Spring Song on the Passion*
60 *Stond Wel, Moder, vnder Rode*
61 *Iesu, for Þi Muchele Miht*
62 *I Syke When Y Singe*
63 *An Autumn Song*
66 *Blessed Be Þou, Leuedy*
67 *The Five Joys of the Virgin*
69 *A Prayer for Deliverance*
73 *God, Þat Al Þis Myhtes May*
92 *The Way of Christ's Love*

SECULAR VERSE (Brook nos. 3–9, 11–12, 14, 19, 24–25, 30, 32)

28 *Annot and John*

Introduction

APPENDIX. *N. R. Ker's corrigenda to the facsimile*

A sheet typewritten by N. R. Ker, dated May 23, 1975, survives among the papers of R. H. Robbins at the Robbins Library, University of Rochester, Rochester, New York. It is unclear whether Ker sent it to Robbins intending it for the unfinished volume of essays on MS Harley 2253 or simply for Robbins's information. The following lines reproduce Ker's corrigenda.[31] I am grateful to Russell Peck for allowing me to peruse Robbins's file on the Harley MS.

Corrigenda to the Facsimile
Neil Ker   (23 May 1975)

The least I can do is to spend ten minutes on errors and additions to my introduction. I think most of them have been pointed out in reviews.

p x.	Ed. Wright not Jubinal[32]
p x.	Nos 10–17 were printed by Wright in Archaeological Journal 1 (1845) 64–66.
p. xi	No. 26. The rhyme scheme is abababab.
p. xi.	No. 45. The rhyme scheme is aabaabccbccbedde.
p. xii.	No. 54 f. 76 not 75v.
p. xv	No. 110 f. 136 not 136v. No. 111 Cf. Latin in BL Addit 33382, Art 32
p. xvi	No. 114 was printed by Whitaker, History of Whalley i (1872) 156–58 from BL Addit 10374, ff. 145v (1147 ? a slip ?)(–147)
p. xvii.	Disposition of the text. Add that on f. 73 he looked ahead to see how No 47 went before finishing No 46.
p xviii	footnote 4. Soc Antiq 119 need not be strictly contemporary.
p xxii[33]	Broken g is fairly common back to f. 130

---

[31] The user of the facsimile may add four more corrigenda not listed by Ker:

    p. x   No. 8. The metrical form is *ababababcdc*, the ninth line being a one-stress bob (see Mary Dove's discussion in this volume, p. 331).

    p. xv No. 86. Read "L., p. 342," not "L., p. 432."

    p. xv No. 113. For the journal title, read "*Philosophie*," not "*Philologie*."

    p. xvi No. 116. For Hardy, *Descr. cat.*, read "no. 1023," not "no. 1054."

[32] Ker has mistakenly reversed the editors' names. No. 9 (on p. x) is edited by Jubinal (1.40–49), not by Wright, as cited.

[33] Footnote 22.

p. xxiii. I am not sure of my facts here. Christopher Hohler pointed out to me in 1964 already that there is yet another line of verse on fol. 6v of Royal. 'Virgo parens natum tibi Thomam redde beatum' which might, as he suggested, refer to Thomas of Lancaster. Is it in the main hand or not? If it isn't then I did all right to neglect it. If it is I should have mentioned it. It is something I must check on in B.L.

Scribe and Provenance

Carter Revard

In 1965 N. R. Ker summarized facts and provided crucial new information on the provenance of London, British Library MS Harley 2253, and in 1975 the editors of *Fouke le Fitz Waryn* repeated the process.[1] From their accounts, the Harley scribe (that is, the copyist of fols. 49–140) seemed linked to a baron or a bishop, each of national importance: Roger Mortimer of Wigmore, first earl of March (1286–1330), and Adam Orleton, bishop of Hereford (1317–27). However, research by the present writer since 1975 has turned up a series of forty-one dated holographs in this scribe's hand that show he worked as a "conveyancer" producing legal charters in and near Ludlow from 1314 to at least 1349. Four of the holographs are now in the British Library (BL), London, thirty-six are in the Shropshire Records and Research Centre (SRR), Shrewsbury, and one is in the Bodleian Library, Oxford.[2] They do not reveal directly the scribe's name, without which we must make

---

[1] N.R. Ker, into., *Facsimile of British Museum MS. Harley 2253*, EETS o.s. 255 (London, 1965), pp. ix–xxiii; E. J. Hathaway, P. T. Ricketts, C. A. Robson, and A. D. Wilshere, eds., *Fouke le Fitz Waryn* (hereafter *FFW*), ANTS 26–28 (Oxford, 1975), pp. xxxvi–liii. I offer thanks to Alan Robson for many helpful discussions, and to Dr. Ker for expert advice on paleographical matters.

[2] For help generously given, patiently and efficiently, I am very grateful to the excellent staff of the Salop Record Office; to Miss Penelope Morgan and the Hereford Cathedral Library; and to librarians and staffs of the Bodleian Library, Oxford, and the British Library and London Public Record Office, Cambridge University Library, Worcester Cathedral, and the County Record Offices of Hereford, Worcester, and Hampshire; as also the librarians of Merton, University, Balliol, St. John's, and All Souls colleges at Oxford, and of Corpus Christi and Caius colleges at Cambridge; and to librarians of Trinity College and University College, Dublin, the University of Wales at Aberystwyth, and Washington University, St. Louis. Help on paleographic questions has come from Malcolm Parkes and T. J. Brown, and A. I. Doyle found time in a crowded evening to solve one cryptic signature; I am most grateful to them. Many helpful suggestions came from Norman Davis, Roger Highfield, and Douglas Gray, and indispensable guidance on historical matters from G. A. Holmes, J. R. Maddicott, David Cox, and Christopher Hohler of the Courtauld Institute. Correspondence with Derek Pearsall and Elizabeth Salter clarified certain points; Theo Stemmler of the University of Mannheim, and his colleagues and students, proved most graciously helpful.

inferences from them, and from masses of other documents and information obtained subsequent to their discovery, as to the probable identity of this scribe and his patrons. Being dated, however, the holographs do illustrate changes in his handwriting from 1314 to 1349, thus letting us date his work in the three manuscripts where his hand appears, and allowing a chronological view of how his professional and personal interests developed in those thirty-five years.

More than a hundred names of persons appear in the holographs. See Index of Names (below, pp. 101–07). Preliminary study of the Ludlow milieu of these, and of the Harley scribe's peers and colleagues, lets us understand to some extent the interplay of interests and circumstances reflected in the contents of his manuscripts (BL MSS Harley 2253, Royal 12.C.xii, and Harley 273), and thus clarifies the function or *raison d'etre* of each manuscript.

Over twenty years of research has not allowed identification beyond doubt of this scribe or of his patrons. However, from the documentary evidence in combination with that of his three manuscripts, he appears most likely to have served as parish chaplain in Virgin's Chapel in the parish Church of St. Bartholomew there. If so, his most likely patrons would have been the lady of Richard's Castle, Joan Mortimer (1291–1341), co-heiress of the barony of Burford of which this castle was the *caput*, and her son Sir John Talbot (ca. 1318–55). Yet some documentary evidence suggests his patrons may have included certain other local families of county-magnate status with holdings precisely where the scribe wrote most of his extant legal documents: the Ludlows of Stokesay Castle, very wealthy wool merchants risen to knighthood (with strong ties to the Hodnets, LeStranges, FitzWarins, and FitzAlan earls of Arundel), who held in free socage half of Overton, where the scribe wrote almost half of his legal documents; and the similar if less wealthy Cheynes of Cheyney Longville, some of whom were tenants not only in the area south of Ludlow where the scribe worked, but also north of it, near the village of Edgton where the scribe wrote a 1343 deed, and also near Wistanstow (the scribe copied a life of St. Wistan onto the last page of Harley 2253). It is also possible — though in 1999 this seems to me much less likely than it seemed in 1980 — that he was a servitor of the Mortimers of

Alan Wilshere saved me from some blunders; Mary Dove and Charity Scott-Stokes helped on Anglo-Norman poems; Susan Cavanaugh and Clifford Peterson offered generous help. Financial help came from the Graduate School of Washington University, the American Philosophical Society, and the British Academy; I am grateful. Rossell Hope Robbins was extraordinary in conceiving and supporting this work. I offer thanks to Talbot Donaldson, for whom many years ago I first looked at Harley 2253 — though I must exonerate him and another martyr, Prof. Stella Revard, from any responsibility for the results. Finally, my debt to the intelligence, patience, and generosity of Susanna Fein for her assistance with getting this essay into printable shape, I can only say is very great indeed, and I thank her and Russell Peck for their unfailing courtesy and good cheer over the long haul.

Wigmore: perhaps an Ace, an Orleton, or someone else from among local well-to-do burgess/merchant/franklin families whose sons included chaplains, lawyers, monks, and baronial retainers. He might just have sprung from the knightly Lingen family discussed by E. J. Dobson in relation to the authorship and manuscripts of *Ancrene Wisse*. Finally, he might have been relatively independent, a member of a local family of burgess or franklin status carrying on his parochial and legal duties and producing his manuscripts in part for himself and in part for the unusually literate household of such a merchant/franklin/burgess family.

The "bastard feudalism" that tied clergy, gentry, burgesses, and barons into a network of relationships is reflected in the political poems of Harley 2253 and Royal 12.C.xii. Thus, while the scribe appears to have been of secular clerical status and may have served a newly gentle household, his probable family and connections cover a wide social and geographic range, from Ludlow chaplains to the Mortimer earls of March and the FitzAlan earls of Arundel.

Research to 1975

Before Ker's magisterial contribution in his 1964 facsimile of Harley 2253, scholars had shown that it is a West Midlands manuscript, linked by lives of local saints to Hereford and Leominster (in Herefordshire) and to Wistanstow (in southern Shropshire). They had shown that it contains one poem dated ca. 1338 (the Latin and French protest against wool seizure and high taxes [no. 114; fols. 137v–138v]), and thus was not copied before ca. 1340. They had noted that its flyleaves contain fragments of an account roll with Irish place-names which (on its dorso) has portions of the Hereford Cathedral Ordinal, with the Irish roll being in another scribe's hand but the ordinal in the main scribe's hand. Ker added several important pieces of information: first, that the Harley scribe had also copied much of BL MS Royal 12.C.xii, and next, that in this second volume the scribe's hand shows an earlier and a later style. Since the earlier style is used in items datable to 1322–26, it is clear that the scribe did not adopt the later style until after 1326. Since Harley 2253 is entirely in the later style, it must have been copied after 1326 and not completed before 1338–40.[3]

---

[3] Ker, *Facsimile*, pp. xx–xxiii. The earlier scholars include Thomas Wright, who cited the localizing lives of saints (Ethelbert of Hereford, Etfrid of Leominster, Wistan of Wistanstow; nos. 18, 98, 116), and pointed out that since an elegy for Edward I is included (no. 47), the manuscript's *terminus a quo* had to be 1307, suggesting that its scribe was "some secular clerk connected with the priory of Leominster" (*Specimens of Lyric Poetry, Composed in England in the Reign of Edward the First*, Percy Society 4 [1842; repr. New York, 1965], p. vii). In 1953 Isabel S. T. Aspin

Next, Ker established links between the scribe and the castle and town of Ludlow, and
— apparently — to the powerful baronial family of Mortimer of Wigmore, which after
1308 held the castle and half the town and had alternate presentation (with the Verduns)
to the Ludlow parish Church of St. Laurence. These links appear partly in the flyleaves
of Harley 2253, partly in the French prose ancestral romance of *Fouke le Fitz Waryn*
which the scribe copied into Royal. In this romance the scribe shows detailed knowledge
of Ludlow Castle and its chapels, and of Ludlow town and environs. For example, at one
point in copying *Fouke*, he inserted above the line information concerning the dedication
date and indulgences to those praying in the castle's Magdalene Chapel.[4] Before 1308
Ludlow Castle and half the town had been held by Sir Geoffrey de Genville; in that year
he granted these to his granddaughter Joan and her husband Roger Mortimer, along with
Irish lands in Trim. It is, as Ker shows, precisely these Irish lands in Trim that are
mentioned in the flyleaves of Harley 2253, which record the expenses of a large household
for a week in March (probably 1309).[5] Among recorded expenses is the gift of a salmon
to Sir Geoffrey, showing that this visit preceded his death in 1314. The roll is not in our
scribe's hand but rather in one that Ker judged to be somewhat earlier. The Harley scribe
had access to this old roll, used its dorso at one point for drafting portions of a revision of
the Hereford Cathedral Ordinal, and eventually made it into the binding leaves for Harley
2253.

One would expect that access to such a document implied service in the household
whose expenses it records, but we must remember two facts: we do not *know* this
household was a Mortimer one, and there were ways other than service for getting hold
of such an old roll. That it is a Mortimer document seems likely, however, from the fact
that one name in the roll — Fort (mentioned three times as buying items for the household)
— is the same as that of a certain Richard le Fort, who served Roger Mortimer of

---

extended the *terminus a quo* to 1338 by showing that the poem protesting taxes and wool seizure
(no. 114) referred to events of that time (*Anglo-Norman Political Songs*, ANTS 11 [Oxford, 1953],
pp. 105–07). Editors of the New Palaeographical Society (*Facsimiles of Ancient Manuscripts etc.*,
1st series [London, 1912], pl. 241) showed that the flyleaves' fragment of material relating to
Hereford Cathedral was extracts from its ordinal. Theo Stemmler has done important work on the
stylistics of the Middle English alliterative lyrics in relation to date, and on the dating evidence,
e.g., in "Zur Datierung des MS. Harley 2253," *Anglia* 80 (1962): 111–18.

[4] See *FFW*, 13.30–31, and notes on pp. 76, 137. The passage in Royal 12.C.xii is on fol. 37v.
More detailed knowledge of Ludlow Castle's layout, and of the lesser chapels within its walls, is
shown by the romance-redactor (e.g., *FFW* 16.30), presumably the Chapel of St. Peter, for which
compare *Calendar of Patent Rolls Preserved in the Public Record Office* (hereafter *CPR*) *1350–54*
(London, 1891–1916), p. 223, and *CPR 1354–58*, pp. 87, 311.

[5] Ker, *Facsimile*, pp. xxii–xiii.

Wigmore as chaplain, was presented by him to two benefices,[6] and accompanied Mortimer to Ireland in 1316–17. Nevertheless, there were other Ludlow-area magnates with Irish interests who could have been in Ireland with a large household at the time the old roll was being made: the Verduns, for example, or the Bykenores (after Sir Thomas, by marriage, became lord of Richard's Castle just south of Ludlow). And it is certainly true that such household documents could go astray: in 1310, for instance, Roger Mortimer's clerk Thomas Ace was assaulted by Roger Foliot and William de Sparchford, who took Mortimer's deeds and charters from Ace in Stretton (Church Stretton, north of Ludlow on the way to Shrewsbury).[7]

---

[6] Neen Sollars in 1314 and Ludlow in 1326 — though he held the latter only until 1328, being succeeded then by John Evesham as rector of Ludlow. For the career of Richard le Fort, see: W.W. Capes, ed., *Registrum Ricardi de Swinfield, episcopi Herefordensis*, Canterbury and York Society 6 (1909), p. 543; A. T. Bannister, ed., *Registrum Ade de Orleton, episcopi Herefordensis*, Canterbury and York Society 5 (1908), pp. 389, 391; *CPR 1313–17*, pp. 620, 650; *Calendar of Fine Rolls Preserved in the Public Record Office* (hereafter *CFR*) *1312–27* (London, 1911), p. 239 (April 21, 1324); and Oxford, Bodleian Library MS Blakeway 3, p. 14. For John Evesham and the presentation to Ludlow, see: Oxford, Bodleian Library MS Blakeway 3, p. 14; W. W. Capes, ed., *Registrum Thome de Charltone, episcopi Herefordensis*, Canterbury and York Society 9 (1913), p. 75; and *CPR 1327–30*, pp. 254, 273. Evesham remained rector of Ludlow until at least 1365, and probably until a succeeding rector was presented in 1369: J. H. Parry, ed., *Registrum Ludowici de Charltone, episcopi Herefordensis*, Canterbury and York Society 14 (1913), pp. 24–27; compare also A. C. Wood, ed., *Registrum Simonis de Langham, Cantuariensis Archiepiscopi*, Canterbury and York Society 53 (1956), p. 322. For the careers of the Verduns, see "G. E. C," *The Complete Peerage of England, Scotland, Ireland, Great Britain, and the United Kingdom*, 2nd ed., 13 vols. (London, 1910–59), 12.246–52; for Sir Thomas Bykenore and Richard's Castle, ibid., "Mortimer of Richard's Castle," 9.256–66. The Verduns, with extensive Irish lands, held half of Ludlow and had alternate presentation to the parish church there.

[7] Roger Foliot, cleric, was surely related to Thomas Foliot, merchant of Ludlow, and Thomas Ace was also of a family of Ludlow merchants and burgesses and chaplains. For the appointment of Roger Foliot as attorney for the Irish affairs of Roger Mortimer of Wigmore, see *CPR 1307–13*, p. 32 (dated 1308). For Ace's appointment by August 6, 1309, and the assault in 1310, see *CPR 1307–13*, pp. 240, 254. Ace was attorney for other Ludlow-area or Hereford diocese magnates serving in Ireland about this time: on March 19, 1308, for Walter de Thornbury, going to Ireland to take up appointment as Chancellor of the Exchequer; on October 1, 1310, for numerous retainers of Mortimer then in Ireland with him (*CPR 1307–13*, pp. 56, 283). Ace had a considerable career later as a Mortimer clerk and judge-administrator. Regarding the identity of William de Sparchford, cleric, it may be of related interest that one of the Harley scribe's documents records a release from legal claims by Henry de Sparchford, cleric, to the wife of a Mortimer supporter exiled in 1330 (see Appendix 2, **#26**).

Returning to Ker's work, we note that he discovered another pointer to scribal interest in Hereford Cathedral and its bishops in Royal 12.C.xii, fol. 6v, where are copied seal-mottoes of two Hereford bishops, Richard Swinfield (1283–1317) and Adam Orleton (1317–27). Orleton was subsequently translated to Worcester (1327–33) and then to Winchester (1333–45). The consensus in 1965, when Ker published his evidence, was that Orleton was a political protégé of Mortimer, while more recent work suggests that these men's close conjunction does not necessarily indicate that the lesser Orleton was satellite to the greater Mortimer.[8] Certainly the two cooperated in the overthrow of Edward II in 1326, after which Orleton served in the royal administration controlled by Mortimer until the latter's fall in 1330. A scribe with ties to Mortimer might easily have had links also to Orleton and to Hereford Cathedral. Thus the manuscripts could plausibly be thought to have had both bishop and baron as patrons, whether simultaneously or sequentially.

In 1975 just this suggestion was made by the editors of *Fouke le Fitz Waryn*: the Harley scribe began, they suggested, as secretary and tutor in a baronial retinue, compiling and copying during this period the earlier "booklets" of Royal 12.C.xii. Later he sought ecclesiastical preferment, obtaining it as a canon of Hereford and familiar of Bishop Orleton, perhaps going with Orleton to Worcester in 1327. The transition from baron's man to bishop's could reasonably have occurred either in 1322, when Mortimer was put in the Tower for his leading role in the Lancastrian rebellion, or in 1330 when Mortimer was hanged. A stronger link to Ludlow and thus, perhaps, to the Mortimers, was also reported by the *Fouke* editors: the fact (first discovered by Christopher Hohler of the Courtauld Institute) that the Harley scribe's hand appears in still a third manuscript, BL MS Harley 273, in which there is a calendar wherein is rubricated the dedication date of the Ludlow parish Church of St. Laurence, indicating that the manuscript's owner used it in that church.[9] These editors, noting in Royal the episcopal seal-mottoes and a moral maxim in rhyme ("*Finita uita, finit amicus ita*"), went beyond the facts in a bit of romantic speculation, suggesting that the maxim may be the "last advice given to the younger man

---

[8] Roy Martin Haines, *The Church and Politics in Fourteenth-Century England: The Career of Adam Orleton c. 1275–1345* (Cambridge, 1978); see also Haines's edition of the *Calendar of the Register of Adam de Orleton, Bishop of Worcester, 1327–1333* (London, 1979) and his more recent *Archbishop John Stratford: Political Revolutionary and Champion of the Liberties of the English Church ca. 1275/80–1348* (Toronto, 1986), which provides important additions and corrections to this history. In 1975 Orleton's Worcester register was made available for my inspection by Miss Henderson of the Worcester Record Office, to whom I am most grateful.

[9] Hohler's discovery was reported in *FFW*, p. xxxviii. The contents of Harley 273 are listed in H. Wanley, D. Casley, et al., *A Catalogue of the Harleian Manuscripts in the British Museum* (1759; rev. and repr. 4 vols. London, 1808–12), 1.102, noting the rubrication of the dedication date of Ludlow parish Church of St. Laurence.

by Bishop Adam before his death in 1345; in any case the *amicus* must be his lifelong patron and hero."[10]

However romantic, this notion seemed in 1975 highly plausible. Such ties would have meant that the Harley scribe moved among the wealthiest, most powerful and sophisticated people of his time, and not just in the Ludlow or West Midlands area. Orleton and Mortimer were of national importance. Orleton, doctor of both canon and civil law, was a papal chaplain who advanced the causes of the Hereford diocese, including that for canonization of St. Thomas Cantilupe in 1320; he was sent many times on royal diplomacy to Paris and to the papal curia in Avignon; and to judge from a list of books mentioned as in his hands during one trip to France, he had intellectual interests as well as political and diplomatic and legal skills. He was certainly a survivor. Having served Edward II before 1320, he was an important figure in the Mortimer-controlled royal administrations of 1326–30. He not only survived Mortimer's fall and execution; he managed thereafter to get himself advanced once more to a richer see (Winchester), continuing in diplomatic work for Edward III during the 1330s.[11]

As for Mortimer, his Luciferian career is well known. One of the wealthiest and most powerful barons in England, he served Edward II as Irish commander, then led the Marcher Barons' upheaval in 1321, joined Thomas of Lancaster's doomed rebellion in 1321–22, was imprisoned for life in the Tower in 1322, but drugged his jailers and escaped to France in 1323. When Edward II later sent his queen, Isabella, over to Paris to negotiate with the King of France, Mortimer became her lover, used her aid to build an invasion force, and returned to England with her to overthrow Edward, hang his own old enemies (the Despensers, the earl of Arundel, and others), and rule from behind the throne for four years, getting himself named first earl of March. In 1330, however, he was captured by the young Edward III and his allies in Nottingham Castle — in the Queen Mother's bedroom, it seems — and was disgraced and executed. He was survived by his widow Joan Genville Mortimer (granddaughter of Sir Geoffrey), who retained in dower Ludlow Castle and her manor of Stanton Lacy north of Ludlow, and who lived until 1356 — much of the time, apparently, in the Ludlow area.[12]

With such patrons the Harley scribe would have had plenty of educational travel, access to cultured courtly circles, and — to say the least — an exciting life. One would expect from him the kind of sophisticated manuscript that Harley 2253 certainly is, whether its patron was the baron or the bishop. Even if made only for the scribe himself, it would have

---

[10] *FFW*, pp. xlii–xliii.

[11] Haines, *Archbishop John Stratford*, p. 188

[12] For Mortimer, see May McKisack, *The Fourteenth Century 1307–1399* (Oxford, 1959), pp. 58–88 *passim*, supplemented by Haines, *Archbishop John Stratford*, pp. 197–220 *passim*.

had to suit a man who, on the above assumptions, was either much at Avignon with Orleton or much at court with Mortimer.

Alas, the documentary discoveries since 1975 have not supported such a view of scribe or patrons. There had been serious difficulties apparent, indeed, before the documentary discoveries, and we may adduce these before showing what the new evidence consists of. Mortimer patronage, in the first place, seems hardly compatible with certain pieces that our scribe copied into Harley 2253. *A Song of Lewes* and *Lament for Simon de Montfort* (nos. 23, 24), both praise the Montfortians, with the latter mentioning especially Hugh Despenser, yet the Mortimers were key enemies of de Montfort in 1264–65, helping Prince Edward escape from the barons before the battle of Evesham, and profitting largely from de Montfort's overthrow at this battle; and during 1318–30 the Mortimers were deadly foes of the Despensers.[13] Would a manuscript under Mortimer patronage, or even one copied by a cleric in Mortimer service, have included such praise of their enemies not only from the old days of 1264–65, but from the very recent ones of 1318–30?

In the second place, why would Mortimer have wanted a piece such as the Middle English poem celebrating the Flemish insurrection (no. 48; fols. 73v–74v)? The heroes of that poem are the Flemish weavers. As R. H. Robbins has pointed out, it was their need for English wool that led to an alliance between the Count of Flanders and the English King Edward I, which provoked the French to invade Flanders, imprison its nobles, and govern the country so harshly that a revolt erupted, led by Peter de Conyng, master of the cloth-weavers, and John Breydel, master of the butchers.[14] The poem exults over the defeat of French knights by Flemish burghers. It is difficult to see why a partisan of Mortimer, or of Bishop Orleton, would be interested in having a poem celebrating a 1302 defeat of French aristocrats by Flemish burghers, especially since it was being copied after 1331. Presumably it could be part of the English nationalist fervor of the beginnings of the Hundred Years' War, launched by Edward III in 1337–38, but one would expect an Orleton or Mortimer servant to have selected a more elegant poem, perhaps one celebrating victories by more aristocratic Englishmen. And one must recall too that there is another poem in Harley 2253 in which the wool trade is of great importance — the poem *Against the King's Taxes* (no. 114; fols. 137v–138v). Bishop Orleton could have had reasons for interest in this French and Latin protest against the French; he was active in

---

[13] McKisack, p. 61; see also J. R. Maddicott, *Thomas of Lancaster 1307–1322: A Study in the Reign of Edward II* (Oxford, 1970), pp. 258–68, 304–08. Note, however, that during the 1330s, when Harley 2253 was being shaped perhaps, marriages to reconcile some of the old enemies were being arranged.

[14] R. H. Robbins, *Historical Poems of the XIVth and XVth Centuries* (New York, 1959), pp. 9–13, 250–52.

the subsequent crisis.[15] Even so, the presence of both *The Flemish Insurrection* and *Against the King's Taxes* points to a concern with the wool trade and an interest in keeping open the ties to Flemish clothiers, as well as a bitterness about property taxes of 1338 and an exultation about burghers' victories of 1302.

Though the evidence of these two items is hardly of great weight, it seems to militate against Orleton and Mortimer as patrons and to suggest someone directly concerned with the 1337–41 crisis over English wool and the efforts to finance Edward III's war by its sales.[16] Even more puzzling is the presence of the ancestral romance *Fouke le Fitz Waryn* in one of the Harley scribe's books, in his own hand. Nowhere that I have been able to search is there any reason to believe that a FitzWarin was connected with either Orleton or Mortimer, during the period 1322–49 at least. In early 1322, indeed, Fulk FitzWarin led the royal forces holding Bridgnorth when Mortimer burned that town, just before Mortimer's surrender (January 23); and in 1330 Fulk had to flee England as reputed adherent of the earl of Kent in an anti-Mortimer "rebellion" (Appendix 1). Yet the Harley scribe has copied a romance celebrating the unjust exile and triumphant return of the ancestral Fulk FitzWarin — and, as will be seen, he copied it in part before 1330, in part after 1330, showing continued interest in FitzWarins over the period 1320–40 at least. No Mortimer or Orleton servant would have had special reason for this.

In sum, we have a scribe who had access to the Irish account roll that likely came from Mortimer archives, who had reason to copy onto its dorso portions of the Hereford Cathedral Ordinal. The man knew Ludlow Castle and its chapels and the environs of Ludlow intimately. He had reason to copy seal-mottoes of Hereford bishops Swinfield and Orleton into a book of his during the 1320s. He also had reason to copy poems in praise of Simon de Montfort and Hugh Despenser into another book of his about 1340, along with other pieces showing deep interest in wool and in ties with Flanders. He was apparently a strong supporter of the cause of Thomas of Lancaster in 1322, since he copied into Royal 12.C.xii (fol. 1) a collection of liturgical pieces honoring Thomas as a saint. He must have had a special interest in the FitzWarin family, sufficient that he obtained an older verse romance and turned it into a prose tale with local color additions, a task lasting

---

[15] In 1340–41 England was wracked by severe economic and political difficulties of which many were direct outgrowths of Edward III's heavy taxes and wool prices. The complicated political struggles then involved Bishop Adam Orleton on one side and Archbishop of Canterbury John Stratford on the other, their rivalry being in part personal, it seems. For the historical context, see Haines, *Archbishop John Stratford*, pp. 125–26, and G. L. Harriss, *King, Parliament, and Public Finance in Medieval England to 1369* (Oxford, 1975), pp. 231–312, especially pp. 250–52.

[16] See E. B. Fryde, *Studies in Medieval Trade and Finance* (London, 1983) and *William de la Pole, Merchant and King's Banker (1366)* (London, 1988).

for some time, from well before to well after 1330. Obviously, he must have had cause to select the three *vitae* included in Harley 2253 (nos. 18, 98, 116), those of the local saints Ethelbert of Hereford, Etfrid of Leominster, and Wistan of Wistanstow, and it is the last who, we may assume, would be the least commonly cultivated — St. Ethelbert being patron of the diocesan cathedral and St. Etfrid of a town with a large Benedictine priory, while Wistanstow is merely a small village some ten miles northwest of Ludlow.

Discovery of Dated Holographs by the Harley Scribe

From 1974 to 1976 I sought documents in the hand of the Harley scribe, on the assumption that the scribe was in the household of either Roger Mortimer or Adam Orleton, or both. Examination of large numbers of documents from their retinues produced, however, no positive results.[17]

In July 1976, while preparing to order certain items listed in the British Library's *Index to Charters and Rolls*, I noticed that in addition to certain items from Bishop Orleton's chancery there was one item involving a John Orleton, burgess of Ludlow: BL Addit. ch. 41301, in which Howell Vaughan conveyed a moiety of Ludford Manor (just across the River Teme south of Ludlow) to John Orleton. There was also a 1338 charter by which a John de la Chapele conveyed a meadow in Ludford to the Ludlow Hospital of St. John Baptist (BL Addit. ch. 41302). Since the Harley scribe was closely acquainted with Ludlow, interested in Bishop Orleton, and knew the chapels of Ludlow Castle, I ordered

---

[17] For Orleton, much documentary material is extant. I have examined the scribal hands, for instance, in his episcopal registers at Hereford, Worcester, and Winchester, as well as in letters, receipts, and the like now preserved in Hereford Cathedral, the British Library (hereafter BL), and the London Public Record Office (hereafter PRO). I have also looked at the episcopal registers of other bishops of Hereford — Cantilupe, Swinfield, Charlton, and Trillek — in search of the Harley scribe's hand.

Mortimer documents are not so concentrated, but I have viewed a number of letters from his household in the London PRO: *Ancient Correspondence of Chancery and Exchequer* items dating ca. 1306–27 include S.C. 1/19:133; 28:31, 32; 30:162; 35:195; 36:148, 149. There are numerous legal charters from the Mortimer manor of Stanton Lacy just north of Ludlow, ca. 1250–1350, extant in the Shropshire Records and Research Centre (hereafter SRR), the BL, the Bodleian Library (Craven Papers), and the London PRO, which I have examined — e.g., BL Addit. chs. 8333–8360, 41371–41376. One can never be sure of seeing all the relevant evidence; what I have been able to view of Mortimer household documents lacks any pointers to the Harley scribe and has no evidence of his actual hand. Location of Mortimer archives at present has been summarized in R. R. Davies, *Lordship and Society in the March of Wales 1282–1400* (Oxford, 1978), pp. 5–7 and nn. 22–24.

these two charters for inspection along with those others involving Bishop Orleton. It was only the two from Ludford/Ludlow that turned out to be in the hand of the Harley scribe. As later became clear, the Ludlow Orletons were merchants connected primarily with the wool trade and cannot be shown to be related to Bishop Orleton, while the Chapeles were a prominent family in Ludlow from the early thirteenth century who by 1338 were not necessarily "chaplains."[18]

Once these two holographs were found, on July 14, 1976, it was clear where to search for others. To date, a total of forty-one holographs (and two fragments) have been discovered, out of the thousands of such legal documents from Shropshire and Herefordshire that have been examined (with a good many more from Cheshire, Worcestershire, and elsewhere).[19] All forty-one of these dated holographs are here reproduced (Plates 1–27) and their contents described (Appendix 2, below, pp. 91–100). Others may yet be found.[20] The real work, however, was begun only by the finding of the

---

[18] Persons named "de Orleton" occur in Ludlow from at least the mid-thirteenth century. The earliest extant record of the Ludlow palmers' guild, compiled over a considerable period from early Henry III to early Edward I (i.e., ca. 1230–80) has been edited by Rev. W. C. Sparrow, "The Palmers' Gild of Ludlow," *Transactions of the Shropshire Archaeological and Natural History Society* 1 (1878), 333–94. According to Sparrow, the record shows that a William Orleton granted 2½ d annual rent to the guild, Roger Orleton gave 8d, and Richard Orleton gave 4d (p. 382), while Ludlow-area charters dating from at least 1295 forward name Orletons as principals or witnesses. To cite only a few, SRR 356/MT/172, 1194, and 1208 (dating from 1295–1317) attest to Orletons holding land in Ludlow or the village of Overton about 1½ miles south of Ludlow. Nothing in any of the documents I have examined indicates that the Ludlow Orletons are related by blood to Bishop Adam Orleton or the Hereford Orletons to whom Haines has concluded the bishop belongs (*Calendar*, p. 2).

As for the family of Chapeles of Ludlow, Ludford and nearby, they also go back into the thirteenth century as a family of merchants and burgesses for whom "de Capella" was early a patronym. In 1302–03 Walter de la Chapele was witness on SRR 356/MT/166 and 1211 (his brother Stephen also occurs in 166): in 1310 we find Roger de Capella in 356/MT/168, and in 1314 Roger de la Chapele's son John de Chapele occurs in 356/MT/314; again in 1327 John is in 356/MT/474, and in July 1338 we find both John de Chapele and his brother Thomas in 356/MT/565.

[19] Help in this search came particularly from Miss Jancey in the Herefordshire Record Office, Miss Henderson in the Worcestershire Record Office, and the archivists in the Chester Record Office at the Town Hall and the Castle, as well as at the London PRO and the BL.

[20] If the scribe of Harley 2253 had ties to the Ludlows of Stokesay, and through them to the earls of Arundel, it is possible that there are items in his hand in Arundel Castle archives, which I have not yet examined. In December 1979 the Pottesman Purchase by the SRR contained three more deeds in the Harley scribe's hand (**#3, #11, #19**; now SRR 4032/1/29, 13, 14), and as a result of discovering these, I found a fourth additional item in his hand (**#33**; SRR 465/54). In July 1988

holographs — of which the last one was discovered in 1988. This work was, in the first instance, paleographic analysis to be sure that we have but one scribe and that the man who wrote the holographs *is* the scribe of Harley 2253, Royal 12.C.xii, and Harley 273. In the second, it was study of the documents' contents and contexts to determine the Harley scribe's employers and his places and dates of work, to infer patterns of relationships among the persons for whom and with whom he worked, and to reach conclusions with regard to the scribe's status, career, and — if possible — family and patrons. And finally, the task was to apply these conclusions to the questions of provenance and *raison d'etre* of the Harley scribe's three manuscripts.

Dating the Harley Scribe's Texts by Paleographic Analysis

Identification of holograph-scribe with manuscript-scribe may begin by noting the full and exact match of features between Harley 2253 and the holographs of 1331–49, and particularly the correspondence of the 1340 items to most pages of Harley 2253. The most unusual features of the Harley scribe's hand, as was shown by Ker, the *Fouke* editors, and Malcolm Parkes,[21] are the flat-bottomed g and the stroke over *i* made with a double hook, and these features may be seen in (for instance) **#27** (dated 1338; Plate 18), where the flat-bottomed g (*ego*, line 1) and the double-hooked *i*-stroke (*integre*, line 6) are apparent; or **#22** (dated 1333; Plate 15), where in line 1 the double-hooked *i*-stroke appears in *Sciant*, *futuri*, *Rogeri*, *presenti*, and the flat-bottomed g in *ego*, *Hugo*, *Rogeri* of the same line.

But while a flat-bottomed g is found in all the holographs, the hooked *i*-stroke is not. Indeed, we do not find a hooked *i*-stroke in any of the nineteen holographs dated from 1314–29, though we find it in all those from 1331–49. Could we have two different scribes here? The answer is no, we have one scribe who changed between 1329 and 1331, going from an earlier curving *i*-stroke to the later hooked one. Ker had pointed out that the scribe of Harley 2253 had an earlier style with this curving *i*-stroke, and we are now able to say

---

another purchase of deeds by the SRR proved to contain **#37** (SRR 5075/42). These discoveries (see Appendix 2) must make one believe that there are very likely other items extant in this man's hand, and of course these could be in almost any collection of medieval documents. Given that the Ludlows had relatives and ties in Oxford, Northampton, Chipping Campden, and Much Markley areas in the period 1300–50, it remains possible that items from these areas could contain charters or letters in the scribe's hand. I am grateful, for permission to publish photographs of Ludlow Borough documents, to the Ludlow Town Council, the South Shropshire District Council, and Lord Plymouth.

[21] Ker, *Facsimile*, pp. xviii–xx; *FFW*, pp. xxxviii–xxxix; Malcolm B. Parkes, *English Cursive Book Hands 1250–1500* (1969; repr. Berkeley, 1979), p. 1 (ii) and pp. xv, 1.

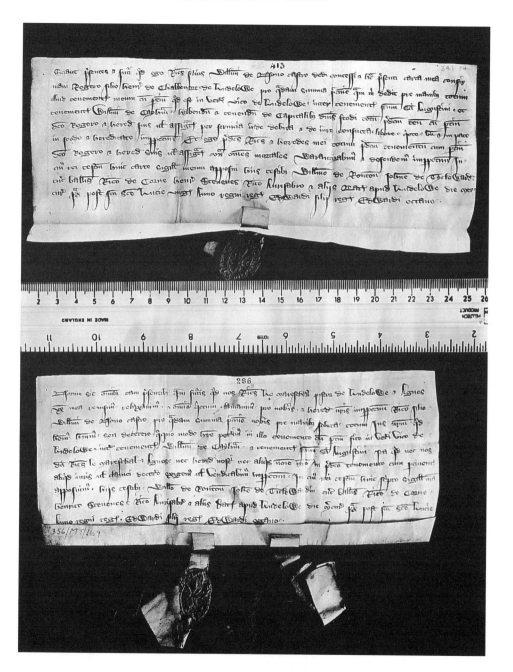

PLATE 1. (top) **#2**: SRR 356/MT/170 (Ludlow, December 18, 1314);
(bottom) **#1**: SRR 356/MT/169 (Ludlow, December 18, 1314).
By permission of the Ludlow Town Council and the South Shropshire District.

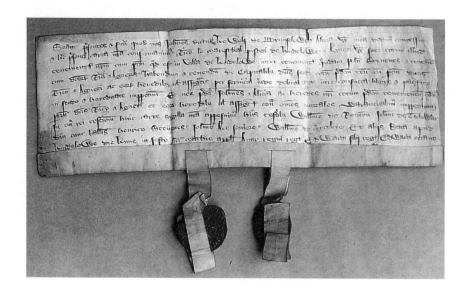

PLATE 2. (top) #3: SRR 4032/1/29 (Ludlow, Monday, February 24, 1315)
PLATE 3. (bottom) Seals on #3: SRR 4032/1/29 (Ludlow, Monday, February 24, 1315).
By permission of the Ludlow Town Council and the South Shropshire District.

PLATE 4. (top) #8: SRR 356/MT/1213 (Overton, Saturday, May 7, 1317);
(bottom) #4: SRR 356/MT/554 (Ludlow, Tuesday, February 24, 1316).
By permission of the Ludlow Town Council and the South Shropshire District.

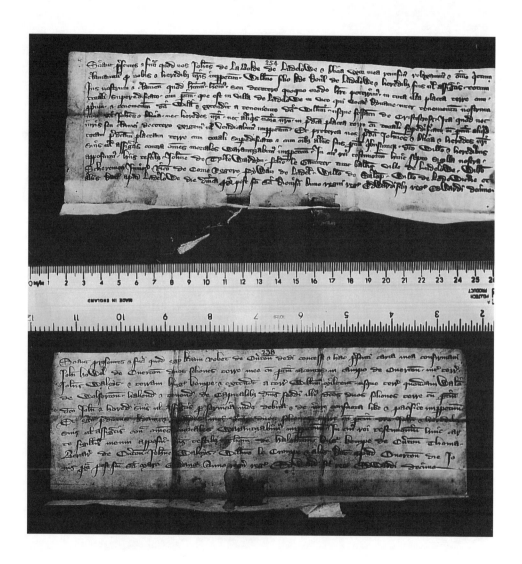

PLATE 5. (top) **#5**: SRR 356/MT/471 (Ludlow, Sunday, October 10, 1316);
(bottom) **#6**: SRR 356/MT/1217 (Overton, Thursday, April 28, 1317).
By permission of the Ludlow Town Council and the South Shropshire District.

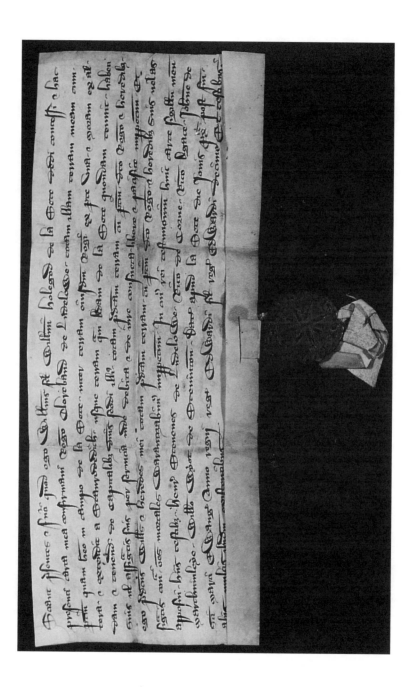

PLATE 6. #7: BL Addit. ch. 41336 (Sheet, April 28, 1317).
By permission of The British Library.

PLATE 7. (top) **#9**: SRR 356/MT/1221 (Overton, Sunday, March 5, 1318);
(bottom) **#12**: SRR 356/MT/1195 (Overton, Monday, April 13, 1321).
By permission of the Ludlow Town Council and the South Shropshire District.

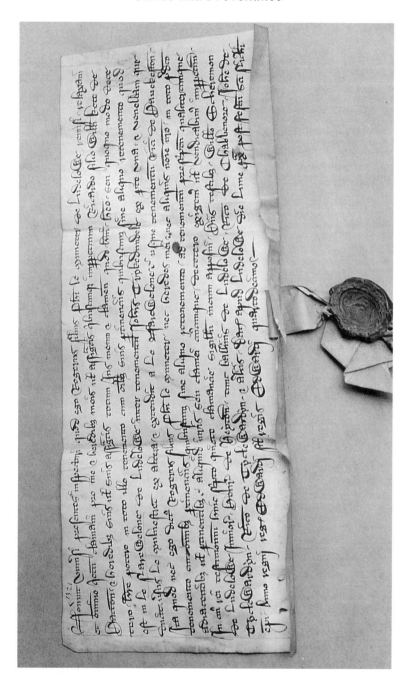

PLATE 8. **#11**: SRR 4032/1/13 (Ludlow, Monday, December 8, 1320).
By permission of the Ludlow Town Council and the South Shropshire District.

PLATE 9. (top) **#10**: SRR 356/MT/555 (Ludlow, April 18, 1320);
(bottom) **#13**: SRR 356/MT/1225 (Overton, Monday, July 6, 1321).
By permission of the Ludlow Town Council and the South Shropshire District.

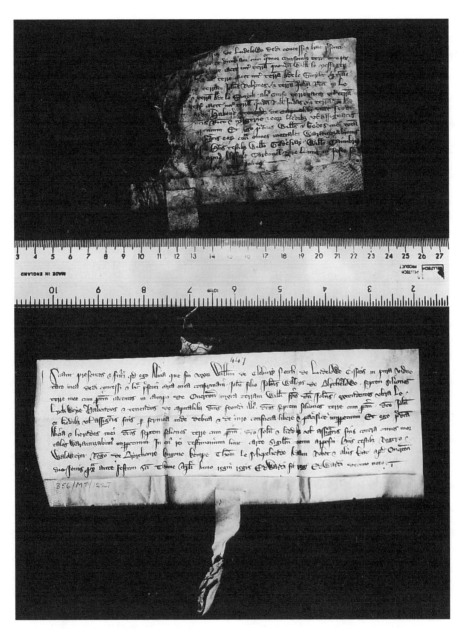

PLATE 10. (top) **#14**: SRR 356/MT/791 (Ashford Carbonel, Monday, feast of ?,
16 Edw II [from July 8, 1322, to July 7, 1323]);
(bottom) **#15**: SRR 356/MT/1227 (Overton, Thursday, December 19, 1325).
By permission of the Ludlow Town Council and the South Shropshire District.

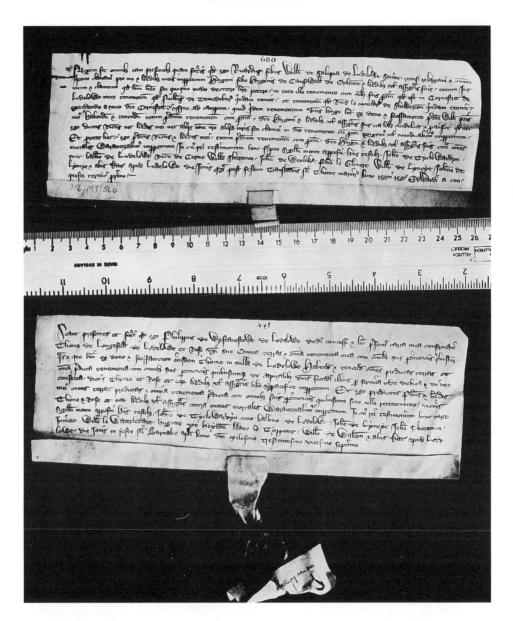

PLATE 11. (top) **#17**: SRR 356/MT/560 (Ludlow, Thursday, July 9, 1327);
(bottom) **#16**: SRR 356/MT/796 (Ludlow, Thursday, June 11, 1327); and
#16a: fragmentary deed, cut to make attached seal-strip.
By permission of the Ludlow Town Council and the South Shropshire District.

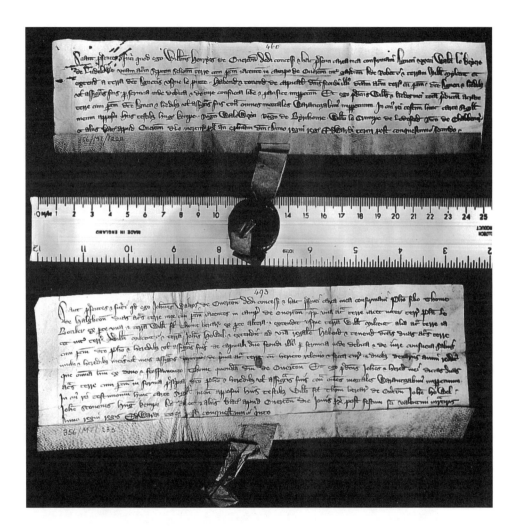

PLATE 12. (top) **#18**: SRR 356/MT/1228 (Overton, Wednesday, January 4, 1329);
(bottom) **#20**: SRR 356/MT/1230 (Overton, Thursday, February 21, 1331).
By permission of the Ludlow Town Council and the South Shropshire District.

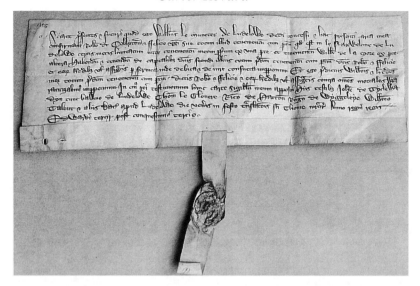

PLATE 13. (top) **#19**: SRR 4032/1/14 (Ludlow, July 7, 1329); and
#19a: fragmentary deed, cut to make attached seal-strip.
By permission of the Ludlow Town Council and the South Shropshire District.
PLATE 14. (bottom) **#21**: BL Addit. ch. 4130l (Ludford, Monday, August 5, 1331).
By permission of The British Library.

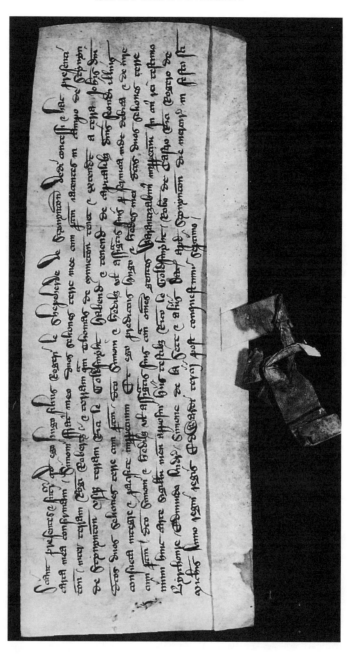

PLATE 15. **#22**: BL Addit. ch. 41316 (Steventon, Wednesday, September 29, 1333).
By permission of The British Library.

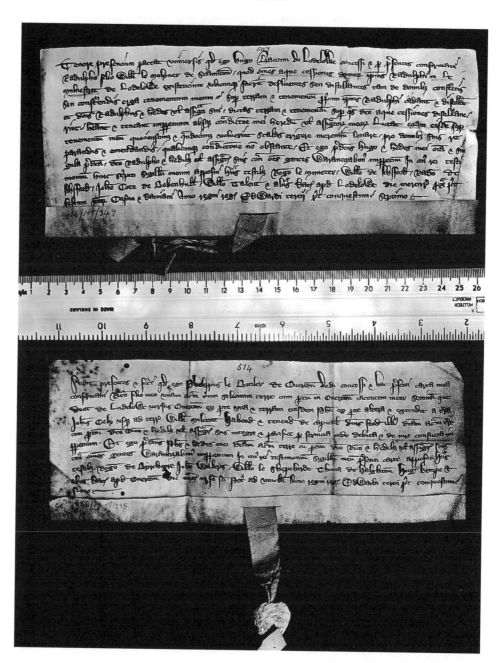

PLATE 16. (top) **#23**: SRR 356/MT/349 (Ludlow, Wednesday, September 29, 1333);
(bottom) **#25**: SRR 356/MT/1235 (Overton, Tuesday, August 1, 1335).
By permission of the Ludlow Town Council and the South Shropshire District.

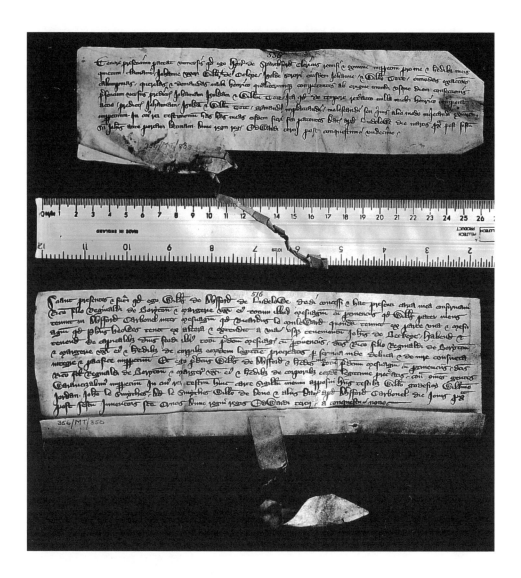

PLATE 17. (top) **#26**: SRR 356/MT/808 (Ludlow, Tuesday, May 13, 1337);
(bottom) **#24**: SRR 356/MT/350 (Ashford Carbonel, Thursday, May 4, 1335).
By permission of the Ludlow Town Council and the South Shropshire District.

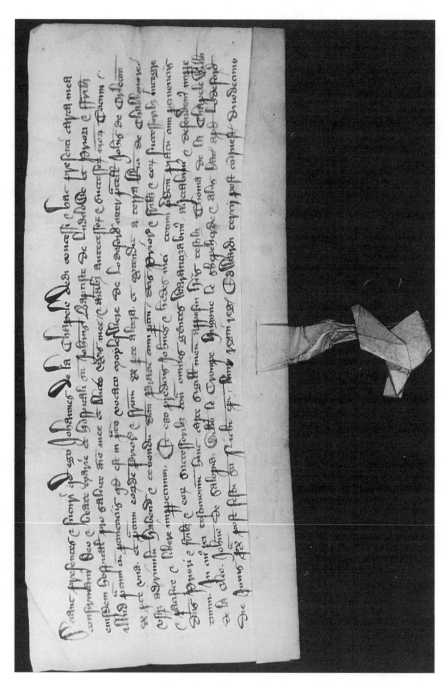

PLATE 18. **#27**: BL Addit. ch. 41302 (Ludford, December 10, 1338).
By permission of The British Library.

Scribe and Provenance

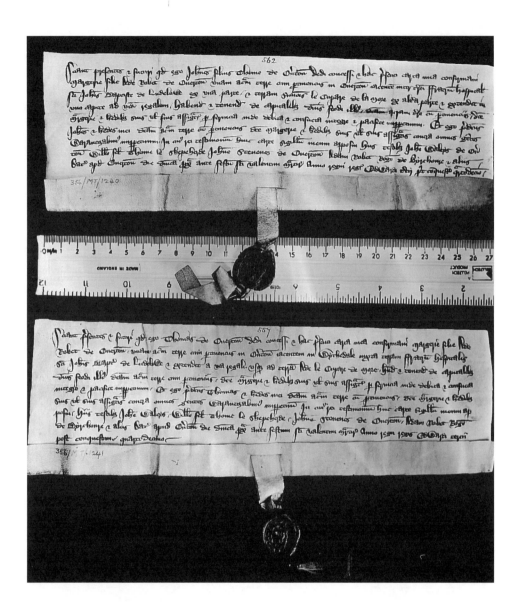

PLATE 19. (top) **#28**: SRR 356/MT/1240 (Overton, Sunday, February 13, 1340);
(bottom) **#29**: SRR 356/MT/1241 (Overton, Sunday, February 13, 1340).
By permission of the Ludlow Town Council and the South Shropshire District.

49

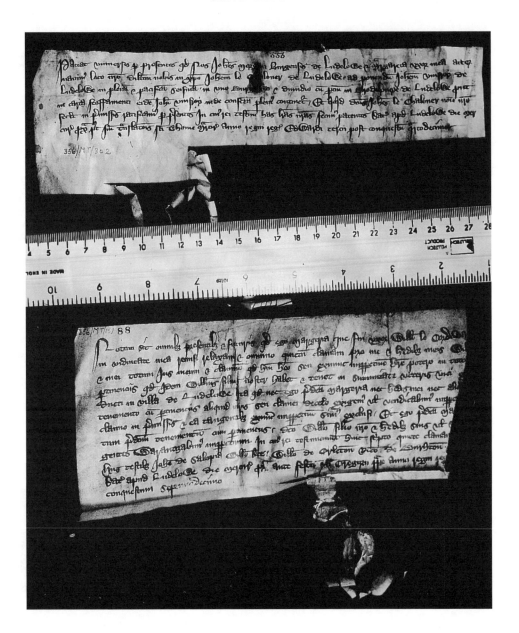

PLATE 20. (top) **#30**: SRR 356/MT/302 (Ludlow, Wednesday, July 12, 1340);
(bottom) **#34**: SRR 356/MT/157 (Ludlow, Wednesday, March 5, 1343).
By permission of the Ludlow Town Council and the South Shropshire District.

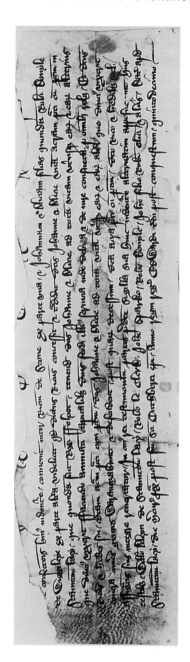

PLATE 21. **#31**: Bodleian Library, Craven Papers, vol. 63, fol. 6r, item 21
(Stanton Lacy, Wednesday, March 21, 1341).
By permission of the Bodleian Library, Oxford.

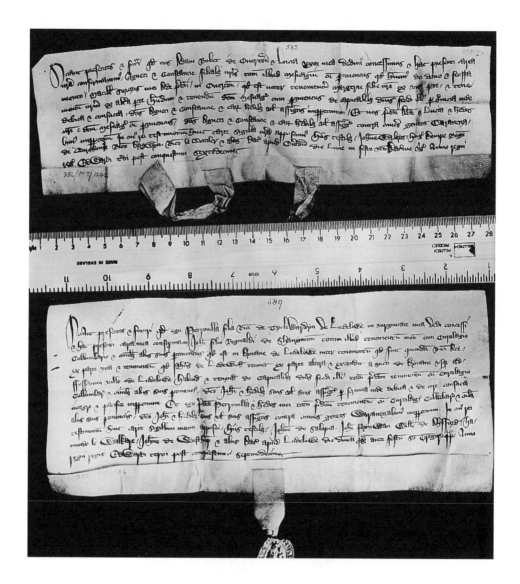

PLATE 22. (top) **#32**: SRR 356/MT/1242 (Overton, Monday, November 25, 1342); (bottom) **#35**: SRR 356/MT/478b (Ludlow, Sunday, March 9, 1343).
By permission of the Ludlow Town Council and the South Shropshire District.

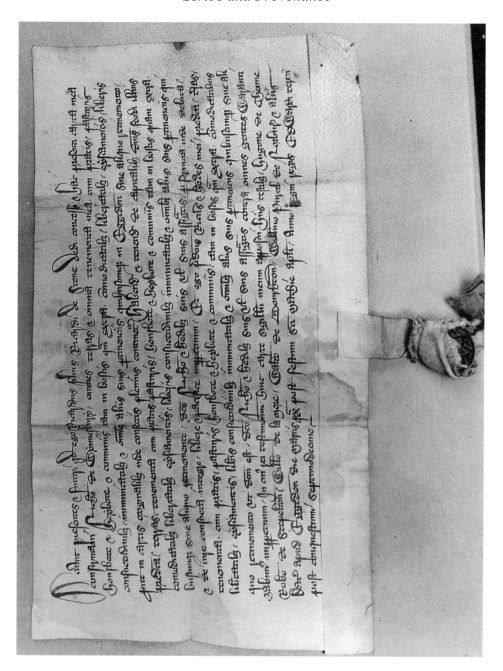

PLATE 23. **#33**: SRR 465/54 (Edgton, Tuesday, February 25, 1343).
By permission of the Ludlow Town Council and the South Shropshire District.

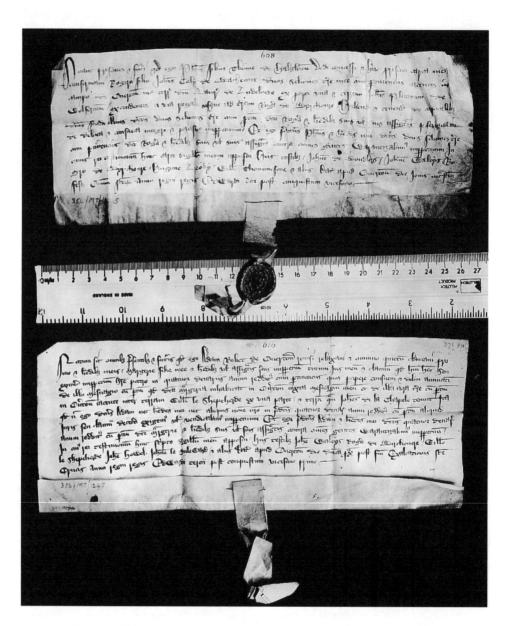

PLATE 24. (top) **#36**: SRR 356/MT/1245 (Overton, Thursday, November 2, 1346);
(bottom) **#39**: SRR 356/MT/1247 (Overton, Sunday, September 16, 1347).
By permission of the Ludlow Town Council and the South Shropshire District.

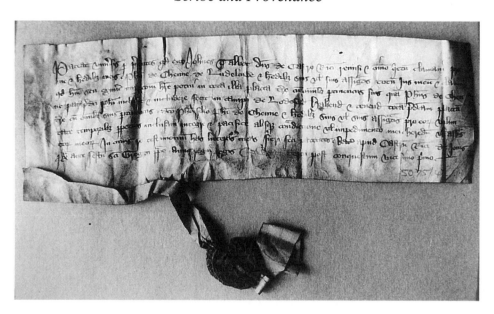

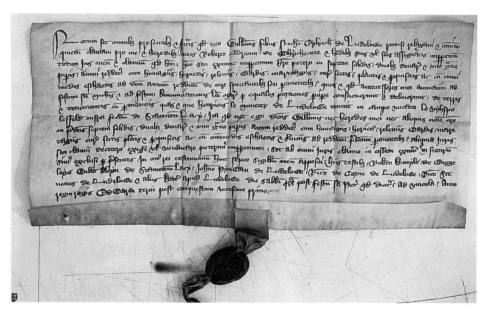

PLATE 25. (top) #37: SRR 5075/42 (Richard's Castle, Thursday, March 8, 1347)
By permission of the Ludlow Town Council and the South Shropshire District.
PLATE 26. (bottom) #38: SRR 20/5/76 (Ludlow, Saturday, August 4, 1347).
By permission of Lord Plymouth.

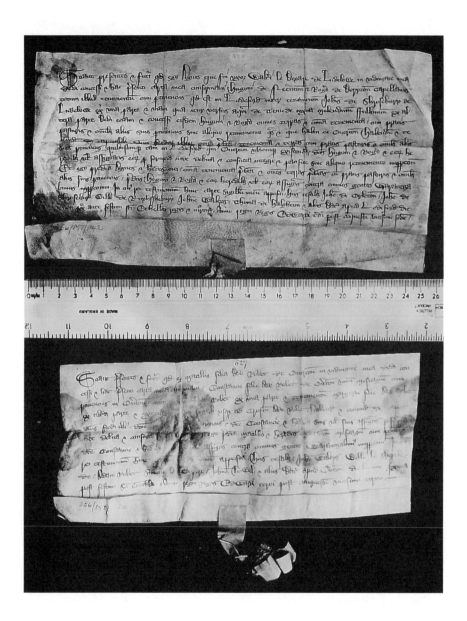

PLATE 27. (top) **#40**: SRR 356/MT/1142 (Ludford, May 18, 1348);
(bottom) **#41**: SRR 356/MT/1250 (Overton, April 13, 1349).
By permission of the Ludlow Town Council and the South Shropshire District.

just when the change of style (on this feature) occurred. Ker showed that the Harley scribe used the earlier curved stroke in portions of Royal 12.C.xii, but the later hooked *i* for other parts of Royal and in all of Harley 2253.

The example serves to illustrate our procedure for each of the criterial features by which the scribe's changes of style may be dated (see Table below, p. 59) — where feature *5a* is the earlier curving *i*-stroke and *5b* the later hooked one. In the column under *5a*, checkmarks occur from 1314–29 to show that this feature is present in every one of those holographs; under *5b* for those dates, however, no checkmarks occur, showing that no instances of the hooked *i* are present in any holograph from 1314–29. For the nineteen later holographs (1331–49) the columns contain numbers to indicate how many instances of *5a* or *5b* are found in each holograph: for instance in the two 1331 holographs, **#20** (Plate 12) has ten instances of *5a* and nine of *5b*, while **#21** (Plate 14) contains sixteen occurrences of *5a* and one hundred seventeen of *5b*.

The neatness with which the data can be sorted on this criterion — the kind of *i*-stroke — is such that we can say with fair certainty that any writing by the Harley scribe containing only *5a* is pre-1331, while any that contains some *5b* is post-1329. By this criterion, the "earlier" portions of Royal 12.C.xii are pre-1331, and all of Harley 2253 is post-1329, as are the "later" portions of Royal.

As is apparent from the Table, analysis of the holographs has established a number of such criterial features. The earliest changes in the scribe's hand are those at the left, numbers *1a*, *1b*, *1c*, and later changes are arranged in successive columns to the right as *2a*, *2b*, etc. Thus, feature *1a* is a form of capital *L* with hump-backed foot and split ascender, while feature *1b* retains the split ascender but has a smooth foot. Feature *1b* occurs first in 1316 (**#4**: *Laurencio*, *Ludelowe*, lines 2, 9), alongside the later *1c* (**#4**: *Le*, line 8; Plate 4), which has neither split ascender nor humped foot. Feature *1b* then disappears until 1346 (**#36**: *Laur[encii] de Ludelowe*, *Leoky*, lines 3, 9; Plate 24). Feature *1a* is therefore critical for literary texts in this hand, marking them as pre-1316, while *1b* probably marks them as about 1316, and *1c* as probably post-1316. (Instances of *1a*, *1b*, and *1c* are in the Plates.[22])

---

[22] Instances of the earliest form of *L* (*1a*) are found in **#1** in *Le*, *Ludelowe*, and *Lucie* (lines 1, 5, 9); other instances in the holograph of same date as this, **#2** (December 18, 1314), appear in *Ludelowe* and *Lucie* (lines 2, 3, 9, 10); see Plate 1. The latest occurrence of *1a* in the holographs is in **#3** (February 24, 1315, from Ludlow), in *Le*, *Ludelowe*, *Lune* (lines 1, 2, 3, 19); see Plate 2.

Instances of *1b* occur, in the holographs, mostly in **#4** (Plate 4), whose date is thus crucial for determining when the Harley scribe used this form. Unluckily, parts of the dating clause in **#4** are faded or missing. Decipherment is possible, however. First, we can read the year under ultraviolet as *nono*, meaning it is 9 Edward II, that is from July 8, 1315, through July 7, 1316. Since the weekday is shortly before the Feast of St. Mathias, the month must be February, which means the

No pages of either Royal 12.C.xii or Harley 2253 contain *1a*, but certain pages of Harley 273 do (fols. 181v–194r, 195v–197v, among others), and we may date those portions of Harley 273 (a final segment of the *Manuel des péchés* and all of the *Purgatoire s. Patrice*) as copied in 1314 or 1315. Elsewhere in Harley 273, however, we find work in the scribe's later style, for example, on fol. 85v some charms appear to be in a manner datable to ca. 1318–25, while on fol. 7v two indulgenced prayers (one from Pope John XXII, elected in 1316) look like holographs of 1318–21. It thus appears that the scribe's work in Harley 273 includes items done at various times over a considerable period, ca. 1314–29, even though there are not features indicating a date of post-1329 for any of the bits in his hand in this manuscript. Even a fifteen-year span of use would imply that Harley 273 was his own book or easily accessible in a way suggesting familial ownership if not personal possession by the scribe.

With Royal 12.C.xii there is also a wide range of copying dates for its different portions, from ca. 1316–40. As Parkes and the *Fouke* editors showed, its eight component "booklets" were acquired, copied, or assembled at different times.[23] The earliest one copied is fols. 62–68, containing the *Short Metrical Chronicle*, of which the final datable reference is to the death of Piers Gaveston in 1312. Paleographically, it can be assigned to ca. 1316–17, since it contains no *1a* but a mixture of *1b* and *1c* corresponding to holograph #4 (Plate 4) and also contains a mixture of *2a* and *2b* such as does not occur in any holograph later than 1320. It contains only the other paleographic features that are "early" rather than late: *3a*, *4a*, *5a*, *7a*, and a mixture of *8a* with *8b*. The holographic evi-

---

year must be 1316. In 1316, a leap year, the Feast of St. Mathias fell on February 25. Of the weekday we can just barely see the scribe ended it with a flourish, such as he used on either the abbreviated form of either Wednesday (*Mercur'*, as in **#1**, **#2**, **#18**, **#23**, **#30**, and **#34**), or Tuesday (*Mart'*, as in **#25**, line 9; he wrote out *martis* in **#26** and **#33**, lines 6 and 15, respectively). Since in 1316 February 25 fell on a Wednesday, it would make better sense for the scribe to have dated a document the day before that, i.e., on Tuesday, February 24, rather than the week before, Wednesday, February 18. Hence, we may conclude with fair certainty that **#4** is dated Tuesday, February 24, 1316. When we observe that in this holograph the scribe uses the "intermediate" form of *L* (*1b*) in *Laurencio, Lu-, Ludelowe* (lines 2, 9), while also using the later form *1c* in *Le Gaunter* (line 8), we seem justified in assuming that on February 24, 1316 the scribe was changing his manner of making *L* from *1a* to *1c*, and was using the intermediary *1b*, usually, but occasionally beginning to use *1c*.

The Harley scribe did revert to his earlier *1b* form in two very late holographs, however. In **#36** (November 2, 1346), he uses *1b* in *Laur' de Ludelowe, Leoky* (lines 2, 9; Plate 24). Again in **#40** (May 18, 1348), *Ludelowe, Lodeford* (lines 1, 3, 4) contain *1b*, while *Lodeford* (line 13) has form *1c* (Plate 27).

[23] See *FFW*, pp. xliv–liii.

Scribe and Provenance

TABLE. *Criterial changes in dated holographs*

No.	Date	L 1a	L 1b	L 1c	N 2a	N 2b	S 3a	S 3b	Split Ascenders 4a (Yes)	Split Ascenders 4b (No)	i 5a	i 5b	g 6a	g 6b	2-shaped r 7a	2-shaped r 7b	v-shaped r 8a	v-shaped r 8b	v-shaped r 8c	B 9a	B 9b
#1	1314	x			x		x		x		x		x		x		x				
#2	1314	x			x		x		x		x		x		x		x				
#3	1315	x					x			x	x		x		x		x	x			x
#4	1316		x	x			x			x	x		x		x		x				
#5	1316			x			x		x		x		x		x		x	x		x	
#6	1317			x			x			x	x		x		x			x		x	
#7	1317			x			x		x		x		x		x			x			
#8	1317			x			x		x		x		x		x			x		x	
#9	1318			x			x		x		x		x		x			x		x	
#10	1320			x			x		x		x		x		x		x	x		x	
#11	1320			x	x	x	x		x		x		x	1	x		x	x			
#12	1321			x		x	x		x		x		x		x		x	x		x	
#13	1321			x			x		x		x		x		x		x	x		x	
#14	1322-3			x			x		x		x		x		x			x			
#15	1325			x		x		x	x		x		x	1	x		x	x		x	
#16	1327			x				x	1		x		x	1	1			x		x	
#17	1327			x		x	x		x		x		x		2			x			
#18	1329			x				x	1		x		x		x			x		x	
#19	1329			x			x		x		x		x	1	2			x			
#20	1331							x		x	10	9	14	1	1			x		x	
#21	1331			x		x	x			x	16	117	28	1				x			
#22	1333			x				x		x	4	25	12	2				x		x	
#23	1333			x						x	7	23	14	1	2			x		x	
#24	1335			x			x			x	4	3	19	2				x		x	
#25	1335			x		x	x			x	7	2	10	2				x		x	
#26	1337			x			x			x	5	10	5					x			
#27	1338			x			x			x	11	5	6		1			x	x	x	
#28	1340			x			x			x	6	1	14			1		x	x	x	x
#29	1340			x			x			x	4	1	10	5		1		x	x		x
#30	1340			x		x	x			x	1	1	7			1		x	x	x	x
#31	1341			x			x			x	3	4	9					x			
#32	1342			x			x			x	4	1	14	3	1	4		x	x		x
#33	1343			x			x			x	22	22	12	3		9			x		x
#34	1343			x		x	x			x	4	5	8			5			x		x
#35	1343						x			x	5	6	11	4		1			x		
#36	1346		x				x			x	6	8	5	12					x		x
#37	1347						x			x	5	4	6	1		2		8	9		
#38	1347			x		x	x			x	13	10	18	10		3		20	20		1
#39	1347					x	x			x	2	3	4	12		3			x		x
#40	1348		x			x	x			x	3	5	18	2		4			x		
#41	1349			x			x	x		x	3	1	5	4					x		

dence thus confirms Ker's judgment that "the chronicle looks paleographically older than anything else [in Royal] and stops at 1312. It may well have been written not much later."[24] As Ker further points out, other items in Royal can be dated from their contents as late as 1338, and paleographic features confirm such dates, showing that, as Ker put it, "Royal was being added to over a number of years," ca. 1316–40.

For our purposes the most important dating within Royal is of the earlier and later portions of *Fouke*. The scribe began copying it on fol. 33, but broke off in the middle of line 28 on fol. 53r. Up to that point his style is clearly pre-1331, the only question being how much before 1331 he copied this section. By comparison with the holographs, it appears to be a product of the period 1321–29, most resembling items of 1325–29. It is later than 1316, since it contains no *1a* and usually has *1c*. It may belong to ca. 1325 since it contains mostly *3a* rather than *3b*, and the latter (sigmoid form of capital *S*, without vertical bar) appears to have become the nearly exclusive form used in holographs from 1325 onward, though in 1348 and 1349 the earlier *3a* is found. It has a few split ascenders (*4a*), and this too suggests it is not so late as 1329 but better matches the style of 1323–27. It has nearly all *8b*, again suggesting it is later than 1320–22, and perhaps pointing to 1325–27. It has only *5a*, no *5b*, showing it is pre-1331. Its particular form of curving *i*-stroke, its *virgula suspensiva*, and other features appear to match most closely the holographs of 1325–29, and if one had to choose the likeliest period it would be ca. 1325–27, though there are arguable reasons for a slightly earlier or slightly later date.[25]

---

[24] Ker, *Facsimile*, p. xxi.

[25] To judge from the single criterion of whether split ascenders on *l*, *b*, *h* appear in the Harley scribe's work, the earlier portion of *FFW* would seem to date from 1321–25 rather than from 1327–30. In the holographs, for instance, split ascenders are fairly common from 1317 through 1325, but thereafter appear only once in a document of 1327, and never in documents of 1329 or later. The scribe's use of split ascenders from May 7, 1317, through July 7, 1329, nearly always on the letter *l*, is as follows:

TOTALS

1	May 7, 1317	#8 SRR 356/MT/1213	*ul* 2
4	Mar. 5, 1318	#9 SRR 356/MT/1221	*howel* 2, *Chapele* 3, *ul* 4, 6
3	Apr. 18, 1320	#10 SRR 356/MT/555	*Coterel* 1, *ul* 8, 10
12	Dec. 8, 1320	#11 SRR 4032/1/13	*filuis* 1, *ul* 2, 3, 9 (twice), *omnibus* 4, *Ludelowe* 5, *aliquid* 9, *Heyton* 11, *aliis* 12, *Nicholai* 12, *fil.* 13
4	Apr. 13, 1321	#12 SRR 356/MT/1195	*simul* 6, *ul* 6, 7, *nichil* 6
1	1322–23	#14 SRR 356/MT/791	*Carbonel* 13 (document damaged, half missing)
4	Dec. 19, 1325	#15 SRR 356/MT/1227	*Clebury* 1, *Waleys* 2, *Blythelowe* 2, *Habendes* 4

The later portion of *Fouke* is clearly post-1329, as shown by the presence of *5b* (hooked *i*-stroke). It is impossible to say just how much after 1329 it was copied. However, it does not match very closely the two holographs from 1331, being less formal and calligraphic, a little more coarse and rapid in appearance. In these respects, it looks more like texts from 1333–40, though we may simply have a case of a long prose text being finished hastily after a considerable delay for some reason, and being written less carefully than a legal charter would be. In any event, the difference in appearance between earlier and later portions of *Fouke* appears to require a dating of ca. 1327 for the earlier and ca. 1333 for the later work. The interval might have been shorter — from, say, 1329 to 1331 — but it does not seem possible for it to have been a matter of a few months. The break had to be long enough for the change from earlier to later style to be quite pronounced, and a good guess would be that it was from ca. 1327–29 to at least 1333–35 (Appendix 3). In general appearance, the later portion of *Fouke* is perhaps closest to the two holographs of 1335, **#24** and **#25** (Plates 16, 17).

Finally, we may consider the dating of Harley 2253 on paleographic grounds. As Ker remarked, "Harley does not look as if it was written over a long period of years, but the last dozen leaves, perhaps from the point where the scribe begins to use a horizontal line to bound his writing at the top of the page, may well be a few years later than the rest."[26]

0	June 11, 1327	**#16** SRR 356/MT/796	no split ascenders
1	July 9, 1327	**#17** SRR 356/MT/560	*Habendum* 6
0	Jan. 4, 1329	**#18** SRR 356/MT/1228	no split ascenders
0	July 7, 1329	**#19** SRR 4032/1/14	no split ascenders

By way of comparison with the latest portion of the part of *FFW* copied in the Harley scribe's earlier manner, we may examine the split ascenders on fol. 53r, lines 1–27: there, we find 8 instances of split ascenders (*oyl* 4, *yl* 10, *bel* 10, *chevalers*15, *cel* 18, *quil* 20, *ql* 21, 26) occurring in some 360 words. This means that the scribe, just before he broke off copying *FFW*, averaged about one split ascender every 45 words. In the documents, those from 1318 through 1325 contain a total of about 1118 words, with 31 split ascenders, one every 36 words. This is also the average for the 1321 documents alone (9 splits in 338 words, an average of 37), and the 1325 document has abut 160 words, 4 splits, averaging 40 words per split.

It seems quite clear that the scribe changed his habits between 1325 and 1327, and that so far as the use of split ascenders is criterial, we can say that the earlier portion of *FFW* was copied before 1327. This date is in accord with the historical evidence from the first booklet in Royal 12.C.xii, fols. 1–7, where the presence of the piece honoring Thomas of Lancaster (fol. 1) must show that the booklet was begun no earlier than 1322, while the prophecy for 1325, altered to 1326 (fol. 6), tells us that the last portion of this booklet was not completed before 1326. These pages of Royal are most like the Harley scribe's work in the first portion of *FFW*, and most like the documents of 1321–27 of course. My guess would be that he copied *FFW* to fol. 53r in 1325–27.

[26] Ker, *Facsimile*, p. xxii.

61

All of Harley 2253 is post-1329 (criteria *5a*, *5b*), and much of it most closely resembles the holographs of 1340, but the scribe did not change his manner drastically between 1331 and 1340, so it is not easy to assign more precise dating to particular pages of Harley. However, the Table shows that certain features do change beginning about 1338 — these being the forms of 2-shaped *r* (*7a*, *7b*), v-shaped *r* (*8a*, *8b*, *8c*), and the forms of capital *B* (*9a*, *9b*). We already have a *terminus a quo* of 1338 for one item in Harley 2253, the poem *Against the King's Taxes* (no. 114),[27] and we may assume that the two items following this were copied later than 1338 also, though they are not internally datable, being religious items: we therefore have *Against the King's Taxes* at fols. 137v–138v, *Contemplacioun de la Passioun Iesu Crist* (no. 115) at fols. 138v–140r, and *De martirio sancti Wistani* (no. 116) on fol. 140v. We may now compare these with the holographs for the criterial features *7a*, *7b*, *8a*, *8b*, *8c*, *9a*, *9b*.

As shown in the Table, the earlier 2-shaped *r* occurs as the exclusive form in earlier holographs, and the first clear instance of the later calligraphic variant *7b* is in 1340: *7a* is exemplified in **#1** (December 18, 1314; Plate 1), *pistor*, line 1, and *7b* in **#28** and **#29** (both February 13, 1340; Plate 19), *More*, line 3. The most frequent and pronounced use of *7b* is in the 1342–43 holographs, and *7a* does not appear in them after 1342. Comparing with Harley 2253, we notice that in *Against the King's Taxes* there is a form almost intermediate between *7a* and *7b*, but the resemblance is more to *7a* in most instances (fol. 137v, lines 23, 24, 35; fol. 138r, lines 3, 19, 20, 22, 23, 27, 31, 37; fol. 138v, lines 4, 10, 11, 12). The conclusion is that *Against the King's Taxes* on this feature looks closer to 1338 than to 1340, but of course 1340 is possible. The subsequent items, however, show a tendency to use *7b* more often. In the *Contemplacioun*, *8b* occurs in *t'oreysoun* (fol. 139r, line 2), but *7a* in *moruz*, *reporta*, *hors* (fol. 139r, lines 4, 16, 32). In the same work on the next page (fol. 139v), *7b* occurs two times (lines 9, 29), *7a* three times (lines 6, 15, 19). And on fol. 140r, in the last portion of this *Contemplacioun*, only *7b* occurs (*vncore*, *hors*, *mort*, *cors*, lines 3, 21, 25, 26). These instances are fairly close in appearance to the occurrences of *7b* in the 1342–43 holographs. And finally, in the last text, *De martirio sancti Wistani* (fol. 140v), there are seven instances of *7b* and none of *7a*, and these are identical to the instances of *7b* in holographs from 1346, 1347, and 1348.[28]

---

[27] For discussion of this poem and its date, see E. B. Fryde, "Parliament and the French War, 1336–1340, " in his *Studies*, pp. 250–69, especially pp. 263–64 and n. 71. It is further explored by Harriss, *King*, pp. 250–52, and well discussed by J. R. Maddicott in "Poems of Social Protest in Early Fourteenth-Century England," in *England in the Fourteenth Century: Proceedings of the 1985 Harlaxton Symposium*, ed. W. M. Ormrod (Woodbridge, Suffolk, 1986), pp. 130–44.

[28] For *7b* on fol. 140v of Harley 2253 (counting title as line 1): *vxorem* 5, *patre* 8, *vxore* 14, *mortuus* 16, *dolores* 17, *immortalem* 18, *vxorem* 22, *Corpus* 29.

The criterial features of the 2-shaped *r* seem, then, to indicate that *Against the King's Taxes* was copied ca. 1338–40, or at least before 1342, and that the following folios of Harley 2253 (fols. 139 and 140) are post-1340, with the *Contemplacioun* copy being ca. 1342 and *De martirio sancti Wistani* perhaps 1343–48. These dates are the same as we deduce from another criterial feature, the v-shaped *r*. As the Table shows, the Harley scribe had an early form of this that was shallow and rather round-bottomed (*8a*), which by the 1320s was supplanted by a more sharp-pointed and crisp variant, still not extending below the line (*8b*), but this in turn gradually developed a deeper extension that by 1338 had some instances reaching well below the line (*8c*). Like *7b*, *8c* seems to have begun as a calligraphic variant. The scribe uses both *8b* and *8c* in the holographs of 1338–42, with *8c* favored for top lines and bottom lines.[29]

One finds *8c* rarely in Harley 2253 outside of its final folios. It occurs as a *litera notabilior* in the title of *King Horn* (no. 70; fol. 83r) and in top lines (for example, fol. 54ra, line 1, *regis*, *rege*). When we look at the later folios, we find that in *Against the King's Taxes* certain words on fol. 138v contain *8c*: *freyt*, *d'argent*, *parare*, *pacare*, *seruare*, *errores* (lines 1, 2, 4, 8, 9). Here the long-stemmed *r* resembles more closely those in the holographs of 1338–42. In the following text, *Contemplacioun de la Passioun Iesu Crist*, we find *8c* in the bottom-line words on fol. 139r but rarely within the text. In contrast, the final text, *De martirio sancti Wistani* (fol. 140v), has *8c* throughout. Once

---

[29] See, for instance, **#27** (December 10, 1338, from Ludford), where the long-stemmed *8c* appears in *confirmaui*, *futuri*, *presenti*, and *carta*, but in line 2 the shorter *8b* appears in *confirmaui*, *Marie*, *Priori*, and the rest of the charter (Plate 18). In **#28** and **#29** (both February 13, 1340, from Overton; Plate 19) we find relatively few of the long *8c* forms: in **#28**, line 1, *8c* appears in *futuri*, *carta*, but the shorter *8b* in *confirmaui*, *presentes* (these are, however, extended slightly below the line, as are most of the *8b* instances in this document); in **#29** all but one of the *r*'s are *8c* in line 1: *futuri*, *Ouerton*, *carta*, *Margerie* show *8c*, and only *confirmaui* has *8b*. This proportion holds elsewhere in **#29**, so we note that in two documents written on the same day and from the same place (Overton), the second uses the later more ornamental *r*-form much more than the first. In a third item from six months later than these, **#30** (July 12, 1340, from Ludlow; Plate 20), the scribe shortens the *8c* form and uses a good many of *8b* forms, probably because this is a six-line power of attorney rather than a large formal charter; but he does use a few longer forms (*Margareta* 1, *ratificamus* 5, and in the bottom line *cur'*, *regni*, *reg'*). In **#32** (November 25, 1342, from Overton), we find many ornamental 2-shaped *r*'s where we might expect the long-stemmed ones (*presenti* 1), but there are instances of *8c* (*carta* 1, *regni* 8, *reg'* 9), the rest being *8b* (Plate 22).

It is in the documents from 1343 that *8c* forms are common in the body of the text as well as in first and last lines. Holograph **#33** is consciously calligraphic, as befits a solemn document, and nearly all its *r*-forms are *7b* and *8c* (Plate 23). To a great extent this is true also of **#34** and **#35**, done within a few weeks of **#33** (Plates 20, 22). Obviously, in late February and early March of 1343, the scribe was at his professional best, and most careful.

again, the forms of *8b*, *8c* correspond in date to those of *7a*, *7b*, showing that fols. 137v–140r are ca. 1338–42, but that fol. 140v is later, probably 1343–49, being almost precisely like the 1346–47 holographs.[30]

The final criterial feature is capital *B*, of which an upright form (*9a*) was used to 1340 and a later cursive and more squat form (*9b*) favored 1342–49. The scribe used *9b* in *Brunselowe* (line 1) in the 1315 holograph **#3** (not discovered until July 31, 1980; Plate 2), so we must conclude that the cursive *9b* was always an option, but in all of the other pre-1340 legal documents the more formal *9a* was used. In most of Harley 2253 only *9a* appears, with *9b* the exclusive variant only on fol. 140v (lines 11, 21, 23, 26). So far as the form of *B* is criterial, then, it suggests that all of Harley 2253 was copied by ca. 1340–42 except for fol. 140v, which is most like the holographs of 1346–47, as already stated.

Limited by space, we cannot here discuss fully the nature and contents of the Harley scribe's holographs (but see Appendix 2), the individuals and groups who are the principals in them, and their social milieu and interrelations. I hope to offer more detail in a book on the Harley scribe now in progress. For the present, having dated the various portions of each of the scribe's manuscripts, we may use this knowledge to sketch the scribe's developing intellectual and professional interests during his career.

---

[30] The difference between work of 1342–43 and that of 1346–48, in the holographs, appears distinctly in the 2-shaped *r*. In 1343 particularly this *7b* form is crisp, ornamental, and fluently made with no messy jointure-marks where the extension below that line was added, but in 1347 the 2-shape has become more narrow and laterally compressed, the lower spike is more vertically extended rather than curving crescent downward to the left. For comparison, we may cite **#33** (Plate 23), *presentes*, *presenti* (line 1) versus **#39** (Plate 24) *quatuor* (lines 6, 7); in **#39** *quatuor* (line 3) is more like the 2-shaped *r* of **#33**, but its lower spike is longer though curved.

In **#40** (May 18, 1348, from Ludford; Plate 27) the form of *7b* in *vxor* (line 1), *Lodeford* (lines 3, 8) is again more vertical, compressed, and unevenly formed than in the 1343 deeds. There are no instances of *7b* in the 1346 or 1349 documents.

A close comparison of Harley 2253, fol. 140v, with the documents shows that so far as the shape of *7b* is concerned., fol. 140v contains forms matching almost exactly the 1347–48 documents' instances of *7b*. If I had to judge just when the Harley scribe wrote fol. 140v, it would be 1347 or thereafter, and N. R. Ker has suggested that it was written very nearly at the same time as **#39** — that is, about September 1347. (In a letter of October 5, 1980, to the present writer, he writes: "I am perfectly prepared to think that f. 140v was written in about the middle of September 1347.") I had earlier thought the best date might be 1343–46, but close study has convinced me that Dr. Ker is — as would be expected — precisely right.

Scribe and Provenance

The Harley Scribe's Training and Interests as Educed from the Manuscripts

The Harley scribe's three books differ in make-up and function. Harley 273 was made for devotional and instructive purposes. Royal 12.C.xii is in part the Harley scribe's commonplace book, though much of it is also instructive and devotional, and only indirectly reveals personal interests. Harley 2253 is, in contrast, an anthology carefully selected and structured to comprise a wide range of interests: aesthetic in the rhyme-craft of its lyrics; religious and devotional in its *vitae*, hymns, and prayers; political in its protests of royal and seignorial prises, taxes, and purveyances. Since our focus is on the provenance of Harley 2253, it is the political pieces we shall view most closely, for they are likely clues to the probable patrons. As necessary context to these, however, his two earlier books need scrutiny for pointers to his career and developing interests.

The manuscripts show the Harley scribe to be trilingual, and the holographs show him knowledgeable in law. Such skills point to certain kinds of social status and training, while the range of texts which he copied or assembled illuminates both his professional and personal interests and, therefore, the *raisons d'etre* of his manuscripts. His legal charters were produced from forms such as those still extant in London, BL MS Harley 274, so his training was very much like that given by Thomas Sampson, who provided such training in Oxford, ca. 1346–1409. What Sampson taught, as he put it, was "how to keep the reckoning of his lord's expenditure and write his letters," which Sampson claimed he could teach in six months or so if the student paid him well and was diligent. Textbooks used by Sampson — letterbooks and formularies — survive, and a model letter in one of them shows us what a young scribe was, or aspired to be. This letter tells of a young man who, having "gone up to Oxford to read for a degree in arts," subsequently hears from his father that the earl of W. is "prepared to take the young man into his service the following year," and the father adjures his son to put himself under the tutelage of Thomas Sampson in "writing, composition, and accounting," and so that he can be sure of good teaching, "to pay his master 100 shillings."[31]

---

[31] H. G. Richardson, "Business Training in Medieval Oxford," *American Historical Review* 46 (1941): 259–80; the quotes appear on pp. 259–60. See also Richardson's other articles: "An Oxford Teacher of the Fifteenth Century," *Bulletin of the John Rylands Library* 23 (1939): 436–57; and "Letters of the Oxford *Dictatores*," in *Formularies Which Bear on the History of Oxford 1204–1420*, ed. H. E. Salter, W. A. Pantin, and H. G. Richardson, Oxford Historical Society, n.s. 5 (Oxford, 1942), pp. 329–450. In the latter, Richardson cites the collection of formularies by an Oxford "business-school" teacher, William Kingsmill, in which there is introduced "a boy of twelve, the son of the hostess of an Oxford inn, who is attending a school kept by Kingsmill, where he is learning writing, composition, bookkeeping, and spoken French. The boy expects to become an apprentice in London" (p. 341 and n. 4). For Cistercian formularies, see the same article, pp.

Lest such studies be thought extremely perfunctory and illiberal, we may recall here that the medieval letter-writing arts were highly developed, as James J. Murphy's work illustrates.[32] Certain textbook collections intended by Thomas Sampson for use in teaching these arts have survived, and one of them will illustrate such a cleric's curriculum: Cambridge, University Library MS Ee.iv.20, which now has three parts. In Part I we find treatises on conveyancing and on wills; a tract on the office of coroner; the office of clerk in a noble household; precedents for bills and writs; precedents in a seignorial court; and a tract on Latin composition. In Part II there are a treatise on French composition; French vocabularies; the *Orthographia Gallica*; verb conjugations in French and Latin; a French tract on heraldry.[33] In Part III there is another tract on French composition. We see that "business training" involved much grammar and rhetoric: letters from a noble or mercantile household, addressed perhaps to other nobles or to ecclesiastical prelates as well as to other merchants, had to be, however formulaic, as elegant as possible. Moreover, keeping accounts and supervising households would sometimes involve such officials in legal matters.

That such "secretaries" of noble households could indeed copy manuscripts, rather than handle purely business tasks of correspondence and account-keeping and legal matters, is shown from an example of the next century, in France. As C. E. Pickford has shown, a certain Barthelemi Cousinet, *secretaire* to the Duke of Nemours, testified that during his final two years in the duke's service he did little else but copy romances and devotional books, but he did use his spare time to "expedier requestes, mandemens, assignacions et autres lectres pactentes tant aux officiers du Duc de Nemours que aux autres ses subgetz pour les communs affaires" [draw up and send the requests, orders, assignments, and other letters patent, both to officials and others of the Duke de Nemours's subjects, concerning the Duke's business affairs].[34] Malcolm Parkes has shown in rich detail how such

---

279–328.

[32] James J. Murphy, *Rhetoric in the Middle Ages: A History of Rhetorical Theory from Saint Augustine to the Renaissance* (Berkeley, 1974) and (ed.) *Medieval Eloquence: Studies in the Theory and Practice of Medieval Rhetoric* (Berkeley, 1978); in the former, Chap. 5, "*Ars dictaminis*: The Art of Letter-Writing," pp. 194–269; in the latter, the essay by C. B. Faulhaber, "The *Summa Dictaminis* of Guido Faba," pp. 85–111.

[33] In Harley 2253 there is a whole page (fol. 131r) listing the arms of kings.

[34] C. E. Pickford, "A Fifteenth-Century Copyist and His Patron," in *A Medieval Miscellany, Presented to Eugene Vinaver*, ed. F. Whitehead, A. H. Diverres, and F. E. Sutcliffe (Manchester, 1965), pp. 245–62, at p. 257. Compare the 1347 letters patent provided by the Harley scribe for John, Lord Talbot of Richard's Castle, now SRR 5075/42 (see Appendix 2, **#37**).

combined literary and business scrivening is implicit in the very existence of so many manuscripts that are, as is Harley 2253, in the "business" script.[35]

There are obvious models of such scribes, both family factotums and professional scriveners, laid out in prosopographic detail by Norman Davis and A. I. Doyle. Davis sketches the career of James Gloys, who was a priest serving the Pastons from at least 1448 to his death in 1473, "performing general clerical and estate duties as well as acting as chaplain."[36] Gloys was rewarded only a year before his death by presentation to the benefice of Stokesby, and he served as a "special confidant" to old Margaret, the redoubtable wife of John Paston I, in her widowhood. In contrast to this family priest is the professional scrivener William Ebesham, who wrote one letter for John Paston II, many legal documents (copied several times over on paper and on parchment), and also much of the "Great Book" which John Paston II commissioned. His work for the Pastons was apparently early in his career (1468), and Doyle has traced his manuscript copying for other patrons to at least 1497. Ebesham did not simply live near the Pastons and do work there; he worked for them both at their Norfolk estates and while he was living in London, doing both their legal and their literary work; and for other patrons — particularly the monks of Westminster Abbey — he copied books of mainly devotional and theological material. His books, as Doyle summarizes them, were "made at different times, with different materials, embracing different matter and envisaging different readers."[37]

It would therefore be perfectly usual for a cleric-chaplain to assemble a book such as Harley 273, as did the Harley scribe about 1314–15. This manuscript was more gathered than copied by him, but his earliest work in it shows him to be interested in matter that a young priest or chaplain would need. At fols. 113–197, where his earliest work is found, there is a textura copy (not in his hand) of the *Manuel des péchés* which apparently lacked its final portion; the Harley scribe has copied its final segment (fols. 181v–191v) and added a neat tabular schema, also in Latin, of the venial and mortal sins involving swearing (fol. 190vb). Following this, he collaborated with a second scribe in copying the *Purgatoire s. Patrice* (fols. 191v–197v) — a French verse romance in which a knight observes the torments in purgatory. The Harley scribe copied lines 1–372, 551–858 of this piece; the other scribe did lines 373–550. Other places where his work appears in this early section are in the bottom margins of fols. 114v and 116v, where he has copied Latin verses

---

[35] M. B. Parkes, "The Literacy of the Laity," in *Literature and Western Civilization [vol. 2:] The Mediaeval World*, ed. David Daiches and A. K. Thorlby (London, 1973), pp. 555–77.

[36] Norman Davis, ed., *Paston Letters and Papers of the Fifteenth Century*, 3 vols. (Oxford, 1971–76), 1.lxxvi.

[37] A. I. Doyle, "The Work of a Late Fifteenth-Century Scribe, William Ebesham," *Bulletin of the John Rylands Library* 39 (1956–57): 298–325, at p. 308.

on the length of Adam's stay in hell (which he later copied in part into Royal 12.C.xii, fol. 6v) and on the Credo. Since the *Manuel des péchés* is a handbook of the kind episcopal constitutions prescribed — its contents including what priests needed to teach their parishioners with regard to doctrine and admonition — and since it includes many exempla usable for preaching purposes — these exempla being carefully marked with marginal glosses "*in ex.*" — it is obvious that the Harley scribe in 1314–15 was obtaining and in part copying material needed by a candidate for ordination and aspirant to a benefice. The schema on swearing suggests a confessor or one training to act as a confessor. The Harley scribe's marginalia at fols. 114v and 116v of the *Manuel* point to his actually studying those parts of it that he did not himself copy. The picture we get is of a young man in clerical orders beyond the minor orders or aspiring to be so ordained to acolyte or subdeacon, in 1314–15.

There are other texts in the scribe's hand in Harley 273, from a later date, that show his devotional and medical interests. At fol. 7r he copied two indulgenced prayers from popes Urban IV and John XXII. Since the latter was elevated in 1316, obviously the scribe's copy postdates that; paleographically it looks to be from ca. 1318–21. At fols. 85v and 112v, the scribe has copied charms against fever, wounds, and bleeding, again in writing datable to a period later than 1316 — that of fol. 85v perhaps 1317–21, while that of fol. 112v is perhaps a bit later than that. These pieces show that the Harley scribe still had Harley 273 in his possession and was treating it as his book, copying devotional and other material into blank pages or columns of it at least ten years later than the earliest work in it by him. We find small scraps and pieces elsewhere that confirm this: at fol. 81ra (last two lines) he has added "*Issinc fine Bestaire damours*"; on fol. 85va (line 17) he wrote "*Explicit*" at the end of the short French prose piece *Twelve Rules of Friendship* (in textura); and on fol. 214v (line 35, left margin) he supplied a corrective gloss on dismal days to the text (in textura) which had omitted them: "*In mayo .iiij. / dies .vij.xv. / xvj.xxj. / In aug .ii dies. / ix.xx.*"[38]

For further consideration of the Harley scribe's interests and career, the one remaining scrap is of some importance: at fols. 81r–85r Harley 273 contains a textura copy of Bishop Grosseteste's *Rules* for the management of a seignorial household, and at fol. 82ra (line 35) the scribe has completed a line omitted in the original, writing in "*Ce serra ix^e quart(er)s*" to specify the correct amount of grain involved in the sowing and management of arable demesne land, the topic under discussion at that point in the *Rules*. On the same page (margin to left of line 30) he wrote "*xxvii*" as clarifying gloss for the numeral

---

[38] He copied into Royal 12.C.xii, fol. 90v, a listing of the dismal days that agrees with this corrected version in Harley 273, and in Royal turned the Latin into French prose and wrote out the numerals as words to avoid mistakes. It seems he was using that portion of Harley 273 as a *pecia* to make his own "text" here.

obscurely written within the line there.[39] That the Harley scribe wanted a copy of Grosseteste's *Rules* points to his being interested in serving within or even managing a large household; that he made such additions and corrections proves that he paid minute attention to its text precisely where it concerns how to manage the farming of demesne land. Such interests in demesne management and household rules in a man otherwise studying or teaching doctrine, hearing confession, and perhaps preaching point, I suggest, to a household cleric and chaplain. A parson with glebe would, of course, want to study and practice some farming, but Grosseteste's *Rules* were originally written for the countess of Lincoln, and thus meant as an outline of procedures for a person handling a large estate.[40]

During 1314–28, then — to sum up the evidence in Harley 273 — the Harley scribe was obtaining and in part copying texts devotional, penitential, and administrative, combining study of priestly learning and tasks with interest in demesne and in estate or household management. The fact that Harley 273 also contains a calendar with the dedication date of Ludlow parish Church of St. Laurence rubricated (fols. 1–6) tells us that the scribe's early studies were done either in Ludlow or by a man closely connected with Ludlow, and this inference is corroborated by his holographs from 1314. Finally, in Harley 273 there is also an illuminated Psalter, Benedicite, Te Deum, Credo, Litany, Office for Virgin Mary, and Placebo (incomplete) at fols. 8r–69v, all in textura. The Psalter in French suggests that this was a book for a secular rather than a regular cleric, and the collection of these items suggests further the book's being primarily for devotional and secondarily for professional administrative purposes of its compiler. That he was interested in private meditation is made likely by the exercises in Latin keyed to diagrams of right and left hands (fols. 110r–112r) that follow a treatise on confession and penance and precede one on the Seven Gifts of the Holy Spirit.

Turning now to Royal 12.C.xii, we find it includes several kinds of matter not present in Harley 273: history, political texts, games, recipes, prophecies, texts on prognostication

---

[39] It is notable that the scribe's textura copies of Richard de Fournival's *Bestiaire d'amour* and Bishop Grosseteste's *Rules* are not separately presented texts: *Bestiaire* ends at fol. 81ra, and *Rules* begins on the same page (fol. 81rb). *Bestiaire* is finely illustrated with pen drawings (see, for example, the frontispiece to this volume), whereas *Rules* is plain text (almost entirely). This fact is of interest since the "continuity" of *Bestiaire* and *Rules* suggests that literary, doctrinal, and "practical" texts were not isolated or pigeonholed as separate.

[40] Alice de Lacy, countess of Lincoln, was the widow of Thomas of Lancaster. Some time before November 10, 1324, she married Eubelo LeStrange, whose sister-in-law, Isolda LeStrange of Knockin, was served in 1320 by Richard Ludlow of Stokesay, a lawyer and portioner in Westbury, 1308–21 (Hamon LeStrange, *LeStrange Records: A Chronicle of the Early LeStranges of Norfolk and the March of Wales A.D. 1100–1310* [London, 1916], pp. 271–86; 274).

and interpretation of dreams, and ancestral romance. The *Short Metrical Chronicle* (fols. 62–68) was copied ca. 1316 and is the Harley scribe's earliest work in this book. Perhaps the year after he copied this, or a little later, he obtained a doctrinal and devotional treatise, the *Merour d'eglise* (fols. 17–30, with chapter headings in his hand), and a tract on the mass (fols. 30v–32v, of which the last five lines may be in his hand). The *Chronicle* is a spare, versified history of England that ends with the death of Piers Gaveston in 1312, so it appears the Harley scribe wanted a history brought very nearly up to the present. At the same time he was going on with the devotional and doctrinal studies that we saw in Harley 273. About 1322–27, he copied two other pieces that show his interest in history could be both personal and political: the liturgical collection honoring Thomas of Lancaster as a saint (fol. 1), which must have been copied after 1322 since Lancaster was executed in that year (it closely resembles the 1321–25 holographs), and *Fouke*, of which the earlier folios (fol. 33r to fol. 53r, line 21) match the handwriting of the 1321–27 holographs and most closely resemble those of 1325–27. From this 1322–27 period we have in fact the entire commonplace booklet of fols. 1–7, which includes a prophecy for 1293 and another for 1325, corrected to 1326; recipes for dyeing linen; a Latin satire on avaricious clerics (which could be assumed to point to some rather stiff competition for benefices and household appointments or legal assignments); verses on phlebotomy; rules for interpreting dreams; hymns to the Virgin Mary; lines on the death of St. Thomas Becket; and so on. Some of these pieces are copied by the Harley scribe from elsewhere: two lines on the length of Adam's stay in hell (fol. 6v), for instance, he had earlier copied into Harley 273 (fol. 112v), while the lines on phlebotomy occur twice in Royal.[41]

The commonplace booklet of fols. 1–7 therefore shows him recopying scraps that he had elsewhere written as part of longer works, adding political, satiric, and devotional items, as well as household recipes (linen-dyeing) and the like. Since he was at about this time copying *Fouke*, the impression one gains is of a man who had obtained preferment but who was not entirely pleased with national affairs, perhaps being a follower or partisan of Thomas of Lancaster. His interests and studies during the period 1322–27 show up also in fols. 77–107, a booklet whose handwriting seems later rather than earlier in this period, even at a few places resembling the 1329–30 work. The texts are all in the Harley scribe's hand, and most of the booklet is concerned with prognostications, medical notes, palmistry, and *sortes*. These may have been further studies that a cleric or priest might want for his household or parish duties, rather than being merely personal interests. One item, the Latin prose *Somnia Danielis* on interpreting dreams (fols. 81v–86r), is a source for the unique English verse treatise on dreams found in Harley 2253 (no. 85; fols.

---

[41] Fol. 91r, lines 3 ff., are also at fol. 5va, lines 18 ff.; fol. 91r, lines 18 ff., occur again on fol. 7r, lines 18 ff.

119ra–121ra).[42] The Latin piece has its contents arranged by alphabetic order — e.g., dreams involving *arma* precede those involving *aves*; of course, when the tract is translated, the English verses leap from *Arms* (fighting) to *Birds*, and in many cases the result is an apparent hodgepodge.

Another item in Royal is a textura copy of *Ami et Amile* (fols. 69r–76v). The scribe has not annotated it, but on the final blank page (fol. 76v) he copied two items:[43] a hymn to Mary, which paleographically is datable (by its curved *i*-stroke) as *earlier* than 1331; and a poem on the vanity of human life, which is datable *after* 1330 (hooked *i*-stroke, most closely similar to holographs of 1331–35). Since *Ami et Amile* is the very popular and moral romance on the classic friendship unto death of two knights, it continues the earlier interest in friendship shown in Harley 273's *Twelve Rules of Friendship*, which will recur in Harley 2253's *Enseignement sur les amis* (no. 26; fols. 61v–62v). Just as a priest's or chaplain's book might be expected to include a good deal on the subject of *amour*, including the pros and cons of the love of women (with cons getting more space), so it would be sure to have some didactic pieces on true friendship and on gracious manners — in other words, courtesy literature. The Harley scribe obtained the textura copy of *Ami and Amile* before 1331, as shown by the hymn copied before 1331 on fol. 76v, and after 1330 he then copied the poem on the vanity of human life below the hymn; so the booklet was in his hands, and presumably part of his reading, during the 1320s, probably 1325–30.

The Harley scribe was still assembling and copying parts of Royal in the next decade: fols. 8–16 and 53–61 are paleographically post-1331, and the prophecies in fols. 8–16 date from 1335 and 1338. He also resumed copying *Fouke* (onto fols. 53–61) in the 1330s, after a break of up to ten years (ca. ?1328–38). The division occurs just in the middle of a scene in which Fouke by a clever disguise and ruse is about to capture the villainous King John. Obviously the Harley scribe was not working on a commission or a deadline; this break and resumption would seem to show a personal or familial interest in the text rather than a professional scrivener's concern, the kind of interest suited to a man producing *Fouke* for himself or his patron-household rather than for a remote patron.[44]

As for the separate booklet that is now fols. 8–16, it is a miscellany containing a collection of mathematical problems, puzzles, and cooking recipes (the puzzles in Latin, the recipes in French); prophecies relating to the early years of Edward III and to the year 1337 or 1338; and a "fictitious letter from a Christian in the East describing the rise of the false Christ in the summer 1335," as the *Fouke* editors describe it (p. xlix). Paleographically it looks to be 1335–40, and its items show the Harley scribe interested in the study

---

[42] On the dream treatise in Harley 2253, see Helen Phillips's essay in this volume (pp. 241–59).

[43] See Ker, *Facsimile*, p. xx and nn. 4–5 there.

[44] For hypotheses as to why the Harley scribe broke off copying when he did, see Appendix 3.

or teaching of mathematics (though some of these are party-game mathematical puzzles); in prophetical and prognosticative material pertinent to the 1330s; and in good eating and cookery for a household, during the decade 1331–40 or so.[45] Evidently his late-1320s interest in palmistry, *sortes*, and prophecies had carried over into the 1330s. The final booklet of Royal (in its present format), fols. 108–23, contains the *Liber experimentarius*, astrological *sortes* translated from Arabic, and is not in the scribe's hand. We cannot be sure whether this piece dates from 1330 or later because the scribe did not annotate it.

To summarize the Harley scribe's work in Royal 12.C.xii during ca. 1316–40: from about 1316–22 he copied material involving English history and doctrinal or devotional topics (*Chronicle*, *Merour*, tract on the Mass). During 1322–27 he copied the first part of

---

[45] Space forbids all but bare mention here of the items in fols. 8–16. The French recipes could only have been for a quite wealthy if not noble household; an English translation of them is found in Friar William Herebert of Hereford's manuscript, London, BL Addit. MS 46919. A Magister Walter de Lodelowe was head of Queen Isabella's kitchen in 1334–36 (*CPR 1330–34*, p. 538; *CPR 1334–38*, p. 101), but in July 1336 was replaced by another man. Another item copied into this booklet of Royal 12.C.xii (fol. 16v) in the 1330s or so is a version (incomplete by loss of leaf) of the story of the "Miraculous Oil of St. Thomas Beckett," perhaps in relation to the diplomacy between English and French as they moved towards beginning the Hundred Years' War. Among the diplomats in these and earlier negotiations was Adam Orleton, successively bishop of Hereford (1317–27), Worcester (1327–33), and Winchester (1334–45). In 1319 Edward II had sent Orleton to Avignon to try and persuade Pope John XXII to obtain papal sanction for this "miraculous oil," whose legend tells that the Virgin Mary gave it to Becket while he was in exile, along with a prophecy that in future it would be used to consecrate a certain English king. Orleton took with him on this 1319 mission Thomas Talbot, younger clerical brother of Richard Talbot of Richard's Castle. The pope politely refused to give the oil any special sanction, so Edward II could not use it (as he had wished) to gain extra stature in his struggles with barons at home and French rivals abroad (who themselves had the superior chrism-oil of Charlemagne). I suggest that in the 1330s Edward III, who would assert his claim to the French throne in 1340, was considering use of the Becket oil for similar prestige. Pope John XXII died in 1334, so the new pope (so I suppose Edward and his diplomats hoped) might sanction the oil, which then could be used in a coronation of Edward III as king of France as well as of England. That would perhaps have been contemplated as to occur sometime after his 1338 invasion of France, his election as vicar of the Holy Roman Emperor, and his adoption of the title of King of France. The Becket oil was also considered for use by later kings of England (Richard II, Henry IV) since it came with a prophecy of great European power as well as splendid English reign. See J. R. S. Phillips, "Edward II and the Prophets," in *England in the Fourteenth Century*, ed. Ormrod, especially pp. 196–202. In the above scenario, one may suggest that the scribe was most likely to have copied the Becket piece about 1337–41, a date which fits its handwriting well.

Fouke and a good many prophetic, prognosticative, physiognomic, and psychological works, as well as certain political items (*Thomas of Lancaster*) and others pointing to interest in episcopal affairs (seal-mottoes of bishops of Swinfield and Orleton). About 1327–30 he worked most on prognostication and dream interpretation, but he had by then obtained the courtesy literature apparent in *Ami et Amile* (and in Harley 273's *Twelve Rules of Friendship*). Throughout 1322–30 he copied, now and then, hymns and devotional items. During the period 1338–41 or so, he returned to and completed copying *Fouke*, as well as prophetic or other pieces for the period 1327–38, and he also copied mathematical problems and cookery-recipes which point, I believe, to his being the member of a household to which his knowledge of these might be useful.

Chronologically, the later work in Royal (1331–40) overlaps, probably, with at least some of that in Harley 2253, and in at least one instance a text he copied into Royal in Latin (*Somnia Danielis*) was put into an English version for Harley 2253 (*A Bok of Sweuenyng*, no. 85). It seems likely that most of Royal, being in French or Latin, is aimed at a securely literate audience, whereas Harley 2253 has a good deal of English and might presuppose therefore listeners or readers unlikely to know Latin or French (in some members at least). This argument, however, is weaker than it might seem: since the English poems in Harley 2253 are unusually ornate and intricately wrought, quite possibly we have here early instances of a Chaucerian kind of effort at embellishment of the native tongue — and an audience who, knowing Latin and French, would the better appreciate a skillful use of English. Such a view would imply Harley 2253 to be, among other things, a deliberate display of the art of composing in English. This would be true even if the Harley scribe had simply culled the "best" alliterative poetry from all over England, and composed none himself. In fact, however, some of the "Harley Lyrics" are in dialects matching that of the Ludlow area, and he himself might therefore have composed such a piece as *Alysoun* (no. 29; fol. 63v).

We have here already begun discussing the contents of Harley 2253, but its amorous and religious lyrics offer but weak evidence as to its provenance, so we may now turn to its political and historical pieces. These show that the manuscript reflects the events of the political and social crisis of 1340–41, and the poems chosen by its compiler offer views of the political scene that closely match those of the earl of Arundel and his group during that crisis. They also suffer complaints that seem especially close to those we might expect of someone like Sir Laurence Ludlow of Stokesay Castle, considering his personal circumstances at the time, circumstances of abuse and harassments by royal officials and judges.

The Political Poems as Clues to the Scribe's Provenance and Patrons

Just as the Harley scribe had previously copied into Royal 12.C.xii the "liturgical" pieces that treat Thomas of Lancaster as a saint (ca. 1322–27), the political poems in Harley 2253 consistently champion the Lancastrian and ecclesiastical positions as applied to events and struggles of 1338–42 — particularly as these positions were argued in 1340–41 by some of the king's home council, notably Richard FitzAlan, earl of Arundel.[46] The home council's handling of affairs during the king's campaigns in France was under heavy attack by the king and his counsellors (Kilsby, Darcy) from the time the king returned in late 1340 through much of 1341. As detailed by G. L. Harriss, Arundel and others had to defend their efforts to raise the exorbitant taxes and levies which had been granted the king, while at the same time they were explaining to the king the national destitution and resistance rising almost to rebellion that had prevented their sending the king enough money to keep his French campaigns going.[47] Harriss assigns to 1338–39 the Harley 2253 poem *Against the King's Taxes*, as had Isabel Aspin, N. R. Ker, and E. B. Fryde,[48] and he points out that it is not mere tirade but a "coherent indictment of the level of taxation as unnecessary and harmful to the common good, and . . . a charge of fundamental misgovernment" which "in language and argument . . . *strikingly anticipates the petitions of the Commons in Parliament in 1340*," pointing for instance to "the likelihood of a peasant rising" and thus showing "*the mood of the lesser landowning classes in England*" (emphases mine).

Of course, the date and social events referred to by this poem have been well known since Aspin edited it in her 1953 *Anglo-Norman Political Poems*, and it is no new proposal that it was composed in 1338–39, nor any surprise that it should have been copied soon after the events. But it is a little more surprising, on the surface, that certain other political poems were copied into Harley 2253 at the same time, when they were certainly composed much earlier: *A Song of Lewes* and *Lament for Simon de Montfort* (nos. 23, 24) in

---

[46] An excellent account of the crisis of 1340–41, with special attention to the church-versus-state dimension, is given by Haines, *Archbishop John Stratford*, pp. 278–327. Stratford held — and voiced — almost precisely the positions, and cited the same royal abuses, as are found in the political poems of Harley 2253. Stratford had been head of the king's home council while Edward was fighting in France in 1338–40, but Edward on his sudden return not only sacked Stratford but tried to prosecute him. Relying on his clerical status and citing Becket as a model, Stratford managed to avoid imprisonment or worse.

[47] The course of events is presented in Harriss, *King*, pp. 231–312, supplemented by T. H. Lloyd, *The English Wool Trade in the Middle Ages* (Cambridge, 1977), pp. 144–92.

[48] Harriss, *King*, pp. 250–52; Aspin, *AN Political Songs*, pp. 105–07; Ker, *Facsimile*, p. xxin6; Fryde, *Studies*, pp. 250–69, especially pp. 263–64 and n. 71.

1264–67; *The Flemish Insurrection* (no. 48) in 1302; *The Execution of Sir Simon Fraser* (no. 25) in 1306; and *Trailbaston* (no. 80) in 1305–07. The last of these, however, turns out to be very pertinent to events of 1341, and we may discuss it as a clue to the manuscript's general political viewpoint at that date.[49]

The names of the justices of trailbaston in Harley 2253 (fol. 113v) show that the poem was composed soon after the original statutes of Edward I authorizing such commissions of justices to go into the provinces and hear and determine a wide range of criminal offenses (1305), for the poem names Martyn, Knoville, Spigurnel, and Belflour, men sent into the South Western shires in 1306–07. These commissions of trailbaston (or oyer and terminer), according to J. R. Maddicott,

> largely took the place of the eyre as the judicial arm of government in the shires. . . . in the fines and amercements which they imposed, eyre and trailbaston contributed much to the financing of the King's government and its unpopularity.[50]

The poem testifies to the unpopularity; its speaker exclaims: "Saving the king himself, damn whoever granted such a commission!" ("Salue le roi meismes, de dieu eit maleysoun / Qe a deprimes graunta tiel commissioun" [lines 6–7; fol. 113vb]).

In 1341, however, this was not merely an old complaint trotted out as interesting bygones, for it was in April of 1341 that Edward III set up general commissions of trailbaston specifically to compel local officials and communities to pay large fines in order not to have to pay the exorbitant taxes and purveyances and levies which were being demanded of them in 1340–41 as part of the financing for Edward's wars in France. Edward was furious at having been forced to return from France in November 1340, with his campaign a fiasco which had run out of revenues, and he set about punishing those he held responsible and taking steps to raise funds such as he needed. In 1341 the commons of England were suffering from destitution after storms and diseases of crops and cattle had wiped out many small farmers, even as the Parliament had been compelled to grant Edward an extraordinary tax of a ninth of every lamb, fleece, and sheaf, and this following three years running of a tax on movables of a fifteenth, with results that are documented in the *Inquisiciones nonarum* and (if it was composed at that time) described in Harley 2253's *Song of the Husbandman* (no. 31; fol. 64r). The king in 1340–41 was using the legal instruments of oyer and terminer and trailbaston as "a blunt instrument for

---

[49] See Carter Revard, "The Outlaw's Song of Trailbaston," in *Medieval Outlaws: Ten Tales in Modern English*, ed. Thomas H. Ohlgren (Stroud, Gloucestershire, 1998), pp. 99–105, 302–04, 329–31.

[50] J. R. Maddicott, *Law and Lordship: Royal Justices as Retainers in Thirteenth- and Fourteenth-Century England*, Past and Present Society Supplement 4 (Oxford, 1978), pp. 2–3.

establishing communal culpability as the pretext for large collective fines," and it was "towards the people that the trailbaston commission was directed."[51] In January 1341 Edward commanded that the ninth be levied not only on the laity's lands but on those of the church,[52] in direct contradiction to what had been decreed the previous July (1340) by his own regent council while Edward was in France. This action might well be behind the line in *Song of the Husbandman*, "Meni of religioun me halt hem ful hene" (no. 31; line 29), especially since Archbishop Stratford at this time, being Edward's chancellor, was under severe attack and claiming clerical privilege as his cause.

The Harley scribe's copying of *Trailbaston*, then, would be extremely pertinent to events of 1340–41, and since the king's commissions of trailbaston were sent out in April 1341, the poem might well have been dusted off and updated later that year — about when Sir Laurence Ludlow of Stokesay Castle began to find himself in very hot water over the wool collection in Shropshire. A chief magnate on the king's council at this time was the earl of Arundel, who was responsible to some extent for the management of English affairs in 1338–41, and thus under implied attack for the failure to produce revenues as promised in support of Edward's French wars.[53] Harriss points out that Edward's actions in late 1340 and 1341 directly attacked the "administration of the council during the past twelve months," in particular "*its cooperation with parliament and its responsiveness to public opinion*" (emphasis mine). The magnates with Arundel, though not actually against Edward himself, were in 1340–41 effectively promoting the Lancastrian idea that to govern well the king needed a council of barons and magnates whose advice and consent were necessary to royal action, an idea that had roots in the 1258–67 struggles between Montfortians and royalists, and later in the 1311–12 Ordinances and struggle over Gaveston, as well as in the 1321–22 rebellion and the 1327–28 arrangements for a council to assist the young Edward III. But according to Harriss, in 1340 "the home council had received plenary power *on the petition of the Commons* who saw it as the means of rescuing the community from royal exactions."[54] And when Edward, on November 30, 1340, returned to England furiously determined to deal with the council for not having provided his financial needs in France, he at once dismissed or imprisoned the members

---

[51] Harriss, *King*, pp. 287–88.

[52] See John J. Thompson's account of this tax on the church in his discussion of the biblical stories, found in this volume (pp. 286–87).

[53] The part played by Arundel and his uncle by marriage, John de Warenne earl of Surrey (who died in 1347, and whose lands and title Arundel eventually inherited), has been discussed by Bertie Wilkinson, "The Protest of the Earls of Arundel and Surrey in the Crisis of 1341," *English Historical Review* 46 (1931): 177–93.

[54] Harriss, *King*, p. 273. Emphasis mine.

of the council — besides Stratford, the earls of Surrey, Lancaster, Arundel, Huntingdon, Hereford, and Pembroke, and the lords Bassett, Wake, Despenser, and Burghersh.[55] When Archbishop Stratford, who as Edward's chancellor had to defend himself against the attack for the failures of 1340–41, cited the fate of Edward II as an explicit warning to Edward III of what could happen to kings who lost their people's hearts through evil counsellors, it was to events of 1328–30 that he made reference, recalling

> how, through certain councillors, the King had nearly lost the hearts of the people, but had then been delivered so that thereafter through the good counsel of prelates, peers, the great and wise of the council, he had . . . won the people's trust.[56]

We see therefore that in 1340–41 the barons were fighting not only to defend their actions of the past few years, but saw those actions as related both to the struggles of 1258–67 and of 1311, 1322, and 1326. We also see that when the king issued new commissions of trailbaston in 1341, the old poem from 1305–07 became highly relevant to current events.

Circumstantial Evidence as to the Harley Scribe's Patrons

To examine reasons why the Harley scribe would copy an ancestral romance honoring the FitzWarins into a book which otherwise contains his more personal and professional collection of materials, we may point out that the family with the closest feudal connections to the FitzWarins in the Ludlow area seems to be the Ludlows of Stokesay Castle, some eight miles northwest of Ludlow.[57] Shortly before 1300 Sir William Ludlow, scion of a wealthy wool merchant (Laurence de Ludlow), married Matilda (Maud) de Hodnet, heiress to all the lands of William de Hodnet, including the castle of Hodnet, manors of Westbury (near the FitzWarin castle of Alberbury and Alberbury Priory, which was founded by the hero of *Fouke le Fitz Waryn*) and Welbache and Moston among others — the last two being manors which were held by the FitzWarins. Among the heroic figures loyally and courageously sharing Fouke's exile and fights against King John in the romance is Baldwin de Hodnet, ancestor of Maud Hodnet. Thus, the son and heir of William Ludlow and Maud Hodnet, born about 1301, would have been a suitable recipient

---

[55] Harriss, *King*, p. 283; see Haines, *Archbishop John Stratford*, pp. 281–82.

[56] Harriss, *King*, p. 289.

[57] As discussed earlier in this essay, the Cheynes of Cheyney Longville seem to have had many dealings with the FitzWarins, but I have not discovered in their case such familial ties as those between Ludlows and FitzWarins. Similarly, it is possible that Joan Talbot, lady of Richard's Castle, and her son Sir John Talbot had such ties, but I have not traced any if they did exist.

of a copy of *Fouke le Fitz Waryn*, especially if he were to be sent to fight in Scotland in the summer of 1322, knighted and serve as M.P. in Shropshire in 1324–25, and married in about 1326 to a woman named Hawise, the name of the first Fouke's wife (Hawise de Dinan). In the romance Baldwin de Hodnet is referred to as a *cousin* of Fouke, and there is evidence that this may be historically accurate.[58] The Ludlows of Stokesay, from ca. 1300, controlled the advowson of Wistanstow, which is just a little more than two miles north of Stokesay Castle.[59] It can be shown that both FitzWarins and Ludlows of Stokesay appear to have had connections to the earls of Arundel, and that the Ludlows had marital and feudal ties to the LeStranges also.

Descended from a companion of Fulk FitzWarin, Sir Laurence Ludlow is therefore someone who might be expected to have shown an interest in the romance of *Fouke le Fitz Waryn*, and even to have wanted a copy of it made for the household, in about 1324–26. Experiencing his first military service in 1322, he was knighted and married in 1324–26, summoned to the king's council at Westminster in 1325, the father of a son and heir in 1327, and made M.P. for Shropshire in 1328. In considering the politics of Harley 2253 in this light, poems praising Simon de Montfort and mentioning the Despensers with honor would also be very apposite to a manuscript being completed in the Ludlow household in 1341. Further, the Harley 2253 poem on trailbaston suits Sir Laurence's problems of the time in striking fashion.

Sir Laurence had been named to collect the Shropshire wool in 1339 and again in 1341. The second time he apparently found it not possible, and there was acrimony over the charge by merchants who had contracted to buy the wool that the Shropshire collectors had supplied bad wool or used false weights.[60] But the king's men were very active in overseeing this process of collection, and commissions of oyer and terminer were issued in each county on June 20, 1341, to hear complaints about collectors or receivers of the wool. On December 8, 1341, all the Shropshire collectors were cited as negligent; on January 30, 1342, Sir Laurence was attached for nondelivery; and on March 28, his arrest was ordered. He was said to have borne himself negligently and contemptuously and to have contemned the whole thing as much as he could.[61] All of his lands and goods were to be seized into the king's hand until he produced the assigned amounts of wool.

---

[58] Robert William Eyton, *Antiquities of Shropshire*, 12 vols. (London, 1854–60), 9.328, gives four reasons (including coats of arms) for believing Hodnets began as a cadet branch of the FitzWarins. See also, in this regard, Appendix 3 below.

[59] Cheyney Longville is also an easy walk from Wistanstow and a short ride from Edgton, where the scribe wrote a 1343 deed (**#33**; Plate 23).

[60] Lloyd, *English Wool Trade*, pp. 161–62.

[61] *CFR 1337–47*, p. 254; *CPR 1340–43*, pp. 368, 422, 445.

Sir Laurence had been in trouble with the courts before: in 1332, accused of taking cattle belonging to a Mortimer follower, William de Ocle,[62] he was pardoned at the earl of Arundel's request. Further, he was later to be outlawed, in 1345, at the suit of John Wyard, on charges of trespass and assault; Wyard, like Ocle, was one of Mortimer's men, as was his brother Robert Wyard.[63] In 1330, before Mortimer's fall, Wyard had himself seized a war-horse belonging to Fulk FitzWarin, so that the troubles which Ludlow had with Wyard were between a Mortimer man and an Arundel one.[64] We may guess, therefore, that there was some matter from the 1330s that John Wyard brought up against Sir Laurence Ludlow, and that a long process beginning with this resulted in Ludlow's outlawry of 1345–48.

In 1341–42, then, Sir Laurence was on the one hand being asked to collect the king's wool for him, and on the other — quite probably — being accused of old actions against Wyard that would get him outlawed presently; and the wool collection itself went so badly that it resulted in his arrest and seizure of his lands and goods in March of 1342 (or at least the order for this). Yet he had also served the king in the Scottish wars in 1322 and was summoned again to them in 1344 (though excused from this it seems[65]). He was therefore bound to have felt, in 1341–42, that he had fought for the king, handled the king's business, and collected the king's moneys, and yet was being arrested, his land and goods attached, and himself threatened with outlawry by a person — Wyard — who had been the king's enemy.

If we now examine the assertions of the speaker in the poem of *Trailbaston*, we can see how well they fit the case of Ludlow in 1341–42.[66] The speaker begins by saying that if

---

[62] In 1337 the Harley scribe wrote a release in form of letters patent by Henry de Sparchford, *clericus*, of all exactions, calumnies, quarrels, and demands which he might have, for all time, against Johanna, wife of William de Ocle, her sister Isolda, and a certain William Tote, pledging not to sue or molest or disturb them in any fashion (**#26**; Plate 17).

[63] *CFR 1327–37*, pp. 76, 89, 121, 197, 217– 219, 222, 226; *CFR 1347–56*, pp. 128, 180, 183, 237, 381, 402, 411.

[64] *Calendar of Inquistions Miscellaneous (Chancery) Preserved in the Public Record Office* (hereafter *CIMC*) (London, 1916), 2.1255, p. 307 (January 31, 1331).

[65] *Rotuli Scotiae*, 2 vols. (London, 1814, 1819), 1.307a, 333b; his father Sir William Ludlow was summoned to Scotland for the king in 1311 and 1315 (pp. 97b, 145b).

[66] There were a good many gentlemen and knights whom the *Trailbaston* poem could fit — both when it was composed (ca. 1305–07) and when it was copied (ca. 1341–42). When it was composed, the evidence from actual trailbaston court rolls in Hereford (London PRO, JUST 1/306) and in Shrewsbury (London PRO, JUST 1/744, 745, 746) would fit such a man as William of Billebury, chamberlain of Maud, wife of Hugh Mortimer, lord of Richard's Castle. I have discussed Richard's Castle people in Revard, "Outlaw Song," pp. 100, 302, and also in Carter Revard,

he corrects his servant ("garcoun") with a blow or two, the servant will sue a writ and get him arrested, and before the speaker can get out of prison, he will have to pay a huge ransom, besides a "guerdon," to the sheriff (lines 9–16; fol. 113vb). "Saving the king himself," he says, "God damn those who first granted such a commission!" (lines 6–7). He is therefore going to betake himself to the greenwood, "le bois de Belregard," where there is neither falsehood nor bad law (lines 18–19); but the "male doseynes" and "fauce bouches" have indicted him for robberies and other misdeeds, so that he cannot be given help or hospitality by his friends (lines 21–24):[67]

> I have served my lord king in peace and war, in Flanders and Scotland and in his land of Gascony, but now I cannot even raise a loan ["cheuisaunce fere"]; I have spent my time in vain to serve such a man, if these evil jurors will not amend themselves so that I can ride or walk in my own country. (lines 25–30)

It is notable also that in lines 49–52 (fol. 114r) the speaker points out that monks and merchants should curse those who ordained the trailbaston commissions, for with the outlawry of men forcing them to plunder travellers, the royal letters of protection (given to monks and merchants on their travels) will be worthless and they will be robbed without recompense ("sauntz regerdoun"). He also claims that tonsured clerics are threatened with being hauled before these justices, handed over to the bishop to be purged, and given "trop dure penaunce," so these men ought to join him in the woods, a better place than the bishop's prison (lines 57–66). Rich people are at ransom, the poors ones dwindle away ("a escolage"), he says (line 72). If he himself knows more of law than do his accusers, they will claim he is hatching a conspiracy (lines 89–90). In short, according to the poet, nearly every kind of man is bedevilled by the articles of trailbaston: knight, clerk, merchant, monk, lawyer.

We have seen, then, that the two Montfortian poems and *Trailbaston* fit the political crisis of 1340–41, and that *Against the King's Taxes*, composed 1338–39, is like the others in being a protest from the point of view of the popular and baronial home council party, of which the earl of Arundel was a leader. Though composed in one version ca. 1305–07, *Trailbaston* is well suited to the period 1341–42 and also to the personal circumstances of Sir Laurence Ludlow at that time.

As for the other political pieces in Harley 2253, it is at once easy to see general reasons for inclusion of *The Flemish Insurrection* and *The Execution of Sir Simon Fraser* but less

---

"'Annote and Johon,' Harley 2253, and *The Book of Secrets*," *English Language Notes* 36 (1999): 5–19, especially nn. 17–24 (pp. 16–19).

[67] We may recall here the accusations against Sir Laurence Ludlow for taking William de Ocle's cattle, as well as the attachment of his goods for the wool levy's failure.

easy to see any special connection between them and the Ludlows or Arundel. Though composed in 1302 and 1306, respectively, they would obviously be relevant at a time of war or hostility between England, Scotland, and France — which would be true a good many times between 1302 and 1350. Both Sir Laurence Ludlow and his father were summoned to the Scottish wars at times, and Ludlow certainly went there in 1322. Further, Sir Laurence was overseas and probably in France in 1346–47, and we may guess he was there or in Gascony on other occasions. The poem on the execution of Sir Simon Fraser might have been used as a recruiting or battle-eve song for any of the Scottish campaigns from 1322 through 1339; among Ludlow-area lords the Talbots were stalwart campaigners in Scotland in this period, while Richard, earl of Arundel led the campaigns of 1337–38 there.[68] Similarly, *The Flemish Insurrection*, suited to England's mood at the start of the Hundred Years' War, would have fit well with Ludlow family interests in the wool trade and Flanders, since it is the Flemish weavers and fullers whose defeat of the French aristocrats is celebrated in the poem with special relish. In 1339 Sir Laurence Ludlow was a wool collector for Shropshire, and Sir William FitzWarin was licensed to ship wool to the Antwerp staple.[69]

In short, the political poems of Harley 2253 are compatible with patronage of the Harley scribe and his manuscript by the Ludlows of Stokesay, most particularly by Sir Laurence Ludlow. Nothing in the rest of the manuscript forbids or works against such a view.

Later Ownership of Harley 273 as Clue to Patronage and Provenance

Nothing that further clarifies location or ownership of Royal 12.C.xii or Harley 2253 after ca. 1349 can be offered here. Royal 12.C.xii was later owned by John, Lord Lumley

---

[68] See *Rotuli Scotiae*, 1.331b, 332b, for summons to Talbot, Arundel, Fulk FitzWarin, John LeStrange in 1335. For the earl of Arundel's leadership in 1337–38, see N. B. Lewis, "The Recruitment and Organization of a Contract Army, May to November 1337," *Bulletin of the Institute for Historical Research* 37 (1964): 1–19, especially pp. 4, 13n2, 13n3.

[69] Sir William FitzWarin was a knight of Queen Philippa's household, fought as a banneret in the 1339–46 campaigns, and was an early Knight of the Garter. For names of wool collectors and merchants in 1337–46, see the *Calendar of Close Rolls Preserved in the Public Record Office* (London, 1892–1954) (hereafter *CCR*): *1337–39*, pp. 120, 148, 169, 268, 307, 348; *1339–41*, pp. 524, 555–56, 592; *1341–43*, pp. 574–75; and *1343–46*, pp. 138, 140, 151–53, 156, 176, 217, 266, 573–74, 593, 601, 647, 649. The license to ship wool to Flanders in 1339 as a way of paying Sir William FitzWarin is mentioned in *CFR 1337–47*, pp. 120, 169, 307; compare *CCR 1341–43*, pp. 574–75, for further payment to him from wool sales in 1342. He was paid also from proceeds of the ninth in 1340 (*CCR 1339–41*, p. 524).

(later sixteenth century), and Harley 273 can be traced to a fifteenth-century Londoner, John Clerk. C. E. Wright pointed out that the name "John Clerk," found in a flyleaf of Harley 273, is that of a man appointed apothecary for life to King Edward IV in 1462, who was also warden of the London Company of Grocers in 1467 and 1475.[70] The post of Apothecary Royal was not merely titular; on May 9, 1464, Clerk was paid £87 18s 7½d "for certain physic supplied for the said king's use, and administered to him under the advice of the said king's physicians."[71] Clerk left on the flyleaves of Harley 273 some fragments for accounts for wine purchases and such, showing that he had Harley 273 with him on his business.[72]

How did Harley 273, with a Ludlow calendar and in the possession of a Ludlow-area cleric and legal scrivener from 1314–30 or so (at least), get to London and into the hands of a royal apothecary in 1462–80 or so? Perhaps the answer lies in the fact that Edward IV, during his boyhood, lived in Ludlow and was tutored there by Sir Richard Croft of Croft Castle, Herefordshire. One of his first acts after becoming king was to grant Ludlow a charter as a royal borough (1461). Conceivably, John Clerk could have had Ludlow roots and his appointment as royal apothecary could have come from prior acquaintance — perhaps between Clerk and one of Edward's retainers. One of these retainers, Sir John Cheyne, might have had Ludlow origins of his own: Cheyney Longville is in Wistanstow parish, just across the River Onny from Wistanstow, while Norton (sometimes called Norton Cheyney) is 5 km southeast and 2½ km east of Stokesay Castle.[73]

---

[70] C. E. Wright, *Fontes Harleiani: A Study of the Sources of the Harleian Collection of Manuscripts* (London, 1972), p. 105.

[71] *Issues of the Exchequer*, qtd. from A. R. Myers, ed., *The Household of Edward IV: The Black Book and the Ordinance of 1478* (Manchester, 1959), p. 245n186.

[72] Grocers might deal in a wide range of merchandise, as Sylvia Thrupp points out: "The grocers retailed miscellaneous small wares as well as spice and medicines . . ." (*The Merchant Class of Medieval London* [Ann Arbor, 1948], p. 7). It seems clear that John Clerk was a well-to-do man who obtained a prestigious appointment from the king soon after Edward IV attained the throne, and went on to become the head of his fraternity in London. As royal apothecary, he had a daily fee of 8d and a yearly robe at Christmas. The ordinance of Edward IV's household, the *Liber Niger*, tells us that he could dine in the royal hall or chamber if he were of the number of yeomen of the chamber, when and as often as the usher of the chamber should assign; he was to take "wages and clothyng . . . lyke to other yomen," which implies he wore the king's livery; and there was a "half bed" for him in the chambers, with payment for his medicines and ingredients coming from the jewelhouse by oversight of the royal physician and chamberlain. However, he was assigned "nother grome nor page, but if ony able grome be in the ewry" (Myers, *Household*, p. 125).

[73] From at least 1296 to 1327 a Roger Cheyne held lands under the Cliffords in Norton (W. G. D. Fletcher, "The Shropshire Lay Subsidy Roll of 1327, Munslow Hundred," *Transactions of the*

Scribe and Provenance

We do not know whether the later Sir John Cheyne, who was in the household of Edward IV at the same time as the apothecary-grocer John Clerk, was one of the Ludlow-area Cheynes. There were certainly a number of Cheynes in the royal household in 1350–1400, and several among these — Sir Edmund Cheyne, a keeper of the Isle of Guernsey; John Cheyne, a justice in Cambridge; Thomas and Hugh Cheyne, king's yeomen — were rewarded with various offices and places in the king's gift, such as lands in Devon, Buckinghamshire, and elsewhere. Hugh was made keeper of Shrewsbury Castle, suggesting a Shropshire provenance.[74] This Sir John Cheyne, Edward IV's retainer, served as chamber-squire to the king from 1471, was captain of a fleet against France in 1472, and in 1475 was one of two hostages left by Edward in France as guarantee that he would take his army back from France to England. Cheyne was promised a pension from the French that year, but no record of his receiving it is extant. His service to Edward continued, and he was Master of the Henchmen in the royal household, which meant that Cheyne was in charge of teaching young courtiers and wards of the king courtly duties and graces, including "sondry langages and othyr lernynges vertuous . . . to herping, to pype, sing, daunce, and . . . comunicacion and other formez curiall, after the booke of vrbanitie."[75] Cheyne's loyalty to Edward IV survived the king's death in 1483; in the next year, after having led a rebellion against Richard III, Cheyne was attainted for treason.[76]

We do not know, however, whether John Clerk, grocer and apothecary, was close to Sir John Cheyne — though they certainly would have known each other and been at times in the royal chambers together. The name "Clerk," of course, is very common, and "John" extremely so. We are thus on shaky ground in tracing a path from Ludlow ca. 1350 to London of 1461–83.

Shropshire Archaeological and Natural History Society, 2nd ser., 4 [1892], 301). In 1343 one of the wool merchants of Ludlow licensed to export wool was Philip Cheyne (*CCR 1343–46*, p. 138), though the amount he was allowed (£19 4s) was the least of the six Ludlow merchants' allowances, the highest (to Richard Orleton) being over £334 (*CCR 1343–46*, p. 152). Philip Cheyne and his son Philip held an enclosed *platea* of land in Ludford fields, in which in 1347 Sir John Talbot, lord of Richard's Castle, quitclaimed all rights to the son, said to be "of Ludlow." This quitclaim, now SRO 5075/42, is in the hand of the Harley scribe (#**37**; Plate 25).

[74] *CPR 1354–58*, pp. 106, 230, 497, 550, 562; *CPR 1358–61*, pp. 60, 100, 103, 235, 551, 583; *CPR 1364–67*, pp. 62, 83, 103, 160, 169, 214–15, 418, 442; *CPR 1377–81*, pp. 247–48, 349, 490; *CPR 1399–1401*, pp. 60, 111, 130, 415.

[75] *Liber Niger*, qtd. Richard Firth Green, *Poets and Princepleasers: Literature and the English Court in the Late Middle Ages* (Toronto, 1980), p. 81.

[76] Myers, *Household*, pp. 199, 263; C. L. Scofield, *Life and Reign of Edward the Fourth, King of England and France and Lord of Ireland*, 2 vols. (New York, 1923), 2.29, 142, 147–49, 157, 335; Charles Ross, *Edward IV* (Berkeley, 1974), p. 329.

Still, Edward IV was heir to the Mortimers, which is why he was brought up in Ludlow, and there was a family in the Mortimer manor of Stanton Lacy whose name was Clerk, as recorded in documents from the time of Henry III onward. The progenitor was Robert Constable of Stanton Lacy, named in three grants as father of Robertus Clericus of Stanton Lacy.[77] The mother seems to be Edith, daughter of Alan Capellanus of Stanton Lacy.[78] There was a second son of Robert Constable named Roger, who appears as granting his brother Robert Cleric an acre of land in Stanton Lacy, and who was later father of William de la Hale and grandfather of John, Thomas Capellanus, Cecilia, and Alicia of Stanton Lacy.[79]

Obviously, we have a family here who live exactly where they would have access both to Ludlow (town and castle) and to the Mortimer lands in Stanton Lacy. They spring from a constable of Stanton Lacy when it was in the hands of Walter and Gilbert de Lacy. They remain landholders there and remain either clerics or Clerks or both at least as late as 1335. In 1335 we find them granting land to Mortimer's lawyer and retainer Thomas Ace, the very man who was appointed lawyer when Mortimer and wife Joan were going to Ireland in 1309–10. Moreover, they are to some extent neighbors and being witnessed for by a Cheyne about 1300 or later. It would be a good assignment to trace Ludlow and Stanton Lacy records between 1335–1480 to see whether this family appear there through

---

[77] BL Addit. chs. 8337, 8344, 8351. Robert Cleric fathered a son also called Robert Cleric; the *Hundred Rolls* record that in 1255 Stanton Lacy jurors included Robertus Clericus de Doddemore, probably the father, and in 1274, a juror for Ludlow hundred was Robertus Clericus, either father or son (pp. 98–100), while in 1297 is a chirograph (London, BL Addit. ch. 8352) by which Alicia, daughter of William le Harper of Stanton Lacy concedes to Robert, son of Robert Cleric of Stanton Lacy, and to Johanna his wife her tenement in Stanton Lacy. A brother, John Clericus, also flourished 1307–34, and a sister, Isabella de Stoke, appears in 1334 (London, BL Addit. chs. 8656, 8657, 8658), while in 1335 Robert le Clerke of Stanton Lacy granted to Thomas Ace of Ludlow meadowland in Stanton Lacy (London, BL Addit. ch. 8359). It is also the case that for three charters from Stanton Lacy or nearby — two of which involve a Clerk — a Cheyne serves as witness: in London, BL Addit. ch. 8332 (temp. Henry III), Hugo de Cheyne; in London, BL Addit. chs. 8346 and 8348 (temp. Edward I), Roger de Cheyne. The first of these is a grant of lands in Bache, the two others being grants from John Sparke and his wife Juliana of Stanton Lacy to John dictus Clericus of Burele of a tenement in Siefton (just up Corvedale from Stanton Lacy), and then from John Clericus of Borleye to his son John of this tenement, with Roger de Cheyne witnessing both these transactions.

[78] London, BL Addit. ch. 8343.

[79] London, BL Addit. chs. 8337, 8345, 8349.

the whole period and can be linked to Edward IV's apothecary John Clerk, and whether the latter could be connected with Edward's henchman Sir John Cheyne.[80]

It is possible to trace a man named Richard le Clerk as connected directly with Stokesay in the 1330s. Richard Clericus de Stokesay was ordained acolyte at Ledbury on May 21, 1334; a Richard, son of Henry Clerk de Onibury (near to Stokesay, and between it and Stanton Lacy), was papally provided to a benefice in the gift of Hurley Priory, and ordained subdeacon at Bishop's Castle on September 21, 1336, and deacon on June 14, 1337 in Hereford Cathedral,[81] while in 1336 a Richard le Clerk was presented by the king to the benefice of Rock (Aka) in Stanton Lacy (this being then in royal custody as guardian of the Mortimer heir, a minor), and he exchanged Rock in 1340 for the rectory

---

[80] There are more complications to be registered here. In London, BL Addit. ch. 8347 (temp. Edward I), Robert of Stoke in Stanton Lacy, for two marks of silver, grants to Reginald called Cleric, dwelling in Oswaldestree, two acres of land in Stanton, the witnesses being Masters Richard and Reginald de Heyton, Robert Cleric, and others. "Oswaldestree" is in fact Oswestry, and a man living there is likely to have been in the service of the earl of Arundel (though a FitzWarin might be his patron). Reginald Clerk might therefore have been one of this Stanton Lacy family who obtained service with the earl. Secondly, *CCR 1296–1302* records that John de Lodelawe, William de Lodelawe, and Reginald le Clerk of Osewaldstete acknowledged a debt to Henry, Thomas, and Idonis Cosyn of 85 marks, to be levied in default of payment in their lands and chattels in Shropshire (p. 299). Perhaps the two sons of Laurence Ludlow (d. 1294) were in some enterprise with Reginald le Clerk, of the Stanton Lacy family, who was living in Oswestry.

And finally, *CPR 1272–1281* records that Reginald de Staunton was clerk to the merchant Nicholas de Ludlow and (with Nicholas's son Laurence) was co-executor of Nicholas's will on August 20, 1279, when they were empowered to recover and receive all debts and chattels due to Nicholas (p. 325). The king commanded that the mayors of Ypres, Ghent, St. Omer, and Bruges deliver Nicholas's goods in those cities to the executors. As the king's merchant, Nicholas had been one of the two envoys to recover from Flanders the enormous amounts due to English merchants from the count of Flanders after the trade wars of 1270–74 (Lloyd, *English Wool Trade*, pp. 25–39). In November 1277 Nicholas reported having gotten over £2,000 of this, but the remnant was not finally recovered until ten years later — eight years after his death (*CPR 1272–81*, p. 247; Lloyd, p. 39).

While Nicholas and his son were dealing in large sums, the lord of Ludlow Castle and half the town (as well as of extensive Irish estates) was Sir Geoffrey de Genville, who had married the Lacy heiress. In 1278, when Sir Geoffrey was going to Ireland, he appointed as attorney in England for two years a certain Richard de Lodelawe. In 1280, when Sir Geoffrey and his wife Matilda went to Lorraine, they appointed the same Richard de Lodelawe as their attorney in Ireland for three years (*CPR 1272–81*, pp. 279, 364).

[81] Capes, ed., *Registrum Thome de Charltone*, pp. 81, 83, 143, 168, 173.

of St. Helen's, Worcester.[82] By 1347 Richard, rector of St. Helen's, was old and ill, and a co-adjustor was appointed by Bishop Bransford of Worcester.[83]

These final notes have shown us that the Clerks of Stanton Lacy were a family with holdings there from the early thirteenth century, springing from a man who was constable of Stanton Lacy. One of them (Reginald Clerk) appears to have been connected with the Ludlows of Stokesay, being co-executor with Laurence Ludlow of Nicholas Ludlow's will, and also with Oswestry as perhaps cleric to the earl of Arundel when Laurence Ludlow's son Sir William was in some way involved there.[84] One of the Clerks of Stanton Lacy granted land there to Thomas Ace, the lawyer-administrator who handled Mortimer documents, in 1335. On two charters involving a John Clerk, Roger de Cheyne is a witness, and Cheyney Longville (seat of these lesser gentry and wool merchants of Ludlow) is very close to Stokesay and to Stanton Lacy.

There may, then, have been a direct line from Ludlow in 1300–50, when the Harley scribe was copying his manuscripts and producing legal documents in the area, to the royal court of Edward IV in 1461–83, when Sir John Cheyne was his Master of Henchmen and Squire of the Body, and when John Clerk was Royal Apothecary and Warden of the London Grocers' Company. We cannot, at present, know for certain whether the Harley scribe was himself a Ludlow, a Clerk, or a Cheyne, and we cannot be sure he worked for the Ludlows of Stokesay — but considerable evidence shows that he did produce Harley 2253 as a household book, quite possibly for the Ludlows of Stokesay.

---

[82] Capes, ed., *Registrum Thome de Charltone*, pp. 81, 83.

[83] Haines, *Calendar*, pp. 152–53 (July 9, 1347).

[84] And while Thomas Wynnesbury was bailiff there. On the Wynnesbury connection, see Appendix 1.

Scribe and Provenance

APPENDIX 1. *The FitzWarins and the Mortimers*

Fulk FitzWarin was a paid retainer of Thomas of Lancaster, receiving a 200-mark annuity in 1318–19, but "was the commander of the royal cavalry on the Boroughbridge campaign."[85] He was not the only Lancastrian retainer to change just before the final crisis in 1321–22, for Fulk LeStrange (another Shropshire baron) was still with Lancaster as late as December 1321, but obeyed a royal summons to appear at Coventry on February 28, 1322, and in May was appointed seneschal of Aquitaine. Roger Mortimer of Wigmore and his uncle of Chirk had surrendered to Edward II in Shrewsbury in January, after having attacked and burned Bridgnorth when Fulk FitzWarin was holding it for the king.

Obviously the Mortimers and FitzWarins would have had no good reason to have been friendly, therefore, in the period 1322–26, that is, while Mortimer was in the Tower or in exile. Yet that was precisely when the Harley scribe (on paleographic evidence) began copying *Fouke le Fitz Waryn*. On the other hand, it looks at first sight puzzling that the scribe would also have copied into Royal 12.C.xii in that period the liturgical pieces honoring Thomas of Lancaster as a martyr (fol. 1). There were, however, two FitzWarins on the Contrariant side: the *Calendar of Close Rolls 1318–23* (March 9, 1323) records that Nicholas le fizWarin had found mainpernors and his lands and issues were restored; he had worn robes of William FitzWarin, "then a rebel" (p. 633). This was apparently Sir William FitzWarin, a Knight Banneret, who fought against the king at Boroughbridge, but was later summoned to parliament (in 1342) and became Knight of the Garter as the twenty-sixth member (in 1349), and who lived until 1361.[86] Another man of this name was the holder of 2½ knights' fees at Upton Warin in Worcestershire (about three miles northwest of Droitwich), and he is the man whom Charles Moor identifies as the captive at Boroughbridge.[87] Moor notes that Sir William was pardoned in 1318 as adherent of Thomas of Lancaster, captured at Boroughbridge on March 16, 1322, and pardoned for his rebellion on April 15. On March 26, 1324, he was given protection to go overseas with Edmund, earl of Kent.

The association with the earl of Kent in 1324 seems to connect Sir William FitzWarin with the events of 1330 as they affected his kinsman Sir Fulk FitzWarin. In March 1330 Mortimer had Kent arrested and executed, and he accused Fulk of adhering to Kent. Fulk's sons, Fulk and Ioun, were arrested and imprisoned in Shrewsbury, two of Mortimer's men came to seize Fulk's chattels at

---

[85] Maddicott, *Thomas of Lancaster*, pp. 296, 304–05.

[86] "G. E. C.," *Complete Peerage*, 2.535 (Appendix B), and 2.599 (Appendix C). We may doubt whether all these accomplishments belong to a single man, since there were at least two William FitzWarins in the period.

[87] Charles Moor, *Knights of Edward I*, Harleian Society 80–84 (London 1929–32), p. 69, under "FitzWarin, William," no. 4.

Wantage (a war-horse was seized there in March 1330 by John Wyard and John de Alcestre[88]), and Fulk himself fled to avoid arrest. Not until November 26, 1330, was Fulk given safe-conduct to return to England, where on December 8 he was cleared of the charges; obviously, this followed the overthrow and execution of Mortimer in October-November.[89]

These facts show that in 1322 Mortimer and Fulk FitzWarin were opponents; that during 1323–26 while Mortimer was in exile and threatening return to overthrow Edward, Fulk and William FitzWarin were royal servants; that in 1327–30 there was at best tolerance followed by mortal enmity; and that only after Mortimer tried to arrest Fulk as traitor and was himself overthrown, was Fulk restored to a position of power and favor. We may now demonstrate that royal favor was shown particularly to Sir William FitzWarin, *le Frere* — probably the brother of Sir Fulk,[90] perhaps Boroughbridge captive. In 1330 Sir William FitzWarin, *le Frere*, was appointed keeper of the royal Castle of Montgomery, and in 1332 this office was granted to him for life.[91] This office had been obtained for Queen Isabella during Mortimer's ascendancy, and on February 6, 1330, Isabella granted its reversion (on her death) to Mortimer — but he forfeited it as traitor that fall.[92] Obviously, a royal plum which Mortimer had plucked was now being handed to a royal supporter, Sir William FitzWarin, who held the constableship of Montgomery until 1355, when it was recovered by Mortimer's grandson Roger Mortimer, second earl of March. At that time the king granted Sir William, as compensation, an annual pension of 100 marks from the Exchequer.[93]

More tokens of royal favor went to William FitzWarin: in 1355 his son John was granted £20 annuity to maintain his status as knight, "which he has taken at the king's command," until John should succeed to his father's estate.[94] Much earlier, in 1337, Sir William's daughter, Iseult, is shown to have been married to Robert de Rochesford and jointly enfeoffed with him in two Essex manors and extensive marshlands and in the advowson of the church of Rochesford, in an arrangement which looks very much as if it were made under the auspices of Queen Philippa, since the lands are in the honor of Rayleigh which was in Philippa's hands.[95] Also in 1337 there was a royal grant to William FitzWarin of £19 10s from the farm of land in Ilchester which was part of

---

[88] *CIMC*, 2.1255, p. 307.

[89] "G. E. C.," *Complete Peerage*, 5.497–99.

[90] "G. E. C.," *Complete Peerage*, 5.512 n. *c.*

[91] *CFR 1327–37*, pp. 209, 316; see also William Rees, ed., *Calendar of Ancient Petitions Relating to Wales* (Lampeter, 1975), pp. 101–02, and references therein.

[92] *CFR 1327–37*, p. 168.

[93] *CFR 1354–58*, p. 267; see also *CPR 1358–61*, p. 267 (August 21, 1359).

[94] *CPR 1354–58*, p. 170.

[95] *Calendar of Inquisitions Post Mortem and Other Analogous Documents Preserved in the Public Record Office* (hereafter *CIPM*) (London, 1904), 8.134, p. 80 (March 12, 1337).

the earldom of Cornwall, recently vacant by death of Prince John of Eltham.[96] These favors point to the likelihood that Sir William FitzWarin was a knight serving in a royal household, and this is confirmed by records of the Scottish wars showing that he was a household knight of Queen Philippa who led five esquires and seven mounted archers during November 1334 to February 1335, and led forty men-at-arms and forty mounted archers from June to September 1335.[97]

Sir William FitzWarin's wife was Amice, daughter of Henry de Haddon, who brought him land in Dorset.[98] If he was brother to the Fulk FitzWarin who led the royal cavalry at Boroughbridge and who died in 1336, then he was uncle to the Fulk FitzWarin who was that man's son and heir. This younger Fulk was imprisoned at Shrewsbury by Mortimer's men in 1330, released with his father from charges of treason later that year, and went on to fight with the king against the French at Crecy and Calais in 1346–47.[99] When this younger Fulk died in 1349 of the Black Death, along with his wife Eleanor, they left as son and heir another Fulk, only seven years old, and the king granted custody of him and wardship of his estates to his great-uncle Sir William FitzWarin.[100] Sir William leased custody of Whittington Castle and Hundred (Fulk's castle) to Sir James Audley, and later Fulk was married to Audley's daughter Margaret.[101] Sir William FitzWarin died in 1361 holding lands in Wilton, Bereford, and Stanton FitzWarren, Wiltshire, and in Somerset. His heir was then said to be a minor in the king's custody, so his son John, who had been given the pension in 1335 by the king, was presumably dead by 1361.[102]

In sum, the Fitzwarins can be found between 1322 and 1361 as royal courtiers and knights, but not associated with Roger Mortimer of Wigmore 1322–30, and not particularly with Mortimer family members either then or later. They were in the retinue of Thomas of Lancaster between 1310 and 1322, and it would appear that their feudal allegiances were — like those of their relatives and in-laws the LeStranges, Hodnets, and Corbets — to the earls of Arundel and of Hereford, rather than to Mortimer.

Among lesser knights one finds the Wynnesburys associated with them: for example, on February 4, 1331, when keeping of certain castles and lands forfeited by the Mortimers was given to Thomas Cloune, parson of Hopesay (the advowson of which was held by the earl of Arundel), those who mainprised for Thomas Cloune were Fulk FitzWarin and Thomas de Wynnesbury le Fuitz. During the 1320s Thomas Wynnesbury *pere* had served the earl of Arundel as deputy justice of North

---

[96] *CIPM*, 8.69, p. 42 (January 12, 1337).

[97] Ranald Nicholson, *Edward III and the Scots 1327–1335* (Oxford, 1965), pp. 245–49, Appendices I, IV.

[98] *CIPM*, 9.106, pp. 94–95 (August 20, 1348).

[99] "G. E. C.," *Complete Peerage*, 5.499–500.

[100] *CIPM*, 9.177, p. 163 (August 20, 1349).

[101] *CFR 1347–56*, pp. 256, 282; "G. E. C.," *Complete Peerage*, 5.500.

[102] *CFR 1356–58*, pp. 182, 241; *CIPM*, 10.83.

Wales, and a Wynnesbury had been the earl of Arundel's bailiff at Oswestry earlier,[103] while in 1350 Richard Wynnesbury was an attorney for Mabel FitzWarin, Sir William's sister.[104]

In 1343 the Harley scribe wrote **#33** (Plate 23), in which Richard de Stone grants all his lands in Edgton (northeast of Ludlow, on the way to Montgomery) to Nicholas de Wynnesbury. We may further note that the Ludlows of Stokesay had ties through Maud Hodnet (who married Sir William Ludlow in about 1300) to the FitzWarins, were under patronage of the earls of Arundel, and were associated with the bailiffs at Oswestry when Wynnesburys were there. Furthermore, the Ludlows were hereditary stewards of Montgomery Castle (through the marriage of Maud Hodnet) at the time when Sir William FitzWarin or Sir Fulk FitzWarin had the keeping of Montgomery Castle. The evidence is thus clear that the FitzWarins had good reason not to be associated with Mortimers, 1322–40, but were linked to other families who can be shown to have connections with the Harley scribe during that period: the Wynnesburys, the Ludlows of Stokesay, and the earls of Arundel.

---

[103] *CFR 1327–37*, p. 231; *CIMC*, 2.667, 669, 732, 746, 784, 1282.

[104] *CPR 1348–50*, p. 489.

Scribe and Provenance

APPENDIX 2. *Calendar of deeds in the Harley scribe's hand*

Deeds **#7**, **#21**, **#22**, and **#27** are in London among the British Library Additional Charters. Deed **#31** is among the Craven Papers in the Bodleian Library, Oxford, which presumably derive from the Ludlows of Stokesay. The remaining thirty-six deeds are in the Shropshire Records and Research Centre in Shrewsbury, in five different collections there:

(1) Ludlow Palmers' Guild: SRR 356 (**#1**, **#2**, **#4–#6**, **#8–#10**, **#12–#18**, **#20**, **#23–#26**, **#28–#30**, **#32**, **#34–#36**, **#39–#41**). Each of these deeds was written before the land or fee involved was acquired by the Ludlow Palmers' Guild, so the Harley scribe was not writing them as a chaplain or clerk for the Palmers' Guild. When later owners of the properties deeded them to the Guild, it acquired these earlier deeds of tenure and ownership that had been written in his hand.

(2) Pottesman Purchase deeds: SRR 4032/1/29, 13, 14 (**#3**, **#11**, **#19**).

(3) Phillips Purchase (Sheriff Ledwyche deeds): SRR 5075/42 (**#31**).

(4) Sandford of the Isle deeds: SRR 465/54 (**#33**).

(5) Oakly Park deeds (Fishpool Farm): SRR 20/5/76 (**#38**).

Beyond these forty-one documents, there are two fragments in the Harley scribe's hand, which are here referred to as **#16a** and **#19a**. Both are in the Shropshire Records and Research Centre, the first attached to a Palmers' Guild deed (**#16**; Plate 11), the second attached to the Pottesman Purchase deed (**#19**; Plate 13).

#1 SRR 356/MT/169. Ludlow, December 18, 1314.

Quitclaim: *Richard le Mareschal, pistor, of Ludlow, and his wife Agnes* release to *Richard son of William de Nouo Castro*, for a certain sum *pre manibus*, all their rights in a tenement in Old Street, Ludlow, between the tenement of *William de Cayham* on one side and the tenement of the *Austin Friars* on the other. Witnesses: *William de Routon* and *John de Ticlewardin, then bailiffs of Ludlow; Richard de Corue, Henry Steuenes, Richard Aurifaber*, "and others." Seals (attached by two separate strips) of *Richard* and of *Agnes le Mareschal*.

#2 SRR 356/MT/170. Ludlow, December 18, 1314.

Grant in fee simple with warranty: *Richard son of William de Nouo Castro* grants the Ludlow tenement described in **#1** (above), for a certain sum paid to him *pre manibus*, to *Roger son of Henry de Chabbenore of Ludlow*. **Witnesses as in #1**; seal of *Richard son of William de Nouo Castro* attached.

#3 SRR 4032/1/29. Ludlow, February 24, 1315.

Grant in fee simple with warranty: *John dictus Le Wolf of Brunselowe* and *his wife Alice* to *Richard le Mareschal, pistor, of Ludlow, and his wife Agnes*, a tenement in Ludlow between the tenement of *the late Philip Steuenes* and the tenement of said Richard and Agnes. Witnesses:

William de Routon & John de Ticlewardin, then bailiffs of Ludlow; Henry Steuenes, John Ace (senior); William de Marceleye; "and others." Seals of *John Le Wolf & wife.*

#4   SRR 356/MT/554. Ludlow, February 24, 1316.

Grant in fee simple with warranty (mutilated at left margin, rubbed and faded to right of center down whole document; dating portion legible under ultraviolet): *Henry son of Philip son of Stephen* to his *brother Laurence*, his tenement in Corve Street, Ludlow, between the tenements of *John de Clunton* and *John de Kinton*. Seal missing (flap attached). Witnesses: *John de Tyclewardin and Philip le Gaunter, then bailiffs of Ludlow; [?Matthew] de Pywan; John de [Wen]lake; Hugo de Heyton*; "and others."

#5   SRR 356/MT/471. Ludlow, October 10, 1316.

Quitclaim with warranty: *John de la Bolde of Ludlow and his wife Alice* release to *William son of Adam Doul of Ludlow* and his heirs or assignees, all rights and claims in a *platea* of land with all its edifices in Dynan *vico*, Ludlow, between the tenements of *John and Alice* on one side and of said *William* on the other, extending from William's tenement to the ditch of Cristescroft. Seals missing from two seal-strips. Witnesses: *John de Tyclewardyn and Philip le Gaunter, then bailiffs of Ludlow; William Scheremon Junior; Richard de Corue; Roger Pywan of Ludelowe; William de Salop; William de Ledewiche*; "and others."

#6   SRR 356/MT/1217. Overton, April 28, 1317.

Grant with warranty: *Adam Robet of Ouerton*, to *John Howel of Ouerton*, two selions of Adam's land in Overton Field, between the land of *John Waleys* and that of *Hugo Kempe*; extending from the land of *William Milcent* to that of *the late Walter de Wolferton*. Seal missing from seal-strip. Witnesses: *Thomas de Halghton; Hugo Kempe of Ouerton; Thomas Bercarius of Ouerton; John Waleys; William le Crompe*; "and others."

#7   BL Addit. ch. 41336. Sheet, April 28, 1317.

Grant with warranty: *William son of William Holegod of Sheet (la Sete)* to *Roger Clerebaud of Ludelowe*, all his land in the field of Sheet between the land of the aforesaid Roger on one side, and the moors on the other; extending from Stanrodedich to the land which *Adam de la Sete* once held. Seal attached. Witnesses: *Henry Steuenes of Ludelowe; Richard de Corue; Richard Agace; John de Marchumlye; William Wyot of Steuinton.*

#8   SRR 356/MT/1213. Overton, May 7, 1317.

Quitclaim: *Thomas dominus of Ouerton* releases to *John Howel of Ouerton* all rights in two acres and seven selions in Overton Fields between land of said John [Howel] and that of *Richard de Chabbenore*, and extending from the land of *William le Crompe* to that of *Thomas de Halghton*; also, certain ploughlands (*cursonibus*) in Overton Fields between land of the grantor [Thomas] and that of said John Howel, extending from the land of *the late Agnes de Ludelowe* and *Roger Waleweyn* to *Muchele Brademore*. Seal missing. Witnesses: *Hugo Kempe; Thomas Bercarius; William de Crompe; Adam Robet; Walter Tinctore*; "and others."

#9 SRR 356/MT/1221. Overton, March 5, 1318.

Grant with warranty: *William le Crompe of Lodeford [Ludford]* to *John Howel of Ouerton*, three selions of land in Overton Fields between the land of the Ludlow Hospital of St. John Baptist, and that of *Thomas de la Chapele*, extending from the garden of said John Howel to the land of *the late Agnes de Ludelowe*. Witnesses: *Thomas dominus of Ouerton; Thomas Bercarius of Ouerton; Hugo Kempe; Adam Robet; John Waleys*; "and others."

#10 SRR 356/MT/555. Ludlow, April 18, 1320.

Grant with warranty: *Cristiana, daughter of William Coterel of Ludlow* to *Thomas son of Robert de Buterlye*, her shop with a solar chamber and *celario* adjacent; and the reversion of a latrine held by *Henry Mynch* for life; all these properties are in Corve Stret, Ludlow, between the tenements of *John de Wenlake* and *Henry Mynch*, and extending from Corve Street to the tenement of Henry Mynch. Seal and seal-strip missing; date faded but legible under ultraviolet. Witnesses: *William Scheremon Junior, then bailiff of Ludlow; John de Wenloke; Philip le Glōuere; William de Lyneye; H[ugo] de Heyton*; "and others."

#11 SRR 4032/1/13. Ludlow, December 8, 1320.

Quitclaim: *Roger son of Philip le Muneter of Ludlow* releases to *Richard son of William Kete of Hatton* and his heirs and assigns, all rights and claims in a tenement in *le Narewelone* of Ludlow, between the tenement of *John Trykedundele* and the lane (*venella*) that leads toward Mill Street, extending from *le narwelone* to the tenement of *Richard de Hauekeston*. Seal (damaged) attached. Witnesses: *William Scheremon Junior of Ludlow and Henry de Heyton, then bailiffs of Ludlow; Richard de Chabbenore; John de Tyclewardyn; Richard de Tyclewardyn*; "and others."

#12 SRR 356/MT/1195. Overton, April 13, 1321.

Quitclaim: *William son of Henry Owen* releases to *William de Hamenasch*, for a certain sum *pre manibus*, all rights in four acres of land in Overton which had belonged to *the late Henry father of William Owen*, and which the said William de Hamenasch had purchased of *John de Lyneye*, as specified in the charter of feoffment made by John. Seal missing from seal-strip. Witnesses: *John de Boudlers; Robert his brother; Thomas de Ouerton; Hugo Kempe; William de Greote*; "and others."

#13 SRR 356/MT/1225. Overton, Monday, July 6, 1321.

Grant with warranty: *Thomas dominus de Ouerton* to *Philip le Botiler of Ouerton and Agnes Vorst his wife*, one acre and three selions of land called *le Hedaker* in Overton Fields, between the land of *William le Waterledare* and that of *Robert le Muneter*; and extending from the land of *John Coly* to that of *William Milcent*. Seal-strip, but seal ruined. Witnesses: *William Carbonel; Thomas Bercarius of Ouerton; Hugo Kempe; Roger de Byrchoure; Roger Waleweyn*; "and others."

#14 SRR 356/MT/791. Ashford Carbonel, 16 Edw II (deed mutilated; regnal year is from July 8, 1322 to July 7, 1323).

Grant with warranty: Left half of document is damaged, and over a third is missing. The remnant makes clear that a certain *William* has granted to a certain *Richard and Margerie* and their heirs [implying they are married] certain portions of land [evidently] in Ashford Carbonel. Of the acre and a half of land with four "courses" (*cursonibus*), one part lies between the land of *William le Messager* and that of [name lost], another portion between the land of *Adam le Smyht* and that of [name lost], a third part is between the lands of *John Robynes* and *Richard in le [?]*, a fourth piece between the lands of *[?] de Hynton* and that of *Adam le Smyht*, a fifth between lands of *the late Robert Judas* and *Adam [?]*. Seal. Witnesses: *William Godefroy; William Caumbrey* [the rest are lost].

#15 SRR 356/MT/1227. Overton, December 19, 1325.

Grant with warranty: *Alice widow of William de Clebury North of Ludelowe* to *John son of John Waleys of Blythelowe*, seven selions of land in Overton Fields, next to the land of *William brother of said John*, and extending beyond Le Lychweye. Seal lost from seal-strip. Witnesses: *Roger Waleweyn; Roger de Byrchoure; Hugo Kempe; Thomas le Schepeherde; Adam Robet*; "and others."

#16 SRR 356/MT/796. Ludlow, June 11, 1327.

Grant with warranty: *Philip de Wystanstowe of Ludlow* to *Thomas de Longefeld of Ludlow and Rose his wife*, all lands and tenements in Ludlow which Philip had by gift and feoffment of the said Thomas. Seal. Witnesses: *John de Tyclewardyn, then bailiff of Ludlow; John de Lyneye; John Scheremon Junior; William le Waterledare; Hugo de Heyton; Alan le Typpour; William de Walton*; "and others."

[**#16a** The seal-strip attached to **#16** is cut from a deed written by the Harley scribe; no details of names or dates are apparent, but one can read the first word of the first line, *Sciant*, and the beginning of the second line, *me de Longe*. The fragment may be from a spoiled draft of **#16** itself, whose grantee is *Thomas* (dative *Thome*) *de Longefeld*: in **#16** *Thome* begins the second line, so perhaps in the spoiled deed *Tho-* (at the end of line 1) was completed by *-me* (at the beginning of line 2). In any case, the seal-strip was cut from the top of a deed in this scribe's hand.]

#17 SRR 356/MT/560. Ludlow, July 9, 1327.

Quitclaim with warranty: *Richard son of William de Salopia Senior* [it is Richard who is "senior"] to *Hugo son of Hugo de Causewalle of Orleton*, all rights in a tenement in Corve Street, Ludlow, between the tenement of the late *Nicholas de Temedebury* and one lately held by *Richard le Voulare of Schelderton*, extending from Corve Street to the *campum*. This tenement Hugo had by gift and feoffment of *Richard de Salopia's father William* and Richard now releases all rights in it to Hugo. Witnesses: *John de Tyclewardyn, then bailiff of Ludlow; Richard de Corue; William Scheremon; John de Wenloke; Philip le Glouere; William de Lyneye; John de Lyneye*; "and others."

#18 SRR 356/MT/1228. Overton, January 4, 1329.

Grant with warranty: *William Henryes of Ouerton* to *Agnes wife of Walter le Deyere of Ludlow*, an acre and seven selions of land in Overton Fields, between the garden of *Adam Robet* and the land of *William Mylcent*, extending from the land of the said Agnes to the pit. Seal. Witnesses: *Hugo Kempe; Roger Waleweyn; Roger de Byrchoure; William le Crumpe of Lodeford; Richard de Chabbenore*; "and others."

#19 SRR 4032/1/14. Ludlow, July 7, 1329.

Grant with warranty: *William le Muneter of Ludelowe* to *Robert de Coblyton and Felicia his wife*, the tenement in *le Narewelone* of Ludlow between William's tenement and that of *William de la More*. Seal ruined; its still-attached seal-strip is **#19a**. Witnesses: *John de Tyclewardyn, then bailiff of Ludlow; Thomas le Glouere; Richard de Hatton; Roger de Wyggeleye; William Talent*; "and others."

[**#19a** The seal-strip's fragmentary deed records a grant to *Laurence de Lodelowe* of lands in the village of Coston, date lost. Legible portions of its first two lines are: *Sciant presentes & futuri q. . . de Costone dedi concessi & hac presenti carta. . . aurencio de Ludelowe p. . . in villa* [added above line: *in Coston*] *[j]acente inter terram Hugonis*. It may have been the addition of *in Coston* above the line that "spoiled" the deed: there were strict rules against interlineations in such charters so a lawyer might have got this one disallowed as "doctored." If the deed was written about 1329 — the date of **#19** — the *Laurence de Ludelowe* in it must be Sir Laurence Ludlow of Stokesay.]

#20 SRR 356/MT/1230. Overton, February 21, 1331.

Grant with warranty: *John Waleys of Ouerton* to *Philip son of Thomas de Halghton*, two acres in Overton Fields — one acre between lands of *Philip le Botiler* and *William son of Thomas Bercarius* extending to the land of *William Milcent*; a second acre between the lands of *William Milcent* and *John Howel*, extending to the King's Way. Seal-strip missing. Witnesses: *William son of Thomas Bercarius of Ouerton; John Howel; John Steuenes; Hugo Kempe; Adam Robet*; "and others."

#21 BL Addit. ch. 41301. Ludford, August 5, 1331.

Grant with warranty: *Howel Vahchan lord of a moiety of all the demesne (*dominium) and *manor of Lodeford and his wife Joanna* to *John de Orleton burgess of Ludelowe and his wife Agnes*, a moiety of the lordship and manor of Ludford, with specified rents and services and customs due from named tenants; and with the reversion of a moiety of all the land which *Alice widow of Nicholas de Routon* holds in Ludford as dower, when she shall die. Rents are 18s 1d plus a pound of cumin and a half-pound of pepper, due at the feast of the Annunciation (March 25) and of St. Michael (September 29). Tenants owing rents are: *Thomas de la Chapele* (7s 1 d, a fourth of a pound of pepper); *William son of William le Waterledare* (6d); *Nicholas Miller* (*Molendenarius*) (6d); *William de Lyneye and his wife Alice* (15d); *William Modbert* (6d); *Roger le Masoun* (6d); *Roger lord of Sheet* for his millpond in Sheet (half a penny); *Philip de Cheyne* for the land that was *Roger de Brustowe*'s (12d and a pound of cumin); also from *Philip de Cheyne* (21d for the land that was *Henry le Muneter*'s); *Robert Douyle* (12d); *Thomas Pynwan* (2d); *William le Crumpe* (12d); *Hugo le Shepeherde* (3d); *William de la Cleo* (20d, a halfpenny, and a quarter-pound of pepper); *Alice widow of Nicholas de Routon* (1d annually for her dower-land in Ludford). The manor-moiety and lordship includes, along with the above rents and services, the lands, pastures, woods, mill and millpond and running waters, homages, fidelities, reliefs, wards, marriages, suit of court, hedges, and all other commodities, issues and emoluments due and services owed to the manor-lord. Two seals apposed, both damaged. Witnesses: *William de Billebur[y]; John le Boudlers; Henry de Halghton; William le Crumpe of Lodeford; Richard de Chabbenore*; "and others."

#22 BL Addit. ch. 41316. Steventon, September 29, 1333.

Grant with warranty: *Hugo son of Roger le Shepeherde of Styuynton* to *Simon his brother*, two selions of his land in Styuynton Field between the land of *Roger Roberts* and that of *Thomas de Muneton*, extending from the land of *John dominus de Styuynton* to that of *Richard le Goldsmyht*. Witnesses: *Richard le Goldsmyht; Robert de Castro Ricardi; Roger de Byrchoure; Edmund Andrews; Simon de la Sete*; "and others."

#23 SRR 356/MT/349. Ludlow, September 29, 1333.

Grant and license with warranty: from *Hugo Bacoun of Ludlow* to *Ralph son of William le Molyner of Staunton*, of all the buildings, flowing waters (springing or passing), of the said Ralph in Mill Street, Ludlow, and all buildings to be constructed or already constructed; with license when Ralph pleases to erect steps and make repairs as desired. Witnesses: *Roger le Muneter; William de Ahsford; Ralph de Ahsford; John Cote of Bokenhulle; William Talent*; "and others."

#24 SRR 356/MT/350. Ashford Carbonel, May 4, 1335.

Grant with warranty: *William de Ahsford of Ludlow* to *Richard son of Reginald de Boryton and Margerie wife of Richard*, a messuage which *William father of William* had held in Ashford Carbonel, between the messuages of *the late Richard le Muleward* and *Philip Heowes*, extending from the road to the tenement of *John de Beckeye*. Seal. Witnesses: *William Godefroye; William Jordan; John le Smythes; Adam le Smythes; William de Dene*; "and others."

#25 SRR 356/MT/1235. Overton, August 1, 1335.

Grant with warranty: *Philip le Botiler of Ouerton* to *his son Richard*, one acre and three selions of land in Overton between the *semita* leading from Ludlow toward Overton, and the land of the aforesaid Philip; and extending from the land of *John Coly* to that of *William Milcent*. Seal. Witnesses: *Roger de Byrchoure; John Waleys; William le Shepeherde; Thomas de Halghton; Hugo Kempe*; "and others."

#26 SRR 356/MT/808. Ludlow, May 13, 1337.

Release in form of letters patent from legal claims and grievances: *Henry de Sparchford, clericus*, remits and quitclaims, from now in perpetuity, for himself and his heirs, all *exactiones, calumpnias, querelas, & demandas* which he might have had power in any way to press, from the origin of the world to the day on which this document was confected, against *Johanna wife of William de Ocleye, her sister Isolda*, and *William Tote*, so that from this time Henry shall not implead, molest, bring charges, or in any manner disturb them from this time forward. In which matter, these letters patent have been made as testimony.

#27 BL Addit. ch. 41302. Ludford, December 10, 1338.

Grant with warranty: *John de la Chapele* to *the Hospital of St. John the Baptist of Ludelowe, and its prior and brethren*, for the good of his soul and that of *his wife Alice* and those of his ancestors and successors, a meadow in the area called Moyleswere of Lodeford, between the small meadow (*pratella*) of *John de Orleton* and the meadow of *the prior and brethren of the Hospital*, extending from the land of *Richard de Chabbenore* to the brook. Seal destroyed. Witnesses: *Thomas de la Chapele; William de la Cleo; John de Salopia; William le Crompe; Hugo le Shepeherde*; "and others."

#28 SRR 356/MT/1240. Overton, February 13, 1340.

Grant with warranty: *John son of Thomas de Ouerton* to *Margerie daughter of Adam Robet of Ouerton*, an acre of land in Overton between the land of *the Hospital of St. John Baptist in Ludelowe* and that of *Simon le Cupare de la More*, extending *in uno capite* to the King's Way. Seal. Witnesses: *John Waleys of Ouerton; William son of Thomas le Shepeherde; John Steuenes of Ouerton; Adam Robet; Roger de Byrchoure*; "and others."

#29 SRR 356/MT/1241. Overton, February 13, 1340.

Grant with warranty: *Thomas de Ouerton* to *Margerie daughter of Adam Robet of Ouerton*, an acre in Overton, in Wythedale next to the land of *the Hospital of St. John Baptist of Ludelowe*, extending from the King's Way to the land of *Adam le Cupare of More*. Seal. Witnesses: *John Waleys; William son of Thomas le Shepherde; John Steuenes of Ouerton; Adam Robet; Roger de Byrchoure*; "and others."

#30 SRR 356/MT/302. Ludlow, July 12, 1340.

Power of attorney in form of letters patent, by which *John Morgan, burgess of Ludelowe, and his wife Margaret* attorn *John le Chaloner of Ludelowe* as their proxy to put *John Vmfroy of Ludelowe* in seisin of a burgage and a half in Brodelyneye (Broad Linney Street) in Ludlow, as detailed in a charter of feoffment to John Vmfroy. In which matter these letters patent are testimony.

#31 Bodleian Library, Craven Papers, vol. 63, fol. 6r, item 21. Stanton Lacy, March 21, 1341.

Indenture with warranty: convention between *Richard de Stone* on the one part, and *Johanna and Alice daughters of the late Robert Douyle of Wiggeleye* on the other, that Richard has conceded and sold (*tradidit*) to them one acre of meadow with appurtenances in Stanton Lacy, which once was *Roger Folyot*'s. To be held by Johanna and Alice for the life of either and each, so long as either lives, rendering annually rents and services for the capital demesne of fee as custom and law require. After their decease, said acre of meadow etc. shall revert wholly to the said Richard de Stone and his heirs or assigns. Witnesses: *William Aleyn of Staunton Lacy; Robert le Clerke; John Sparke; Robert Douyle; John son of Robert le Clerke*; "and others."

#32 SRR 356/MT/1242. Overton, November 25, 1342.

Grant with warranty: *Adam Robet of Ouerton and his wife Lucy* to *Agnes and Constance their daughters*, a messuage (which Adam and Lucy had of feoffment from *Matilda sister of Adam*) in Overton, between the tenement of *their daughter Margery* and their own tenement. Seals lost. Witnesses: *John Waleys; Hugo Kempe; Roger de Birchoure; Richard Dygwyn; Richard le Botiler*; "and others."

#33 SRR 465/54. Edgton, February 25, 1343.

Grant with warranty: *Richard son of Richard de Stone* to *Nicholas de Wynnesbury*, all his tenements with meadows, pastures, *housbote & heybote* and commons in woods and elsewhere, all commodities, liberties, easements, customary rights and immunities etc. in Edgton (Eggedon), as fully specified in the original charters made concerning this. Seal. Witnesses: *Hugo de Chenne; Robert de Stepelton; William de la More; Walter de Bourhton; William Purcel of Norbur[y]*; "and others."

#34 SRR 356/MT/157. Ludlow, March 5, 1343.

Quitclaim with warranty: *Margerie widow of William le Cordwainer* releases all claims for herself and heirs or assigns to *William her son* (so referred to in lines 4 and 8), in a tenement at the top of Old Street in Ludlow (*in summitate veteris vici . . . in villa de Ludelowe*). Witnesses: *John de Salopia; William Ace; William de Orleton; Richard de Burhton.* The right side of the document has been torn or cut away, and the missing third part likely gave the names of one or more other witnesses, and details on the location of the document. Seal.

#35 SRR 356/MT/478b. Ludlow, March 9, 1343.

Grant with warranty: *Petronilla daughter of Richard de Tyclewardyn of Ludelowe* to *John son of Regnald de Shauynton*, all her tenement in Dynane de Ludelowe with curtilage, dovecote, and other appurtenances, between the tenement of *the late Richard Ace* and that of *Philip de Ledewich*, extending from Dynane Street (*a vico de Dynane*) to the ditch of the town of Ludlow. Seal. Witnesses: *John de Salopia; John Pynwan; William de Ahsford; Hamundus le Walkare; John de Westhop*; "and others."

#36 SRR 356/MT/1245. Overton, November 2, 1346.

Grant with warranty: *Philip son of Thomas de Halghton* to *Roger son of John Coly of Bachecote*, two selions of his land on Overton Field between the land of *Sir Laurence de Ludelowe* on one side and that of *John Plotimon of Wolferton*, extending from the King's Way to the land of *Roger de Byrchoure*. Seal. Witnesses: *John de Boudlers; John Waleys; Roger de Byrchoure; Hugo Leoky; William Thommesone*; "and others."

#37 SRR 5075/42. Richard's Castle, March 8, 1347.

Quiclaim in form of letters patent: *John Talbot, lord of Richard's Castle*, releases and quitclaims to *Philip de Chenne of Ludlow* all rights in a *platea* of land in Lodeford Field which had been enclosed by *Philip's father*. Seal.

#38 SRR 20/5/76. Ludlow, August 4, 1347.

Quitclaim: *William son of Nicholas Eylrich[e] of Ludelowe* quitclaims for himself and heirs to *Robert Broun of Whychecote* all rights and claims in 7s 2d and one grain of pepper annual rent, with homages, heriots, reliefs, wards, marriages, suit of court, pleas and perquisites and all manner of escheats making up that rent, which William's ancestors had received semiannually at Annunciation and Michaelmas for the lands and tenements and appurtenances which *Henry le Muneter* of Ludelow held in the field called *Le Vyhspolesfeld* within the fee of Stanton Lacy. Seal. Witnesses: *Robert Douyle de Wiggeleye; William Aleyn of Staunton Lacy; John Pynwan of Ludelowe; Richard de Corue of Ludelowe; Richard Steuenes of Ludelowe*; "and others."

#39 SRR 356/MT/1247. Overton, September 16, 1347.

Quitclaim with warranty: *Adam Robet of Ouerton* to *his daughter Margerie* and her heirs and assigns, all rights and claims in 4d annual rent from a messuage which Margery inhabits in Overton next to Adam's messuage, and from the water-land in Overton between the land of *William le Shepherde* and that of *John de la Chapele*. Witnesses: *John Waleys; Roger de Birchouere; William le Shepeherde; John Howel; John le Muleward*; "and others."

#40 SRR 356/MT/1142. Ludford, May 18, 1348.

Grant with warranty: *Agnes, widow of Walter le Deyare of Ludelowe*, to *Hugo de Neenton and Roger de Doryton, chaplains*, all that tenement with appurtenances in Lodeford between the tenement of *John de Shrosebury of Ludelowe* on one side, and the way toward the River Teme next to the fulling mill on the other. She also gives to Hugo and Roger all lands and tenements (with meadows, pastures, etc.) which she has held in Overton. Witnesses: *John de Orleton; John de Shrosebury; William de Ruyhsshebury; John Waleys; Thomas de Halghton*; "and others."

#41 SRR 356/MT/1250. Overton, April 13, 1349.

Grant with warranty: *Matilda daughter of Adam Robet of Ouerton widow* to *Constance daughter of Adam Robet of Ouerton*, a messuage in Overton between [the croft?] (document is damaged and faded here) of *Adam Robet* and the tenement of *Margery, Adam's daughter*, extending from the King's Way to the croft of *Adam Robet*. Witnesses: *John Waleys; William le Shepeherde; Adam Robet; Simon le Cupere; John Howel*; "and others."

Index of Names

[?] de Hynton **#14**

Ace *see* John, Richard, William

Adam [?] **#14**

Adam de la Sete **#7**

Adam Doul of Ludlow **#5**

Adam le Cupare of More **#29**

Adam le Smyht (Smythes) **#14**, **#24**

Adam Robet (of Ouerton) **#6**, **#8**, **#9**, **#15**, **#18**, **#20**, **#28**, **#29**, **#32**, **#39**, **#41**

Agace *see* Richard

Agnes daughter of Adam Robet of Ouerton and his wife Lucy **#32**

Agnes de Ludlow **#8**, **#9**

Agnes Vorst wife of Philip le Botiler of Ouerton **#13**

Agnes wife of John Orleton burgess of Ludlow **#21**

Agnes wife of Richard le Mareschal pistor of Ludlow **#1**, **#3**

Agnes wife of Walter le Deyere (Deyare) of Ludlow **#18**, **#40**

Ahsford *see* Ralph, William

Alan le Typpour **#16**

Aleyn *see* William

Alice daughter of Robert Douyle of Wiggeleye **#31**

Alice wife of John de la Bolde of Ludlow **#5**

Alice wife of John de la Chapele **#27**

Alice wife of John dictus Le Wolf of Brunselowe **#3**

Alice wife of Nicholas de Routon **#21**

Alice wife of William de Clebury North of Ludlow **#15**

Alice wife of William de Lyneye **#21**

Andrews *see* Edmund

Aurifaber *see* Richard

Austin Friars **#1**

Bachecote *see* John, Roger

Bacoun *see* Hugo

Beckeye *see* John

Bercarius *see* Thomas, William

Billebur[y] *see* William

Birchou(e)re (Byrchoure) *see* Roger

Blythelowe *see* John, William

Bokenhulle *see* John

Bolde *see* Alice, John

Boryton *see* Margerie, Reginald, Richard

Botiler *see* Agnes, Philip, Richard, Richard son of Richard

Boudlers *see* John de, John le, Robert

B(o)urhton *see* Richard, Walter

Brademore *see* Muchele

Broun *see* Richard

Brunselowe *see* Alice, John

Brustowe *see* Roger

Buterlye *see* Robert, Thomas

Carbonel *see* William

Castro Ricardi (Richard's Castle) *see* John, Richard

Caumbrey *see* William

Causewalle *see* Hugo, Hugo son of Hugo, Richard

Cayham *see* William

Chabbenore *see* Henry, Richard, Roger

Chaloner *see* John

Chapele *see* Alice, John, Thomas

Cheyne (Chenne) *see* Hugo, Philip

Clebury *see* Alice, William

Cleo *see* William

Clerebaud *see* Roger

Clerke *see* John, Robert

Clunton *see* John

Coblyton *see* Felicia, Robert

Joanna wife of Howel Vahchan of Lodeford **#21**

Joanna wife of William de Ocleye **#26**

John Ace (senior) **#3**

John Coly (of Bachecote) **#13**, **#25**, **#36**

John Cote of Bokenhulle **#23**

John de Beckeye **#24**

John de Boudlers **#12**, **#36** (cp. J. le Boudlers)

John de Clunton **#4**

John de Kinton **#4**

John de la Bolde of Ludlow **#5**

John de la Chapele **#27**, **#39**

John de Lyneye **#12**, **#16**, **#17**

John de Marchumlye **#7**

John de Orleton **#21**, **#27**, **#40**

John de Salopia **#27**, **#34**, **#35**

John de Shrosebury of Ludlow **#40**

John de Ticlewardin (Tyclewardyn) (bailiff of Ludlow) **#1**, **#3**, **#4**, **#5**, **#11**, **#16**, **#17**, **#19**

John de Wenlake (Wenloke) **#4**, **#10**, **#17**

John de Westhop **#35**

John dictus Le Wolf of Brunselowe **#3**

John dominus de Styuynton **#22**

John Howel (of Ouerton) **#6**, **#8**, **#9**, **#20**, **#39**, **#41**

John le Boudlers **#21** (cp. J. de Boudlers)

John le Chaloner of Ludlow **#30**

John le Muleward **#39**

John le Smythes **#24**

John Morgan burgess of Ludlow **#30**

John Plotimon of Wolferton **#36**

John Pynwan (of Ludlow) **#35**, **#38**

John Robynes **#14**

John Scheremon Junior **#16**

John son of John Waleys of Blythelowe **#15** (cp. J. Waleys)

John son of Reginald de Shauynton **#35**

John son of Robert le Clerke **#31**

John son of Thomas de Ouerton **#28**

John Sparke **#31**

John Steuenes (of Ouerton) **#20**, **#28**, **#29**

John Talbot lord of Richard's Castle **#37**

John the Baptist *see* Hospital

John Trykedundele **#11**

John Vmfroy of Ludlow **#30**

John Waleys **#6**, **#9**, **#25**, **#29**, **#32**, **#36**, **#39**, **#40**, **#41**

John Waleys of Blythelowe **#15**

John Waleys of Ouerton **#20**, **#28**

Jordan *see* William

Judas *see* Robert

Kempe *see* Hugo

Kete *see* Richard, William

Kinton *see* John

Laurence de Ludlow (*dominus*) **#19a**, **#36**

Laurence son of Philip son of Stephen **#4**

Ledewich *see* Philip, William

Leoky *see* Hugo

Lodeford *see* Howel, Joanna, William

Longefeld *see* Rose, Thomas

Lucy wife of Adam Robet of Ouerton **#32**

Ludlow (surname) *see* Agnes, Laurence

Lyneye *see* Alice, John, William

Marceleye *see* William

Marchumlye *see* John

Mareschal *see* Agnes, Richard

Margaret wife of John Morgan burgess of Ludlow **#30**

Margerie daughter of Adam Robet of Ouerton (and his wife Lucy) **#28**, **#29**, **#32**, **#39**, **#41**

Margerie wife of Richard (son of Reginald de Boryton) **#14**, **#24**

Margerie wife of William le Cordwainer **#34**

Masoun *see* Roger

Matilda daughter of Adam Robet of Ouerton **#41**

Matilda sister of Adam Robet of Ouerton **#32**

[?Matthew] de Pywan **#4**

Messager *see* William

Milcent (Mylcent) *see* William

Miller (Molendarius) *see* Nicholas

Modbert *see* William

Molyner *see* Ralph, William

More *see* Adam, Simon, William

Morgan *see* John, Margaret

Muchele Brademore **#8**

Muleward *see* John, Richard

Muneter *see* Henry, Philip, Robert, Roger, William

Muneton *see* Thomas

Mynch *see* Henry

Neenton *see* Hugo

Nicholas de Routon **#21**

Nicholas de Temedebury **#17**

Nicholas de Wynnesbury **#33**

Nicholas Eylrich[e] of Ludlow **#38**

Nicholas Miller (Molendenarius) **#21**

Norbury *see* William

Nouo Castro *see* Richard, William

Ocleye *see* Isolda, Joanna, William

Orleton *see* Agnes, Hugo, Hugo son of Hugo, John, William

Ouerton (surname) *see* John son of Thomas, Thomas, Thomas dominus

Owen *see* Henry, William

Petronilla daughter of Richard de Tyclewardyn of Ludlow **#35**

Philip de Cheyne (Chenne) (of Ludlow) **#21, #37**

Philip de Ledewich **#35**

Philip de Wystanstowe of Ludlow **#16**

Philip Heowes **#24**

Philip le Botiler (of Ouerton) **#13, #20, #25**

Philip le Gaunter bailiff of Ludlow **#4, #5**

Philip le Glouere **#10, #17**

Philip le Muneter of Ludlow **#11**

Philip son of Stephen **#4**

Philip son of Thomas de Halghton **#20, #36**

Philip Steuenes **#3**

Plotiman *see* John

Purcel *see* William

Pynwan *see* John, Thomas

Pywan *see* ?Matthew, Roger

Ralph de Ahsford **#23**

Ralph son of William le Molyner of Staunton **#23**

Reginald de Boryton **#24**

Reginald de Shauynton **#35**

Richard **#14** (probably R. son of Reginald de Boryton)

Richard Ace **#35**

Richard Agace **#7**

Richard Aurifaber **#1**

Richard de Burhton **#34**

Richard de Chabbenore **#8, #11, #18, #21, #27**

Richard de Corue (of Ludlow) **#1, #5, #7, #17, #38**

Richard de Hauekeston **#11**

Richard de Salopia son of William **#17**

Richard de Stone **#31, #33**

Richard de Tyclewardyn of Ludlow **#35** (cp. R. Tyclewardyn)

Richard Dygwyn **#32**

Richard in le [?] **#14**

Richard le Botiler **#32** (cp. R. son of Philip)

Richard le Goldsmyht **#22**

Richard le Hatton **#19** (cp. R. son of William Kete)

Richard le Mareschal pistor of Ludlow **#1**, **#3**

Richard le Muleward **#24**

Richard le Voulare of Schelderton **#17**

Richard's Castle (Castro Ricardi) *see* John Talbot, Robert

Richard son of Philip le Botiler of Ouerton **#25** (cp. R. le Botiler)

Richard son of Reginald de Boryton ?**#14**, **#24**

Richard son of Richard de Stone **#33**

Richard son of William de Causewalle of Orleton **#17**

Richard son of William de Nouo Castro **#1**, **#2**

Richard son of William Kete of Hatton **#11** (cp. R. de Hatton)

Richard Steuenes of Ludlow **#38**

Richard Tyclewardyn **#11**

Robert Broun of Whychecote **#38**

Robert de Boudlers **#12**

Robert de Buterlye **#10**

Robert de Castro Ricardi **#22**

Robert de Coblyton **#19**

Robert de Stepelton **#33**

Robert Douyle (de Wiggeleye) **#21**, **#31**, **#38**

Robert Judas **#14**

Robert le Clerke **#31**

Robert le Muneter **#13**, **#23**

Roberts *see* Roger

Robet *see* Adam, Agnes, Constance, Lucy, Margerie, Matilda

Robynes *see* John

Roger Clerebaud of Ludlow **#7**

Roger de Birchou(e)re (Byrchoure) **#13**, **#15**, **#18**, **#22**, **#25**, **#28**, **#29**, **#32**, **#36**, **#39**

Roger de Brustowe **#21**

Roger de Doryton chaplain **#40**

Roger de Wyggeleye **#19**

Roger Folyot **#31**

Roger le Masoun **#21**

Roger le Shepeherde of Styuynton **#22**

Roger lord of Sheet **#21**

Roger Pywan of Ludlow **#5**

Roger Roberts **#22**

Roger son of Henry de Chabbenore of Ludlow **#2**

Roger son of John Coly of Bachecote **#36**

Roger son of Philip le Muneter of Ludlow **#11**

Roger Waleweyn **#8**, **#13**, **#15**, **#18**

Rose wife of Thomas de Longefeld of Ludlow **#16**

Routon *see* Alice, Nicholas, William

Ruyhsshebury *see* William

Salop(ia) *see* John, Richard, William

Schelderton *see* Richard

Scheremon *see* John, William

Sete (Sheet) *see* Adam, Roger, Simon, William

Shauynton *see* John, Reginald

Shepeherde (Schepeherde) *see* Hugo, Hugo son of Roger, Roger, Simon, Thomas, William, William son of Thomas

Shrosebury *see* John

Simon de la Sete **#22**

Simon le Cupere (Cupare de la More) **#28**, **#41**

Simon son of Roger le Shepeherde of
Styuynton **#22**

Smyht (Smythes) *see* Adam, John

Sparchford *see* Henry

Spark *see* John

St. John the Baptist *see* Hospital

Staunton (Staunton Lacy) *see* Ralph, Robert,
William

Stepelton *see* Robert

Stephen father of Philip father of Henry and
Laurence **#4**

Steuenes *see* Henry, John, Philip, Richard

Stone *see* Richard, Richard son of Richard

Styuynton (Steuinton) *see* Hugo, John,
Roger, Simon, William

Talbot *see* John

Talent *see* William

Temedebury *see* Nicholas

Thomas Bercarius (of Ouerton) **#6, #8, #9,
#13, #20** (cp. T. le S(c)hepeherde)

Thomas de Halghton **#6, #8, #20, #25, #36,
#40**

Thomas de la Chapele **#9, #21, #27**

Thomas de Longefeld of Ludlow **#16, #16a**

Thomas de Muneton **#22**

Thomas de Ouerton **#12, #28, #29** (cp. T.
dominus)

Thomas dominus de Ouerton **#8, #9, #13** (cp.
T. de Ouerton)

Thomas le Glouere **#19**

Thomas le S(c)hepeherde **#15, #28, #29** (cp.
T. Bercarius)

Thomas Pynwan **#21**

Thomas son of Robert de Buterlye **#10**

Thommesone *see* William

Ticlewardin (Tyclewardyn) *see* John,
Petronilla, Richard

Tinctore *see* Walter

Tote *see* William

Trykedundele *see* John

Typpour *see* Alan

Vahchan *see* Howel, Joanna

Vmfroy *see* John

Vorst *see* Agnes

Voulare *see* Richard

Waleweyn *see* Roger

Waleys *see* John, William

Walkare *see* Hamundus

Walter de Bourhton **#33**

Walter de Wolferton **#6**

Walter le Deyere (Deyare) of Ludlow **#18,
#40** (cp. W. Tinctore)

Walter Tinctore **#8** (cp W. le Deyere)

Walton *see* William

Waterledere *see* William, William son of
William

Wenlake (Wenloke) *see* John

Westhop *see* John

Whychecote *see* Richard

Wiggeleye (Wyggeleye) *see* Alice, Joanna,
Robert, Roger

William **#14** (probably W. de Ahsford)

William Ace **#34**

William Aleyn of Staunton Lacy **#31, #38**

William Carbonel **#13**

William Caumbrey **#14**

William Coterel of Ludlow **#10**

William de Ahsford (son of William) (of
Ludlow) ?**#14, #23, #24, #35**

William de Billebur[y] **#21**

William de Causewalle of Orleton **#17**

William de Cayham **#1**

William de Clebury North of Ludlow **#15**

William de Dene **#24**

William de Greote **#12**

William de Hamenasch **#12**

William de la Cleo **#21**, **#27**

William de la More **#19**, **#33**

William de Ledewiche **#5**

William de Lyneye **#10**, **#17**, **#21**

William de Marceleye **#3**

William de Nouo Castro **#1**, **#2**

William de Ocleye **#26**

William de Orleton **#34**

William de Routon bailiff of Ludlow **#1**, **#3**

William de Ruyhsshebury **#40**

William de Salop **#5** (cp. W. father of Richard)

William father of Richard de Salopia **#17** (cp. W. de Salop)

William father of William de Ahsford of Ludlow **#24** (cp. W. de Ahsford)

William Godefroy(e) **#14**, **#24**

William Henryes of Ouerton **#18**

William Holegod of Sheet (la Sete) **#7**

William Jordan **#24**

William Kete of Hatton **#11**

William le Cordwainer **#34**

William le Crompe (Crumpe) (of Lodeford) **#6**, **#8**, **#9**, **#18**, **#21**, **#27**

William le Messager **#14**

William le Molyner of Staunton **#23**

William le Muneter of Ludlow **#19**

William le Shepeherde **#25**, **#39**, **#41** (cp. W. son of Thomas)

William le Walton **#16**

William le Waterledare **#13**, **#16**, **#21**

William Milcent (Mylcent) **#6**, **#13**, **#18**, **#20**, **#25**

William Modbert **#21**

William Purcel of Norbur[y] **#33**

William Scheremon **#17**

William Scheremon Junior (bailiff of Ludlow) **#5**, **#10**, **#11**

William son of Adam Doul of Ludlow **#5**

William son of Henry Owen **#12**

William son of John Waleys of Blythelowe **#15**

William son of Nicholas Eylrich[e] of Ludlow **#38**

William son of Thomas Bercarius **#20**

William son of Thomas le Shepeherde **#28**, **#29** (cp. W. le Shepeherde)

William son of William Holegod of Sheet (la Sete) **#7**

William son of William le Waterledare **#21**

William Talent **#19**, **#23**

William Thommesone **#36**

William Tote **#26**

William Wyot of Steuinton **#7**

Wolf *see* Alice, John

Wolferton *see* John, Walter

Wynnesbury *see* Nicholas

Wyot *see* William

Wystanstowe *see* Philip

APPENDIX 3. *Historical background possibly relevant to the interrupted copying of* Fouke le Fitz Waryn

Paleographically it is difficult to date the second portion of *Fouke le Fitz Waryn* precisely. I can propose here, however, two speculative scenarios leading to an interruption of the scribe's copying in about 1327–31. The first involves the fortunes of the FitzWarin family and rests on an assumption that disruptions must have occurred in 1330 to FitzWarin archives and chattels, causing a copy of *Fouke le Fitz Waryn* to be removed from easy access by the Harley scribe. As detailed in Appendix 1, the FitzWarins, connected to the earl of Kent, were forced into exile or prison in the period March to December 1330 — Sir Fulk fleeing overseas, his sons Fulk and John being imprisoned in Shrewsbury. If the Harley scribe served a Ludlow-area household that had ties to the FitzWarins in some fashion, it is easy to imagine that when Mortimer's men seized such items as a FitzWarin war-horse at Wantage, they might also have confiscated a romance in Shrewsbury or Alberbury which the scribe had been using to make his prose redaction.

The second possible scenario assumes a different source for the original of *Fouke le Fitz Waryn*: the archives of Maud Hodnet Ludlow, who lived until 1347. A certain cleric, John de Routon, was at law in the Common Pleas with Maud Hodnet in 1327–29. He sued her for a claimed debt of 6 marks, and she sued him for allegedly breaking into a certain chest of hers in Shrewsbury and taking out of it not only goods and chattels (gold rings, a silver cup, a silk girdle), but certain muniments and charters, one of these being that by which Fulk FitzWarin had enfeoffed Baldwin de Hodnet of the manors of Welbache and Moston, and of the services of the free tenants of Coton-by-Tern.[105] The date of these suits ranges from Michaelmas Term, 1 Edward III (CP 40/270), to Hilary Term, 3 Edward III (CP 40/275) — that is, from October 1327 to January 1329. It would seem obvious that if the cleric John de Routon took away family charters and jewelry, he might also have taken a family romance from that same chest, and the date at which he took the charters and jewels is just about the date at which the Harley scribe ceased copying *Fouke*, so far as paleographic indicators suggest. The date of disruption of Hodnet archives matches better the break in copying of *Fouke* than does the disruption date of FitzWarin archives, that is, 1327 as opposed to 1330.

It must be added that if John de Routon himself were the Harley scribe, he might have been alienated from Maud Hodnet, 1326–30s, and lost access to the verse romance of *Fouke le Fitz Waryn* thereby. It seems not too likely that he would have been suing for a debt of 6 marks, and broken a family chest of muniments, had he not been a household cleric or feed retainer of some kind. Perhaps the court rolls of Shropshire might tell us more of the relationship between him and the Ludlows of Stokesay, or perhaps between him and the Fitzwarins or others.

---

[105] London PRO, CP 40/270, m. 78; CP 40/272, m. 108; CP 40/273, m. 46; CP 40/274, m. 140d; CP 40/275, m. 322d.

Finally, the break may have been due not to an absence of the exemplar, but rather to political fear. When the Lancastrians broke with Mortimer in 1328 (Mortimer and Isabella ruling with increasing severity from 1328 to 1330), it became clear that the anti-Mortimer party was under suspicion. Even though Fulk FitzWarin had held responsible positions as magistrate, he was arrested in early 1330 and would have been executed like the earl of Kent, except that he fled overseas. Not until Mortimer was overthrown and hanged in late 1330 did Fulk dare come back to England. A Ludlow-area scribe might not have wanted to be caught copying a pro-FitzWarin romance during the regime of Roger Mortimer of Wigmore, who was lord of Ludlow Castle. So a break from ca. 1328 to at least 1331 might well have stemmed from a life-protecting political caution.

Miscellany or Anthology?
The Structure of Medieval Manuscripts:
MS Harley 2253, for Example[1]

Theo Stemmler

I

The importance of Harley 2253 can hardly be overrated and is comparable to that of few other medieval English manuscripts — Digby 86, Cotton Nero A.x, or Trinity College Cambridge 323. We would look at medieval English poetry quite differently if the scribe of Harley 2253 had not preserved so many poetical items for posterity, as this manuscript contains the majority of all extant secular love lyrics in Middle English before Chaucer and a good many political poems recorded in no other manuscript.

This manuscript, however, does not only contain English lyrics but a bewildering variety of literary genres in English, Latin, and French: debates, legends, fabliaux, dream lore, prayers, proverbs. This catholic taste of the compiler has led most scholars to the belief that Harley 2253 is a hotchpotch of texts copied at random without any discernible order: the *Sammelhandschrift* appears to be a *Sammelsurium*. The unison of the critical voices is impressive. Karl Böddeker, one of the earliest editors of texts from this manuscript, claims:

> The Ms. Harley 2253 is a motley collection of poetic and prose texts in Latin, Anglo-French, and Old English [*sic*], which alternate without rhyme or reason.[2]

Half a century later Carleton Brown goes out of his way to pinpoint the disorder of the manuscript contents:

---

[1] Originally published under the same title in *Zeitschrift für Anglistik und Amerikanistik* 39 (1991): 231–37; this study is reprinted, with revisions, by permission of the publisher.

[2] "Das Ms. Harley 2253 ist ein Sammelwerk eigentümlicher Art. Lateinische, anglo-französische und altenglische Abschnitte, Poesie und Prosa wechseln in regelloser Folge," in *Altenglische Dichtungen des MS. Harl. 2253*, ed. Karl Böddeker (1878; repr. Amsterdam, 1969), p. III.

No arrangement is discernible in the contents of the book. French and English prose and verse are interspersed without apparent plan. Secular and religious pieces follow indiscriminately.[3]

In 1948 G. L. Brook follows the beaten track — though more cautiously than Brown:

The contents of the manuscript are very miscellaneous.[4]

Even more cautious — to the point of ambiguity — are Derek Pearsall's statements on this matter. In his survey of Harley 2253 he characterizes it as being "essentially a miscellany" only to call it "essentially an anthology" some pages later.[5]

I am not of the opinion that we should use the terms *miscellany* and *anthology* indiscriminately. On the contrary, I shall use their different meanings to make my point clear.

II

In my contribution to *Essays on Harley 2253* (edited by the late R. H. Robbins but never published), I opposed the prevalent scholarly opinion by claiming that "the texts are copied in a certain order."[6] Before I elaborate on this assertion, I shall mention a second voice crying in the wilderness — heard two years after mine and belonging to Carter Revard, whose relentless research has thrown so much new light on the Harley scribe.

Whilst all earlier critics disputed that Harley 2253 had any order at all, Revard discovered an extremely subtle plan in its organization — not only a "principled selection of items" but "a principled arrangement of them."[7] He discerns

not merely a selection of opposites but — frequently — a juxtaposition of them, a dialectic arrangement that implies the compiler's ironic awareness of the double view.[8]

---

[3] Carleton Brown, ed., *English Lyrics of the XIIIth Century* (Oxford, 1932), p. xxxvi.

[4] G. L. Brook, ed., *The Harley Lyrics: The Middle English Lyrics of MS. Harley 2253*, 4th ed. (Manchester 1968), p. 1.

[5] Derek Pearsall, *Old and Middle English Poetry* (London, 1977), pp. 120, 132.

[6] Theo Stemmler, "Reassessment of a Dissertation," in *Essays in Harley 2253*, ed. Rossell Hope Robbins (1980; not published), pp. 17ff. of the typescript.

[7] Carter Revard, "*Gilote et Johane*: An Interlude in B. L. MS. Harley 2253," *Studies in Philology* 79 (1982): 122–46, at p. 127

[8] Revard, "*Gilote et Johane*," p. 130.

Because of the "deliberate placement of its pieces in mutually illuminating relationships," Revard even compares the manuscript to *The Canterbury Tales*.[9] I shall discuss Revard's theory below but emphasize from the outset that it is not corroborated by the manuscript.

As to my own position, I prefer to steer a middle course between the extremes. I try to show that Harley 2253 is neither a miscellany — a somewhat arbitrary, casual collection of texts — nor a well-wrought book carefully made up of mutually corresponding parts. Rather, it is an anthology, a careful collection selected as representative specimens of various genres.

III

The compiler of a medieval anthology could apply very different parameters for establishing a certain order of the texts which were at his disposal and which he wanted to copy into the manuscript: author (one author/several authors), language (Latin/vernacular), form (prose/verse), genre (lyric/narrative/drama), content (religious/secular). Below these general organizing principles range more specific ones, e.g., alliterative school (section "authors"), English (section "language"), rhyme royal (section "form"), miracle play (section "drama"), erotic text (section "content"), etc. These sections in the semantic hierarchy are then further subdivided into groups such as: Saint Catherine plays (group "miracle plays"), obscene texts (group "erotic texts"), etc.

Apart from these logically produced decisions, associatively generated links might influence the arrangement of the texts: verbal or phrasal correspondences between various texts can induce the compiler to put these items into one group (see Figure 1).

IV

In compiling the contents of Harley 2253, fols. 49–140, the Harley scribe used almost all the parameters discussed above. He did not consider groupings according to authors for the simple reason that all the pieces in the manuscript are anonymous. His approach to the texts at his disposal betrays the pragmatic flexibility of a compiler, not the systematic rigidity of an editor. The overriding principle he considered for the arrangement of his material is the distinction between verse and prose.

---

[9] Revard, "*Gilote et Johane*," p. 138.

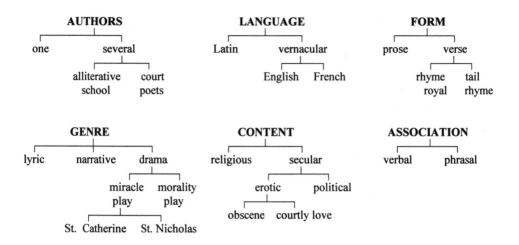

FIGURE 1. *Potential organizing principles for an anthology (in selection)*

As a matter of fact, the first part of the manuscript (fols. 49r–128v) consists of eighty-one items (nos. 8–9, 18, 20–93)[10] written in verse with only seven exceptions.[11] In contrast, the second part (fols. 128v–140v) contains twenty-five texts (nos. 94–116), twenty-three in prose and only two in verse.

These two metrical pieces are the only ostensible exceptions to the compiler's plan in the second part. No. 102 (*Gloria in exelsis Deo* in French) is surrounded by various prose prayers. Perhaps the scribe took this text at first sight for the well-known liturgical piece in prose. Similarly, the other misfit, no. 114 (*Against the King's Taxes*), was erroneously placed into the prose section: when ordering his material, the scribe was perhaps misled by the incipit "Dieu roy de mageste," which at first sight might be the beginning of a religious text, and thus be appropriate to a group of almost exclusively religious pieces.

Here another organizing principle becomes apparent: the second part of the manuscript contains only religious/didactic texts. Thus two parameters — form and content —

---

[10] I have adopted the numbering of N. R. Ker, intro., *Facsimile of British Museum MS. Harley 2253*, EETS o.s. 255 (London, 1965), pp. ix–xvi.

[11] Nine items (nos. 10–17, 19) are later additions and not counted among the eighty-one works. The seven prose works are nos. 18, 38, 39, 71, 72, 90, 91. No. 18 is probably a later addition, too: the leaves on which this item is copied are exceptional in having horizontal ruling.

reinforce the homogeneity of this part. Moreover, only French and Latin texts appear in this section.

The first part of the manuscript is less streamlined and may be generally characterized as a sequence of several text-groups arranged according to varying principles. After a rather isolated introductory piece — the *ABC a femmes* — follows the first coherent group of three texts, nos. 9, 21, 22 (fols. 51r–58v). Their common denominator is the sub-genre "debate." No. 9 is a French *débat* beginning:

> Un grant *estrif* oy l'autrer
> Entre Este e sire Yuer. (lines 1–2; fol. 51ra)

The next piece, no. 20, is not a debate but a French poem on winter:

> Qvant voy la reuenue
> D'*yuer* qe si me argue. (lines 1–2; fol. 55ra)

The theme connects it with the preceding text and is the reason for its inclusion among this group. The following *Harrowing of Hell* (no. 21) is not a debate either — but it does begin like one:

> Alle herkneþ to me nou
> A *strif* wolle y tellen ou. (lines 1–2; fol. 55va)

The final piece of the group (no. 22) makes the scribe's intention clear. A debate between Body and Soul, it begins like the preceding nos. 9 and 21:

> In a þestri stude y stod
> A lutel *strif* to here. (lines 1–2; fol. 57r)

The second group of poems (fols. 58v–62v) is rather loosely knit together and comprises political and moralizing texts (nos. 23–27). No. 23 (*A Song of Lewes*) has perhaps been put at the head of the group because its first line furnishes an associative link with the preceding piece:

> Sitteþ alle stille ant *herkneþ* to me. (line 1; fol. 58v)

Nos. 23 and 24 are strongly linked by their content, which deals with the baronial opposition under Henry III. The death of Simon de Montfort, lamented in no. 24, induces the scribe to insert two poems on the futility of human life (nos. 24a, 24b). The following poem (no. 25) treats the death of Simon Fraser, another historical figure.

The remaining three poems of the group (nos. 25a, 26, 27) — if they belong to it at all — are only loosely connected with each other and with the preceding texts. The common denominator is their didactic, moralizing tone. There is, however, a curious link between no. 25a (*On the Follies of Fashion*) and the preceding political poem (*The Execution of Sir Simon Fraser*). The last rhyme word of no. 25 obviously reminded the compiler of an otherwise totally different poem using the same rhymes in its first stanza. By way of this association, he grouped both poems together:

no. 25:   . . . tprot scot for þi *strif*
     Hang vp þyn hachet ant þi *knyf*
     Whil him lasteth þe *lyf*
        Wiþ þe longe shonkes. (lines 230–33; fol. 61v)

no. 25a: Lord that lenest vs *lyf*
     Ant lokest vch an lede
     Forte cocke wiþ *knyf*
     Nast þou none nede
     Boþe wepmon & *wyf*
     Sore mowe drede
     Lest þou be sturne wiþ *strif*
     For bone þat þou bede. (lines 1–4; fol. 61v)

Or is this kind of linking an indication that the compiler was also the author — at least of some poems in the manuscript?

The third group of texts (fols. 63r–67r) comprises nine pieces (nos. 28–36) ordered according to language, genre, and contents: all the texts are written in English, seven are love lyrics, and eight deal with women. Only two items seem to be exotic: no. 31, because it is a political poem (*Song of the Husbandman*), and no. 32, because it is the legend of a saint (*Marina*). Perhaps the former was placed here as an ironic complement to the preceding no. 30 (*The Lover's Complaint*). *Song of the Husbandman* contains the complaints not of a love-stricken man but of a poor oppressed peasant:

Ich herde men vpo mold *make muche mon.* (line 1; fol. 64r)

This sounds like a sarcastic comment on the preceding erotic complaint:

Wiþ longyng y am lad
On molde y waxe mad
A maide marreþ me
Y grede y grone vnglad. (lines 1–4; fol. 63v)

Miscellany or Anthology?

The following legend of *Marina* has no connection with the preceding political poem but, as praise of a woman, fits well into the group. Moreover, it does have links with the following poem (no. 33, *The Poet's Repentance*): in both texts the importance of Mary is emphasized.

The last three texts of the group belong together, and not only because they are love lyrics. Nos. 34 and 35 (*The Fair Maid of Ribblesdale* and *The Meeting in the Wood*) each begin in the manner of a *chanson d'aventure*:

no. 34: Mosti *ryden* by Rybbesdale (line 1; fol. 66v);

no. 35: In a fryht as y con *fare* fremede (line 1; fol. 66v).

In all three lyrics the woman's beauty is praised at the beginning: "the feyrest on" (no. 34, line 4); "a wel feyr fenge" (no. 35, line 2); "A wayle whyt" (no. 36, line 1).

The third group is followed by eleven texts which do not form a homogeneous whole: some are isolated (no. 40, *Satire on the Consistory Courts*, and no. 46, *Blow, Northerne Wynd*); some appear as pairs only loosely connected by their content (nos. 38, 39 [French prose travel pieces], and nos. 47, 48 [English political poems]). Four texts, however, are combined to form one larger unit. Nos. 41, 43, 44, and 45 have been grouped together for metrical reasons: they are written in the same stanza-form *aabccbddbeeb*.[12] Moreover, all four poems — *The Labourers in the Vineyard, Spring, Advice to Women,* and *An Old Man's Prayer* — are characterized by heavy alliteration. The various metrical and stylistic correspondences are so striking that common authorship may be supposed.

This only partly homogeneous fourth group is succeeded by a large assemblage of rather neatly arranged texts (fols. 70r–83r). It begins with no. 49 (*Les Joies de Notre-Dame*, incipit "Marie pur toun enfaunt") and ends with no. 69 (*A Prayer for Deliverance*, incipit "Mayden moder milde"), comprising twenty-one texts in all. Sixteen are written in English; five in French.[13] The compiler achieves the astonishing homogeneity of this group by using two main parameters: genre and content. Twenty items are lyrics; one item is a longer poem. Sixteen of these lyrics are religious pieces; four are secular love lyrics. Moreover, all the religious lyrics deal with very similar subject matter: themes relating to Jesus and the Virgin Mary.

---

[12] In no. 45 this stanza pattern regularly alternates with a shorter stanza *abaab*.

[13] Nos. 55 and 69 are macaronic poems where — besides English — French (nos. 55, 69) and Latin (no. 55) are used.

The presence of the four love lyrics in this group of predominantly religious poems has been deftly explained by Revard as a juxtaposition of opposites.[14] Though religious and secular love are obviously not quite the same phenomena, their representation in poetry is often very similar. This dissimilar similarity is ubiquitous in medieval manuscripts and does not necessarily indicate a contrasting arrangement on the part of the compiler. Moreover, Christian theology and poetry contain many paradoxes and oxymora, as do medieval love lyrics: Mary is mother *and* virgin; God is triune; love is sweet *and* bitter, etc. In medieval religious and erotic texts the "juxtaposition of opposites" is endemic. Revard's argumentation, therefore, needs detailed proof: verbal correspondences or oppositions. Otherwise the "dialectic arrangement" may be a chance result.

As a matter of fact, there are literal correspondences which unite the secular lyrics with the religious pieces surrounding them. An important element in nos. 53 (religious: *A Spring Song on the Passion*, incipit "When y se blosmes springe"), 54 and 55 (both secular: *Ferroy chaunsoun* and *Dum ludis floribus*), and 56 (religious: *Quant fu en ma iuuente*) are prayers to God, the Virgin Mary, and St. Thomas. These are the links between all four poems:

> no. 53:   Iesu milde ant suete
> Y synge þe mi song
> Ofte y þe grete
> Ant *preye þe* among
> Let me sunnes lete. (lines 41–45, fol. 76r)

> no. 54:   *Ie pri a Dieu e seint Thomas*
> Qe il la pardoigne le trespas. (lines 8–9, fol. 76r)

> no. 55:   *Dieu la moi doint* sua misericordia
> Beyser e fere que secuntur alia. (lines 15–16, fol. 76r)

> no. 56:   *Priez la virgine* que ele vus seit aydaunt
> A Iesu nostre creatour que est soun douz enfaunt. (lines 83–86, fol. 77r)

Other motives led the compiler to include the secular lyrics no. 64 (*De Clerico et Puella*) and no. 65 (*When þe Nyhtegale Singes*) in this group of religious texts. Perhaps he was struck by some literal correspondences between these poems; moreover, nos. 64, 65, and 66 (*Blessed be Þou, Leuedy*) are written in the same stanza form. In nos. 63 (*An Autumn Song*) and 64 the beautiful bright appearance of women is described:

---

[14] Revard, "*Gilote et Johane*," pp. 134–38.

no. 63:   Ne is no quene so stark ne stour
             Ne no *leuedy so bryht* in bour . . .
             Þah þou be whyt ant *bryth on ble*. (lines 4–5, 56, fol. 80rb)

no. 64:   My deþ y loue my lyf ich hate for a *leuedy shene*
             Heo is brith so daies liht þat is on me wel sene. (lines 1–2, fol. 80v)

Both written on folio 81r, the secular no. 65 and the following religious no. 66 share many features: they are variations on the theme of earthly and heavenly love. Thus the secular lyric is fully integrated into this otherwise religious section:

no. 65:   *Ich haue siked moni syk* lemmon for þin ore (line 6; fol. 80v);

no. 66:   *Ofte y syke* ant serewe among may y neuer blynne (line 7; fol. 81r);

no. 65:   So muchel y þenke vpon þe þat *al y waxe grene* (line 16; fol. 81r);

no. 66:   Myne þohtes leuedy *makeþ me ful wan* (line 9; fol. 81r).

After the fifth group no coherent plan may be discerned. The remaining twenty-four texts (nos. 70–93) are either completely isolated or arranged in pairs — the smallest possible units. There is only one exception to this observation. Nos. 76, 77, and 78 — *Le Dit des femmes*, *Le Blasme des femmes*, and *De la femme et de la pie* (fols. 110v–112r) — are grouped according to the same topic: the praise or criticism of women.

Otherwise, several texts are coupled according to genre or content: Nos. 71 and 72 deal with biblical lore (the Anglo-Norman Bible stories and the books of the Bible listed); nos. 73 and 74 are meditative poems (*God, Þat Al Þis Myhtes May* and *Sayings of St. Bernard*); nos. 75 and 75a are fabliaux (*Le Jongleur d'Ely et le Roi d'Angleterre* and *Les Trois Dames qui trouverent un vit*). In one case such a coupling has been obviously provoked by a banal — even bizarre — verbal association which overrules all difference of genre and content. The last piece of the fifth group, the religious lyric *A Prayer for Deliverance* (no. 69), ends with a reference to Christ's Passion:

He was ycrouned *kynge*
Pur nostre redempcioun.
Whose wol me *synge*
Auera grant pardoun. (lines 45–48; fol. 83r)

The following romance of *King Horn* (no. 70) begins:

Alle heo ben blyþe
Þat to my song ylyþe
A songe ychulle ou *singe*
Of Allof þe gode *kynge*. (lines 1–4; fol. 83r)

When he had written down no. 69, its three-beat lilt and its last English rhyme-words *kynge/synge* reminded the compiler of the romance which began very similarly.

Apart from the final pair of texts (no. 92, *The Way of Christ's Love*, and no. 93, *The Way of Woman's Love*), I observe a growing degree of disparateness toward the end of the first part. Nos. 84–91 have not been arranged: they were obviously written down in the haphazard order in which they became accessible to the compiler.

V

Our survey has shown that MS Harley 2253 displays no traces of a sustained organizing principle. Such a consistent arrangement of the texts would have been improbable anyway: the compiler worked over a couple of years (from ca. 1330 to 1347)[15] and was certainly not provided with all 106 texts from the outset. Since several groups, however, have been discernibly arranged, this manuscript is an anthology rather than a miscellany. The range of parameters applied by the compiler is wide (see Figure 2). Among these, the proportion of associative grouping — hitherto neglected procedure — seems unexpectedly high.

It would be expedient to approach other manuscripts with the same intention of gaining an insight into a compiler's psychology.

---

[15] Carter Revard, "Richard Hurd and MS. Harley 2253," *Notes and Queries,* n.s. 26 (1979): 200.

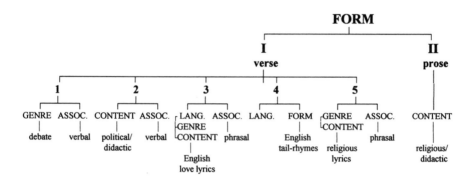

FIGURE 2. *Organizing principles used for MS Harley 2253*

An "Electric Stream": The Religious Contents[1]

Michael P. Kuczynski

What one describes and evaluates as the religious contents of MS Harley 2253 will depend on one's definition of the terms "religious" and "contents." So before I offer my own description and evaluation of Harley's religious contents, I should like to pose some definitions.

First, the easier term, "contents." Everything bound between the modern boards of Harley 2253 has some status, no matter how incidental, as part of its contents. So, for instance, an exhaustive survey of Harley's religious contents would have to note the Latin moralism N. R. Ker records from the book's back flyleaf (fol. 141v; Plate):

> Bonum est nobis credere sicut mater nostra ecclesia silicet vniversalis ecclesia credit et militare Deo in illa vocacione in qua vocauit nos Cristus.[2]

> [It is good for us to believe just as our mother the Church, that is, the universal Church, believes, and to fight for God in that vocation to which Christ has called us.]

This is advice of which even Chaucer's Wife of Bath, that good churchgoing woman, might approve. It is not written by Harley's famous scribe but by an anonymous fifteenth-century hand. Nevertheless, it may record a pious response by a late medieval reader to the multiform religious material in Harley, and it certainly deserves mention and perhaps magnification as one of the "small" rather than "large" religious contents of the manuscript.[3]

---

[1] I am grateful to the British Library, London, for permission to examine, quote, and reproduce materials from MS Harley 2253, and to the Bodleian Library, Oxford, the John Rylands Library of the University of Manchester, the National Library of Scotland, and the Tulane University Library for permission to examine and quote from materials in their care.

[2] N. R. Ker, intro., *Facsimile of British Museum MS. Harley 2253*, EETS o.s. 255 (London, 1965), p. xvi.

[3] The scribe signals his moralism with a cursive *nota*. He begins with a careful capital *B* and regularly spaces his text across the bottom margin of the book's last page, giving the statement a certain formality. Perhaps he meant it, amid the religious tumult of the fifteenth century, as a

Michael P. Kuczynski

It is difficult, for example, to miss the significance of one of Harley's longest religious items, a series of Old Testament stories in French prose (no. 71) that fills fols. 92v–105r of the book. Many of Harley's religious items, however, are much briefer and seemingly more perfunctory, for instance, lists of angels (no. 100) and of prayers drawn from the Psalms (e.g., no. 111), or immediately after the Old Testament stories, a table of the books of the Bible with notes on the interpretation of Hebrew names and the length of a cubit (no. 72). One of Harley's slighter religious contents is not a text at all but a picture: a distinctive cross drawn at the center of fol. 132r in the gap between two pieces of religious prose. The preceding text is a Latin letter describing the history and contents of a famous *arca* or coffer of relics in the Camara Santa at Oviedo (no. 97), and the following one is a Latin life of St. Etfrid (d. ca. 675), a Northumbrian priest who visited Mercia, converted King Merewald, and became the first superior of Leominster Priory (no. 98). These items, on first glance, are liable to mean less to the modern eye than they did to the medieval hand that wrote or drew them, or to the patron who may have directed their execution.

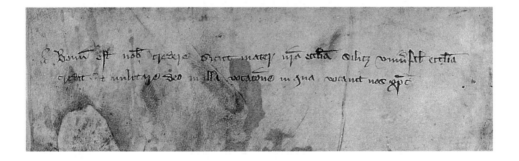

PLATE. *MS Harley 2253, fol. 141v (detail)*.
By permission of The British Library.

Harley's religious items comprise, numerically, over half of the book's texts. And yet, despite their heft, anyone who deals with them will be struck by the irony that even the

---

conservative coda to Harley. (Harley's less incidental religious contents are strictly orthodox.) The moralism certainly reinforces the idea of submission to the Church's teachings and the distinction between lay and clerical roles within the Church.

substantial religious items are far less valued by modern scholars than are the book's secular materials.[4] Much has been written about Harley's French fabliaux and its impressive secular lyrics. Less has been said, however, about the apothegms of the Desert Fathers, *Vitas patrum* (no. 1), that take up Harley's earliest pages (fols. 1–22), or about the book's fine Middle English religious poems, damned with faint praise by G. L. Brook in the introduction to his famous anthology, *The Harley Lyrics*.[5] Such writing does not appeal to the modern temper, though one should recall the thrilling if peculiar "electric stream" that passes through Dorothea in *Middlemarch*, when she hears of Casaubon's collection of pamphlets on the early Church.[6] *Vitas patrum,* its author explains, was not written for clerks, but for pious medieval layfolk, who evidently had a taste for writings about Eastern Christianity:

> Nient pur les clers mes pur la laie gent,
> Que par le rumanz le entendent uniement.[7]

[Not for clerics but for layfolk, that they might understand all of it in French.]

It is probably a sign of clerkly copying in the first four late-thirteenth-century quires of Harley (not reproduced in Ker's facsimile) that the opening line of this couplet gets omitted there. Nevertheless, the point about *Vitas patrum* stands: written in French rhyming couplets, it was a text that could be used for moral deliberation by those who had no Latin. And, although the history of its association with Harley's famous fourteenth-century folios is obscure,[8] it might have been bound with them because these, too, exhibit eclectic didactic tastes.

My use of the term "didactic" begs the question of how that tricky adjective "religious" is to be understood in this essay. The *OED* defines "religious," in the first instance, with

---

[4] This is to some extent understandable given that many of Harley's secular materials exist only in this single copy. See, on this point, Derek Pearsall, *Old English and Middle English Poetry* (London, 1977), p. 120.

[5] G. L. Brook, ed., *The Harley Lyrics: The Middle English Lyrics of MS. Harley 2253*, 4th ed. (Manchester, 1968), pp. 1, 14–17.

[6] George Eliot, *Middlemarch: A Study of Provincial Life*, ed. Margaret Harris and Judith Johnston (London, 1997), p. 34.

[7] Brother Basilides Andrew O'Connor, ed., *Henry D'Arci's "Vitas Patrum": A Thirteenth-Century Anglo-Norman Rimed Translation of the "Verba seniorum"* (Washington, D.C., 1949), p. 1, lines 8–9.

[8] Ker, *Facsimile*, p. xx.

reference to people in religion — that is, clerics. Thomas Wright argued that "some secular clerk" wrote Harley,[9] and Karl Böddeker suggested that he was a *vagans*.[10] All of Harley's religious items can be traced back ultimately to clerical origins: for instance, the Latin saints' lives (nos. 18, 98, 116); questions for the dying attributed to St. Anselm of Canterbury (no. 113); and the French prose directions for contemplation keyed to the monastic hours (no. 115). But their manuscript status in Harley suggests that they may have been assembled to address the needs of nonclerics, too, a lay readership anxious after the watershed Fourth Lateran Council for materials on the devout life. The Council, called by Innocent III in 1215, mandated annual confession for all the faithful and established officially the doctrine of transubstantiation, thereby stressing careful preparation for yearly reception of the Eucharist. It also reemphasized the role of bishops as teachers.[11] One result was a vigorous increase in the production of instructive and edifying materials for clergy and laity, those for layfolk getting translated into the vernacular. Harley's religious contents witness to two healthy vernaculars in fourteenth-century England: Middle English and Anglo-Norman. Indeed, one of its impressive religious poems, a lyrical prayer to the Virgin (no. 69), combines the two languages in macaronic format. As a group, the manuscript's religious lyrics, which Brook and others approach from an almost exclusively aesthetic perspective, are better viewed as didactic structures. Their artfulness is a means of deploying spiritual information — sometimes particular points of doctrine (although this is rare), more often rhetorical models for personal prayer and meditation. While it is true, as Brook writes, that most of Harley's religious poems "are prayers to the Virgin and Christ,"[12] within that narrow designation there is considerable literary variety. The best of Harley's religious poetry and some of its religious prose could have appealed to its compiler first on an artful or merely exotic level: one thinks, for instance, of the romance elements of the Old Testament stories of Joseph and Moses — not out of place in a manuscript that also contains a copy of *King Horn* (no. 70) — or of the descriptions of sites in the Holy Land contained in nos. 38 and 95. Even in these cases, however, an instructional or expository aim underlies the literary appeal of

---

[9] Thomas Wright, ed., *Specimens of Lyric Poetry, Composed in England in the Reign of Edward the First*, Percy Society 4 (1842; repr. New York, 1965), p. vii.

[10] Karl Böddeker, ed., *Altenglische Dichtungen des MS. Harl. 2253* (1878; repr. Amsterdam, 1969), p. iii.

[11] See "Lateran Councils," in *The Oxford Dictionary of the Christian Church*, ed. F. L. Cross (London, 1958), pp. 787–88. For the influence of the Council on the production of AN religious materials, see M. Dominica Legge, *Anglo-Norman Literature and Its Background* (Oxford, 1963), pp. 206–42.

[12] Brook, ed., *Harley Lyrics*, p. 17.

the material and provides an important cultural context for lyrics that have typically been isolated by modern anthologies from their manuscript and its less glamorous religious offerings. Like much of the pious literature produced in the wake of the Lateran Council, many of Harley's religious items are interesting because they are traditional in terms of content and innovative in their use of vernaculars.

In this essay I group and discuss Harley's religious contents under four headings: *Biblical Materials*, including paraphrases from the Bible, materials possibly used for Bible study, and two instances of Middle English verse based on biblical texts or incidents; *Hagiography*, including *Vitas patrum*, French prose saints' lives adapted from the Bible, three Latin saints' lives, and one Middle English legend; *Matters of Practical Religion*, including admonitory matter, instructions on prayer, model prayers, and miscellaneous instructional materials (e.g., reasons for fasting on Friday, no. 106); and *Religious Lyrics*, poems of praise and meditation. These classifications are not ideal, overlapping as they do at several points. For example, *Gloria in excelsis Deo* in French verse (no. 102) is, strictly speaking, a biblical and liturgical paraphrase, but since it concludes with an "amen" and appears in the manuscript's later pages with instructions on prayer, I place it under *Matters of Practical Religion* rather than under *Biblical Materials*. In discussing these subgroups, I do not have the space to take up each item in question, but I try to elaborate on representative texts from each group with an eye to matters of scribal treatment as well as content.

Biblical Materials

In the mid-fourteenth century when Harley 2253 was copied, there was no Middle English translation of the Vulgate Bible in circulation, but there was an Anglo-Norman version.[13] In terms of production values, scribes accorded the Anglo-Norman Bible the same kind of care and respect later shown to the Wycliffite version, at least in its better copies. Some detached leaves from a pocket-sized Anglo-Norman Bible (from the Parabolae Salomonis [Proverbs]), now in the Rare Book Department, Tulane University, are written in double-column format in a small but handsome textura, on uterine vellum, with alternating blue and red paraph marks, careful corrections, and even a couple of glosses. The display qualities of the leaves are equivalent to those in Latin Bibles from the same period.

There were also Anglo-Norman biblical paraphrases available, for instance, a verse Genesis, another poem based on Genesis and Exodus (which was then translated into

---

[13] See Johan Vising, *Anglo-Norman Language and Literature* (London, 1923), p. 71.

prose), a metrical psalter, and individual psalms in Anglo-Norman (e.g., the Miserere [Ps. 50] in London, Lambeth Palace Library MS 522).[14] As noted above, one of Harley's longest religious items is a series of Old Testament prose paraphrases in French (no. 71), stories drawn from Genesis, Exodus, and Numbers. The narratives begin with the story of Jacob and Esau and proceed sequentially to the story of Phineas (paraph marks in the texts often, but not always, signal formal chapter divisions):

fol. 92v	Genesis 27–36, Jacob and Esau
fols. 93r–95v	Genesis 37–50, the story of Jacob
fol. 95v	Exodus 2, the birth of Moses
fol. 96v	Exodus 3, the burning bush
fol. 97r–v	Exodus 7–12, the ten plagues in Egypt
fols. 97v–98r	Exodus 13, passage through the Red Sea
	Exodus 15, the canticle of Miriam
	Exodus 16, manna in the desert
	Exodus 18–20, the Ten Commandments
fol. 98v	Exodus 31, design of the Ark of the Covenant
fols. 98v–99r	Exodus 32, the golden calf
fol. 99v	Exodus 34, Moses' "horns"
fols. 99v–100r	Numbers 1–2, the twelve tribes of Israel
fols. 100v–101r	Numbers 11, God feeds the people again
	Numbers 12, Miriam stricken with leprosy
	Numbers 13, spies sent into Canaan
fol. 101v	Numbers 15, rules for temple offerings
fols. 101v–102r	Numbers 16, the rebellions of Korah
	Numbers 17, Aaron's rod
fol. 102v	Numbers 19, the red heifer
fols. 102v–103r	Numbers 20, Aaron forbidden entry to the Promised Land
	Numbers 21, battle against the Canaanites
fols. 103v–104r	Numbers 22–24, the story of Balaam
fols. 104v–105r	Numbers 25, Phineas's murder of the Midianite woman and her Israelite lover

---

[14] See Jean Bonnard, *Les Traductions de la Bible en vers français au Moyen Âge* (Paris, 1884).

Paul Meyer associates Harley's paraphrases with a French abridgment of Genesis through Job that survives in multiple fifteenth-century copies.[15] Whatever the source, it is tempting to imagine Harley's compiler selecting materials because of their inherent narrative appeal or even sensationalism, such as the story in Numbers 12 of how God afflicts Miriam, Aaron's sister, with leprosy for murmuring against Moses, or the final story of how Phineas surprises the Midianite woman and her Israelite lover together in bed and runs them both through with a dagger. Geoffrey Hartman observes that the stern realism of Numbers and parts of Exodus and Genesis is a helpful qualifier to the attractive "spiritualizing of redemption" in Christianity,[16] and much of this realism certainly gets carried over to these pages of Harley. On the other hand, the stories copied here may simply have been those the scribe had at hand in his exemplar. It is worth observing how the paraphrases skirt elaborate technical information, such as the actual measurements of, building materials for, and appearance of the Ark of the Covenant in Exodus 26. Instead, they concentrate on major Old Testament plotlines, much as popularized or children's Bibles do today.

One notes, too, an occasional effort in the paraphrases, which are usually close to the Vulgate, to play up marvelous elements in the Old Testament stories and, in one case, to connect these with New Testament events. For instance, the paraphrase of Exodus 3 describes how Moses sees on Mount Horeb a burning bush illumined by a "merueillouse flaume," whereas the Vulgate simply says that the bush was burning (*Apparuitque ei Dominus in flamma ignis de medio rubi*, Exod. 3.2). And in describing the cloud that surrounds Mount Sinai when Moses meets God there (Exod. 19), the paraphrase writer thinks of the cloud around Mount Tabor, on which Moses and Elijah appear with Christ during his transfiguration (Matt. 17.5). In this last detail, there may even be an amateur effort at typology. These features of the French paraphrases are probably not the invention of Harley's compiler, but they do suggest the kind of interest in biblical narrative that he might have shared with other medieval writers and readers.

The scribal details in the biblical stories are also noteworthy. First, on fol. 97v the scribe interrupts the stories to provide a list — in the form of an awkward Latin rhyming couplet — of the ten plagues of Egypt (Exod. 7–11). The list stands out because it is in textura

---

[15] Paul Meyer, review of S. Berger, *La Bible française au Moyen Âge*, and Jean Bonnard, *Les Traductions de la Bible en vers français au Moyen Âge*, *Romania* 17 (1885): 140. On Peter Comester's twelfth-century *Historia scholastica* as a possible source, see A. D. Wilshere, "The Anglo-Norman Bible Stories in MS Harley 2253," *Forum for Modern Language Studies* 24 (1988): 78–89. For a qualification of Wilshere's argument, see John J. Thompson's essay in this volume.

[16] See Geoffrey H. Hartman, "Numbers," in *Congregation: Contemporary Writers Read the Jewish Bible*, ed. David Rosenberg (San Diego, 1987), p. 42.

letters slightly larger than the cursive hand used for the stories themselves. Also, it omits the third from last plague, of locusts, perhaps because of scribal eyeskip from *Locusta* in the exemplar to *Brutus caligo*, the penultimate plague:

> Sanguis. rana. culex. musce. pecus. ulcera. grando.
> Brutus. caligo. Mors opt[i]mere necando.
>
> [Blood, frog, gnats, flies, cattle, boils, hail;
> A heavy mist, death of the firstborn.]

Several of these terms are not the Latin words for the plagues in the Vulgate, perhaps because the list had some extrabiblical origin in one of the commentators, or because the original Latin was metrically intractable. The list is crudely mnemonic, that is, it is a summary statement of the extended narrative of the plagues that a reader might easily pick out on the page and memorize.

Second, although glosses are rare in Harley, three appear in the biblical paraphrases: a flourished *nota* at the start of Numbers, where the names of the twelve tribes of Israel occur ("De lygnange de Ruben, etc.," fol. 99v); and a simpler *nota* plus the name "Leuy." next to "le lignange Leuy" in the text (fol. 100r). In the paraphrased story of the golden calf, the subsequent massacre of Israelites carried out by the sons of Levi receives emphasis. The attention drawn to the Levites, the priestly class, in these biblical paraphrases and glosses might, then, point to a clerical hand in the copying of Harley.

Harley contains several other religious items that may have been collected because of their usefulness to Bible study. By Bible study I do not mean the formal exegesis of the commentators, which sought to penetrate the veil of Scripture's literal sense to expose its spiritual and mystical ones. Rather, I mean pious interest in biblical incident and persons by clerics and layfolk alike, which might be an end in itself (an edifying *curiositas*) or which under the right circumstances might provoke prayer and meditation. One such item appears on the verso of the final page of French biblical paraphrases, a table of the canonical books of Scripture headed *Nomina librorum bibliotece* (no. 72). The scribe distinguishes each biblical book by giving its title a separate paraph mark, with the exception of the Pentateuch. These five books, Genesis, Exodus, Leviticus, Numbers, and Deuteronomy, are bracketed and marked "Libri legales." Books that consist of more than one part are so marked: thus, for instance, Kings ("Regum") is designated as having four books, and Corinthians ("Ad Corinthios") as consisting of two epistles. The table may have been copied simply because fol. 105v (the final verso of the quire) was blank. It serves, however, to give a comprehensive sense of the great book from which the foregoing narratives were excerpted.

As Ker notes, the books listed are those usually found in thirteenth-century Bibles.[17] There is, however, an anomaly: the Psalter appears at the end of the list, immediately after the Apocalypse and just before two notes, one on interpreting Hebrew names and the other on the length of a cubit. The anomaly may have arisen because of the Psalter's special independence as a biblical book throughout the Middle Ages. It was the Church's prayerbook, the common property of all the faithful, and it was often copied and commented on separately from the rest of Scripture. Furthermore, the commentators regarded the Psalms as a digest of the wisdom of all Scripture, a kind of Bible in miniature. As the fourteenth-century mystic, Richard Rolle, explains the matter in the prologue to his *English Psalter*, the Psalter

> is perfeccioun of dyuyne pagyne, for it contenys all that other bokes draghes langly [set forth at length], that is, the lare [teachings] of the ald testament & of the new.[18]

Or the anomaly may have arisen from a simple copying error. The entry for Job, the book that immediately precedes the Psalter in canonical order, seems to be written in Harley's table over an erasure, suggesting scribal confusion. Had the scribe missed "Job" in the initial copying due to eyeskip, writing first "Psalterium" and then "Parabolae Salomonis" (the book immediately after the Psalter), he might have felt adding it here and moving "Psalterium" to the end justifiable on grounds explained above. The reason for the anomaly, though, is obscure. It may be relevant, however, that the Psalms figure so prominently in the practical matter on prayer concentrated in Harley's later leaves (especially in nos. 101, 110, and 111, lists of psalms appropriate for various occasions).

Other Harley texts useful to Bible study include three guides to pilgrim sites in the Holy Land (nos. 38, 39, and 95), a letter authenticating a coffer of relics at Oviedo (no. 97), and, maybe strangest of all, a French prose description of Christ's physical appearance, said to be derived from the chronicles of Rome (no. 91). It is possible that texts such as Harley's extract from Jacques de Vitry's thirteenth-century *Historia orientalis* (no. 95), with its descriptions of Alexandria, Babylon, and Damascus, had a merely exotic appeal for the book's compiler. More likely, however, this material satisfied a deeper spiritual need. Like the maps and photographs appended to modern study Bibles, these descriptions realize imaginatively for those who read them a biblical landscape they may never visit.

---

[17] Ker, *Facsimile*, p. xiii.

[18] H. R. Bramley, ed., *The Psalter, or Psalms of David and Certain Canticles, with a Translation and Exposition in English by Richard Rolle of Hampole* (Oxford, 1884), p. 4. Compare Rolle's main source, Peter Lombard's twelfth-century *catena* on the Psalms (J.-P. Migne, ed., *PL* 191:57).

As we will see in Harley's emotional lyrics on Christ's Passion, mid-fourteenth-century religion valued the affective element in prayer. Even bald geographical description could aid the meditative process of *compositio loci*, the mind's effort to project itself, during prayer, to the scene of particular biblical events. And the content of the Harley extract from *Historia orientalis* is not undetailed. It mentions, for example, a famous image of the Blessed Virgin painted at Constantinople and the martyrdom of the Evangelist Matthew (fol. 130r), just as the Latin letter authenticating the Oviedo coffer lists its contents, many of which (like the *arca* itself, fashioned by disciples of the twelve apostles) bring the reader closer to the reality behind biblical texts. Here is earth from the Mount of Olives, hair with which Mary Magdalene wiped the feet of Christ, a right sandal belonging to St. Peter, and a stone from Mount Sinai, where Moses spoke with God. As moderns, we find devotion to such materials a mark of credulity. For medievals, however, these objects authenticated by the Church and writings about them were talismans, that is, magical links with the real biblical past and with real sacred persons.

In the thirteenth and fourteenth centuries, Christian piety, especially its emotional component, increasingly focused on Christ's human nature and his person, and the Gospel narratives were augmented to provide more details about Christ's life on earth. Some of Harley's biblical materials reflect this interest. For instance, in the book's thirteenth-century part there are two such works: an extract on the Passion from a versified Bible history by Herman of Valenciennes (no. 2) and a French prose version of the so-called *Gospel of Nicodemus* (or *Acts of Pilate*, a text that also circulated in Middle English[19]; no. 3). The latter is a fourth-century apocryphal work that draws heavily on the canonical Gospels but supplements them with additional, purportedly eyewitness detail. It contains, for instance, an account of Christ's descent into hell, a legendary biblical event treated in one of Harley's Middle English verse pieces, *The Harrowing of Hell* (no. 21).[20]

---

[19] See William Henry Hulme, ed., *The Middle-English Harrowing of Hell and Gospel of Nicodemus*, EETS e.s. 100 (London, 1907).

[20] This item occurs in an earlier version (*IMEV* 185) in Oxford, Bodleian Library MS Digby 86, a "commonplace book" (according to one scholar) that contains, like Harley, AN and ME materials. Other religious items it shares with Harley are a debate between the body and soul (*IMEV* 1461); *Stond Wel, Moder, vnder Rode* (*IMEV* 3211); *Suete Iesu, King of Blysse* (*IMEV* 3236); and *Sayings of St. Bernard* (*IMEV* 3310). The body-soul debate is discussed in Karl Reichl's and Helen Phillips's essays in this volume; the other poems shared by Harley and Digby I discuss in this essay. For the term "commonplace book" with reference to Digby, and a survey of the MS's contents and provenance, see B. D. H. Miller, "The Early History of Bodleian MS Digby 86," *Annuale Mediaevale* 4 (1963): 23–56. On the similarities between Harley and Digby, see also the essay by Marilyn Corrie in this volume.

Harley's lyrics on the Passion (discussed below) offer a more vivid, if at times more lurid, testament to this development in late medieval piety. But imaginative interest in Christ's humanity was not confined for the later Middle Ages to Jesus' sufferings on the Cross. The Evangelists are reticent about Jesus' boyhood, so apocryphal stories developed about his hidden years and were translated into visual material culture in manuscript miniatures and even on wall tiles.[21] While none of the four Gospels contains a description of Christ's appearance, one does appear in an extended passage of rhythmical French prose in Harley, *La Destinccioun de la estature Iesu Crist Nostre Seigneur* (no. 91), presumably authenticated by its opening reference to "en auncien estoire de Rome." The description anticipates the glamorizing tendency in nineteenth-century religious art, such as Holman Hunt's *The Light of the World*, where Christ is beautifully handsome. Like late medieval panel portraits of Jesus, the text may have served a devotional or meditative purpose, and it in fact survives in Middle English appended to a treatise on temptation ("This lore that folewith techith crist in parable to his children") in Manchester, John Rylands Library, English MS 412:

> Hit is red in the stories and cronycles of Rome, that Our lord Ihesu Crist was callid of the people a prophete of trouthe. He was of a seemly stature and gladsome, havyng worshipfull chere and gladsome, insomuche that al men that behelde hym lovid hym and dred hym.
>
> His heer was of the coloure of walnotys, hangyng dooune playne almost to the eryn, crispn somwhat and yolowe. And from the erys to his shuldren they were shynyng And lightly mevyng. And he had a faire shode in the myddes of his hedde, after the maner and vsage of men of nasareth. He had a playne forehed, moost clere, withoute any ryvelyng [wrinkling] in his face or any spotte. And therwithalle it was faire and honestly rody. Ne ther was no defaute of his mouthe ne of his nose. And he had a thyk berde, full of here, like in coloure to the heere of his hed. But his was not full long. And in the chyn it was double forkyd. He had faire gray eyen and clere.
>
> In all the makyng of his body he was evyn and right. He had also armes and hondis delectable and faire to sight, and in speche he was grete in voice, selde spekyng and sobrely. As the prophecye saith of hym, "Worthely he was faire, and semely in shapp, passyng all the childern of women" (Ps. 44.3). (fol. 49v)

In both the French and English, the passage proceeds in the plainest of styles to describe a paragon who inspired both love and respect. The psalmist's prophecy with which the text concludes, explicitly attributed to David in the Harleian text ("a bon droit dit le prophete Dauid"), lends credibility to the hyperbole: what the writer describes was already forecast before Christ's birth by the most eloquent of Old Testament seers.

---

[21] See, for example, Elizabeth S. Eames, *English Medieval Tiles* (Cambridge, Mass., 1985), p. 23 pl. 24.

Two of Harley's Middle English religious poems are based on biblical material. *The Harrowing of Hell* (no. 21) is a closet drama,[22] describing Christ's descent into limbo after his death on the cross. Here, he releases from the devil's grip those virtuous Old and New Testament figures who believed but died before Christ's redemptive act: Adam, Eve, Abraham, David, John the Baptist, and Moses. The poem opens with an appeal to its audience to listen to the speaker's account of "A strif . . . / Of Iesu ant of Sathan" (lines 2–3; fol. 55v). There is a debate between Christ and Satan, during which Satan argues like a lawyer that mankind belongs to him because he bought Adam in fair exchange for an apple:

> Whose buyþ any þyng
> Hit is hys ant hys offspryng.
> Adam hungry com me to
> Monrade dude y him me do.
> For on appel Ich ȝef hym,
> He is myn ant al hys kin. (lines 85–90; fol. 56ra)

Christ responds, however, that the apple — indeed the apple tree — belonged to him because he fashioned them, and he asks how Satan presumes to make a profit from someone else's possessions:

> Hou myhstest þou on eny wyse
> Of oþer monnes þyng mak marchandise?
> Seþþe he wes boht wyþ myn
> Wyþ resoun wolle Ich hauen hym. (lines 95–98)

The dialogue deliberately places Christ's claim in a legal context to distinguish it from Satan's irrational plea, which masks his use of force ("Þe deuel heuede so muche pouste / Þat alle mosten to helle te," lines 7–8; fol. 55va). But as in medieval paintings of the Harrowing, where hell's gates fall open at Christ's slightest touch, the "strif" here is really no contest at all. Satan is a ridiculous figure whose authority, such as it is, cannot keep the drama's only extrabiblical character, "Janitor" (hell's doorkeeper), from fleeing:

> Ich haue herd wordes stronge
> Ne dar Y her no lengore stonde.

---

[22] Halliwell felt, by contrast, that the play was meant for performance. See J. O. Halliwell, ed. and trans., *The Harrowing of Hell: A Miracle-Play Written in the Reign of Edward the Second* (London, 1840), p. 3.

Kepe þe gates whose may,
Y lete hem stonde ant renne away! (lines 140–44; fol. 56rb)

Aside from this moment of comedy, the poem's most interesting passages are the speeches
by each of the worthies Christ has come to release, signalled in the manuscript margins by
their names. (These appear at the ends of lines, hidden on the inside margin of fol. 56va,
because of the scribe's confusion of format with fol. 56rb.) The speeches of John the
Baptist and Moses, which the poet reserves for last, are especially poignant, given the
special biblical authority of these figures as harbinger and lawgiver, respectively. For
instance,

Louerd Crist Icham Iohan
Þat þe folewede in flum Iordan.
Tuelf moneþ is agon
Þat Y þolede martirdom.
Þou sendest me þe ryhte wey
Into helle forte sey
Þat þou Crist Godes sone
Sone shuldest to helle come
Forto lesen of helle pyne
Alle þat þou holdest þyne. (lines 207–16; fol. 56va–b)

The poetry is wooden. By its directness, however, it compels the penitential prayer with
which the drama concludes. Perhaps the poet recalled, and wants his reader to remember,
Christ's extravagant praise for the Baptist after his imprisonment ("Amongst those that are
born of women, there is not a greater prophet than John the Baptist," Luke 7.28). If John
suffered in good faith not only martyrdom but his term in limbo, why should we not avoid
hell and win heaven by perfecting ourselves, with the help of divine grace?

Let vs neuer þider come.
Louerd for þi muchele grace
Graunte vs in heouene one place.
Let vs neuer be forloren,
For no sunne Crist ycoren. (lines 240–44; fol. 56vb)

Like so much of the religious verse in Harley, the Middle English *Harrowing of Hell* is
both an expression of and inducement to penitential prayer.

The Labourers in the Vineyard (no. 41) is a lyric paraphrase of one of Christ's more
troubling parables, the story of the vineyard owner in Matthew 20.1–16 who hires workers
throughout the day, only at day's end to give each the same wage for different amounts

of work. When those who began work earliest murmur against their employer, calling him unfair, he delivers a stern rebuke: they were in no way mistreated. Christ explains that the vineyard owner is God and that in the kingdom of heaven the last shall be first, and the first last.

The Middle English poem begins in an offhand manner, with a metonymy attributing the story to Matthew the Evangelist himself rather than to Christ in St. Matthew's gospel:

> Of a mon Matheu þohte,
> Þo he þe wynȝord whrohte,
> Ant wrot hit on ys boc. (lines 1–3; fol. 70vb)

The directness and colloquial tone move the story instantly from the biblical past to the poet's present, implying not only the immediate relevance of the gospel to contemporary moral concerns, but also encouraging the reader's identification with the sentiments of the worker (here singular, "þis mon," line 55) who feels cheated. His thoughts, conflated with the narrator's, sound like the simple, honest dialect expressions of Thomas Hardy's peasants, or of churl figures who appear in the Middle English mystery plays:

> For ryht were þat me raht
> Þe mon þat al day wraht
> Þe more mede anyht. (lines 34–36)

Against these too human grumblings, the poet sets the categorical response of God, the vineyard owner:

> To alle þat euer hider eode
> To do today my neode
> Ichulle be wraþþelees. (lines 46–48; fol. 71rb)

"Wraþþelees" implies, as the biblical judgment does not ("Is it not lawful for me to do what I will?," Matt. 20.15), a suspicious motive behind the speaker's plea for fairness: he does not simply want what is his but begrudges his neighbor something. Like the faithful rather than the prodigal son, he prefers invidious comparisons and judgment to the Father-God's generous love.

In a marvelous poetic turn, the lyric's final stanza goes beyond biblical paraphrase as the narrator identifies for a moment with the outraged laborer. He complains that the world does him wrong, that he is "rooles ase þe roo" (invoking an Old Testament analogy for his anxious spirit; compare Ps. 41.2), and he represents the frustrated worker sympathetically (like the narrator, he longs for something more!), only to pull the reader up short in the poem's final line:

Þis mon þat Matheu ȝef
A peny þat wes so bref,
    Þis frely folk vnfete,
ȝet he ȝyrnden more,
Ant saide he come wel ȝore,
    Ant gonne is loue forlete. (lines 55–60)

The entire final stanza is a counsel to penitential humility. The narrator admits his dissatisfaction with life but implies that to blame God for life's disappointments might result in the loss of divine affection. The poem confronts, at once, the ache of human restlessness (which Aquinas interprets as a reflex of man's longing for God) and the need for submission. God's ways, after all, are not man's. *The Labourers in the Vineyard*, while not Harley's best religious poem, progresses from New Testament story to sorrowful piety in a movement similar to that found in *The Harrowing of Hell*, and, more deftly than that poem, it illustrates the Bible's didactic hold on the fourteenth-century imagination.

Hagiography

There are nine hagiographic texts distributed throughout Harley 2253: in the first four thirteenth-century quires, the French *Vitas patrum*, mentioned above, along with French prose narratives of the martyrdoms of St. John the Evangelist, St. John the Baptist, St. Bartholomew, and St. Peter (nos. 4–7);[23] and in the fourteenth-century quires, three Latin *vitae* — the lives of St. Ethelbert (no. 18), St. Etfrid (no. 98), and St. Wistan (no. 116) — and a Middle English *vita* of an obscure female saint, St. Marina (no. 32).

The French materials are of no high literary significance, but they do attest to a strong didactic impulse behind the conjoining of Harley's two parts. As B. A. O'Connor notes in the introduction to his edition of *Vitas patrum*, its author, compelled by an "unrelieved didactic purpose . . . fashioned not poetry, but verse."[24] The work's meter is painfully regular, and its rhymes heavily repetitive. As the opening lines of *Vitas patrum* indicate, the author wrote for the greater glory of God, Mary, and the saints, composing "un sermun" [a discourse] in which he plays the role of anonymous teacher. Another copy of

---

[23] For editions of the French saints' lives, see Delbert W. Russell, ed., *Légendier apostolique anglo-normand: Édition critique, introduction et notes* (Montreal, 1989).

[24] O'Connor, *Vitas Patrum*, p. xxxii. On the real author of *Vitas patrum*, thought by O'Connor to have been Henry D'Arci, but probably a London priest, see Keith V. Sinclair, "The Translations of the *Vitas patrum*, *Thaïs*, *Antichrist*, and *Vision de saint Paul* Made for Anglo-Norman Templars: Some Neglected Literary Considerations," *Speculum* 72 (1997): 762.

the text, in Paris, Bibliothèque Nationale MS fr. 24862, appears between an extended French commentary on the Book of Proverbs and a French sermon on Pentecost.[25] Like biblical commentary, proverbial wisdom, and homily, *Vitas patrum* aims to teach rather than to please. Indeed, as O'Connor observes, the text known as *Vitas patrum* translates only a small part of the Latin *Vitae patrum*, neglecting exotic biographical materials about the Desert Fathers and travel diaries of those who visited them in favor of the *Verba seniorum* or *Apophthegmata*, the sayings or teachings of the Fathers, although more of the exotic material is included in the Harley than in the Paris copy.[26] (Chapter headings throughout the Paris copy of the text, lacking in Harley, underscore the work's didactic character — for instance, "De penitentia," "De mala societate," "De opere e oratione," and "De pena eterna.")

Unlike *Vitas patrum*, Harley's three Latin saints' lives do indeed concentrate on incident, for each of these saints is a local hero, honored in some way for his connection with Mercian history. St. Ethelbert (d. 794) is the most famous, a king of the East Angles who was beheaded on the order of Offa, king of Mercia, because he was perceived as a political rival. Ethelbert became patron of Hereford Cathedral, where some of his relics repose. St. Etfrid (d. ca. 675) was a Northumbrian priest known for his preaching abilities, who traveled south and converted King Merewald of Mercia. Merewald, in turn, established in 660 Leominster Priory, where Etfrid served as head. And St. Wistan, whose life is the last substantial religious item in Harley, was grandson of King Wiglaf of Mercia. He was assassinated in 849 for opposing the marriage of his widowed mother to his godfather because of their spiritual kinship.

These three legends indicate a clear Herefordshire provenance for Harley 2253. As Wright puts it in the preface to his nineteenth-century edition of Harley's lyrics, the lives "could hardly have been collected together by any one who was not residing in, and interested in the monastic establishments of, Herefordshire."[27] Wright goes further, however, giving priority to the life of St. Etfrid because of its local peculiarity and because a large cross appears above its title on fol. 132r; he argues that Harley's compiler must have been a clerk connected with Leominster Priory.[28] Ker, contesting this view, notes that the cross may in fact conclude the previous item, the letter authenticating the Oviedo *arca*,

---

[25] O'Connor, *Vitas Patrum*, p. xxii.

[26] O'Connor, *Vitas Patrum*, p. xiii–xiv; see also pp. 160–224, where O'Connor reproduces the texts unique to Harley.

[27] Wright, *Specimens*, p. vi.

[28] Wright, *Specimens*, p. 7.

and he usefully complicates the issue of provenance by discussing household accounts information from Harley's binding leaves.[29]

Matters of manuscript provenance are beyond the scope of this essay and have, at any rate, been clarified by Carter Revard's investigations.[30] In Wright's belated defense, however, one might observe that the Harley cross cannot be safely joined to either the *arca* letter or the St. Etfrid legend, and it may have been intended as a devout, iconographic link between them. Moreover, although Wright does not provide such manuscript details in his preface, St. Etfrid's legend is the only Harley saint's life with reader-friendly marginal apparatus: the scribe numbers its seven chapters in the margins and, on the inside margin of fol. 133a, signals the founding date of Leominster Priory with a gloss, "Anno domini vj^elx." These details, of course, do not really support Wright's claims about Harley's provenance. They do, however, distinguish St. Etfrid's legend from the other two Harley saints' lives and perhaps underscore the scribe's special interest in it.

From a literary point of view, none of the three lives commands attention, although each is clearly intended to edify. The St. Etfrid legend is over almost as soon as its prologue concludes, with praise for the saint as "vir doctrina clarus, et vita magnificus" and a brief account of how he preached the word of God to Merewald and his people ("verbum Dei predicans regem et eius gentem"), converting them from paganism to Christianity (fol. 132r). There is one nice typological touch in the story, when the author compares Merewald's prophetic dream to one Joseph interpreted for Pharaoh (fol. 132v). Other than this, however, the point is to build up Leominster via its association with the saint.

St. Wistan's legend in Harley, which Ker describes as an "abbreviation" of the *vita* in the *Chronicon abbatiae de Evesham*,[31] is in fact merely an episode from this life, the martyrdom itself, with an appended reference to Wistan's most splendid miracle, the shaft of light ("columpna lucis") emitted from the place of his death for thirty days following his murder. Thus the scribe aptly titles his work, in the upper margin of fol. 140v, *De martirio sancti Wistani*. As Ker explains, the scribe or his source sets forth, whereas the *Chronicon* life does not, Wistan's genealogy — his relationship to Wiglaf of Mercia. All of the dialogue in the *Chronicon* life gets omitted, however, including Wistan's passionate, Hamlet-like speech against marriage to his mother, which concludes with high-minded appeals to New Testament tradition and canon law. Also

---

[29] Ker, *Facsimile*, pp. xxii–xxiii.

[30] See Carter Revard's essay in this volume, and the footnotes to his article *"Gilote et Johane:* An Interlude in B. L. MS. Harley 2253," *Studies in Philology* 79 (1982): 122–46.

[31] Ker, *Facsimile*, p. xvi. For the fuller text, see W. D. Macray, ed., *Chronicon abbatiae de Evesham, ad annum 1418*, Rolls Series 29 (London, 1863), pp. 326–32.

omitted are two typological analogies for Wistan's dilemma, the examples of Job and John the Baptist.

Similar pruning occurs in Harley's *Vita sancti Ethelberti* (no. 18). This text Ker describes as an "abbreviation" of a *passio* in Cambridge, Corpus Christi College MS 303, a shorter and different version of Ethelbert's legend than the more famous one by Giraldus Cambrensis.[32] It appears, however, to be an abbreviation and conflation of the two texts, largely the Corpus *passio*, but possessing in its later parts significant interpolations from Cambrensis's text. In the early sections from Corpus, the adapter eliminates most of the dialogue, concentrating on incident. In the later sections, where the interpolations from Cambrensis appear, the adapter retains more direct speech. This gives special prominence to an episode in the final chapter of Harley's version ("Tercio vero nocte, etc."; fol. 54va), when St. Ethelbert appears to a noble named Brithfrid, asking him to move his body to a monastery near a place named "Status Waye," or Hereford.[33] In other words, the adapter of Harley's version may have intended to make the Hereford connection with St. Ethelbert's legend more pointed. And this, in turn, might have made his version of the story more attractive to Harley's compiler. Beyond the local interest, however, the legend of St. Ethelbert seems to have had a genuine pious appeal to the Harley scribe, since later in the manuscript's process of compilation (the item's ink is lighter than that used for the *vita*), he filled some blank space after the legend with a moving Latin prayer (no. 19). It opens with these parallel entreaties:

> Anima Cristi sanctifica me;
> Corpus Cristi salua me;
> Sanguis Cristi inebria me;
> Aqua lateris Cristi laua me;
> Passio Cristi co[n]forta me. (fol. 54vb)

This prayer, in its emotional simplicity, reminds us that medieval saints' lives often reenact the Passion of Christ himself and invite readers to participate in the Passion by following the path of humilty. Also, *Anima Cristi sanctifica me* reveals that Harley's compiler understood the double value of prayers: as pious self-expressions and meditative models, texts worth both saying and recording.[34]

---

[32] Ker, *Facsimile*, p. x. For the two source texts, see M. R. James, "Two Lives of St. Ethelbert, King and Martyr," *English Historical Review* 32 (1917): 214–44.

[33] James, "Two Lives," p. 219.

[34] On the probable source for the prayer, see Ker, *Facsimile*, p. x.

The legend of St. Marina (no. 32) deserves special notice as the only Middle English saint's life in Harley and as the *vita* of a female saint in a manuscript that contains a fair amount of scurrilous antifeminist material.[35] (This material, by the way, medieval clerkly culture might have classed as "religious," since many of its attacks take the high road of moral accusation. But one nineteenth-century reader of *De conjuge non ducenda* [no. 83], one of Harley's antifeminist diatribes, spoke for many when he scrawled above the title of the Latin text in a book at the Tulane University Library,[36] "A brutal piece of Monkish foulness, worse than any Classical smuttishness. Luther is here justified.")

Although her *vita* does not merit a heading in the manuscript, Marina's legend recoups many of women's losses in the pages of Harley. She was the daughter of a man who, being devout, entered a monastery after his wife's death. How the father became widowed results in some (probably unintended) comedy at the start of the legend. The pious soul, still married, prays to God for some special "vertu / Þe fend to shende ant is myht" (lines 12–13; fol. 64va), with this result:

> Ant God to seruen þat is best ryht
> Hit bifel is wyf wes ded,
> Ant he biþohte him such a reed
> He wolde be monk in alle wyse
> Ant ȝelden him to Godes seruise. (lines 14–18; fol. 64va)

Missing his child, however, he pleads with his abbot to bring her to the monastery, lying about her sex. While living there, Marina develops a reputation for piety and herself becomes a monk, advancing in the monastery's ranks. Her fortunes take a turn for the worse, however, when she is accused by a local woman of fathering her child and is thrust out of the monastery to care for the infant, despite her pathetic prayers to Mary and to Christ:

> "Ich habbe ysunged merci Y crie
> Þou me help, Sone Marie.

---

[35] For the background to Marina's legend, see Donald Atwater with Catherine Rachel John, *The Penguin Dictionary of Saints*, 3rd ed. (London, 1995), p. 239. For another ME version ("hou seynt Maryne was diffamed") from the Vernon MS (Oxford, Bodleian Library MS Eng. poet. a.1), see Carl Horstmann, ed., "Die Evangelien-Geschichten der Homiliensammlung des Ms. Vernon," *Archiv für das Studium der neueren Sprachen und Literaturen* 57 (1876): 241–61.

[36] The writing occurs in a library copy of Thomas Wright, ed., *The Latin Poems Commonly Attributed to Walter Mapes*, Camden Society 16 (1841; repr. New York, 1968), pp. 77–85.

Help me, ȝef þi wille beo,
Louerd þat restest on Rode-treo." (lines 119–22; fol. 65ra)

Marina's patience under adversity and her care for the child are appropriately placed in
a manuscript that contains both French and English poems in praise of the Virgin, who
incidentally, we learn at the start of this story, was the object of her father's special
devotion: once widowed, "Marie milde to wyf he ches" (line 20; fol. 64va).

The narrative, like many medieval saints' lives, is at once edifying and sensational.
Indeed, it concludes with quite a dramatic discovery scene. After her death, Marina's sex
is revealed, and the monks and woman who wronged her do penance. The until now self-
effacing narrator joins in, concluding the legend with a prayer:

To þilke blisse God vs sende
Þat lesteþ euer wiþouten ende.
He þat made ant wrot þis vie
Ant hyre haþ in memorie,
From shome Crist him shilde.
Leuedi, ȝef þi wille be,
Þou haue merci of me
For loue of þine childe. Amen. (lines 225–32; fol. 65vb)

Whether "he who made and wrote this life" refers to Harley's scribe as translator or simple
copyist is unclear. But the concluding prayer reminds us that one of hagiography's appeals
in the Middle Ages was the dream of innocent victimization it encouraged readers to
participate in as a means of recovering, through renewed piety, their lost virtue.[37]

Matters of Practical Religion

In addition to literary inducements to piety in the form of biblical materials and
hagiography, Harley contains a great deal of information on practical religious matters.
This is of two types: admonitory texts, which sometimes try to shock the reader into good
living, and instructions on prayer, sometimes model prayers, designed to educate readers
in pious self-expression.

Among Harley's admonitory pieces there are: a short French stanza warning against the
folly of *charnel amour*, copied in the manuscript just above the Middle English

---

[37] For medieval attitudes toward saints' lives, see Thomas J. Heffernan, *Sacred Biography: Saints
and Their Biographers in the Middle Ages* (New York, 1988).

admonition *Earth upon Earth* (nos. 24a, 24b); a French poem on avoiding pride and the other deadly sins, which uses Lucifer and Adam as powerful exempla (*Vne Petite Parole seigneurs escotez*, no. 59); two Middle English poems, one on the traditional three foes of man, the World, the Flesh, and the Devil — "Middelerd for mon wes mad" (no. 27) — and the other a popular rhymed exhortation, the so-called *Sayings of St. Bernard* (no. 74); and a Latin extract from John of Wales's *Communeloquium* (no. 109), a thirteenth-century compendium for preachers, which compares life and the world ("Mundus") to a game of chess and a chessboard (the white and black squares on the board are likened to man's double state, life and death).[38]

Admonitions can be shrill. Except for the French poem on the sins, however, those in Harley generally avoid this pitfall — even the anxious *Sayings of St. Bernard*, which is more sophisticated than it at first seems. Despite Brook's dismissal of it as a "moralizing jingle,"[39] the brief lyric *Earth upon Earth* engages the reader on both an intellectual and emotional level:

> Erþe toc of erþe, erþe wyþ woh,
> Erþe oþer erþe to þe erþe droh,
> Erþe leyde erþe in erþene þroh,
> Þo heuede erþe of erþe, erþe ynoh. (lines 1–4; fol. 59v)

The riddling quality of the lines keeps the reader's feelings, for a moment, at bay: the punned sense has to be worked out.[40] Yet, even as it is, the term *erþe* rings out at regular intervals, like a death knell, meaning first the earth from which man was made, next the earthly things he accumulates senselessly throughout his life (which, Christ warned, will rust or be consumed by fire), and ultimately the dead earth, man's lifeless body, laid in an earthen grave. The doubling of the noun at the end of the poem's final, weary line, "Þo heuede erþe of erþe, erþe ynoh," drives home the message: man, like the things he chases throughout his life, is nothing. And not even the process of learning this lesson, by deciphering this riddling poem, will impede one's relentless progress to the grave. It may be that the scribe intended the riddle to be read in counterpoint to the more straightforward French admonitions just above it on the page:

---

[38] On John of Wales (fl. in Oxford ca. 1260), see Andrew G. Little, *The Grey Friars in Oxford* (Oxford, 1892), pp. 143–51, and Jenny Swanson, *John of Wales: A Study in the Works and Ideas of a Thirteenth-Century Friar* (Cambridge, 1989).

[39] Brook, ed., *Harley Lyrics*, p. 15.

[40] On the riddling qualities of the poem, see Russell A. Peck, "Public Dreams and Private Myths: Perspectives in Middle English Literature," *PMLA* 90 (1975): 461–68, especially pp. 465–66.

Charnel amour est folie / qe velt amer sagement . . .
Brief delit est lecherie / mes santz fyn dure le torment. (lines 1–2, 7–8; fol. 59v)

[For the one who wants to love wisely, fleshly love is folly . . . The pleasure of lechery is fleeting, but the torment lasts forever.]

In Harley the reader can take his moral medicine directly or not, from the tonalities of the pulpit or those of the poet. Whatever the form, the man who learns from such advice will reject folly and pray for divine help.

The Three Foes of Man begins with something like the repetitive style of Harley's *Earth upon Earth* riddle. The poet uses hyperalliteration to warn man against secret sin, which is certain at Doomsday to be revealed:

Icherde a blisse budel vs bad
  Þe dreri domesdai to drede,
Of sunful sauhting sone be sad
  Þat derne doþ þis derne dede.
    Þah he ben derne done,
  Þis wrakeful werkes vnder wede,
    In soule soteleþ sone.

Sone is sotel as Ich ou sai,
  Þis sake, alþah hit seme suete. (lines 5–13; fol. 62v)

The poem implies that part of sin's sweetness is its hidden quality: if one knew one's sins would be exposed, one would not commit them. One critic identifies the "blisse budel" of these lines as John the Baptist,[41] but we hardly need to be so specific. He might be a Langland-like figure, wandering the world, whose message unexpectedly impresses the poem's speaker. For the speaker, at the start of the second stanza quoted above, takes on the beadle's role. The rest of his poem is moral critique, from which (notably) he does not exempt himself:

In sunne ant sorewe Y am seint,
  Þat siweþ me so fully sore;
My murþe is al wiþ mournyng meind,
  Nay may Ich myþen hit namore. (lines 56–59)

---

[41] Thomas G. Duncan, ed., *Medieval English Lyrics 1200–1400* (Harmondsworth, 1995), p. 207n5.

As so often in Harley's religious texts, injunction of one form or another gives way to admission. The speaker cannot conceal any longer his own guilt: he becomes Everyman, admitting like Haukyn in *Piers Plowman*, "We cannot escape sin!"[42]

The speaker of the *Sayings of St. Bernard* is preachier. He appeals to "ȝe þat wolleþ ou selue yknowe" (fol. 106ra), drawing on Scripture for his stark message,

> Þat mon is worm ant wormes kok
> Ant wormes he shal vede. (lines 8–9; fol. 106ra)

The amplification of the message, however, is more subtle. For instance, in arguing the instability of man's fleshly life, he uses chiasmus to mimic life's reversals:

> Nou þou hast wrong ant nou ryht,
> Nou þou art heuy ant nou lyht,
>   Þou lepest ase a roo.
> Nou þou art sekest ant nou holest,
> Nou þou art rychest ant nou porest.
>   Nis þis muche woo? (lines 37–42; fol. 106va)

Later in the poem, after discussing the changed condition of Lucifer, from archangel to archfiend, the speaker appeals directly to the reader's fear, telling him to beware the devil's hooks. Suddenly, however, there is a long *ubi sunt* passage, which creates pleasant images of "Lordes, ledyes, þat hauekes bere" (line 122; fol. 107ra), only to dispel them like smoke. The final stanzas invoke the spiritual battle topos, a moral commonplace derived from the Pauline epistles, to shore up the reader's courage. A text that could have been repellent instead engages its reader's attention by its violent mixture of styles.

Most of the texts on prayer and model prayers in Harley are concentrated in the book's last quire (fols. 134–140), where they are copied densely on the page, suggesting that they were deliberately assembled as a group, either in the scribe's exemplar or by Harley's compiler himself. They are mixed in this quire with other practical information on Christian devotion, such as a list of angels to think on (no. 100), directions for weekly masses (no. 107), and a list of masses in honor of God and St. Giles (no. 108). One item, a French prose explanation of reasons for the Friday fast (no. 106), lists important Old and New Testament events that occurred on Friday, such as David's slaying of Goliath, the Annunciation, and Christ's death on the Cross. The point, one assumes, is to indicate that

---

[42] "Synne seweþ vs euere" (B version, XIV.326), in George Kane and E. T. Donaldson, eds., *Piers Plowman: The B Version* (London, 1975), p. 533.

Friday abstinence is not arbitrarily imposed and to connect this practice with the memory of key biblical events. The text is a form of elementary Christian education.

Two of Harley's prayer texts have their roots in monastic tradition. One is a series of questions to the dying (no. 113) attributed to St. Anselm of Canterbury (d. 1109), a chief figure in the medieval development of affective prayer.[43] The text begins, on fol. 137r, with the formal title (underlined for prominence) *Hec est doctrina beati Anselmi Cantuariensis archiepiscopi* and a prologue directing the matter below to men and women in religion: "Sic debet frater vel soror proximus vel proxima morti interrogari." Although some of the questions that follow deal exclusively with the religious state, others are applicable to Christian believers in general. In the fuller version printed by J.-P. Migne, the responses to the interrogations are simple but pointed: "Gaudeo," "Poenitet," "Credo," etc. In Harley each question receives a simple affirmative: "Etiam" [Yes, certainly]. In assessing the status of the text in Harley, one should note that the fourteenth and fifteenth centuries witnessed increased adaptation of specialized clerical materials on the Christian life to a lay readership. Many of Richard Rolle's mystical works, for instance, eventually circulated beyond their original audience of nuns to pious layfolk, sometimes getting adapted in the process.[44] St. Anselm's questions to the dying, despite their clerkly origins, could have been used by late medieval laymen or women.

A set of directions for contemplation at the seven hours (no. 115) hearkens all the way back to the traditional organization of monastic prayer by St. Benedict in his rule (sixth century). In the later Middle Ages, however, the Divine Office was adapted to lay needs and became (via the pseudo-Bonaventuran *Meditations on the Life of Christ*) the framework for affective reflection on the events of Christ's Passion, death, and burial. This is the sort of meditation copied out in Harley, where each of the "hours" of the Passion is signalled in the margin by a paraph mark. The reader is told at each hour what to say (e.g., "A houre de nonne dites . . ."), and is guided through an emotional description of Passion events adapted from the Gospels. The mechanical coordination of prayer time and Passion chronology vivifies biblical event (much as Harley's Passion lyrics do),

---

[43] See Sister Benedicta Ward, trans., *The Prayers and Meditations of St. Anselm* (Harmondsworth, 1973), pp. 27–82.

[44] Most notably the *English Psalter*, which survives in thirty-nine fourteenth- and fifteenth-century MSS. But for a smaller instance of such adaptation, see Michael P. Kuczynski, "A Fragment of Richard Rolle's *Form of Living* in MS Bodley 554," *Bodleian Library Record* 15 (1994): 20–32. The main text of the MS is a ME (Wycliffite) psalter, with heavy ME commentary. The *Form* fragment, adapted for a lay readership, appears on a back flyleaf.

encouraging the reader to imagine himself or herself "on the scene." While praying, the devout soul travels the way of the Cross with Christ.

It is impossible to know whether its author intends the text as a strict guide for prayer, to be followed word for word, or as an inducement to meditation, which might by particular devotees be superseded. Certain medieval writers on prayer stress the need to submit to verbal paradigms, as a means of avoiding one's own "idle" words:

> . . . whenne they doth to chyrche fare,
> Thenne bydde hem leve here mony wordes,
> Here ydel speche, and nyce bordes,
> And put a-way alle vanyte,
> And say here pater noster & here ave.[45]

Prayer so conceived is a penitential practice, for it requires a denial of the self. Harley contains a few such prayers, for instance, the poem *Gloria in excelsis Deo* (its title underlined in the manuscript; no. 102). Each of the poem's lines rhyme on the same sound, making it a text easy to memorize. It is akin to other Anglo-Norman translations of biblical and liturgical prayers, such as the rhyming Pater Noster in Cambridge, University Library MS Gg.i.1 (fols. 392vc–393vd).

There are also nonbiblical prayers in Harley clearly meant to be read or recited, aloud or to oneself, word for word: *Anima Cristi sanctifica me* (no. 19), discussed above (to which an indulgence was probably attached); a Latin confession to God the Son (no. 103), requesting perfection in doctrine and true penance ("perfice in me doctrinam tuam et veram confessionem," fol. 134v); and a Latin prayer of preparation before confession (no. 105), requesting the gift of compunction of heart and holy tears ("veram cordis compunccionem et fontem lacrimarum," fol. 135r), two commonplaces of monastic devotion transferred to lay spirituality in the later Middle Ages.[46] There is also a French prose prayer on the Five Joys of the Virgin (no. 104), a devotional paradigm adapted from the Hours of the Blessed Virgin, and a prayer to the Three Kings (no. 108a), who in the Middle Ages were venerated as saints.[47]

---

[45] John Mirk, *Instructions for Parish Priests*, ed. E. Peacock and F. J. Furnivall, EETS o.s. 31 (1868; repr. New York, 1969), p. 9, lines 265–69.

[46] On compunction of heart and holy tears, see Gregory the Great, *Moralia in Iob*, in Migne, ed., *PL* 76:275–77, 291–92; Jean Leclercq, *The Love of Learning and the Desire for God: A Study of Monastic Culture*, trans. Catherine Misrahi (New York, 1974), p. 39; and Sandra McIntire, *The Doctrine of Compunction in Medieval England: Holy Tears* (Lewiston, N.Y., 1990).

[47] See "Magi (in the Bible)," *New Catholic Encyclopedia* (New York, 1967), 9.61–65. For a fifteenth-century charm-like prayer to the Magi, see Eamon Duffy, *The Stripping of the Altars:*

Michael P. Kuczynski

Three sets of instruction on prayer in Harley deal almost exclusively with the Psalter and testify to the preeminence of that biblical book in late medieval devotion. Each item is a list of psalm prayers appropriate to certain conditions or circumstances (nos. 101, 110, 111). They may be connected with regard for the Psalms, even for single words and phrases from certain psalms, as being charm-like in their effects. Consider the following advice from Edinburgh, National Library of Scotland, Advocates MS 19.2.1, copied beneath a Middle English paraphrase of Psalm 50 (fols. 87–89):

> Sic vis delere tua crimina, dic miserere;
> Per miserere mei flectitur ira dei.
>
> [If you want to wipe away your sins, say the *Miserere*;
> through "Miserere mei," God's anger is averted.]

As I mentioned above, the Psalms were the prayerbook of the Church and were regarded as the common property of the faithful. More to the point, here, perhaps, their speaking voice, historically David, was understood tropologically as *ecclesia*, the corporate voice of all believers. In a Wycliffite psalter with Middle English glosses, Oxford, Bodleian Library MS Bodley 554, the glossator makes this point explicit:

> Þis vij salm [*Domine deus meus in te speraui*] mai be expowned gostli, þat it be þe preier of ech man set in bodili turment bi vniust persecucioun, eþer in goostli turment, bi wickid temptacioun of feendis, which man axiþ of god to be delyuerid, and allegiþ his innocence and þe malice of pursueris. *Lire here*. (fol. 2v)

(The gloss derives from Nicholas of Lyra's fourteenth-century *Postillae perpetuae in universam sacra Scripturam*, a favorite Lollard source.) This assumption informs Harley's psalm lists, one of which, for instance, encourages the reader to say the psalms designated for particular purposes with great devotion, at least three times ("Cestes salmes auant nomez serrount dites engeuoillant ou grant deuocioun, e chescun a meynz trois foiz ou plus," fol. 134r; no. 101). The conditions and circumstances for prayer are various. Sometimes, for instance, simply the time of day a particular psalm ought to be said is specified: "Quant vus leuetz de vostre lit, dites, *Deus in nomine tuo*" (Ps. 53). Sometimes the circumstances are more particular. For example, there are psalms prescribed for avoiding temptation (*Iudica me Deus et discerne* [Ps. 42]) and for withstanding adversity ("sept foiz, *Exaudi Deus orationem meam cum deprecor*" [Ps. 63]).

Traditional Religion in England c. 1400–c. 1580 (New Haven, 1992), p. 274.

Many of the psalms recommended in the list on fol. 136v (no. 110) are prescribed "contra inimicos" and "contra aduersarios et maliciosos." It is unclear from the context whether these enemies and adversaries are to be understood as physical or spiritual ones, or both (as in the Lyra gloss quoted above). Behind such prayers, Eamon Duffy explains, "lay a vivid and urgent sense of the reality of the demonic, and the Christian's need for eternal vigilance."[48] This particular list, however, unlike the one on fol. 134r, actually prescribes writing out the psalms in question and wearing them "in brachio," like phylacteries. Also, the list concludes by recommending as a prayer at the elevation of the host (the most important moment at mass for medieval layfolk) "hunc psalmum, *Te Deum laudamus*," one of the Latin hymns routinely assimilated to and copied with the Psalms in medieval Psalters. (Another of Harley's instructions on prayer, copied in the book's final quire, explains the efficacy of some of these hymns [no. 109a].)

The longest and most detailed psalm list in Harley is the third (no. 111), on fol. 136v, attributed in its incipit to St. Hilary of Poitiers (fourth century), presumably because he wrote a commentary on the Psalter, or because of his reputation as a composer of hymns.[49] Here, often, the author recommends more than one psalm for a particular need and quotes not just the Latin cue to the psalm, but the entire opening verse, occasionally slipping over into the second. He is also careful to distinguish in his instructions psalms that begin with the same words, as several of them do — for instance, "*In te Domine speraui* le primer" (Ps. 30) at one point, at another "*In te Domine speraui* le secounde" (Ps. 70). Also noteworthy is his supplementing psalms with common prayers such as the Pater Noster, Ave Maria, and Credo. For instance, he advises those who cannot concentrate ("Quant vus auez de rien songie") to kneel before the crucifix in church and say *Ad Dominum cum tribularer* (Ps. 119), followed by these three prayers. Like one of the other psalm lists discussed above, this one, too, concludes by recommending Te Deum as an elevation prayer (fol. 137r).

Religious Lyrics

None of the poetic materials from Harley discussed above would be classified by critics as lyrics, despite their sometimes literary aspirations and qualities. The term "lyric," as Rosemary Woolf has shown, is associated from the nineteenth century onwards with poems that express their authors' own feelings (she quotes John Ruskin: "Lyric Poetry is

---

[48] See Duffy, *Stripping of the Altars*, pp. 266–67.

[49] For the Latin text of pseudo-Hilary's Psalm commentary, see Migne, ed., *PL* 9:221–908.

the expression by the poet of his own feelings").[50] And, as we have seen, what the Middle Ages found attractive in the Psalms, which are emotional poetry by anyone's standards, was their comprehensive feeling, the sense that their poet spoke his sentiments not only on his own behalf, but for everyone. If the Psalms cannot count as lyric, neither can a versified biblical and liturgical prayer (*Gloria in excelsis Deo*; no. 102), since its sentiments come to its author ready-made, in the Latin text of St. Luke's gospel and the mass. Nor can a poetic prayer like *Anima Cristi sanctifica me* (no. 19), with its mantra-like opening parallelisms. The possibility that a prayer might be repeated verbatim by someone who did not compose it, for an indulgence, would seem *ipso facto* to preclude lyric sincerity.

These assumptions about lyric did not inform the production of Harley's religious poetry. Harley's scribe set the moving penitential poem *God, Þat Al Þis Myhtes May* and the hortatory *Sayings of St. Bernard* (nos. 73, 74) together on the first page of a new quire, I think, because the two texts, however different in literary style, serve the same pious need: each in its own way provokes humility and remorse. Brook, conversely, does not include the *Sayings* in his anthology of Harley's lyric pieces because he regards it (perhaps for good reason) as verse not poetry. His segregation of the two poems, however, obscures their common purpose and implies, maybe unintentionally, that what we should look for in *God, Þat Al Þis Myhtes May* is art rather than religion.[51]

But religion is what Harley's religious lyrics are all about. In one sense, they are the most conventional of poems. Most of them are addressed to the Virgin Mary or Christ, as prayer poems, and they recycle the clichés (a less pejorative term is "topoi") that readers come to expect in religious poetry by the fourteenth century. Many of these topoi, moreover, were already commonplaces in Scripture (preeminently in the repetitive poems of the Psalter), Scripture-based liturgy, and patristic biblical commentaries. So when medieval readers approached such poems, they were attentive not to matters of sincerity (this would be taken for granted in a Passion lyric, otherwise the poem's composition, strictly speaking, would have been idle and sinful[52]), but to circumstances of rhetorical

---

[50] Rosemary Woolf, *The English Religious Lyric in the Middle Ages* (Oxford, 1968), p. 1n1. This book is still the best comprehensive treatment of the religious lyric.

[51] For a related distinction between "religious" and "poetic" emotion, which medieval readers and writers might not have found relevant, see George Kane, *Middle English Literature: A Critical Study of the Romances, the Religious Lyrics, "Piers Plowman"* (London, 1951), p. 138

[52] Compare Thomas Aquinas's remarks on "attentiveness" in prayer in *Summa theologiae*, II–II. Q. 83. Art. 13. I am assuming, here, that the composition of a prayer lyric would itself have been, for its author, an act of prayer. Indeed, one might even speculate that the copying of such materials was for Harley's scribe in part an act of prayer.

arrangement and rearrangement: the new ways in which pious old conventions were being deployed.

For instance, although Harley's two love songs to the crucified Christ, *Suete Iesu, King of Blysse* and *A Spring Song on the Passion* (nos. 50, 53), are not strictly conjoint in the manuscript (they appear on fols. 75rb–75va and 76r, respectively), it is difficult to imagine that they were not sometimes read together, as variations on a theme. That theme, adapted from *fin amour* and biblical materials such as the Song of Solomon, depicted Christ as the soul's spiritual lover in language that flirts with the erotic, as in the opening lines of no. 50:

> Suete Iesu, king of blysse,
> Myn huerte loue, min huerte lisse,
> Þou art suete myd ywisse.
> Wo is him þat þe shal misse! (lines 1–4; fol. 75rb)

The poet might not have approved of Brook's heavy punctuation (reproduced above), which slows the verse considerably and detracts from a sense of breathlessness one gets in the manuscript text. Line 3 is, at once, innocuous and a euphemism: "suete," the reader might wonder, in what sense? Later, following more *fin amour* praise for Christ the Lover, the speaker-soul asks Jesus to open her heart and take up residence there:

> Suete Iesu louerd myn
> My lyf myn huerte al is þin
> Vndo myn herte ant liht þer yn
> Ant wite me from fendes engyn. (lines 25–28; fol. 75va)[53]

The final line here, "and defend me from the fiend's device (or attack)," may allude to a further late medieval development of the Christ the Lover theme, which represented Jesus as a knight who defends the soul under attack.[54] It is not, at any rate, a poetic success. More engaging is the conceit of the open heart, which complicates the sentiment. The poem itself, simply by virtue of its appeal, implies that the speaker's heart is already receptive to divine grace. But it longs for full possession by its Lover, and that the poet describes delicately in the phrase "liht þer yn," language used to represent the mystery of the Incarnation in other Middle English religious lyrics, and in this manuscript's copy of the *Harrowing of Hell*, when the poet speaks of Jesus' pity for hell's captives:

---

[53] See *MED lighten* v.(2), 4a and 4b.

[54] On this topos see Rosemary Woolf, "The Theme of Christ the Lover-Knight in Medieval English Literature," in *Art and Doctrine: Essays on Medieval Literature*, ed. Heather O'Donoghue (London, 1986), pp. 99–117.

Iesu Crist arew hem sore
Ant seide he wolde vacche hem þore.
He lyhte of ys heȝe tour
Into seinte Marie bour.
He wes bore for oure nede,
In þis world in pore wede. (lines 29–34; fol. 55va)

A Spring Song on the Passion (no. 53) is the more intriguing of Harley's love songs to Jesus. The entire first stanza, which describes the speaker's "suete loue-longynge" (line 3) in conventional *fin amour* terms, deliberately conceals the true identity of the soul's lover, until he appears bloody on the cross in the next stanza:

When Y miselue stonde
  Ant wiþ myn eȝen seo
Þurled fot ant honde
  Wiþ grete nayles þreo,
Blody wes ys heued,
On him nes nout bileued
  Þat wes of peynes freo,
Wel wel ohte myn herte
For his loue to smerte
  Ant sike ant sory beo. (lines 11–20; fol. 76r)

Here the poet invokes the traditional *imago pietatis* or depiction of the Man of Sorrows, which Duffy has shown was popular in late medieval churches and devotional books.[55] So that when the speaker-soul says that she herself witnessed Christ's sufferings, she might have provoked in readers their own "eyewitness" testimony. The poem simultaneously expresses the poet's pious mood (via its speaker) and elicits a matching mood in the reader. The details of the pierced foot, three large nails, and bloody head are extrapolated from the Gospel accounts of the crucifixion and were, in their focus, part of a popular medieval meditation on the devices of the Passion, the *arma Christi*.[56] Medieval readers, not feeling required to follow *A Spring Song on the Passion* straight through, might have

---

[55] See Duffy, *Stripping of the Altars*, pp. 134–38, 238–48. Although Duffy is mainly concerned with post-1400 habits, his comments on the Anselmian roots of Passion meditation show that what he has to say is relevant to Harley's materials. On "Christocentric piety" throughout the fourteenth century, see W. A. Pantin, *The English Church in the Fourteenth Century* (Cambridge, 1955), p. 190.

[56] For some picture-poems on this theme, see Douglas Gray, "Medieval English Mystic Lyrics," in *Mysticism and Spirituality in Medieval England*, ed. William F. Pollard and Robert Boenig (Woodbridge, Suffolk, 1997), pp. 203–18.

broken off their reading at this point to engage in penitential prayer, and could even have found models for such prayer in the poem's next or final stanza, or in their Psalters.[57] They might, conversely, have been drawn further into the poem by the author's sly use of the same rhetorical contradiction we just saw in *Suete Iesu, King of Blysse* — his speaker's claim that she cannot respond to Christ even as she registers her deep response in the verse at hand:

> Alas, þat Y ne co[n]
>   Turne to him my þoht
> Ant cheosen him to lemmon;
>   So duere he vs haþ yboht,
> Wiþ woundes deope ant stronge,
> Wiþ peynes sore ant longe;
>   Of loue ne conne we noht.
> His blod þat feol to grounde
> Of hise suete wounde
>   Of peyne vs haþ yboht. (lines 31–40)

The point turns not on the graphic crucifixion imagery, but on the poet's *repetitio* "ne con," "ne conne." The speaker does not know how to choose love of Christ because, presumably like the poem's readers, she knows nothing about true love. "Deus caritas est," St. John writes in his epistle, "God is love" (1 John 4.8). And yet, this love is so different from our everyday kind that man fails to understand it, even while he feels genuine pity for Christ on the Cross. One achievement of many of Harley's religious lyrics is their use of apparently simple pious feeling to inspire the complex, even contradictory thoughts necessary to successful meditation. In medieval devotional practice, the soul had to learn to give over ego-control, to submit passively to the influence of divine grace. This submission is the byproduct of confronting one's own spiritual confusion and helplessness, a confrontation provoked by a lyric such as *A Spring Song on the Passion*.

---

[57] Compare the remarks of St. Anselm concerning his own Latin prayers and meditations, which anticipate the affective piety of many of Harley's religious lyrics: "The purpose of the prayers and meditations which follow is to excite the mind of the reader to the love or fear of God, or to self-examination; hence they are not to be read in a tumult, but quietly, nor cursorily or quickly but slowly and with intense and thoughtful meditation. Nor should the reader trouble about reading the whole of any of them, but only so much as (with God's help) he feels to be satisfying or useful in stirring up his spirit to pray. Nor is it necessary for him to start at the beginning, but wherever he pleases" (qtd. and trans. R. W. Southern, *Saint Anselm and His Biographer: A Study of Monastic Life and Thought, 1059–c. 1130* [Cambridge, 1963], p. 349).

Imaginative concentration on sacred mystery is the ultimate aim of such poetry, but not the local intention of this or that group of poetic stanzas.

The pleasant trick opening of *A Spring Song* serves a meditative purpose that is ethical rather than purely emotional, by implying at the start an essential conflict of values between carnal love and love of God. This conflict, one might argue, is always implied when a medieval poet uses *fin amour* tropes to express spiritual affection. It results from the gap between Christ's selflessness and the human ego, figured touchingly in another of Harley's Passion lyrics, *I Syke When Y Singe* (no. 62), as the actual physical distance between someone observing from ground level the crucifixion (depicted, maybe, on a church rood screen) and the crucified Christ above:

> Þe naylles beþ to stronge,
>   Þe smyþes are to sleye,
> Þou bledest al to longe,
>   Þe tre is al to heyӡe,
> Þe stones beoþ al wete. (lines 31–35; fol. 80ra)

Anaphora and parataxis make the verse seem agitated, to match the speaker's mood. Like the speakers of the other Harley Passion lyrics, this one longs to embrace her Lord, but cannot.

The conflict between human and divine love is strongest, however, between the two Harley lyrics *The Way of Christ's Love* (no. 92) and *The Way of Woman's Love* (no. 93), the first copied above the second on fol. 128r. The two are meant to be read together. They juxtapose the sure love of Christ, demonstrated by his death on the Cross, and the fickle love of woman, each beginning with the same line to play up the antithesis:

> Lvtel wot hit any mon
>   Hou loue hym haueþ ybounde
> Þat for vs o þe rode ron
>   Ant bohte vs wiþ is wounde.
>   Þe loue of him vs haueþ ymaked sounde,
>   Ant ycast þe grimly gost to grounde.
> Euer ant oo, nyht ant day, he haueþ vs in is þohte;
> He nul nout leose þat he so deore bohte. (lines 1–8; fol. 128r)

> Lutel wot hit any mon
>   Hou derne loue may stonde,
> Bote hit were a fre wymmon
>   Þat muche of loue had fonde.
>   Þe loue of hire ne lesteþ nowyht longe;
>   He haueþ me plyht ant wyteþ me wyþ wronge.

Euer ant oo for my leof Icham in grete þohte;
Y þenche on hire þat Y ne seo nout ofte. (lines 1–8; fol. 128r)

Carleton Brown argued, on the basis of manuscript fragments of the two poems, that the religious lyric was adapted from an earlier version of the secular poem.[58] Whether or not this is true, in Harley the two lyrics operate as halves of a poetic whole. Furthermore, Harley's scribe may have intended to give visual priority to the first, sacred half by its more prominent initial capital at the top of the page.

Besides Christ, the other prominent recipient of prayer poetry in Harley is Christ's mother Mary, whose cult was popular in fourteenth-century England and gave rise to a devotional Hours of the Virgin, organized around the scheme of the Five Joys.[59] Mary was mediatrix between man and Christ, someone who could make special entreaty with him because of her status as mother. Thus it behooved the desperate soul to seek her aid. There are no French poems on Christ's Passion in MS Harley 2253, but there are French prayers to the Virgin (nos. 8, 49, 57), for her cult was especially popular in France.

In the first item copied out by Harley's scribe, the *ABC a femmes* (no. 8), Mary is praised in a poem whose successive stanzas follow the alphabet. In the central one, extrapolated from the letter *M*, the epideictic language and imagery derive from the Latin commentators:

Marie, que portastes le salueour,
  Vostre grace vus requer,
Me seiez ayde e socour,
  Pur l'onour de femme sauuer,
Qe portent fruyt de bel colour,
  Noble, douce, ne mie amer;
Gentz qe sount de grant valour,
  Qe le mound gouernent enter,
    Par sen,
Bene soit tiel arbre
Qe tiel fruit porte! Amen. (lines 144–54; fol. 49v)

[Mary, who bore the Savior, I sue for your grace. May you be a help and a consolation to me, as I defend the honor of those women who bear fruit of beautiful color, noble in character, sweet without trace of bitterness — those gentle ones, who are of great worth and who govern the whole world reasonably. Blessed be the tree that bears such fruit! Amen.]

---

[58] Carleton Brown, ed., *English Lyrics of the XIIIth Century* (Oxford, 1932), pp. 235–37.

[59] Duffy, *Stripping of the Altars*, pp. 256–65.

The poet manages to praise Mary superlatively while acknowledging the underlying doctrinal reason for her preeminence: she was the tree that bore that precious fruit, the Savior of the world.[60] *Marie mere al salueour* (no. 57), copied on fol. 77v parallel to a Middle English version of *Dulcis Iesu memoria* (no. 58; not in Brook), a very popular Latin hymn attributed to St. Bernard of Clairvaux,[61] derives its power from the poet's innocuous repetition of the verb "to be":

> Marie mere al salueour
> De totes femmes estes flour,
> Vus estes pleyne de grant docour,
> Vus estes refu al peccheour. (lines 1–4; fol. 77va)

[Mary, mother of the Savior, you are the flower of all women, replete with great sweetness, the refuge of sinners.]

This writer is a master of simplicity. He disappears behind his praise, as a good suppliant should, in one stanza invoking the biblical Ave Maria while working delicate variations on just a few of his own words:

> Aue de totes la plus digne.
> Aue de totes la plus benigne.
> Aue de totes graces signe.
> Pur moi priez que su indigne. (lines 41–44)

[Hail, most praiseworthy of all. Hail, mildest one. Hail, token of every grace. Pray for me, who am undeserving.]

His poem, at least in these lines, has some of the effect of a charm, conjuring up an image of the perfect woman to whom he prays, and ensuring almost magically the success of his prayer.

Three of Harley's religious pieces are organized around the Five Joys (nos. 49, 67, 104), a popular late medieval meditation that, like the Hours of the Passion, works to coordinate

---

[60] On doctrinal attitudes toward Mary in the Middle Ages and the attitudes of the Fathers that informed these, see Woolf, *English Religious Lyric*, especially pp. 115–17.

[61] For the text, see Migne, ed., *PL* 184:1317–20, although the attribution to St. Bernard is denied there. For another ME version, from Glasgow University Library MS V.8.15, see Carleton Brown, ed., *Religious Lyrics of the XIVth Century*, 2nd ed. rev. G. V. Smithers (Oxford, 1957), pp. 111–12.

the progress of prayerful emotion and biblical chronology.[62] (In the fifteenth century the meditation became incorporated into Books of Hours.) These joys, as they occur sequentially in Mary's life, are the Annunciation, the Nativity, the Epiphany, Easter, and Mary's bodily assumption into heaven, this last one having no biblical foundation.[63] Neither of the French items — one a prose meditation (*The Five Joys*, no. 104), the other a rather stiff lyric that pays less attention to Mary than to the power of her Son (*Les Joies de Notre-Dame*, no. 49) — can match the devotional power of the English poem, *The Five Joys of the Virgin* (no. 67). The lyric has a slight textual prominence on fol. 81v of Harley, amid other lyrics to Mary and Christ, because the scribe has drawn a sharp line across the page to distinguish it from the end of the straightforward Marian prayer, *Blessed Be Þou, Leuedy* (no. 66), which precedes it. As Woolf argues, one of the most striking features of this poem is its "informality."[64] It opens, like one of the love songs to Christ discussed above, with the speaker praising his lover in casual *fin amour* terms, only to reveal in stanza two that his lady is the Virgin:

> Þis maiden is suete ant fre of blod
> Briht ant feyr, of milde mod,
> Alle heo mai don vs god
>   Þurh hire bysechynge;
> Of hire he tok fleych ant blod,
>   Iesu heuene kynge. (lines 7–12; fol. 81va)

This revelation wittily converts line 3 of the opening stanza into a famous doctrinal paradox: "Mid herte Y þohte al on a may [maiden]." The Latin Fathers loved the mystery of Mary's simultaneous virginity and motherhood, and medieval poets picked up on this, elaborating the idea for sheer intellectual pleasure. But in some Marian poems, intellectual delight frustrates meditation. The Middle English poet avoids this pitfall by allowing the paradox to emerge gradually. Woolf remarks on the unpleasing, artificial way in which the speaker introduces the theme of the joys:

---

[62] On the history of this meditation, which may have originated in England, see Woolf, *English Religious Lyric*, pp. 134–36.

[63] On the sixth-century origins of this belief, see Cross, ed., *Oxford Dictionary of the Christian Church*, pp. 96–97. In French tradition the Epiphany is sometimes eliminated in favor of Christ's Ascension, as in Harley's item no. 49.

[64] Woolf, *English Religious Lyric*, p. 137.

Nou Y may ʒef Y wole
Þe fif ioyes mynge. (lines 23–24)[65]

But I would argue that the awkwardness fits with the informal air of the poem. What could be a terribly profound liturgical moment becomes instead a playful one.[66] The meditative comes up in the lyric as unexpectedly as the virgin-mother paradox does. As the poem opens, the speaker describes himself riding out "by grene wode to seche play," thinking of his lady, and in this lyric meditation on the Five Joys gets reduced (or elevated?) to the level of inspired game. Like a child stacking his blocks, the poet sets stanza on stanza, and concludes with the plainest of prayers:

Þat heo of vs hauen merci
  Ant þat we ne misse
In þis world to ben holy
  Ant wynne heuene blysse. Amen. (lines 57–60)

One of Harley's most artful religious lyrics, *A Prayer for Deliverance* (no. 69), is a macaronic prayer to the Virgin that combines Middle English and Anglo-Norman in each of its twenty-four lines. Both Brook and Brown print this lyric in alternating short lines of English and French.[67] The editorial arrangement, however, disturbs the subtle parity between English and French on the manuscript page, where only six of the poem's twenty-four lines have a clear virgule at midpoint (fol. 83r).[68] In addition to mixing languages, the poet also combines subgenres of the religious lyric that are kept distinct in other Harley poems: the praise poem to the Virgin and the Passion meditation. Lines 1–8 are pure praise and entreaty, beginning with the virgin-mother paradox discussed above and the speaker's frank self-denigration:

---

[65] Woolf, *English Religious Lyric*, p. 137.

[66] For a crux in the poem's stanza on the second joy, the Nativity, possibly caused by the poet's casualness, see Sister Mary Immaculate, "A Note on 'A Song of the Five Joys,'" *Modern Language Notes* 55 (1940): 249–54.

[67] See Brook, ed., *Harley Lyrics*, pp. 66–68, and Brown, *Eng. Lyr. XIII*, pp. 155–56, respectively.

[68] This suggests that the scribe may have been confused about the format his text should have, or that, confronted with long lines in his exemplar, he began to play the role of editor later in the text (lines 16 ff.), by introducing the virgule. For an edition of the poem that is closer to its MS format, see David L. Jeffrey and Brian J. Levy, eds. and trans., *The Anglo-Norman Lyric: An Anthology* (Toronto, 1990), pp. 41–43.

Mayden moder milde, oiez cel oreysoun.
From shome þou me shilde e de ly malseloun.
For loue of þine childe me menez de tresoun.
Ich wes wod ant wilde ore su en prisoun. (lines 1–4; fol. 83r)

[Kind virgin and mother, listen to this prayer. Protect me from shame and from the devil. On account of your love for Christ, lead me out of temptation. I was mad with sin and reckless, and now am imprisoned.]

The transition from this mood comes abruptly in line 9, with the poet's accounts of Judas's kiss of betrayal (a vivid counterimage to Mary's sure love for Christ) and of the Passion, which Mary herself had to witness:

On stou ase þou stode, pucele, tot pensaunt,
Þou restest þe vnder rode, tou fitz veites pendant;
Þou seʒe is sides of blode, l'alme de ly partaunt;
He ferede vch an fode en mound que fust viuaunt. (lines 13–16)

[In that place where you stood, maid, so thoughtful, waiting beneath the cross, you saw your son hanging. You saw his bloody side and his soul leave his body. He inspired awe in everyone on earth, where he had lived.]

The second line of this stanza exploits macaronic format for emotional effect, as if the poet could not bring himself to state in bald English the grim reality before Mary's eyes, her son hanging from the "rode."

Another of Harley's religious poems, *Stond Wel, Moder, vnder Rode* (no. 60), takes up this same pathetic subject, which medieval churchgoers saw represented above their church altars on rood screens. The lyric is a dialogue between Mary and Christ on the Cross based on the Latin sequence *Stabat iuxta Christi crucem*.[69] Other manuscript contexts for the lyric outside Harley indicate the practical uses such poetry could serve in late medieval religion. On the flyleaves of London, British Library MS Royal 8.F.ii, for instance, its opening stanza is quoted in a Latin sermon. Copies in London, British Library MS Royal 12.E.i and Cambridge, St. John's College MS 111 are accompanied by musical notation, suggesting that the poem may have served as a kind of vernacular hymn.[70]

The poem's force derives from the sharp contrast between Christ's plea that his mother be happy ("blyþe," line 3) over his redemptive death, and Mary's insistence that the

---

[69] Cross, ed., *Oxford Dictionary of the Christian Church*, p. 1285.

[70] For these details, see Brook, ed., *Harley Lyrics*, p. 84.

motherly sorrow she feels is justified. Christ's appeals are to the theological doctrine of satisfaction, Mary's to basic human emotion. Indeed, at the moment of his profoundest suffering on behalf of man, Jesus is cold toward his mother:

> "Moder, þou rewe al of þi bern,
> Þou wosshe awai þe blody tern,
>   Hit doþ me worse þen my ded!"
> "Sone, hou may Y teres werne?
> Y se þe blody stremes erne
>   From þin herte to my fet?" (lines 19–24; fol. 79va)

"My" in the final line of this stanza is a chilling, baroque touch, which confirms the reader's sympathy with Mary's view of the situation. Here the Virgin is no longer mediatrix between man and God, but a surrogate in the poem for the reader meditating outside its frame. The penultimate stanza of the lyric breaks the tension of its earlier lines with the sudden observation, "When he ros, þo fel hire sorewe" — the emotional transformation underscored by the chiasmus and the poet's allusion to the Five Joys scheme. However, even the prayer with which the lyric closes, which starts with a paraphrase of Ave Maria ("Blessed be þou, ful of blysse," line 61; fol. 79vb), cannot dispel the reader's memory of the unresolvable emotional conflict at the poem's core. Like other Harley Passion lyrics, this one is only superficially reassuring. On a deeper level, it is a goad to complex meditative thoughts.

There are other religious poems in Harley that come closer to modern tastes: for instance, a mock penance by a poet who has written against women (*The Poet's Repentance*, no. 33); a satiric prayer delivered in the persona of an old man, suffering from gout (*An Old Man's Prayer*, no. 45); and a brief song set in the cold months of the year, which meditates on the instability of worldly happiness (*A Winter Song*, no. 52):

> Wynter wakeneþ al my care,
> Nou þis leues waxeþ bare;
> Ofte Y sike ant mourne sare
>   When hit comeþ in my þoht
> Of þis worldes ioie hou hit geþ al to noht. (lines 1–5; fol. 75vb)

The lyric, to this point, might have been lifted from Thomas Hardy's *Winter Words*. In the next two stanzas, however, it moves (for us) too far in the direction of traditional moralizing and prayer. Yet this was the point of the natural scene for the anonymous medieval writer who composed the poem.

The impulse to assemble artful *florilegia* of select religious poems from Harley, or of fine passages excerpted from the poems, evades the fact that nearly all of Harley's good religious lyrics, and many of its great ones, are traditional structures (innovative, however, in their confident use of the vernacular) designed for prayer and meditation. They were written as acts of devotion, intended to provoke analogous acts in their audience, and they were probably assembled because Harley's compiler, however refined his taste, shared in some measure their piety. As devotions, they are essentially indissociable from Harley's other religious contents: its Bible stories, saints' lives, instructions on the spiritual life, and admonitory materials. Indeed, seen together with these items rather than in isolation, the lyrics emerge as richer cultural productions. British Library MS Harley 2253 is not exclusively religious in complexion, like the Bodleian Library's famous Vernon MS, but it is heavily so. And it must have been, like Vernon, at times a source of considerable *soulehele* for its medieval scribe and readers.

Authority and Resistance: The Political Verse

John Scattergood

I

The last item but two in MS Harley 2253 is a poem entitled by its latest modern editor *Against the King's Taxes* (no. 114), which appears on fols. 137v–138v.[1] It is written in Anglo-Norman and Latin in a five-line variant of the goliardic stanza *cum auctoritas* and has complex internal rhyming too; the author of this somber but virtuoso piece was evidently highly learned. He was also precise — though he keeps names out of his poem — and knew exactly what he was talking about:

Ore court en Engletere de anno in annum
Le quinzyme dener, pur fere sic commune dampnum;
E fet aualer que soleyent sedere super scannum,
E vendre fet commune gent vaccas, vas et pannum.
  Non placet ad summum quindenum sic dare nummum.

Vne chose est countre foy, vnde gens grauatur,
Que la meyte ne vient al roy in regno quod leuatur.
Pur ce qu'il n'ad tot l'enter prout sibi datur,
La pueple doit le plus doner et sic sincopatur.
  Nam que taxantur regi non omnia dantur.

Vnquore plus greue a simple gent collectio lanarum,
Que vendre fet communement diuicias earum.
Ne puet estre que tiel consail constat Deo carum

---

[1] See Isabel S. T. Aspin, ed. and trans., *Anglo-Norman Political Songs* ANTS 11 (Oxford, 1953), pp. 105–15. I have generally followed Aspin's translation of this poem and others quoted from her excellent edition. For an earlier edition, see Thomas Wright, ed., *The Political Songs of England, from the Reign of John to That of Edward II*, intro. Peter Coss (1839; repr. Cambridge, 1996), pp. 182–87, where, however, the poem is attributed to the reign of Edward I.

Issi destrure le pouerail pondus per amarum.
  Non est lex sana quod regi sit mea lana.

Vncore est plus outre peis, vt testantur gentes,
En le sac deus per ou treis per vim retinentes.
A quy remeindra cele leyne? Quidam respondentes
Que ia n'auera roy ne reygne set tantum colligentes.
  Pondus lanarum tam falsum constat amarum. (lines 11–30; fols. 137v–138r)

[Now the fifteenth runs in England year after year, thus doing harm to all; by it those who were wont to sit upon the bench have come down in the world; and common folk must sell their cows, their utensils, and even clothing. It is ill-pleasing thus to pay the fifteenth to the uttermost farthing.

One thing (above all) is dishonest, whereby the people are oppressed; not half the tribute raised in the land reaches the king. Because he does not receive the tax in its entirety just as it is granted to him, the people must pay the more, and thus they are cut short. For all that is levied is not surrendered to the king.

Still more hard on simple folk is the wool collection; commonly it makes them sell their possessions. It cannot be that such a measure, crushing the poor under a grievous load, is pleasing to God. The law that makes my wool the king's is no just law.

An even greater offence, as men bear witness, is that they forcibly keep back two or three stones weight in the sack. To whom will this wool go? Some reply that never shall king nor country get it, but only the wool collectors. Such a false weight of wool is a calamity.]

In order to finance his war with France, Edward III had to raise considerable amounts of money, which he attempted to do in part by direct taxation and in part by levies on wool exports. In the autumn parliaments of 1333 and 1334, tenths and fifteenths were granted. In 1336 a grant of a tenth and a fifteenth was passed in the March parliament, and at the great council at Nottingham in the autumn a similar grant was made, as well as two-tenths from the clergy. A year later in September 1337, the great council of Westminster gave a tenth and a fifteenth for three years, and the convocation of Canterbury and York committed the clergy to a similar grant. Hence, the poet's complaint that the "quinzyme" has been levied year after year ("de anno in annum," lines 11–12). But the money thus raised was insufficient: besides needing to put his own armies in the field, Edward III had promised financial support to his allies in the Low Countries. So he sought to exploit England's prime export commodity — wool. In the autumn of 1336, an assembly of merchants had granted an increase of the wool tax in the form of a subsidy of 20 shillings and a loan of 20 shillings on the sack. And in the summer of 1337, the king had come to an agreement with the principal wool contractors that, in return for a monopoly that would cut out foreign buyers, they would agree to buy and export 30,000 sacks of wool for the king's use — half the profits to go to the king. This is the "collectio lanarum" (line 21) to which the poet objects. The poem is not a generalized diatribe but is specific and focused: it sets out a reaction to Edward III's adventurist policies against France in 1337 and afterwards. And it may be possible to refine its significance a little more precisely. The poet deplores those who made the king go abroad ("Celi qe ly fist passer partes transmarinas," line 4), so it must have been written in or after 1338. And line 13, which deals with the king's bringing down of those who were accustomed to sit on benches ("E fet aualer que soleyent sedere super scannum"), may refer to Edward III's dismissal of his judges in 1340.[2]

But the broader political attitudes which the poem evinces are more interesting. It is significant that there is no criticism of the king, though there is criticism of the war. The poet opens his poem with a prayer that the king and his household should not be undone ("perire," line 2). He has been deceived into the war by his councillors: he is a young knight ("ieouene bachiler," line 38; fol. 138r) who is incapable of trickery and who has been misled. That he has crossed the sea is the result of those who are false ("falsis," line 5), and it is likely to cause his ruin: great ills ("grantz mals," line 3) will be the result. Much of the responsibility for this is attributed to an evil councillor ("maueis consiler," line 37), who has been variously identified with John Stratford, archbishop of Canterbury, Edward III's chancellor,[3] or William Kilsby, who was promoted to be keeper of the privy seal in 1337.[4] But a precise identification is arguably less important in terms of the dynamic of the poem than the accusation itself, for the poet consistently proposes that the king has been ill served by a number of more minor officials: not all of what is demanded from the fifteenth goes to the king (lines 18–20); the collectors misappropriate some of the wool (lines 28–30). None of this, it is implied, is the fault of the king, but of those around him. Those with power and influence look after themselves and have no regard for the wider community. People are not treated equally. He suggests that the rich get exemptions from the taxation by gift or favor ("dono vel fauore," line 47), and that the poor might rise against the king if they had a leader ("s'ils vssent chief quod vellent leuare," line 64). The oppressive taxes, he argues, have ruined trade by taking money out of the economy:

> Yl y a tant escarcete monete inter gentes.
> Qe houme puet en marche quam parci sunt ementes,
> Tot eyt houme drap ou blee, porcos vel bidentes,

---

[2] For the implications of this crisis for the funding of Edward III's wars with France, see generally May McKisack, *The Fourteenth Century 1307–1399* (Oxford, 1959), pp. 152–81.

[3] See Aspin, ed., *AN Political Songs*, p. 115.

[4] This was the suggestion of K. B. McFarlane; see N. R. Ker, intro., *Facsimile of British Museum MS. Harley 2253*, EETS o.s. 255 (London, 1965), p. xxin6.

Rien leuer en verite, tam multi sunt egentes.
  Gens non est leta cum sit tam parca moneta. (lines 66–70; fol. 138r)

[There is a desperate shortage of cash among the people. At market the buyers are so few that in fact a man can do no business, although he may have cloth or corn, pigs or sheep to sell, because so many are destitute. The people are not cheerful when money is so scarce.]

The war, he says, is too costly, since those engaged in it cannot maintain themselves from the incomes of their lands, and since it is immoral to live on what others provide (lines 76–79). He is not against the king, but he is against the war. In his final stanza he regrets the failure to maintain peace: disturbers of the peace should be brought low, and God is asked to confirm and grant brotherly love between the kings ("confermez e grantez inter reges amores," lines 81–85; fol. 138v). Two cardinals had been sent to try to effect a peace between Edward III and Philip VI in 1337, but their mission had ended in failure — much to the poet's disappointment.

The poem clearly, in part at least, has a clerical agenda. Another copy of it appears in London, British Library MS Additional 10374, fols. 145v–147r. This manuscript, "liber loci benedicti de Whalley," is a cartulary of the Cistercian house at Whalley (Lancashire).[5] It contains documents that date from between 1306 and 1346. A Cistercian abbey was founded at Stanlaw (Lancashire) in 1178. It was translated to Whalley and reconsecrated in 1306 under the patronage of Henry de Lacy, third earl of Lincoln (d. 1311) — which probably explains why the items in this manuscript begin in 1306. Like other cartularies, it contains copies of documents that the house thought were significant — sermons, letters, legal instruments, contracts, and so on. But there are also two poems in Anglo-Norman — one a sardonic piece against David II of Scotland and Philip VI, after the former's defeat and capture at the battle of Neville's Cross in 1346, and the other a variant version of *Against the King's Taxes*. This version omits stanzas 4, 6, 9, 10, and 16 from the Harley version and shows other interesting variations. It objects to the levy of the fifteenth, and to the *collectio lanarum* — and it is worth noting in this connection that Whalley Abbey was involved in the wool trade, and that among the documents preserved in the cartulary are various contracts for the sale and delivery of wool. But the Whalley version generally omits those stanzas which contain criticism of the rich, and it says nothing against those

---

[5] See Thomas Dunham Whitaker, *A History of the Original Parish of Whalley and the Honour of Clitheroe . . .*, 3rd ed. (London, 1801), pp. 120–22 for the poem. For much of what follows in this paragraph, I am indebted to this book. The Whalley text of this poem was first noticed, among modern scholars, by J. R. Maddicott, "Poems of Social Protest in Early Fourteenth-Century England," in *England in the Fourteenth Century: Proceedings of the 1985 Harlaxton Symposium*, ed. W. M. Ormrod (Woodbridge, Suffolk, 1986), pp. 137–38.

involved in military activities in France — perhaps because there was a desire not to upset the monastery's patrons.

All this serves to throw into relief a significant aspect of the MS Harley 2253 version: it is in manner and style by no means a popular poem, yet it has a populist agenda. The poem purports to speak for the common people ("commune gent," line 14), for the people in general ("gens," "pueple," lines 16, 19), and for the poor ("simple gent," "pouerail," lines 21, 24). The poet, at least in the fiction of the poem, is one of them: he speaks of his own wool ("mea lana," line 25). And the injustice of the exactions, which fall principally on those least able to pay, is something he feels personally. But the sentiments in lines 6–7 are particularly interesting — that the king should not act unless "la commune" is willing to consent to it — because parliament, particularly the magnates in parliament, constantly sought concessions from the king in return for the grants which enabled him to pursue the war in France, concessions that effectively, though not formally, curtailed royal power. Edward III had promised in 1331 that "the matters which touch us and the estate of the realm are to be disposed of by the common counsel of the great men of our realm and in no other manner," but he sometimes acted outside this agreement.[6] Matters came to a head in the constitutional crisis of 1341 in which Stratford consistently argued that Edward III was acting, in his policy of waging war in France, against the interests of the common people by relying on a clique of ill-informed and self-seeking advisors instead of on the advice of the wise lords and prelates of his council. As has been shown, this poem reiterates these sentiments. Edward III practically accused Stratford of treason in his intemperate "libellus famosus" and barred him from the parliament that met Monday, April 23, 1341, but Stratford insisted that he should be judged not alone by the king but by his peers in parliament ("in pleno parliamento").[7] Therefore, in insisting that the voice of the "commune" be heard in the shaping of national policy, this poet also reflects and intervenes in the constitutional debate of the years around the opening of the Hundred Years' War.

This short, esoteric, clever poem in many ways defines the political agenda of MS Harley 2253. It dates from the lifetime of the copyist, unlike a number of other datable political items, and it is included presumably because it meant something to him or to the person who organized the production of the book. And the book is organized to a degree. Though its contents may be miscellaneous, they are set out, locally at least, in a manner

---

[6] See V. H. H. Green, *The Later Plantagenets: A Survey of English History between 1307 and 1485* (London, 1955), p. 144.

[7] See McKisack, *Fourteenth Century*, p. 177. I am much indebted to her account of the struggle between Edward III and Stratford.

that suggests that someone thought seriously about their interrelationships.[8] It has often been pointed out that the political verses appear sporadically throughout the manuscript but are generally, though not totally, in a chronological order — the earlier in date, the earlier they appear in the manuscript.[9] It has been proposed that MS Harley 2253 was written in at least two parts:

> Harley does not look as if it was written over a long period of years, but the last dozen leaves, perhaps from the point where the scribe begins to use a horizontal line to bound his writing at the top of the page, may well be a few years later than the rest.

So N. R. Ker.[10] But this is highly questionable: the copyist had used a horizontal line to bound the writing at the top of the page on fols. 53r, 54r, 98r, 99r, 106r, so he can hardly be said to begin to use it for fols. 128r onwards.[11] The manuscript looks as though it is organized and effected without substantial changes of mind or direction. And the complex agenda of *Against the King's Taxes* is that of the political verses in general.[12] It sets forth a generally nationalist set of ideas, a sense of England the nation, and the poems are generally favorable to the king, but not uncritically so. They are, however, suspicious of the king's power and prerogatives, of his officials, and of the fairness of the exactions and taxes levied upon the people. They are also resistant to the encroachments of centrality in the form of the travelling judges and ecclesiastical courts. There is evidence of a regionalism that cuts across the broader nationalist attitudes of the poems. Attempts to centralize and organize England are frequently greeted with a deep-seated skepticism and a resistance that is traditional and local in its ethos — though nobody who set forth these

---

[8] See Theo Stemmler's essay in this volume.

[9] See Aspin, ed., *AN Political Songs*, pp. 106–07; Thorlac Turville-Petre, *England the Nation: Language, Literature, and National Identity, 1290–1340* (Oxford, 1996), p. 195.

[10] See Ker, *Facsimile*, p. xxii.

[11] I derive this information from the facsimile.

[12] There is no general account of the political verses of MS Harley 2253. For useful comments on some of the poems, see Arthur K. Moore, *The Secular Lyric in Middle English* (Lexington, 1951); Rossell Hope Robbins, "Middle English Poems of Protest," *Anglia* 78 (1960): 193–203; V. J. Scattergood, *Politics and Poetry in the Fifteenth Century* (London, 1971), pp. 351–53; George Kane, "Some Fourteenth-Century 'Political' Poems," in *Medieval English Religious and Ethical Literature: Essays in Honour of G. H. Russell*, ed. Gregory Kratzmann and James Simpson (Woodbridge, Suffolk, 1986), pp. 82–91; Maddicott, "Poems of Social Protest," pp. 130–44; and Turville-Petre, *England the Nation*, pp. 195–203.

sentiments would have thought of himself as anything other than a loyal Englishman, and certainly not as a traitor or as a rebel.

II

The nationalist agenda appears most strikingly in the poems relating to the last years of the reign of Edward I. It is highly probable that these poems were preserved not simply because of an antiquarian interest, but rather because the copyist or the compiler of MS Harley 2253 saw similarities between the wars in which Edward III was engaged and those fought by Edward I thirty years earlier against the same enemies — the French and the Scots.

On fol. 73r–v appears *The Death of Edward I* (no. 47), an admiring elegy written in English, of which a fragmentary version has survived in Cambridge University Library MS Additional 4407.[13] Another version of the poem, written in Anglo-Norman, with a different ordering of stanzas, appears in Cambridge University Library MS Gg.i.1.[14] Which is the original and which the translation is difficult to decide, though the English poem appears to be more populist: the French poet addresses his audience as "seignurs" while the English version has "Alle þat beoþ of huerte trewe" (line 1). The poem opens with an announcement of its mood rather than its subject: it is a song "Of duel þat deþ haþ diht vs newe" (line 3). In the second stanza it is revealed that the death is that of Edward I, and the poet praises him in fairly routine terms: his reputation ("nome") was known throughout the world; he was the "trewest mon of alle þinge"; he was skilled and astute ("war ant wys") in war (lines 12–14). And the poet closes his poem in much the same terms: even if his tongue were made of steel and his heart of brass, he says (perhaps echoing *Aeneid* 6.625–27), it would be impossible to relate wholly his "godnesse" or to celebrate his full achievements as a "conquerour" (lines 83–85).

But the poem does not for the most part deal in generalities. It addresses instead three specific but related themes, on which the poet appears to have special information. In the first place, he celebrates Edward I as having a strong sense of England the nation: "al Englond" (line 9) ought to know of the king's death, he says, because of his glories; on his

---

[13] Rossell Hope Robbins, ed., *Historical Poems of the XIVth and XVth Centuries* (New York, 1959), pp. 21–24. For the fragmentary version, see W. W. Skeat, "Elegy on the Death of King Edward I from a New MS.," *Modern Language Review* 7 (1912): 149–50.

[14] For the French poem, see Aspin, ed., *AN Political Songs*, pp. 79–89; she prints the English text from MS Harley 2253 on pp. 90–92. For a careful comparison of the French text with the two English versions, see pp. 81–82. See also Turville-Petre, *England the Nation*, pp. 203–04.

deathbed the king had instructed "clerkes, knyhtes, barouns" that they should "to Engelonde be trewe" and had commended his son to them as a successor,

> Helpeþ mi sone ant crouneþ him newe,
>   For he is nest to buen ycore. (lines 23–24; fol. 73r)

The poet writes this as if he were a witness to it, but to what occasion, if any, he refers is unclear. The poem was evidently written after the coronation of Edward II on February 25, 1308, and the nationalist feeling of the poem extends into the poet's hopes for the new king who has "al Engelond forte wisse ant diht": he should be just to his "pore men"; he should listen to "good consail"; and "gode knyhtes" should not fail him (lines 73–80). But in parallel to this celebration of Edward I as the guide and protector of the English nation comes a second view of him as the champion of Christendom. In the deathbed speech given him by the poet, he bequeaths his heart to the Holy Land and wills that "four-score knyhtes al of pris" should be equipped "to wynne þe croiz" by undertaking the crusade that he wanted to pursue but could not because of the pressures of constant wars in Europe (lines 25–32). There is corroborative evidence for this — though the number of knights to be equipped varies from source to source.[15] The poet projects this view of Edward I in four stanzas that purport to give what seems to be an eyewitness account of the reaction of Pope Clement V to the news of the English king's death. On receiving the messenger's letter, he praises Edward I as the "flour" of Christendom and then retires to his "chau[m]bre" overcome with grief (lines 48–49). He orders a mass to be said in which he expresses the wish that Edward II might continue his father's crusading ambitions:

> "Kyng Edward, honoured þou be!
> God lene þi sone come after þe
>   Bringe to ende þat þou has bygonne;
> Þe holy crois ymad of tre,
>   So fain þou woldest hit han ywonne." (lines 60–64; fol. 73v)

Though a number of chronicles speak of the distress of Clement V at Edward I's death, none has quite this story, and it has been suggested that it may either be an eyewitness account or have come through one of the English attendants of Archbishop Winchelsea,

---

[15] Nicholas Trivet says that Edward I bequeathed his heart to the Holy Land and stipulated that 100 knights should go there for a year to fight for Christendom: see T. Hog, ed., *Annales sex regum Angliae* (London, 1945), pp. 413–14. Thomas Walsingham, on the other hand, says that he paid £32,000 for 140 knights to take his heart to the Holy Land: see Thomas Walsingham, *Historia Anglicana*, ed. H. T. Riley, 2 vols., Rolls Series 28 (London, 1863, 1864), 1.114–15.

who was at the papal court at Poitiers (see line 57) at the time of the English king's death.[16] Whatever accuracy may be in the poet's account, however, his political judgment appears to have been flawed. Though there were others, including the contemporary poet Adam Davy, who predicted that Edward II might undertake a crusade, he never did, and, instead of sending his father's heart to the Holy Land, he had him buried in Westminster Abbey on October 27, 1307.[17] So there may be here an element of wishfulness, that is, a desire to form a policy by predicting it. Nor is there much contemporary corroboration of the third strand of the poem's argument — that the blame for Edward I's failure to undertake a crusade was to be laid at the door of the French:

> Kyng of Fraunce, þou heuedest sunne,
>   Þat þou þe counsail woldest fonde,
> To latte þe wille of Kyng Edward
>   To wende to þe Holy Londe . . . (lines 33–36; fol. 73r)

It is certainly true that Edward I had asked Boniface VIII in 1295 to prevail on Philip IV ("the Fair") to observe his undertakings of nonaggression to the English crown and had promised a crusade against the Saracens if peace in Europe could be established. But according to some chronicle sources Edward I blamed the Scottish wars for his delay, and indeed he died while on his way to Scotland on what was his third campaign.[18]

Immediately following this lament comes *The Flemish Insurrection* (no. 48; fols. 73v–74v), a celebration of the victory of the Flemish burghers, mainly the men of Bruges, against the French army under Robert, count of Artois, at the battle of Courtrai in 1302.[19] It dates from five years earlier than the poem on Edward I's death, but it appears to pick up and echo some of the anti-French sentiments of the preceding poem. Events in the Low Countries were always of interest to the English because the prosperous Flemish textile industry relied principally on English wool, and, in its turn, England was a market for finished cloth: the clothmaking towns of the Low Countries were a significant factor in English trade and politics. Guy of Dampierre, count of Flanders, allied himself to Edward I, but Philip IV, through superior military force, asserted his sovereignty over Flanders. At the truce of Vyve-Saint-Bavon in 1298, the count ceded his power, and James of

---

[16] See Aspin, ed., *AN Political Songs*, p. 89.

[17] See my essay "Adam Davy's *Dreams* and Edward II," in John Scattergood, *Reading the Past: Essays on Medieval and Renaissance Literature* (Dublin, 1996), pp. 52–60; and J. R. S. Phillips, "Edward II and the Prophets," in *England in the Fourteenth Century*, ed. Ormrod, pp. 189–201.

[18] See, for example, Walsingham, *Historia Anglicana*, 1.114–15.

[19] Robbins, ed., *Historical Poems*, pp. 9–13.

Chatillon became the overlord of Flanders. This situation was not acceptable for very long to the Flemings, however, and in May 1302 the burghers of Bruges, under Peter de Conyng, master of the clothweavers, and John Breydel, master of the butchers, organized a rising against the French garrison there — the "Matins of Bruges." Other cities in Flanders, following this example, rose against their overlords. A punitive force was organized under the command of Robert, count of Artois, who had enjoyed some support in Flemish towns, but it was decisively defeated at the battle of Courtrai on July 11, 1302. The battle was fought on marshy ground, which disadvantaged the heavily armed French forces. Another French army, assembled and led by Philip IV, made no significant inroads into Flanders, and it was not until 1305 that the Flemish towns came to terms with the French. The success of the Flemings against their French overlords was a temporary one, but it was lovingly dwelt on by this anonymous poet, whose poem is assiduously preserved by the copyist of this manuscript.

The poem essentially tells the story of the insurrection in a more or less chronological order, but it is interestingly angled. It contains all the relevant historical data: the harsh "statuz newe" (line 9) of the French king; the election by the Flemings of Peter de Conyng as "heuere kyng" and "huere cheueuteyn" (lines 19–20); the massacre of the garrison in Bruges (lines 23–32), the organization of and preparations for the battle of Courtrai (lines 49–72); the battle itself with an account of the outcome (lines 74–104); and its inconclusive aftermath (lines 105–12). The poem is not, however, an attempt to relate the facts of history; it offers, rather, a version of events in the shape of various literary forms. Writing in jaunty tail-rhyme, the poet begins as if he were an oral narrator embarking on a romance: "Lustneþ, lordinges, boþe ʒonge ant olde . . ." (line 1). But it is a parody of romance, and its victims are the French. When Philip IV calls together his war-leaders to organize the punitive expedition against the Flemings, the poet refers to them as "dousse pers" (line 50) as if this were a story from the Charlemagne cycle. The lords are given high-sounding oaths: one promises the king that they will bring the Flemings back to Paris in captivity "By þousendes fyue" (line 64); another vows "We shule flo þe Conyng, ant make roste is loyne" (line 69) — a grim bilingual pun, for though "conyng" in Flemish means "king," in French it means "rabbit." But these boasts of the "proude" French come to nothing and are merely a prelude to their discomfiture. What astonished contemporaries about the battle of Courtrai was that a well-equipped army, led by aristocrats — the natural *bellatores* of their society — could be defeated by Flemish city militias. The clerical author of *Flores historiarum* puts it as follows, not without a certain amount of malicious delight:

Miroque modo, pedestribus equestres, domini subditis, lanarum textoribus, acies loricata, firmamentum formidini, regnum municipio, non valebat resistere.[20]

[And in a wondrous manner, mounted knights were not strong enough to withstand those on foot, lords their subjects, a mail-clad army weavers of wool, the strong the fearful, kingly rule a city.]

Normally the English had a low view of Flemish military prowess — one has only to think of Sir Thopas, Chaucer's burlesque knight from the Poperinghe in West Flanders, or the Flemings who attacked the English at the siege of Calais (1436), according to one poet, as "fersli as lyons of Cotteswold" (i.e., sheep).[21] And this disparagement is not entirely absent from *The Flemish Insurrection*, but the lack of military sophistication of the citizen militias is used as a stick to beat the French. Everywhere in the poem the status of the French leaders and the number of their army are insisted upon:

Seuene eorles ant fourti barouns ytolde,
Fyftene hundred knyhtes proude ant swyþe bolde,
Sixti þousent swyers among ȝunge ant old . . . (lines 73–75; fol. 74r)

Everywhere there is emphasis on the fact that they were mounted on "rouncin" and "stede" (line 84). The Flemish force, by contrast, is made up of "ane few ffullaris" (line 122) — and yet they are victorious. The Flemish do not observe the norms of medieval war; they want neither "raunsoun ne ware" (line 86) for their prisoners but execute them. This is the fate of Robert of Artois:

Þenne seyþ þe eorl of Artois, "Y ȝelde me to þe,
Peter Conyng by þi nome, ȝef þou art hende ant fre,
Þat Y ne haue no shame ne no vylte,
    Þat Y ne be noud ded." (lines 89–92; fol. 74v)

But a "bocher," perhaps meant to be John Breydel, replies and says that the earl will never again see the king of France, nor will he be allowed to eat bread in prison in Bruges, and he is killed (lines 93–96). The chivalric pride of the French is brought low by townsmen

---

[20] See Henry Richards Luard, ed., *Flores historiarum*, 3 vols., Rolls Series 95 (1890; repr. Weisbaden, 1965), 3.111–12, 306–08. The quotation is from p. 308.

[21] For Sir Thopas, see *The Riverside Chaucer*, ed. Larry D. Benson et al. (Boston, 1987), VII [B²] 671–996. For disparagement of the Flemish militias at the siege of Calais, see *Mockery of the Flemings*, in Robbins, ed., *Historical Poems*, pp. 83–86; and more generally, Scattergood, *Politics and Poetry*, pp. 83–96.

who operate by other value systems. And related to this, perhaps, is the linguistic mockery, for the poet uses snatches of French: a relieving force, described as a "gret mounde" goes towards Bruges "pas pur pas" (lines 35–36); one of Philip IV's noblemen swears "par la goule de" (line 61), and another threatens "Nus ne lerrum en vie chanoun ne moyne" (line 66). When this poem was written, French was still a status language in England, and the poet no doubt derived some satisfaction from mocking the French language as well as the French themselves; he possibly defined his own nationalism in part by the English language, which he uses in a particularly demotic and colloquial way. One of its features is the reductive use of proverbial expressions: the French are bought and sold like beasts on market day (lines 3–4), or caught like birds in nets or snares (line 83).[22] As he reviews the story of the battle of Courtrai, the author of the *Flores historiarum* is clear about what it means: it demonstrates the "inglorius" nature of Philip IV and is an example of his unutterable shame ("ineffabili ignominia").[23] The English poet likewise stresses the "shame" (lines 121, 127) that the French have brought upon themselves, and in this he allies himself with the writers of political *sirventes* who see it as their prime function to memorialize the shame of defeated enemies.

The ending of the poem also draws some of its energy from prophecy. The poet reminds Pope Boniface VIII of his degradation of two cardinals of the Colonna family in 1294, advises him to go to Rome to put things right, and warns him that unless he behaves "wysloker" he may lose "lond ant lede" and even his papal crown (lines 113–20). And he prophesies that if the Prince of Wales, Edward of Caernavon, lives, the French king will sorely be sorry for his imprisonment of the count of Flanders, "Wiþ tresoun vntrewe" (line 132), unless he makes amends for it — exposing, in the final stanza, the English nationalism that underlies the poem. Quite what, if anything, these prophecies mean in precise terms is hard to say. But it is clear that the poet senses a volatility in European politics, a time of change, and feels that events are moving in a direction favorable to the English.

The Execution of Sir Simon Fraser (no. 25), which is likewise heavily nationalistic but directed primarily against the Scots, appears much earlier in the manuscript, on fols. 59v–61v, though it dates from four years later and must have been written in the autumn of 1306 after the battle of Methven or Kirkencliff.[24] It purports to be a topical eyewitness account, and its author was certainly well-informed about events in London, where the trial and execution of the Scottish rebels took place. The author presents himself as an oral performer, a purveyor of news: "Lystneþ, lordynges, a newe song Ichulle bigynne . . ."

---

[22] For these proverbs, see B. J. Whiting and H. W. Whiting, *Proverbs, Sentences, and Proverbial Phrases from English Writings Mainly before 1500* (Cambridge, Mass., 1968), B637 and B310.

[23] See Luard, ed., *Flores historiarum*, 3.308.

[24] Robbins, ed., *Historical Poems*, pp. 14–21.

(line 1). And it seems to have been the "newe" which generated the poem — a particularly gruesome form of execution first used by the English on Sir William Wallace on August 23, 1305, and on Sir Simon Fraser on September 7, 1306.[25] These two executions frame the poem. It takes as its starting point "Þe heuedes o Londone Brugge whose con yknawe" (line 10) — that is, the heads of Wallace and Fraser displayed there. In the next stanza comes a brief description of the earlier execution:

> Þe Waleis wos todrawe, seþþe he wos anhonge,
> Al quic biheueded, ys bowels ybrend,
> Þe heued to Londone Brugge wos send
>   To abyde. (lines 18–21; fol. 59v)

And practically the whole of the second half of the poem (lines 105–216) is taken up with an account of the capture, trial, and execution of Fraser. It concentrates unremittingly on the degrading details of his punishment. He was "yfetered weel" with iron and steel as he was brought from Scotland (lines 110–12). When he entered London at Newgate his legs were "yfetered . . . vnder his horse wombe" and "mankled were ys honde" (lines 121–22), and on his head was placed "a gerland of leues . . . of grene" so that he should be "yknowe" for a traitor (lines 116–20). After his trial and condemnation he was drawn on a bullock's hide (lines 162–63). As he came from the Tower of London through Cheapside to be executed, he was drawn with "feteres" and "gyues," dressed in sackcloth (lines 177–81). His execution is in all respects like the previous one:

> Þo he com to galewes, furst he wes anhonge
> Al quic byheueded, þah him þohte longe.
> Seþþe he wes yopened, is bowels ybrend;
> Þe heued to Londone Brugge wes send
>   To shonde. (lines 185–89; fol. 61r)

The poet uses the same rhymes and much of the same vocabulary. But the repetition is part of the point: it establishes a pattern of shame ("shonde") and humiliation to which the "traytours of Scotland" (lines 2, 225) are subjected. Fraser's head stands above the bridge, says the poet, "ffaste bi Waleis" (lines 201–02) — thus closing the circle of the poem's action, though he adds three more triumphalist stanzas on more general political matters.

"The public execution is to be understood not only as a judicial, but also as a political ritual. It belongs, even in minor cases, to the ceremonies by which power is manifested."

---

[25] See George James Aungier, ed., *Croniques de London, depuis l'an 44 Hen. III. jusqu'a l'an 17 Edw. III*, Camden Society 28 (1844; repr. New York, 1968), p. 32.

So Michel Foucault.[26] And many of the incidental gestures of the poem disclose both the political intentions of the particular types of execution devised for the defeated Scots, and the agenda of the poem itself. The executions are designed to demonstrate English power and to arouse fear in the Scots. Wallace was executed, says the poet, "to warny alle þe gentilmen" of Scotland (line 17); his body was quartered and sent to four towns in the North "huere myrour to be," to give them something on which to think, so that "monie myhten se / Ant drede" (lines 25–29). They are to provide a visual lesson for the ambitious and treacherous Scots: the Scottish leaders "wenden han buen kynges," but, says the poet, it would have been better if they had reconciled themselves to being "barouns" and living in God's law, peacefully, in their allotted stations (lines 11–13). There is a whole series of examples of the "ffalsnesse ant swykedom" (line 170) of the Scots, when oaths of fealty were sworn to Edward I but never kept (lines 24, 33–40, 42, and so on). And a litany of other shortcomings are attributed to the Scots: they were "vnwis" to oppose the will of the English king (line 54), and despite all their efforts "lutel pris wonne" (line 88). Events demonstrate, the poem asserts, that all resistance to Edward I is futile. And, in any case, Robert Bruce, the king of Scotland, was not a very impressive ruler — really just a temporary, holiday king from a summer game:

> Hii þat him crounede proude were ant bolde;
> Hii maden kyng of somere, so hii ner ne sholde;
> Hii setten on ys heued a croune of rede golde,
> Ant token him a kyne-ȝerde (so me kyng sholde)
>   To deme.
>   Þo he wes set in see,
>   Lutel god couþe he,
>   Kyne-riche to ȝeme. (lines 65–72; fol. 60r)

Despite his coronation, says the poet, "Kyng Hobbe" is a fugitive, living a hunted and marginalized existence on the "mures" (lines 73–74), which is derogative in a punning way — "Hobbe" being both a familiar diminutive form of Robert and a generic name for a rustic or clown and a hobgoblin or sprite. Nor will the help of Charles IV of France, who promised to support the Scots "wiþ myht ant wiþ streynþe" (lines 227–28), amount to anything while Edward I "longe shonkes" is alive (lines 232–33).

But the English king was ill when this poem was written (he died the following year) — hence, perhaps, the stress given to the achievements of Edward of Caernavon, Aymer de Valence, earl of Pembroke, and others. The poet appears to be trying to persuade

---

[26] Michel Foucault, *Discipline and Punish: The Birth of the Prison*, trans. Alan Sheridan (London, 1977), p. 47.

himself and his audience that even without Edward I England would have war leaders capable of destroying its enemies and of securing it against foreign aggression. But there may be a more subtle subtext: the executions which are so dwelt upon may have been meant to be a "myrour" not only to the Scots but to the populace of England too. It may be that they are designed to make the common people of England "se / Ant drede" (lines 28–29). The poet makes the point that the spectacle of Fraser's degradation and execution was popular: "Moni mon of Engelond" came to London "Forto se Symond" (lines 182–84). And, in a revealing passage, the poet tries to define the appropriate public reaction, that is, to define the response of his audience under the guise of describing it:

> Moni wes þe wyues chil þat þeron lokeþ a day,
>> And seide alas,
>> Þat he wes ibore
>> Ant so villiche forlore
> So feir mon ase he was. (lines 196–200; fol. 61r)

This is a lesson in the futility and inadvisability of ambition and treachery, an argument for acceptance of the status quo, and a reinforcement of the power of the establishment, which extends beyond the Scots to an English populace that was becoming increasingly lawless and restive. So the triumphalism of this poem may be qualified by a degree of anxiety.

The most quizzical of the poems on the Scottish wars in MS Harley 2253 is *The Prophecy of Thomas of Erceldoune* (no. 90), which appears on fol. 127rb–va.[27] It is presented by its heading as an answer to a question by the countess of Dunbar to Thomas of Erceldoune, a noted Scottish prophet, as to when the war between England and Scotland might end ("prendreit fyn") — and the conditional tense is important, because the reply is enigmatical and inconclusive: it consists of a series of conditional statements beginning "When . . ." They move between the implausible and the unlikely. Most are utterly general and vague, but some contain place-names that suggest more precision — though in exactly what terms is not easy to be certain about. The agenda of the poem is, however, despairing, and this is communicated by a number of statements that indicate that the war will end only when the world is changed by some cataclysmic set of circumstances. Some of these are cultural *impossibilia*:

> When Londyon ys forest, ant forest ys felde . . .
> When Rokesbourh nys no burgh ant market is at Forwyleye. (lines 3, 7; fol. 127rb)

---

[27] Robbins, ed., *Historical Poems*, p. 29.

Some are moral:

> When mon is leuere oþermones þyng þen is owen . . .
> When ryþt ant wrong ascenteþ togedere. (lines 2, 14; fol. 127rb–va)

Other lines, however, suggest other things. The prediction "When Scottes flen so faste, þat for faute of ship, hy drouneþ hemselue" (line 16; fol. 127va) recalls the poem on Sir Simon Fraser on the events of 1306 and the drowning of the fleeing Scots:

> So hii weren byset on eueruche halue,
> Somme slaye were, ant somme dreynte hemselue,
> Sire Iohan of Lyndeseye nolde nout abyde,
> He wod into þe water, his feren him bysyde,
> To adrenche. (lines 97–101; fol. 60v)

On the other hand, the line "When Bambourne ys donged wyþ dede men" (line 9; fol. 127rb) might suggest an occasion in 1314 at around the time of the battle of Bannockburn. The poem ends with a question, which is answered after a fashion:

> Whenne shal þis be? Nouþer in þine tyme ne in myne,
> Ah comen ant gon wiþinne twenty wynter ant one. (lines 17–18; fol. 127va)

Twenty-one may not be a number to be taken too literally, but if it is exact, and if the reference to Bannockburn is the latest in the poem, this might indicate a date for it of about 1335, roughly the same as the later political verses in the manuscript. If so, it might testify to the war-weariness of these years.

III

Among the many poems in MS Harley 2253 that question royal authority and the king's prerogative, those dealing with Sir Simon de Montfort and the Barons' Wars[28] are the clearest and most focused.

Henry III's flamboyant and rather arbitrary rule had long been the subject of criticisms to which he failed to respond before matters came to a head when seven of his most important barons, supported by many others and a lot of knights, confronted him in Westminster Hall on April 30, 1258. They demanded a radical reform of the way in which

---

[28] For a comprehensive account, see J. R. Maddicott, *Simon de Montfort* (Cambridge, 1994).

England was ruled: henceforth the king should answer to "le commun d'Engleterre," which the barons claimed to represent. As M. T. Clanchy puts it,

> two political philosophies, both with deep medieval roots, were therefore in conflict in 1258. On one side stood the sacred authoritarian monarchy, championed by Henry III, and on the other communal custom and baronial rights, championed by Simon de Montfort.[29]

Initially the king had few choices in the matter: the barons came to Westminster armed and well-supported, so Henry III and his son, the Lord Edward, prudently took the oaths required of them and bound themselves to the commune. In the Provisions of Oxford drawn up in June 1258, the barons spelled out the shape of their radical proposals: that wide powers should be invested in a permanent council of fifteen people appointed jointly by the king and his supporters and the barons and theirs; that these fifteen men and twelve elected from the commune should form "parlementz" to meet regularly three times a year; that public officials (chancellor, justiciar, treasurer) should be appointed annually; and much besides. They also asked for reforms in the church. "Taken together, the Provisions of Oxford reduced the authority of the king of England to that of a figurehead, directed by the council which was answerable to the commune."[30] Again, Henry III had no choice but to comply. Proclamations were issued to the shires, some in English, stipulating that whatever "vre rædesmen" (i.e., the council) or the "loandes folk" (i.e., the commune) decide should be accepted, and that these decisions should be, for the benefit of the country, "stedefæst and ilestinde in alle þinge a butan ænde."[31]

But Henry III had no intention of conceding this diminishment of his royal prerogatives "a butan ænde" or otherwise. He sought to divide the barons from each other. He disrupted parliaments by absence abroad. He successfully petitioned the Pope in 1261 for release from his oaths on the grounds that they had been made under duress. And in 1264 he succeeded in persuading the barons to allow the issues between him and them to be arbitrated upon by Louis IX, king of France. Henry III had ceded his claims to France north of the Loire and in Poitou at the Peace of Paris in 1259, and this may well have weighed with the French king. In any case, it would have been difficult for a monarch, however unbiased, to have accepted proposals that sought to establish, as a matter of constitutional policy, the diminishment of royal rights. He found so decisively for Henry

---

[29] M. T. Clanchy, *England and Its Rulers 1066–1272: Foreign Lordship and National Identity* (Glasgow, 1983), p. 270.

[30] Clanchy, *England and Its Rulers*, p. 273.

[31] For a text of the proclamation, see Bruce Dickins and R. M. Wilson, eds., *Early Middle English Texts*, 3rd ed. (London, 1956), pp. 7–9.

III that it appeared he had not listened to the baronial case. The decision was meant to end the matter, but it had the opposite effect: it exacerbated the conflict and practically guaranteed that there would be civil war.

Initially the barons had a lot of support, and Henry III and his adherents were extremely unpopular — all of which is reflected in the many political verses of the period. *Song of the Peace with England*, preserved in Paris, Bibliothèque Nationale MS fr. 837, is a satirical account of English plans to regain lands in northern France.[32] Early in the poem the author draws his audience's attention to the absurdity of the situation:

> Sinor, tendez a mai; ne devez pas rier:
> Ce navel que je port doit tout le mont crier . . . (lines 13–14)

[Lords, listen to me; you must not laugh: the whole world ought to cry out at the news which I bring . . .]

He then recounts a debate, held at London, amongst the English lords about how they might recover their French possessions. If the French king had heard it, he says, they would have had a great fright ("grant poentement," line 19). But this is all ironic: the high-sounding speeches enunciating chivalric vows are undercut by the coarse and demotic language in which they are made:

> Le bon rai d'Ingleter se traina a .i. apart,
> Li et Trichart sa frer, irrous comme lipart.
> Il suspire de cul, si se claima a l'art
> "Hui Diex! com puis-je voir de Normandi ma part?" (lines 29–32)

[The good king of England takes himself to one side, he and Richard his brother, as angry as leopards. He sighs from his behind, and exclaims with alacrity, "Oh God! how can I get my part of Normandy?"]

Here the allusion to the leopards in the English royal coat of arms coexists with the coarse phrase "suspire de cul," and the version used for Richard of Cornwall's name contains a deliberately derogatory pun: "trichart" means traitor. The poem is written in deliberately rough and, at times, ungrammatical French, so it may be tempting to see it as a metropolitan travesty of the provincial English. Simon de Montfort appears fleetingly yet interestingly in the poem. He is the only person to urge caution:

---

[32] Wright, ed., *Political Songs*, pp. 63–68.

"Se vous aler seur leus, il se voudra dafandre:
Toute ta paveillons metre feu a la cendre.
Il n'a si vaelant qui l'ose mi atendre;
Mult sarra maubali qui le Francois puet prendre." (lines 57–60)

["If you go against them, they will wish to defend themselves: he (the French king) will burn all your tents to ashes. There is no man so brave who dare wait for him; those whom the French can take prisoner will be very uncomfortable."]

For his advice de Montfort is threatened and called a piece of excrement ("merdaele," line 66), yet his is the only sensible voice. This distinguishes him and isolates him from the general derision, so perhaps the poem is of English origin and written by one of his supporters. He is certainly the hero of most of the verses supporting the baronial cause. In the fragmentary poem called *The Song of the Barons*, a laudatory roll call of their adherents that seems to date from about 1263,[33] appears the following verse that puns on his name:

Il est apele de Montfort,
Il est el mond et si est fort,
    Si ad grant chevalerie;
Ce voir, et je m'acort:
Il eime dreit, et het le tort,
    Si avera la mestrie. (lines 37–42)

[He is called de Montfort: he is in the world and he is strong, and great is his prowess; this is the truth and I concur: he loves right and hates wrong, and he will get the upper hand.]

For the principled stand that he took in seeking to curb royal power and to broaden the power base of constitutional government, this unbending aristocratic Frenchman became something like an English popular hero.

When the baronial forces beat the king's army on May 14, 1264, the supporters of de Montfort celebrated, some of them in verse. The most comprehensive account of the baronial position at this point appears in the 968 lines of *Carmen de Bello Lewensi*, a somber moralizing work that contrasts the high principles of the barons with the deceit and treachery of the royal party.[34] It treats de Montfort as the agent of God who has freed the English from their oppressors:

---

[33] Wright, ed., *Political Songs*, pp. 59–63.

[34] See C. L. Kingsford, ed., *The Song of Lewes* (1890; repr. Brussels, 1963). There is also a text in Wright, ed., *Political Songs*, pp. 72–121. Both include translations.

Benedicat dominus S de monte-forti!
Suis nichilominus natis et cohorti!
Qui se magnanimiter exponentes morti,
Pugnaverunt fortiter, condolentes sorti
Anglicorum flebili, qui subpeditati
Modo vix narrabili, peneque privati
Cunctis libertatibus, immo sua vita,
Sub duris principibus languerunt, ita,
Ut israelitica plebs sub pharaone,
Gemens sub tyrannica devastatione. (lines 65–74)

[May the Lord bless Simon de Montfort, his sons and his army, who, exposing themselves bravely to death, fought valiantly, pitying the lamentable lot of the English who, trodden under foot in a manner scarcely to be described, and almost deprived of all their liberties, nay, of their life, had languished under hard rulers, like the people of Israel under Pharaoh, groaning under a tyrannical devastation.]

This is a highly learned, literary poem: in his opening line the poet refers to the pen ("calamus") with which he writes.

Nothing could be further from this tone than *A Song of Lewes* (no. 23), which appears in MS Harley 2253, fols. 58v–59r.[35] Its opening line establishes a possibly fictive mode of oral performance to an essentially listening audience: "Sitteþ alle stille ant herkneþ to me" (line 1), and it proceeds in a language that is appropriately demotic. It is the earliest surviving English *sirventes*, a mocking poem against defeated enemies. The issues that caused de Montfort to take up arms against his king are not mentioned or alluded to: this is a highly personalized version of events. Its hero is de Montfort, and, notably, it omits all reference to Henry III, so the king is spared its vituperation. Instead, its principal villain is Richard of Cornwall, brother of Henry III, king of the Romans, and leader of the royal forces. He was captured at the battle and afterwards imprisoned in his own castle at Wallingford, a fact of which the poet reminds him (lines 10–11), along with Lord Edward, who was moved to Dover after the beginning of 1265 (line 40). Though Richard of Cornwall survived, his character is systematically assassinated. He is repeatedly called "þe kyng of Alemaigne," but the activities the poet mentions serve to degrade him: he asked £30,000 to make "pees in þe countre" between the king and the barons (line 4); though he led the king's army, he spent all his money on "swyuyng" [fornication] (line 9); he took refuge in a windmill during the battle (lines 16–18, 20–21). The refrain of the poem alludes to his treachery in breaking an oath he had taken at Canterbury to abide by the

---

[35] Dickins and Wilson, eds., *Early ME Texts*, pp. 10–12.

Provisions of Oxford and utilizes the pun on *Richard/trichard* which had been used in an earlier pro-baronial poem:

> Richard, þah þou be euer trichard
> Tricchen shalt þou neuermore. (lines 6–7, etc.; fols. 58v–59r)

Subsidiary targets in the poem include John de Warenne, earl of Surrey, and Sir Hugh Bigod, a former justiciar and one of the original seven rebels — both of whom escaped from Lewes to France, much to the disappointment of the poet (lines 28–32, 34–38), and, he says, of Simon de Montfort.[36] But the last stanza attacks the Lord Edward in direct terms:

> Be þe luef, be þe loht, Sire Edward,
> Þou shalt ride sporeles o þy lyard
> Al þe ryhte way to Douere ward;
> Shalt þou neuermore breke foreward,
>   Ant þat reweþ sore.
> Edward, þou dudest ase a shreward,
>   Forsoke þyn emes lore. (lines 38–44; fol. 59r)

The allusion to ignoring an uncle's teaching takes one back to the traditional notion in heroic society of a close relationship between uncles and nephews (de Montfort was Edward's uncle by marriage). The giving of spurs was part of the institution of knighthood and to be deprived of them was axiomatically a disgrace. And "lyard" was a derogatory term for a horse — certainly not the sort of mount a "kyng" ought to have. The poet constantly uses the word "neuermore," as if there were no chance that the royalist cause might recover, but in this he was mistaken.

Briefly, de Montfort and the barons controlled the country, Henry III, and the Lord Edward. But de Montfort's support drifted away and the royalist fortunes revived. On August 4, 1265, at the battle of Evesham, de Montfort was defeated, killed, and his body dismembered. The king's forces under Lord Edward ruthlessly hunted down de Montfort's major supporters and had them executed or imprisoned. Immediately following the English verses on Lewes in MS Harley 2253 comes an Anglo-Norman *Lament for Simon*

---

[36] On the desertion of some of de Montfort's original supporters, see the verses preserved in William de Rishanger's chronicle of the Barons' Wars printed by Wright, ed., *Political Songs*, pp. 121–24. Bigod is urged "pactam serva sanu" [keep your argument] — advice that was ignored.

de Montfort (no. 24; fol. 59r–v), which again proposes itself as being orally delivered and reviews the situation after the defeat of the barons:[37]

> Chaunter m'estoit,
> Mon cuer le voit,
> En vn dure langage;
> Tut en ploraunt
> Fust fet le chaunt
> De nostre duz baronage,
> Qe pur la pees
> Si loynz apres
> Se lesserent detrere,
> Lur cors trencher
> E demenbrer
> Pur saluer Engletere.
>   Ore est ocys
>   La flur de pris,
>   Qe taunt sauoit de guere,
>   Ly quens Mountfort;
>   Sa dure mort
>   Molt enplorra la terre. (lines 1–18; fol. 59r)

[I must sing, my heart wishes it, in a grievous strain; in tears was made the song of our gentle baronage, who for the sake of the peace so long deferred, let themselves be torn asunder, their bodies hacked and dismembered to save England. Now he is slain, the flower of fame, who was so versed in warfare, Montfort the earl; the whole land bewailed his cruel death.]

He mentions Hugh Despenser, the "tres noble iustice" (line 57), and Henry, Simon de Montfort's eldest son, and prays for those supporters who are committed and detained in harsh prison (lines 153–56). But he has nothing good to say about the royal supporters: because of the fact that they brought loyalty and truth to nothing, the king, who is a deceitful man ("losenger") and a fool ("fol"), will be able to reign again (lines 127–38). Most interesting, however, is the way in which the poet seeks to memorialize de Montfort with the standard tropes of the consolatory elegy[38] and to make him into a martyr ("Le seint martir") for peace and justice (lines 75–76): he compares him with Thomas Becket ("ly martyr / De Caunterbyr," lines 40–41); he mentions the hair shirt de Montfort was

---

[37] Aspin, ed., *AN Political Songs*, pp. 24–35.

[38] For a study of these conventions, see V. J. Scattergood, "Skelton and the Elegy," *Proceedings of the Royal Irish Academy* 84, C 10 (1984): 333–47.

found to be wearing at his death ("heyre," line 93); and affirms that he is certain of everlasting life (lines 148–50). In fact, a cult grew up associated with his name. He was revered as a saint and martyr, and it was believed he could work miracles. A record of these miracles appears in London, British Library MS Cotton Vespasian A.vi, along with a life of him and a prayer to be said for him as protector of the English ("protector gentis Angliae").[39]

In the Anglo-Norman poem Simon's "heir" is prayed for — possibly Aumery, since he is described as "l'enfant" (line 112), though it is hard to see how he could be called an heir since he had elder brothers living. Perhaps the poet means Guy de Montfort, who escaped from prison after the battle and avenged his father's death on Henry of Almain, the heir of Richard of Cornwall, by murdering him in Italy in 1271. The divisions created by the Barons' War did not end with the defeat of de Montfort. Nor did the constitutional issues — particularly those relating to the "commune" and the curbing of royal power — disappear from the political agenda, which is perhaps why the compiler of MS Harley 2253 did not think it inappropriate to preserve poems about events that took place more than half a century earlier.

IV

Scattered throughout MS Harley 2253, in no particular order that can be established, appear other poems that express resistance to royal authority in other ways. They are not so much attacks on the king as questionings of the increasingly determined attempts to establish some kind of centralized control in England, or, at a more local level, grumbles about the repressiveness of officials.

It is hard to establish a definite context for most of these poems, but it is easiest in the case of the outlaw's song of *Trailbaston* (no. 80), which appears on fols. 113vb–114v.[40] It was written probably about 1305 or a little later in monorhyming Anglo-Norman quatrains by somebody from the South West of England, who depicts himself, fictively or otherwise, as an outlaw living in the romanticized forest of "Belregard" (line 19). He has written his poem on parchment so that it may be preserved, and thrown it on the high-road so that it may be found and read (lines 99–100). It has been suggested that the author was a cleric because at one point he talks about benefit of clergy and the bishop's prison (lines 59–64), but his own version of himself is as one who has served his king in

---

[39] See Wright, ed., *Political Songs*, pp. 124–25.

[40] Aspin, ed., *AN Political Songs*, pp. 67–78.

Flanders, Scotland, and Gascony (lines 25–26), so he may be a former soldier.[41] All his problems he blames on the newly enacted "trailbaston" ordinances of 1305:

> Ce sunt les articles de Trayllebastoun.
> Salue le roi meismes, de Dieu eit maleysoun
> Qe a de primes graunta tiel commissioun:
> Quar en ascuns des pointz n'est mie resoun. (lines 5–8; fol. 113vb)

[These are the articles of Trailbaston. Saving the king himself, may he have God's curse who first of all granted such a commission; for there is no sense of right in some of its points.]

These ordinances were set in place to enable the prosecution and punishment of armed bands of robbers whose standard *modus operandi* involved violence with clubs and staves: according to Ralph B. Pugh, "trailbaston" meant "club-carrying" and "applied both to the offence and the offender."[42] The outlaw in this poem has fallen victim to the new law. He has been indicted falsely, he says, "De male robberies e autre mauestee" [Of wicked robberies and other misdeeds] (lines 21–24), and his neighbors speak of him as a member of an outlaw band ("compagnie," line 86), but he has never deliberately murdered anybody or stolen to do anybody any harm (lines 95–96). The new ordinances cause crime, he argues, rather than prevent it, because men would rather become outlaws than submit themselves to the officials of the law and possible imprisonment, and "Quar pur doute de prisone meint laroun serra" [Because of fear of prison many a man will become a thief] (line 44; fol 114r). He cannot give himself up, he says, because he is under sentence of death, and he is not rich enough to buy himself his freedom (lines 73–76). Yet he wishes to come to peace in his own area amongst his own kinsmen. Typically and unsurprisingly, he expects a pardon so that he can resume his life within society: "Vncore attendroy grace e orroi gent parler" [Yet I shall get pardon and hear people speak] (line 77; fol. 114v).[43]

The outlaw's reaction to the new ordinances and those carrying them out is aggressive and violent. In one stanza he names four of the commissioners charged with implementing

---

[41] For studies of this poem, see Maurice Keen, *The Outlaws of Medieval Legend* (London, 1961), pp. 204–05; R. B. Dobson and J. Taylor, eds., *Rymes of Robyn Hood: An Introduction to the English Outlaw* (London, 1976), pp. 250–54, for a discussion and translation; and my essay, "*The Tale of Gamelyn*: The Noble Robber as Provincial Hero," in Scattergood, *Reading the Past*, pp. 100–03.

[42] See Ralph B. Pugh, ed., *Calendar of London Trailbaston Trials under Commissions of 1305 and 1306* (London, 1975), p. 4.

[43] On the comparative ease with which pardons could be obtained, see John Bellamy, *Crime and Public Order in England in the Later Middle Ages* (London, 1973), pp. 190–98.

the trailbaston ordinances in the South West of England: the two South Westerners, William Martyn and William de Knoville, are called "gent de piete" [pious men], but the two Midlanders, Henry de Spigurnel and Roger Belflour, are "gent de cruelte" [cruel men] (lines 33–35) and are threatened with violence, which the outlaw calls a "game":

> Ie lur appre[n]droy le giw de Traylebastoun,
> E lur bruseroy l'eschyne e le cropoun,
> Les bras e les jambes, ce serreit resoun,
> La lange lur toudroy e la bouche ensoun. (lines 37–40; fol. 114r)

> [I will teach them the game of Trailbaston, and I will break their back and rump, their arms and their legs, it would be right; I will cut out their tongue and their mouth in the bargain.]

He has a similar attitude towards jurors: "Si ie les pus ateindre la teste lur froi voler" [I will make their heads fly if I can get at them] (line 31; fol. 113vb). There is more than a little irony here because the sort of physical violence he promises is one of the things the commissions were designed to stamp out. But violence is part of the outlaw's way of life, and he resents anything and anyone who questions this.[44] Interestingly, at one point, he puts forth a case, expressed as hypothetical, which makes it clear that, for him, the law is not an embodiment of moral and ethical principles by which society chooses to regulate itself, nor an instrument that exists to protect human rights, but something that threatens his lifestyle and behavorial norms:

> Sire, si ie voderoi mon garsoun chastier
> De vne buffe ou de deus, pur ly amender,
> Sur moi betera bille, e me frad atachier,
> E auant qe isse de prisone raunsoun grant doner. (lines 9–12; fol. 113vb)

> [Sir, if I want to punish my boy with a cuff or two, to correct him, he will take out a summons against me, and have me attached and made to pay a big ransom before I get out of prison.]

He may have to pay a fine of 40 shillings, and then there is the expense of rewarding the sheriff for not putting him into a deep dungeon (lines 13–15). His readers are asked to consider whether it is reasonable that he be treated thus for punishing a servant by beating him: "Ore agardez seigneurs, est ce resoun?" (line 16). A trailbaston commissioner, or

---

[44] On the intimidation of jurors, see Bellamy, *Crime and Public Order*, pp. 19, 21, 125; and Barbara A. Hanawalt, *Crime and Conflict in English Communities, 1300–1348* (Cambridge, Mass., 1979), p. 51.

187

indeed anybody who believed that the physical ill-treatment of servants was wrong, might have answered "yes" to his question, but that is not the answer the outlaw expects. Unwittingly, he lays bare the violence that is implicit, and sometimes explicit, in hierarchical relationships. But more obviously here he resents the intrusion of the law into his affairs and is prepared to resist it by violent confrontation or evasion. By his own standards, which he expects to be those of his readers, he has done nothing wrong. He is an unfortunate man, he maintains, oppressed by bad laws and malicious accusations that have disrupted his traditional value system and way of life. The spirit of provincial resistance, possibly ironized, to a centralized legal system which it sees as intrusive, breathes from every line of this poem.

The protest in this poem is precise and specific. That in *Song of the Husbandman* (no. 31), which appears rather incongruously on fol. 64r following a sequence of love lyrics, is more general, and dates ranging from 1300, 1315–17, and 1340 have been suggested for its composition.[45] It is a somber, intricately crafted poem recording agrarian grievances, and its main targets are the king's tax collectors and various local officials, but no names are mentioned. The opening is indicative of the poem's procedure:

> Ich herde men vpo mold make muche mon,
>   Hou he beþ itened of here tilyynge:
>
> Gode ʒeres ant corn boþe beþ agon;
>   Ne kepeþ here no sawe ne no song synge.[46]

The poet reports what he hears, and though a single voice appears to articulate the complaint, plural forms are used ("we," "vs," "oure") along with the speaker's "Ich": he claims to speak on behalf of a whole class of poor tenant farmers, and his experience is also theirs. So the poem's strategy is to generalize the complaints to make them universal. The "good years" and the plentiful harvests have gone, according to the poem, because of the weight of exchequer taxation and the overbearing venality of the collectors:

> ʒet comeþ budeles, wiþ ful muche bost:
>   "Greyþe me seluer to þe grene wax;

---

[45] For a brief discussion of the date, favoring 1340, see Maddicott, "Poems of Social Protest," p. 132. Maddicott had earlier proposed a date of 1315–17, the years of the great famine, in *The English Peasantry and the Demands of the Crown, 1294–1341*, Past and Present Society Supplement 1 (Oxford, 1975), pp. 3, 7, 13. See Richard Newhauser's essay in this volume.

[46] Lines 1–4; fol. 64r. Robbins, ed. *Historical Poems*, pp. 7–9, where a date of 1300 is given.

Þou art writen y my writ, þat þou wel wost!"
  Mo þen ten siþen told Y my tax. (lines 37–40)

Always "þe furþe þeni mot to þe kynge" (line 8), he complains, and in order to pay he has to sell some of his tools ("mi bil ant my borstax," line 44), his mare (line 54), and his corn before it is ripe (line 46). And as if this were not enough, there are the local manorial officials to contend with, the bailiff, and those in charge of the lord's fences and forest timber:

Þe hayward heteþ vs harm to habben of his;
  Þe bailif bockneþ vs bale ant weneþ wel do;
Þe wodeward waiteþ vs wo, þat lokeþ vnder rys;
  Ne mai vs ryse no rest, rycheis ne ro.
Þus me pileþ þe pore, þat is of lute pris.
  Nede in swot ant in swynk swynde mot swo. (lines 15–20)

And then there are fierce storms ("wickede wederes," line 70), which rot the corn "er we repe" (line 68). This is a poem of despair and frustration, most of which is blamed on officialdom of one sort or another, which purports to speak for an agrarian group whose livelihood is threatened: "Forþi mi lond leye liþ ant leorneþ to slepe" (line 64). No solution is offered nor is any action proposed, certainly nothing approaching revolt. This is simply complaint and the registering of protest, and the speaker can look forward to nothing except beggary (line 68) if things continue.

The relationship between officialdom and the peasantry is treated in a wittier and more indirect way in *The Man in the Moon* (no. 81), which appears on fols. 114v–115r immediately following the Anglo-Norman verses on trailbaston, presumably because both poems deal with fugitives from justice. It reinterprets, in contemporary terms, the well-known folk story that the man in the moon is a peasant with a dog and a thornbush:

Wher he were o þe feld pycchynde stake,
  For hope of ys þornes to dutten is doren,
He mot myd is twybyl oþer trous make
  Oþer al is dayes werk þer were yloren.[47]

In order to repair and close the gaps ("doren") in his hedges, the peasant has planted a quickset hedge and has had to cut brushwood ("trous") with his double-edged axe so that he can cover the shoots of his new hedge to protect them from cattle and sheep which may

---

[47] Lines 13–16; fol. 115r. G. L. Brook, ed., *The Harley Lyrics: The Middle English Lyrics of MS. Harley 2253*, 4th ed. (Manchester, 1968), pp. 69–70.

eat them, so that his day's work will not be wasted. But the lord's hedgekeeper ("hayward") has caught him illegally cutting wood, and he has been forced to give a pledge ("wed," line 24) as security for paying a fine.[48] Rather than face his punishment, however, the peasant has fled the manor, says the poet, and taken refuge in the moon. The poet offers to help the fugitive peasant by inviting the manorial official to his home, getting him drunk, and recovering the pledge:

> We shule preye þe haywart hom to vr hous
>   Ant maken hym at heyse for þe maystry,
> Drynke to hym deorly of fol god bous,
>   Ant oure dame Douse shal sitten hym by.
> When þat he is dronke ase a dreynt mous,
>   Þenne we schule borewe þe wed ate bayly. (lines 27–32)

This is not an ordinary political poem, though the situation it imagines — a peasant has fled the manor for an offense against the vert — is not an unusual one. And the poet has sympathy with the starved and hunted outlaw, who experiences "muche chele" in the frost and gets his clothes torn by thorns (lines 5–6). But the protest here against officialdom is very mild. The poet seems to suggest that the best way to deal with the peasant's plight is to exploit the human weaknesses of the representatives of manorial authority — here in terms of drink and women.

V

Not entirely dissimilar to these verses dealing with intrusive officialdom are those which address the problems associated with bastard feudalism — the abuses of livery and maintenance, the difficulties of controlling retinues, and the overbearing behavior of the indentured retainers of lords and their servants towards the vulnerable common people. Traditional tenurial relationships weakened with the break-up of feudal patterns of demesne farming. In place of the old relationships between lords and vassals based on serfdom emerged new types of arrangement based on contracts freely negotiated. The arrangement could be highly formal and involve precise definitions of the scale of a retainer's service and the extent of his recompenses, or highly informal and involve simply a promise by a powerful magnate to be "good lord" to lesser men — which is to say, he might seek to promote their interests in return for some sort of service or help if it were needed. Late medieval legislation, particularly the statute of 1390, sought to define various

---

[48] See R. J. Menner, "The Man in the Moon and Hedging," *Journal of English and Germanic Philology* 48 (1949): 1–14; Scattergood, *Politics and Poetry*, pp. 351–53.

categories of retainer: one group consisted of resident household retainers, estate managers, legal advisers, and the like; a second consisted of those who agreed by written indenture to serve a particular lord in peace and war under certain conditions; and a third, more amorphous category included those who had no written contract but accepted the lord's fees and wore his livery in return for certain services.[49] Retainers of lords, particularly those in the third category, were frequently criticized in medieval literature. In the Wakefield *Second Shepherds' Pageant*, for example, there are complaints about the overbearing behavior of those wearing livery ("a broche, a paynt slefe," line 28), who are supported "thrugh mantenance" of "men that are gretter" (lines 35–36):

> We ar so hamyd,
> ffor-taxed and ramyd,
> We are mayde hand tamyd,
> With thyse gentlery men. [50]

The appearance of such criticisms in a play-text, which had presumably been looked over by the city authorities and the clergy, suggests that such sentiments were not only commonplace but at certain levels acceptable.

In the poems in MS Harley 2253 the problems associated with bastard feudalism and retinues are never directly addressed. They are, however, discernible presences in at least three texts. The most orthodox objections appear in the most unusual place — in a love poem. *Blow, Northerne Wynd* (no. 46), which appears on fols. 72va–73rb, opens with a laudatory *descriptio* of the poet's beloved in the conventionally correct head-to-foot manner recommended by the rhetorical handbooks (lines 5–38), and continues with an *effictio* detailing her moral qualities (lines 39–54).[51] It is constructed in the social terms of a formal complaint to an overlord, Love, about the way in which the lady and her servants have injured the speaker: she has taken into her possession ("hent in honde," line

---

[49] *The Statutes of the Realm*, 11 vols. (1810–28; repr. London, 1963), 2.75. There is a good discussion of this legislation in N. B. Lewis, "The Organization of Indentured Retinues in Fourteenth-Century England," in *Essays in Medieval History*, ed. R. W. Southern (London, 1968), pp. 200–12 (essay first published in 1954). For a more general treatment of this important topic, see J. M. W. Bean, *From Lord to Patron: Lordship in Late Medieval England* (Manchester, 1989).

[50] George England and Alfred W. Pollard, eds., *The Towneley Plays*, EETS e.s. 71 (1897; repr. Millwood, N.Y., 1996), pp. 116–18, lines 15–18.

[51] Brook, ed., *Harley Lyrics*, pp. 48–50. For the rhetorical basis of the description, see D. S. Brewer, "The Ideal of Feminine Beauty in Medieval Literature, especially 'Harley Lyrics', Chaucer, and Some Elizabethans," *Modern Language Review* 50 (1955): 257–69.

57) his heart, and her seven knights have brought him to grief against the peace (line 62).
He further complains that two of them have threatened to imprison him and to kill him:

> To Loue Y putte pleyntes mo,
> Hou Sykyng me haþ siwed so,
> Ant eke þoht me þrat to slo
>   Wiþ maistry, ȝef he myhte,
> Ant Serewe sore in balful bende
> Þat he wolde for þis hende
> Me lede to my lyues ende
>   Vnlahfulliche in lyhte. (lines 63–70; fol. 73ra)

It is not uncommon in the poetry of *fin amour* for the lover to cast himself in the role of
a feudal inferior. But here the quasi-legal language suggests a more precisely articulated
and imagined situation. And Love's judgment, given perhaps from the bench ("bord," line
72) is a standard quasi-legal one: the lover must recover what has been taken from him,
his "huerte hele" (line 74), and ask for compensation ("bote," line 77). The allegory is
sustained by the running image of a social complaint.

Immediately preceding this poem, on fol. 72ra–va, comes *An Old Man's Prayer* (no.
45), and the positioning of these poems together in MS Harley 2253 suggests that the
compiler may have seen a similarity between them. Like the love poem, the old man's
complaint is ostensibly a fairly commonplace performance; it deals with the *incommoda*
of old age: physical decline, loss of status and influence, awareness of sin, fear of death.
But again, as I have shown elsewhere, there is a precise social dimension to the poem, an
articulation which imagines a particular situation.[52] The complaint is made in a hall, and
the old man compares himself and his situation to that of a "hirmon halt in hous" and a
"heued hounte in halle" (lines 84–85), that is, to a haughty retainer in the house or a head
huntsman in the hall — so he is evidently meant to be a retainer.[53] Both of these were
household positions, but he appears to be imagined as someone who agreed by indenture
to serve his lord in peace and war: the usual provision of rations while in the lord's service
and livery, which are always mentioned in the indentures, are alluded to in the reference
to those who "founden me mete ant cloht" (line 44). Horses are mentioned several times
in the poem, and indentures are very specific on what a retainer is meant to provide by

---

[52] See John Scattergood, "*An Old Man's Prayer* and Bastard Feudalism," in *Expedition nach der Wahrheit: Poems, Essays, and Papers in Honour of Theo Stemmler*, ed. Stefan Horlacher and Marion Islinger (Heidelberg, 1996), pp. 119–30.

[53] Brook, ed., *Harley Lyrics*, pp. 46–48.

way of horses and how they are meant to be fed and stabled when being used in the lord's service. But the old man is now too infirm to ride:

> Faste Y wes on horse heh
>   Ant werede worly wede;
> Nou is faren al my feh,
> Wiþ serewe þat Ich euer seh,
>   A staf ys nou my stede. (lines 30–34; fol. 72ra)

He is evidently meant to be somebody who served a greater lord, who also had his own household, and who in the days of his prosperity lived in great wickedness:

> Whil mi lif wes luþer ant lees;
> Glotonie mi glemon wes,
>   Wiþ me he wonede a while;
> Prude wes my plowe-fere,
> Lecherie my lauendere;
>   Wiþ hem is Gabbe ant Gyle.
> Coueytise myn keyes bere,
> Niþe ant Onde were mi fere,
>   Þat bueþ folkes fyle;
> Lyare wes mi latymer,
> Sleuthe ant Slep mi bedyuer,
>   Þat weneþ me vmbe while. (lines 52–63; fol. 72rb)

He evidently had a treasurer (line 58), a secretary (line 61), chamber companions (line 62), a minstrel (line 53), and a mistress, euphemistically called a "laundress" (line 56) — but this is all in the past. He now limps about his lord's hall (line 36), little regarded (lines 22–23, 45), and called an encumbrance who clutters the hall floor ("fulle-flet") and a good-for-nothing looker into the fire ("waynoun wayteglede," lines 16–17). The usual accusations against the overbearing pride of indentured retainers appear in the poem, but satire is twisted into a modified kind of sympathy: this is a salutary reminder of what happens when a retainer grows old and loses his usefulness.[54]

There is no such complexity, no such indirectness, however, in *Satire on the Retinues of the Great* (no. 88), which appears on fols. 124va–125r. This is a direct, abusive attack on the servants of indentured retainers rather than on the retainers themselves, particularly on grooms to whom the standard indentures refer as part of the retainer's entourage: since

---

[54] See Barbara A. Hanawalt, *The Ties That Bound: Peasant Families in Medieval England* (Oxford, 1986), pp. 227–36, for "retirement contracts."

much was made of the provision for horses, there had to be plenty of grooms to look after them. The poem has all the linguistic inventiveness of the traditional flyting, a highly colloquial tone, and a very demotic register:

> Of rybaudz Y ryme ant rede o my rolle,
> Of gedelynges, gromes, of Colyn ant of Colle,
> Harlotes, hors-knaues, bi pate ant by polle;
> To deuel Ich hem tolyure ant take to tolle![55]

The opening appears to promise a quasi-official listing of servants in a manorial account roll or the like, a head count "bi pate ant bi polle," but the only names that appear are "Colyn" and "Colle," both derogatory traditional names for a countryman (Latin *colinus*). Instead, the poet reads off a list of insults: they are hatched from horses' dung (line 7); they drink before dawn (line 14) and eat before cock-crow (line 17); they are vermin-infested (line 12) and scabby (lines 22–24). He throws in what he says are proverbs: the devil made his foodstore in the stomachs of grooms (line 16). He uses jokes. Why did Christ walk and not ride? So that he would need "no grom to go by ys syde" (line 35), to whose complaints and gossip and cursing he would have to listen. What lies behind this invective is difficult to discern with absolute certainty, but it seems to be a sense that this class of person, the grooms or attendants of retainers, have been given an importance beyond their deserving. The poet in his second stanza refers to the "boste" of "pale-freiours ant pages ant boyes" (line 6), and towards the end of the poem, appropriately considering its fictive form as an account roll, he draws up a kind of balance sheet:

> Whose rykeneþ wiþ knaues huere coustage,
> Þe luþernesse of þe ladde, þe prude of þe page,
> Þah he ȝeue hem cattes dryt to huere companage,
> ȝet hym shulde arewen of þe arrerage. (lines 29–32; fol. 125r)

If one calculated the wages of such servants against their wickedness and pride, he says, one would be in arrears even if one cut down on their food costs by giving them cat's excrement as the relish ("companage") with their bread. The French culinary term and the English colloquialism neatly define the poet's view of the gap between the aspirations of grooms and his estimate of their worth.

---

[55] Lines 1–4; fol. 124va. Thorlac Turville-Petre, ed., *Alliterative Poetry of the Later Middle Ages: An Anthology* (Washington D.C., 1989), pp. 34–35. For some comments on the poem, see Scattergood, *"An Old Man's Prayer,"* pp. 128–29.

VI

Something must be said finally about the anticlerical satires in the manuscript — though the contents of MS Harley 2253 would not as a whole support the view that the compiler of the manuscript was anything other than an observer of the religious norms of the fourteenth century. The two poems reveal a high degree of specific knowledge on their chosen subjects, but in tone they are very different.

The *Ordre de bel ayse* (no. 86; fols. 121ra–122va) is written in French short couplets in a mocking, ironic manner. Not particularly original, it satirizes the religious orders by drawing on what David Knowles has called the "floating body of commonplaces" that had been current since the late twelfth century.[56] Yet the poet shapes his material in an interesting way, pretending to have invented a new religious order whose rule, which he writes, consists of points from already existing orders. Instead of poverty, chastity, and obedience, this order is dedicated to wealthy ease, sexual license, and permissiveness — as, by implication, are those orders it imitates. It is to have double houses, like the Gilbertines of Sempringham, but there are to be no moats or walls and the brothers and sisters are to have free access to each other "a lur pleysyr" [at their pleasure] (line 47).[57] They are to imitate the drinking habits of Beverly — either those of the secular canons or, more likely, the Dominican friars:

Pur beyure bien a mangier,
E pus apres desqu'a soper,
E apres a collatioun . . . (lines 63–65; fol. 121va)

[to drink deeply at meals, and then afterwards until supper, and afterwards at collation . . .]

Like the Hospitallers, who are "molt corteis cheualers" [very courtly knights] (line 72), the members of the order are to have long, well-fitting robes and shoes, and are to ride fat, easy-paced palfreys. They are to eat a lot like regular canons — "char" [meat] five days a week and six if they have guests (lines 86–94) — and like the "moyne neirs" (line 95, here possibly the Cluniacs), they can drink as much as they like. If one should have a hangover, "Yl dormira grant matinee" [He shall sleep late in the morning] (line 111; fol. 121vb). In imitation of the secular canons, it is strictly commanded that each brother should play "le giw d'amour" [the game of love] (line 126) at least once before matins and once afterwards, and if he should do it a third time, he should be without blame and the

---

[56] David Knowles, *The Monastic Order in England* (Cambridge, 1949), p. 677.

[57] Aspin, ed., *AN Political Songs*, pp. 130–42.

195

reputation of the order should stand undiminished. Like the Carthusians, the brothers of the "the order of fair ease" are to have private cells:

> Si doit chescun a sa fenestre
> Del herber auer, pur solas,
> E la suere entre ces bras,
> E estre enclos priuement
> Pur suruenue de la gent. (lines 162–66; fol. 122ra)

[And each must have at his window some plants for solace, and the sister in his arms, and be shut up in privacy for fear of people dropping in.]

Like the Minorite friars, the brothers should always, when away from the abbey, take lodging with the "chief baroun ou chiualer" or with the "chief persone ou prestre" rather than with a "poure houme" (lines 178–84). And when preaching, they should imitate the Dominican friars and do it only indoors ("dedenz mesoun," line 208) and only after a meal. In matters of discipline and promotion, he stipulates that the order should follow the practice of the Augustinians. A provincial shall inquire into everyone's behavior: those who are found wanting shall be punished "priuement" (line 231), and those who have best followed the rule shall be "mis en dignete" and promoted to be abbots and priors for their "humilite" (lines 235–38). So the poem is ironic to the end.

But because it deals essentially through irony, it is difficult to discern precisely its agenda. Clearly the author thinks that the religious orders have grown away from their original ideals of promoting the ascetic life and have declined into ease and sloth — not uncommon charges, which are repeated over the centuries. But there may be more to his criticisms. Near the beginning of the poem he defines who shall be eligible to enter the imaginary order and who shall be expressly excluded:

> De l'ordre vus dirroi la soume,
> Quar en l'ordre est meint prodhoume
> E meinte bele e bone dame;
> En cel ordre sunt sanz blame
> Esquiers, vadletz e serjauntz.
> Mes a ribaldz e a pesauntz
> Est l'ordre del tot defendu;
> Qe ia nul ne soit rescu,
> Quar il frount a l'ordre hounte. (lines 15–23; fol. 121ra)

[I will tell you the whole story of the order, for in it is many a worthy man and many a beautiful and fair woman; in this order, without blame, belong squires, pages, and men at arms.

But to rascals and peasants the order is totally forbidden; none may ever enter into it, for they would disgrace the order.]

Only the socially elevated, the influential, the wealthy, those belonging to the court can get into the monastery, and the lower orders are to be kept out.[58] The implication is that the powerful rich have appropriated the religious orders and remade them for their own advantage and in their own images.

The tone of *Satire on the Consistory Courts* (no. 40; fols. 70va, 71ra, 71va) is quite different, as is its subject matter: it is an intricately written diatribe against the operation of consistory courts, here in a case which involves extramarital fornication and an enforced marriage. What precisely is at issue is not exactly clear, but enough emerges between the lines of the diatribe to suggest a narrative. The fictive speaker has had a sexual relationship with a "mai" (line 4) and is brought before the court because of it, but he wishes to escape the consequences:

> Of scaþe Y wold me skere
> Ant fleo from my fere.[59]

The court officials accuse him of his sexual misdemeanor ("sugge ase Y folht tok," line 52) with the girl, and they produce her and someone else as witnesses, summoned by the court crier:

> Þer stont vp a ȝeolumon, ȝeȝeþ wiþ a ȝerde,
> Ant hat out an heh þat al þe hyrt herde,
>   Ant cleopeþ Magge ant Malle . . . (lines 55–57; fol. 71ra)

His mistress "scrynkeþ for shome" (line 59) because of what she is forced to admit. But she shrieks and screams for justice, too, that his lying ("gabbyng," line 62) should not be allowed to deceive the court and that he be forced to marry her: "me wedde ant welde to

---

[58] Contrast the close of the dystopian satire *The Land of Cockaygne*, where the monastic "land of plenty" is open only to peasants:

Whose wl com þat lond to,
ful grete penance he mot do:
Seue ȝere in swine-is dritte
he mote wade, wol ȝe iwitte,
al anon vp to þe chynne,
so he schal þe lond winne. (lines 177–82)

Robbins, ed., *Historical Poems*, pp. 121–27.

[59] Lines 15–16; fol. 70va. Turville-Petre, ed., *Alliterative Poetry*, pp. 28–31.

wyf" (line 64). He does not wish to marry her and finds her ugly — "Vncomely vnder calle" (line 60) — a reversal of the usual laudatory alliterating epithet of love poetry. But he is so threatened ("þrat," line 69) that he has to concede. He is first driven like a dog round the church and the marketplace, to his own shame and that of his family (lines 82–84), which probably means that he was whipped — a common enough punishment for fornication.[60] Then he is forced to marry the girl:

> A pruest proud ase a po
> Seþþe weddeþ vs bo.
> Wyde heo worcheþ vs wo
>   For wymmene ware! (lines 87–90; fol. 71va)

The last phrase means "because of the private parts of women," but it has commercial overtones as well and alludes to what in financial terms his escapade has cost him (compare lines 73–75).

Yet for all its antifeminism the poem has other targets that are political. One has to do with overbearing officialdom. The poem is full of officials, and their number in contrast to the single complainant makes the point. There is the judge, "an old cherl in a blake hure" (line 19), and the clerks of the court who are ready to record what is deleterious to the narrator, "mo þen fourti him byfore" (line 23), and then the "somenours syexe oþer seuene" (line 37). And these officials are, in the second place, corrupt: the judge and his clerks require "mede" (line 29); the summoners are characterized as misrepresenting ("mysmotinde," line 38) men. But, perhaps most important, a third theme has to do with learning and literacy, both of which are seen as inimical to the speaker because they are the property of officialdom. Since he has little or no access to them, they render him powerless. The opening of the poem proposes a truth "universally acknowledged":

> Ne mai no lewed lued libben in londe,
> Be he neuer in hyrt so hauer of honde,
>   So lered vs biledes . . . (lines 1–3; fol. 70va)

---

[60] See the typical entry from the proceedings of the court of a rural dean in Hanbury (Worcestershire) in 1300: "Nicholas Veredarius fornicated for the second time with Evette Pinyng. The woman appears and confesses and renounces her sin and is whipped in the usual way once through the marketplace. The man confesses and is whipped in the usual way. He did penance. The woman withdrew . . ." (Harry Rothwell, ed., *English Historical Documents [vol. 4:] 1189–1327* [London, 1975], p. 724). For another case of a woman who is whipped five times round the marketplace and round the church "as is customary," see p. 718.

No matter how skilled with his hands, the unlearned ("lewed") man is overcome by those who are learned ("lerede"), by which the poet means learned in writing. Books and writing are the means by which the ecclesiastical establishment overbears him: what seem to be the court registers are brought in (line 13); the clerks are ready "my bales to breuen" and write with their pens on the parchment (lines 23–27); summoners, who are hated by retainers and servants bring forth their rolls (lines 39–40); and they swear on a "bok," possibly the Bible, that he is guilty (lines 51–52). At one point the speaker says,

> ȝef Y am wreint in heore write,
> Þenne am Y bacbite (lines 33–34),

which means, "if I am entered in their documents I am defamed." The literal sense of "bacbite," bitten from behind, is important here because it suggests the way in which the speaker thinks that the case deployed against him by means of literacy and documents is somehow unfair. Though the author of the poem is stunningly proficient in the medium, his fictive narrator suggests that literacy and written documents are regarded as instruments of oppression and power by those who have no access to them.[61]

VII

And this suspicion of the new, this atavistic conservatism, is characteristic of most of the political verse in MS Harley 2253. It is doubtful whether the "commune" on whose behalf some of these poems appear to speak — or, for that matter, the poets themselves — could have defined very precisely what exactly were the values they cherished and wished to live by, except for a general loyalty to the king and the nation. But they are clear about what they think is threatening them: high levels of government taxation to support foreign adventurism; an increasingly centralized system of authority and the perceived corruption of those officials who administered it; the intrusion of the law both secular and religious into affairs regarded as private; "bastard feudalism" and its self-seeking agents and beneficiaries; and the intelligentsia and the new culture of literacy and record keeping.

This conservatism is evident even in poems only marginally political — such as *On the Follies of Fashion* (no. 25a), which appears on fol. 61v. Ostensibly the poet objects to the fashion of "boses" (stylish buns of hair at either cheek) in contemporary women's coiffure:

---

[61] For evidence of a distrust of writing, see M. T. Clanchy, *From Memory to Written Record: England 1066–1307*, 2nd ed. (Oxford, 1993), pp. 185–96.

ȝef þer lyþ a loket by er ouþer eȝe
Þat mot wiþ worse be wet for lac of oþer leȝe,
Þe bout and þe barbet wyþ frountel shule feȝe.
Habbe he a fauce filet he halt hire hed heȝe
   To shewe
    Þat heo be kud ant knewe
   For strompet in rybaudes rewe.[62]

This is informed and precise criticism, for much of the language is technical: "loket" is a lovelock or curl of hair; "leȝe" is lye used as a cosmetic; "bout" is perhaps the curved part of the headdress passing round the back of the head; the "barbet" is the pleated cloth worn over or under the chin so as to cover the neck and bosom; the "frountel" is an ornament for the forehead; and the "filet" is a ribbon or band of cloth worn round the head to keep the hair in place or, as here, used as an ornament. The poet's objection to this new fashion is in part aesthetic. The effect of "boses" was to give an appearance of width to the face by emphasizing the sides, and the poet describes this in derogatory terms: "He sitteþ ase a slat swyn þat hongeþ is eren" (line 23). In part, though, it is moral.[63] Both men's and women's fashionable dress was seen as conducive to lechery, hence the accusation that the woman is a whore in the company of dissolute people (line 35). But the poem is really driven by the author's perception that these new fashions are a threat to social order. Originally, he says, "boses" were devised "leuedis to honoure" (lines 15–16), that is, for upper-class women. Now, however, because of "prude" (line 8), every "strumpet," "screwe," or "gigelot" (lines 11, 13, 17, 18, 25) imitates them and causes the devil to rejoice (lines 26–28). In 1337 the first piece of sumptuary legislation appeared in England, a very limited law but one having the preservation of social distinctions as its central conceptual basis: it forbade the wearing of fur in clothes to all "only except" the royal family, prelates, earls, barons, knights, ladies, and "people of holy church which may expend by year £100 in their benefices."[64] This, however, set the pattern for subsequent, more far-reaching acts in that it defined what it was possible to wear both in terms of social class and income.[65] The poet of the MS Harley 2253 fashion satire sees a threat in

---

[62] Lines 29–35; fol. 61v. Turville-Petre, ed., *Alliterative Poetry*, pp. 12–13.

[63] See my essay "Fashion and Morality in the Late Middle Ages," in Scattergood, *Reading the Past*, pp. 240–57, where the whole tradition of fashion satire is discussed.

[64] *Statutes of the Realm*, 1.280–81.

[65] For a brief account of later sumptuary legislation, see my essay, "Fashion and Morality," in Scattergood, *Reading the Past*, pp. 244–57. For a more general account, see Frances Elizabeth Baldwin, *Sumptuary Legislation and Personal Regulation in England* (Baltimore, 1926). For the fashions, see Stella Mary Newton, *Fashion in the Age of the Black Prince: A Study of the Years*

the imitation of an originally upper-class fashion by women who are not "ladies." "Al hit comeþ in declyn" (line 25), he says, and this sense of things going to the bad is characteristic of the political and quasi-political verses in the manuscript. Much was changing in the period covered by these poems. Old certainties were being questioned, and a new order was emerging in all sorts of areas — political, economic, and social. The poems in MS Harley 2253 constitute a sporadic but often highly informed chronicle of comment on and resistance to these changes.

1340–1365 (Woodbridge, Suffolk, 1980).

Historicity and Complaint in *Song of the Husbandman*

Richard Newhauser

Historicisms, new and old, remain literary criticism's most productive procedures for anchoring a text so that it does not float entirely clear into absolute subjectivity or theoretical "contextlessness." As Paul Strohm has written:

> Th[e] emphasis on the contingency of texts, their reliance on a material reality beyond their own bounds, is my rejoinder to those notions of textuality that would view language and text as all there is, as our sole point of access to past events and their understanding.[1]

Yet no one would argue that any historicism is a panacea. On the one hand, the type of self-styled historical criticism of medieval literature known as "Robertsonianism" long has been rejected for requiring an unambiguous, universalist, and literal understanding of theological doctrine which is remarkable in its avoidance of the multivalence inherent in all texts.[2] On the other hand, any historicism must ultimately capitulate before the theoretical impossibility of reconstructing perfectly that multivalence of discourse over the historical distance between the present moment and the Middle Ages. And yet, despite the dogmatic truth of this assertion, it is undeniable that various types of historical procedures have succeeded in excavating, to whatever degree, contexts of meaning within texts that might otherwise have lain forever undiscovered by later audiences. It may be true that the practice of historicism has generally divorced modern hermeneutics from political engagement,[3] yet if we are to read medieval literature historically, we must also be prepared to unearth a textuality in which historicity and politics themselves are hardly ends in themselves; we must be ready to admit into our habits of reading a literature in

---

[1] Paul Strohm, *Hochon's Arrow: The Social Imagination of Fourteenth-Century Texts* (Princeton, 1992), p. 7.

[2] See Lee Patterson, *Negotiating the Past: The Historical Understanding of Medieval Literature* (Madison, 1987), pp. 32–34.

[3] Rita Copeland, "Introduction: Dissenting Critical Practices," in *Criticism and Dissent in the Middle Ages*, ed. Rita Copeland (Cambridge, 1996), p. 2.

which context is pretext and what appear to be topical allusions are doorways to a universal realm. Rather than a call to arms, such allusions can amount to a statement of an eternal "theodicy."[4] It is precisely this kind of literature — in which a lack of topicality contributes to the very point of the text — that thrived in the midst of the consciousness of vast social and economic changes underway in England in the later Middle Ages, and that expressed itself in an endless series of complaints about the decline of the world, the growth of vice and its ability to turn everything upside down, and the disruption of the moral order.[5] Concrete details within the authors' time-bound poetic framework were, of course, an essential element of these works — as they are of all poetry — but in this literature the historically limited details from later medieval England did not expend themselves in topicality: they served the purposes of the poet as theodicean. In consequence, complaint literature of the type to be examined here subsumed itself into the corporate discourse of an orthodox theology that saw human suffering in those times as one in a series of proofs of God's omnipotent control.[6]

Lyrics on the general theme of a complaint against the abuses or moral decline of the times have taken a special place in discussions of what have been called "political" and "protest" poems in Middle English. At best, they have been read as a discrete part of "the vast medieval literature of reproof that ranges from comprehensive works like *Handlyng Synne* down to lyrics and epigrams a few lines long."[7] Although framed in explicitly moral terms and maintaining a perspective that is truly *sub specie aeternitatis*, such poems sometimes still are read as comments on historically identifiable incidents, perhaps because they employ historical details that might seem to be topical references. Some

---

[4] For ME poetry of this type as a theodicy, that is, a demonstration of, and acceptance of, God's justice wherein the presence of evil is seen to contain within itself the promise of its ultimate punishment (naming the evils of human beings in this life looks ahead to their punishment on the day of justice), see George Kane, "Some Fourteenth-Century 'Political' Poems," in *Medieval English Religious and Ethical Literature: Essays in Honour of G. H. Russell*, ed. Gregory Kratzmann and James Simpson (Woodbridge, Suffolk, 1986), p. 89. See also the more general observation of the lack of topicality in moral complaints by Joseph R. Keller, "The Triumph of Vice: A Formal Approach to the Medieval Complaint against the Times," *Annuale Mediaevale* 10 (1969): 120–37; repr. in *Die englische Satire*, ed. Wolfgang Weiss (Darmstadt, 1982), pp. 103–23, at pp. 105–06.

[5] See Richard Firth Green, "John Ball's Letters: Literary History and Historical Literature," in *Chaucer's England: Literature in Historical Context*, ed. Barbara A. Hanawalt (Minneapolis, 1992), p. 189.

[6] Derek Pearsall, "The Timelessness of *The Simonie*," in *Individuality and Achievement in Middle English Poetry*, ed. O. S. Pickering (Woodbridge, Suffolk, 1997), pp. 64–65.

[7] John Peter, *Complaint and Satire in Early English Literature* (Oxford, 1956), p. 3.

critics, beyond that, also have purported to find in this literature not simply a condemnation of the growth of vice in the world but, rather, a call "for social reform here and now."[8] And because these lyrics have been perceived as a unit, they are dealt with most often in the aggregate. One finds, that is to say, that among the pieces in MS Harley 2253, *Song of the Husbandman* (no. 31; fol. 64r), *Satire on the Consistory Courts* (no. 40; fols. 70va, 71ra, 71va), and *Satire on the Retinues of the Great* (no. 88; fols. 124va–125r) are most frequently mentioned and discussed (briefly) together.[9] Each one suffers by this treatment, for while they are all complaints that eschew direct political engagement for the timeless perspective inscribed in the language of moral outrage, they differ widely in their objects and methods of attack, and in the amounts and types of emotional response they demand from a reader. One should note, as well, that another poem found in MS Harley 2253, *The Man in the Moon* (no. 81; fols. 114v–115r), contains an implicit complaint about haywards and bailiffs, though it has not generally been discussed among the group of three "historical" poems. Unlike such a poem as *Song of the Husbandman*, however, *The Man in the Moon* deals with the agents of oppression in late medieval rural England not by transforming the historical details of its complaint into a theodicy, but by employing the weapon of satirical humor.[10]

Although fleetingly mentioned in numerous studies, *Song of the Husbandman* is a complaint about which there exists no apparent critical consensus concerning its literary qualities and its historicity. J. P. Oakden felt that "in diction and style it is extremely crude" and that "the poem d[oes] not come from a literary artist, . . . [but] from a simple

---

[8] Thomas J. Elliott, "Middle English Complaints against the Times: To Contemn the World or To Reform It?" *Annuale Mediaevale* 14 (1973): 34. See also Rossell Hope Robbins's view that although complaint poems use the terminology of doctrine, they "are really political," in "Middle English Poems of Protest," *Anglia* 78 (1960): 193; but compare the same author's "Dissent in Middle English Literature: The Spirit of (Thirteen) Seventy-Six," *Medievalia et Humanistica*, n.s. 9 (1979): 28, where the use in complaint poems of more *topoi* than topicality is said to make them "devaluated as expressions of protest."

[9] All have been edited by Rossell Hope Robbins in *Historical Poems of the XIVth and XVth Centuries* (New York, 1959), pp. 7–9, 24–27, and 27–29, respectively. The three lyrics have been printed more recently in Thorlac Turville-Petre, ed., *Alliterative Poetry of the Later Middle Ages: An Anthology* (Washington, D.C., 1989), pp. 17–20, 28–31, and 34–35; and in Elisabeth Danninger, ed., *Sieben politische Gedichte der Hs. B.L. Harley 2253* (Würzburg, 1980), pp. 49–56, 104–11, and 213–16.

[10] G. L. Brook, ed., *The Harley Lyrics: The Middle English Lyrics of MS. Harley 2253*, 4th ed. (Manchester, 1968), pp. 69–70.

peasant."[11] Not so, claimed Arthur K. Moore, who brought the author up a notch on the social ladder. For Moore, the poet "seems to be one of that class of relatively prosperous tenant farmers coming into prominence" in the early fourteenth century, whose poem is actually "a poignant revelation of [his] own 'cares ful colde.'"[12] Carter Revard cast serious doubt on the prosperity of the speaker's estate by noting that he identifies himself as a "cotter," that is, "the lowest-ranking, in worldly and in social status, of the landholding men who farmed a medieval manor for their overlord."[13] Following G. R. Owst, Derek Pearsall shifted the author to a different estate when he suggested that the lyric was written by a friar or by one of the "humbler clerics" who were the successors to the friars in the fourteenth century.[14] More recently, Pearsall returned the discussion to its early stages represented by Moore's view, by noting that the oppressions complained about are visited upon "well-to-do tenant farmers, not 'peasants,' to judge by the kinds of transaction mentioned and the sums of money involved."[15] Finally, Oakden's judgment concerning the poem's lack of artistry was rejected roundly by John Scattergood, who wrote that "In technique the poem is highly accomplished — the rhyme scheme is demanding, the alliteration heavy and the poet uses the device of stanza-linking fairly consistently."[16] These critics' pronouncements not only represent the gamut of opinions about the lyric and the perhaps futile speculation about the status of its author, but, with some exceptions, they demonstrate the widespread willingness to read the text as social commentary and to see in it identifiable and topically specific events that the poet felt were in need of protesting.

The situation of the poem's alleged historicity becomes most evident in the many attempts which have been made to provide it with a verifiable date of composition. In his early edition of *Song of the Husbandman*, Thomas Wright put the poem firmly in the reign of Edward I (1272–1307) and defended this date by noting that:

> Edward endeavoured to call off the vigour of his subjects from domestic sedition to foreign wars. But the expenses dependent upon the latter only added to the many burdens

---

[11] J. P. Oakden, *Alliterative Poetry in Middle English*, 2 vols. (1930, 1935; repr. Hamden, Conn., 1968), 2.10.

[12] Arthur K. Moore, *The Secular Lyric in Middle English* (Lexington, 1951), pp. 85–87.

[13] Carter Revard, "The Medieval Growl: Some Aspects of Middle English Satire" (Ph.D. diss., Yale University, 1958), p. 24.

[14] Derek Pearsall, *Old English and Middle English Poetry* (London, 1977), p. 123. See also G. R. Owst, *Literature and Pulpit in Medieval England*, 2nd ed. (New York, 1961), pp. 218–25.

[15] Pearsall, "Timelessness," p. 68.

[16] V. J. Scattergood, *Politics and Poetry in the Fifteenth Century* (London, 1971), p. 351.

under which the English peasantry laboured; and it is now that we begin to find the complaints of the latter vented in the shape of popular songs.[17]

At one time most critics accepted Wright's judgment — Rossell Hope Robbins even went so far as to give the poem the nearly exact date of 1300 — but in his dissertation Theo Stemmler rejected this dating on stylistic grounds and suggested instead that the poem was written around 1340 and in no case could be earlier than 1320.[18]

Stemmler, Scattergood, and others who have argued for the poem's stylistic complexity are on firm ground. The poem's verse form is fairly unusual. It is similar to, though more consistent than, another poem in the Harley MS, *The Meeting in the Wood* (no. 35; fols. 66v–67r).[19] Both lyrics use an alternation of eight-line stanzas and four-line codas, with the following rhyme scheme: *abababab/abab*. In addition, both exhibit frequent stanza linking, accomplished most often by the repetition of a single word at the end of one stanza or coda and at the beginning of the next poetic unit. *Song of the Husbandman* lacks this device only at lines 32–33, 36–37, 44–45, and 60–61. The alliteration in both poems is also very marked, though it is not, as Pearsall claimed at one point, "normally *aa/aa*."[20] In fact, as is common in the alliterating English poems found in the Harley MS, there is no unvaryingly consistent or normal pattern of alliteration here. There are almost as many *xa/aa* verses in this lyric as there are *aa/aa*, and the number of *aa/ax*, *aa/xa*, *ax/aa*, and *aa/bb* lines is almost equal to these two. Such complex and relatively unusual stanza patterning is hard to imagine as the work of a poet with no training; its intricacy demonstrates that continuum of alliterative production which culminated in the complexity of a poem like *Pearl*.[21] It seems highly unlikely, therefore, that this poem was written by a peasant or even a poor tenant farmer. But it seems impossible to go beyond this essentially negative finding in speculation about the poet's occupation, though some member of the lower clergy, of course, would fit the poet's literacy. Thus, the recognition of the poem's stylistic refinement and the poet's nebulous position in the medieval English

---

[17] Thomas Wright, *Political Songs of England, from the Reign of John to That of Edward II*, intro. Peter Coss (1839; repr. Cambridge, 1996), p. 148. Rossell Hope Robbins's dating of "ca. 1300" is found in his "Poems Dealing with Contemporary Conditions," in *A Manual of the Writings in Middle English 1050–1500*, ed. J. Burke Severs and Albert E. Hartung, 10 vols. (New Haven, 1967–99), 5.1404.

[18] Theo Stemmler, *Die englischen Liebesgedichte des MS. Harley 2253* (Bonn, 1962), p. 33.

[19] Brook, ed., *Harley Lyrics*, pp. 39–40.

[20] Pearsall, *OE and ME Poetry*, p. 123.

[21] Derek Pearsall, "The Origins of the Alliterative Revival," in *The Alliterative Tradition in the Fourteenth Century*, ed. Bernard S. Levy and Paul E. Szarmach (Kent, Ohio, 1981), pp. 3–4.

social hierarchy also will not allow us the luxury of a simple and specific answer to the question of the poem's date.

Wright undoubtedly was responding to the narrator's complaints about taxes when he set it in the reign of Edward I. Further reflection on the poem's date generally has centered around what is taken as the historicity of its complaints about bad weather, its projection of a meager harvest, and its laments about how heavy taxes add to these natural disasters. Here, too, there is little unanimity among interpreters of the poem, regardless of whether they are, foremost, literary critics or historians. Carter Revard adduced — from the mention of crops ruined by floods, the famine expected to follow, the exceptionally high taxes, and the harsh treatment not only of the peasantry but especially of the clergy — that all of these laments could refer only to the autumn of 1294.[22] The most striking famine of the early fourteenth century, however, took place in the years 1315–16,[23] and, as J. R. Maddicott and G. L. Harriss have pointed out, looking only at the first quarter of the fourteenth century, taxes were heavier between 1314 and 1319 than during any other period since 1297, which would make this sequence of some six years in the early fourteenth century appropriate as the time of composition of *Song of the Husbandman*.[24]

Yet, unlike the openly partisan political poems in MS Harley 2253, such as *A Song of Lewes* (no. 23; fol. 59r–v) or *The Execution of Sir Simon Fraser* (no. 25; fols. 59v–61v),[25] each of which deals with a singular and unmistakable historical event of some national magnitude, *Song of the Husbandman* complains about conditions which are applicable in a general way. Without an identifiable political event to limit the range of topicality in the poem, there is little to offer as a criterion to choose between the attempts at dating already mentioned, nor much to hinder us from finding another appropriate estimate for the period of composition. Such verses as "For euer þe furþe peni mot to þe kynge" (line 8) and the complaint about "cachereles" [petty tax officials] (line 50) might seem at first glance to be a response to the consistently high taxes under Edward I. It is known, for example, that from 1294 to 1296 the burden of tallages was especially heavy, and that when, in 1297, Edward levied an eighth on movables in the counties and a fifth on movables in urban areas and the royal demesne, the Council revoked these levies and granted a ninth

---

[22] Revard, "Medieval Growl," pp. 59–63.

[23] E. B. Fryde, *Peasants and Landlords in Later Medieval England: c. 1380–c. 1585* (New York, 1996), p. 12.

[24] J. R. Maddicott, *The English Peasantry and the Demands of the Crown, 1294–1341*, Past and Present Society Supplement 1 (Oxford, 1975), pp. 3–13; G. L. Harriss, *King, Parliament, and Public Finance in Medieval England to 1369* (Oxford, 1975), pp. 113–14. Compare Turville-Petre, *Alliterative Poetry*, p. 17.

[25] On these two poems, see Robbins, "Poems," 5.1404, 1405.

instead.[26] Nowhere, however, is there a mention under any king of England of a tax as high as one-fourth, though if the "furþe peni" refers to royal tallage as well as the wool collection, for example, then there is the distinct possibility that the combined taxes were equal to a fourth — but this would be true in any number of years during the earlier fourteenth century.

Still, there is nothing about the high rate of taxation itself that would place the poem in the reign of Edward I. In fact, Wright's argument along these lines for another poem in the Harley MS, the Anglo-Norman and Latin *Against the King's Taxes* (no. 114; fols. 137v–138v), has been demonstrated to be in need of revision. The complaint in the following stanza, though it speaks of a percent of tallage different from that in *Song of the Husbandman*, is a lament about the constancy and burden of taxation that is similar to what one finds in the English poem. It also bemoans the fact, as does its Middle English equivalent, that the poor are forced to sell the very means of their production simply to remain alive. Even so, historians and literary scholars have argued on the grounds of decisive internal evidence that *Against the King's Taxes* dates from around 1340:

Ore court en Engletere de anno in annum
Le quinzyme dener, pur fere sic commune dampnum;
E fet aualer que soleyent sedere super scannum,
E vendre fet commune gent vaccas, vas et pannum.
  Non placet ad summum quindenum sic dare nummum. (lines 11–15; fol. 137v)

[Now the fifteenth runs in England year after year, thus doing harm to all; by it those who were wont to sit upon the bench have come down in the world; and common folk must sell their cows, their utensils, and even clothing. It is ill-pleasing thus to pay the fifteenth to the uttermost farthing.][27]

Indeed, the similarity between this poem and *Song of the Husbandman*, coupled with the fact that both lyrics are transmitted uniquely in MS Harley 2253, has been used to argue for a later date of composition for the Middle English poem, that is to say, a date closer

---

[26] See Harriss, *King*, pp. 62–65, 74; James Field Willard, *Parliamentary Taxes on Personal Property, 1290 to 1334: A Study in Medieval Financial Administration* (Cambridge, Mass., 1934); and Sydney Knox Mitchell, *Taxation in Medieval England*, ed. Sidney Painter (New Haven, 1951), pp. 360–81.

[27] Isabel S. T. Aspin, ed. and trans., *Anglo-Norman Political Songs*, ANTS 11 (Oxford, 1953), pp. 109, 112. On the date of this poem see J. R. Maddicott, "Poems of Social Protest in Early Fourteenth-Century England," in *England in the Fourteenth Century: Proceedings of the 1985 Harlaxton Symposium*, ed. W. M. Ormrod (Woodbridge, Suffolk, 1986), p. 132.

to the period of the manuscript's compilation (ca. 1338–42 for most of the contents).[28] Thus, revising his earlier determination of the date of the poem as falling in the period 1315–17, Maddicott has come to consider the years just preceding 1340 as the more appropriate time frame for the composition of *Song of the Husbandman* because, as he now argues, from 1336–41 "the weight of taxation may have been greater than at any other time in the Middle Ages,"[29] and because this burden ran concurrently with an extraordinary famine in 1340, such as the one which the poet anticipates following the climatic disasters mentioned near the end of the poem.[30]

Certainly, a date close to that of the compilation of the manuscript brings a satisfaction of its own, but the search for historicity in topical references in the poem now has brought us a triple satisfaction, which of course is none at all: (1) 1294; (2) ca. 1315–17; or (3) some time around 1338–40. Obviously, the mere fact of a complaint against taxes or a lament of disastrous weather is not enough to situate the poem in the reign of any monarch — Edward I, II, or III — let alone specify its date to an exact year. The point is that such complaints, as much else in *Song of the Husbandman*, were common throughout the late thirteenth and early fourteenth centuries and cannot be used as the only grounds for dating a poem that nowhere employs identifiable topical allusions.[31] As was mentioned before, this lack of topicality contributes to the point the poet wishes to make.

Whether it is from 1294, ca. 1315–17, or around 1340, the poem is an early English representative of complaint that does not merely depict the plight of the oppressed rural worker; in one fashion or another, it actually takes his point of view and involves the reader in that perspective. Many of the poems that are called complaints are not this specific. A large number of these are simple catalogs that merely list the vices now triumphant in a world turned upside-down. In such poems the personifications listed in clear fashion are keys to the meaning. What is emphasized is the universal and abstract nature of moral imperfection itself, not the social appearance of evil as evidence of God's control, singled out for complaint, as in *Song of the Husbandman*. The following example of a verse catalogue of vices points out the fairly static nature of this type of poetry:

---

[28] Carter Revard, "Richard Hurd and MS. Harley 2253," *Notes and Queries*, n.s. 26 (1979): 199–202; "Three More Holographs in the Hand of the Scribe of MS. Harley 2253 in Shrewsbury," *Notes and Queries*, n.s. 28 (1981): 199–200; "The Scribe of MS. Harley 2253," *Notes and Queries*, n.s. 29 (1982): 62–63.

[29] Maddicott, *English Peasantry*, p. 45.

[30] Maddicott, "Poems," p. 143; for the earlier dating, see Maddicott, *English Peasantry*, p. 13.

[31] Note the criticism of some scholars' treatment of ambiguous allusions even in more historically specific political poems by Laura Kendrick, "On Reading Medieval Political Verse: Two Partisan Poems from the Reign of Edward II," *Mediaevalia* 5 (1979): 184.

Lex lyth doun over al, fallax fraus fallit ubique;
Ant love nys bot smal, quia gens se gestat inique.
Wo walketh wyde, quoniam movet ira potentes:
Ryht con nout ryde, quia vadit ad insipientes.[32]

[Law lies down everywhere, false Deceit deceives everywhere; and Love is only subdued, because people carry on wickedly. Woe walks widely, because Anger moves those who have power: Right cannot ride, since it goes over to those who are ignorant.]

Yet, even these lines can be related to verses at the center of *Song of the Husbandman*, where we read that:

Þus Wil walkeþ in lond, ant Lawe is forlore,
  Ant al is piked of þe pore, þe prikyares prude. (lines 23–24; fol. 64r)

In fact, the *Husbandman* poet strategically has placed such abstractions in the context of a conventional social complaint as a way of summing up his overriding concerns. They locate the social criticism of the poem in a moral context, while in the even more general *Song of the Times* the moral context floats free of any anchoring whatsoever.

Of those complaints that are less abstract about the object of their reproach, more than a few take the rural poor as examples of unjust oppression. In *Mult est diables curteis* (dated 1200–50), for example, one reads that after the clerks and knights, God created the *villein* to produce food for the others. The *villein* is happy only when he can work with his hands, and yet "En un jur pert quanque ad amé" [In one day he loses whatever he has amassed] (line 30).[33] The Anglo-Norman poem, in the fashion of a catalogue, is precise in the object of its reproof — it goes on to criticize the Templars and Knights of the Hospital — yet it is satiric and detached, unimpassioned in its criticism of the social order. In contrast to this, *Song of the Husbandman* gives more voice to the loss incurred by the *villein* — "Bote euer þe leuest we leoseþ alast" (line 12; fol. 64r) — and not merely because it is couched in the first-person plural; the alliterative emphasis reinforces the point that here it is the dearest thing that is lost. Beyond that, as the poet goes on to explain, it is all the more grievous to lose what one possesses when one has little to begin with (compare lines 13 and 14). Indeed, the English poet's compassionate view of those suffering from poverty has been taken as typical of the interests of those families in the

---

[32] *Song on the Times*, lines 13–16; Wright, ed., *Political Songs*, p. 251. These lines are from London, British Library MS Royal 12.C.xii, which also contains the Harley scribe's hand (see N. R. Ker, intro., *Facsimile of British Museum MS. Harley 2253,* EETS o.s. 255 [London, 1965], pp. xx–xxi).

[33] Aspin, ed., *AN Political Songs*, pp. 119, 124.

South West Midlands who could have served as the patrons of MS Harley 2253.[34] If there is topicality to be associated with this poem, in other words, it might be found in the procedure of selection and reception which led to the inclusion of this piece of verse in an anthology that surely was meant to appeal to the tastes and predilections, political and otherwise, of its patrons. Yet, one must always keep in mind that composition and reception are two very different processes.

There are purely English poems, too, that provide parallels to the interests, if not to the presentation of those interests, in *Song of the Husbandman*. Bailiffs, beadles, and other minor officials are frequent objects of scorn in English complaints. The conventionality of such laments might be illustrated from a number of sources, though two may suffice. In *The Simonie* (ca. 1325) one reads the following:

> And baillifs and bedeles vnder þe shirreue,
> Euerich fondeþ hu he may pore men most greue.
> Þe pore men beþ oueral somouned on assise,
> And þe riche sholen sitte at hom, and þer wole siluer rise
>   To shon.[35]

As the author of *Handlyng Synne* mentions in regard to some of these same officials, the oppression of the powerless can be attributed to the moral lapses of "lordynges cunseylours, wykked legystrys or fals a-countours,"[36] though in Robert of Brunne's translation these lapses are of importance chiefly for the explicit lessons they can teach. This kind of didactic intent is wholly foreign to *Song of the Husbandman*. Its concern, in any immediate terms, is not with verbalizing a punishment for the offenders but, rather, with involving the reader in the despair of the lyric persona himself.

Yet, the poetic contexts of earlier Anglo-Norman and English literature do go hand in hand with the homiletic and theological interests of the English church. In satire and complaint, as Owst put it, "we touch at once the profoundest and most abiding influence of the English pulpit."[37] In the churchman's preaching and moral evaluation of sin, one can

---

[34] Thorlac Turville-Petre, *England the Nation: Language, Literature, and National Identity, 1290–1340* (Oxford, 1996), pp. 197–98.

[35] Dan Embree and Elizabeth Urquhart, eds., *The Simonie: A Parallel-Text Edition*, Middle English Texts 24 (Heidelberg, 1991), p. 92, lines 337–41. The poem also appears in James M. Dean, ed., *Medieval English Political Writings* (Kalamazoo, Mich., 1996), pp. 193–212, 227–36.

[36] Frederick J. Furnivall, ed., *Robert of Brunne's Handlyng Synne,* EETS o.s. 119, 123 (1901, 1903; repr. Millwood, N.Y., 1978), p. 177, lines 5407–08.

[37] Owst, *Literature and Pulpit*, p. 213.

find the general topics for many of the conventions in poetry of complaint in the thirteenth and fourteenth centuries. It is, in particular, under the general heading of Avarice — in writings by, for example, John Bromyard (to name only one important English author of popular preaching materials), as well as in a host of vernacular treatises — that one can find the topics and some of the very images and characters used in *Song of the Husbandman*; in a few instances one finds verbal parallels as well. The combination, borrowing, and remixing of some frequently found phrases and terms in preaching treatises and complaint verse demonstrate the essentially oral nature of preaching discourse, which served as the common medium of moral analysis connecting pulpit addresses, popular treatises, preaching aids, and the versified literature of complaint.[38] One might object, as has Richard Green in reference to John Ball's letters, that the fact of complaint literature's conventionality cannot by itself allow us to argue that it is not topically relevant.[39] By their external and internal contexts, Ball's letters necessitate a direct connection with a verifiable event in English history. Such a connection is, however, only tangential to most of the literature of complaint under examination here. Taken together with the cluster of other conventional complaints in the thirteenth and fourteenth centuries, *Song of the Husbandman* can serve as a valid witness to the widespread resentment against oppression and the specific agents of oppression mentioned in the poem, but without necessitating our discovery of topical allusions in any particular verse.[40]

Of the myriad subcategories that *Avaritia* had acquired by the fourteenth century, the ones that are of interest when examining *Song of the Husbandman* concern taxation, *aquisitio mala*, *rapina*, and usury. It already had become a commonplace to chastise lords for burdening their subjects with heavy taxes before the poet of *Song of the Husbandman* began work on this poem. Robert of Flamborough had set out, early in the thirteenth century, some rules of thumb for lords to follow in their taxation policies.[41] By the late thirteenth century and from then on to the end of the Middle Ages, Latin ecclesiastical literature and preaching texts regularly included many accusations against any and all harsh lords who plundered the poorer people and made them pay exorbitant taxes.[42] *A*

---

[38] See Siegfried Wenzel, *Preachers, Poets, and the Early English Lyric* (Princeton, 1986), pp. 205–08.

[39] Green, "John Ball's Letters," pp. 188–89.

[40] For some guidelines in dealing with the conventions of a conservative literature, see Richard Newhauser, *The Treatise on Vices and Virtues in Latin and the Vernacular* (Turnhout, 1993), pp. 165–66.

[41] See J. J. Francis Firth, ed., *Robert of Flamborough's Liber poenitentialis* (Toronto, 1971), pp. 186–87.

[42] John Bromyard, *Summa praedicantium* (Venice, 1586), chapter on *furtum*.

Myrour to Lewde Men and Wymmen (ca. 1375–1425) can be taken as typical of the vernacular voices in this chorus of conventional invectives:

> Coueitous lordes beþ þei þat byreueþ and bynemeþ here pouere tenantes and oþere her good aӡenst þaire wille, and taxith & pileþ here bonde tenauntes & oþere oþerwise [þan þe seruice] acustomed [of] her holdyng askeþ. Þei beþ worthi to be cleped raueynoures.[43]

Song of the Husbandman lies close to this conventional attitude found in preaching manuals and penitential works, an attitude also well represented by Chaucer's Parson when he speaks of the covetous impulse "thurgh whiche men been distreyned by taylages, custumes, and cariages, moore than hire duetee or resoun is."[44] It is altogether in keeping, thus, that the poet includes in his complaint the fact that "Mo þen ten siþen told Y my tax" (line 40). In fact, the complaint about taxes, as with most of the topics in *Song of the Husbandman*, functions as a continuous *leitmotiv*, important for structural purposes more than for its historicity. It is mentioned at four points in the progress of the poem. First, it helps complete the initial stanza by intensifying the bitterness of the boon-work required of the farmer (lines 7–8), then it appears with the coming of the beadle who demands a payment of fines (line 40) and again in reference to the master beadle (line 51), and finally it is mentioned in a return to the opening concern with the king (line 63). This return acts as a way of setting limits for and emphasizing the futility of the speaker's position. His needs are set within the bounds of the king's needs.

The petty officials mentioned throughout the poem also are discussed frequently in the manuals dealing with avarice under the rubric of "illegal acquisition." It is in this way that Chaucer's Parson speaks of the lords who

> taken . . . of hire bonde-men amercimentz, . . . / Of whiche amercimentz and raunsonynge of boonde-men somme lordes stywardes seyn that it is rightful, for as muche as a cherl hath no temporeel thyng that it ne is his lordes, as they seyn.[45]

In the same way, *Song of the Husbandman* represents the bailiff who "bockneþ vs bale ant weneþ wel do" (line 16). These petty officials and their abuse of position were a constant source of irritation to all those over whom they had control and also a constant source of complaint in moral literature. Owst prints an excerpt from one sermon of the fourteenth

---

[43] Venetia Nelson, ed., *A Myrour to Lewde Men and Wymmen: A Prose Version of the "Speculum vitae,"* Middle English Texts 14 (Heidelberg, 1981), p. 135 (in chapter on *Auaricia*).

[44] ParsT X [I] 751 (*The Riverside Chaucer*, ed. Larry D. Benson et al. [Boston, 1987], p. 313).

[45] ParsT X [I] 751–52 (*Riverside Chaucer*, p. 313).

century that angrily denounces "fals bedels and baylyes, fals heywardes and iaylers."[46] The appearance of these same officials in the poem works, in effect, as another repetitive motif, providing a reminder of the conventional abuses with which the estate laborer must contend. The beadle, bailiff, and hayward are familiar figures from other writings and complaints, though the woodward is, in English poetry of this time, a figure not altogether common in complaints about the abuses or moral decline of the times. In any case, it is precisely because these minor officials were in the position to do so much harm on the manors — by guarding too zealously the land enclosed by hedges or by keeping too firm a grasp on wood used for kindling — that they were such an irritation to the poorer ranks of farmers. Nevertheless, the citations from the conventional literature of the moral tradition from the end of the thirteenth century to the beginning of the fifteenth century underscore the fact that it is unnecessary to search for topicality in a complaint poem that is ultimately universally moral in its perspective.

Finally, *rapina* [theft] and usury are two other categories of avarice that are well represented in the poet's analysis of the moral decline of the times. The fourteenth-century English translation of the *Somme le roi* defines the second bough of *rapina* as made up of the following:

> wikkede lordes, be þei knyȝtes or oþere, þat pilen þe pore folke . . . and make hem paye gret amendes for litle trespas . . .[47]

A close verbal parallel to this is found in *Song of the Husbandman*: "Þus me pileþ þe pore, þat is of lute pris" (line 19; fol. 64r). In the same way, the *Book of Vices and Virtues* defines usury in merchants as a sin wherein the businessman buys something for half of what it is worth and then sells it for twice what it cost him. As an example of this kind of practice, it lists those who "bien þe corn in gras."[48] In *Song of the Husbandman* one of the complaints represented by the poet is that:

> Ich mot legge my wed wel ȝef Y wolle,
> Oþer sulle mi corn on gras þat is grene. (lines 45–46; fol. 64r)

The parallels in language are obvious, though one does not have to argue either for a pastoral work as the direct source of the lyric complaint, or for *Song of the Husbandman*

---

[46] Owst, *Literature and Pulpit*, p. 324.

[47] W. Nelson Francis, ed., *The Book of Vices and Virtues, A Fourteenth Century Translation of the "Somme le roi" of Lorens d'Orléans*, EETS o.s. 217 (1942; repr. London, 1968), p. 34.

[48] Francis, ed., *Book of Vices and Virtues*, p. 32.

as an influence on medieval English popular theology. The point is simply that the theological texts and the lyric are both part of the same discourse: both are illustrations of the dominance of avarice and its negative effects in the imagination of English writers of the later Middle Ages, and both are located in an essentially moral literature.

While the preaching manuals, sermons, and other works on the Seven Deadly Sins provided the general topics for discussion in *Song of the Husbandman*, its unique organizing principle is seen in the way it unites the particular objects of reproach with general abstractions drawn from the simpler, category-type complaint poetry. This association of material is accomplished in a way that escalates the sense of hopelessness and despair enveloping the poem from its outset. The lyric moves generally from one loss to the next: from despair at the hands of the king and his appointed officials; to despair occasioned by the manor lord and *his* appointed officials; to the general hopelessness of one's situation when confronted with an abstraction such as will or falsehood; and finally, to something as ubiquitous as bad weather. Indeed, the singular focus on unrelieved complaint may account for the placement of the poem in MS Harley 2253, as Stemmler has argued, where it may be read as a type of commentary in contrast to the preceding poem of erotic complaint.[49] Moreover, it should be noticed that at key points in the complaint of *Song of the Husbandman* — that is, near its middle section and at its end — the conventionality of reproach resolves itself into an abstraction. Thus, the actions of tax collector, bailiff, woodward, and hayward are seen as aspects of Will, walking freely in the land, and of Falsehood, getting fat from others' labor (lines 31–32). In the same way, by the end of the poem it is not merely woe and misery that the poet feels, but Woe and Misery themselves who have awakened in the world (lines 71–72).

The poet does not speak for himself alone, nor does he attempt to represent only one voice. If this poem is to work as though in touch with the universality and timelessness of moral reproach, it not only must address itself to a specified and limited group; it must draw in other readers by engaging them imaginatively in the poem's complaint. *Song of the Husbandman* does this by including, in effect, every personal pronoun in the English language. It is, then, not only the *Ich* of the poem who hears and responds to all people's complaints. It is not only *þou* who is put down in the beadle's writ. It is the reader, too, who becomes involved in these actions. The poet seems always careful to include himself and the reader in that group most suffering at the hands of the rich and their officers in a vast display of a theodicy, as the poet moves from one topic of complaint to the next in an almost inevitable fashion. It is decisive for the poetic effectiveness of the lyric, that is to say, that although it is the poet who says his home must become bare before he can pay the tax officials, although it is he who must sell his horse and give a bribe, it is *vs* whom

---

[49] See Theo Stemmler's 1991 article reprinted in this volume (p. 116).

the green wax grieves and *vs* whom the officials accompanying moral dissolution are hunting as a hound does the hare.[50]

---

[50] Note, as well, the appeal to "vs" in *Satire on the Consistory Courts*, and the interesting discussion of this poem in Thorlac Turville-Petre, "English Quaint and Strange in 'Ne mai no lewed lued,'" in *Individuality and Achievement*, ed. Pickering, pp. 73–83, especially p. 79.

Debate Verse

Karl Reichl

"One of the oldest Latin debate poems," writes Hans Walther in his study of medieval Latin debate poetry, "treats the topic of the battle between summer and winter, which recurs in almost all literatures."[1] Walther adds references to Middle High German, Old French, Hebrew, Arabic, and Turkish debate poems on this subject, references which could doubtless be enlarged. The ubiquity of this theme, not only in literary but also in oral traditions and in folklore, precludes the search for sources: "in the case of these poems, there is no reason to think of a literary imitation of existing models, unless we are dealing with direct translations, because this subject matter emerged on its own at all times and among all peoples."[2] The "grant estrif" between "Esté and Yver" in the Harley MS is hence a specimen of an unusually widespread type of poem, which is in medieval literature, as Walther points out, first represented by the *Conflictus Veris et Hiemis*, a poem dating from around 800, which was formerly erroneously attributed to Alcuin.[3] While in this *conflictus* Winter and Spring argue about the coming of the cuckoo, messenger of spring, in other medieval Latin debate poems of this type, Winter and

---

[1] "Eines der ältesten lateinischen Streitgedichte behandelt den in fast allen Literaturen wiederkehrenden Stoff des Kampfes zwischen Sommer und Winter" (Hans Walther, *Das Streitgedicht in der lateinischen Literatur des Mittelalters*, Quellen und Untersuchungen 5.2, 2nd ed. rev. Paul Gerhard Schmidt [Hildesheim, 1984], p. 34).

[2] "An literarische Anlehnung an vorhandene Muster ist, wo nicht direkte Übersetzungen vorliegen, hier am wenigsten zu denken, da allen Zeiten und Völkern sich dieser Stoff von selbst darbot" (Walther, *Das Streitgedicht*, p. 34).

[3] The poem is printed in F. J. E. Raby, ed., *The Oxford Book of Medieval Latin Verse* (hereafter *OBMLV*) (Oxford, 1959), pp. 99–101 (no. 75); Raby characterizes it as follows: "This Eclogue, which was once ascribed to Alcuin, may be of Irish authorship. Its subject is a poetical debate between Spring and Winter whether the cuckoo should come or not. The shepherds Palaemon and Daphnis preside at the contest. They decide that the cuckoo, the shepherds' friend, shall come" (p. 465). See also F. J. E. Raby, *A History of Secular Latin Poetry in the Middle Ages*, 2nd ed., 2 vols. (Oxford, 1957), 1.208–09.

Summer (rather than Spring) dispute about their respective importance and power. This is also the theme of the Harley poem *De l'Yver et de l'Esté* (no. 9; fols. 51ra–52va).[4]

This poem consists basically of the speeches of the two opponents, who are only briefly introduced by the narrator (lines 1–4):

> Un grant estrif oy l'autr'er
> Entre Este et sire Yuer,
> Ly quieux auereit la seignurie. (lines 1–3; fol. 51ra)

[I heard a heavy dispute the other day between Summer and Sir Winter about who should have supremacy.]

Winter begins the debate, stressing that the bad weather he brings hinders everybody in their work and allows nobody, not even king or duke, to till the soil (lines 5–24). Summer replies that this kind of behavior speaks rather against than for Winter (lines 25–60):

> Vus n'auez cure d'autre vie,
> Fors fere mal e freyterye
> A tote gent. (lines 52–54; fol. 51rb)

[You care for no other life than to do evil and violence to everybody.]

"But if it was not for my help," retorts Winter, "you would die of hunger." He accuses Summer of laziness and keeping flies, lizards, adders, toads, and stinking snakes in his retinue (lines 61–90). Summer parries these accusations by stressing his own bounty as opposed to Winter's miserliness and greed (lines 91–147): "I nourish men and give them

---

[4] Item numbers are from N. R. Ker, intro., *Facsimile of British Museum MS. Harley 2253*, EETS o.s. 255 (London, 1965), pp. ix–xvi. The poem is listed in Arthur Långfors's register of incipits (*Les Incipit des poèmes français antérieurs au XVIᵉ siècle: Répertoire bibliographique* [Paris, 1971], p. 423) and in Johan Vising's inventory of Anglo-Norman texts (*Anglo-Norman Language and Literature* [hereafter *ANLL*] [London, 1923], p. 73 [no. 366]); see also Robert Bossuat, *Manuel bibliographique de la littérature française du Moyen Âge* (Melun, 1951), p. 245 (no. 2639). It is edited in Achille Jubinal, *Nouveau Recueil de contes, dits, fabliaux et autres pièces inédites des XIIIᵉ, XIVᵉ et XVᵉ siècles*, 2 vols. (Paris, 1839, 1842), 2.40–49, and, more recently, with an English translation, in Michel-André Bossy, *Medieval Debate Poetry: Vernacular Works* (New York, 1987), pp. 2–15. I am quoting from Bossy's text, which I have, however, checked against the MS. Translations are my own.

pleasure, I let wheat and vegetables grow and wine ripen." Winter, on the other hand, is both immoderate and destructive:

> Quar en vus n'est point de mesure
> Tant come vyn ou ceruoise dure,
>   En verite.
> Par vos tempestes, gresils, plues, ventz,
> Vous anuyez totes gentz,
>   Sauntz faucete. (lines 118–23; fol. 51va)

[For in you is no moderation as long as wine and beer last, in truth. By your thunderstorms, hail storms, rain showers, and gusts of wind you annoy everybody without fail.]

Summer as the bringer of plenty should therefore predominate over gluttonous Winter. Winter does not agree to leave the pride of place to Summer (lines 148–93): Summer's retainers are Daunz Poydras [Sir Littlecloth], Maymont, and Sweyn,[5] loafers who sleep all morning. But Winter's retainers are no such weaklings: they can endure the cold and eat hearty food rather than dainties like raspberries. "Your retainers," concludes Winter, "are evil-doers, they are thieves and murderers and pride themselves with their love affairs" ("se fount coyntes d'amours," line 188; fol. 52ra): you should be hanged if judged properly."

Despite these weighty accusations, it is Summer who wins the contest (lines 194–287). He accuses Winter of being more poisonous than a snake, while he, Summer, nourishes everybody, knights as well as clerics ("Chiualers, clerks ensement," line 207), indeed all of God's creatures, great and small, the powerful as well as the poor:

> Quanque ie faz de noreture,
> Tot est pur Dieu creature,
>   Petit e grant. (lines 218–20; fol. 52rb)

[When I provide nourishment, it is all for God's creatures, small and big.]

While Summer sustains life, Winter kills. And as to Winter's noble lineage, he is descended from Lucifer, whose relation and friend he is ("Vus estes son parent e son dru," line 233). Summer, on the other hand, has been sent from paradise to chase Winter out of the country and bring improvement to the people:

---

[5] The MS has *sweyn* (fol. 51b) and not, as both Jubinal and Bossy print, *swyn*.

Ie su de parais transmys
Pur vus remuer del pays
   E gent amender. (lines 239–4)

[I have been sent from paradise to chase you out of the country and improve the people.]

Summer causes the nightingale to sing, the trees to flower and to bear fruit, the orchards to bloom and sprout and flower:

Ie faz russinole chaunter,
Arbres floryr, fruit porter,
   Sauntz countredit.[6]
Ie faz floryr le verger,
Fueil e flur novel porter,
   A grant delit. (lines 242–47)

[I make the nightingale sing, the tree flower and bear fruit, without any doubt. I make the orchard bloom and bear new leaves and flowers, to (everybody's) great delight.]

And if Summer did not make the wheat grow and the fruit ripen, what would Winter do? His followers would have neither white wine nor red wine ("clare") nor spiced wine ("piement") to drink (line 263). So, obviously, it is possible to live without Winter, but certainly not without Summer. And Summer ends the debate by inviting the listeners, and in particular the maidens, to give their judgment:

Seigneurs e dames, ore emparlez,
Que nos paroles oy auez
   Apertement.
E vus, puceles, que tant amez,
Ie vus requer que vus rendez
   Le iugement. (lines 272–77; fol. 52va)

[Lords and Ladies, now speak out, you who have heard our words openly. And you, maidens, who have so much love, I entreat you that you give the judgment.]

The most interesting feature of this debate is its metrical form. While Winter speaks in octosyllabic couplets, Summer uses a more intricate metrical pattern: concatenations of six-line stanzas, rhyming *aabaab*, *ccdccd*, *eefeef*, etc., with two octosyllabic and a third

---

[6] Bossy prints *contredit* (Jubinal has correctly *countredit*).

four-syllable line (as exemplified in the quotations above).[7] This change of meter is unusual, both in French and in Latin. It is, however, found in one of the Latin debates between Winter and Summer edited by Hans Walther, the *Altercatio Yemis et Estatis* beginning with "Phebus libram perlustrabat / media temperie."[8] Walther gives the following characterization of this metrical change: "The form of this poem is very interesting: there is an alternation between stanzas in goliardic lines and stanzas with four fifteen-syllable lines; the former as the lighter and airier stanzas have characteristically been put into the mouth of Summer, while Winter speaks in the heavier fifteen-syllable lines."[9] Although Summer in the Harley poem does not use the goliardic line but rather a form of the tail-rhyme stanza, the latter shares with the goliardic line the switching between a longer and a shorter line. As to its content this Latin *altercatio* shows some basic similarities with the Harley poem (Winter and Summer use similar arguments), but is otherwise in its frame-story and learned trimmings quite different. Closer to the Harley poem is another Latin debate poem edited by Walther, the *Conflictus Hyemis et Estatis*.[10] Winter accuses Summer of bringing forth vermin and tempting people to engage in love adventures while Summer counters with accusations of ugliness and gluttony. In the end Reason declares Summer the winner of the contest.

Similar arguments are also found in the two versions of another French *débat*, edited by Anatole de Montaiglon.[11] After a *chanson d'aventure* introduction (only found in the

---

[7] The poem is far from regular, a fact generally observed of AN verse. The octosyllabic lines are in their majority eight-syllable lines (with masculine ending) or nine-syllable lines (in the case of feminine endings); while four syllables seem to be the norm with the four-syllable lines (generally with masculine ending), a number of lines have only three syllables.

[8] Incipit in Hans Walther, *Initia carminum ac versuum Medii Aevi posterioris Latinorum: Alphabetisches Verzeichnis der Versanfänge mittellateinischer Dichtungen*, 2nd ed. (Göttingen, 1969), no. 14091. The poem, preserved in a thirteenth-century MS (Göttingen, Universitäts-bibliothek MS theol. 105), is edited in Walther, *Das Streitgedicht*, pp. 191–203.

[9] "Die Form des Gedichtes is sehr interessant: es wechseln Vagantenstrophen mit Strophen von je 4 Fünfzehnsilbern; die ersteren als die leichteren und luftigeren sind bezeichnenderweise dem Sommer in den Mund gelegt, während der Winter in den schweren Fünfzehnsilbern spricht" (Walther, *Das Streitgedicht*, p. 37).

[10] Walther prints two versions: see incipit "Taurum sol intrauerat, / iui spaciatum" (*Initia carminum*, no. 19032); editions of versions A and B are found in *Das Streitgedicht*, pp. 203–06, 206–09, respectively. For a third debate poem (*Initia carminum*, no. 15059), see *Das Streitgedicht*, pp. 209–11, and A. G. Rigg, *A Glastonbury Miscellany of the Fifteenth Century: A Descriptive Index of Trinity College, Cambridge, MS. O.9.38* (London, 1968), p. 68.

[11] For the shorter version (from early prints), see Anatole de Montaiglon, ed., *Recueil de poesies françoises des XVᵉ et XVIᵉ siècles, morales, facétieuses, historiques*, 13 vols. (Paris, 1855–78),

longer poem) Summer and Winter introduce one another: Winter brags that he makes rain and snow and causes rich men to wear fur coats; Summer, however, counters that he brings forth a rich harvest of wheat, good wine and sweet fruit ("beaux bledz, bons vins et doux fruitz," line 26).[12] Criticism of the other and self-praise run along very much the same lines as in the Harley poem: Winter removes Summer's vermin, Summer makes everything flower and the nightingale sing; Winter is proud of the coziness he brings to warm houses with plenty of food, while Summer retorts:

> Yver, tu n'as desir que de ta pance emplir;
> Mieux vault en ung vergier dessus l'herbe gesir,
> En acollant sa mye, et baiser à loisir,
> Que le feu où te chauffes, qui ne fait qu'envieillir.[13]

[Winter, your only desire is to fill your belly; it is much better to lie in an orchard on the grass, embracing one's beloved and kissing at leisure, than next to the fire where you warm yourself and which only makes one age.]

And so they continue their dispute, till Winter mentions that the greatest feast, Christmas, is celebrated in his season. But, adds Summer, it is a season which makes all poor people, including the divine Infant, tremble with cold. Winter agrees to this and proposes to pray to the Lord that he give us warmth after the cold, a prayer which Summer seconds, concluding that they should both make their peace: "Prions luy par sa grace qu'ayons bon finement" [Let us pray to him that by his grace we may have a good ending] (line 100).[14]

Although all the poems mentioned differ somewhat in the arguments exchanged between the contestants, they resemble one another in their general tenor: Winter brings coldness and bad weather, but also warmth into the houses; it is the season of food at rich feasts

---

6.190–95 (incipit "Chascun de ma venue doit estre esjouyssans" [spoken by Summer]); for the longer version (from a fifteenth-century MS), ibid., 10.41–49 (incipit "L'Autrier par ung matin, sur la rive de Sainne"). Neither of these poems is listed in Långfors.

[12] Poem A (Montaiglon, ed., *Recueil de poesies*, 6.192). The *chanson d'aventure* typically begins with the speaker riding out to seek adventure and his encounter with some person (generally a woman); he overhears the person's monologue (generally a complaint) or dialogue with someone else or enters himself into a dialogue with the person. In ME, many of these poems are of a religious nature, with the speaker meeting the Virgin; see Helen Estabrook Sandison, *The "Chanson d'aventure" in Middle English* (Bryn Mawr, 1913).

[13] Poem A (Montaiglon, ed., *Recueil de poesies*, 6.193).

[14] Poem A (Montaiglon, ed., *Recueil de poesies*, 6.195).

(which leads to the accusation of gluttony) and of warm clothes and fur coats (and hence of advantage to the rich rather than the poor); Summer brings the singing of birds and the flowering of vegetation, leading to a rich harvest; it is the season of warmth (and hence of vermin), and it is also the season of love (and hence of sin). The accusation of vermin, for instance, is a striking detail which is found in the *Conflictus Hyemis et Estatis* as well as in the French debates, including the Harley poem.[15] It is also found in a sixteenth-century English debate which is so closely modeled on the two French poems edited by Anatole de Montaiglon (in particular poem B) that it must be considered a translation:

> Wynter.
> SOMER, yf that I were not, thou sholdest be made full lene,
> By many a beste venymus, of the which I make the clene.
> Of snakes, adders, & stynkynge wormes & of many a flie,
> From the I make clere delyuerance by my great curtesye.[16]

---

[15] Compare lines 2 and 3 of stanza 46 in the *Altercatio Yemis et Estatis*: "angues, ranas et bufones, muscas atque pulices, / bruchos, uespas, teredones, locustas et culices" [serpents, frogs and toads, flies and fleas, caterpillars, wasps, wood-worms, grasshoppers, and gnats] (edited by Walther, *Das Streitgedicht*, p. 196); or in Poem A (Montaiglon, ed., *Recueil de poesies*, 6.192):

Esté, se je n'estoye, tu ne durerois mie
De bestes venimeuses, de quoy je te nettye,
De Mouches et de vers, punaises et d'arignie;
Je t'en fais delivrance par ma grant courtoisie.
[Summer, if it were not for me, you would never survive the vermin of which I make you clean, or the flies and worms, bed-bugs and spiders; I deliver you from these through my great courteousness.]

[16] This poem, entitled *The Debate and Stryfe between Somer and Winter*, was printed by Laurens Andrew "at the sygne of seynt John Evangelyst in saynt Martyns parysshe besyde Charynge crosse." The print is not dated; it is reprinted in W. Carew Hazlitt, ed., *Remains of the Early Popular Poetry of England*, 4 vols. (London, 1864–66), 3.29–39. The title page has a woodcut, which is reproduced in Hazlitt's edition (p. 31) and described by him as "representing in the centre a tree, in the branches of which sits a dove of hybrid aspect, and of dimensions slightly out of proportion to the tree itself, and on either side a figure; one of an old man closely wrapped up to typify *Winter*, and the other of a young spark, who might have sat for *the Knave of Clubs*, habited in light costume, with a hawk on his fist, and a sword at his side. This gallant is of course intended to symbolize *Summer* . . ." (p. 29).

Some of these arguments, one might add, are not limited to these particular figures: they are also exchanged between the Owl and the Nightingale in the Middle English debate poem, where the two birds in addition to whatever else they stand for are also quite clearly associated with Winter and Summer, respectively.[17] The "grant estrif" in the Harley MS is firmly linked to Latin as well as vernacular debates between Winter and Summer. In view of its metrical similarity to the *Conflictus Hyemis et Estatis*, one wonders whether one should not place it in a goliardic, or at any rate clerical, context. The attribution of the poem to Nicholas Bozon (fl. 1320–50), first made by Johan Vising and later supported by M. Dominica Legge, ties in with this assumption.[18] On the other hand, there is no positive evidence on which this attribution rests apart from a hunch on Vising's part. However close the Harley poem might be to the medieval Latin tradition, and hence however likely Nicholas Bozon's authorship, it is well to remember that all these poems also reveal a popular inspiration, which makes source-hunting difficult, as stressed by Hans Walther (see above) and also F. J. E. Raby:

> The persistence of this [classical] rhetorical tradition is a fact that must be reckoned with, and yet it is difficult to deny that the subjects of many of the later debates had their roots in popular song and story. Such influences are suspected in the early *Conflictus Veris and Hiemis*, and, in spite of the classical learning displayed, in those 'conflicts' which belong to the age of the developed medieval Latin lyric.[19]

There is one other poem in the Harley MS which has been attributed to Nicholas Bozon, the satirical misogynous poem *De la femme et de la pie* (no. 78; fol. 112ra–b), a not very flattering comparison of women with magpies.[20] Nicholas Bozon is also credited with the

---

[17] This was pointed out most convincingly by Herbert Hässler, *"The Owl and the Nightingale" und die literarischen Bestrebungen des 12. und 13. Jahrhunderts* (Frankfurt a. M., 1942), pp. 21–24; compare E. G. Stanley, ed., *The Owl and the Nightingale* (London, 1960), pp. 25–27.

[18] According to Vising, "probably by Nicole Bozon" (*ANLL*, p. 72); compare the discussion of Bozon's works in M. Dominica Legge, *Anglo-Norman Literature and Its Background* (Oxford, 1963), pp. 229–32, where she notes, "A Debate between Winter and Summer is in varied form. Winter uses the octosyllabic couplet, Summer a six-line stanza" (p. 230). This poem is not listed, however, in the entry on Nicholas Bozon in Robert Bossuat, Louis Pichard, and Guy Raynaud de Lage, *Dictionnaire des lettres françaises: Le Moyen Âge*, 2nd ed., rev. Geneviève Hasenohr and Michel Zink (Paris, 1992), pp. 1069–70.

[19] Raby, *History*, 2.282; see his section on "The Poetical Debate," 2.282–308.

[20] Långfors, *Les Incipit*, p. 142; Vising, *ANLL*, no. 282. The poem is printed in Thomas Wright, ed., *Specimens of Lyric Poetry, Composed in England in the Reign of Edward the First*, Percy Society 4 (1842; repr. New York, 1965), pp. 107–09; compare also August Wulff, *Die*

authorship of another French debate poem, the *Desputeison de l'ame et du corps*.[21] This poem stands in the tradition of the Latin *Visio Philiberti*, a text which was extremely popular in the Middle Ages, with imitations also in Middle English.[22] The Harley MS contains a Middle English debate between Body and Soul on fols. 57r–58v (no. 22), an older version which does not go back to the *Visio Philiberti* but continues, via the so-called Worcester fragments, themes already found in Old English. The Harley MS shares this version with two important miscellanies of the thirteenth century, Cambridge, Trinity College MS B.14.39, and Oxford, Bodleian Library MS Digby 86.[23] While the *Visio Philiberti* and its imitations present a spirited debate on the question of guilt between the

---

frauenfeindlichen Dichtungen in den romanischen Literaturen des Mittelalters bis zum Ende des XIII. Jahrhunderts (Halle a. S., 1914).

[21] Incipit "Si cum jeo ju en un lit / La voiz oÿ de un esperit"; Vising, *ANLL*, no. 361; Bossuat, *Manuel*, no. 3365; Långfors, *Les Incipit*, p. 363; the poem is in six-line tail-rhyme stanzas. See W. Linnow, ed., *Þe Desputisoun bitwen þe Bodi and þe Soule* (Erlangen, 1889), pp. 115–16; it is edited by Edmund Stengel, "Desputeison de l'ame et du corps, ein anglo-normannisches Gedicht," *Zeitschrift für romanische Philologie* 4 (1880): 74–80.

[22] On the versions and MSS of the *Visio Philiberti*, see Walther, *Das Streitgedicht*, pp. 211–14; version A, with the incipit "Noctis sub silentio tempore brumali" (Walther, *Initia carminum*, no. 11894) is printed in Thomas Wright, ed., *The Latin Poems Commonly Attributed to Walter Mapes*, Camden Society 16 (1841; repr. New York, 1968), pp. 95–106. An AN version (incipit "Un samedi par nuit, endormi en mun lit"; Långfors, *Les Incipit*, p. 433) is found ibid., pp. 321–33 (for a parallel text edition, see Hermann Varnhagen, "Das altfranzösische Gedicht 'Un samedi par nuit,'" in Linnow, ed., *Þe Desputisoun*, pp. 113–96). On the relationship between the *Visio Philiberti*, an earlier Latin debate between Body and Soul, and the French debate "Un Samedi," see Robert W. Ackerman, "The Debate of the Body and Soul and Parochial Christianity," *Speculum* 37 (1962): 541–65, at pp. 543–44. The ME version modeled on the *Visio* (incipit "Als I lay in a winteris nyt"; *IMEV* 351) is also found in Wright's edition, pp. 334–39 (MS Laud 108) and pp. 340–46 (Vernon MS); see also Linnow, ed., pp. 24–105 (critical edition) and John W. Conlee, ed., *Middle English Debate Poetry: A Critical Anthology* (East Lansing, Mich., 1991), pp. 18–49. For a general survey of medieval Body and Soul poems, see Michel-André Bossy, "Medieval Debates of Body and Soul," *Comparative Literature* 28 (1976): 144–63 (with further bibliographical references).

[23] The Harley text (*IMEV* 1461) is printed in Wright, ed., *Latin Poems*, pp. 346–49, and Karl Böddeker, ed., *Altenglische Dichtungen des MS. Harl. 2253* (1878; repr. Amsterdam, 1969), pp. 233–34; for an edition of all three texts, see my dissertation, Karl Reichl, ed., *Religiöse Dichtung im englischen Hochmittelalter: Untersuchung und Edition der Handschrift B. 14. 39 des Trinity College in Cambridge* (Munich, 1973), pp. 339–65; for an edition of the Bodley version, see Conlee, *ME Debate Poetry*, pp. 10–17. For the Worcester fragments, see Douglas Moffatt, ed., *The Soul's Address to the Body: The Worcester Fragments* (East Lansing, Mich., 1987).

dead body of a knight and his soul about to leave the corpse, the Harley poem is more of a dialogue than a debate, tending even towards a monologue. The narrator overhears the Soul addressing the Body laid out on a bier, reminding him of his former wickedness and power and asking him, where all his glories are now (the widespread *ubi sunt* motif). The Body replies repeatedly to leave him alone: he realizes that it is too late now and that he must decay and be the food of worms and other vermin. The poem continues with the Soul's description of the *signa* preceeding the Last Judgment and ends with a description of the putrefying corpse; the introductory narrative frame is not taken up again.[24] When one compares the Harley text to the Digby and Trinity versions, it emerges that Harley shows the greatest number of changes and textual corruptions, with a number of stanzas missing or incomplete; it is also the latest text of the three.[25]

The two debate poems of the Harley MS mentioned so far are both representatives of a widely diffused medieval type, the debate between Summer and Winter on the one hand and the debate between Body and Soul on the other, but they are, notwithstanding their common classification as debates, fairly different in the way the protagonists of the poems argue with one another. The debate between Summer and Winter is a vivid and fast-moving debate between two personifications, who attack one another as persons as well as in regard to various principles and patterns of behavior for which they stand. The Harley Body and Soul poem is, despite its dialogue form, basically a moralizing sermon, reminding the Body — and hence the reader — of human transience and warning him of the dire results of a sinful life. The two poems attest to the popularity as well as the variety of the debate setting in medieval literature, also stressed by Raby for medieval Latin debate poetry: "If we look at these debates as a whole, we are struck by the immense variety of theme, of poetical form, and of manner, all bearing witness to the great hold which this setting had on the imagination of medieval versifiers."[26]

But variety is not exhausted by these two poems, although they are the poems in the Harley MS which conform most clearly to the poetical debate defined, as in medieval Latin, as a dialogue between two (or more) persons (including personifications and animals) on some issue (or issues) for which one speaker's position is opposed by the other speaker (or speakers). The genre is represented *par excellence* by the French debate between Winter and Summer — and similar debates in Middle English, like that between Owl and Nightingale or, on the question of women (blame or praise), between Thrush and

---

[24] On the *ubi sunt* motif, see James E. Cross, "'Ubi Sunt' Passages in Old English — Sources and Relationships," *Vetenskaps-Societeten i Lund Årsbok* (1956): 25–44; on the *signa ante iudicium*, see W. W. Heist, *The Fifteen Signs Before Doomsday* (East Lansing, Mich., 1952).

[25] See Reichl, *Religiöse Dichtung*, p. 342, and the parallel edition ibid.

[26] Raby, *History*, 2.308.

Nightingale.[27] There is no generally accepted definition of debate poetry, and every general discussion or survey marks a somewhat different territory. Hans Walther, focusing on debate poetry in medieval Latin, distinguishes various types of debate poetry on the basis of their topics: (1) debates on popular themes (among them the debates between Winter and Summer and Body and Soul), (2) on classical themes (as the debate between Ajax and Ulysses), (3) debates of a theological-dogmatic nature (such as Peter Abelard's *Dialogus inter Philosophum, Judaeum et Christianum*), (4) of a theological-moral nature (with personifications like Philosophia vs. Fortuna or Divinitas vs. Humanitas and comprising the various debates between Virtues and Vices), (5) legal school debates, (6) debates on questions concerning love (like the *Altercatio Phyllidis et Florae*, see below), (7) debates on the opposition between the estates and on the antagonism between the monastic orders, and (8) political debates on topics like the investiture.[28] As to Middle English debate poetry, Francis Lee Utley proposes a basic dichotomy between "Religious and Didactic Dialogues" and "Debates on Love and Women," differentiating in each group (rather mechanically) between the various types of protagonists: supernatural figures, abstractions, birds, and human beings.[29] I think the distinction between debates concerned with ideas or principles and debates on questions of love is an important one. Of course, the notion of a debate implies in either case some kind of alternation between statement and counter-statement, thesis and antithesis; however much the contending parties might become emotionally involved in the debate (and hence abusive in their language), a debate is based on arguments and proofs and obeys the laws of rational discourse. But in the love debates, in particular those belonging to lyric genres such as the

---

[27] Also transmitted in MS Digby 86 (*IMEV* 3222); there are a number of editions, among them Bruce Dickins and R. M. Wilson, eds., *Early Middle English Texts*, 3rd ed. (London, 1956), pp. 71–76, and Conlee, *ME Debate Poetry*, pp. 237–48; for a modern English translation (in the context of other medieval texts on the praise and blame of women), see Alcuin Blamires, ed., *Woman Defamed and Woman Defended: An Anthology of Medieval Texts* (Oxford, 1992), pp. 222–28.

[28] Walther, *Das Streitgedicht*, pp. 34–184; see also the additions by Schmidt in the reprint edition, pp. 257–82.

[29] See Francis Lee Utley, "VII. Dialogues, Debates, and Catechisms," in *A Manual of the Writings in Middle English 1050–1500*, ed. J. Burke Severs and Albert E. Hartung, 10 vols. (New Haven, 1967–99), 3.669–745, 829–902. For a (fairly inclusive) survey of ME debate poetry, see also Thomas L. Reed, Jr., *Middle English Debate Poetry and the Aesthetics of Irresolution* (Columbia, Mo., 1990), pp. 153–218. For a classification of French debate poems, see Pierre-Yves Badel, "Le Débat," in *Grundriß der romanischen Literaturen des Mittelalters*, ed. Hans Robert Jauss, Erich Kohler, and H. U. Gumbrecht, vol. 8.1: *La Littérature française aux XIVe et XVe siècles (partie historique)*, ed. Daniel Poirion (Heidelberg, 1988), pp. 95–110.

pastourelle (see below), the argumentation is part of an emotional not just a rational response to love. They are lyrics, in form and spirit, and as such quite different from the disputations between personifications or animal protagonists, however much they might smack of the language of the schools.

The question of women, raised in Nicholas Bozon's *De la femme et de la pie* and in the Middle English debate between Thrush and Nightingale, is also the topic of a French dialogue poem in the Harley MS (*Gilote et Johane*, no. 37; fols. 67va–68va), in which, at least initially, two points of view, that of a permissive young woman and of a coy virgin, clash.[30] A young knight, on a May morning, overhears two young women conversing on the question of love. Gilote has a lover, while Johane is still a virgin; the latter warns her friend of her sinfulness and urges her to get married. Gilote, however, retorts that sin is with us from birth anyway and marriage an inconvenience: if she gets tired of her lover she can go and find a new one. Johane asserts that virginity is the most perfect goodness ("la fyn de tote bounte," line 76; fol. 67vb) as is witnessed by Mary and the virgin saints in heaven. Gilote, however, remains unimpressed: she points out to Johane that she has no right to compare herself to Mary and the saints in heaven, given that she is very earthly indeed, and that besides God has commanded man to multiply and give souls to heaven. Johane agrees but finds that procreation should take place in marriage and not outside marriage. Gilote is still of the opinion that marriage is a bad thing and adduces the example of Mary Magdalen who despite her sinfulness was forgiven in the end: God loves a repenting sinner more than a virgin. With Johane's remark that there is a difference between sinning and sinning on purpose, the discussion takes a somewhat theological turn. Gilote counters that every Christian who asks forgiveness, no matter what his sin, will be forgiven. This clinches the case for Johane, who is convinced by her friend's arguments and is now eager to know how she can deal with her parents if they find out that she too has a lover. As Gilote has some good advice on this issue (ask your mother to intercede with your father and just let your father swear at you), Johane finds a "bel bachiler" as lover (line 178). When Gilote asks her how she likes this new life, Johane expresses her enthusiasm for the play of love. The poem continues with a new scene: the two wanton damsels are one day asked for advice by a young married woman who is deeply dissatisfied with her husband. Gilote recommends a young "clersoun" (line 247), whom she is willing to find for the woman. When the woman remonstrates that this is sin and that the birth of a child might have unpleasant consequences, Gilote has an answer for everything and succeeds in convincing the woman to get the satisfaction she cannot find

---

[30] Incipit "En May par vne matyne s'en ala iuer" (the poem fills eight columns; there is an extra leaf between fols. 67 and 68); Långfors, *Les Incipit*, p. 129. The poem is in Jubinal, ed., *Nouveau Recueil*, 2.28–39. I am quoting from Jubinal's edition, checked against the MS.

with her husband outside the bonds of marriage. This verdict meets with general approval, and the two *damoiseles* go round preaching their ideas in England, Ireland, and elsewhere, settling down in the town of Pount-Freint (line 340, perhaps Pontefract in Western Yorkshire). The poem ends by stating that it was composed in Winchester in the twenty-ninth year of King Edward's reign (Edward I), the son of King Henry (III), i.e., in 1301.[31]

As the summary of the poem shows, the exchange of arguments gives place in the course of the poem to bawdy details (the husband's failings and the joys of love) and comic situations; what started out as a debate poem takes on more and more the character of a fabliau. And this is indeed what the text calls the poem: "C'est vne bourde de reheyter la gent," [This is a comic tale to amuse people] (line 342; fol. 68va). Hence the poem fits both into the generic framework of the debate and of the fabliau. The Harley MS is a rich source for French fabliaux, of which one other text might be mentioned in the context of debate poetry. This is the dialogue between the King of England and the Jongleur of Ely (*Le Jongleur d'Ely et le Roi d'Angleterre*, no. 75; fols. 107va–109vb).[32] One day, a "jongleur" (or "menestrel"), his drum ("tabour") round his neck, finds himself in the presence of the king and his retinue on a meadow near London. When the king asks him who he is, the jongleur answers, "I am my lord's person." "And who is your lord?" "My lady's baron." "And who is your lady" "My lord's wife." (lines 32–36). The dialogue continues in this way, with the jongleur often playing on the semantic ambiguity of

---

[31] C'est vne bourde de reheyter la gent,

    A Wyncestre fet verroiement,

    Le mois de Septembre le iour quinsyme,

    Le an roy Edward vyntenuefyme,

    Le fitz roy Henry qe ama sainte eglise,

    E quant vus auez lu tote ceste aprise,

    Priez a Dieu de ciel, roy glorious,

    Qe il eit merci, piete de nous. (lines 242–49; fol. 68va)

[This is a comic tale to amuse people, composed at Winchester in truth, in the month of September, on the fifteenth day, in the twenty-ninth year of King Edward, the son of King Henry, who loved holy church, and when you have read this adventure, pray to God in heaven, the glorious King, that he have mercy and pity on us.]

[32] Incipit "Seygnours escotes vn petit / Si orrez vn tres bon desduit"; Långfors, *Les Incipit*, p. 368. The poem is printed in Anatole de Montaiglon and Gaston Raynaud, eds., *Recueil général et complet des fabliaux des XIIIᵉ et XIVᵉ siècles*, 6 vols. (1872–90; repr. New York, 1964), 2.242–256 (no. 52); it is listed as no. 117 in Joseph Bédier's list of fabliaux (*Les Fabliaux: Études de littérature populaire et d'histoire littéraire du moyen âge*, 6th ed. [Paris, 1964], p. 439). I am quoting from Montaiglon and Raynaud's edition, checked against the MS.

different words. When asked for example what the water which flows near Ely is called ("apeler") he replies that there is no need to call the water; it comes of its own accord (lines 51–54). When the king proposes to buy the jongleur's nag (lines 60–61), he again answers the king's questions about the horse in this facetious manner. In answer to the king's question as to his way of life, the jongleur gives a vivid description of his profession (lines 163–202). When the king remains unconvinced, the jongleur shows him that a life in jest is of as much worth as a reasonable and courtly life ("Ataunt valt viure en folye / Come en sen ou corteysie," lines 211–12; fol. 108va): whatever one does, whatever one wears, however one looks, people will always criticize you (lines 209–401):

> Si i'ay la barbe long pendaunt:
> "Est cesti cheure ou pelrynaunt?"
> E si ie n'ay barbe: "Par seint Michel!
> Cesti n'est mie madle, mes femmel."
> E si ie su long e graunt,
> Ie serroi apele geaunt;
> E si petitz sei de estat,
> Serroi apele naym et mat.
> Dieu! come le siecle est malore,
> Qe nul puet viure sanz estre blame![33]

[If I have a long, drooping beard, (they will say:) "Is this a goat or a pilgrim?" And if I do not have a beard: "By St. Michael, this is not a male, but a female!" And if I am tall and big, I would be called a giant; and if I am of small stature, I would be called a dwarf and weakling. God, how this world is accursed, so that no one can live without being blamed!]

The king is deeply impressed by the jongleur's wisdom and asks him what advice he can give him. "Good measure" is the jongleur's answer:

> Qy par mesure tote ryen fra
> Ia prudhome ne l'y blamera.[34]

[Who does everything with good measure will never be blamed by a sensible man.]

---

[33] Montaiglon and Raynaud, eds., *Recueil général*, 2.255 (the edition has erroneously *matle* in line 387), lines 384–93; fol. 109va.

[34] Montaiglon and Raynaud, eds., *Recueil général*, 2.256, lines 416–17; fol. 109vb.

Beginning as a light-hearted and jocular dialogue, the poem develops a satirical and moralizing strain when the jongleur shows the king in his jestful manner a mirror of man and society. Humor serves in the end a deeper purpose than simply the provocation of laughter through punning and tomfoolery.

Apart from these poems there is a completely different type of poetic debate current in medieval poetry, the dialogue between two lovers, antagonistic at first and possibly in agreement at the end. Here, disagreement and argument do not concern some principle or idea (virginity vs. carnal love, the love of knight vs. the love of cleric, the benefit of summer vs. that of winter, etc.) but rather the opposed wishes and attitudes of the two speakers, the male protagonist wishing to make love to his female interlocutor, and the woman refusing (at least at first) the man's advances. This is the classic situation of the medieval pastourelle, with a knight chancing to meet a beautiful shepherdess, with whom he falls in love and whom he tries to seduce, sometimes, but by no means always, with success.[35] The Harley pastourelle *The Meeting in the Wood* (no. 35; fols. 66v–67r) is an example of this genre, represented by only a few poems in Middle English.[36] It has been much discussed, in particular as the lyric poses a number of textual problems. It begins with the speaker riding out and encountering a beautiful girl in *chanson d'aventure* fashion, a "burde briht" (line 6), glistening like gleaming gold (line 3). When the man asks the girl who she is (line 5), he is told to leave her alone (lines 7–8). The dialogue begins at line 9, with the speaker offering the girl clothes as a reward for her love, a common motif in French pastourelles (lines 9–12). The girl scornfully refuses the offer (lines

---

[35] For a discussion of the French pastourelle, see Pierre Bec, *La Lyrique française au moyen-âge (XIIᵉ-XIIIᵉ siècles): Contributions à une typologie des genres poétiques médiévaux. Études et textes*, 2 vols. (Paris, 1977, 1978), 1.119–36; and Michel Zink, *La Pastourelle: Poésie et folklore au moyen âge* (Paris, 1972). A convenient collection of medieval texts with English translations is William D. Paden, ed. and trans., *The Medieval Pastourelle*, 2 vols. (New York, 1987).

[36] Incipit "In a fryht as Y con fare fremede" (*IMEV* 1449). For editions and discussions, see *inter alia* Böddeker, ed., *Altenglische Dichtungen*, pp. 158–60; Theo Stemmler, ed., *Die englischen Liebesgedichte des MS. Harley 2253* (Bonn, 1962), pp. 147–54; G. L. Brook, ed., *The Harley Lyrics: The Middle Lyrics of MS. Harley 2253*, 4th ed. (Manchester, 1968), pp. 39–40; J. A. W. Bennett and G. V. Smithers, eds., *Early Middle English Verse and Prose* (hereafter *EMEVP*), 2nd ed. (Oxford, 1968), pp. 116–17; Conlee, *ME Debate Poetry*, pp. 295–99; and Thomas G. Duncan, ed., *Medieval English Lyrics 1200–1400* (hereafter *MEL*) (Harmondsworth, 1995), pp. 25–27. I have discussed this pastourelle in the context of other ME pastourelles in Karl Reichl, "Popular Poetry and Courtly Lyric: The Middle English Pastourelle," *REAL: The Yearbook of Research in English and American Literature* 5 (1987): 33–61. I am quoting from Brook's edition, but interpret the poem as suggested in my article (on p. 46 of this article, read *yclope* in line 37 of the poem).

13–20), and when the man affirms his trustworthiness (he will keep his promises [lines 21–28]), the girl remains unconvinced and only foresees inconstancy on the part of the man (lines 29–36). It is from line 37 onwards that the poem becomes obscure. It is not even quite certain whether the girl yields or not. Most critics agree that the male speaker is successful in the end, but how this change of heart in the girl is brought about is controversial. The solution hinges on the interpretation of the last two stanzas: Who is speaking? Is anything missing, and if so, what and where? According to one reading of the poem, the girl is speaking in stanza six (lines 37–44), realizing rather suddenly that it is better to make love to a well-dressed lover than be married to some wretch, adding then in the last stanza (lines 45–48) rather wistfully that she cannot avoid her destiny anyway, although a "man without guile" (or possibly "love-play without guile," as suggested by Peter Dronke; line 48) might be preferable.[37] This casting of parts would mean that the poem ends in a monologue (lines 29–48), which seems rather unlikely, also in view of the technique of the *coblas capfinadas* (the beginning of a stanza taking up the end of the previous stanza), a technique which generally entails a change of speakers. If, however, stanza six is put into the man's mouth, line 40 will have to be emended: instead of "Þah he me slowe, ne myhti him asluppe," we have to read "Þah he *þe* slowe, ne *myhtu* him asluppe," an emendation proposed by Rosemary Woolf, which makes good sense.[38] The male speaker would hence suggest to the girl that it is preferable to make love to him than to be married unhappily, even if a jealous husband might in the end beat her up. However, whether it is the girl or man who speaks the sixth stanza (or, for that matter, the girl and the man, as suggested by Peter Dronke),[39] the last stanza (spoken by the girl) seems to indicate that the man is successful in the end:

> "Mid shupping ne mey hit me ashunche;
> Nes Y neuer wycche ne wyle;
> Ych am a maide, þat me ofþunche;
> Luef me were gome boute gyle." (lines 45–48; fol. 67r)

---

[37] For the translation of *gome* as "game," see Peter Dronke, review of Stemmler's *Die englischen Liebesgedichte des MS. Harley 2253*, *Medium Ævum* 32 (1963): 146–50, at p. 150.

[38] Rosemary Woolf, "The Construction of *In a fryht as y con fare fremede*," *Medium Ævum* 38 (1969): 55–59, at p. 57.

[39] Dronke proposes that the first half of the stanza is spoken by the girl, the second half by the man (review, p. 150).

Unfortunately, this last stanza contains also a number of cruxes. In line 45, "shupping" is ambiguous and "ashunche" is a *hapax legomenon*. A translation of the last lines, accepted by a number of editors and commentators, would be:[40]

> By shape-shifting I/one cannot avoid it [God's decree, fate]; I was never witch nor sorceress [who could transform herself]; I am a maiden, and that bothers me; I would prefer a man (love-play?) without guile.

The Harley MS contains a second Middle English poem of a similar nature, the lyric entitled by a number of editors *De Clerico et Puella* (no. 64; fol. 80v).[41] This poem is not actually a pastourelle: it lacks both the frame-story (the *chanson d'aventure* introduction) and the usual protagonists, knight and shepherdess (although occasionally other figures are also found in genuine pastourelles). It shares with the pastourelle, however, the seduction dialogue between man and woman. The male speaker turns out to be a "clerk" ("Do wey, þou clerc," line 9; "Whil Y wes a clerc in scole," line 29; "Þou semest wel to ben a clerc," line 33), while the female speaker is addressed as "leuedy shene" (line 1), "Suete ledy" (lines 21, 32), and "my suete lemmon" (lines 8, 16). The word *clericus* has many meanings in the Middle Ages; it could be a cleric in higher or lower orders or simply a student or someone who has been to school.[42] While the *clericus* entreats his sweetheart to have pity on him and return his love (lines 1–8), the girl at first rebuffs him as a fool who will only get into trouble if caught in her bower (lines 9–12). When the lover retorts that it would bring shame on the girl's reputation if he died of love (lines 13–16), he is once again told to be quiet, as all her relatives keep an eye on her and would give both him and her a beating should the lovers get caught (lines 17–20). The clerk brings about a change of mind in the girl when he reminds her of a previous occasion when they kissed fifty times in a window (lines 21–24). This brings back memories in the girl of her love to a "clerk al par amours" (lines 25–28). "And I am just such a clerk," continues the lover, assuring the girl of his own knowledge in the lore of love and appealing once more to her

---

[40] See Stemmler, ed., *Die englischen Liebesgedichte*, p. 150; Dronke, review, p. 150; Bennett and Smithers, eds., *EMEVP*, p. 325; Celia Sisam and Kenneth Sisam, eds., *The Oxford Book of Medieval English Verse* (Oxford, 1970), p. 117; and Duncan, ed., *MEL*, pp. 27, 191.

[41] Incipit "My deþ Y loue my lyf Ich hate for a leuedy shene" (*IMEV* 2236); edited *inter alia* in Böddeker, ed., *Altenglische Dichtungen*, pp. 171–73; Brook, ed., *Harley Lyrics*, pp. 62–63; Carleton Brown, ed., *English Lyrics of the XIIIth Century* (Oxford, 1932), pp. 152–54; Dickins and Wilson, eds., *Early ME Texts*, pp. 121–22; Bennett and Smithers, eds., *EMEVP*, pp. 124–26; and Duncan, ed., *MEL*, pp. 29–31.

[42] Compare *MED*, s.v. *clerk*.

pity (lines 29–32). This convinces the girl, who will not be held back any more by either parents or relatives from loving the clerk and doing his will (lines 33–36).

The poem is somewhat obscure in stanzas six and seven (lines 21–28): while the clerk reminds the girl of their previous intimacy, the girl seems to be reminded of her love to another *clericus*. Karl Böddeker thinks (rather implausibly) that the girl's reminiscences in stanza seven are accompanied by the fifty kisses mentioned in stanza six. Thomas Duncan interprets the girl's mention of a previous clerk as lover as a reference to the very person she is speaking to, which is possible and would somewhat attenuate the girl's free and easy lifestyle. Francis Lee Utley is uncertain whether the *clericus* is identical with the speaker, while J. A. W. Bennett and G. V. Smithers comment simply that this poem is "intermittently cryptic."[43] On the surface, the girl is not alluding to the speaker of the poem in stanza seven, but it would make good sense if she did, as according to the clerk there has been intimacy between the two at an earlier date. His rhetoric certainly carries the day, although what exactly the girl means when she says "þou spekest so stille" (line 33), if indeed this is what she said, is once again matter for speculation. The manuscript definitely reads "stille," but some editors have preferred to read "scille."[44] The manuscript form makes good sense, as Middle English *stille*, both the adjective and the adverb, comprise a range of meanings which fit here, from "quietly" ("soft-spoken") to "secretively," a sense according well with the demands of *derne love*, demands to which the clerk has actually alluded in stanza six, when he spoke of the concealment of love and the woes of love (line 24).[45]

---

[43] Böddeker, ed., *Altenglische Dichtungen*, p. 173, note to line 25: "Die Fortsezung des Wechselgespräches von diesem Verse ab haben wir uns von den 50 Küssen begleitet zu denken"; Duncan, ed., *MEL*, pp. 192–93: "Whether moved by such a hint, or rather, as the next stanza suggests, by the memory of their previous love, the girl, now, suddenly and dramatically, changes her attitude from scorn to affection"; Utley, "VII. Dialogues," 3.727: ". . . and she yields to him (or recognizes him as her former lover?)"; Bennett and Smithers, eds., *EMEVP*, p. 109. See also David Lampe, "Courtly Matters and Courtly Eyes: Two Thirteenth Century Middle English Debate Poems," in *The Thirteenth Century*, ed. Kathleen Ashley, SUNY Binghamton Center for Medieval and Early Renaissance Studies, *Acta* 3 (1976): 79–93.

[44] Thus Brown, ed., *Eng. Lyr. XIII*, p. 154, and Dickins and Wilson, eds., *Early ME Texts*, p. 122. The latter comment: "*scille*, 'eloquently'. But Brook [*Harley Lyrics*, p. 85] points out that OE *sc* in this text is otherwise regularly represented by *sh-* and prefers to read the MS *stille* 'softly', though this, perhaps, hardly gives the sense required" (p. 230). On ME *shille*, see *MED* s.v. *shil(le* adj. and adv. — On the emendation *fer from [bour]* (Brown) or *fer from [hom]* (Böddeker, Brook, Dickins and Wilson, Bennett and Smithers, Duncan) in line 31, see the editions cited in note 41.

[45] See *MED*, s.v. *stille* adj. and adv.

With the male speaker of this poem a goliardic element is introduced which tallies with Gilote's advice to the unhappy married woman to seek the consolation of a *clersoun* (see above). In that poem the love of both a *chivaler* and a *clersoun* was sought, but in goliardic poetry the love of a *clericus* is understandably preferred by the love-sick maidens to that of the *miles*. When Amor's judges Usus and Natura decide the dispute between Phyllis, who loves a knight, and Flora, who loves a cleric, they have to give pride of place, according to science and usage, to the love of the *clericus*:

> secundum scientiam et secundum morem
> ad amorem clericum dicunt aptiorem.[46]

[According to science and usage, clerks are said to be better fitted for love (than knights).]

Similarly the verdict in the *Love Council of Remiremont* is in favor of clerical love and excommunicates all those who prefer the love of knights.[47] In the medieval Latin pastourelles it is often implied that the speaker is a *clericus*, although he might not always be successful. In one of the pastourelles in the *Carmina Burana* the speaker is resting in the cool shade of an olive tree in the heat of summer — in a place more beautiful than even Plato could have painted ("stilo non pinxisset Plato / loca gratiora") — when he sees a pretty *pastorella*: "Stay, I will give myself and all I have to you!" But she answers (with arguments found also in *De Clerico et Puella*):

> Que respondit verbo brevi:
> "Ludos viri non assuevi.
> Sunt parentes michi sevi;
> Mater longioris evi

---

[46] *Carmen Buranum* 92 (*Altercatio Phyllidis et Florae*) fully edited in Alfons Hilka and Otto Schumann, eds., *Carmina Burana: Die Lieder der Benediktbeurer Handschrift. Zweisprachige Ausgabe*, trans. Carl Fischer and Hugo Kuhn (Zurich, 1974), pp. 310–29; partially edited in Raby, *OBMLV*, pp. 312–16, at p. 316.

[47] On the *Altercatio Phyllidis et Florae*, the *Love Council of Remiremont* and a third Latin poem on this topic, see Raby, *History*, 2.290–97. For the text of the *Love Council* (with German translation), see Karl Langosch, ed. and trans., *Weib, Wein und Würfelspiel: Vagantenlieder Lateinisch/Deutsch* (Frankfurt, 1969), pp. 106–29.

Irascetur pro re levi.
Parce nunc in hora!"[48]

[The girl answers in few words: "I am not used to men's plays. I have stern parents; my mother of advanced age gets angry for nothing. Leave off at this time!"]

While the lover comes away empty-handed in this poem, in another lyric of the Benedikt-beuren collection (with an inverted *chanson d'aventure* introduction: it is the *puella* who goes out in the morning), he is actually invited by the shepherdess to make love to her:

Exiit diluculo
    rustica puella
Cum grege, cum baculo,
    cum lana novella.

Sunt in grege parvulo
    ovis et asella,
Vitula cum vitulo,
    caper et capella.

Conspexit in cespite
    scolarem sedere:
"Quid tu facis, domine?
    veni mecum ludere!"[49]

[Early in the morning a farmer maiden went out with her herd, a stick, and a new woolen dress.There are in the small herd a sheep and a donkey, a she-calf and a he-calf, a billy-goat and a she-goat. She saw the student sitting on the grass: "What are you doing, sir? Come and play with me!"]

Although the Harley poem *De Clerico et Puella* can be placed in the context of the vernacular tradition of the pastourelle, it also points to goliardic poetry as a source of inspiration. This is also typical of the other poems discussed here: they attest no doubt to the popularity of debate poetry in the vernacular literatures of medieval England but they also partake in the wider tradition of European debate poetry, both in the vernacular

---

[48] *Carmen Buranum* 79, incipit "Estivali sub fervore" (Hilka and Schumann, eds., *Carmina Burana*, pp. 262–63).

[49] *Carmen Buranum* 90 (Hilka and Schumann, eds., *Carmina Burana*, pp. 302–03; Raby, ed., *OBMLV*, pp. 327–28). On these poems, see also Raby, *History*, 2.271–74.

languages and in medieval Latin. The choice of a clerk as lover implies the question of the respective value of the love of clerk and knight. But the debate on the merits of different lovers or different conceptions of love is not actually found in any of the Middle English debate poems extant. What was dear to the composers of the Provençal *tenso* and *partimen* did apparently not catch the interest of Middle English poets.[50] This is partly explainable by the fact that a number of these love debates are concerned with different styles of love poetry and are actually composed by known poets, who contend with one another in verse. This is a form of poetry which presupposes a far more sophisticated literary scene (with self-assured poetic individualities) than can be assumed for thirteenth-century England. This is not to say that a number of Harley poems — and the pastourelle *The Meeting in the Wood* is one of them — do not exhibit a high level of metrical and stylistic polish (alliteration, stanza-linking techniques, rhyme schemes, diction etc.). But the English poems (and most of the others) are anonymous and difficult to place in a definite socio-cultural context. It is only at a later time, with the emergence of a generation of poets who were both self-confident and proud of their individuality, that the spirit of the *tenso* is matched in English, or rather in Middle Scots: in the vigorous *Flyting of Dunbar and Kennedy* from the fifteenth/sixteenth century. What the debate poems do make clear, however, is the participation of thirteenth-century (and early fourteenth-century) England in mainstream European literary traditions, vernacular as well as medieval Latin, even if the full extent of this participation cannot be known on account of the fragmentary nature of what has been transmitted.

---

[50] Four of these love debates (two Provençal and two French) are edited and translated in Bossy, *Medieval Debate Poetry*, pp. 140–61; on the Provençal genre of the *tenso*, see David J. Jones, *La Tenson provençale: Étude d'un genre poétique, suivie d'une édition critique de quatre tensons et d'une liste complète des tensons provençales* (Paris, 1934).

Dreams and Dream Lore

Helen Phillips

ȝef þou etest of thystles ȝurne,
Þy fomon þe freteþ on uche hurne.[1]

Did medieval people often dream of eating thistles? Probably no more than other people, though the subject matter of dreaming and the expectations of the forms dreams will take, as well as theories about their significance, differ in different cultures. This item in the Harley 2253 *A Bok of Sweuenyng* (no. 85; fols. 119ra–121rb) is typical of the text's content in drawing on inherited written tradition rather than real-life evidence. It is one of the Middle English versions of a widely known dreambook, which was in existence in Greek by the fourth century, usually known by the title *Somnia* (or *Somniale*) *Danielis*.[2]

Dreams and medieval dream lore are important elements in two other texts in Harley 2253: in the Body and Soul debate *In a Þestri Stude* (no. 22; fols. 57r–58v), which is a dream vision, and in the romance *King Horn* (no. 70; fols. 83r–92v), where dreams are a

---

[1] If you are eating thistles eagerly [in your dream], your enemies on every side are hurting you (*A Bok of Sweuenyng*, lines 137–39; fol. 119vb). The *Bok* is printed by Max Förster, ed., "Beiträge zur mittelalterlichen Volkskunde V," *Archiv für das Studium der neueren Sprachen und Literaturen* 127 (1911): 31–84 (text on pp. 36–46), and by Thomas Wright and James Orchard Halliwell, eds., *Reliquiae Antiquae*, 2 vols. (London, 1841, 1843), 1.261–68. Text and translations are mine.

[2] On dreambooks and their influence, see Rachel G. Giblin, "Middle English Dreams and Dreams Books" (M.A. diss., University of Liverpool, 1971). The *Somnia* perhaps originated as a Latin text, though the earliest extant Latin text postdates the earliest Greek. On dates and origins, see Lawrence T. Martin, "The Earliest Versions of the Latin *Somniale Danielis*," *Manuscripta* 23 (1979): 131–41; and Klaus Speckenbach, "Die Deutschen Traumbücher des Mittelalters" and "Die Deutsche *Somniale Danielis* — Rezeption," in *Träume und Kräuter: Studien zur Petroneller "Circa instans"-Handschrift und zu den Deutschen Traumbücher des Mittelalters*, ed. Nigel F. Palmer and Klaus Speckenbach (Cologne, 1990), pp. 123–27, 128–49. Steven R. Fischer, ed., *The Complete Medieval Dreambook: A Multilingual, Alphabetical "Somnia Danielis" Collation* (Bern, 1982), lists or describes seventy-three *Somnia* manuscripts, including the text in Oxford, Bodleian Library MS 581, an illuminated presentation copy for Richard II.

central part not only of the plot but also of the poem's imagery and its presentation of psychological meaning. Although these three Harley texts differ greatly from each other, each is a representative of one of the major forms in which dreams occur in medieval literature (dream lore, dream vision, and dreams within narratives), and there are also aspects in which, as this essay will show, they resemble and illuminate each other.

A Bok Of Sweuenyng

The Latin *Somnia*, the source of *A Bok of Sweuenyng*, survives in many manuscripts, the earliest dating from the ninth or tenth century. There are vernacular versions in medieval French, medieval Welsh, Old English, Old Icelandic, and other languages.[3] Textual corruption, rationalizations, and modifications produced many variants over the centuries. This is illustrated in the Latin versions of the dream interpretation cited above: it may be thistles (*carduos, cardones*), coals (*carbones*), hinges (*cardines*), or flesh (*carnes*, including *carnes humanas*), and rationalization also produced new dreams where, for example, "carbones" were merely "seen," or where living or extinct coals signified the enemies.[4] The thistle dream also typifies the metaphoric link which often underlies interpretations: here thistles parallel malice, and eating them parallels the "fretting" ("devouring," "destroying," "hurting") by enemies. That interpretation is, however, itself a reformulation of the original metaphoric link, which seems to have existed between thistles in the mouth and enemies' sharp words: "Kardones comedere, inimici tui de te male loquentur" [To eat thistles means that your enemies will speak ill of you]. The same basic metaphor is found in another, possibly late, *Somnia* item: "Super spinas ambulare significat inimicorum destructionem" [To walk on thorns means the destruction of enemies].[5] The late Middle English prose version, *The Interpretacions of Daniel the Prophete*, has a variant: "To be hurte in þe fete wiþ þornes, ouer-comyng of enemyes."[6]

---

[3] On the *Somnia* dreambooks, see Steven R. Fischer, *The Dream in the Middle High German Epic* (Bern, 1978), and Steven F. Kruger, *Dreaming in the Middle Ages* (Cambridge, 1992), pp. 7–16.

[4] For some of the variants, see Fischer, ed., *Complete Medieval Dreambook*, p. 145, and Lawrence T. Martin, ed., *Somniale Danielis: An Edition of a Medieval Latin Dream Interpretation Handbook* (Frankfurt, 1981), p. 112.

[5] *Somnia Danielis* printed by Bartholomaeus Guldenbeck, ca. 1475; see Fischer, ed., *Complete Medieval Dreambook*, p. 145.

[6] *The Interpretacions of Daniel the Prophete* appears in Cambridge, Trinity College MS O.9.37 and two other MSS; it is edited by Förster, "Beiträge . . . V," pp. 53–83, and Carl F. Bühler, "Two Middle English Texts of the *Somniale Danielis*," *Anglia* 80 (1962): 264–73.

There are other important traditions of dream interpretation from the Near East and Europe,[7] one of them originating from the *Oneirocriticon* attributed to Artemidorus, ca. 200 AD.[8] This and the *Somnia Danielis* undoubtedly contain material from even earlier dream lore. It contains more varied and detailed descriptions of dreams than the emblematic descriptions in the *Somnia* and sometimes takes into account the dreamer's age, wealth, or emotional state. A third category of divination was lunar dreambooks, where interpretation depended on the phase of the moon when the dream occurred, and a fourth category was dream chancebooks, where the dreamer opened a Bible at random to light on the meaning of the dream.[9] Fifteenth- and sixteenth-century printers produced dreambooks of many kinds, including dreambooks which claimed to diagnose the causes of illnesses, an Aristotelian tradition in which the late medieval period showed revived interest; Steven R. Fischer points to Pertelote's style of interpretation in Chaucer's Nun's Priest's Tale as typical of this late medieval fashion in physiological dream interpretation.[10]

The *Somnia Danielis* was alphabetical. Though the text was subject to variations, misinterpretations, rationalizations, additions, and omissions, the original Latin alphabetical order tends to survive in vernacular translations. The first items in the oldest extant form are:

> Aves in somnis qui contra se pugnare viderit, iracundiam significat.
> Aves in somnis apprehendere, lucrum significat.
> Agnos vel hedos habere, consolationem significat.
> Arma in somnis portare honorem significat.
> Arma in somnis perdere aut frangere, dampnum significat.
> Aves perdere, dampnum significat.
> Arbores cum fructibus videre, lucrum expertum significat.[11]

> [(To see) in sleep birds who fight against oneself signifies anger. To catch birds in sleep signifies profit. To have lambs or goats signifies comfort. To carry arms in sleep signifies honor. To lose or break weapons signifies a harm. To lose birds signifies harm. To see trees full of fruit signifies certain profit.]

---

[7] See Förster, ed., "Beiträge . . . V," and "Beiträge zur mittelalterlichen Volkskunde IV," *Archiv für das Studium der neueren Sprachen und Literaturen* 125 (1910): 39–70; Kruger, *Dreaming*, pp. 7–16.

[8] Artemidorus, *The Interpretation of Dreams: Oneirocritica by Artemidorus*, trans. Robert J. White, Noyes Classical Studies (Park Ridge, N.J., 1975).

[9] See Fischer, *Dream in MHG Epic*, pp. 24–36.

[10] Fischer, ed., *Complete Medieval Dreambook*, p. 29.

[11] Förster, ed., "Beiträge . . . V," p. 53.

The Interpretacions of Daniel the Prophete keeps alphabetical order, prefacing each English item with a Latin keyword:

> Aves. A man that dremeth, that birds ffyghten with hym: it betokneth wrath.
> Aves. A man that dremeth that he letyth byrdys gon: it be-tokneth wynnyng. etc.[12]

A Bok of Sweuenyng keeps for the most part the *Somnia* order, though without the alphabetical keywords. Its first items illustrate well how readily a text of this kind undergoes mutation:

> Mon þat bryddes syþ slepynde
> Him is toward gret wynnynge.
> Mon þat meteþ of lomb ant got,
> Þat tokneþ confort, God yt wot!
> Mon þat þuncheþ he brekeþ armes,
> Þat ywis bytokneþ harmes.
> Mon þat syþ tren blowe [blossom] ant bere
> Bitokneþ wynnyng ant no lere [loss]. (lines 13–20; fol. 119ra)

Comparison with the *Somnia* version above shows how the *Aves* and *Arma* items have coalesced here into single items. Another fourteenth-century English dreambook, *Danyelles Dremys*, which is very much condensed, illustrates rationalization well: obviously based on a Latin text with *carnes* for the thistles dream, it has the homely "to ete roste fleshe by-tokeneth harme."[13]

Belief in divination, including the prophetic meaning of dreams, was often condemned as superstition and even necromancy by the Church.[14] The text we find in the Harley MS frames the dream interpretations carefully with religious sanctions. It begins with a preface which, in different forms, is common in *b*-type *Somnia* texts (see below). This version claims the interpretations derive from David's interpretations of dreams for princes when he was "in a cyte / Of Babyloyne," that David was a "prophete of gret pris," and that his ability to interpret dreams correctly came from the Holy Spirit (lines 3–12; fol. 119ra).

---

[12] Bühler, "Two ME Texts," p. 271.

[13] Text in Bühler, "Two ME Texts," pp. 265–68, who points out that it seems to be a selection of dream items taken from a *Somnia* textual branch which survives in fifteenth-century Latin, German, and Italian printed editions; the German and Italian versions also have the meat explicitly roasted.

[14] See Lynn Thorndike, *A History of Magic and Experimental Science*, 8 vols. (New York, 1923–58), 2.162–64, on John of Salisbury's scathing attack on interpretations attributed to Daniel.

"Dauid" in Harley is a mistake for Daniel. The Book of Daniel itself (2.26–28) presents Daniel's dream interpretations as gifts of the true God, superceding the interpretations of the pagan Babylonians. In the Harley text three validating strategies are succinctly combined: it invokes associations with the astrological fame of the Babylonians, the Old Testament divine gifts of prophecy, and the Christian concept of the Holy Spirit as the inspiration of the Christian God. At the end the Harley text states that no man can tell the true meaning of dreams except "þe heuene kyng" and concludes with a prayer that he protect us and shield us from our foe (lines 336–39; fol. 121rb). The Harley text takes more care than some *Somnia* dreambooks to package its material in a directly Christian way. Some *Somnia* prologues say that all Daniel's knowledge came from God, which the text in Harley reworks for its conclusion.[15]

Despite the air of unity this Christian frame gives *A Bok of Sweuenyng*, it actually contains items from two different Middle English versions of the *Somnia Danielis* run together. The first series goes up to the equivalent of *N* in the Latin alphabetical series, then the briefer second series of items begins at "Tren wiþ frut whose siþ [whoever sees] . . ." (equivalent to *Arbores*, line 175; fol. 120ra) and contains a selection of items up to *Z*. It uses slightly different styles for the items. Whereas the first series has a preference for items in the style "Mon þat of cartes met, / Of dedemon tidyng he het" (lines 29–30; fol. 119ra), or the "ȝef þou . . ." formula found in the thistles example above, the shorter second series tends to use "whose syþ." The thistles item appears in this second text as: "Þistles eten whose him [himself] syþ / Euel speche of fon [foes] þat byþ" (lines 223–24; fol. 120rb). The interpretation of the thistles dream in the second series is closer to the original metaphorical link: enemies speaking evil — sharp words in the mouth — rather than "fretting" the dreamer.

The *Somnia* tradition divides into two main branches, *a* and *b*: *a*, perhaps the earlier, had from an early date a longer list of dreams; *b*, among other distinctive features, lacks or bowdlerizes dreams with a taboo element. For example, sleeping with a sister (*concumbere* in a sexual sense) may become *recumbere*, "to recline to eat" with a sister, or disappears entirely. The distinctness of the two strands is, however, obscured by the general tendency of these texts, over time and through translation, to change, merge, develop, or shorten their material. *A Bok of Sweuenyng* includes an *a* incest dream in its second half, "wiþ soster have to donne . . ." (line 221), while the *Somnia b* "cum virgine nubare" (less respectable variant *b* "cum meretrice") appears as "Wiþ maide wedded

---

[15] *The Interpretacions of Daniel the Prophete* has "Here be-gynnen the interpretacions of Daniel the prophete to hym shewid in Babilone be the holy gost of mennys dremys in slepyng"; text edited by Förster, "Beiträge . . . V," pp. 52–80, and Bühler, "Two ME Texts," pp. 271–72.

whose him syþ" (line 211). Both versions are said to signify anxiety.[16] Fischer argues that some *Somnia* items tally with modern psychological theories: for example, sleeping with one's mother signifies safety, and a dream of whipping signifies that good will follow (neither example occurs in Harley).[17] An alternative explanation in such cases, however, would be the quite common dreambook practice of offering reassuring interpretations to frightening dreams. Harley, for example, has "ʒef þou wiþ dedemon spext, / Muche joie þe is next" (lines 161–62; fol. 120ra). This positive interpretation seems to go right back to the early *Somnia*. The similarly sanguine interpretation of the preceding Harley dream — "Mon þat þuncheþ he ded ys, / Newe hous ant comfort shal buen his" (lines 159–60) — probably has, however, a different origin and is a cheerful reformulation of a more disturbing Latin original, which employed the style of metaphoric parallel we have already seen with the thistle dream: "Migrare de seculo, habitationem in dissolutionem mutabit." To pass away out of this world is metaphorically to change one's house for a decayed ruin. The *Interpretacions* version of this is: "Migrare. To passen out of the world in thi sleep, be-toknith to changen thi stondyng other thi dwellyng."[18] This enshrines the image of death as a change of house (which is an important motif in the Body and Soul tradition discussed later in this essay). It appears also to be related to the *Somnia* interpretation of the dream of flying, where flying signifies a move (lines 300–01; fol. 120vb). Perhaps behind it lies also the ancient cultural expectation that one important form dreams will take will be the journey to the next world, a form best known from *Somnium Scipionis*. The dreambooks' tendency to interpret positively dreams about the frightening subjects of ghosts and conversations with the dead — a Harley example is "Whose þe dede spekeþ wyþ, / Fader oþer moder . . . / Þat is muche ioie ant blis" (lines 215–16, 218; fol. 120rb) — perhaps similarly reflects the prevalence in classical literature and dream theory of the belief that one of the other categories of meaningful dreams is a meeting with the ghost of a dead kinsperson, or other authority figure, who can bring information about the fate of the dead or the future.[19]

Despite its susceptibility to error, variation, and development, the dreambook tradition remained a relatively self-contained genre, catering to the perennial market for a user-friendly index of dream interpretations. The texts show little influence from, or common ground with, more learned dream lore, such as Macrobius's *Commentary on Somnium*

---

[16] See Fischer, ed., *Complete Medieval Dreambook*, pp. 4–12, and, for variants, Martin, ed., *Somniale Danielis*, pp. 114–15.

[17] Fischer, *Dream in MHG Epic*, p. 8.

[18] See Fischer, ed., *Complete Medieval Dreambook*, p. 57, for the variants of this *Migrare* item.

[19] See A. C. Spearing, *Medieval Dream Poetry* (Cambridge, 1976), pp. 1–18. Examples include Cicero, *Somnium Scipionis*, *Aeneid* 6, and *Odyssey* 11.

Scipionis, and no influence from the medieval Christian genre of messages from the dead to the living concerning purgatory or requests for prayers which, as Jacques Le Goff shows, developed particularly from the thirteenth century on in exempla and pious tales.[20] Specifically Christian content is rare and seems to be an addition to the original, primarily secular and perhaps pre-Christian, concept of a compendium of dream topics. The Harley text, for example, has as its penultimate item a dream of seeing God, which signifies good deeds (lines 306–09; fol. 120vb). Seeing a cross or talking to the Virgin Mary occasionally figures in fifteenth-century texts, and Fischer shows that completely new dreams in a fifteenth-century German *Somnia* were drawn from Joseph's dreams in Genesis 37 and also from two literary texts, the *Nibelungenlied* (Uota's dream) and *Meier Helmbrecht*.[21] The dreams about washing hands and dirty hands, which go back to earlier *Somnia* tradition, might derive, I suggest, from the Jewish custom of washing hands to free oneself from guilt, a gesture which in the Gospels is used to exonerate Pilate from Jesus' condemnation to death.[22]

Are there discernible influences from the dreambooks on literature? Fischer examines their possible influence on dreams in medieval German literature, and Pierre Jonin suggests their influence on Iseult's dream in the forest of Morrois in the Béroul *Tristan*.[23] The dreams of dirty hands, signifying sin and shame, in Harley (lines 151–54; fol. 119vb), and of washing one's hands, signifying freeing oneself from sins and crimes, which is a *Somnia* dream but not in Harley, represent a metaphorical tradition which clearly lies behind the famous scene of Lady Macbeth's sleepwalking and guilty dreams. The dream interpretation which states that seeing carts foretells news of a death may have some link with the ominous associations of the cart in Chrétien de Troyes' *Chevalier de la charette* (lines 320–429), or both may reflect the same background: David J. Shirt argues that

---

[20] Jacques Le Goff, *The Birth of Purgatory*, trans. Arthur Goldhammer (Chicago, 1984).

[21] Fischer, ed., *Complete Medieval Dreambook*, pp. 9–10.

[22] For Old Testament background, see Deut. 2.1–9, and Pss. 26.6 and 73.13. Handwashing like this and its symbolism is distinct from ritual bathing of the whole body in *mikva'ot*. I am grateful to Stuart Dyas for help on this topic.

[23] Fischer, *Dream in MHG Epic*; Pierre Jonin, "Le songe d'Iseult dans la forêt du Morrois," *Le Moyen Âge* 64 (1958): 103–13. Gabriel Turville-Petre at first discounted the idea of influence in Old Icelandic literature ("Dreams in Icelandic Tradition," *Folklore* 69 [1958]: 93–111), but after discovering an Old Icelandic version of the *Somnia*, he modified this extreme position while remaining uncertain about influence: see "Dream Symbols in Old Icelandic Literature," in *Festschrift Walter Baetke*, ed. Kurt Rudolph (Weimar, 1966), pp. 343–54; and "An Icelandic Version of the *Somniale Danielis*," in *Nordica et Anglica: Studies in Honor of Stefan Einarsson*, ed. Allan H. Orrick (The Hague, 1968), pp. 19–36.

Chrétien was drawing on an English custom of carts used as tumbrels, specifically to carry prisoners condemned to death.[24] Carters are also loosely linked to dangers of death and damnation in Chaucer's Friar's and Knight's tales.[25] Rachel G. Giblin suggests other possible examples of influence on Chaucer.[26] Dragons are not in the *Somnia* tradition, but Karl Heinz Göller speculated that the *Oneirocritica* interpretation of a dragon seen in dream as an emperor might have been part of the imaginative background to Arthur's dream of the bear and the dragon in the alliterative *Morte Arthure*. Since the *Oneirocritica* was not well known in the medieval period, the more obvious source is probably the national symbolism of the Welsh dragon as Arthur, British king.[27] Towards the end of *A Bok of Sweuenyng* appears a cluster of dreams of dramatic events in the heavens signifying political events, such as suns clear or dark (peace or peril to kings), a red sun (bloodshed), falling stars (great battle), and earthquake (harm in that area), which clearly reflect the widespread belief in such portents as found in texts from Plutarch to Shakespeare. Included here are two moons seen in the evening, signifying "Chaunge of kyng oþer prince" (lines 286–87, 292–93; fol. 120vb). King Arthur's dream of his house falling in Layamon's *Brut*, discussed below, perhaps reflects *Somnia* interpretations that link falling or burning houses to slander or curse. Falling into a ditch is a warning that "blame" may follow (lines 101–02; fol. 119va).[28] Could this have influenced Julian of Norwich's allegory of Adam's fall as a tumble into a ditch?[29] These suggestions, some of which may appear tenuous at best, seem nonetheless worth making partly because the *Somnia*

---

[24] David J. Shirt, "Chrétien de Troyes et une coutume anglaise," *Romania* 94 (1973): 178–95; and Chrétien de Troyes, *Lancelot (Le Chevalier de la charette)*, ed. Mario Roques (Paris, 1958), pp. 320–429.

[25] FriT III [D] 1536–70, KnT I [A] 2021–23; see *The Riverside Chaucer*, ed. Larry D. Benson et al. (Boston, 1987), pp. 126, 52, respectively. I am indebted to Russell Peck who points out that the "fare-carte" in *Troilus and Criseyde* 5.1162 (*Riverside Chaucer*, p. 575), perhaps a cart for carrying the dead, may have ominous associations in the context of the death of Troilus and Criseyde's love.

[26] See, for example, Giblin, "ME Dreams," pp. 91–92, on WBPro III [D] 577–81.

[27] Karl Heinz Göller, "The Dream of the Dragon and the Bear," in *The Alliterative Morte Arthure: A Reassessment of the Poem*, ed. Karl Heinz Göller (Cambridge, 1981), pp. 130–39. The dream is also found in sources with Welsh origins: see Elaine C. Southward, "Arthur's Dream," *Speculum* 18 (1943): 247–51.

[28] Fischer, ed., *Complete Medieval Dreambook*, pp. 58–59.

[29] Long version of the *Revelation*, chapter 51; see Julian of Norwich, *Showings*, ed. Edmund Colledge and James Walsh (New York, 1978).

Danielis material appears, from the number of manuscripts, to have been so widely known that it is likely to have formed part of writers' often unconscious lexicon of images.

Though dreambooks may have contributed thus to the heritage of imagery, their typically unsophisticated approach to dreams, their content, and their significance does not often seem to have appealed to poets as sources for complete dreams or dream explanations in romances and other narratives, despite the fact that significant dreams are common there and the dream is itself also a major narrative form in medieval literature. Yet, just as authors of dream visions may mention Macrobius, but in practice show little interest in using his dream categories creatively,[30] romance writers devising dreams for their psychological, symbolic, and narrative effect eschew for the most part the dreambooks' compendium of dreams and interpretations and instead offer readers dreams that provoke curiosity and retain, even when a dream's meaning for the plot is detected, an element of mysteriousness quite absent from dream lore. The approach to dreaming in the dream lore tradition is, in short, so limited and lacking in profundity that, though dreambooks like *A Bok of Sweuenyng* are of interest in indicating the traditional storehouse of images and associations from which imaginative writers sometimes drew their literary dreams, the creative power of dreams in poetry and romance comes from elsewhere. Dream lore may have provided the starting point; it is rarely the source of what is significant about a dream within its literary context. The description of Arthur's dream of his hall collapsing under him, in Layamon's *Brut* (lines 13980–4015), for example, may certainly reflect the dreambooks, and the sort of association found in *A Bok of Sweuenyng*:

> ȝef þin hous falleþ mid þe wowe [wall],
> Þe worþ harm ant eken howe [anxiety]. (lines 77–78; fol. 119rb)

A hall is obvious metonymy for a lord's power and the loyalty of his household and retainers, but the fact that Arthur is astride his hall in his dream, as if riding a horse, resists simple interpretation. (Is it, however — if we are thinking about starting points for an imaginative process — a coincidence that dreams about horses follow dreams about houses in the *Somnia* tradition?) The dream of riding the house joins the sensation of collapse to Arthur's own body, the royal person but also a distressed human tossing in nightmare-ridden sleep.

---

[30] See Helen Phillips and Nick Havely, eds., *Chaucer's Dream Poetry* (London, 1997), pp. 3–9.

King Horn

King Horn, which appears in Harley 2253 (fols. 83r–92v), Oxford, Bodleian Library MS Laud Misc. 108 (fols. 219v–228r), and Cambridge, Cambridge University Library MS Gg. iv.27 (2) (fols. 6r–13r), provides an excellent example of a complex symbolic dream. Rymenhild dreams, during her long-drawn-out attempt to win Horn as her husband, that she has cast a net into the sea but a large fish has torn the net so that she cannot be sure of catching the fish she wants (lines 658–64). Like most dreams in romances, this account is first and foremost a comment on an emotional state, here the princess' anxiety that it will be hard (like catching a slippery fish in the ocean) to get her father to agree to a low-born bridgroom. It also excites the reader with suspense to await a future danger, in this case the treachery of Fikenhild which results in Horn being exiled. It clearly also has sexual symbolism. Besides all this, however, it has a puzzling quality and, as is not uncommon in medieval narrative, the explicit explanation offered within the text, here by Horn (that she is dreaming of fears that he will betray her), is, if one may use the phrase, a red herring. At first the reader may suppose the big fish is Horn himself, especially since the dream occurs around the time of the young lovers' first sexual encounter.[31] It is only as events unwind that the reader deduces that the destructive big fish is either Fikenhild or the king, and later Fikenhild also fits another element of the dream's imagery, in the role of the unwanted fish Rymenhild fears: the unwanted bridegroom who threatens to usurp Horn's place in her bed.

This first dream plays a powerful role amid the repetitions and symmetries that distinguish the skillful design of *Horn*. Its maritime subject fits in with the voyages that are central to the plot, and Rymenhild's second dream will also be concerned with danger and the sea.[32] Susan Crane traces the importance of the sea in *Horn* and comments:

> The strongest natural force in *King Horn* is the sea. The sea's power dominates all but
> Horn himself . . . Horn's control over the elemental power of the sea demonstrates his

---

[31] Jennifer Fellows, ed., *Of Love and Chivalry: An Anthology of Middle English Romance* (London, 1993), p. 275 (note to lines 658–64), who points out that the author may have been inspired by the sexual image of fish and net in *The Romance of Horn*, laisse 192. The Harley text of *King Horn* is printed in J. Rawson Lumby, ed., *King Horn, Floris and Blauncheflur, The Assumption of Our Lady*, 2nd ed. rev. George H. McKnight, EETS o.s. 14 (1901; repr. Bungay, Suffolk, 1962), pp. 1–69. Line numbers derive from this edition.

[32] Susan Crane, *Insular Romance: Politics, Faith and Culture in Anglo-Norman and Middle English Literature* (Berkeley, 1986), pp. 12–27.

superiority in the absence of an impressive set of social accomplishments for him to master.[33]

We shall see his control of the sea particularly in the passage containing Rymenhild's second dream. But the images of this first dream will themselves also reappear and be creatively extended later in the narrative; indeed, we can see the second dream as one of the offshoots of this first dream, whose elements prove to have an inexhaustible abundance of potential meanings. When Horn comes back in the nick of time, disguised as a beggar in the hall (lines 1091–1296; fols. 89r–90v), and asks Rymenhild for a drink from her horn, he announces himself not a beggar but a fisherman who has returned to look and see if there are any fish in the net he left on a fair strand seven years ago. His enigmatic speech is a cluster of images that take up and develop further the symbolic potential of the first dream. He will, he says, drink only out of a white cup, not a brown bowl (Rymenhild, of course, is symbolically this white cup). He throws his ring into her ceremonial horn, the symbol of herself sexually and as lady of the household, for her to find — so that she recognizes her true love by peering into the cup as if she too were a fisherman looking into the ocean. Later, as Horn moves towards the achievement of his kingdom and his plan of marrying Rymenhild, and as she waits in mounting anxiety, menaced by Fikenhild's plots, Horn dreams another dream: she will be taken onto a ship that begins to lurch; in danger of drowning, she struggles to reach "with hire honde" the dry land but is beaten back by the hilt of Fikenhild's sword (lines 1521–30; fol. 91v). This dream precipitates the final rapid climax as Horn rushes back to rescue Rymenhild from Fikenhild's sea-girt fortress (lines 1547–1624; fol. 92r–v). The events of the dream are in reality reversed by the hero's expertise: he now brings Rymenhild from her danger amid the sea back to dry land (lines 1617–18; fol. 92r); his sword — its point, not a hilt — is used against Fikenhild, to save Rymenhild from his power, and the sea is the means of their escape rather than of Rymenhild's imprisonment:

> Þe see bigan to flowen
> Ant hy faste to rowen.
> Hire aryueden vnder reme [came to shore] . . .
> Horn eode to ryue [sailed]
> Þe wynd him con wel dryue . . .[34]

---

[33] Crane, *Insular Romance*, pp. 31–32.

[34] Lines 1621–23, 1631–32; fol. 92v; see Fellows, ed., *Of Love and Chivalry*, p. 40.

Such references to the speed of sea and wind, part of the network of sea allusions throughout the text, parallel the rapid pace and movement of the narrative, passing between the kingdoms of Sudenne, Westernesse, and Ireland. In Horn's dream of Rymenhild's imprisonment as her attempt to escape from a capsizing ship (lines 1521–30), "with hire honde" perhaps means swimming rather than pulling onto shore; it may be relevant that in the *Somnia* dreambook tradition swimming sometimes denotes anxiety or *impedimentum grave* [severe difficulty], and dreaming of fish is also interpreted as *impedimentum*.[35] Dreambook interpretations, however, could, at best, have contributed no more than a basic association of themes to the *Horn* poet: the multiple meanings the dreams have within that text go far beyond such single denotations.

The *Horn* poet's use of dreams for symbolic and structural power that extends throughout the text is not an isolated case in medieval romance. Dreams in romances often have ambiguous elements and wide resonances in the narrative. Arthur's two dreams in the alliterative *Morte Arthure* have something of the same multivalence. Of Arthur's second dream of wandering through a wood, menaced by wild beasts and meeting Fortune, Mary Hamel observes — in words that apply just as well to *Horn* — that the dream is "central to the meaning of the poem and pivotal to its structure."[36] Far from being merely brief episodes with only single functions — to herald the treachery of Fikenhild in one case and to warn of Rymenhild's imprisonment in the other — *Horn*'s two sea-centered dreams are integrated into the dominant themes of the text. Rymenhild's dream of her net, the sea, and the fish, in particular, comes to span the whole structure, and it contains within itself both the endless uncertainty and restlessness of the plot and the structural coherence and emotional unity which, at the same time, shape this very carefully designed romance.

In a Þestri Stude

The Harley 2253 *In a Þestri Stude* (fols. 57r–58v) is a Body and Soul debate[37] found also in Oxford, Bodleian Library MS Digby 86 (fols. 195v–200r), and Cambridge, Trinity

---

[35] See Fischer, ed., *Complete Medieval Dreambook*, pp. 71, 143.

[36] Mary Hamel, ed., *Morte Arthure: A Critical Edition*, Garland Medieval Texts 9 (New York, 1984), p. 44.

[37] Thomas Wright, ed., *The Latin Poems Commonly Attributed to Walter Mapes*, Camden Society 16 (1841; repr. New York, 1968), pp. 346–49.

College MS 323 (fol. 29v).[38] It is mostly in four-line monorhyme stanzas, interspersed with single couplets in the final section unique to Harley (see below).[39] The Body and Soul tradition, whose origins go back to the early Christian period, contains considerable variety of forms: debates where both entities speak; addresses by the soul alone, complaining of the harm the body's sins have done to the soul's fate after death; related dialogues — for example, between worms and the body; dialogues that take place after death; and dialogues about ascetic and nonascetic lifestyles within this life. The Old English Body and Soul poem, extant in a long and a short version, is not a debate; only souls speak. In the long version (*Soul and Body I* in the Vercelli Book) a damned soul first upbraids its body for lack of self-control, and then a saved soul speaks in gratitude to its body.[40] The twelfth-century *Soul's Address to the Body* is a text in seven fragments. Another twelfth-century poem, *The Grave*, may also be an address by a soul; it is a speech to a body about the "house" it will now lie in and the lonely state of decay it will endure.[41] Material of this kind is also found in sermons.[42] Two Latin poems, *Nuper huiuscemodi visionem somnii* (ca. 1190?) and *Noctis sub silentio* (early thirteenth century),[43] influenced the extant Middle English debates, including *In a Þestri Stude*. Rosemary Woolf provides a valuable discussion of medieval texts, including Body and Soul debates, that present voices from the grave, and Takami Matsuda explores them as developments from homiletic tradition.[44]

These poems dramatizing the fate of the soul can all be seen to be, essentially, visions: the speeches and debates of Body and Soul take place in a realm beyond that of normal human time and space, but, as is common with medieval literary visions, they are not

---

[38] John W. Conlee, ed., *Middle English Debate Poetry: A Critical Anthology* (East Lansing, Mich., 1991), pp. 10–17; also in Wright, ed., *Latin Poems*, pp. 246–49.

[39] On Body and Soul debates in general, see Hans Walther, *Das Streitgedicht in der lateinischen Literatur des Mittelalters*, Quellen und Untersuchungen 5.2 (Munich, 1920), pp. 63–88; Douglas Moffatt, ed. and trans., *The Old English "Soul and Body"* (Wolfeboro, N.H., 1990), pp. 28–44.

[40] *Soul and Body I*, Vercelli Book; *Soul and Body II*, Exeter Book. See Douglas Moffatt, ed., *The Soul's Address to the Body: The Worcester Fragments* (East Lansing, Mich., 1987), and Moffatt, ed., *OE "Soul and Body."*

[41] Conlee, ed., *ME Debate Poetry*, pp. 3–6.

[42] See Moffatt, ed., *OE "Soul and Body,"* pp. 28–35; and Robert W. Ackerman, "The Debate of the Body and Soul and Parochial Christianity," *Speculum* 37 (1962): 544.

[43] Ackerman, "*Debate*," p. 544.

[44] Rosemary Woolf, *The English Religious Lyric in the Middle Ages* (Oxford, 1968), pp. 67–103, 326–30, 401–06; Takami Matsuda, *Death and Purgatory in Middle English Didactic Poetry* (Woodbridge, Suffolk, 1997), pp. 130–46.

necessarily explicitly designated as dreams. A variety of kinds of framing device is used. The texts in which the narrator, while in this life, is granted a vision (sometimes literally, rather, an overhearing) revealing truths about life after death belong to the wider general category of journeys to the next world already mentioned. *Nuper huiuscemodi visionem somnii* purports to tell the dream of a cleric who sees the soul leave the body and overhears its speech criticizing the body while standing by its coffin, and then a long speech in reply by the body. After a final complaint by the soul, demons attack it and take it to hell. *Noctis sub silentio*, like the English *Als I Lay* based on it, describes the narrator's dream on a winter night of a soul standing by a bier, lamenting the harm the body has done to it. In the English *Als I Lay* the bier holds the corpse of a "mody kny3t." Here there is a longer exchange of short speeches, creating more of a dialogue, and this is also true of the Middle English and Old French versions.

The dark place in which the narrator stands at the beginning of *In a Þestri Stude* is unspecific and suggests not only the nighttime when dreams come and the darkness of the grave, but also that indefinite mental area where vision and allegory are enacted. Its gloom and fear prefigure also the soul's future misery in hell.[45] The Middle English debates use colloquial idioms and exclamation to create an almost theatrical effect of a close emotional relationship breaking apart under the forces of anger, recrimination, and terror, just as the genre of Body and Soul debate itself centers on the doctrine that human identity involves two entities that ultimately belong to different realms of being and will separate from each other to face different fates. The body in *In a Þestri Stude* is not given strong arguments and its tone is petulent rather than reasoned. There is a more sober style and more theological sophistication in Latin Body and Soul debates. As Robert W. Ackerman shows, *Nuper huiuscemodi visionem somnii* allows the body's arguments "at least as much theological sophistication as had Anima."[46] He links the greater emotional vehemence of the English debates and their relative lack of concern for purely theological disputation to the movement in the Church after 1215 to educate both laity and parish priests in matters of faith, and particularly to inculcate the importance of contrition and confession.

There are Latin Body and Soul dialogues with a different focus — those that discuss the arguments for and against an ascetic approach to life — which do not present the furious acrimony nor the generally pathetic characterization of the body, as found in the English debates.[47] These are debates about flesh and spirit or the celibate and married states, within life, rather than debates between a soul and body after death. In *O Caro, cara vilitas* (ca.

---

[45] Conlee, ed., *ME Debate Poetry*, p. 11, suggests possible influence from Matt. 1.27 and Job 33.15–17.

[46] Ackerman, "*Debate*," p. 543.

[47] See the texts printed in Walther, *Das Streitgedicht*, pp. 215–21.

1200?), we are offered sophisticated arguments from Flesh, for example, that the Creator must have wished humanity to enjoy the good things of creation, and that the creation of humanity in two sexes indicates God's will that humanity should enjoy sexual relationships, and Spirit agrees at the close that a man who is not bound by rules of celibacy may enjoy legitimate sexual union for the sake of offspring, but not fornication. Finally, Reason adjudicates as judge, warning Flesh to stay subject to his judgment and to Spirit, in order to keep dangerous tendencies under control. In contrast, the postmortem Body and Soul debates, especially vernacular ones, exploit material images more.

As is typical of texts of this type, *In a Þestri Stude* provides a context for a number of traditional mutability themes. One stanza uses the *ubi sunt* motif: "Body, wher aren þy solers, þi castles, ant þy toures . . . ?" (line 37; fol. 57r). Another invokes the common image of the grave as a move to an uncomfortably constructed house, an image which, we have seen, also appears in the dreambook tradition: "Min hous ys maked of erþe, yturnd ys al to kare" (line 43; fol. 57v); "Min hous is maked of cleie, þw woues [walls] beþ colde and bare" (Digby text, line 51).

The literature and art that warns humans of their mutability tended to focus particularly on the degradation of those who in this world were rich and powerful. This is found already in the ancient sources of some of the medieval topoi: "Where are the princes of the people?" (Baruch 3.16); "What profit to us is pride?" (Wisdom 5.8). Medieval parishioners of all classes saw Last Judgment scenes and other didactic mutability motifs depicted in their churches where the rich and powerful were prominent among those being consigned ignominiously to hell.[48] The sins of the wealthy deceased are sometimes presented as social sins that are reprehensible because they harm other people: deceptions, extortions, perversion of justice, lack of charity. But above all they are treated as spiritual sins — pride, gluttony, worldliness — which harm the perpetrator's personal chances of salvation in the afterlife.[49] These two attitudes to sin are not rigidly separated in medieval mutability literature, for the social sins also imperil the individual soul in the afterlife, but in general in medieval Christian moral warnings it is the consequences for the sinner's soul that are of primary interest since eternal damnation is more serious than temporary

---

[48] See T. S. R. Boase, "King Death," in *The Flowering of the Middle Ages*, ed. Joan Evans (London, 1966), pp. 203–44.

[49] At Doomsday, as depicted in the mystery plays, Jesus — like the bridegroom in the Parable of the Bridegroom — does, however, judge souls according to whether they performed the Seven Works of Mercy to their fellow human beings. A few Doom paintings concentrate on the Works of Mercy versus Seven Deadly Sins, rather than just the contrast between the saved and the damned (E. Clive Rouse, *Medieval Wallpaintings*, 4th ed. [Princes Risborough, 1990], pp. 56–65).

earthly deprivation.[50] Nevertheless, mutability literature is one of the areas of medieval culture that provides a vehicle for criticism of the rich and powerful, not only in relation to their own spiritual health but in their relationships with those subject to them. While the two Latin poems mentioned above concentrate mostly on the loss of former glory and luxury, each also condemns deceptions practiced by the deceased, and *Noctis sub silentio* warns the dead man that, because he was not a father to the poor but a robber, he will suffer after death (lines 89–90).

In a Þestri Stude uses the structure, common in medieval dialogue poems, of allotting one stanza to each speaker alternately. This design, in a culture where literature was still largely orally performed and written texts lacked quotation marks, makes it possible to deduce where shifts between speakers occur even without speech indicators like "he said"/"she said." Dialogue in the first half of the poem gives way at line 52[51] to a sermon-like monologue by the soul about the Last Judgment. The Harley text ends with a passage, missing in Digby, describing the soul's misery in hell and the body's "endeles" rotting in the earth, and with warnings: we shall all die, be we never so proud, and lie outside in snow, frost, showers, and mist; only deeds done for love of God will be causes of pride then (lines 113–17; fol. 58r). We shall move from our houses of lime and stone to "a bour þat is oure long hom" (lines 118–20; fol. 58r–v), a motif we saw in the dreambook tradition. The Harley text ends with a couplet addressed by the narrator to the audience, taken from the "When the turf is thy tower" tradition:[52]

> When the flor is at þy rug [backbone], þe rof ys at þy neose,
> Al þis wolrdes [*sic*] blisse nis nout worþ a peose (lines 123–24; fol. 58v),

and with a prayer: only the mercy of Jesus can save us from catastrophe; may Christ bring us all to be with his saints (lines 125–27).

Here the sins of the body — conceived as a rich member of the ruling class — fall into two categories: one is heedless absorption in worldliness, summed up in conventional terms, for example, furs and purple silk, fine horses, playing, hunting, beautiful clothes and tapestries, towers and elegant rooms (lines 14–15, 37–39); the other is oppression of the lower classes. He has been unjust in his own manorial courts, extorting money from

---

[50] To modern ethical sensibilities it seems, after all, strange that there should be a head sin of Wrath (*Ira*) in the Seven Deadly Sins, rather than of Cruelty: Cruelty figures but as a subdivision of *Ira*. The Seven Deadly Sins are essentially a scheme based on the concept of the fate of the individual soul; in contrast, the Ten Commandments unite duty to God and duty to neighbor and society.

[51] Digby text, line 57.

[52] See Woolf, *English Religious Lyric*, pp. 67–68.

his tenants, threatening poor men, and robbing them of their inheritance (lines 5–6, 22–24, 31). These past false judgments, threats, and removal of due inheritance, perpetrated by him against his fellow men, will be matched by the judgment and the threat of loss of heaven in his own future encounter with God the judge. Verbally, the poem is tightly constructed. The word *dome* recurs throughout it in a variety of contexts, including the earthly "false domes" of the landowner "in halle" (lines 5–6), Jesus' "hard domes" (line 84; held, as the Digby text visualizes it [lines 87, 100], in God's "halle" before the saved enter his "halle" in paradise), as well as the worms' "domes" over who wins the body's flesh (Digby text, line 27). Just as the landowner turned right to wrong — "Falsnesse ant swykedom thou wrohstes ful ryue" and "Turne ryht to wronge þou louedest al to mukel" (lines 7, 23) — being "false" in judgments and words, so he himself will be overturned from his high status and "heye parage" (lines 6, 21–22, 32). He will fall despite his "heye boures" and "toures heye," and at Judgment only the "treu" will be safe (lines 37, 39, 56, 114). He moves from grand "toures" to the earthen house of the grave, from fine clothes and tapestries to cold bare sides and walls. His knightly hunting of wild beasts of prey (boars and lions) is juxtaposed — as if both are instances of the same lordly aggression — with his threats and predatory robbery of the poor, but then the landowner becomes himself in the next line the victim of predators as the worms eat his flesh. Digby seems to offer at times a text closer to the original conception and more tightly integrated in thematic terms. In line 50 Harley has "wondres fele ant ryue" before Doomsday, but, since there are seven of them, Digby's reading, "tuo miracles and fiue" (line 58), is more likely to be original. The theme of Christ's wounds also comes across more strongly in Digby than in Harley, and the themes of the cross, atonement, and wounds are interwoven skillfully. This verbal coherence creates a strong sense of worldly and spiritual dualities, matching events in this life to those in the next and underlining the poem's message of the inevitability of retribution.

Woolf pointed out that medieval lyrics on death use the arts of poetry to evoke an emotional response, above all of fear which we would rather not feel. To overcome this resistance, they often use more overt artfulness and poetic virtuosity than other kinds of religious verse; even within the medieval tradition of affective piety, they are in this sense closer to sermons than poetry.[53] In this poem the body's grumpy reluctance to pay heed to what the soul wants to tell dramatizes that assumption of a generic predisposition in the audience for texts of this type not to want to hear to what they teach:

"Wrecche gost, þou wen away, hou long shal þi strift laste?" (line 25; fol. 57r)

---

[53] Woolf, *English Religious Lyric*, pp. 67–68.

"Wen auuei nou, vrec ghost, mid þine longe tale,
Me is vo i-nou þei þou ne houpreide mi bale . . ."
"Þei þou chide niȝt and dai, ne sege Ich þe namore."[54]

In fact, after Body has expressed its sulky protests, Soul launches into an uninterrupted sermon on the Last Judgment (lines 44–96). It describes the signs that will come before Doomsday, Christ showing his Cross, summoning the saved to paradise, and sending Satan to hell. The motif of reluctant pupil continues in this sermon section: Soul asks Body why it was never mindful of the Creator (lines 45–46); admonishes "Bodi, wyld þou nou lythe [listen], and Y wol telle þe . . ." (line 49); and warns that at the Judgment it will be too late to cavil:

"We mowe þer noud chyde, ne haue wordes stronge" (line 83)
"Ne halt þe nout to chide ne holde domes strong." (Digby text, line 89)

It is not uncommon for the Digby text to be more adversarial in wording, as here, and the verbal repetitions on the theme of judgment are slightly stronger in Digby.

The message of the urgency of penitence and reform that is expressed through this device of the soul trying to penetrate didactically the body's unresponsiveness is also expressed through a manipulation of time (past, present, and future) in the text, something that is typical of these poems from beyond the grave. Since Body and Soul signify two aspects of those who receive the teaching, the fictional "now" of their exchange represents the future for the living audience. It is that time after death when bodies and souls can speak in some symbolic, archetypal space about their real theological relationship, seen now tardily in its full clarity for the first time. The fictional past over which the two speakers contend, the sins of the body, represents the lesson for the audience, a warning of what to avoid. And the fictional future, the vision of Judgment, gives urgency to the lesson. The poem's constant shifting between the three fictional times is itself expressive of the lessons of mutability and of the inevitability of judgment. Body complains: "Nou aren mi dawes done, Y wende ha lyued ay!" (line 19). Though the body is being used in that last statement specifically to voice foolish assumptions for didactic purposes, a more general sense of overturning the expected is central to Body and Soul debates. The later variations on the form continue to create surprises: in the fifteenth-century *Disputacione betwyx the Body and the Wormes* it is not a soul but worms that vilify the body. In mutability art, whether the cadaver tomb, the Soul and Body debate, or skeletons dragging away or dancing with the living, the contemptuous exposure of the body's powerless and humiliating state is a displacement of an attack on the audience's physicality in the

---

[54] Digby text, lines 41–42, 52. A line similar to the last one occurs in Harley (line 46; fol. 57v).

interests of preaching spirituality to them. They are devices that present a sharply divided choice to the audience. The putrid bodies, like the cadaver tombs, the petulent body under attack from its soul, or the skeleton figures of Death, do not really represent the deceased so much as aspects of the life of those who are still alive, which the artist is anxious to denigrate. Their role is to warn.

How Man's Flesh Complained to God against Christ is a fifteenth-century variation on the theme which reverses the usual power balance, at least on the literal level, so that it is the body who takes on the tone of injured superiority usually adopted by the soul against the body.[55] It laments that the soul has deserted it to dwell with Jesus, having become disgusted with the body's worldliness and sins. The text also wittily adopts the topos of Jesus as Lover, here an adulterous lover, derived originally from exegesis of the Song of Songs as the Bridegroom wooing the soul; by focalizing the text from the disgruntled viewpoint of the body, it draws attention to the body's foolish inability to see the truth as it really is. God replies that it has caused its own misery but Jesus will save it from hell and purgatory if it repents, does good deeds, accepts whatever God sends in meekness, and helps the poor. This unconventional complaint by the body against the soul's preference for a spiritually advantageous lifestyle and partner conveys the same message that underlies other, more conventional, irate complaints in the Body and Soul tradition: body and soul are distinct and they tend towards opposed goals. The soul finds the body's proclivities distasteful and harmful to its own heavenly destiny; the body is slow to accept the lesson that humans need to reject worldly pleasures and turn to penance in order to avoid misery after death. It teaches the same message as *In a Þestri Stude* and employs in an original fashion the same dramatic situation of fraught and emotional quarrelling between partners who were formerly related.

All three Harley texts discussed here are English texts with known French analogues, and two also are English versions of Latin works of extremely wide distribution. This multilingual context is, of course, typical of the Harley material, and it is perhaps typical of the extraordinary range of the manuscript that it should include examples of the three main forms of medieval dream lore and of the literary use of dreams: the dream as a framing device in *In a Þestri Stude*, the dream as a thematic and structural element in romance, and the dream as a representative of the widely popular *Somnia Danielis* guide to the interpretation of dreams.

---

[55] Printed in J. Kail, ed., *Twenty-Six Political and Other Poems*, Part 1, EETS o.s. 124 (1904; repr. Millwood, N.Y., 1973), pp. 89–95.

Authors, Anthologists,
and Franciscan Spirituality

David L. Jeffrey

It is at the very least unlikely, as G. L. Brook tells us, that all the lyrics in London, British Library MS Harley 2253 are the work of the same poet.[1] The Harley MS is an anthology of poems, saints' lives, condensations from scriptural exegesis, catechetical material, political propaganda, romance, and recipes. A great majority of the one hundred twenty-one items in the manuscript still stand as anonymous. In our attempt to understand Harley 2253 as an anthology, therefore, we are left with difficult problems in trying to establish those traditions or personal considerations which have governed its collection and preservation. For one thing, there would appear to have been both thirteenth- and fourteenth-century layers to the materials in the anthology.[2] For another, the poems collected represent a considerable variety of dialects.[3] Further, the diversity of the manuscript's total contents takes it out of the category of either simple poetic miscellany (e.g., of the sort represented by some medieval Italian or German *laudario* manuscripts), or explicit English handbook of *pastoralia* (e.g., most manuscripts of the *Dormi secure* or *Fasciculus morum* type) from which come so many other medieval English lyric poems.[4]

---

[1] G. L. Brook, ed., *The Harley Lyrics: The Middle English Lyrics of MS. Harley 2253*, 4th ed. (Manchester, 1968), p. 2.

[2] Folios 1r–48v; 49r–140v. See N. R. Ker, intro., *Facsimile of British Museum MS. Harley 2253*, EETS o.s. 255 (London, 1965), pp. ix, xviii–xix. Ker's numbered list of contents appears on pp. ix–xvi.

[3] G. L. Brook, "The Original Dialects of the Harley Lyrics," *Leeds Studies in English* 2 (1933): 38–61.

[4] For a discussion of Harley 2253 in relationship to "friar miscellanies," see David L. Jeffrey, *The Early English Lyric and Franciscan Spirituality* (Lincoln, 1975), pp. 205–14. *Laudario* MSS are essentially songbooks, comprising lyrics with or without accompanying music. Friars of the Franciscan order especially made these as an aide to their mendicant evangelizing. The *Dormi secure* MS was a more inclusive preacher's prompt book, containing sermon outlines, homilies, anecdotes for illustration, materials for catechesis, and, intermittently, poems.

261

Finally, Harley 2253 contains poems not only from a variety of sources, but sources which have appeared to many readers to represent conflicting and contradictory sensibilities.[5] Yet despite all of the apparent (and not atypical) haphazardry of organization in the manuscript's table of contents, I believe that there are principles governing some of the inclusions which, when traced out a little, can help us to infer something more definite about the authors and the anthologist of fols. 49–140, as well as to be more confident about the motivations and purposes which may have created and preserved this extraordinarily valuable medieval book.

First of all, as Rossell Hope Robbins observed in 1952, Harley 2253 "clearly contains work by friars, since half its poems are duplicated in manuscripts belonging to friars."[6] In fact, if we place the manuscript in relation to others of what he calls "friar miscellanies," we will discover that Harley 2253 shares several poems with manuscripts whose provenance is basically Franciscan. Robbins himself came to think that these "miscellanies," although bearing strong evidences of mendicant influence, were much more generally used, and that they were even added to, modified, and edited by secular priests and others who could make use of them. In making ascriptions, one is usually speaking of prevalent influence, in this sense, rather than provenance in the strict sense of the word. Without then trying to argue a narrow case for provenance for each of these related manuscripts, since I have already hazarded that elsewhere,[7] let me simply itemize: the Harley MS shares eight poems with Oxford, Bodleian Library MS Digby 86 (nos. 21, 22, 50, 60, 68, 73, 89, 104); two with the Auchinleck MS (Edinburgh, National Library of Scotland Advocates MS 19.2.1) as well as Digby 86 (nos. 21, 89); one with Trinity College Cambridge MS 323 and Digby 86 (*In a Þestri Stude*, no. 22); one with BL MS Harley 913 (Kildare MS) (*Earth upon Earth*, no. 24b); one with BL MS Royal 2.F.viii (*A Spring Song on the Passion*, no. 53); one with Cambridge, Saint John's College MS 111, BL MSS Royal 8.F.ii and 12.E.i, and Dublin, Trinity College MS 301, as well as Digby 86 (*Stond Wel, Moder, vnder Rode*, no. 60); one with Oxford, Bodleian Library MS Digby 2 (*I Syke When Y Singe*, no. 62); and one with the apparently Franciscan BL MS Egerton 613 (*Blessed Be Þou, Leuedy*, no. 66). Of these manuscripts, Digby 86, TCC 323, Harley 913, Digby 2, and Egerton 613 are almost certainly to be ascribed to the dominant influence of the Franciscans,[8] so that the least that can be said of Harley 2253 in this

---

[5] Brook, ed., *Harley Lyrics*, pp. 16–17, 26.

[6] Rossell Hope Robbins, ed., *Secular Lyrics of the XIVth and XVth Centuries* (Oxford, 1952), p. xviii.

[7] Jeffrey, *Early English Lyric*, pp. 207–13.

[8] Compare Robbins, ed., *Secular Lyrics*, p. xviii. B. D. H. Miller has argued that MS Digby 86 was a secular compilation for a domestic household ("The Early History of Bodleian MS Digby

respect is that it contains a good deal of work which has been otherwise preserved by Franciscan friars or those sympathetic to their style.

With due caution, we can go a bit further. Aside from compatible traits of spirituality, to which I will turn momentarily, it is evident that the writer of at least one of the Anglo-Norman poems must have been sympathetic to the cause of Simon de Montfort, as was also the fourteenth-century Harley scribe-anthologist. *Lament for Simon de Montfort* (no. 24) is highly charged with party feeling, and, as Isabel S. T. Aspin has noted, the poem is more than likely to have been authored by one of his Franciscan admirers who — at some political risk — made Simon de Montfort a kind of martyr.[9] The English poem on that same subject, *A Song of Lewes* (no. 23), is no less a witness to the same sympathies. In addition, Harley 2253 contains a well-known Anglo-Norman poem by Franciscan friar Nicole de Bohun (i.e., Nicholas Bozon), *De la femme et de la pie* (no. 78); an Anglo-Norman paraphrase of a pseudo-Bonaventuran meditation on the Passion (no. 115); a free translation into English of a poem by Jacopone da Todi (*Stond Wel, Moder, vnder Rode*, no. 60); and a Latin prose extract from the *Communiloquium* by John of Wales (no. 109), who is yet another important Franciscan author of the thirteenth century. On the face of

---

86," *Annuale Mediaevale* 4 [1963]: 23–56). I have argued elsewhere in some detail that the nature of many elements in the compilation suggests that the compiler was notably responsive to Franciscan influence (Jeffrey, *Early English Lyric*, pp. 203–07). In a related argument, the editors of *Fouke le Fitz Waryn* note that both of these trilingual MSS (Digby 86 and Harley 2253) "contain much that would appeal to the laity; yet there are many elements, prayers, indulgences, liturgical lessons in Latin, which betray the hand of a priestly compiler" (E. J. Hathaway, P. T. Ricketts, C. A. Robson, and A. D. Wilshere, eds., *Fouke le Fitz Waryn*, ANTS 26–28 [Oxford, 1975], p. xl). Friars often attached themselves to notable families, especially in the fourteenth century, and as Hathaway et al. speculate, this may have been especially true when a cleric had in his secular days "belonged to the baronial world" (p. xli). See also David L. Jeffrey and Brian J. Levy, eds. and trans., *The Anglo-Norman Lyric: An Anthology* (Toronto, 1990), pp. 4–6; but compare Marilyn Corrie, "The Compilation of Oxford, Bodleian Library, MS Digby 86," *Medium Ævum* 66 (1997): 236–49; also Judith Tschann and M. B. Parkes, intro., *Facsimile of Oxford, Bodleian Library, MS Digby 86*, EETS s.s. 16 (Oxford, 1996).

[9] See Isabel S. T. Aspin, ed. and trans., *Anglo-Norman Political Songs*, ANTS 11 (Oxford, 1953), p. 26. Simon de Montfort's sons were educated by the Franciscans, and Stevenson notes that after Montfort's death "fratres Minores . . . materium loquendi sumentes de vita ejus, ex optimis gestis ejus venerandam de illo ediderunt hystoriam, scilicet lectiones . . . et alia que pertinent ad decus unius martirus et honorem" [Friars Minor . . . gathered up oral reports of his life, and, out of his best and most honorable deeds, constructed a history, . . . undoubtedly selecting out those items most appropriate to the dignity and singular honor of a martyr] (J. Stevenson, ed., *Chronicle of Melrose* [Edinburgh, 1935], p. 212; translation mine).

it, then, there is clear evidence of important Franciscan contributions to the composition of our anthology.

The manuscript which seems most to resemble Harley 2253 in the structuring and arrangement of its contents, and which is perhaps closest to it in date among the major "friar miscellanies," is Harley 913, the Franciscan Kildare MS. Dated about 1325, it is a collection by friars of verse and prose in Latin, Anglo-Norman, and English, written in different hands.[10] While it lacks the saints' lives of Harley 2253, it has much of the diversity of writing there represented, including even the recipes for preparation of pigments for an illuminator of manuscripts — a further clue to the provenance of both manuscripts.[11] We know about the Kildare MS that it began its history among Anglo-Irish friars in the southeast of Ireland. We can fairly conclude that it was for a time the miscellany of one convent or other in that area (Kildare, Waterford, or even Dublin are the likely candidates). And we know that in the sixteenth century it passed into middle-class private ownership. N. R. Ker, Aspin, and Brook, among others, have projected compatible histories for Harley 2253 and Hereford, save that the precise affiliations of authors, scribe, and the earliest private owners have not yet been established.[12]

One way to determine something further about these questions is simply to subject the poems themselves to such an analysis as might reveal any peculiar themes, concerns, or stylistic traditions. If then the poems could be identified with others whose authorship is better known, they might at least be connected to an authorial tradition. When we so evaluate the religious lyrics in Harley 2253, the result is to strengthen substantially the case for a general Franciscan spiritual influence.

The spiritual style and typical motifs of Franciscan vernacular poetry of the period are emphatically present in the manuscript, not only in its excellent version of Jacopone da Todi's *Stabat mater iuxta crucem* (no. 60), but also in such poems as *The Labourers in the Vineyard*; *Iesu Crist, Heouene Kyng*; *Iesu, for Þi Muchele Miht*; and *I Syke When Y Singe*

---

[10] W. Heuser, ed., *Die Kildare Gedichte: Die altesten mittelenglischen Denkmaler in anglo-irischen Uberlieferung* (1904; repr. Darmstadt, 1965), pp. 4, 13–19. See also E. B. Fitzmaurice and A. G. Little, *Materials for the History of the Franciscan Province of Ireland, A.D. 1230–1450* (Manchester, 1920), pp. 121–26.

[11] In Harley 913, *Modus distemperandi colores ad illuminandos libros*, including "De temperatura azori" (fol. 52r); in Harley 2253, "Vor te tempren Asure," second in a list of recipes (no. 11; fol. 52va; Von Henning Keller, ed., "Die me. Rezepte des Ms. Harley 2253," *Archiv für das Studium der neueren Sprachen und Literaturen* 207 [1970]: 94–100).

[12] Ker, *Facsimile*, pp. xxii–xxiii; Aspin, ed., *AN Political Songs*, p. 24; Brook, ed., *Harley Lyrics*, p. 3; and M. Dominica Legge, *Anglo-Norman Literature and Its Background* (Oxford, 1963), pp. 81–84.

(nos. 41, 51, 61, 62). The particular features which achieve prominence in Franciscan spirituality, as opposed to less emotional and hyperbolic medieval spiritual traditions, are (as I have suggested elsewhere) an emphasis on Scripture, on the humanity of Christ, on affectual response evoked through an appeal to the senses, and on the sacramental grace which accrues to emotional identification and contrition.[13] These characteristics, modelled on the pseudo-Bonaventuran *Meditations on the Life of Christ* as in other Franciscan meditations,[14] are prominent, even in an opening stanza of one of the best of the Harley lyrics:

Iesu, for þi muchele miht,
  Þou ȝef vs of þi grace,
Þat we mowe dai ant nyht
  Þenken o þi face.
In myn herte hit doþ me god
When Y þenke on Iesu blod,
  Þat ran doun bi ys syde,
From is herte doun to is fot;
For ous he spradde is herte blod,
  His wondes were so wyde.[15]

The forceful engagement of contrition-evoking, affective contemplation of Christ on the Cross, beginning with his face, is wrought in such a way as to encourage spiritual "conformity," and expresses the characteristic Franciscan teaching that all sacramental grace is invested in the Passion.[16] It is here that we may locate the Franciscans' repeated assertion that grace, like the Cross itself, is a paradox. Alexander of Hales, for example, develops two principles with respect to the grace appropriate to each sacrament. The first is that sacramental grace has as its font of efficacy a particular virtue of the Passion of Christ; the second is that by sacramental grace one becomes conformed to the "suffered Christ."[17] The first principle relates specifically to the removal of eternal punishment; that is, the grace of each sacrament relates to a virtue of the Passion in such a way as to create

---

[13] Jeffrey, *Early English Lyric*, pp. 43–82.

[14] For a full bibliography, the reader should consult John V. Fleming, *An Introduction to the Franciscan Literature of the Middle Ages* (Chicago, 1977), pp. 190–234.

[15] Lines 1–10; fol. 79vb. Brook, ed., *Harley Lyrics*, pp. 57–58.

[16] See Alexander of Hales, *Glossa in quatuor libros sententiarum Petri Lombardi*, 4 vols. (Florence, 1951–57), 4.14.210, 4.16.253.

[17] See K. F. Lynch, "The Doctrine of Alexander Hales on the Nature of Sacramental Grace," *Franciscan Studies* 19 (1959): 354–55, 364.

a purgatorial effect like that of the sacrament of penance.[18] The remission of actual guilt and the stricture of human weakness depends on an infusion of grace by God, while the remission of punishment (as in *A Winter Song*, no. 52), or the granting of the "carentia temporalis visionis Dei" [temporal vision of God (hitherto) denied] (as in *Iesu, for Þi Muchele Miht*) finds its causality in the Passion of Christ: "virtus Passionis Christi delevit poenam originalis pecatti" [the virtue of Christ's Passion is the remission of original sin].[19] The second principle is simply that by a consistently renewed encounter with the sacramental grace inherent in the virtues of the Passion, we become conformed to the *rejectedness* of the suffered Christ, and so identified, reconciled to the Cross.

In Franciscan spirituality contrition itself (the object of these poems) becomes sacramental[20] in this sense. A poem like *Iesu, for Þi Muchele Miht* invites grace through an affectual response — identification — gracefully turning the whole poem to its larger purpose:

> Mon, ful muchel he louede þe,
> When he wolde make þe fre
> Ant bicome þi broþer.[21]

The poem, like so many Franciscan meditations, is actually built on paradox, that essence of Christian theology which it was the particular joy of the Franciscans to celebrate in every conceivable form, from their name itself — Friars Minor ("He that is least among you all, the same is held to be great," Luke 9.48) — to their radical views concerning poverty. From the poet's initial reminder, known in prayer, that Christ's strength ("muchele miht") is made known — by grace — in apparent weakness (thus he thinks on Christ's tortured face on the Cross), there springs a reciprocity similarly paradoxical: the poet's heart is made to feel whole by contemplating how Christ's heart burst, how his life-blood ran "From is herte doun to is fot" (line 8). But the poem resolves in paradoxes exchanged: Christ's might is made known in his love shown to us in our weakness and sin,

---

[18] Alexander of Hales, *Glossa*, 4.22.382: "Praetera, virtus Passionis Christi delevit poenam originalis peccati, et baptismus ex virtute gratiae delet culpam, et ita plena remissio quod culpam et poenam fit praetur resurrectionem Christi" [Accordingly, the virtue of Christ's Passion expiates the penalty for original sin, and the virtue of grace of baptism removes the (burden of) guilt; following the resurrection of Christ, therefore, full remission of both guilt and penalty have been accomplished].

[19] Lynch, "Doctrine," pp. 340–41.

[20] Alexander of Hales, *Glossa*, 4.22.382.

[21] Lines 48–50. Brook, ed., *Harley Lyrics*, p. 59.

and his bondage to the Cross becomes an incongruous invitation to an identification by virtue of which Christ in his suffering and bondage grants us freedom, conjoining disparities and becoming our brother.

Not all the Harley poems of this type are so finely tempered from a theological point of view, but very many — whether Anglo-Norman or English — reflect the principal emotional and theological character of Franciscan spirituality. *I Syke When Y Singe* is exemplary of the purely affective and vivid pictorial tendency of Franciscan poetry:

> Þe naylles beþ to stronge,
>   Þe smyþes are to sleye,
> Þou bledest al to longe,
>   Þe tre is al to heyȝe,
> Þe stones beoþ al wete.
> Alas! Iesu, þe suete,
>   For nou frend hast þou non
> Bote seint Iohan mournynde
> Ant Marie wepynde
>   For pyne þat þe ys on.[22]

An Autumn Song (no. 63) is, on the other hand, a beautiful penitential lyric whose integration of natural imagery with spiritual reflection to produce contrition joins *A Winter Song* and *A Spring Song on the Passion* in a well-established tradition: the aesthetic is Bonaventuran, but the language has its roots in the poems of Jacopone da Todi and even in the canticle of Saint Francis himself.[23]

Yet if the authors of many of the poems are certainly influenced by Franciscan spirituality, and others are themselves Franciscans, the fact of these inclusions does not necessarily speak definitively concerning the background of the anthologist-scribe. Some of the clues are apparently contradictory. One obvious objection which might arise against an ascription of the anthologizing of Harley 2253 to a Franciscan is that it contains the poem *The Man in the Moon* (no. 81), which has antifraternal overtones, specifically, in fact, satirizing sluggardy "ase a grey frere" (line 19).[24] It should be remembered, however, that the most assuredly Franciscan Kildare MS contains a much more specific and virulent

---

[22] Lines 31–40; fol. 80ra. Brook, ed., *Harley Lyrics*, pp. 59–60.

[23] Jacopone da Todi, *Laudi*, ed. Franca Ageno (Florence, 1953); and Marion A. Habig, ed., *St. Francis of Assisi: Writings and Early Biographies* (Chicago, 1973), pp. 127–34.

[24] Brook, ed., *Harley Lyrics*, p. 70.

antifraternal satire in its *Epistola principis regionis Gehennalis* (fol. 32v).[25] The friars were not adverse to including such items, either for sometime admonition of their own faults, or, more likely, for the same sorts of reasons that they collected, as in Kildare, heretical and blasphemous parodies of the mass and Scripture. The presence of *The Man in the Moon* is thus not by itself substantially contradictory to an argument for Franciscan influence nor even provenance of this manuscript.

For all that, I would not wish, despite so many indications of Franciscan authorship for a large portion of the contents, to argue exclusively for Franciscan provenance or especially for a Franciscan anthologist for Harley 2253. Until recently it has generally been thought that the domestic records of an important Irish household (Ardmulghan), which occur on front and back flyleaves of the manuscript, an inscribed association with Saint Ethelbert, and ordinals copied according to the Hereford breviary, might associate the manuscript with Thomas de Charlton, bishop of Hereford, who was appointed by Edward II Justice of Ireland sometime between 1337 and 1340.[26] The inclusion in the manuscript of such poems as the English elegy *The Death of Edward I* (no. 47) and the macaronic French and Latin *Against the King's Taxes* (no. 114), which would seem to have had most relevance to lords in a position to ease the burden on the victims, suggests that the collection could have been made by someone associated with one of the principal families, such as the Leominsters, the Ludlows, or the Bohuns.[27]

Humphrey de Bohun, the tenth earl of Hereford (1336–61), was succeeded by his nephew Humphrey, patron of the famous Bohun psalters. The family was known for its patronage of Augustinian friars: the convent of Augustianian friars in London was founded by an earlier Humphrey of Hereford (in 1253) and the church rebuilt by Humphrey IX and much assisted by Humphrey X. The Augustinians were, among the other orders of friars, most responsive and sympathetic to the spirituality of the Franciscans. They were also great collectors and preparers of books, as witnessed in their

---

[25] *The Land of Cokaygne* has been thought also to be an attack on friars, but Thomas J. Garbáty has suggested that the satire was written by a Franciscan of the Athlone friars (Ath Luain, ca. 1224) and directed against the Cistercians of the neighboring abbey ("Studies in the Franciscan 'The Land of Cokaygne' in the Kildare MS.," *Franziskanische Studien* 45 [1963]: 139–53). See also Fitzmaurice and Little, *Materials*, p. 21.

[26] See the discussion by Ker, *Facsimile*, p. xxii.

[27] Compare Sabino Casieri, ed., *Canti e liriche medioevali inglesi dal MS. Harley 2253* (Milan, 1962), who argues for a courtly audience for the MS, one familiar with the traditions of Provençal and Norman lyric verse and likely to be associated with Edward I (p. 7). Compare here Ker's suggestion that the MS might be further associated with Adam of Orleton, bishop of Hereford after Charlton (p. xxiii).

great library at nearby Llanthony (from which come so many Lambeth Palace manuscripts), and as a reconstructed catalogue will show, they freely collected Franciscan materials among others.[28] One Austin friar, John Erghome, who actually dedicated work to Humphrey Bohun XI (1361–72), left his personal library to the Austin friary at York, a library more than incidentally rich in Franciscan books by writers such as Bonaventure, Robert Grosseteste, Bartholomaeus Anglicus, as well as miscellanies, homiletical collections, and pseudo-Bonaventuran passions.[29] In this light alone, it is certainly possible that the Harley scribe, as anthologist of so many Franciscan poems, might prove to have been, in some as yet undocumented fashion, an Augustinian friar attendant upon Bishop Thomas de Charlton, of the Bohun patronage, or even a secular priest in the employ of an important area family.[30]

There remains a possibility that the anthologist responsible for this miscellany was in fact himself a Franciscan. Ardmulghan is very close to Kildare, and the striking parallels between Harley 2253 and Harley 913 may owe to more than coincidence. While the date of the Ardmulghan accounts is earlier than the time of Charlton (this date would seem to be not much before 1325, the date of the Kildare MS), that portion is, after all, only a binding picked up as available. The bulk of the manuscript (fols. 49–140), that portion containing the greatest Franciscan influence, is written in the same early mid-century hand that transcribed the Hereford ordinals.[31] The question we might yet ask is: what could have taken the Harley scribe to the southwest of Ireland between 1328 and 1340? A first conjecture might well be that the anthologist was a friar in the retinue of Bishop Thomas de Charlton, who was there at just that time as Lord Justice. It is far from certain, however, that such a scribe would be an Austin. The Bohun family patronage extended handsomely to the Franciscans as well, and it may not be without significance for the history of Harley 2253 that Eleanor de Bohun, daughter of Earl Humphrey X and grandmother of Edward I, became in 1327 countess of Ormonde. Her husband founded the Carrickbeg friary of Franciscans in 1336, a friary which — had it ever been completed — would have been

---

[28] See Robert Reinsch, "Mitteilungen aus einer französiscen Handscrift des Lambeth Palace zu London," *Archiv für das Studium der neueren Sprachen und Literaturen* 63 (1880): 51–96.

[29] Erghome dedicated his *Prophecy of John Bridlington* to Humphrey de Bohun XI. For the library, see M. R. James, "The Catalogue of the Library of the Augustinian Friars at York, Now First Edited from the MS. at Trinity College, Dublin," in *Fasciculus Ioanni Willis Clark dicatus* (Canterbury, 1909), pp. 16–21, who published the remains of the York Austin catalogue.

[30] See the essay by Carter Revard in this volume, "Scribe and Provenance."

[31] Ker (*Facsimile*, p. xxii); Ker further notes that the Harley scribe also copied part of MS Royal 12.C.xii, and that he demonstrates in his transcription that he is "an educated scribe" (p. xix). On the scribe's possible background, see also notes 8 and 29 above.

proximate to both Kildare and Ardmulghan. When Eleanor died in 1363, she left a total of £2915 80s 5d, largely to a number of friaries in England and Ireland, and first among those were the Franciscan friaries of Nenaugh and Carrickbeg.[32] Bohun patronage in the likely districts of influence for Harley 2253 is indeed considerable, and it encompasses both Franciscans and Augustinians.[33] But these suggesions offer no more than an insight into the sympathies of what may be, at least in general terms, the patron group for the manuscript. Regretfully, they cannot definitively assure us whether the anthologist was an Augustinian, a Franciscan, or merely a sympathetic secular scribe in the retinue of the Bohuns or their bishop.

As for the *authors* of the poems in Harley 2253, I think we can conclude that many, though certainly not all, were Franciscan friars. For the others — including the Cistercian Thomas of Lancaster (no. 7), the translated Bernard of Clairvaux (*Dulcis Iesu memoria*, no. 58), Jacques de Vitry (no. 95), and Anselm of Canterbury (no. 113) — we must observe that these are authors who turn up regularly in Franciscan manuscripts and who are, indeed, the principal sources in Franciscan works such as the pseudo-Bonaventuran *Meditations* (where Bernard, Jacques, and Anselm are all quoted). Thus they are far from incongruent with a sensibility that would approve the Franciscan inclusions. The final anthologist-scribe may himself elude us: his taste, however, is one which the Franciscans, most readily among the orders of friars, would have heartily approved.

---

[32] Fitzmaurice and Little, *Materials*, p. 149.

[33] One tantalizing suggestion — and it is no more than that — potentially linking the Bohuns, Franciscan patronage, and Harley 2253 is the inclusion in the MS of work by Nicole de Bohun (Boȝun). This particular Friar Minor's work has, of course, become well known, especially for his poems in that great Franciscan miscellany, MS Phillips 8336 (now BL Addit. MS 46919) and for his *Contes moralisés*. See Paul Meyer, "Notice et extraits du MS. 8336 de la Bibliothèque de Sir Thomas Phillips à Cheltenham," *Romania* 13 (1884): 497–541; and also the edition of Bohun's *Contes moralisés* by L. T. Smith and P. Meyer (Paris, 1889). Bohun's name was not "Bozon"; what transcribers have often taken for a modern *z* is, in fact, a yogh, and phonetically *h* in "Bohun" (Edmund Colledge, ed., *The Latin Poems of Richard Ledrede, O.F.M., Bishop of Ossory, 1317–1360* [Toronto, 1974], p. xxxv). In fact, the name is most often written "Bohun" or "Boioun" in the various MSS in which his work appears. Friars in the fourteenth century almost invariably drop their surnames, taking a place-name instead. Bohun's preservation of this important family name, and also the fact that he was most active in the first third of the fourteenth century, may yet prove to be useful to scholars wishing to trace the patronage of the Bohun family to categories of MSS other than the famous illustrated psalters already bearing their name. Compare *Histoire Littéraire de la France* 36 (1924): 400–02; and M. R. James and E. G. Miller, *The Bohun Manuscripts* (Oxford, 1936).

"Frankis rimes here I redd, / Communlik in ilk[a] sted . . .": The French Bible Stories in Harley 2253

John J. Thompson

The quotation in my title is taken from near the end of the 270-line prologue attached to the late thirteenth-century Middle English biblical compilation known as the *Cursor Mundi*.[1] Having just stated that his work has been rendered in English "for the commun at vnderstand" (line 236), the *Cursor Mundi* poet next explains, in a particularly controlled and purposeful manner, why he has apparently chosen not to follow the prevailing linguistic currents in the literary world he knows best. At lines 237–38, quoted above, the poet concedes that French verse can be found all over the place. Neither the precise type of French verse nor even its country of origin are specified. By suggesting that such verse can be found "communlik in ilk[a] sted," however, the poet highlights the fact that, although English may have often seemed of greater utilitarian value than French, it was not the main vernacular literary language current in this Northern English poet's world. The French language, in both its continental and Anglo-Norman forms, was pretty clearly the main vernacular language of culture in his version of "Ingland the nacion" (line 241).[2]

Both the *Cursor Mundi* poet's robustly expressed preference for the English language and his comments on its relative socio-linguistic status must obviously be granted some important place in the history of English as an emerging national literary vernacular.[3] But

---

[1] All references to *Cursor Mundi* are to the edition by Richard Morris, 7 vols., EETS o.s. 57, 59, 62, 66, 68, 99, 101 (1874–93; repr. Oxford, 1961–66).

[2] For further discussion, see John J. Thompson, "The *Cursor Mundi*, the 'Inglis tong,' and 'Romance,'" in *Readings in Medieval English Romance*, ed. Carol M. Meale (Woodbridge, Suffolk, 1994), pp. 99–120. For the status of AN at this time as an artificial language of culture rather than a spoken vernacular, see Ian Short, "Bilingualism in Anglo-Norman England," *Romance Philology* 33 (1980): 467–79.

[3] This point has been made most forcibly by Thorlac Turville-Petre, *England the Nation: Language, Literature, and National Identity, 1290–1340* (Oxford, 1996). In the textual tradition represented by the four extant *Cursor Mundi* MSS of the so-called "Southern Version," however,

it is important not to forget that there are likely to have been many other late medieval biblical writers, compilers, and scribes who responded quite differently to the perceived interests and needs of their reading and listening audiences in England. An interesting case in point is offered by the activities of the anonymous Harley 2253 compilers and copyists known as "Scribe A" and "Scribe B": both apparently worked as copyists within a few years of each other and possibly in the same general geographical area, but Scribe A probably also worked separately from Scribe B on the small samples of vernacular biblical material that are now extant in the trilingual Harley 2253 collection.[4]

If we choose to borrow the parlance adopted by the *Cursor Mundi* poet at lines 20061–64 (when it suited his purposes to divide "Ingland the nacion" into two distinctive Middle English dialect regions: the North — "our aun" — and the South), then it is clear that Harley Scribes A and B can both be described as "Southerners." There is nothing to suggest that either of the Harley copyists knew the *Cursor Mundi* biblical version, of course, but it is worth noting that they not only shared some of the *Cursor Mundi* poet's declared narrative interests but probably also enjoyed access to some of the same types of biblical sources. For example, a few of the noncanonical narrative embellishments found in Scribe B's selection of Anglo-Norman biblical stories are similar to those preserved in the *Cursor Mundi* narrative, pointing to the likelihood that both writers used as a source the widely known and influential Latin biblical version known as Peter Comestor's *Historia scholastica*. And at around the same period in the late thirteenth century that the *Cursor Mundi* prologue was being imaginatively conceived, Harley Scribe A used as one of his exemplars a characteristically "English" version of the continental French biblical adaptation compiled by Herman of Valenciennes, the textual features of which will be discussed further below. Besides being a major vernacular source for the *Cursor Mundi*, this late twelfth-century *Bible* inspired many other experimental vernacular biblical

---

the poet's comments on the French language have been tactfully edited out of the poem, presumably because they have failed to match the sociolinguistic experience of certain other fourteenth-century English speakers; see John J. Thompson, *The "Cursor Mundi": Poem, Texts and Contexts*, Medium Ævum Monographs New Series 19 (Oxford, 1998), pp. 50–51.

[4] For the identification and dating of the two hands, see N. R. Ker, intro., *Facsimile of British Museum MS. Harley 2253*, EETS o.s. 255 (London, 1965), pp. xvi (Scribe A), xviii–xxii (Scribe B, including discussion of this scribe's contribution to Royal MS 12.C.xii). I follow Ker (p. ixn4) in assuming that the titles added later to items 1–7 in the opening section of Harley 2253 are probably the work of Scribe B. All codicological evidence cited as evidence in this essay has been checked by my own examination of the MSS in question.

writings in both France and England.[5] As such, Herman's work may well have been one of the examples that the *Cursor Mundi* poet had in mind when he chose to comment in his prologue on the ubiquitous presence and relative popularity of French verse in England.

Harley Scribe A and the Opening Section of MS Harley 2253

Before commenting further on the background and context of the French-language biblical stories and related material copied by Harley Scribes A and B, some preliminary estimate of the likely nature and extent of Scribe A's activities as a vernacular literary compiler can be gained from the available codicological evidence. The most important point here is that the Harley 2253 collection probably took on its present trilingual "shape" because of the copying/compiling activities of Scribe B, and some time after Scribe A had already transcribed the material, all in French, that is now preserved at the head of the manuscript. Folios 1–48 preserve Scribe A's entire written contribution to the Harley 2253 collection. It is probably safe to assume that his book-producing activities were fascicular in character since, as my diagram shows, this opening manuscript section was originally formed from two thematically related but physically and textually distinctive quire units: the first comprises two quires, $\mathbf{a}^{12}$ and $\mathbf{b}^{10}$ (fols. 1–22), and the second a further two specially tailored quires, $\mathbf{c}^{12}$ and $\mathbf{d}^{12+2}$ (fols. 23–48).[6] It is Scribe A's disposition of material in these quires that suggests the manner in which he approached the task of providing a religious reading program for an English audience who obviously preferred such reading to be in the French language.

Quires $\mathbf{a}$ and $\mathbf{b}$ preserve Scribe A's copy of a text entitled *Vitas patrum*, now the opening item in the manuscript (no. 1).[7] The *Vitas patrum* is an Anglo-Norman versified rendering (in rhyming couplets, with individual lines often approximating to alexandrines) of austere and moralistic material associated with the accumulated wisdom of the Desert Fathers. Its material is largely derived from the portion of the Latin *Vitae patrum* known as the *Verba seniorum* or *Apophthegmata* — the supposed "kernel" of the desert tradition

---

[5] A summary account appears in Thompson, *The "Cursor Mundi,"* pp. 109–21; see also discussion and further bibliographical reference below.

[6] My account of the Harley 2253 quiring follows the details given in Ker, *Facsimile*, p. xvi.

[7] All text and line references to *Vitas patrum* are to *Henri d'Arci's "Vitas Patrum": A Thirteenth-Century Anglo-Norman Translation of the "Verba seniorum,"* ed. Brother Basilides Andrew O'Connor (Washington, D.C., 1949). O'Connor believed, erroneously, that the *Vitas patrum* was written by (rather than for) Henri d'Arci, on which point see M. Dominica Legge, *Anglo-Norman Literature and Its Background* (Oxford, 1963), pp. 191–92.

TABLE. *Scribe A's mini-anthology in MS Harley 2253*

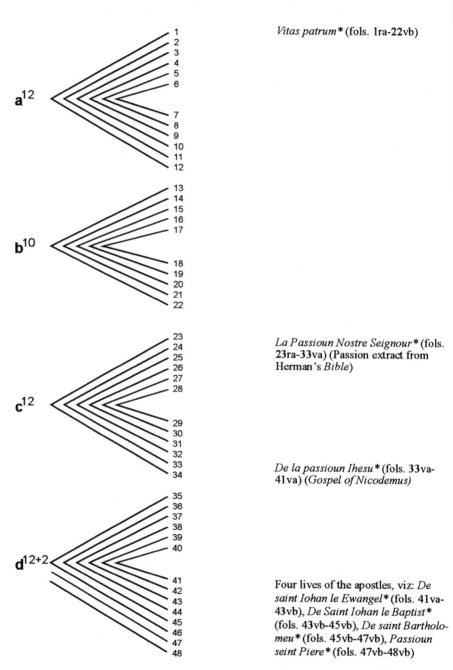

Vitas patrum * (fols. 1ra-22vb)

La Passioun Nostre Seignour * (fols. 23ra-33va) (Passion extract from Herman's *Bible*)

De la passioun Ihesu * (fols. 33va-41va) (*Gospel of Nicodemus*)

Four lives of the apostles, viz: *De saint Iohan le Ewangel* * (fols. 41va-43vb), *De Saint Iohan le Baptist* * (fols. 43vb-45vb), *De saint Bartholo-meu* * (fols. 45vb-47vb), *Passioun seint Piere* * (fols. 47vb-48vb)

* indicates manuscript title

— to which was early appended an account of the life of Thaïs, the reformed Egyptian prostitute whose conversion by Paphnutius led to her own hermetic enclosure. It is fortunate that another text of the *Vitas patrum* is preserved in Paris, Bibliothèque Nationale MS fr. 24862, since this mid-thirteenth-century version (also copied in England) offers a fuller account than Harley 2253 of the Anglo-Norman poem's genesis. Having formally announced that his work is "un sermun" (line 4) and should be called "*Vitas patrum*" (line 5; the title later adopted in the Harley MS heading on fol. 1r for this item), the anonymous author goes on to explain that he was divinely inspired to translate his text

> Al Temple de la Bruere tut veraiment,
> Nient pur les clers mes pur la laie gent. (lines 7–8)

[at Temple Bruer, in truth, not for the clergy but for layfolk]

Both of these lines are omitted from the Harley text. Also missing is an epilogue where the writer explains that he has made this work for "Henri d'Arici, frere del Temple Salemun" (line 6919) and that he intends the *Vitas patrum* to be the first of a small series of other translated works that will include his rendering of the coming of Antichrist (referred to by title at line 6931), and his account of the pains of St. Paul upon his descent into hell (referred to at line 6938). Copies of the last two eschatological works (both written in alexandrines) are now preserved in sequence alongside the *Vitas patrum* in BN MS fr. 24862.[8]

The Harley text of the *Vitas patrum* ends with space to spare on fol. 22vb, in a quire that was probably constructed to contain the material that was actually copied, but, perhaps, very little else. Since the remaining space would probably have been sufficient to copy the epilogue, it is possible that Scribe A may well have had a hand in tailoring the material he inherited from his *Vitas patrum* source to suit the different perceived requirements of his intended audience. The concerns of these later English readers and listeners were presumably somewhat more varied than the established hermitic and eschatological preoccupations of the original Anglo-Norman compiler or those of Henri d'Arci and his austere lay male colleagues in late twelfth-century Lincolnshire. Codicological evidence also lends support to the view that it was Scribe A who appended the Harley text of the *Vitas patrum* to a style of vernacular reading program quite different from the one that the

---

[8] Although the St. Paul item was subject to some later metrical reworking, both texts were originally written in alexandrines. The poem on the Antichrist is also found in Manchester, John Rylands Library MS French 6, for which see the discussion below (MS E). Both texts are edited and discussed by R. C. D. Perman, "Henri d'Arci: The Shorter Works," in *Studies in Medieval French Presented to Alfred Ewert in Honour of His Seventieth Birthday* (Oxford, 1961), pp. 279–321.

original compiler envisaged and that was then faithfully executed in BN MS fr. 24862. That different style of mini-anthology was orginally formed by adding two new quires, **c** and **d** (fols. 23–48), in which Scribe A has preserved diverse French vernacular biblical material centering on the life and Passion of Christ and the lives and martyrdoms of four apostles: John the Evangelist, John the Baptist, Bartholomew, and Peter.

The biblical and hagiographical mini-anthology that was thus formed by adding quires **c–d** comprises a verse extract from the Passion section of Herman's *Bible* (no. 2), to which has been appended a copy of the short "A" version of the *Évangile de Nicodème* (no. 3), followed by a text of the prose *Légendier apostolique anglo-normand* (nos. 4–7).[9] This cluster of material has its strongest textual links with configurations of similar vernacular material in two other late thirteenth-century manuscript collections copied in England. These are Paris, Bibliothèque Nationale MS fr. 19525 (hereafter referred to as P), and London, British Library MS Egerton 2710 to which the fragment that is now Manchester, John Rylands Library MS French 6 also once belonged (hereafter, both manuscripts will be referred to as E).[10] At a cursory glance, both P and E might be described as more miscellaneous or "mixed" religious collections than is Harley Scribe A's mini-anthology, but all three exhibit an extraordinarily strong shared interest in the same vernacular biblical and legendary items. All three manuscripts preserve closely matching extracts of the material from Herman's *Bible*, the prose *Évangile de Nicodème*, and the *Légendier apostolique anglo-normand*. In addition, P and E each preserve a prose Life of St. Paul derived from the same Anglo-Norman legendary source; an account of the Virgin's Assumption belonging to the version found in Herman's *Bible*;[11] the *Vie de saint Laurent* taken from the prose *Legende dorée*; the anonymous twelfth-century verse sermon known as *Grant mal fist Adam*; and Guischart de Beaulieu's verse *Sermon* (sometimes referred to as the *Romaunz de temtacioun de secle*). E also preserves the only other extant text of

---

[9] In the following discussion, I refer to the texts (and line numberings where relevant) in the modern editions of these items: Ina Spiele, ed., *Li Romanz de Dieu et de sa mere d'Herman de Valenciennes, chanoine et prêtre (XIIᵉ siècle)* (Leiden, 1975); Alvin E. Ford, ed., *L'Évangile de Nicodème: Les versions courtes en ancien français et en prose* (Geneva, 1973); and Delbert W. Russell, ed., *Légendier apostolique anglo-normand: Édition critique, introduction et notes* (Montreal, 1989).

[10] A description of the MSS and bibliographical information on their contents appear in Russell, ed., *Légendier*, pp. 15–19.

[11] In view of the manner in which certain other biographical information has been lost from these copies of Herman (for which see the discussion below and n. 19), it is worth noting that, in E, this Assumption poem, and another item, the *Vie de Madeleine*, are both attributed to one "Willemme." Presumably this represents an anglicized version of the AN writer Guillaume le Clerc's name, associated elsewhere with four other items in this MS.

the *Poème sur l'Antéchrist*, the item promised by the *Vitas patrum* compiler and supplied in BN MS fr. 24862 but now also notable for its nonappearance in the opening section of the Harley 2253 collection.

Among this welter of French biblical treatments and related legendary, hagiographical, and didactic material, it is striking that the items associated with Herman de Valenciennes, and (less certainly) the roughly contemporary *Sermon* attributed to Guischart de Beaulieu, testify to the continuing English fascination with *chanson de geste* and romance-style courtly treatments of biblical and related themes, a fashion that Herman himself seems to have been one of the first vernacular writers to exploit.[12] At roughly the same time as Harley Scribe A and other anonymous English compilers and copyists had selected and copied the narrative material from Herman described above, we can also say that the *Cursor Mundi* poet, in the North of England, and the Middle English poet of *Iacob and Iosep*, in the South West, were each independently employing Herman's *Bible* as a major source for their pioneering Middle English biblical narratives.[13] Such examples reveal the dramatic impact that the twelfth-century French poet's lively and informed approach to retelling biblical stories must have had on the socially and geographically diverse vernacular audiences for French-style biblical adaptations in late thirteenth-century England.

No fewer than thirty-five manuscripts containing Herman's *Bible* are identified in the poem's most recent modern edition, where the extracts in Harley 2253, P, and E are correctly listed among the eight extant texts of known English origin.[14] Whereas Harley 2253 preserves material corresponding to lines 4820–6662 of Herman's *Bible*, the

---

[12] For the manner in which Guischart's rather somber sermon was packaged with an eye to current polite literary tastes, see Legge, *AN Literature*, pp. 134–38. The general tendency of French biblical poets to imitate secular literary fashion is remarked upon in J. R. Smeets, "Les Traductions-adaptations versifiées de la Bible en ancien français," in *Les Genres littéraires dans les sources théologiques et philosophiques médiévales*, Publications de l'institute d'Études Médiévales (Louvain-La-Neuve, 1982), pp. 249–58.

[13] Details in Spiele, ed., *Li Romanz de Dieu*, pp. 34–35 (*Iacob and Iosep*); and Thompson, *The "Cursor Mundi,"* pp. 109–21 (*Cursor Mundi*).

[14] Spiele, ed., *Li Romanz de Dieu*, pp. 144–59. In Spiele's summary P is listed as MS 5, Harley 2253 as MS 20, and E as MS 22. The other five MSS of known English provenance are Paris, BN MS fr. 24387 (MS 8) and MS nouv. acq. fr. 4503 (MS 10); London, BL MSS Harley 5234 (MS 21) and Royal 13.A.xxi (MS 24); and Cheltenham, Phillips 4156 (MS 27); *pace* Spiele, p. 159, where only seven MSS are listed. For further corrections to Spiele's account of P, E, and Harley 2253, see also the following note and n. 20 below.

equivalent material in P and E consists of lines 4820–6957.[15] The copies of both the Passion and the Assumption narratives from Herman in P and E are textually closely related to each other; as far as it has proved possible to tell, the text of the Herman extract in Harley 2253 is also more nearly related to P and E than to any other extant version.[16] In short, the Herman extracts in all three manuscripts seem to have been ultimately derived from the same English anthologizing tradition.

The account of Christ's Passion in Herman's *Bible* may well have held some particular attraction for later anthologizers because it consists largely of a tissue of translated biblical borrowings woven together from the narrative details preserved in Matthew, Luke, and John. It has recently been suggested that Herman probably found such biblical passages in a missal or a breviary, as the Gospel readings for Lent, from the Thursday after the fourth Sunday in Lent until Holy Thursday.[17] At this obvious narrative high point in his poem, the French poet rarely strayed far from the biblical version of events presumably found in his liturgical exemplar. At one particularly dramatic narrative moment, however, he obviously could not resist placing his translated version of an eighth-century processional hymn for Palm Sunday in the mouths of the exultant inhabitants of Jerusalem as Christ enters their city (lines 5507–28).[18] On a few other occasions, his account also points out the larger significance of New Testament events by careful historical recapitulation (lines 5326–448, 5507–53, 5663–94). And, at another extraordinary moment, Herman pauses to comment on his own background and purpose in writing vernacular religious history (lines 5593–662).

The extracts in Harley 2253, P, and E all fail to record the precise details concerning the poet's family background provided in some other copies at lines 5608–22.[19] On the other

---

[15] Unlike the Herman extracts in P and E, the Harley 2253 borrowing ceases at line 6662 (*pace* Spiele, ed., *Li Romanz de Dieu*, p. 150). By coincidence, it was at precisely the same place that the *Cursor Mundi* poet also seems to have ceased using Herman as his major vernacular source. Line 6662 in Harley (fol. 32va) marks the point where Herman finally turns from biblical events as they are recorded in the Gospel narrative (here, Luke 13.14) and incorporates material in the form of a vernacular *planctus* to describe the lamentation of the inhabitants of Jerusalem following Christ's death.

[16] Confirmed by my textual collation of the MS copies I have been able to examine; see also the studies of the MS tradition listed and summarized in Spiele, ed., *Li Romanz de Dieu*, pp. 158–59.

[17] Spiele, ed., *Li Romanz de Dieu*, pp. 37–45.

[18] Spiele, ed., *Li Romanz de Dieu*, p. 44.

[19] The various attempts to assign authorship of Herman's Assumption narrative to someone else may well also have some bearing on this common failure to record Herman's biographical information in the extant copies. If the evidence of the MSS is to be trusted, the former feature was

hand, however, all three manuscripts originally contained lines 5640–47, where the impeccable pedigree of Herman's work is underlined by the French poet's stated deep regard for Henry II:

Il fu rois d'Angleterre et quens de Normendie,
Gale et Escoce tint trestout en sa baillie.[20]

[He was king of England and count of Normandy; he held Wales and Scotland completely in his power.]

By the time of his death in 1189, Henry enjoyed an established reputation in both England and France as a patron of several vernacular works, including a number written according to *chanson de geste* and romance patterns. Not all of the relevant extant manuscript copies preserve Herman's eulogy for Henry, but the importance placed on his role in setting the cultural patterns of twelfth-century England and France and securing the French vernacular as a suitable medium for biblical translation can hardly be doubted.[21] Nor can there be much reason to doubt that the sentiment expressed in these lines is an attempt to anchor Herman's vernacular biblical version in a late center of royal power and influence. Such an association can only have enhanced the prestige and authority of Herman's work among francophone audiences on both sides of the English Channel, including the earliest audiences for the Harley Scribe A's copy. The respectable pedigree of Herman's poem must have been a major factor in ensuring that it became a favorite target for literary anthologizers keen to provide their listeners and readers with material from a high quality biblical adaptation as part of a larger and more varied vernacular reading program.

---

a particularly English phenomenon: thus MS P credits one "Willem*me*" with writing the Assumption poem (see also n. 11 above); MS E names "Richard" as its author; while the Harley 5234 copy of the Assumption poem suggests "Thomas" as its preferred candidate.

[20] Lines 5641–42 in Spiele, ed., *Li Romanz de Dieu*, p. 315. On the 3 MSS, see Spiele, pp. 145, 150, 151, where it is stated that the lines referring to Henry (her section G) are absent from these copies. (Because of physical damage to the MS, the text in P ends abruptly at line 5641 on fol. 197v, recommencing on fol. 198r at line 6395.)

[21] On the general topic of Henry's patronage, see Elizabeth Salter, *England and International: Studies in the Literature, Art and Patronage of Medieval England*, ed. Derek Pearsall and Nicolette Zeeman (Cambridge, 1988), pp. 20–25; also John J. Thompson, "The Governance of the English Tongue: The *Cursor Mundi* and Its French Tradition," in *Individuality and Achievement in Middle English Poetry*, ed. O. S. Pickering (Woodbridge, Suffolk, 1997), p. 27.

John J. Thompson

Harley Scribe B and the Old Testament Biblical Stories in MS Harley 2253

About a generation after Scribe A had completed the work that now forms the opening "biblical" section of MS Harley 2253, the main Harley copyist, Scribe B, included among the many other items that have given this trilingual collection its unique "shape" a selection of Old Testament stories in Anglo-Norman prose (no. 71). Given both the range and quality of other items copied by the main Harley scribe, also the number of other apparently more ambitious vernacular biblical adaptations to have survived from the period, it is hardly surprising that relatively little modern critical attention has been paid to the episodes from Genesis, Exodus, and Numbers recorded by Scribe B on fols. 92v–105r. A. D. Wilshere, in the only significant published study of this item to date, characterizes it as a relatively free, sometimes confused, and mostly uninspired rendering of material from the Vulgate and Peter Comestor's *Historia scholastica*. Furthermore, on the basis of certain orthographical, phonological, and syntactical textual features shared with Harley Scribe B's text of the prose *Fouke le Fitz Waryn* in London, British Library MS Royal 12.C.xii, he hazards the opinion that the scribe and the author of both items were probably the same person.[22] Some of the linguistic evidence adduced to support such a conclusion is occasionally amenable to more than one interpretation, of course, but the recovery of the substratum influence of English on the individual form of Anglo-Norman prose used in both the Harley biblical text and *Fouke le Fitz Waryn* is particularly persuasive, indicating the deep involvement of at least one anglophone writer in the transmission of material written in the artificial literary language. That writer is likely to have been Harley Scribe B, who will be referred to throughout the following discussion as the "Harley redactor."

The Harley redactor's suspected adaptation of the Bible stories betrays, for Wilshere, "his erratic performance as a narrator, his unevenness of form, and his comparative insensitivity to poetic imagery."[23] Such a conclusion is doubly disappointing, first because of the "freshness and vigour" critics have always associated with *Fouke le Fitz Waryn* — perhaps forcing one to question momentarily whether the Bible stories really could have been written by the same hand — and second, because it seems at variance with our sense of the liveliness, inventiveness, and general literary interests evinced by his compiling and

---

[22] A. D. Wilshere, "The Anglo-Norman Bible Stories in MS Harley 2253," *Forum for Modern Language Studies* 24 (1988): 78–89, at p. 87; his comments should be read in the context of the extended linguistic analysis of the *Fouke le Fitz Waryn* text in the edition by E. J. Hathaway, P. T. Ricketts, C. A. Robson, and A. D. Wilshere, *Fouke le Fitz Waryn*, ANTS 26–28 (Oxford, 1975), pp. lii–cxvi.

[23] Wilshere, "AN Bible Stories," p. 88.

copying activities elsewhere in Harley 2253 and Royal 12.C.xii. The latter detail will doubtless be discussed at length by many of the other contributors to this volume. Since the Harley redactor's reputation as a scribe and book compiler must now be wedded to our sense of the quality and purpose of his biblical writing, some further critical examination of the manner in which the stories themselves have been shaped and presented is obviously warranted.

In all that follows, it is important to rid ourselves of the notion that the Harley Bible stories represent a bungled or incompetent attempt to produce a literal vernacular translation of a Vulgate/Comestor biblical version. While it is true that the text preserves a number of careless errors consistent with the view that the Harley 2253 version may be a prematurely completed and partially uncorrected treatment of biblical material, comparison with other French and English biblical adaptations of the Pentateuch suggests that it was possibly written as an experimental item, perhaps with some singular motive in mind. The question of what that singular motive might have been is an interesting one. In common with most other vernacular biblical treatments of the time, for example, the Harley 2253 redactor's interest in Old Testament narrative patterning meant that he simply ignored Leviticus, the third book of Moses which mainly deals with legislative matters. Nor was he any more concerned than most contemporary vernacular biblical writers with teasing out the ontological implications of God's revelation in Exodus 3.13: *Ego sum qui sum*, or entering into theological debate on other minutiae concerning the laws and ordinances set out in the books of the Bible he chose to summarize. More interestingly, perhaps, in the light of the stipulations of the Fourth Lateran Council (1215), he was not prepared to allow his storytelling to be interrupted by the requirement to render the fundamental tenets of the Christian faith in a form that would be readily understood by an unlearned lay audience.[24]

The Harley redactor was not even interested in dealing with the opening chapters of Genesis. Instead his text begins with a call for attention, followed immediately by a rapid survey of the familiar biblical stories that will *not* be included in this abbreviated version:

> Seigneurs vus oy auetz molt souent diuerses estoyres de la bible, que plusors sunt de Adam, Seth, Noe, Habraham, Ysaac, e Iacob e autres plusours de queux ore leysyr me est de parler . . . (fol. 92v).

---

[24] Similarly to the example set by Herman de Valenciennes, for example, the Harley redactor resisted the didactic impulse to present a rendition of the Ten Commandments in his drastically abbreviated version of Exodus 17–30; it is interesting to compare the manner in which the *Cursor Mundi* poet almost intuitively provided his own ten-line English version of the decalogue in his version of Exodus, at lines 6471–80, especially since he had been relying solely on Herman as his source for the story before this point.

[Sirs, you have very often heard various biblical stories, for many of them are about Adam, Seth, Noah, Abraham, Isaac, and Jacob, and many others, of which I now have occasion to speak . . .]

Having presupposed that his intended audience will have knowledge of or access to most of the best-known Genesis stories from some other, more extended biblical version, his narrative focuses on the story of Joseph, opening with a drastically edited version of Genesis 29.32–35, 30.1–24. Near the end of this rapid genealogical summary, it is stated that Leah was the mother of Joseph and Benjamin, a mistake followed three lines later in the manuscript by a correct reference to Rachel as Joseph's mother (fol. 92v). Since Harley Scribe B later made good several other brief moments of carelessness elsewhere in his text, it seems likely that this one simply escaped his attention at the stage when he was correcting his copy.[25]

Perhaps the most interesting feature of the intelligently condensed version of Genesis 37–50 offered in the Harley text is the detail of Joseph's attempted seduction by Pharaoh's queen, rather than Potiphar's wife (fol. 93r). Although Wilshere assumes that this deviation from the version of the story found in the Vulgate and Comestor is the redactor's mistake and "an unfortunate lapse,"[26] the same detail concerning the Queen of Egypt is found in Herman's *Bible* and several other vernacular biblical adaptations, including the Middle English *Iacob and Iosep*, which was partly based on Herman.[27] Both versions of the seduction story have a long history and seem to have been widely current in both England and France. It seems not unlikely, then, that, on this occasion, a significant narrative detail in the Harley text was derived from another unknown source that had momentarily taken the place of the Vulgate/ Comestor biblical version.

The Harley redactor's possible reliance on an intermediary text that was itself dependent on the Vulgate and Comestor may well explain why his work sometimes reads like a garbled version of its presumed Latin sources. Although the parallels between the Harley version and Herman's *Bible* are never close enough to enable us to identify Herman as that

---

[25] Scribal self-corrections over erased text or by a later insertion can now be detected on fols. 93v, 95r, 96v, 99v, 101r, 104r, 104v; see also n. 32.

[26] Wilshere, "AN Bible Stories," p. 79.

[27] See n. 13, also lines 195–245 in Napier's edition (Arthur S. Napier, ed., *Iacob and Iosep, a Middle English Poem of the Thirteenth Century* [Oxford, 1916]) and the general survey in Frederic E. Faverty, "Legends of Joseph in Old and Middle English," *PMLA* 43 (1928): 79–104. By contrast, the *Cursor Mundi* poet much preferred the story of Potiphar's wife, the Comestor version of which he seems to have expanded with relish into an extraordinary illustration of the dangers and excesses of careless love (lines 4259–420).

likely intermediary, it is worth noting one other interesting similarity in their treatments of the Joseph story. As such, both Herman and the Harley redactor describe how Joseph's brothers instantly kneel before their unrecognized younger sibling when they come to Egypt.[28] Although the detail of the kneeling brothers is not found in either the Vulgate or Comestor, it is prominently featured in the Harley text, where, as in Herman, it represents the brothers' instinctive recognition of Joseph's greater worth (fols. 93v–94r). But other minor and often unique narrative embellishments to his Latin sources show that the Harley redactor need hardly have relied on his reading of Herman to discover such an obvious and simple "romance-style" motif.[29] It seems far more likely that it was the Harley redactor's wider leisure-time reading experience that made him aware of the expectations of an English audience naturally drawn to "la chanson de geste, le roman, et la vie de saint."[30]

The singularity of the Harley redactor's interests and motives in treating these biblical stories is perhaps most clearly hinted at by the manuscript rubrication of his text. On fol. 99v, the word "Nota" in the margin, written in red ink, draws the reader's eye to the section of the text where the genealogical pedigree of the tribes of Israel found in Numbers 1.5–15 is outlined, the redactor having first emphasized that the Levites are not included in the list (compare Num. 1.47). A second marginal note in red on fol. 100r marks the point corresponding to Numbers 1.46, where the total number of Israelites ready to go to war is recorded correctly as "vj^c mil iij mil v.c.L.," and where it is noted for a second time that the tally has omitted the Levites. The same issue is highlighted a few lines later by the only other marginal notation in the entire item, again written in red, which simply reads "Leuy" (fol. 100r).

The last-mentioned notation draws the reader's attention to the summary account (in just thirteen manuscript lines) of the details given in Numbers 1–4. The summary was probably taken from Comestor[31] and reveals the Harley redactor's particular interest in highlighting the special priestly responsibilities God granted the tribe of Levy as the guardians of the

---

[28] The same detail is found in the *Cursor Mundi* version at line 4816.

[29] A good example is the description of Joseph's new wife Asneth as "vne pucele molt gente la file Putyfares (vn grant mestre e prestre de la ley egipciene), engendre a Helyopoleos vne riche cyte" [a very beautiful young girl, daughter of Potipherah (who was himself a powerful lord and priest of the Egyptian religion), born in Heliopolis, a great city] (fol. 93v). Such details are not found in Comestor or the Vulgate. It is also interesting that the Harley redactor inserted this additional information over an earlier erasure in his text. For knowledge of the Asneth story in England and France, see the useful survey in Russell A. Peck, ed., *Heroic Women from the Old Testament in Middle English Verse* (Kalamazoo, Mich., 1991), pp. 1–21.

[30] Spiele, ed., *Li Romanz de Dieu*, p. 1.

[31] Compare J.-P Migne, ed., *PL* 198:1218–19.

tabernacle. His preoccupation with the rights and privileges of the priestly caste had already been signalled during the story of Joseph when he chose to paraphrase Genesis 47.22, describing how Joseph was able to buy up all the land of Egypt for Pharaoh, with the exception of the land belonging to the temples. The text in question was copied on four lines in the bottom margin of fol. 95r, accompanied by a caret mark, in red, which signals that the passage was probably added to the Harley text as some kind of an afterthought. A similar mark in the outer margin of the main text, about halfway down the page, indicates the point at which the late addition might now most properly be inserted when reading this item. Although there is evidence that the Harley redactor later returned to his text and entered other minor corrections and embellishments over erasures, he elsewhere resisted the temptation to add other marginalia or new material in the bottom margins of his pages.[32]

While obviously anxious to record and highlight the details described above, the Harley redactor was also keen to maintain some distance between his Christian faith and the parallel but strange religious rites of the children of Israel. He does this by strategically inserting a lengthy digression — the only one of its kind in the text — before his account of the rebellion against Moses and the story of Aaron's rod through which God confirmed the role of the priesthood and the law of the tabernacle (Num. 16–17). The digression takes the place of Numbers 15 in the Harley text, but the redactor reminds his audience that their Bible will contain the full details of the sacrificial customs of the people he calls "payen iudeux" (fol. 101v). Having taken a glance at Comestor, his second Latin source, he takes the time to explain with a degree of historical accuracy

> al temps que c'est escrit fut fet, mil aunz cent aunz e trente furent que Iesu Crist primes fust sacrifiez pur nostre pecchie.[33]

> [at the original time of writing, it had been 1130 years since Jesus Christ had been sacrificed for our sin]

---

[32] However the evidence of marginal erasures on fols. 96r, 97r, 98r, 98v, 100v, and 101r suggests that the redactor may have taken some interest in annotating and correcting his translation work as it proceeded.

[33] Fol. 101v. Wilshere, "AN Bible Stories," p. 83, makes a reasonable claim for assuming that this date (1130, to which the thirty-three years of Christ's life should be added) was meant to refer to the date the *Historia scholastica* was written, a point generally supported by Ranulf Higden's entry for the year 1164 in his *Polychronicon* (Trevisa's 1383 translation). The *Polychronicon* includes the information that "þat tyme was maister Peres Comestor in his floures in Fraunce; he wroot a storye of þe eyþer Testament, þat hatte Historia Scolastica" (quoted from James H. Morey, "Peter Comestor, Biblical Paraphrase, and the Medieval Popular Bible," *Speculum* 68 [1993]: 6–35, at p. 25).

Because of that sacrifice so long ago, the Christian church now stands in place of the temple and synagogue of more primitive times. And from now until the end of time, he piously adds, Christians will continue to make their own sacrifice in remembrance of their Creator.

The biblical details that the Harley redactor chose to relate, often in summary fashion, were not always those that attracted other vernacular storytellers dealing with the same widely reworked Old Testament stories. Although often at the expense of the dramatic force of the narrative, such details afforded his readers and listeners some limited opportunity to relate the customs and procedures of the ancient temple, tabernacle, or synagogue in Old Testament times to those of the Christian church in the present day. The *Historia scholastica* itself assumes that the ancient biblical past would hold many points of historical interest for contemporary readers and listeners, of course, and Comestor's influence on the third and fourth books of Ranulf Higden's universal history, the *Polychronicon* (ca. 1327–ca. 1360), is particularly well known.[34] But, in order to understand the likely implications of the Harley redactor's presumed "historical" interest in his biblical stories, it is perhaps more revealing to conclude this discussion by comparing his vernacular efforts to those of the anonymous so-called "Monk of Malmesbury," who is credited with having written the *Vita Edwardi Secundi* in rhythmic Latin prose in the first quarter of the fourteenth century.[35]

The author of the *Vita* was an educated man with legal training, obvious baronial sympathies, and a strong interest in important families and events associated with Hereford and the South West.[36] In writing his memoir of the local disorder, famine, and civil war that, for him, marked Edward II's reign, he almost effortlessly cites biblical quotations in support of his often fairly unguarded political comments. A small detail from his account of Edward's successful 1321–22 campaign to subdue the baronial households in the March offers a convenient example. As the victorious king turns to attack the

---

[34] See John Taylor, *The Universal History of Ranulf Higden* (Oxford, 1966), especially, p. 84; and bibliographical references in Morey, "Peter Comestor," p. 25 (strangely, Comestor's obvious influence on Higden is not mentioned in Antonia Gransden's account of the *Polychronicon* in *Historical Writing in England II: c. 1307 to the Early Sixteenth Century* [Ithaca, 1982], pp. 43–57).

[35] See the text and facing-page translation in the edition by Neil Denholm-Young, *Vita Edwardi Secundi (The Life of Edward the Second)* (London, 1957), to which the page numbering refers. The *Vita* now exists only in a 1729 transcript made by the Oxford antiquarian Thomas Hearne. Its anonymous author was probably a secular clerk, one of several such fourteenth-century historians who took it upon themselves to analyze and record the events of Edward II's reign; see Gransden, *Historical Writing II*, pp. 1–42, especially pp. 3–4.

[36] Denholm-Young, ed., *Vita*, pp. xix–xxviii.

marcher strongholds in the West, the author notes that the calvary was under the command of Fulk FitzWarin.[37] Some version of the FitzWarin ancestral romance may well have provided his apparently intimate knowledge of the characters of Fulks I, II, and III, the founding fathers of the FitzWarin dynasty whose lives also provide the focus for the Anglo-Norman text written by the Harley redactor for Royal 12.C.xii. Fulk VI would hardly have gained much comfort from the account of his family pedigree in the *Vita*, however, since it concludes that a valiant man is often succeeded by one who is less worthy, a sentiment copper-fastened by the *Vita* author's quotation from Romans 9.21.[38]

Elsewhere in his account, the *Vita* author frequently invokes Old and New Testament historical precedents when he wants to underline his reading of the nature and significance of political crises. His account of the threat to the kingdom posed by Piers Gaveston, or by the Scottish war, is sprinkled with biblical allusions.[39] So too is his discussion of the continuing royal threats to church privileges so strenuously resisted by Robert Winchelsey, archbishop of Canterbury. Indeed, it is in his discussion of lay encroachments upon ecclesiastical rights, at two separate points in the *Vita*, that its author betrays his interest in exactly the same biblical passages from Exodus and Numbers that particularly appealed to the Harley redactor. The first of these extended passages takes the form of a panegyric for Winchelsey when he reports the occasion of his death.[40] The *Vita* author alludes to the early years in his archiepiscopate (1294–1303) when Winchelsey and the clergy loyal to him were harried for resisting Edward I's attempts to tax the clergy in the face of the assertion of ecclesiastical privilege in *Clericis laicos*, a papal bull of 1296. Not only has canon law enshrined the rights of the Church in this matter, the *Vita* author indignantly exclaims, but we also have an example from pre-Christian times to show us the proper way forward in the matter: thus even when the Egyptians were starving and put

---

[37] The reference (Denholm-Young, ed., *Vita*, p. 118) is to the sixth FitzWarin to bear the illustrious name (ca. 1277–ca. 1336). See the family pedigree in Hathaway et al., eds., *Fouke le Fitz Waryn*, p. xxiv.

[38] The *Vita* version reads: "Sic figulus iuxta artem suam quedam uasa ad honorem, quedam componit ad contumeliam" (Denholm-Young, ed., *Vita*, p. 118); compare the Douay version: "Or hath not the potter power over the clay, of the same lump, to make one vessel unto honour, and another unto dishonour?" (Rom. 9.21).

[39] The best examples appear in Denholm-Young, ed., *Vita*, pp. 16, 25, 27, 30 (Gaveston), and pp. 54, 56, 76 (Scottish war).

[40] Denholm-Young, ed., *Vita*, pp. 40–42; Winchelsey died in 1313. A convenient and useful account of his life and career is by Jeffrey Howard Denton, *Robert Winchelsey and the Crown, 1294–1313: A Study in the Defence of Ecclesiastical Liberty* (Cambridge, 1980).

themselves under royal control, the priests and guardians of the temples were still allowed to remain free (an allusion to Gen. 47.22).

The second passage that takes up this theme deals with the events of 1316.[41] At this time of famine across Europe and a Scottish war, the English bishops sided with Edward II rather than their clergy in the king's request for ecclesiastical goods to aid the royal cause. Even the granting of an ecclesiastical tenth to the king irritates the *Vita* author since, in his view, neither the Church nor the poor should be despoiled: "Nam bona ecclesiae sunt bona pauperum!" Under Pharaoh, he reminds his readers, the priests were exempt from taxation (a reference to Gen. 47.26). And in the book of Numbers the tribe of the Levites was also granted special privileges as the priests of the children of Israel (Num. 1–4). Let the king remember how Moses and Aaron appeased the anger of the Lord by prayer and sacrifice (Num. 16–17); the king has received the power of the sword from the Church to protect it rather than oppress it, so let his wars be funded instead from the royal treasury.

The concerns of the Harley redactor in retelling biblical stories from Genesis, Exodus, and Numbers would almost certainly have struck a chord with the *Vita* author. In their various ways, both writers demonstrate a particular interest in issues relating to ecclesiastical privileges in biblical times. Both also share some knowledge of the first three generations of the FitzWarin family, although that knowledge manifests itself in different ways in their writings. And since the Harley redactor and Harley Scribe B are likely to have been the same person, the other items copied by him for both the Harley 2253 collection and Royal 12.C.xii show that he often shared the *Vita* author's lively interest in contemporary social and political conditions. Such an interest frequently expressed itself in surprising ways in the three written languages of record in fourteenth-century England around which English cultural attitudes formed. Therefore we need no longer be all that surprised or embarrassed by the survival of the Harley redactor's personal selection of prose biblical stories from Genesis, Exodus, and Numbers on fols. 92v–105r in Harley 2253. His text may sometimes read more like a draft summary than a polished work, yet it also offers its intended readers and listeners a carefully pointed version of biblical history. From the point of view of a fourteenth-century vernacular church propagandist, the historical and political lesson contained in the Harley Bible stories is important and clear enough; it may even have been one that the earliest readers of Harley 2253 knew the third Edward now on the throne of England could only afford to ignore at his peril.[42]

---

[41] Denholm-Young, ed., *Vita*, pp. 76–78.

[42] I am most grateful to my colleagues Evelyn Mullally and Jason O'Rourke for reading an early draft of this essay and making a number of helpful suggestions for improvement. All remaining inaccuracies are solely my responsibility.

Anthologizing Ribaldry:
Five Anglo-Norman Fabliaux

Barbara Nolan

As everyone knows, BL MS Harley 2253 includes a wealth of Middle English lyrics of signal importance to the history of medieval literature in England. Yet very few scholars would be able to name the Anglo-Norman bawdy fictions in Harley. These poems have rarely been studied either in themselves or in their material life as written texts rubbing up against discourses of very different kinds contiguous with them in the manuscript.[1] Nor have they been much discussed as tales composed or redacted in England for Englishmen, or as links to be reckoned with between the continental fabliau tradition and Chaucer. There are reasons for this neglect, one of which is their hybrid linguistic status. Because they are written in the "faus françeis d'Angletere" rather than the "frenssh of Paris," continental scholars have generally side-stepped them.[2] By the same token, since canons

---

[1] For notable exceptions, see Nico van den Boogaard, "Le Fabliau anglo-normand," in *Proceedings [of the] Third International Beast Epic, Fable, and Fabliau Colloquium* (1979), ed. Jan Goossens and Timothy Sodmann (Vienna, 1981), pp. 66–77, and Thomas Corbin Kennedy, ed., "Anglo-Norman Poems about Love, Women, and Sex from British Museum MS Harley 2253" (Ph.D. diss., Columbia University, 1973). Kennedy edits and translates four of the five fabliaux I discuss here (excluding the *Jongleur*) and provides a useful introduction to them.

[2] For the old view of AN as already on its way to being "dead" in the thirteenth century, see M. K. Pope, *From Latin to Modern French with Especial Consideration of Anglo-Norman* (Manchester, 1934), p. 424. This view has, however, been compellingly disputed by William Rothwell. As Rothwell puts it, AN was becoming by the later thirteenth century "a highly sophisticated instrument of English law[,] . . . was embarking on a long and successful career as the language of administration," and "was destined to be used over the whole of the next century and beyond for a wide variety of literary productions . . . from the political satire through adventure yarns to religious allegory and mystical outpourings" ("From Latin to Modern French: Fifty Years On," *Bulletin of the John Rylands University Library of Manchester* 68 [1985]: 192). It is in this context, I believe, that Harley's AN fabliaux deserve investigation. The phrase "faus françeis d'Angletere" is one the Nun of Barking uses to describe the French she knows (Östen Södergard, ed., *La Vie d'Edouard le Confesseur: Poème anglo-normand du XIIᵉ siècle* [Uppsala, 1948], p. 109,

of British literature tend to privilege texts composed in the Middle English of emerging insular nationhood, the Anglo-Norman fabliaux, even when mentioned, remain very little known.[3] None of the Harley fabliaux, moreover, offers us the kind of polished literary "cherles tale" Chaucer gives us, say, in the Miller's Tale. As scribal copies, most if not all of the texts we have are corrupted or truncated in relation to other extant redactions or to the imagined completeness of lost originals. Yet in spite of their imperfections as literary texts, each one of them can teach us a good deal about the fabliau tradition in fourteenth-century England and about the culture, textual and social, that embraced them.

In this essay I interrogate five Harley fabliaux, asking how they participate in the generic tradition with which they are usually identified and what communicative functions they seem to serve in the three interlinked quires of the manuscript that preserves them. Before turning to the tales, though, and the block of quires they occupy, I need to raise two fundamental questions my title begs. The first of these has to do with the assumption that Harley 2253 is, in fact, an anthology involving the scribe's "culling of flowers" and arranging them in order to guide the reading of a particular audience. Each of the Harley tales I discuss reveals its roots in traditions of oral performance. Yet they also participate as written texts in a trilingual English book. Because their ribaldry jostles for attention in the manuscript with religious and secular lyrics, saints' legends, prayers, political satire, treatises on good conduct, and antifeminist diatribes, these tales raise the question for us as to how the scribe copying them might have expected such fictions to function for silent readers. Taking up his stylus to begin each new quire, did he copy texts, including the

---

line 7). It is noteworthy that every one of the AN tales in Harley included in Willem Noomen and Nico van den Boogaard, eds., *Nouveau Recueil complet des fabliaux* (hereafter *NRCF*), 10 vols. (Assen, 1983–98) is described disparagingly as containing all the [unfortunate] characteristics of late AN. Variations of the following comment are used to characterize the Harley texts: "Les graphies sont souvent aberrantes par rapport aux normes continentales, le mètre est irrégulier et certaines rimes n'existent qu'à la faveur d'une prononciation insulaire. . . . En plus, la règle qui interdit de faire suivre deux couplets sur la même rime n'a pas été suivie dans une dizaine de cas" [The spellings are often aberrant in relation to continental norms, the meter is irregular and certain rhymes work only thanks to insular pronunciation. . . . Moreover, the rule that forbids two successive couplets using the same rhyme has been violated in about ten cases] (3.49).

[3] For a refreshing departure from this norm with regard not to fabliaux but to insular romance, see Susan Crane, *Insular Romance: Politics, Faith and Culture in Anglo-Norman and Middle English Literature* (Berkeley, 1986). See especially her introduction for a detailed account of the attitudes on both sides of the Channel that have discouraged critical attention to AN literature generally. A full study of the AN fabliaux — a key vehicle for the transmission of French bawdy tales to England — would include not only the Harley fabliaux, but also those in several other thirteenth- and fourteenth-century English manuscript anthologies like Harley.

fabliaux, in a more or less random order, as some have suggested?[4] Or did he deliberately collate his texts, placing the bawdy tales at particular points in his book in order to enliven a large argument he was developing in and through all of the texts in his codex?

I am not the first to wonder about this question. Both Carter Revard and Susanna Fein have, in different ways, pointed in just this direction.[5] Their arguments, moreover, parallel my own recent work and that of others on continental French manuscripts containing fabliaux, which seem, like Harley, to have been organized dialectically for the sake of instigating ethical debate.[6] In this regard, Harley 2253, mirroring its continental counterparts, provides further evidence that such books were often designed as anthologies — and anthologies of a certain kind. As I mean to demonstrate by looking closely at one independent block of quires in Harley, there can be scant doubt that the Harley scribe aimed to juxtapose key themes within and across generic boundaries and to engage his English audience in responding to their interplay. It would be wrong to imply that either Harley or the French or English fabliau-anthologies like it aspired to the compilatory coherence of great *specula* like those, for instance, by Vincent of Beauvais.[7] Nor do scribes provide narrative or moral frames for their fabliau-anthologies to guide (or complicate) interpretation in the way that poets like Chaucer or sermon writers like Jacques de Vitry do. Yet many of the scribes arranging their materials in anthologies like Harley do seem to have imposed more or less fully one or more strong principles of organization in putting their books together. Of these, the principles of hierarchy,

---

[4] For a succinct account of scholarly opinion on Harley as a "miscellany," see Carter Revard, "*Gilote et Johane*: An Interlude in B. L. MS. Harley 2253," *Studies in Philology* 79 (1982): 127n11.

[5] See Revard, "*Gilote et Johane*," pp. 127, 129; Fein, "A Saint 'Geynest under Gore': Marina and the Love Lyrics of the Seventh Quire" in this volume (pp. 351–70).

[6] For work on this question, see Luciano Rossi, "À propos de l'histoire de quelques recueils de fabliaux: Le Code de Berne," *Le Moyen Français* 13 (1985): 58–94; Jean Rychner, "Deux Copistes au travail: Pour une étude textuelle globale du manuscrit 354 de la Bibliothèque de la Bourgeoisie de Berne," in *Medieval French Textual Studies in Memory of T. B. W. Reid*, ed. Ian Short (London, 1984), pp. 187–218; Richard Trachsler, "Le Recueil Paris, BN ms fr. 12603," *Cultura Neolatina* 54 (1994): 189–211; Keith Busby, "Fabliaux and the New Codicology," forthcoming in a festschrift in honor of Per Nykrog; Barbara Nolan, "Turning Over the Leaves of Medieval Fabliau-Anthologies: The Case of Bibliothèque Nationale MS. Français 2173," *Medieval Perspectives* 8 (1998): 1–31.

[7] On thirteenth-century developments in compilations like Vincent's, see Malcolm B. Parkes, "The Influence of the Concepts of *Ordinatio* and *Compilatio* on the Development of the Book," in *Medieval Learning and Literature: Essays Presented to R. W. Hunt*, ed. J. J. G. Alexander and M. T. Gibson (Oxford, 1975), pp. 115–41.

contrariety,[8] and exemplary mirroring are the most frequent, and all three seem to have entered into the ordering of Harley 2253.

The second question my title begs has to do with the problem of identifying the Harley fabliaux. At least five Harley poems invite labeling under the rubric "fabliau," although only four of them have been admitted into Willem Noomen and Nico van den Boogaard's *Nouveau Recueil complet des fabliaux*. These include: *Les Trois Dames qui troverent un vit* (no. 75a; fol. 110ra–va); *Le Chevalier et la corbaille* (no. 82; fols. 115va–117ra); *Le Dit de la gageure* (no. 84; fol. 118rb–vb); and *Le Chevalier qui fist les cons parler* (no. 87; fols. 122vb–124va). A fifth poem, *Le Jongleur d'Ely et le Roi d'Angleterre* (no. 75; fols. 107va–109vb) — the one Noomen and van den Boogard exclude — has had a more fraught, less stable career among scholars of fabliaux than the other four. Yet its uneven history is more the fault of modern editors and critics than of the poem itself. Indeed, its fate demonstrates an axiom worth repeating about medieval texts, namely, that they rarely if ever conform neatly to the "rules" of a single genre. When Joseph Bédier, confronting the problem of the *Jongleur*'s form, attempted to categorize it in his seminal book on the fabliaux, he struggled visibly to give it a place on his list in spite of its explicit moral interests (to which a counterfeit, pseudo-Anglo-Norman prologue added by an early nineteenth-century editor would have given added emphasis).[9] "The fabliaux," he argues,

---

[8] This principle is given one of its best known formulations by Jean de Meun, himself a master at deploying the principle in the *Roman de la Rose*:

Ainsinc va des contreres choses,
les unes sunt des autres gloses;
et qui l'une an veust defenir,
de l'autre li doit souvenir,
ou ja, par nule antancion,
n'i metra diffinicion;
car qui des .II. n'a connoissance,
ja n'i connoistra differance,
san quoi ne peut venir en place
diffinicion que l'an face. (21543–552)

[Things go by contraries; one is the gloss of the other. If one wants to define one of the pair, he must remember the other, or he will never, by any intention, assign a definition to it; for he who has no understanding of the two will never understand the difference between them, and without this difference no definition that one may make can come to anything.]

Jean de Meun, *Le Roman de la Rose*, ed. Félix Lecoy, 3 vols. (Paris, 1970–75), 3.148; *The Romance of the Rose*, trans. Charles Dahlberg (Princeton, 1983), p. 351.

[9] The first scholar to edit the *Jongleur*, the antiquarian Sir Francis Palgrave, seems to suggest his own sense of its complexity by calling it a "flabel" at one point and a "dit" at another *(Cy ensuyt une chanson moult pitoyable des grievouses oppressions* . . . [London, 1818], pp. xi, xiii). Palgrave

are never moral *dits*; but this is not to say that they must necessarily be immoral; and, without losing their character as joking tales, they can share borders with this neighboring, distinct genre [the moral *dit*]. . . . *Le roi d'Angleterre et le Jongleur d'Ely* is on the edge between the two genres.[10]

Here, as at several points in his study, Bédier's prose seems to suggest his own discomfort with a restrictive generic definition clearly at odds with his sound intuition that many actual fabliaux are ambiguous with regard to their formal affiliations. The *Jongleur*, as a self-proclaimed exercise in ribaldry, not only borders on being a moral *dit*; it also draws into its orbit the forms of the lai, the pedagogical dialogue, and the exemplum. What the

---

also invented an *accessus* of sorts, emphasizing the poem's didactic trajectory: "Cy comence le flabel du Jongleur de Ely et de monseignour le Roy d'Engletere, lequel Jongleur dona counsail al Roy pur sei amender e son estat garder" [Here begins the fabliau of the Jongleur of Ely and my lord the king of England, which jongleur gave advice to the king so as to correct himself and protect his status] (p. xi). In addition, he composed a prologue in pseudo-Anglo-Norman, further privileging the poem's moral function over its bawdy linguistic play. So credible was Palgrave's pious, though counterfeit celebration of the loyal minstrel's truth-telling and wise counsel to the king that it became part of the poem's editorial tradition, repeated (and "corrected"!) in two different French editions published in 1834: Francisque Michel, ed., *La Riote du monde* (Paris, 1834), pp. 27–43; and Abbé Gervais de La Rue, *Essais historiques sur les bardes, les jongleurs et les trouvères normands et anglo-normands*, 3 vols. (Caen, 1834), l. 286–98. In their important *Recueil général et complet des fabliaux des XIIIᵉ et XIVᵉ siècles*, 6 vols. (1872–90; repr. New York, 1964), Anatole de Montaiglon and Gaston Raynaud likewise printed Palgrave's prologue to the *Jongleur*, not realizing that there is not the slightest evidence for it in the MS. When at the end of the nineteenth century Bédier used the Montaiglon-Raynaud edition as the basis for his study, *Les Fabliaux: Études de littérature populaire et d'histoire littéraire du moyen âge* (Paris, 1892), he tested the *Jongleur* — as he did every other bawdy tale — by the rule of his own definition of fabliaux as "contes à rire en vers."

[10] Bédier, *Les Fabliaux*, 6th ed. (Paris, 1964): ". . . les fabliaux ne sont point des dits moraux; mais ce n'est pas dire qu'ils doivent nécessairement être immoraux; et, sans perdre leur caractère de contes plaisants, ils peuvent confiner à ce genre voisin et distinct" (p. 34). The test Bédier puts forward for judging whether the dominant generic mode in a poem is the fabliau or the *dit moral* involves a subjective critical judgment as to emphasis: "In case of difficulty in deciding [between genres], we have to ask ourselves this question: Did the *trouvère* want to create a work by a tale-teller or by a moralist? Has he been drawn to his subject through a story that amused him or, on the contrary, has he imagined the story on account of its moral lesson?" ["En cas d'indécision, nous devons nous poser cette question: si le trouvère a voulu plutôt faire oeuvre de conteur, ou de moraliste; s'il à été attiré vers son sujet par le conte, qui l'amusait, ou s'il a, au contraire, imaginé le conte pour la moralité"] (p. 34).

poet creates in effect is a small anthology of (and debate among) disparate literary kinds, including the bawdy tale.[11] In this respect, moreover, the *Jongleur* — as the first of the five fabliaux in the manuscript — anticipates the comparable generic "anthologizing" also characteristic of the other four. Even more importantly, the *Jongleur* as the *first* fabliau in the anthology provides a defense of ribaldry as an honorable part of Harley's textual universe. The *Jongleur*'s dramatic dialogue, orchestrated by a rowdy minstrel and sanctioned by no less an authority than the king of England, establishes a solid ethical rationale for the other bawdy tales in the scribe's book and also for the several ribald satires that complement them. Bawdy fictions, as the poem's minstrel shows, can freely make fun of complacent illusions about the world, tell the truth about secular treachery, and thereby encourage prudent behavior among the socially and politically powerful.

Block Six of MS Harley 2253: Quires 12, 13, and 14

The block of gatherings in the Harley MS harboring all five of the fabliaux I discuss here exemplifies the scribe's practices in putting his anthology together.[12] His mode of constructing the book, like that of many of his continental counterparts, seems to have involved something like the processes of invention medieval rhetorical handbooks recommended for poets, letter writers, and orators. Starting with a handful of topics, he selects his *materia* from a range of available short texts that embody those themes.[13]

---

[11] In thus weaving elements drawn from other genres into the fabric of his fabliau, the *Jongleur*'s composer is not exceptional either among fablulists in general or among the other authors of the Harley fabliaux. For a fuller discussion of this issue, see Barbara Nolan, "Promiscuous Fictions: Medieval Bawdy Tales and Their Textual Liaisons," in *The Body and the Soul in Medieval Literature*, ed. P. Boitani and A. Torti (Woodbridge, Suffolk, 1999), pp. 79–105.

[12] In the fourteen bifolia that make up Harley's sixth block of gatherings, there are twenty-eight separate texts: twenty of these are in verse, eight in ME and twelve in AN. Of the eight prose texts, four are in AN and two, in Latin; one combines ME with AN, and one, AN with Latin. On the quires and independent blocks of Harley 2253, see the chart appended to Susanna Fein's essay in this volume, pp. 371–76.

[13] A precious Latin notation in another trilingual anthology composed in England in the early fourteenth century — Cambridge University Library MS Gg.i.1 — gives some hints as to how this process of invention and arrangement of parts must have worked both for poets and for scribes. The Latin outline lists the topics a poet might use for composing a poem in praise of women or that an anthologist might use as a guide to selecting verses on the theme of the goodness of women:
Mulier prefertur viro, scilicet:
Materia: Quia Adam factus de limo terre, Eva de costa Ade.

Because the topics characteristically present in such compilations are closely interlinked — mainly having to do with the treacherous way of the world, the problem of human conduct, and the need for salvation — he can move freely from one to the other, knowing that his readers will recognize, delight in, and very likely learn from his particular arrangements of them. Sometimes the scribe orders his texts to articulate affinities between them, and sometimes to emphasize disjunction or contradiction. For readers, the experience is almost bound to be rather that of montage or layering than of anything like linear progress from beginning to end.[14] The Harley block we are about to study offers just such a montage of texts, and the fabliaux within it constitute one of the most striking elements of surprise. A handful of topics guides the choice of texts. The first of these is the problem of sin and salvation, and the block begins and ends with pious texts focused on Christian salvation and the life of the spirit. In between, however, attention is abruptly shifted to much more vexed questions as to how one can best negotiate within the world of ordinary discourse, politics, ecclesiastical abuse, and sexual warfare. How — most of the texts in the block ask, either straightforwardly or satirically — is a gentleman to conduct himself so as to win honor and avoid shame? And how is he to approach the fraught problem of women, honored by God through his own mother Mary, but also deceptive, fickle, lecherous, conniving, and altogether dangerous?

Loco: Quia Adam factus extra paradisum, Eva in paradiso.

In conceptione: Quia mulier concepit Deum, quod homo non potuit.

Apparicione: Quia Christus primo apparuit mulieri post resurrectionem, scilicet Magdalene.

Exaltacione: Quia mulier exaltata est super choros angelorum, scilicet beata Marie. (fol. 392r) [Woman is superior to man, namely: *In (terms of) matter*: Because Adam was made from earth, Eve from Adam's rib. *In (terms of) place*: Because Adam was made outside paradise, Eve within paradise. *In (terms of) conception*: Because woman conceived God, which a man could not do. *In (terms of) apparition*: Because Christ appeared first to a woman after the Resurrection, namely (Mary) Magdalen. *In (terms of) exaltation*: Because a woman has been exalted above the choir of angels, namely Blessed Mary.]

In CUL Gg.i.1, which is an anthology not unlike Harley 2253, this little paradigm in fact follows closely upon a poem praising women, *La Bonté des femmes* (fol. 390v), a poem that uses the Virgin Mary as one key to praising women. Both the Latin outline and the poem, moreover, share the quire's space with pious prayers — the Credo, Pater Noster, and Ave Maria in AN (fol. 392v). In this case, the scribe seems to be laying bare for us a principle of organization not only for this particular quire, but also for his anthology as a whole.

[14] On the idea of layering in the construction of fabliau-anthologies, see Nolan, "Promiscuous Fictions" (note 11 above). On the concept of montage, see also Jacqueline Cerquiligni, "Le Clerc et l'écriture: Le *Voir dit* de Guillaume de Machaut et la définition du dit," in *Literatur in der Gesellschaft des Spätmittelalters*, ed. Hans Ulrich Gumbrecht (Heidelberg, 1980), pp. 151–68.

I say "gentleman" and "he" in talking about the readers the scribe seems to have had in mind because the texts in this block of Harley appear in general to be directed to an audience of upper-class men rather than to a mixed audience. Three conduct books for young men anchor the varied discourses of the three quires: *Urbain le courtois* (no. 79; fols. 112rc–113vc), the last complete poem in Quire 12; the series of prudential aphorisms on conduct in Middle English called *Hending* (no. 89; fols. 125ra–127a), located near the beginning of Quire 14; and the *Enseignements de saint Louis à son fils* (no. 94; fols. 128v–129v), found in the middle of Quire 14. In addition, four verse treatises and a lyric in the three quires raise the question of women, but women viewed entirely from a male point of view. Three of the treatises on women and the lyric damn them, while one treatise alone praises them.[15] Finally, two poems of a different kind, pointing to abuses in the political and religious realms, physically link the quires into a free-standing block. A satire against the trailbaston courts (no. 80; fols. 113vb–114v), spoken by an outlaw who has been forced out of proper society by them, ends the twelfth quire and begins the thirteenth, while a satire against laxity — especially sexual laxity — among monks and nuns (no. 86; fols. 121ra–122va) ends the thirteenth quire and begins the fourteenth. I have deliberately left until last the five fabliaux in the block, and it is to these that I now turn, looking especially at how each one intensifies, plays with, or challenges the thematic program of the block of gatherings it inhabits.

Harley Quire 12 and Its Two Fabliaux

Eight poems and a part of a ninth occupy the four bifolia (fols. 106r–113v) of Harley's twelfth quire, including two fabliaux — *Le Jongleur d'Ely et le Roi d'Angleterre* and *Les Trois Dames qui troverent un vit*. In the quire as a whole the Harley scribe invites his audience to traverse familiar terrain, both sacred and profane. Perhaps honoring a hierarchy of values, he begins the gathering with a simple focus on the sacred before moving to the messiness of the secular. The first two poems of Quire 12 deal with the simplest and most universal of devotional themes — fragile humankind's plight as sinful and the concomitant need for divine mercy. Written in Middle English (surely the mother

---

[15] The five are: *Le Dit des femmes* (praising women), and *Le Blasme des femmes* and Nicholas Bozon's *De la femme et de la pie* (attacking women) (Quire 12; nos. 76–78); an AN misogamist/misogynist verse treatise on Walter Map's *De conjuge non ducenda* (Quire 13; no. 83); and a ME lyric called *The Way of Women's Love* (attacking women) (Quire 14; no. 93). The poem praising women is a variation on a well-known text called *Le Bien des femmes*. Lines taken from this poem appear verbatim not only in Harley's *Le Dit des femmes* but also in its redaction of *Urbain le courtois* (no. 79).

tongue for most of Harley's anticipated audience), the two lyrics address respectively God and those who want to know themselves. In the first poem (no. 73), with God's name as its (and therefore the quire's) first word, the speaker acknowledges the greatness of divine power: "God, þat al þis myhtes may."[16] Against such majesty he confesses himself "þe wrst of alle" (line 16; fol. 106r) — a sinner who can only be saved by God's and Christ's mercy. The second lyric, *Sayings of St. Bernard* (no. 74), explicitly speaking to those "þat wolleþ ouselue yknowe" (line 2; fol. 106r), turns on a catalogue of commonplaces about the frailty of the flesh, the mutability of all things in the transitory world, the threat of the devil, and the need to seek refuge in Christ's cross.[17] The mirror this poem and the one preceding it hold up to devout readers by way of movingly subjective elegy could not be more limpid or more conventional, and their prayerful tone leaves no room for play or irony.

When we move to the very next poem in the gathering, however, the *mise-en-scène* has utterly changed, and so too has the language. The first ribald tale the Harley scribe copied into the twelfth quire of his anthology, *Le Jongleur d'Ely et le Roi d'Angleterre*,[18] draws us abruptly away from God and into the morass of worldly talk with its possibilities for ironic play, riddles, double entendres, punning, scandal, and malevolent gossip. The language, moreover, is not the English of devotional prayer but rather the Anglo-Norman of fourteenth-century upper-class social conversation — a shift that may well provide specific evidence as to the status of the audience the Harley scribe assumed for the fabliaux intercalated in his anthology. This possibility is reinforced by the dramatic situation in the *Jongleur*. It is the king of England himself who participates in a ribald minstrel's impudent language game and, in the end, takes the minstrel as his moral guide. Towards the poem's conclusion, the king humbly puts to him the anguished question:

> "Quei me sauerez vus counsiler
> Coment me pus countener

---

[16] G. L. Brook, ed., *The Harley Lyrics: The Middle English Lyrics of MS. Harley 2253*, 4th ed. (Manchester, 1968), pp. 68–69 (no. 29).

[17] *Sayings of Saint Bernard: Man's Three Foes*, in F. J. Furnivall, ed., *The Minor Poems of the Vernon MS.*, Part 2, EETS o.s. 117 (1901; repr. Millwood, N. Y., 1987), pp. 511–22.

[18] The manuscript gives no title for this poem. Sir Francis Palgrave first named it in his 1818 edition, calling it "le flabel du Jongleur de Ely de monseignour le Roy de Engletere." Michel renamed it in his 1834 edition "Le Roi d'Angleterre et le Jongleur d'Ely" (*La Riote du monde*, p. 28), and Montaiglon and Raynaud in their influential edition followed Michel.

E sauntz blame me garder
Que vm ne me vueille mesparler?" (lines 382–85; fol. 109vb)

["What advice do you have for me concerning how I am to conduct myself in the world and to watch out, without being blamed, so that no one may want to slander me?"]

By accepting a lead role in the fabliau and embracing the lessons the minstrel, as a self-confessed "ribaud," gives him, the king effectively authorizes all of the Harley fabliaux, not for their joking *plaisanteries* alone, but also for the accurate moral vision of the world's ways that their comic play catalyzes. The king's own interactive "reading" of the jongleur's puns, riddles, debauched life — at first reluctant, then enlightened — provides in fact an ethical model of considerable prestige, showing Harley's likely audience of English gentlemen how to read the fabliaux it contains.

Neither the *Jongleur*'s dramatic situation nor its riddling linguistic play nor its declared exemplary function nor its narrative outcome is original. The author of the Harley poem adapts, shortens, streamlines, and clarifies a continental prose fabliau-cum-dialogue, *La Riote du monde* [Debate of the World].[19] In continental versions of the *Riote* an unidentified first-person speaker is riding from Amiens to Corbie when he encounters "le

---

[19] The *Riote* is extant in prose or verse redactions, either whole or fragmentary, in at least five other MSS, and it is therefore not impossible that the *Jongleur* drew on an earlier poetic version, rather than the prose dialogue (the only version available in a printed edition). Three of the prose texts have been edited by J. Ulrich, "*La Riote du monde*," *Zeitschrift für romanische Philologie* 8 (1884): 275–89. Of the MSS containing these, one is a thirteenth-century French fabliau-anthology, Paris, BN MS fr. 1553, a MS at least as carefully organized as Harley; the second is Bern, Bibliothèque de la Bourgeoisie MS 113; and the third is Cambridge, Trinity College MS O.2.45, like Harley, a trilingual anthology, but very likely earlier than Harley by nearly a century. Written in a beautiful AN hand, it once belonged to, and was perhaps written at, Cerne Abbey in Dorset. The AN rendering of *La Riote du monde* in the Cambridge MS, though not in verse, indicates that the French text had already made its way to England by the later thirteenth century. In addition, there is a fragment of a continental French version in octosyllabic couplets extant on the flyleaf of Paris, BN MS fr. 1588. When, in 1834, Michel edited the last lines of this poem, he was not aware of its intimate connection with the prose *Riote*, and Victor LeClerc, in his influential discussion of the fabliaux ("Fabliaux," in *Histoire littéraire de la France*, 39 vols. [Paris, 1895], 23.69–215) perpetuates Michel's misperception, supposing that the poem shares simply its title with the *Riote*. Another AN poetic adaptation appears in London, BL MS Arundel 220, fol. 303v. There is also mention in the table of contents of London, BL MS Arundel 292 of a text, now missing, entitled *De rege et joculatore*, but this work is quite possibly in Latin. The AN poem was translated in the early nineteenth century by J. J. C. Lockhart under the title "The King and the Minstrel of Ely" (in *The Keepsake*, ed. Frederic Mansel Reynolds [London, 1829], pp. 354–59).

roi" (no doubt understood as the king of France) and the joking conversation begins immediately. By contrast, in the Anglo-Norman *Jongleur*, the speaker is identified as a minstrel from Ely, and the monarch with whom he debates is explicitly the king of England. By this means, the *Jongleur* gives us a much more sharply focused dramatic situation than any of the continental redactions we have, and an emphatically English one. It also brings more sharply to the fore the source's underlying argument about the dangers of ordinary social discourse for anyone interested in safeguarding identity and reputation.

Le Jongleur d'Ely et le Roi d'Angleterre, like two other fabliaux in Harley's sixth block, begins as a courtly lai or a romance might. The opening scene has about it the aura of a charming miniature, dramatizing an oft-repeated visual image of a royal patron being entertained by his court minstrel. The king and his household are taking their leisure in an idyllic setting, a meadow near London. This delightful scene proposes to us a *locus amoenus*, a place apart from the responsibilities of court. Into this setting — this cultural space of comfort and security — comes "un menestrel" seeking "merueille e auenture" (line 4).[20] The *Jongleur* poet takes pains to emphasize his protagonist's specific *métier* as a minstrel by having him wear a richly decorated drum around his neck. And this detail only solidifies our expectation that the tale will unfold as many an Arthurian lai and romance does with the visitor proposing a quest or adventure to the king. Although this expectation is deflected for most of the poem, it is not, in the end, disapppointed. Instead of a physical journey from one geographical point to another, the fiction leads the king on a quest through the thick wood of malevolent gossip to arrive at a new level of moral self-awareness. For the better part of the poem, however, the mode of presentation is rather that of a fabliau-cum-dialogue-cum-exemplum than that of a lai. Immediately following the opening tableau, the poet begins to deconstruct his initial icon.

The process of breaking down the romance idyll, of displacing the meadow — metaphor for the world as pastoral haven — with the confused noise of a hostile field full of folk, proceeds in two stages. To begin, the poet deploys the widely diffused medieval genre of the pedagogical dialogue. But this is a dialogue with a difference. When the minstrel comes upon the royal entourage, the king courteously initiates what he anticipates will be the most conventional of conversations with him. Yet the conversation that ensues is anything but conventional. The jongleur refuses to give the expected answers. Instead, using only puns and riddles (the stuff of improvised oral performance), he plays the role of a joking *fableor*. At the very start of the conversation, the king asks a question he presumes will enlighten him as to the minstrel's social identity: "Ou qy este vus, sire

---

[20] All references to the *Jongleur* will be to the edition by Ulrich, "*La Riote*," pp. 275–79, checked against the facsimile of Harley 2253: N. R. Ker, intro., *Facsimile of British Museum MS. Harley 2253*, EETS o.s. 255 (London, 1965); items numbers correspond to Ker's list, pp. ix–xvi.

ioglour?" [Whose man are you, sir jongleur?] (line 10; fol. 107va). Refusing to give either names or facts, the minstrel replies, "Sire, I am [pledged] to my lord." And so the dialogue proceeds with the king questioning, the minstrel evading direct answers:

> "Quy est toun seignur?" fet le roy.
> "Le baroun ma dame, par ma foy."
> "Quy est ta dame, par amour?"
> "Sire, la femme mon seignour." (lines 13–16; fol. 107va)

["Who is your lord?" says the king. "My lady's husband, by my faith." "Who is your lady, for love's sake?" "Sire, my lord's wife."]

Comic as such refusals are — especially if we imagine them performed orally with ventriloquized changes of voice as the debate moves back and forth from the urbane king to the perverse minstrel — they also raise serious questions about reputation. How, in the face of the *riote* or debate that constitutes ordinary discourse in the world, can humans, including the king, protect themselves from slander?

For the first third of the fiction, this argument remains latent, only implicated in the jongleur's bantering play with the king's questions. The king remains the king, and the minstrel, on the other side of a firm social barrier, jokingly mocks his effort to converse according to the rules of social propriety. Yet the security of the king's position (and identity) begins to weaken as the first movement of the poem nears its end. In what becomes an absurd discussion about the minstrel's nag, the king asks about its tongue: "Ditez moi s'il a lange bone?" ["Tell me, does he have a good tongue?"] (line 117; fol. 108ra). While the king wants to know about the horse's literal tongue, the minstrel takes the word *langue* metaphorically as "language." His nag, he says, has never told a lie nor abused the good name of his neighbor nor, he promises, will he ever accuse the king. By innuendo, the minstrel's playful retort exposes a very real threat the king faces to his political position, but at this point it is an innuendo the king fails to hear. His final effort to get at the facts brings him to ask the jongleur, "De quele terre estez vous?" ["What is your native land?"] (line 134; fol. 108rb). With his delight in obfuscating wordplay, the jongleur translates the word *terre* from its metaphoric to its literal sense, "earth, dirt," in declaring:

> "Sire, estez vus tywlers ou potters
> Qe si folement demaundez?
> Pur quoi demandez 'de quele tere'?
> Volez vus de moi potz fere?" (lines 135–38)

["Sire, are you a maker of tiles or a potter that you ask so foolishly? Why do you ask 'of what earth'? Do you want to make a pot out of me?"]

In asking the king what he *is*, the minstrel directly raises the question of the king's identity, and the king fails to understand what is really at issue.

At this point in the fiction, just before the social barriers separating the king from the jongleur begin to collapse, they seem most solidly in place. So irritated does the king become at the minstrel's perverse riddles that he finally protests: "Ie ne prise pas vos dys" ["I do not value your words"] (line 129). Not surprisingly, the jongleur parries the king's put-down: "Ne ie les vos que vaillent pys. / Ie di bourde pur fere gent ryre." ["Nor I yours that are worth less. I tell lying jokes to make people laugh."] (lines 130–31). Now at last, as the king, ever more angry, asks what sort of chap the minstrel is, the dialectical terms of the poem's improbable drama begin to come fully to light. "E qe diables auez vus," he demands,

> "Que si responez a rebours?
> Tiel ribaud ne oy ie vnqe mes.
> Diez de quel maner tu es." (lines 139–42)

["And what devil possesses you that you answer by contradicting? I have never heard such a debauched fellow. Tell (me) what sort you are."]

Once the king puts his question in terms of the minstrel's ribaldry and his profession, the jongleur for the first time in the poem gives a direct answer. He is, he says, part of a company of rowdy fellows who like to eat and drink at the expense of others, who sleep late and prefer as far as they can to occupy themselves in playing, laughing, and enjoying women. So much, the minstrel says provocatively, he can reveal. "More I cannot, on account of crudeness, tell of our debauchery."[21]

Here we are made aware just how fully opposed the poem's two protagonists are, how far apart the cultural space each one normally occupies is from the other's, and how different their languages are. On the one hand, there is the king of England secure in his power and his conviction that he knows who he is, and what correct social behavior is. On the other, there is a "ribaud" — the minstrel-fableor — who respects neither the language that gives the king his sense of power nor the rules of social propriety that seem to order his life. The king confirms this opposition. He cannot condone the jongleur's debauched way of life any more than he can tolerate his riddles, and he says so:

---

[21] "Plus ne pus pur vileynye / Counter de nostre rybaudie" (lines 179–80; fol. 108va).

"Certes ie preise molt petit
Vostre vie ou vostre manere,
Quar ele ne valt mie vne piere.
Pur ce qe vus viuez en folie,
Da[s]heit qe preyse vostre vie." (lines 184–88; fol. 108va)

["Indeed I do not value your life or your sort, for it is not worth a stone. Because you live in folly, cursed be anyone who praises your life."]

Suddenly, though, the jongleur makes a generic shift, giving up his riddling fabliau-performance for a didactically tempered exemplum. And it is the abrupt shift from one genre to another that will enable a moral breakthrough. The questions the jongleur raises, moreover, bear not only on the king, but also on all of the texts in the same manuscript block in Harley, and particularly those dealing with good conduct for young noblemen:

"Quei valt sen ou sauer?
Ataunt valt viure en folye
Come en sen ou corteysie.
Et tot vus mostroi par ensample
Qu'est si large e si aunple
Qe vm ne dirra si noun." (lines 190–96)

["What is knowledge or understanding worth? It is as valuable to live in folly as in good sense or courtesy. I will show you everything by an example that is so broad and so full and so replete with reason that no one will say anything but good (of it)."]

The *ensample* or mirror the jongleur proceeds to hold up to the world's chatter focuses almost but not quite exclusively on the lives and reputations of men. The prudent, the affable, wealthy landowners, spendthrifts, lovers of women and misogynists, the prayerful and the impious, the fat, the thin, those who dress well and those who do not, those with long noses and those with pug noses: no one escapes the gossiper's scalpel. Potentially infinite in length, the list of what the world says is enough to establish the principle. Whatever one is or wishes to be, it will not fail to draw commentary from the malevolent who haunt every nook and cranny of the world's space.

As the minstrel orchestrates his *ensample*, we realize how his absurd game of riddles and puns earlier in the poem deepens the satire on gossip and slander that the example now presents in "straight" language. The riddling fabliau-dialogue of the first section has shown the inadequacy of language as a vehicle for representing even the simplest of facts. The exemplum, then, explicates the dangers in revealing the facts about one's identity to others. The underlying argument against such revelation is simple. The world's continual gossip ever inclines to distort the facts and to destroy reputation. The jongleur's amusing language game, called variously a "bourde" (line 131), a "desduit" (line 2), a "trufle" (line 400) — all terms medieval poets use to describe fabliaux — not only shelters but also enables a moral lesson. Yet, as with most fabliaux, it is a lesson presented more as a fantasy or dream than a realistic account of an actual or verisimilar event. Not only do the meadow and the royal *maisnée* of the opening scene disappear once the jongleur and the king begin to converse, but the king, improbably enough, asks the rowdy low-life minstrel for lessons on how to conduct himself in the world. What the fantasy enables is a utopian breaching of the conventional barriers both social and ethical. Starting from a static, asymmetrical relationship between the English king and the vagabond minstrel, the poem as lai-cum-fabliau-cum dialogue-cum-exemplum moves the two interlocutors to common ground. By the end they have become equals — two human beings faced with the same urgent need to protect themselves and the identities they have constructed against the onslaught of the world's lies.

It is only in the final movement of the poem, after the minstrel has shown the king how difficult it is to sustain what one wants to do in the face of endless, contrarious talk — "Quar nulle rien purroi fere / Qe vm ne trouera le countrere" ["For I can do nothing without someone finding it the opposite"] (lines 378–79; fol. 109vb) — that the king acknowledges the truth of what the jongleur has said. In asking his counsel, he also expresses the fabliau's core ethical concern:

> "Coment me pus countener
> E sauntz blame me egarder
> Que vm ne me vueille mesparler?" (lines 382–85)

["How can I conduct myself and, without blame, watch out so that no one may want to slander me?"]

What the jongleur of Ely teaches the king as the poem comes to its end is much clearer and simpler than the lessons offered in other extant versions of *La Riote du monde*. The Harley poet frees his jongleur to speak directly as a moral authority, one who can even translate his lesson into Latin:

> Qy par mesure tote ryen fra,
> Ia prudhome ne ly blamera
> Par mesure meenement
> Come est escrit apertement
>
> E le latyn est ensi:
> Medium tenuere beati. (lines 394–99)

303

[Whoever does everything according to measure — by measure moderately — will never be blamed by any good man as it is written openly. And the Latin is thus: Blessed is he who holds the middle way.]

Paradoxically, the minstrel's self-professed debauchery, like the transgressive fabliau-debate he orchestrates, is what frees him to attack sacrosanct assumptions about wise and foolish conduct in the world. First he lures the king into condemning him and his ilk for their "folie," and then he shows why his kind of foolishness is a legitimate response to the world's treacheries. By the end we realize that the jongleur's ribald life, like the fabliau we have just read, deliberately attacks the conventional wisdom of society in order to make much-needed revisions:

> Qy cest trufle velt entendre,
> Auke de sen purra aprendre.
> Car vm puet oyr souent
> Sage est qe parle sagement,
> Vn fol parler sagement
> Sage est qe parle sagement
> Fols come parle folement. (lines 400–05)

[Whoever wants to hear this trifle will be able to learn something of good sense from it. For one can often hear a fool speaking wisely. The wise man is the one who speaks wisely, just as a fool speaks foolishly.]

What this ending provides is a way of encompassing the two very different routes to wise speech and wise conduct that the poem offers.

The first of the two routes is the way of moderation and prudence taught by conduct and courtesy books for young men, like the three the Harley scribe includes in the manuscript block we are investigating. The second way to wisdom, however, is the way of the fabliau. Looking at human conduct from a perspective deep within the "riote" or debate of the world with its "changing, flitting" language and talk,[22] the jongleur traffics in ribald oral performance designed to shock: riddles and puns, combative insults, the world's malicious gossip, double entendre, low-life, sexually explicit diction. Paradoxically, by claiming the minstrel's license to use the tactics and language of the fabliau world, he is able (at least in fiction) to maneuver in the king's world and break through his complacency.

---

[22] This quotation is from Chaucer's Parson's Tale X [I] 367 (*The Riverside Chaucer*, ed. Larry D. Benson et al. [Boston, 1987], p. 298).

The text that follows immediately upon *Le Jongleur d'Ely et le Roi d'Angleterre* in Harley's twelfth quire is another fabliau, one that draws us away from the world of men and into the vexed question of women. *Les Trois Dames qui troverent un vit* begins a study (entirely from a male perspective) concerning what one manuscript calls the "bonit[as] et malitia mulierum" [goodness and evil of women].[23] Indeed, it is this subject that occupies almost all the remaining space of the twelfth quire, entering even into the argument of the courtesy book for young men that ends this gathering.[24]

The *Trois Dames* survives in two manuscripts — Harley 2253 and a thirteenth-century French manuscript now in the collection of the Bibliothèque Nationale in Paris.[25] Except for their beginnings and endings, which differ considerably, the texts of the two redactions are quite close. In addition, the two anthologies that contain them include enough texts in common to suggest that their compilers were working according to shared ideas about what kind of book they were making.[26] That the beginnings and endings of the two redactions differ may be simply a matter of chance. One might also speculate, however, that the Harley scribe himself imposed the opening lines on his version of the *Trois Dames*, replacing the more elaborate prologue in the Paris manuscript in order to suit the generic and thematic symmetries of his own anthology. The *Jongleur* ends in the second column of fol. 109v, and the *Trois Dames*, starting at the top of a new folio, begins:

> Puis que de fabler ay comence,
> Ia n'y ert pur moun trauail lesse.
> De trois dames comenceroy,
> Assez brieuement le counteroy,
> Que al mount seint Michel aloient

---

[23] This is the title given to a poem, also contained in this quire of Harley, that is best known as *Le Blasme des femmes* (no. 77). The Latin title appears in Florence, Biblioteca Laurentiana MS Plutarch XLII, fol. 83r.

[24] In her essay in this volume Mary Dove has usefully studied the antifeminist poems per se. Here I focus instead on the ways in which the same material typically functions in anthologies like Harley in the milieu of antifeminist fabliaux, satires, devotional material, and books of conduct for young aristocrats.

[25] Paris, BN MS fr. 1593.

[26] There is, however, a major difference between the two compilations in terms of the way the books were put together. Harley is the work of a single person, both copying and anthologizing all of the texts. BN MS fr. 1593, on the other hand, is constituted of booklets copied by a number of different scribes. What is remarkable is that, in spite of its genuinely miscellaneous character in terms of the way it has been assembled, it nonetheless resembles much more carefully orchestrated anthologies like Harley in terms of the texts and kinds of texts it contains.

En pelrynage come vowe auoyent.
Ne voderount plus demorer
De lur promesse aquiter.[27]

[Since I have begun to tell fables, certainly (fabling) will not be set aside on account of my work. I will begin with the three ladies, I will tell it quite briefly, who were going to Mont St. Michel on pilgrimage as they had vowed. They will not wish to delay any longer in keeping their promise.]

The first two lines of this prologue are borrowed from the beginning of Marie de France's lai *Yonec*:[28]

Puis que des lais ai comencé,
Ja n'iert par mon travail laissé. (lines 1–2)

[Since I have begun some lais, certainly (the work) will not be set aside on account of my work.]

The *Trois Dames*'s English redactor (or the Harley scribe), altering Marie's lines only in terms of the genre named, seems to use them just as Marie had in her collection of lais. The temporal conjunction "puis que" at the beginning of the *Trois Dames*, linked to a task already begun, together with the verb "fabler" (replacing Marie's "des lais"), seems to insist on a generic similarity between the two poems the scribe is just now copying side by side in his book — the *Jongleur* and the *Trois Dames*. If it is the scribe himself who has imported Marie's lines for the start of the *Trois Dames*, we can impute to him a thought-process something like the following: "Since I have just 'fabled' — i.e., given you a fable/fabliau — namely the *Jongleur* — in this quire of my anthology — I will now not shirk from copying another text of the same kind to follow it."

Two other features of the Anglo-Norman prologue to the *Trois Dames* in Harley may also point to scribal interventions — and interventions that, reading backwards in the manuscript, we also find in the prologue to the *Jongleur*. In the *Jongleur*, it will be remembered, an eight-line prologue — exactly the same length as the *Trois Dames* prologue — establishes a much more precise dramatic situation for the poem's two

---

[27] Lines 1–8; fol. 110rb. All references to the *Trois Dames* will be to the diplomatic edition in Noomen and van den Boogaard, eds., *NRCF* 8.274–77, checked against the MS. I have added punctuation where needed.

[28] Per Nykrog pointed this out in his important study *Les Fabliaux*, 2nd ed. (Geneva, 1973), p. 84, calling the borrowing an example of a fabliau citing a lai.

interlocutors than its French sources offer. Both the king and the minstrel are assigned a local English habitation, the action is set in a meadow near London, and the opening scene implicates the generic trajectory of the lai, with the minstrel arriving as if to give the king an adventure or quest. In the *Trois Dames* prologue the locus of the action is likewise made specific and a second generic thrust is hinted to complicate that of the fabliau. Whereas the French redaction of the *Trois Dames* gives no idea as to which "mont" the three ladies are seeking nor in what "pais" it is to be found, the Harley version tells us that the tale's protagonists are making a pilgrimage to Mont St. Michel in Normandy.

For Harley's likely upper-class readership of Englishmen well versed in Anglo-Norman, the pilgrimage site of the abbey church at Mont St. Michel would have been a very familiar one. In addition, both the pilgrimage motif and the reference to Mont St. Michel add to the fiction a generic and thematic richness that is absent in the French version. In fulfilling a vow to make a religious pilgrimage, the three ladies signal the promise of a familiar literary kind — the medieval quest for the heavenly Jerusalem. To be sure, the aura of religious devotion, of vows, of prayerful pilgrimage — hovering over the start of the tale and intermittently recollected through the course of the Anglo-Norman redaction — is countered by the stunningly obscene action that occupies the center. Yet the ending of the Harley poem, which is, like the beginning, quite different from that of its French counterpart, returns us directly, if parodically, to the "devotional" promise of the prologue. The effect of the Anglo-Norman version's generic commingling of pilgrimage and fabliau is to make the poem funnier, more outrageous, and more intently antifeminist than its source. Whether the redactor of Harley's *Trois Dames* is the manuscript's scribe or another Englishman, his urge for brevity ("assez brieuement le counteroy" [line 4]) does not keep him from adding dramatic details to build a devotional leit-motif. The liturgical time references and the delicacy used in describing the "find" at the tale's start, the references to God and the devil, and above all Harley's "sacral" conclusion all intensify the poem's central clash between the profane and the sacred.

The plot of the *Trois Dames* as it unfolds in the Harley poem is easy to summarize. Having set out on their pilgrimage, the ladies travel for two days. On the third day at the liturgical hour of terce, one of them, looking down at the path, finds "vn vit gros et plener / Enuolupe en vn drapel" [a large and ample penis wrapped up in a rag] (lines 14–15; fol. 110ra). What she can see, we are told, is only "le musel" [the forward edge of the rod] (line 16), but she is filled with joy at the find because "ele sauoit quei ce estoit" [she knew what it was] (line 19). As her two companions catch up with her and discover her treasure, they immediately claim their own right to a share in it in language that reaches towards the devotional formulas of pilgrimage:

"Vus sauez bien, se Dieu m'enioie,
Qe nus sumes en ceste voie

Compaignes e bones amyes." (lines 29–31)

["You well know, so God give me joy, that we are companions and friends on this journey."]

The finder, though, not being willing to share what she has found, the three decide to seek a judgment. The judge will be, they decide, the abbess of a nearby convent. When they arrive, the abbess is at mass, as a good religious should be. Eventually she comes into the parlor where the three ladies are seated, and one of the two deprived ladies tells the abbess, the prioress, and the cellarer the story of the object their companion has found.

On hearing the story, the abbess asks to see the object so that she can give a correct judgment. At this, the lady who has been telling the tale asks her friend to bring the *vit* forward, which she does, pulling it from her breast and setting it in front of a "noneyn," who, we are told, "mout le garda de bon oyl" [looked upon it with great favor] (line 85; fol. 110va). Just as we await the judgment as to how the *vit* will be dispensed, the abbess performs a stunning act of rhetorical magic — one that effects a reversal of all the ladies' expectations. Instead of rendering a verdict in the case, she transforms the penis into a "verrous" [bolt] (line 92). The *vit* becomes in her act of linguistic co-optation the lost bolt for her abbey door. With the decisiveness of an administrator, she orders "ma dame Eleyne," whose full white sleeves identify her as a nun (though her name connects her to the infamously lustful Helen of Troy), to take the contested *vit*/bolt and put it back in the place from which it had been taken. And so dame Eleyne does, slipping the penis into her sleeve, leaving the three ladies destitute of "la chose" [the thing], as the text now calls it, over which they had quarreled (line 108).

Before turning to the striking difference between the concluding lesson in the two versions of the *Trois Dames*, we must pause to ask what emphases in the tale, besides that of a religious pilgrimage, separate the Anglo-Norman redaction of the *Trois Dames* from the French version. In the first place, the Harley poem makes the poem's central object — the *vit* — both more prominent and more mysterious. The penis wrapped in a rag is mentioned literally, euphemistically, or figuratively in Harley more than twice as often as it is in the slightly longer French version (118 lines versus 128 lines). It is named a *vit* four times in Harley, but only twice in the Paris text; the euphemism *chose* appears six times in Harley, but only twice in the other. In the Paris manuscript, the abbess' "toraille" represents the only figurative naming of it, while in Harley it is successively named a "trouvure" [find]; a "verrous" [bolt]; and a "relique" [relic]. The much more frequent and varied naming of the male organ in Harley coincides with a great heightening of its importance in the fabliau as a quasi-sacred object of desire for women.

When we compare the very different endings of the two versions, we discover why the Harley redaction interpolates both the pilgrimage motif and the play with diction surrounding the "trouvure." In the Paris version, although the penis greatly delights both the nuns and the three ladies, it is not the inveterate lust of women assumed by Ovid and echoed by medieval clerks that occupies the important concluding lines of the poem. Instead the poet calls his tale an "essample" and explains that its purpose is to admonish men to share what they find with their companions and also not to trust false covetous judges (a moral imported from the second fable of Marie de France's *Ysopet*). By contrast, the Harley redactor makes the supposed quasi-religious allure the penis holds for women the focus of both the tale and its concluding lesson. As he adds the motif of pilgrimage to the ladies' journey, the *vit* becomes, implicitly, the desired goal of the female quest for saving bliss.[29] What seems to interest the English redactor most through the course of the tale is the alternate linguistic (and literal) unveiling and veiling of the "chose" which is the worshipful object of the "holy" women, *all* of whom capitulate to its allure.

The concluding ten lines of the fabliau, then, unique to Harley, insist on this theme in a way that recalls the discussion of obscene language in relation to male genitals in Jean de Meun's *Roman de la Rose*. As the ladies leave the convent, we are told, they agree that they will never again ask for a judgment about such a "chose." Rather, the one who finds it will always keep it "come *relyke* molt desirree / E de totes dames honoree" [as a much desired *relic* honored by all women] (lines 117–18, italics mine; fol. 110va). If the nuns now have their "bolt" as the sexually charged object with which to "lock their door," the ladies have found a new goal for future pilgrimages — namely the *vit* of which they have been so slyly deprived. Indeed, the conclusion of the *Trois Dames* parodically defends the pseudo-religious euphemism that names testicles "reliques" (which Reason rejects in the *Rose*). It is, so the argument goes, a way for women to mask their sexual appetite, at the same time acknowledging their religious devotion to the male organ they universally admire. But there is a further parodic twist. In an important sense, the *vit* wrapped in cloth, separated as it is from a living male body, resembles the bodily parts of revered saints conserved in reliquaries at major medieval pilgrimage sites. In this regard, the comic but also macabre treatment of the detached *vit* as an object of worship plays with the link between the literal and the metaphoric in the euphemism itself. And this link may in turn obliquely raise taboo questions about the pervasive devotion to saints' preserved body parts as relics in the late Middle Ages.

In terms of its place in Harley's twelfth quire, *Les Trois Dames qui troverent un vit*, with its antifeminist, sacrilegious exposure of female lust, introduces a sequence of texts, or better, kinds of texts, that appears frequently in French and English fabliau-anthologies — verse tracts arguing for and against women. The most widely diffused of these is an

---

[29] In this way, the poet links the "trois dames" *as* religious to the nuns at the abbey — the "Mout seinte dames . . . / Que Dieu seruent nuit e iour" [very holy women . . . who serve God night and day] (lines 42–43; fol. 110rb).

antifeminist diatribe called most often *Le Blasme des femmes* (no. 77).[30] In Harley an equally formulaic poem praising women separates the *Blasme* from the *Trois Dames* (*Le Dit des femmes*, no. 76), while a third antifeminist diatribe, *De la femme et de la pie* by Nicholas Bozon (no. 78), comparing women to magpies, follows upon the *Blasme*. It is common in continental anthologies to find such poems praising and blaming women in the company of fabliaux, but not often in so concentrated or deliberate a way. What is striking about Harley's arrangement is the apparent consciousness with which the fabliaux and the verse tracts are placed side by side. It is also noteworthy that the scribe brackets the woman-question in the twelfth quire by returning at its end to a book for and about men — a courtesy book for aristocratic youth. Yet the woman-question is not entirely absent from this tract. *Urbain le courtois* (no. 79) recontextualizes it, both repeating lines from the earlier pro-female *Le Dit des femmes* and offering its own cautionary advice about how to avoid choosing a troublesome wife. By no accident, I think, *Urbain* also returns us to a key theme developed by *Le Jongleur d'Ely et le Roi d'Angleterre*, namely the problem of slanderers. The advice it gives is not identical to the *Jongleur*'s, but complementary to it, offering an immediate pragmatic solution to a difficult situation:

> Si vm vus mesdit de nule part,
> Gardez bien cet art:
> Respounce a ly ne donez
> Mes la place voidez. (lines 300–03; fol. 113va)

[If anyone slanders you, pay attention to this rule: Give him no response but leave the place.]

The satire that fills out the blank space left on the verso of the last leaf of Quire 12 and begins Quire 13 is, like *Urbain*, a poem about and for men. *Trailbaston* (no. 80) is an outlaw poem and its protagonist is, like the minstrel of the *Jongleur*, a self-professed renegade from society, but one who yearns to right the injustices under which he suffers. Like the *Jongleur*, too, *Trailbaston* immediately precedes a fabliau, and one that like the *Trois Dames*, introduces a sequence of antifeminist texts.

Harley Quire 13 and Its Two Fabliaux

When we turn from the end of *Trailbaston*, with which Harley's thirteenth quire begins (fol. 114r), to the first of the two fabliaux that follow it, we find ourselves again in the

---

[30] This is the title given to it in Paris, BN MSS fr. 837 (fol. 192r) and fr. 1593 (fol. 153r). In Harley 2253 a space is left for a title but none is given.

presence of a tale that begins, like the *Jongleur*, as if it might unfold as a lai or a romance. In the fabliau of *Le Chevalier et la corbaille*, however, as with the *Jongleur*, the idealizing trajectory of the courtly lai is displaced by strategies belonging to the fabliau tradition. And, as in the *Jongleur*, it is behavior within the court that requires the transgressive play of fabliau — both linguistic and material — in order to bring balance and justice to the fore. In the case of the *Corbaille*, the dilemma at court has to do with a wealthy baron's oppression of his wife. Having enclosed her narrowly within the walls of his castle, he has her watched day and night by his old wrinkled mother so as to prevent his "property" from theft. Yet in spite of the baron's best efforts, the *châtelaine* "de honor" is in love with a poor but valiant knight to whom she has promised herself. If the *Corbaille* were a straightforward courtly lai, we would expect the story to develop as, say, Marie de France's *Lanval* does. The lovers would be discovered and separated, would undergo the greatest of difficulties, and would at last be reunited by the intervention of supernatural magic. What happens instead in the *Corbaille* draws us directly into the world of fabliau.

Le Chevalier et la corbaille is arguably the most deliciously wicked, aesthetically interesting, and morally satisfying of the bawdy tales in Harley. Extant only in this manuscript, it shows evidence through its rhymes that its author was of insular origin.[31] And it is not impossible that here, as in the case of the *Jongleur* and the *Trois Dames*, the scribe himself has furnished the prologue and ending. The *Corbaille* is a poem fascinating not only in itself but also as it models a generic complexity of the kind we also find both in Chaucer's fabliaux and in his lais. Within the brief compass of 264 lines, the *Corbaille* poet manages a brilliantly incongruous marriage between the sentimental ideals of the courtly lai and the comic material staging typical of fabliaux. And he complicates this generic relationship by drawing on a third form, not literary but juridical in character, namely, the formal curse. In the composition the expected trajectories of all three generic traditions are played out. True love triumphs over what appear to be insurmountable odds. A rough-hewn trick involving the hoisting of the lover in a basket over a castle wall enables him to have sex with his lady love. At the same time, a series of heart-felt formal curses results, as if by divine intervention, in the punishment of the baron's wicked mother. In this secondary plot of vengeance, as in the love story, the fabliau-basket plays a key role. Operating technically just as it had for the lover, it functions in the revenge plot in what appears to be a providential way, assuring that the curses uttered by the poem's teller and the two lovers are precisely fulfilled.

To discover how neatly the poet weaves the genres of the lai, the fabliau, and the curse together in his composition, we first need to trace each discrete trajectory, though it is of course their interaction that gives the poem its particular delight. Let us begin with the

---

[31] Noomen and van den Boogaard, eds., *NRCF*, 9.266.

Corbaille's opening sequence as the text outlines a plot shared by many a courtly lai. The very first lines of the tale proper give us a charming scene of aristocratic life:

> Vn cheualer de grant valour
> E vne dame de honour
> S'entre amerent jadis d'amour
> Leaument ou grant doucour.[32]

[Once upon a time a knight of great courage and a lady of honor loved each other faithfully in great tenderness.]

Every word in this portrait of aristocratic love counts to win our sympathy, and in particular, the four rhyming end-words: *valour, honour, amour, douçour*. Yet immediately we learn what blocks the consummation of perfect love. There is the matter of the lady's husband. As a "ryche baroun," proprietor of a thickly walled and moated castle, he has her narrowly enclosed in a chamber where his malevolent mother watches her constantly. And even, so the poet tells us, if she were not so closely watched, it would be very difficult to approach the beautiful *châtelaine* because too many moats and walls block the way. In the tale's opening argument the poet leaves no doubt that the sordidness in the situation lies not with the would-be adulterous lovers but with the baron, his old mother, and the material castle-walls that support their cruelty. The question thus posed identifies the dilemma as one proper to a courtly lai. How, in the face of so many barriers, is the brave knight to consummate his love with the honorable lady who has promised him her body?

The knight's first approach to his lady is one any lover in a lai (or a fabliau, for that matter) might try. Having languished a long time, he chooses a moment when the wealthy baron is off at a tournament and goes to visit the castle to see his lady. Hospitably received by the porter, he is invited by the lady to her chamber on the pretext that she wishes to consult with him about an "affere" (line 57; fol. 115vb). The two lovers sit together on a carpet and settle down for what the poet calls a "parlement d'amours" (line 66) — a kind of conversation perfectly suited to a courtly lai. But we are immediately made to remember the old woman, keeping her watch close to the lovers. Though the old woman belongs to the "official" world of the aristocracy — the world of social power — it is she, and not the adulterous lovers, whose behavior engenders the need for curses and a fabliau plot. And it is these latter genres, each one with its own trajectory, that the poet will deftly intertwine with the paradigm of the courtly lai.

---

[32] Lines 5–8; fol. 115va. All references to the *Corbaille* will be to Noomen and van den Boogaard, eds., *NRCF*, 9.272–78, checked against the MS.

The first of the curses against the wicked old woman comes from the poet's teller, sympathetic to the two lovers. "May an evil curse kill her!" he declares. This malediction (guiding audience response) is immediately followed by the more specific curses the knight and his lady utter immediately. The knight calls on God to smash the old woman's arm or thigh, or lame or paralyze her, or pull out her tongue so that she might never again speak either lies or truth. In her turn, the lady wishes death and madness on her mother-in-law, hoping at the same time to find a drug to make her deaf. The lovers' curses, juridical rather than literary in character, function as the puns and riddles do in the *Jongleur*, aligning the poem with oral tradition and oral performance. And it is these curses, like the minstrel's linguistic play in the *Jongleur*, that will magically open the way to a just resolution of the moral problem posed by the plot. For the time being, though, the tale suspends the subject of the curses in favor of developing the plot. Only the good knight's advice to his lady ("the evil curse . . . may be able to avenge us. I do not know any other counsel to give you"[33]) hints at their future importance.

As the parliament of love comes to its close, the knight promises the lady that he will enter the castle that very night in order to be together with her. For her part, the lady assures him that she will await his arrival and then she orders wine for her lover.[34] At this point, we have no idea how the knight plans to make his way into the castle once it is closed for the night, remembering what the narrator has told us of the formidable number of walls and the great difficulty involved in penetrating them. Yet the form of the lai set in motion at the very beginning promises that the hero will succeed in his task by surprising means. And so he does.

The means, however, are not those we tend to associate with the supernaturally magical interventions of the lai or with romance heroes. Instead, what takes over is the kind of ingenious material staging that fabliau characters typically deploy to achieve their goals. In the *Corbaille*, though, it is not a bawdy character who designs the farcical "staged-set" for the fabliau, but the noble lover-knight. It is as if the hero of the lai recognizes that he can best undermine the "official" but perverse order of things at court blocking the consummation of his love not by great acts of bravery but rather by playful trickery. And

---

[33] "La male goute, bele amye, / Fet il, nous em pusse venger: / Ie ne vous say autre enseigner!" (lines 90–92; fol. 116ra).

[34] Before the lovers part, the poet interjects an exchange between them that raises religious questions about adulterous love, no doubt to remove even the slightest doubt a reader or listener might have about the goodness of their relationship. It is appropriately the knight, solicitous of his beloved's soul, who asks how the lady can continue to love him, since such love is a great sin. Responding as the heroine of a courtly lai would have to respond, the lady dismisses any thought of sin because perfect love transcends *all* conventional categories.

so he begins to plot his course by scrutinizing his immediate physical surroundings — the castle's hall. At once he descries an opening in one wall giving onto a small shed. The knight calls his squire and orders him to hide in the shed until night has fallen and the castle's inhabitants have gone to bed. Then, he gives the squire further instructions. Under cover of darkness the squire is to make his way to the crenellations atop the castle wall to await the knight's arrival outside the castle wall. Following his master's order, the squire hides himself in the shed, holding in his hand, we are told, a basket.

From this point on, the basket — *la corbaille* — enters into play as the key prop in the working out of all three of the poem's generic trajectories. The basket itself is not described until the moment it is put into use, more than halfway through the story. In the dark, as the knight arrives outside the castle wall, "vne corbaille bien tornee, / De cordes bien auyronee" [a well-shaped basket wrapped round well with ropes] is lowered to the ground, we are told, and the knight settles himself within it (lines 161–64; fol. 116va). The basket holding the knight is then hoisted up by men at the top of the wall and lowered down the other side. Here, with an astonishing economy of means, the poet enables his hero to penetrate the impassable castle walls not by magic or by armed force but simply by means of a hollow bucket. The contrast between the solidity of the walls — articulating the baron's power — and the lightness of the basket serving true love and a poor knight — could not be more striking. A fabliau prop comically displaces the conventional deeds of valor or supernatural intervention as the force enabling the lovers to consummate their love, and so they do. The knight makes his way to his lady's chamber, and the two "do whatever they ought to do" ("E firent quanque fere durent," line 179).

We are not allowed, however, to forget the old mother-in-law and her spying. The *mise-en-scene* the poet creates for the lady's chamber is very amusing, but it reminds us as well just how systematically suspicious and oppressive the mother-in-law is. It also makes possible a spectacularly clever dramatization of the lovers in bed — touched at once by the delicacy of the lai and the sexual frankness of the fabliau. The situation as the poet describes it is this. The *châtelaine*'s bed and her mother-in-law's are less than a meter apart, and the two beds share a single coverlet. Consequently, as the knight makes love to his lady, the coverlet common to the two beds begins to move — and to move violently enough so that the "maveise veille" feels it and asks her "fille" what is going on. Responding with a half-lie, the *châtelaine* explains that she could not resist scratching an itch. While the mother-in-law believes her fib, it is not long before the coverlet again begins to move. The knight, we are told, "Bien sout les coupes le roy doner" (line 200; fol. 116vb), as he continues to take his pleasure. Here a fabliau euphemism for love-making

— "giving the king's blow"[35] — reinforced by the voyeuristic old woman's fabliau conduct, delightfully intersects with the far more delicate image of the rustling coverlet. The interpenetration of the strategies of the lai with those of the fabliau enables the poet to figure ideal *fin amour* and intense, frankly sexual activity as a single complex experience.

Before the love-making signaled by the coverlet comes to an end, though, the old woman begins to suspect the *châtelaine*'s excuse. "Never," she shrewdly guesses, "would a coverlet move thus only on account of scratching" ("Pensa qe vnqe pur graterye / Ne ala le couertour ensi," lines 208–09). Guided by her suspicion (and the mean-spiritedness beneath it), she returns us to the fabliau world and — by no accident — to the basket at its center. Taking an unlit candle she sets out for the kitchen. There she hopes to find a light for her candle so that on her return she can explore what is going on beneath the coverlet. Such a discovery, of course, would bring tragedy to the lovers, ending their romance as well as cutting short the comic fabliau and rendering impotent the curses uttered against the old woman. If she were allowed to expose the lovers by the light of her candle, moreover, the baron's oppressive cruelty and her own, hidden behind their wealth and their castle walls, would certainly continue unchecked.

Instead, by the kind of coincidence that hints at a divine destiny shaping events, the wicked mother-in-law manages, in the middle of the great hall, to trip over the basket in such a way that she falls into it. What happens next defies the laws of verisimilitude but satisfies poetic justice. The same men who had hoisted the lover over the castle walls in the basket now hoist the old woman up. As the basket swings in the moonlight, the squire realizes that it contains not his master but the woman. He and his companions proceed to swing the basket from rafter to rafter, up and down, until they have almost deprived the baron's mother of life. At last, the men controlling the ropes let them go, and the basket holding the old woman crashes to the ground, causing her to fly out onto the floor. Even before the basket has crashed, the poet suggestively links the old woman's punishment to divine intervention by having her suppose that she has been "rauye" by "deables ou autre malfees" [ravished by devils or other evil spirits] (lines 232–33). Rendered mad and nearly speechless by her experience, she makes her way trembling back to her bed. Then, scarcely able to utter the words, she reports to the *châtelaine* her belief that supernatural spirits have caused her traumatic experience: "Malement me ad atornee / Les damos que errerent par nuit" [the demons who wander by night have wickedly tossed me about] (lines 248–49; fol. 117ra). What is remarkable about this, the story's final movement, is that through it the poet returns us to the curses the two lovers had spoken against the baron's

---

[35] On this metaphor, see Roy J. Pearcy, "A Fabliau Crux: *Les Coup le roi*," *French Studies Bulletin* 54 (1995): 1–4. See also Noomen and van den Boogaard, eds., *NRCF*, 9.314, note to line 200.

mother early in the story. In its first appearance in the poem, the fabliau-basket had helped the knight to achieve the impossible — to "break through" the castle's walls — in order to enjoy his lady as a lover in a lai should. Here the same basket enables a "divine" response to his own and the lady's curses against their oppressor. Thanks to the "miracle" of the fiends tossing her in the basket, the old *talevace* is effectively rendered both deaf and dumb.

As the twelve lines ending the poem tell us, the lover is now free to go and come as he pleases to visit his lady. Never again, we learn, will the *châtelaine*'s mother-in-law arise for any reason once she has gone to bed, remembering as she does the battering she has suffered. No matter what she hears, she will remain forever silent. Not surprisingly, in light of its place in the Harley anthology, the very last lines of the poem emphasize the trajectory of the antifeminist fabliau plot rather than that of the lai (which has, nonetheless, its own misogamous argument). In fact, the last two lines actually rename the tale to address the punishment of the cruel old woman. No longer *Le Chevalier et la corbaille*, the fabliau is called at last *De la vielle e de la corbayle*:

> Ataunt finist sauntz nulle fayle
> De la vielle e de la corbayle. (lines 263–64)

[And so ends without anything missing (in the tale) of the old woman and the basket.]

This ending, whether it is the work of the Harley scribe or not (and it may be), leads us directly into the next two antifeminist poems. The first of these is a misogamous, misogynist verse tract, based on Walter Map's *De conjuge non ducenda* (no. 83).[36] The second is the Harley block's fourth fabliau, *Le Dit de la gageure*, a cautionary tale about a vicious wife and one that vies with *Les Trois Dames qui troverent un vit* and *Le Chevalier qui fist le cons parler* as the most crudely obscene of Harley's bawdy fictions. By no accident, I think, we find a striking thematic consonance between the argument of the Anglo-Norman verse *De conjuge* and the two fabliaux flanking it in Harley. Both the *Corbaille* and the *Gageure* imagine for us dysfunctional marriages. In the first case, an aristocratic *châtelain* oppresses his beautiful young wife, and his wicked mother models the merciless women of the *De conjuge* even as she supports her son's misogyny. In the second case — that of the *Gageure* — the wife is the one who makes her marriage a

---

[36] This same poem also appears in a thirteenth-century English MS containing Latin and AN texts, Oxford, Bodleian Library MS Douce 210, which includes in addition a redaction of the courtesy book *Urbain le courtois* and another guide to religious and moral precepts for knights called *Le Chevalier de Dieu*. The scribe of Douce 210 is narrowly ethical and religious in the choice of texts he anthologizes. See Paul Meyer, "Notice du ms. Douce 210 de la Bibliothèque Bodleienne à Oxford," *Bulletin de la Société des anciens textes français* 6 (1880): 46–84.

battlefield, hating her husband's lineage, callously exploiting her cousin to serve her hatred, and reforming only under the pressure of losing a bet. While the *Trois Dames* and the two antifeminist discourses on women in the previous quire had brought to the fore familiar topoi regarding women's vices in general, this triptych of texts paints a much darker portrait of women and, in particular, of wicked mothers-in-law and craven wives.

Like *Le Chevalier et la corbaille*, *Le Dit de la gageure* has no known source or analogue with which we can compare it in terms of either its text or its thematic emphasis.[37] As with the *Jongleur*, the *Trois Dames*, and the *Corbaille*, however, its prologue and its ending may have been either invented or modified by the Harley scribe to suit the formal and thematic needs of his anthology. The six-line prologue calls the tale "Vne fable" (line 1; fol. 118rb), corresponding to the verb "fabler" in the first line of the *Trois Dames*. In this case, as in the *Jongleur*, the *Trois Dames*, and the *Corbaille*, the poet (or perhaps the scribe) gives the fabliau a moral and even an aesthetic respectability by aligning it formally with the highly regarded tradition of the fable. If the prologue focuses intently on the problem the wife causes for the marriage, the cautionary ending — a direct echo of the beginning — shows that she has learned her lesson:

> Vn cheualer iadis estoit
> Que vne tres bele femme auoit,
> *Mais ele n'amoit pas soun lygnage*:
> *De ce ne fist ele que sage.* (lines 5–8; italics mine)

[Once upon a time there was a knight who had a very beautiful wife, *but she did not love his lineage: in this she was not prudent.*]

At the end of the "fable," then, the husband spells out the moral lesson his ungrateful wife has been forced to learn in losing the wager:

> "*E, dame, vus ne fetez mie qe sage*
> *De haier ceux qe sunt de mon lynage,*
> Depus qu ie tendrement
> Aym les vos entierement."[38]

---

[37] Sir Francis Palgrave was the first to name this poem *La Gageure* — "The Wager" — and all subsequent editors have repeated this title. The motif of the wager, often a bet involving a seduction, is very widely diffused in medieval vernacular poetry. See Gaston Paris, "Le Cycle de la *Gageure*," *Romania* 32 (1903): 481–551.

[38] Lines 97–100; italics mine; fol. 118vb. All references to the *Gageure* are to the unpublished edition by Kennedy, *AN Poems*, pp. 230–37, checked against the MS.

["*And, madame, you do not behave prudently at all to hate those of my lineage*, since I tenderly and completely love yours."]

The form of the poem thus shaped by its prologue and its conclusion corresponds to the neatness in the ethical framing given to the other Harley fabliaux. It also mirrors the exemplary shape of comparable antifeminist fables in both Marie de France's *Ysopet* and Peter Alfonsi's conduct book-cum-story collection.[39]

If the prologue and the conclusion of the *Gageure* emphasize the wife's moral failure and the husband's superiority, the tale itself unveils for us unbelievably sordid, sexually explicit, exploitative game-playing in an aristocratic household. The situation of the *Gageure* is this. The knight's squire, who is also his brother (and therefore of his *lynage*), falls in love with the lady's cousin, a "gente meschyne" who is the lady's chambermaiden. When the squire asks for her love, the girl reports his request to her lady in terms familiar in both medieval romance and Ovidian seduction stories. The lover, she says, has requested her *shame* ("hounte," line 20). If the tale *were* a romance, and if the lady were a good wife to her knight or a responsible mentor to her young cousin, steps would be taken to effect a decorous marriage, thereby reinforcing the ties binding the two families. Instead, the lady outdoes even the most unprincipled of the medieval fabliau go-betweens,[40] reinforcing everything said against women in poems like *Le Blasme des femmes* and the antimatrimonial verses immediately preceding the *Gageure* in Harley. As go-between, she uses her young cousin to enable not simply a seduction but a rape, and

---

[39] See, for example, Fables 94 and 95 in Karl Warnke's edition of Marie's fables (*Die Fabeln der Marie de France* [Halle, 1898]). It is noteworthy that in at least one French anthology containing fabliaux, a scribe has intermingled antifeminist fabliaux with Marie's antifeminist fables in such a way that the two forms are presented visually on the page in exactly the same way. Each one begins with a charming miniature, and the exemplary lesson at the end begins with a colored capital. For a discussion of this MS (Paris, BN MS fr. 2173), see Nolan, "Turning over the Leaves," pp. 1–31. See also three antifeminist exempla in the French version of Peter Alfonsi's *Disciplina clericalis* (Edward D. Montgomery, Jr., ed., *Le Chastoiement d'un pere à son fils: A Critical Edition* [Chapel Hill, 1971], pp. 79–87 [lines 1161–451]). It is not irrelevant that the son in the *Chastoiement* approves his father's exempla in terms of their moral edification: "A grant profet li tornereit / Qui tels fableals auques orreit" [It would bring great profit (to) anyone who listened to a few such fabliaux.] (p. 81, lines 1233–34).

[40] I think here particularly of characters like the *Anus* in the Latin *Pamphilus* and its vernacular translation as well as Auberee in the fabliau of that name. For these texts, see Franz G. Becker, ed., *Pamphilus: Prolegomena zum Pamphilus (de amore) und kritische Textausgabe*, in *Mittellateinisches Jahrbuch*, Beiheft 9 (Ratingen, 1972); and *Auberee* in Noomen and van den Boogaard, eds., *NCRF*, 1.163–312.

she does so to embarrass her husband. Advising the girl to test the depth of the squire's love, she tells her to prove his ardor by having him kiss her rear end ("vostre cul beiser premerement," line 31) in private so that no one will blame him. The naive maiden presents this astonishing task to the squire, who (needless to say) accepts it willingly, and she arranges to meet him in the garden under the pear jonette tree to receive the kiss. She then hurries back to report the plan to her mistress. The lady, overjoyed, sends her cousin back to the squire, while she rushes to tell her husband what is about to transpire, inviting him to witness the act.

At once the husband avers that his brother will never perform so villainous an act and bets his wife a cask of wine that he will not. The two then go to the window overlooking the garden. What they witness is an entirely predictable rape, the product of the wife's effort to shame her husband's brother and thereby expose his lineage to shame. Shockingly enough for a late twentieth-century audience, in the poem's argument the rear-end kiss is regarded as an act of "vilanie," while the rape is acceptable as a normal sex act. And it is the wife herself who confirms this point. With a loud cry, horrifying in what it reveals about the hatefulness of the lady, she condemns her unsuspecting, just-raped young cousin of causing her to lose her bet:

> "Gwenchez, trestresse, gwenchez, puteyne!
> Gwenchez, Dieu te doint mal fyn.
> I'ay perdu le tonel de vyn." (lines 86–88; fol. 118vb)

["Pull away, traitor, pull away, whore! Pull away, may God give you a bad end. I have lost the cask of wine."]

Happily, because the wife has lost the bet, she also loses her power to have the last word. In an act of poetic justice like the one that ends the *Corbaille*, her perverse abuse of her young cousin is superseded by her husband's acts of social conscience. He corrects her and arranges his brother's marriage to the girl he has just raped. At the same time, we are assured that the wife has reformed. Henceforth, the poet tells us, she

> ama par tendrour
> Ceux qe soun seygneur ama
> E molt de cuer les honora. (lines 104–06)

[tenderly loved those whom her lord loved and heartily honored them.]

In spite of this fairy tale conclusion, the drama of the perverse wife in the *Gageure*, like the plots of the *Trois Dames* and the *Corbaille*, contradicts the pious praises of women in the earlier *Le Dit des femmes* in Harley and the echoes of them in *Urbain le courtois*. At

319

the same time, it confirms, with all the imaginative force of storytelling, what is alleged against women and marriage in *Le Blasme des femmes*, in *De conjuge non ducenda*, and in three of the other four Harley fabliaux.

Harley Quire 14 and the Fifth Fabliau

The poem that begins on the last leaf of Quire 13 and ends at the beginning of Quire 14 — the *Ordre de bel ayse* (no. 86; fols. 121ra–122va) — brings into the last gathering of Harley's sixth block not just the antifeminist arguments of its textual predecessors in the block, but also the spirit and play of the fabliaux. The *Ordre* is a satire rather than a fabliau, projecting not a story but the rules for an imaginary libertine religious order of men and women. Yet its satiric mode blends comfortably with the fabliau-attitudes towards sexual excesses among contemporary religious dramatized in both the *Trois Dames* and the fabliau we are about to engage — *Le Chevalier qui fist le cons parler* — which follows the *Ordre* in the fourteenth gathering. In the *Ordre*, nearly a third of the poem (71 lines of 248) is given over to the sex lives of the religious in the new order. To solace the sisters, for example, the secular canons will "play the game of love" (lines 122–26). And the sisters, according to the rule, will be obliged to lie on their backs, praying with their faces turned upward, while each friar, imitating the practice of the Carthusians, will have his own cell where he can have a sister in his arms. Limits of space keep us from looking more closely at the *Ordre* here. It is worth observing, however, that the notion of *solas*, used consistently to describe the illicit sex "regularized" in the order of "bel ayse," seems to have provided the scribe with a verbal link between the *Ordre* and the prologue to the fabliau immediately following it.

The last of the fabliaux in block six of Harley and the last fabliau in the anthology, *Le Chevalier qui fist le cons parler*, begins with a prologue that differs substantially from the six other extant redactions (all of them participants in continental fabliau-anthologies).[41] In all six the tale is named a *flabel* or a *fableau* in the first line, and in five of them we are told that minstrels are making good money by trafficking in a genre much in vogue. By contrast, Harley's prologue begins in more courtly tones, capturing the generic complexity of the tale to follow, and reminding us that all of the fabliaux in the English anthology enjoy comparable gentrification:

---

[41] The *Chevalier qui fist* is preserved in: Paris, BN MSS fr. 837 (incomplete), 1593, 19152, and 25545; Bern, Bibliothèque de la Bourgeoisie MS 354; Berlin, Deutsche Staatsbibliotek MS Hamilton 257; and Harley 2253.

Auentures e enseignement
Fount solas molt souent,
E solas fet releggement.
Ce dit Gwaryn que ne ment.
E pur solas demostrer
Vne trufle vueil comencer.[42]

[Adventures and instruction very often provide solace, and solace causes relief from anxiety. This Guerin says who does not lie. And to show forth solace, I want to begin a *trufle*.]

Insistently focused on *solas*, perhaps echoing the repeated notion of "comfortement" in the preceding satire, the opening lines of the *Chevalier qui fist* declare the English redactor's aim to engage readers in just the terms Harry Bailly uses to entice Chaucer's pilgrims to play the Canterbury game. Whether or not the Harley version is the result of memorial transmission, as Jean Rychner has suggested,[43] or of deliberate editing, the tale proper begins, as the other Harley fabliaux do, with an economical *mise-en-scene*. In this case, we meet a valiant, worthy, brave, wise, and handsome *bachiler*, recently knighted on account of his worth, who is nonetheless impoverished because of his extreme generosity. He is served by a squire named Huet, and with Huet, he sets out on a journey to fight in a tournament so as to better his financial situation. The dominant form framing this scenario is, as in the *Jongleur* and the *Corbaille*, that of the Breton romance or lai, though, as Per Nykrog rightly observes, this poem is "un véritable roman breton grossier" [a really crude Breton lai].[44]

In the tale proper the knight and his squire almost immediately come upon the kind of fairy tale landscape typical of Breton romance, but sketched out rather than elaborated: blossoming flowers, sweet fragrances, a fountain, a small, beautiful stream. At this point Huet catches sight of three naked maidens, "Sages, cortoises e tres beles," bathing in the stream (lines 61–63; fol. 123ra). Sending his master on ahead, he stops to steal the clothing the maidens have discarded, and though they cry out, asking him to give back their garments, Huet refuses to do so. The knight, to whom they also cry out, does return their clothes, though in the Harley version all of the ethical discussion between the knight and Huet about courtesy, shame, and the monetary value of the clothing present in other

---

[42] Lines 1–6; fol. 122vb. All references to the *Chevalier qui fist* are from Jean Rychner, ed., *Contribution à l'étude des fabliaux: Variantes, remaniements, dégradations*, 2 vols. (Geneva, 1960), 2.39–79, checked against the MS. See also the diplomatic edition of the Harley text in Noomen and van den Boogaard, eds., *NRCF*, 3.57–156.

[43] Rychner, ed., *Contribution*, 1.117.

[44] Nykrog, *Les Fabliaux*, p. 81

redactions is absent. Instead, the Harley text cuts directly to the action. As a reward for the knight's courtesy to them, each of the three maidens offers him a gift. The first two gifts would be perfectly appropriate in a courtly romance or lai: the eldest maiden promises the knight that he will be honored and loved wherever he goes, and the second tells him that no lady or maiden will refuse his love if he asks for it. The third gift, however, turns us abruptly to the world of fabliau:

> "Bel sire cheualer,
> Qe estes si cortois e si fer,
> Vn doun te vueil ie doner
> Dont meint se doit enmeruiller:
> Ie vus dorroi le poer
> De fere cul e coun parler
> A vostre requeste communement." (lines 99–105; fol. 123b)

> ["Handsome lord knight, you who are so courteous and so bold, I want to give you a gift about which many ought to marvel: I will give you the power to make asses and cunts alike speak at your request."]

Here the Harley text insists on the courtliness of the knight and the marvelousness of the gift in a way that invites laughter at the clash between the two generic trajectories being brought suddenly into intimate contact with each other.[45]

From this point on — nearly a third of the way into the tale — a bawdy fiction as incredible in its details as any in the Harley anthology — produces a series of embarrassing revelations first about a priest, then about a young woman serving a countess, and finally about the countess herself. While the first two revelations bear on the sex lives of the characters, the third one illustrates stock antifeminist arguments about the wiliness of women of the kind found, for example, in *Le Blasme des femmes* and the vernacular *De conjuge non ducenda* in the two previous quires of Harley. What gives the revelations their particular shock value is the hovering presence of the marvelous and the courtly borrowed from the tradition of the Breton lai. The first adventure constitutes a test of the first and third bathing maidens' gifts to the knight. As he and his squire ride forth, they encounter a chaplain who honors him just as the first *damoiselle* had promised. At this, Huet urges his master to make the cunt of the chaplain's mare speak, and so he does, asking the horse's genitalia where the priest is going. "Sire," the mare's cunt replies, "ie

---

[45] The other versions separate the gift of the speaking *cul* from that of the speaking *con*. Arguments could be made in defense of consolidating the two as the culminating third gift, but the continental separation of them makes good sense in terms of the knight's last adventure in the tale.

porte a mesoun le prestre a s'amie" [Lord, I carry the priest home to his girlfriend] (line 126; fol. 123va). The same genital voice also informs the knight that the priest is carrying ten marks to give to his mistress (suggesting that the *amie* is a prostitute). The result of this miracle is the priest's plea to the knight not to shame him, together with his bribe of the ten marks to ensure silence. What the redactor emphasizes (again absent from the other versions) is the knight's gratitude to God for his "merueillouse auenture" (lines 139–44), a gesture that recalls the motives of "auenture," "enseignement," and "solas" of the Harley prologue.

The knight's second and third adventures in the *Chevalier qui fist* turn us to the tale's dominant concern with female lust and trickery. If the fairy-tale-like bathing maidens give the knight gifts that bring him much-needed wealth, the same gifts also expose lascivious and scheming women, and they do so in the environment of a fine castle with all the amenities of a feudal court. Though much of the courtly description of the continental redactions is omitted in the Harley version, there is nonetheless a delightful interweaving of gracious hospitality with frank sexual desire as the knight asks, at supper, for the love of the maiden sitting next to him. The teller delicately occludes the alacrity of her acquiescence with the (mildly ironic) discretion of the brevity topos:

> A quoi dirroi je longement?
> Ele ly graunta soun talent . . .
> Ensemble ou li la nuit cochereit. (lines 169–70, 172; fol. 123vb)

[Why should I talk at length? She granted him his desire . . . went to bed with him that night.]

The maiden's willingness to go right to bed with the knight is, of course, the gift promised to him by the second of the beautiful bathers. The third gift, moreover, follows immediately, as the knight breaks into his love-play with the maiden to ask her cunt the most embarrassing of questions for a courtly *damoiselle*: "Daun coun, . . . / Me diez si vostre dammoisele / Seit vncore pucele" [Lord cunt, . . . tell me if your mistress is still a virgin] (lines 178, 181–82). With its habit of infallible truth-telling (recalling the themes of the *Jongleur*), the cunt replies:

> "Nanyl, syre, certeignement,
> Ele ad eu plus que cent
> Coillouns a soun derere." (lines 183–85)

["Not at all, lord, certainly, she has had more than a hundred testicles at her rear end."]

So dismayed and shamed is the maiden by this revelation that she flees the knight's bed and rushes to report her adventure to the countess. And this confession brings us to the tale's most hard-core fabliau event, precipitated by a wager the ingenious countess makes with the knight: a hundred pounds against his horse that he will not be able to make her cunt speak. With a slight smile, the countess excuses herself, goes to her room, stuffs her "coun" with four pounds of cotton (evoking the image of a cavernous space), and returns to challenge the knight's power. When he asks her cunt a question, no answer comes, but then Huet recalls the second half of the third bather's gift. If the cunt fails to respond, the *cul* will speak in its place. And so it does, explaining what ruse the countess has used to try to trick the knight and thereby win the bet. At this, the whole court condemns the countess, and, with a long hook, the cotton is pulled out. Now the knight asks the cunt directly why it did not respond, and the cunt repeats the explanation the *cul* had given, after which the count orders his wife to make her peace with the knight. With the knight triumphant, the wife embarrassed, he then takes his leave, bringing with him enough money to pay all his debts.

What this concluding sequence permits is a stunningly ungenteel focus on the countess' nether parts, presented as at once enormous and vocal. Her speaking *con* and *cul*, moreover, like the cunt of the chambermaid in bed with the knight earlier, confirm the worst antifeminist fears and suspicions about female sexuality and wiliness. The truths the nether voices reveal are secrets women's mouths would never speak concerning their hidden but insatiable appetite and their inveterate pleasure in playing tricks to win control of men.[46] In this regard, the tale may be seen as a fitting companion to the Harley fabliau of the *Trois Dames* in Quire 12 with its insistent exposition of male genitalia as objects of female devotion. As in the *Trois Dames*, this tale's concluding eight lines are very different from its continental analogues. Here the English redactor returns parodically to the initial trajectory of the Breton romance or lai of his tale, glancing perhaps at Chrétien de Troyes's *Le Chevalier au lion*:

> E quaunt cest auenture fust sue,
> E entre gent oye e vellze,
> Sy ly mistrent vn surnoun
> E le apelerent Cheualer de Coun,
> E son esquier Huet
> Le sournoun de Culet:
> Chyualer de Coun, Huet de Culet.
> Fous y est que plus y met! (lines 285–92; fol. 124va)

---

[46] I am grateful to my colleague, Farzaneh Milani, for helping me to understand the full antifeminist implications of the speaking female organs.

[And when this adventure was known, and heard and seen among the people, they gave him a surname and called him "Knight of the Cunt," and his squire Huet, the surname "Asslet": Knight of the Cunt, Huet of the Asslet. Crazy is he who puts down any more here!]

If indeed the composer of these lines had Chrétien's romance in mind, he would seem to have been thinking both of the "sournoun" given to Yvain and of the poem's final warning against any additions to the story:

Del chevalier al lion fine
Crestiëns son romant issi.
Onques plus dire n'en oï
Ne ja plus e'en orés conter
S'on n'i velt mençogne ajoster.[47]

[Thus Chrétien ends his romance of the Knight of the Lion. I have never heard more of it told and you never will hear more of it told, unless someone wants to add some lie.]

Textual relief from what many readers might regard as a surfeit of bawdiness comes at last, in the fourteenth quire of Harley, through a Middle English guide to practical wisdom written in rhymed stanzas, beginning with the comforting *incipit*: "Mon þat wol of wysdam heren" (fol. 125ra).[48] *Hending*, as this poem is known, is the second conduct book in Harley's sixth block, but, unlike *Urbain* in Quire 12, it is not in any way aristocratic; it is directed rather to the rich and poor alike.[49] Building on a foundation of faith in Christ and contempt for the world, *Hending* compiles a long series of folk proverbs (for example, "Honey licked from a thorn is dearly bought"), includes counsel against choosing the wrong wife, gives advice on the care of the soul, and concludes with a pious prayer to Christ to bring "vs to blisse" (fol. 127ra). The pair of lyrics on the folio following the end of *Hending* (fol. 128r–v), likewise in Middle English, draws together two of the main currents organizing the sixth block, namely, devotion to Christ versus the folly of devotion to women. Presented in the manuscript one after the other, the two poems — as song and

---

[47] David Hult, ed., *Le Chevalier au lion* (Paris, 1994), p. 594, lines 6804–08.

[48] The scribe actually exits from the world of fabliaux by way of a slight ME poem copied onto the blank space of the leaf on which the *Chevalier qui fist* ends, beginning, not incidentally, with the line "Of rybaudz Y ryme" (no. 88; fol. 124va). Among the debauched crowd satirized in this text are the grooms and pages who care for horses. Their very low stock, according to this text, explains why Christ himself, not wanting to put up with their waywardness, did not ride horses.

[49] For an edition of *Hending*, see Thomas Wright and James Orchard Halliwell, eds., *Reliquiae Antiquae*, 2 vols. (London, 1841, 1843), 1.109.

parados (song beside a song) — crystallize one of the largest, most commonplace of debates about love in the later Middle Ages (nos. 92, 93). In the way the two are presented in the manuscript, moreover, the lyric urging gratitude for Christ's saving love takes absolute precedence over the critique of a woman who refuses to requite her lover's suit. As mirror-images of each other, the two lyrics and their refrains express the vast abyss separating the comfort of Christ's ever-present love from the loneliness of the worldly lover yearning for an absent lady.

As if these two lyrics together were intended to punctuate the philosophical argument raised by Harley's sixth block, the rest of the fourteenth quire (which is to say the rest of the block) gives us a series of conventional texts belonging to the official world of the aristocracy, public affairs, and religious devotion. The first of these, the third of the block's courtesy books, is an Anglo-Norman redaction of the pious treatise Saint Louis compiled in Tunis on his deathbed in order to instruct his son in the conduct appropriate to a nobleman.[50] With its strong Christian foundation, Louis's *Enseignements*, like *Hending*, teaches lessons that provide ethical norms against which to measure the divagations of the fabliau world from which we have just emerged — illicit love-making among nuns, monks, priests, and friars; a wicked mother-in-law oppressing a poor knight and a *châtelaine* in love; a wife who despises her husband's family; a countess' genitalia speaking unsavory truth. "Speak no ill of others," King Louis advises his son (and Harley's readers). "Keep yourself from any action that might displease God." "Follow justice." If, as the shape of the Harley anthology hints, every aristocrat were to embrace such a guide (and if most or even all women except the Virgin Mary and her imitators were excluded from the world), then there would be no need to uncover and expose the extravagantly bad behavior of men and women living behind castle and abbey walls. Nor would there be a need for devotional saints' lives and prayers for divine mercy of the kind that conclude Harley's sixth block: first, a Latin life of an Anglo-Saxon bishop-saint, and then a Latin prayer which, according to its Anglo-Norman introduction, will guarantee remission of sins, protection from a bad death, and the assurance of a good end (nos. 98, 99).

That the conventional religious and ethical texts framing the sixth block of Harley seem to "save" the fabliaux (and the scurrilous world they depict) for a genteel audience might be merely a matter of chance. In this essay I have aimed, instead, to show that the ordering of the whole block, and of the fabliaux within it, is rather the result of fairly careful planning. At the same time, I have not meant to suggest that we can recreate exactly what

---

[50] The Harley text is nearly identical to the *text primitif* of the *Enseignements de saint Louis à son fils*, ed. Henri-François Delaborde, "Le Texte primitif des Enseignements de saint Louis à son fils," *Bibliothèque de l'École des Chartres* 73 (1912): 73–100, 237–62.

the scribe had in mind as he selected and copied each of the texts onto the parchment leaves before him, or to argue that no element of chance played a part in his selection. Nor do I make the least claim that there is only one correct or likely reading either of the anthology as a whole or of the individual texts or groups of texts within it. As Chaucer would have put it, "diverse folk diversely they rede." And this axiom would apply especially to the question of reading the Harley fabliaux, whose textual life in the manuscript has been the particular focus of this essay. Far from being marginalized or isolated, however, the five bawdy tales we have looked at seem to participate actively in a universe of discourse the Harley scribe's audience of gentlemen would surely have recognized as familiar, interconnected, and ethically useful. The fabliaux nestled within the sixth block of the manuscript challenge the assurance and comfort of the anthology's "official" discourses, no doubt delighting some readers and shocking others. For the scribe, though, they seem to enjoy an exemplary status in the codex by their implied kinship with clerkly antifeminist treatises, aristocratic conduct books, and even perhaps (in the case of the *Trois Dames* and the *Corbaille*) with Christian devotional materials.

As students of medieval English literature will recognize, Chaucer's *Canterbury Tales*, with its heterogeneous collection of fictions, including fabliaux, offers a discursive universe not altogether unlike the one we have been examining in Harley. To be sure, much in the Harley collection is verse rather than poetry, while Chaucer gives us poetic compositions of rare genius, including his bawdy tales. In addition, his anthology results from authorial rather than scribal choice (though it is put forward *as if* the choices were scribal). Yet there is no great leap between the kind of layered, multivalent intellectual and imaginative experience to which the Harley scribe invites us and the kind of challenge Chaucer offers us in a much more brilliant, aesthetically coherent way in his great Canterbury project. In both cases, the material book, presented as an anthology, virtually requires us to read backwards and forwards, to compare, contrast, and recollect the details of a particular range of well-known texts and kinds of text for the sake of vibrant debate and moral edification.[51]

---

[51] I am grateful to A. C. Spearing and Farzaneh Milani for their valuable criticism of earlier drafts of this essay and to Susanna Fein for her keen eye in preparing the text for publication.

Evading Textual Intimacy: The French Secular Verse

Mary Dove

The French secular verse of London, British Library MS Harley 2253 is still relatively unfamiliar, and even recent discussion of it tends to hark back to old critical debates. David L. Jeffrey and Brian J. Levy, editors of an invaluable anthology of French verse preserved in English manuscripts, regret that Anglo-Norman versification has been such a contentious issue.[1] Nevertheless, they associate the "astonishingly elastic" insular verse of Harley's only all-French love lyric, *Ferroy chaunsoun que bien deit estre oye* (no. 54; fol. 76r), with "vigour," as though insular poets were evincing a manly impatience with syllable-count.[2] I find this hard to reconcile with the considerable subtlety of the *Ferroy chaunsoun* refrain. In the first half the poet asks for God's and St. Thomas (Becket?)'s mercy on the faithless female beloved, and in the second half — with the stress emphatically falling on *ie* [I] — the poet offers her *his* pardon, if she begs him for mercy:

> Ie pri a Dieu e seint Thomas
> Qe il la pardoigne la trespas,
> E ie si verroiement le fas
>   Si ele merci me crye. (lines 8–11, etc.; fol. 76r)

[I pray to God and to St. Thomas that they may pardon her sin, and I shall truly do so if she begs me for mercy.]

This French *carole* and *Alysoun* (no. 29) are the only two lyrics in Harley 2253 written in a verse form specifically associated with the "courtly" lyric, and we have no way of

---

[1] David L. Jeffrey and Brian J. Levy, eds. and trans., *The Anglo-Norman Lyric: An Anthology* (Toronto, 1990), p. 17.

[2] Jeffrey and Levy, eds., *AN Lyric*, p. 20. For their metrical analysis of *Ferroy chaunsoun*, see pp. 253–54; for a general discussion of the relation between AN and continental French versification, see pp. 17–27. Item numbers derive from the list of contents in N. R. Ker, intro., *Facsimile of British Museum MS. Harley 2253*, EETS o.s. 255 (London, 1965), pp. ix–xvi.

knowing whether the resemblance is due to sheer chance or influence (in either direction).[3] Theo Stemmler claimed that the form of the English love lyrics in Harley 2253 owes a great deal to Romance and specifically to Anglo-Norman influence,[4] but, as Peter Dronke countered, the "Harley lyrics" show scarcely any sign of the "formal virtuosity" of the continental love poets.[5] The kinds of complexities Stemmler demonstrates arise, on the one hand, from a common European tradition (lyrical genres, rhetorical figures, narrative voice) and, on the other, from their poets' distinctive exploitation of the English language. Neither the manuscript itself nor the texts edited by Jeffrey and Levy in *The Anglo-Norman Lyric* amount to evidence of a flourishing tradition of French love lyric in England in the fifty years before Harley 2253 was written.[6]

When we consider the French secular verse of Harley 2253 as a whole, it is evident that the compiler(s) did not select on the basis of formal ingenuity or adventurousness.[7] In fact, apart from *Ferroy chaunsoun*, only two of the French secular poems are formally of interest: *Qvant voy la reuenue d'yuer*, a celebration of seasonal foods and drink (no. 20; fol. 55r), and "Qvy a la dame de parays," an alphabet poem in praise of women (*ABC a femmes*, no. 8; fols. 49r–50v). The form of *Qvant voy la reuenue d'yuer* is hard to elicit from the Harley 2253 copy, both because it is written in long lines with the ends of verses and stanzas only occasionally indicated and because the rhymes are often obscured, since it is an Anglo-Norman copy of a continental French original.[8] N. R. Ker admits he finds the rhyme scheme difficult and suggests that the scribe may have found it difficult too.[9]

---

[3] For details of the formal resemblances, see Mary Dove, "A Study of Some of the Lesser-Known Poems of British Museum MS Harley 2253" (Ph.D. diss., University of Cambridge, 1970), p. 285.

[4] Theo Stemmler, ed., *Die englischen Liebesgedichte des MS. Harley 2253* (Bonn, 1962), p. 215.

[5] Peter Dronke, review of Stemmler's *Die englischen Liebesgedichte*, *Medium Ævum* 32 (1963): 147.

[6] M. Dominica Legge's account of the AN love lyric has not been superseded (*Anglo-Norman Literature and Its Background* [Oxford, 1963], pp. 342–61). Most of the lyrics she mentions are accompanied by musical notation in the MSS, and she suggests that the words and music of *chansons* may, in England, normally have been copied onto rolls, which would have little chance of survival (p. 357).

[7] Nos. 75, 75a, 76, 77, 79, 82–84, 86, and 87 are in couplets; no. 9 is in couplets and *rime couée* (Yver speaks in the former and Esté in the latter); no. 24 is in *rime couée* with a refrain; no. 78 is in *rime couée* throughout; no. 80 is in monorhyming quatrains; no. 37 is in monorhyming quatrains and couplets; and no. 26 is in eight-line stanzas rhyming *abababab* (not *ababaaabab*, as Ker states [*Facsimile*, p. xi]).

[8] Bern, Bibliothèque de la Bourgeoisie MS 354, fols. 112v–114r; printed by M. Méon, *Nouveau Receuil de fabliaux et contes inédits*, 2 vols. (Paris, 1823), 1.301–06 (*La Devise aus lechéors*).

[9] Ker, *Facsimile*, p. xvii.

The other copy makes it clear that the stanzas are indeed of varying lengths and that monorhyme and *abab*-rhyme alternate in no fixed pattern.

Both the *ABC a femmes* and the English version of this poem in the Auchinleck MS (Edinburgh, National Library of Scotland MS Advocates 19.2.1, fols. 324r–325v) are in eleven-line stanzas rhyming *ababababcdc*, the ninth line being a one-stress bob.[10] Apart from the bob and the final line (a trimeter), the English text is in iambic tetrameters; in the French text it is difficult to identify any consistent syllabic or stress pattern. A minority of the stanzas are based (more or less) on the syllabic pattern 86868686286; the majority read more readily as accentual verse, the stress pattern being roughly the same as that of the English text. This kind of tension between syllabic and accentual verse is characteristic of French verse written in England in around 1300, and the extreme metrical irregularity of the French *ABC a femmes* would seem to me to suggest that the poet's ear is simultaneously hearing both the four-stress lines of the English text and the 8686 syllabic pattern of a poem like the *Enseignement sur les amis* (no. 26; fols. 61v–62v). If the French text were in any way obscure, or if at any point the sense had obviously been lost, we might guess that the *ABC a femmes* is a later version of what was once a more metrically regular poem, but in fact there is no obscurity at all.[11] There is no reason, then, to suppose that the French poem was written before the English poem, or before the English Harley lyrics.[12]

The English poem, it has been assumed, is the translation,[13] for (I think) two main reasons: first, that at the time F. Holthausen printed the texts in parallel Harley 2253 was

---

[10] The French and English texts are printed in parallel by F. Holthausen, ed., "Die Quelle des mittelenglischen Gedichtes 'Lob der Frauen,'" *Archiv für das Studium der neueren Sprachen und Literaturen* 108 (1902): 288–301. Ker gets the rhyme pattern wrong (*Facsimile*, p. x). The two versions are compared in Dove, "Study," pp. 50–60, and the French text is printed, pp. 95–102.

[11] The one obscure place in the text printed by Thomas Wright (*Specimens of Lyric Poetry, Composed in England in the Reign of Edward the First*, Percy Society 4 [1842; repr. New York, 1965], pp. 1–13) and then Holthausen ("Die Quelle," pp. 289–98) results from a misreading of the MS: for "Quant diensist femme compaigne a houme" read "Quant Dieu fist . . ." (line 164; fol. 49v). This is not noticed by Holthausen among his few corrections to Wright's text, "Nachtrag zu Archiv CVIII, 288ff," *Archiv für das Studium der neueren Sprachen und Literaturen* 110 (1903): 102–03.

[12] The term refers to the verse printed in G. L. Brook, ed., *The Harley Lyrics: The Middle English Lyrics of MS. Harley 2253*, 4th ed. (Manchester, 1968).

[13] Following Holthausen ("Die Quelle," pp. 288–301), Rossell Hope Robbins and John L. Cutler mention the "French original" in Harley 2253 (*Supplement to the Index of Middle English Verse* [Lexington, 1965], no. 552.8), citing F. L. Utley, *The Crooked Rib* (Columbus, Ohio, 1944), p. 42.

dated ca. 1310[14] and the Auchinleck MS anything from twenty to forty years later; secondly, the French text is complete while the English text begins and ends imperfectly. I incline to the view that the *ABC a femmes* is a translation of the English poem, or rather a *remaniement* of the English poem. The short bob (usually two, sometimes three syllables in the French) is characteristic of English poetry written in the Northern Midlands, but not at all characteristic of French poetry.[15] The French counterpart of the bob, the short line introducing the *tornada*, is the four-syllable line made famous by the "Gailhem IX" stanza.[16] Other evidence suggesting that the English poem may be the original is provided by the more effective alphabet-words at *E* ("Eiȝen," eyes, as against "Eux"), *L* ("Luf" as against "L'amour"), *Q* ("Quen" as against "Qvoyntement"), and *S* ("Spice" as against "Si").[17] If I am right that the *ABC a femmes* is an Anglo-Norman *remaniement* of an English lyric (and it seems to me an open question), it would be tempting to see a flourishing tradition of English secular lyric in the North and in the Midlands encouraging poets to compose secular lyrics in similar stanza-forms in French. This would, of course, be the exact opposite of Stemmler's thesis.

***

The pursuit of formal relationships between the Middle English and French secular verse in Harley 2253 soon peters out in pure speculation, so that questions of priority and influence yield to newer literary-historical questions of mediation and negotiation. Editing the trilingual lyric *Dum ludis floribus* (no. 55; fol. 76r), in which French is,

---

[14] Karl Böddeker, ed., *Altenglische Dichtungen des MS. Harl. 2253* (1878; repr. Amsterdam, 1969), p. III.

[15] The dialect of the English text is North East Midland. Examples of the one-foot bob in English poems in Harley 2253 are *The Execution of Sir Simon Fraser* (no. 25) and *On the Follies of Fashion* (no. 25a). The most famous example is, of course, *Sir Gawain and the Green Knight* (North West Midland dialect).

[16] Compare, in Harley 2253, *A Wayle Whyt ase Whalles Bon* (no. 36), a poem imitating the "Gailhem IX" stanza in English, as Dronke points out (review, p. 147). Alfred Jeanroy discusses the "Gailhem IX" stanza in his edition of the poet's works, *Les Chansons de Guillaume IX, duc d'Aquitaine (1071–1127)*, 2nd ed. (Paris, 1927), p. xiii.

[17] We may also note that the bob-lines in the English poem have a much greater impact than do the equivalent French lines: "al our blis were brouȝt on kne / *wel lawe*" (lines 41–42), "Þer never more schal be no griþ / *no bote*" (lines 63–64), "so clot, that liþ in clay yclong / *so sore*" (lines 74–75), "maken oft her leres swet / *wel wete*" (lines 206–07), and "Wolves and houndes to don his masse / *bi niȝt*" (line 229), for instance. Typical French examples are *a dreyt* (line 9), *a tort* (line 42), *dedenȝ* (line 41), *souent* (line 196), and *tot dis* (line 240).

in spite of the opening line, the primary language, Jeffrey and Levy speculate "that the composer is an English wandering scholar . . . learning the French of Paris and its gallant verses and showing off his Latin into the bargain."[18] The poet does indeed claim

> Scrips[i] hec carmina in tabulis,
> Mon ostel est en mi la vile de Paris (lines 17–18),

[I wrote these verses on my note-tablet; I live in a student hostel in Paris.]

but an English (South West Midland?) student at the University of Paris around 1300 hardly qualifies as a *clericus vagans*, even if he does envisage his beloved like Juno among the flowers and desire God mercifully to grant that he may kiss her and do "the other things that follow" (lines 15–16).[19] Writing as if from a lodging-house in Paris, the student-poet may predict he will die if his girl denies him sex, but the presumptive *tabula* on which he writes his short-term verses can only be encountered by way of the page of a codex, a codex that could not have been written without at least relative stability of employment, cultural contacts permitting texts to be exchanged, interest in the conservation of texts, and expectation of the continuing value of certain texts in a specific social context.

To put sexual desire where love of God should be is in medieval terms "inordinaat," but disorder of this kind surely does not signify lack of a fixed abode or permanent employment. Rather, it implies a context in which the proper ordering of love is so securely agreed that the idea of disorder can be safely enjoyed. The trilingualism of *Dum ludis floribus* must suggest either that the perceived context for its performance/circulation was a male and educated one, or that the perceived context was one in which the male and educated element would enjoy understanding what the female and non-Latin-literate element could not understand. The two lines of English with which the poem ends suggest the latter:

---

[18] Jeffrey and Levy, eds., *AN Lyric*, p. 249. The "wandering" clerk-poets were first identified as a group by German scholars, as in the title of W. Giesebrecht's ground-breaking discussion, "Die Vaganten oder Goliardi und ihre Lieder," in *Allgemeine Monatschrift für Wissenschaft und Literatur* (Braunschweig, 1853), pp. 10–43. The term was popularized in English by Helen Waddell, *The Wandering Scholars* (London, 1927). Böddeker, the first editor of the collected English lyrics of Harley 2253, portrayed their scribe as a wandering scholar who sought the shelter of the cloister after a life of restless roaming (*Altenglische Dichtungen*, p. III).

[19] I read *velud Lacinia* as "like the Lacinian woman," i.e., Juno. Jeffrey and Levy translate the first line "While my mistress disports herself in flowers" (*AN Lyric*, p. 248), although the verb is certainly second person singular. *Que* (line 16) is Latin, not French.

May Y sugge namore so [uv]el me is,[20]
3ef Hi de3e for loue of hire, duel hit ys. (lines 19–20; fol. 76r)

If *Dum ludis floribus* offers itself as a transgressive *jeu d'esprit*, the context in which it is preserved invites us to ponder that self-assessment. What kind of discourse of sexuality do the French secular poems of Harley 2253 participate in? The *Dum ludis floribus* poet's girl is set apart among the flowers and in her non-Latinity from the world of the schools, but the poet of the *ABC a femmes* offers women an alternative schooling:

Ie froi a femmes vn ABC
  A l'escole si eles vueillent aler.
Celes que sunt lettree
  As autres purront recorder
Coment eles sunt honoree. (lines 14–18; fol. 49r)

[I shall compose an alphabet for women, should they wish to go to school. Those who are literate will be able to tell the others how they are held in honor.]

Those women who can read (French) are offered the chance to go to school to learn what is being said about women, by men, and to pass on to their illiterate sisters the news that they are by all men held in honour, "En dreyture sauntz fauser / De nulle" [as is only right, no one denying it] (lines 19–20). The trope recognizes women's desire for the education they are denied, but permits them to be interested in one subject only, themselves, reflected through men and doubly distorted because the curriculum shows them only what they want to see, preserving them "de tote blame" [from all reproach] (line 25). Doubtless the *ABC a femmes* assumes a knowledge of misogynistic alphabet poems such as "Audite alphabetica / Cantica sophistica," continuing "Bilingwis [double-tongued] . . . / Cruenta [blood-guilty] . . . / Dolosa [treacherous] . . ." etc.[21]

The *ABC a femmes* belongs to what I shall call the *propretés des femmes* (the characteristics of women, "what women are like") discourse, involving in its late medieval

---

[20] The MS reads *wel*, which I interpet as *uvel*. Jeffrey and Levy translate this line "I should say no more and quit while I'm behind" (*AN Lyric*, p. 249), but I take the literal meaning to be "I can say no more, I am in such a sorry state."

[21] Julius Feifalik, ed., *Sitzungsberichte der Kaiserlichen Akademie der Wissenschaften*, Phil.-Hist. Classe 36, II (Vienna, 1861), pp. 164–66; see also August Wulff, *Die frauenfeindlichen Dichtungen in den romanischen Literaturen des Mittelalters bis zum End des XIII. Jahrhunderts* (Halle a. S., 1914), pp. 56–57.

manifestation both *blasme* [accusation, reproach] and praise.[22] I take the category-name from the Cambridge text of the poem *Le Blasme des femmes*: "Ici commencent les propretés des femmes en romaunz,"[23] an incipit implying that this *dit* was perceived to derive from Latin accounts of the *proprietates mulieris* such as that in Oxford, Bodleian Library MS Bodley 57 (ca. 1300). There, the question "Quid est mulier?" [What is woman?] is answered:

Humana abusio, insatiabilis bestia, continua sollicitudo, indesinens pugna, cotidianum dampnum, domus tempestatis, castitatis impedimentum, incontinentis viri naufragium (etc.).[24]

[Incorrectly termed "human," she is an insatiable beast, continuous anxiety, an unceasing battle, daily loss, the dwelling-place of storm, an obstacle to chastity, shipwreck for the incontinent man.]

To be sure, the poet of the *ABC a femmes* owns his text as a "poy enueysure" [a little pleasantry] (line 24); to take it seriously against the grain is not to deny the barbed yet graceful wit its original readers/hearers, female and male, must have enjoyed. Wit, grace, barbs, and a mixed audience do not, however, sufficiently account for the phenomenon of the *propretés des femmes*.

Five of the French secular poems of Harley 2253 concern what women are like: "Qvy a la dame de parays" (*ABC a femmes*, no. 8); "Seignours e dames ore escotez" (*Le Dit des femmes*, no. 76); "Quy femme prent a compagnie" (*Le Blasme des femmes*, no. 77); "Femmes a la pye" (Nicholas Bozon's *De la femme et de la pie*, no. 78); and "Bene soit Dieu omnipotent" (*De conjuge non ducenda*, no. 83). Another two French secular poems of Harley 2253 contain related material: "En May par vne matyne s'en ala iuer" (*Gilote et Johane*, no. 37) and "Vn sage homme de grant valour" (*Urbain le courtois*, no. 79). Moreover, at least five of the English poems of Harley 2253 can be associated with the *propretés des femmes* discourse: "Lord þat lenest vs lyf" (*On the Follies of Fashion*, no. 25a), "Weping haueþ myn wonges wet" (*The Poet's Repentance*, no. 33), "In a fryht as Y con fare fremede" (*The Meeting in the Wood*, no. 35), "In May hit murgeþ when hit

---

[22] A useful summary of the classical and patristic origins of this tradition can be found in Wulff, *Die frauenfeindlichen Dichtungen*, pp. 1–18. See also Dove, "Study," pp. 7–14, and for some interesting and less frequently encountered references, R. F. Bennett, *The Early Dominicans: Studies in Thirteenth-Century Dominican History* (Cambridge, 1937), p. 121.

[23] Cambridge, Cambridge University Library MS Gg.i.1, fol. 627r–v; Gloria K. Fiero, Wendy Pfeffer, and Mathé Allain, eds. and trans. in *Three Medieval Views of Women* (New Haven, 1989), pp. 120–42.

[24] Fol. 20v. See Paul Meyer, "Notice du MS Bodley 57," *Romania* 35 (1906): 576; compare also Wulff, *Die frauenfeindlichen Dichtungen*, pp. 28–32.

dawes" (*Advice to Women*, no. 44), and "Mon þat wol of wisdam heren" (*Hending*, no. 89). Among the Latin contents of Harley 2253, *propretés des femmes* material occurs in the extract from John of Wales's *Communeloquium* (no. 109). The queen in the game of chess "vadit oblique et capit vndique indirecte, quia cum auarissimum sit genus mulierum" [moves obliquely and takes indirectly on all sides, because the nature of women is extremely avaricious] (fol. 135v).[25] Avarice is one of the charges characteristically levelled against women in *propretés des femmes* poems: "Les plus riches fet payn querauntz" [(She) makes the richest men beggars] (line 22; fol. 111va), claims the poet of *Le Blasme des femmes*.[26]

At the end of the *ABC a femmes*, the poet envisages women turning pale as they leave the public room for the private chamber in order to give birth, a pallor men have caused:

> Lur colour pur nus empire
> De sale en chau[m]bre quant eles vont. (lines 309–10; fol. 50v)

[Their complexion dims on our account when they go from the hall to their bedchamber.]

He had earlier claimed that

> Ou va femme la vet ioie;
> Ele ne va pas soule (lines 21–22; fol. 49r),

[Where woman goes, there goes joy; she does not go alone.]

but woman's constant companion, joy (that is, man's joy in her sexual company) has led ineluctably to her life's danger. As we should expect, most *propretés des femmes* texts include material directly relating to marriage. This may be in the form of debate motifs, virginity versus marriage debate (*De conjuge non ducenda* is of this type),[27] marriage versus promiscuity debate (such as *L'Estrif de deus dames* in Oxford, Bodleian Library MS Digby 86, fols. 192v–195r[28]), or, in the case of *Gilote et Johane*, debate between all

---

[25] Compare *Communeloquium (Summa collationum)* (Paris, 1516), pt. i, dist. x, cap. 7; fol. xxix.

[26] See Fiero et al., eds., *Three Medieval Views*, p. 123.

[27] See particularly the notes to part I of M. W. Bloomfield's article, "*Piers Plowman* and the Three Grades of Chastity," *Anglia* 76 (1958): 227–45.

[28] Edmund Stengel, ed., *Codicem manu scriptum Digby 86 in Bibliotheca Bodleiana asservatum* (Halle, 1871), pp. 84–93; see also the text in Paris, BN MS fr. 837, fols. 338r–339v, Achille Jubinal, ed., *Nouveau Receuil de contes, dits, fabliaux et autres pièces inédites des XIIIe, XIVe et XVe siècles*, 2 vols. (Paris, 1839, 1842), 2.73–82.

three options (virginity is personified by Johane, promiscuity by Gilote, and marriage by "Uxor" [Wife]). Marriage may also be represented in the *propretés des femmes* in the form of topoi such as the *Minnesklaven* "(male) slaves of love," made famous by *Sir Gawain and the Green Knight,*[29] or *mal mariage* warnings about the kind of woman not to wed and about the kinds of behavior to avoid in marriage.

The *mal mariage* topos is particularly associated with the literature of proverbial wisdom passed from father to son. In Harley 2253 we have an example in *Urbain le courtois* (no. 79):

> Prenez femme de honours
> E que soit de bon mours,
> E veiez qe ele seit sage
> Que tei ne peyse la mariage . . .
> Quei que vostre femme vus die
> Trop ne la creyez mye,
> Si ele ne seit profitable
> Saunz mensonge ou fable[30]

[Take to wife a worthy woman with good habits, and make sure that she is wise, so that marriage may not be a burden to you . . . Do not place too much trust in anything your wife says to you, unless it is both useful and true.][31]

"Do not trust your wife"[32] provides the starting point for two versions of the *dit* known as *Le Blasme des femmes*:

---

[29] J. R. R. Tolkien and E. V. Gordon, eds., *Sir Gawain and the Green Knight*, 2nd ed. rev. Norman Davis (Oxford, 1967), pp. 66–67 (lines 2414–28), discussed by Mary Dove, "Gawain and the *Blasme des Femmes* Tradition," *Medium Ævum* 41 (1972): 20–26. On the topos, see Friedrich Maurer, "Der Topos von der *Minnesklaven*," *Deutsche Viertejahrsschrift für Literaturwissenschaft und Geistesgeschichte* 27 (1953): 182–206.

[30] Lines 328–31, 334–37; fol. 113va. There are nine texts of *Urbain li courtois*, but lines 334–37 are found only in the Harley MS, which is not used for H. Rosamond Parsons's edition, "Anglo-Norman Books of Courtesy and Nurture," *PMLA* 44 (1929): 383–455.

[31] The *mal mariage* topos is also found in *Hending*, lines 113–24 and 264–69 (lines found only in the Harley MS).

[32] We may recall here Adam's words to Eve, "Jo te crerrai, tu es ma per" [I shall trust you, you are my companion/equal], and Figura's words to Adam, "Ta mollier creïs plus que mei" [You trust your wife more than me] (P. Studer, ed., *Le Mystère d'Adam* [Manchester, 1918], p. 17, line 313, and p. 21, line 423, respectively).

Ne est mie saie qui femme creyt
Morte ou vive qu'ele qui seyt. (Digby text)

[He who trusts women, whether she is alive or dead, is not at all wise.]

Mult fait graunte folie
Qui femme crest en ceste vie. (Douce text)

[Whoever trusts a woman in this world is a very great fool.]

The same idea occurs in all nine versions at some point in the poem.[33] In Harley 2253 the equivocal opening of the poem immediately suggests a marriage debate:[34]

Quy femme prent a compagnie
Veiez si il fet sen ou folye (lines 1–2; fol. 111rb)

[See if the man who takes a woman as a companion is doing a wise or foolish thing.]

All the texts of *Le Blasme des femmes* (except Douce) introduce the *Minnesklaven* topos. The Cambridge and Florence texts remind us of what happened to Adam, the first of woman's victims:

Puis que li monde fust furmé
Comenca femme cruealté. (Cambridge text, lines 33–34)

[Woman began to be cruel as soon as the world had been made.]

The other versions all mention Solomon, Samson, and Constantine, and the Harley, Digby, and Westminster Abbey texts refer to Hippocrates as well:

---

[33] Digby 86 (fols. 113v–114r) and Oxford, Bodleian Library Douce 210 (fol. 49v). The Douce text is not mentioned in Fiero et al., eds., *Three Medieval Views* (see pp. 12–16 for the other eight texts), or elsewhere; it is printed by Dove, "Study," pp. 75–76. CUL Gg.i.1, fol. 627r, reads "Ki femme ou femine creit / sa mort brace e sa mort beit" [Whoever trusts any woman embraces and drinks his death] (lines 7–8).

[34] The Florence text (entitled *Tractatus de bonitate et malitia mulierum*), the two Paris texts, and the Rouen text of *Le Blasme de femmes* (Fiero et al., *Three Medieval Views*, p. 12) begin in the same way as Harley 2253; the text in London, Westminster Abbey MS 21 (entitled *Le Dit de la condition des femmes*) begins "Uns homs qui se marie / Voiez [etc.]" (fol. 35v).

> . . . ly bon myr Ypocras
> Qe tant sauoit de medicyne artz
> Fust par sa femme descu.[35]

[The good doctor Hippocrates, who knew so much about the skills of medicine, was deceived by his wife.]

Consequently, Harley 2253 (and five other texts of *Le Blasme des femmes*) give instructions on how to render a wife a tolerable companion:

> Mes, quy vodera femme ioyr,
> Ie ly dirroi sauntz mentyr
> Qu'il ly donast poy a manger
> E mal a vestir e a chaucer
> E la batist menu e souent:
> Donqe freit il de femme son talent.[36]

[Further, I shall say without a lie to the man who would like to enjoy a wife that he should give her little to eat and poor clothing and shoes, and that he should beat her little and often: after that, he will be able to do what he likes with her.]

The first seven stanzas of Franciscan friar Nicholas Bozon's poem *De la femme et de la pie* (no. 78; fol. 112ra–b) reproach women in general, not just married women, but the rest of the poem talks specifically about the unattractive habits of wives, by way of an extended comparison between the characteristics of women and magpies.[37] This can be seen as an elaboration of the topos of woman-as-animal found in Latin accounts of the *proprietates mulieris*; in Bodley 57 woman is "animal pessimum . . . aspis insanabilis" [the worst of animals, a viper whose bite is incurable]. All but two of the versions of *Le Blasme des femmes* include the woman-as-animal topos: in Harley 2253, the section begins

> Femme est lyoun pur deuorer,
> Femme est gopil pur gent deceyure. (lines 38–39; fol. 111va)

---

[35] Harley text, lines 85–87. The Westminster Abbey text provides details of how Hippocrates was poisoned by his wife and thrown on a dunghill (lines 99–111, text unprinted).

[36] Lines 63–68; fol. 111vb. The other texts including these lines are the Digby text, the two Paris texts, and the Rouen and Westminster Abbey texts.

[37] Ed. from BL Addit. MS 46919, fol. 75r–v, by Jeffrey and Levy, eds., *AN Lyric*, pp. 223–29; Dove prints the Harley and Additional texts in parallel ("Study," pp. 86–88). On Bozon, see also *AN Lyric*, pp. 14–16.

[Woman is a lion in devouring, a fox in deceiving people.],

while the Douce text, after the opening couplet about the folly of trusting a woman, compares her with the serpent, lizard, and basilisk, "that with one single look puts to death a hundred thousand men" (lines 9–10).[38] The text of *De la femme e de la pie* in Harley 2253, as Jeffrey and Levy note, includes three added lines (disrupting the stanza pattern)[39] in which the male reader/ hearer is directly warned against wedlock:

> Pur icele gyse
> Ie lou que vm se auyse
>   Auaunt qu'il soit mary. (lines 49–51; fol. 112rb)

[Therefore I recommend that a man should think carefully before getting married.]

Le Blasme des femmes in Digby 86 is tacked onto the fabliau *Les Quatre Souhés s. Martin*,[40] as though at some point a scribe had taken the ending of the Paris text of the fabliau —

> Qui miex croit sa fame que lui
> Sovent l'en vient honte et anui (lines 199–200)

[Shame and harm often come to the man who trusts his wife more than himself] —

as a cue, and the fabliau and the *dit* had come to circulate together.[41] Similarly, in Douce 210 *Le Blasme des femmes* follows on from *De conjuge non ducenda* (in French) with only a marginal *nota* to mark the transition. As the title suggests, *De conjuge non ducenda*

---

[38] The woman-as-animal topos in Harley 2253 ends at line 48 (CUL Gg.i.1 has a better reading than Harley at lines 71–72; Fiero et al., eds., *Three Medieval Views*, p. 124); the topos is not found in Paris, BN MS fr. 1593 or in Westminster Abbey MS 21.

[39] Jeffrey and Levy, eds., *AN Lyric*, p. 228.

[40] As noted by Fiero et al., eds., *Three Medieval Views*, p. 13.

[41] *Les Quatre Souhés*, Digby 86, fols. 113r–114r in Stengel, ed., *Codicem manu scriptum Digby 86*, pp. 36–38. The text in Paris, BN MS fr. 837, fols. 189r–190r, is printed in Anatole de Montaiglon and Gaston Raynaud, eds., *Receuil général et complet des fabliaux des XIIIᵉ et XIVᵉ siècles*, 6 vols. (1872–90; repr. New York, 1964), 5.201–07; quotation, 5.207. The ending of the Bern text resembles the end of the Paris text (see 5.368).

is another warning against marriage: three "angels" in the form of three eminent medieval ecclesiasts advise Gawain of the miseries of married life.[42]

The poem (no. 83; fols. 117ra–118rb) is a mock-debate; the three voices, like the Trinity, all speak with one sense (Latin text, lines 29–30). In the French translation there is the added joke that Gawain pretends he is expecting to hear arguments encouraging a man to want to marry and estimates that the angels are doing a very poor job:

> Veiez ci poure comencement
> A doner houme bon talent
> De femme prendre en esposaille!
> N'est mie bone, ie dy sauntz faille. (lines 61–64; fol. 117va)

[See here a feeble start at making a man desirous of taking a woman in marriage! I say for sure, it is no good at all.]

But the message of the poem is unequivocal, at least in the Latin, and in the French text in Douce 210: "Gardez vous de mariage" [Beware of marriage] (line 286). In Harley 2253, however, the reading is "Gardez vus de mal mariage" (line 166; fol. 118ra), a reading weakening the whole impact of the argument, which does not allow for the possibility of anything *but* a "bad marriage." Interestingly, however, it suggests that some reader of *De conjuge non ducenda* has linked the advice given to the young Gawain by the experienced "angels" with the advice given by the old man to his son.

Returning, then, to *Urbain le courtois* (no. 79; fols. 112rc–113vb), in which we have already noticed the inclusion of the *mal mariage* topos, four texts of this poem (not including Harley 2253) culminate in material relating to *Le Blasme des femmes*.[43] Some "fole gent" [foolish fellows] realize all their assets in order to buy their women clothes and delicate foods, but a woman's greed — unlike a man's purse — is inexhaustible:

> Tant cum la bours puet durer
> Amur de femme poez aver,

---

[42] The Latin original is printed in A. G. Rigg, ed., *Gawain on Marriage: The Textual Tradition of the "De Coniuge Non Ducenda" with Critical Edition and Translation* (Toronto, 1986). Rigg describes the Harley 2253 redaction on pp. 102–03. The French poem is more fully discussed in Dove, "Study," pp. 40–49, and the Harley and Douce texts are printed in parallel (pp. 77–85).

[43] CUL Gg.i.1, fols. 6v–7v; Douce 210, fols. 43r–45r; Cambridge, Trinity College MS O.1.17, fols. 265r–266r; and Oxford, Bodleian Library MS Bodley 9, fols. 55v–58r. All these texts contain texts of the "Earlier Version," according to Parsons ("AN Books," pp. 398–408).

E quant la bourse si est close
De femme averez une glose.[44]

[As long as the money-bag holds out, you can have a woman's love, and when the money-bag is shut up, you will get a brush-off.]

We have seen how misogynistic *propretés des femmes* material circulates through the French secular verse of Harley 2253 and through the French secular verse of some related French and English manuscripts (Cambridge, Cambridge University Library MS Gg.i.1; Oxford, Bodleian Library MSS Digby 86 and Douce 210; London, British Library MS Additional 46919; Paris, Bibliothèque Nationale MSS fr. 837 and fr. 1593; and Bern, Bibliothèque de la Bourgeoisie MS 354). The praise of women that is an element of the *propretés des femmes* textual complex is also represented in Harley 2253 and in these other manuscripts. Unlike *blasme* poems, however, praise poems do not constitute a poetic corpus whose parts can be fairly freely interchanged and combined. Sometimes praise-of-women texts simply, and flatly, contradict *blasme*. The opening lines from the Harley *Le Blasme des femmes*, meaning "See if a man who takes a woman as a companion is doing a wise or foolish thing" (quoted above), become in the Bern version of *Le Bien des femmes*:

Je l'ai oi, c'est veritez,
Sa compeignie valt assez. (lines 9–10)

[I have heard, it is the truth, her company is worth a lot.]

And the next lines in Harley,

Qy en femme despent sa cure
Oiez sa mort e sa dreiture (lines 3–4; fol. 111rb)

[Hear the death and judgment of the man who devotes his care to a woman],

become:

---

[44] CUL Gg.i.1, lines 177–80. There is a marginal *nota* on fol. 7v; see Parsons's "Earlier Version," lines 231–34 ("AN Books," p. 407). Parsons glosses *glose* "speech, words" (p. 454); in context it seems to mean "empty words."

Il fait mult bien selonc nature
Qui en fame despant sa cure[45]

[The man who devotes his care to a woman acts very well, in accordance with nature].

Such verse is worth nothing unless the reader/hearer mentally supplies the *blasme* text that is being rewritten[46] — but the same is not true in reverse. I cannot agree with F. L. Utley that *blasme* material always implies the possibility of its opposite, or that *blasme* and praise of women are exact counterparts.[47]

Each praise poem is a separate and discrete apologia. The impersonal *blasme* material is countered by scholastic and pseudo-scholastic arguments, by proverbs, by arguments drawn from experience and from common sense, and by courtly assertions of woman's pre-eminence. The compiler of Harley 2253 evidently thought of *Le Dit des femmes* and *Le Blasme des femmes* as related texts, for they are juxtaposed in the manuscript (nos. 76, 77, respectively; fol. 110vb–111vb),[48] but the Harley *Le Dit des*

---

[45] Lines 11–12; Bern 354, incipit "Oez seignor ie n'otroi pas" (fol. 174r). Thomas Wright prints lines 1–16 only (*Anecdota literaria: A Collection of Short Poems in English, Latin and French* [London 1844], pp. 97–99); the full text is printed by Dove, "Study," pp. 92–94. The poem in BN MS fr. 837 called *Le Bien des femmes*, incipit "Qui que des fames vous mesdie" (fol. 193r), is a different text (Fiero et al., eds., *Three Medieval Views*, pp. 106–18). The Harley 2253 *Le Dit des femmes*, incipit "Seignours e dames ore escotez" (fols. 110v–111r), is again a different text (Bern and Harley share just one couplet: lines 79–80 = lines 33–34).

[46] The same can be said about the introduction of the *Minnesklaven* topos in the English text of the *ABC a femmes*:

& y were as douhti a swai(n)
as was Samson, er he w(as schorn),
or al so wiȝt as was Waw(ain)
or Salomon þat was (wisest born)
ȝete wald me nouȝt (þinke gain)
þat wiman schuld (be sent at morn)
to go on feld in snow (and rain) (lines 243–49).

See further Dove, "Study," p. 22.

[47] Utley, *Crooked Rib*, p. 38.

[48] Carter Revard sees this juxtaposition as a pairing of opposites characteristic of Harley 2253 as a whole ("*Gilote et Johane*: An Interlude in B. L. MS. Harley 2253," *Studies in Philology* 79 [1982]: 131).

femmes is an intimate-seeming celebration of two interrelated concepts, God's high regard for woman and woman's innate courtliness:[49]

> . . . Dieu les fist par grant cure.
> Le noun de femme lur dona
> Pur sa mere qe taunt ama,
> E pus les fist bones e pleynes de bounte
> E beles sauntz iniquite. (lines 10–14; fol. 110vb)

[God made them with exquisite care, and gave them the name "woman" for the sake of his mother whom he loved so much, and afterwards he made them full of goodness, beautiful and guiltless.]

The same point, with the same opening words, opens the discussion of the folly of those who abuse women, for

> Deus les fist, par grant leysir,
> Pur seruyr gentz a pleysyr. (lines 67–68; fol. 111ra)

[God made them, and took a long time over it, so that they might be a means of delight to man.]

Whatever a woman may do, she will never see hell's torment (lines 101–02), but the man who has the temerity and folly to abuse her will never reach paradise, because "Dieu ne eyme qe femme het" [God does not love the man who hates woman] (line 49). How can this be heresy, the poet would seem to be mock-innocently asking, when I am defending woman to the hilt?

Blasme texts present themselves as impersonal and authoritative; praise texts present themselves as personal and grounded in *preef*. "What women are like" is obscured both by the *blasme* and the praise aspects of the *propretés des femmes* discourse, which might be seen as an even more than usually unacceptable version of the woman-as-devil/woman-as-angel bifurcation,[50] since these texts actually claim as their subject matter what women

---

[49] There is a more extensive comparison of this poem with the Harley 2253 *Le Blasme des femmes* in Dove, "Study," pp. 33–40.

[50] In Harley's *Le Jongleur d'Ely et le Roi d'Angleterre* (no. 75) there is an explicit recognition of the fact that if a woman behaves graciously she is regarded as a whore, while if she behaves with some restraint she is regarded as intolerably haughty (lines 306–21); compare also Nicholas Bozon, *La Bonté des femmes*, ed. L. T. Smith and P. Meyer, *Les Contes moralisés de Nicole Bozon* (Paris, 1889), pp. xxxiii–xli (lines 79–96). See also Dove, "Study," pp. 110–11.

are like. In Johan Vising's and Keith V. Sinclair's classifications of Anglo-Norman literature (I do not underestimate the difficulties of classification), poems about women are included in the category "satirical and humorous pieces," while *Urbain le courtois* is included in the category "didactic and moral works, proverbs."[51] Yet, as we have seen, *propretés des femme* material circulates both along with and within *Urbain le courtois*, and there are many *blasme* proverbs, including "Femme siet vn art plus que le deable" [Woman is craftier than the devil], the final line of *Le Blasme des femmes* in Harley 2253, included in all nine versions of this poem. In the fabliau *Dame Jouenne*, this proverb is cited by Jouenne, in relation to herself — "J'ai un art plus que deable" — and approved as true by her husband: "Jouenne, ce n'est mie fable!" [Jouenne, that is unquestionably true!] (lines 45–46).[52]

Jeffrey and Levy describe *Da la femme et de la pie* (and presumably would so describe other *blasme* verse) as "secular social satire, depicting the stock humorous character of the wife as nag, whore, cheat and deceiver of gullible men," its aim being "to amuse."[53] In their introduction, they problematize this by claiming that it is characteristic of medieval perception that "the humorous or satiric predicament is the common lot open to a common remedy rather than a separate predicament from which the poet is aloof or removed in some way."[54] But their "common lot" signifies "common to men," and the "common remedy" — for instance, "do not trust a woman" — is available to men only. Is it possible to contextualize the *propretés des femmes* in a way that does not exclude women, or suppose that laughter was the natural response to these texts? We may note that in Douce 210 *De conjuge non ducenda* and *Le Blasme des femmes* are the only "secular" texts, which suggests they may have been included in this South West Midlands manuscript for something other than their satiric or amusement value.[55]

---

[51] Johan Vising, *Anglo-Norman Language and Literature* (London, 1923); Keith V. Sinclair, *French Devotional Texts of the Middle Ages: A Bibliographic Manuscript Guide* and *First Supplement* (Westport, Conn., 1979, 1982); *Second Supplement* (New York, 1988).

[52] Arthur Långfors, ed., "*Le Dit de Dame Jouenne*: Version inédite du fabliau du *Pré Tondu*," *Romania* 45 (1918–19): 102–07, from Paris, BN MS fr. 24432, fols. 412r–414v (quotation, p. 103, lines 45–46).

[53] Jeffrey and Levy, eds., *AN Lyric*, p. 227.

[54] Jeffrey and Levy, eds., *AN Lyric*, p. 17.

[55] Douce 210 contains *Le Roman de Philosophie [La Romance Dame Fortune]* of Simon de Freine, a canon of Hereford, fols. 51v–59v (John E. Matzke, ed., *Les Oeuvres de Simund de Freine* [Paris, 1909], pp. 1–60). This romance is a free adaptation of Boethius's *Consolation of Philosophy*. The contents of the MS are described in full by Paul Meyer, "Notice du ms. Douce 210 de la Bibliothèque Bodleienne à Oxford," *Bulletin de la Société des anciens textes français* 6 (1880):

Editors Gloria K. Fiero, Wendy Pfeffer, and Mathé Allain link French *blasme* verse with woman's growing prominence in public urban life in the thirteenth century, suggesting that the writer of *Le Blasme des femmes* "had in mind a particularly aggressive category of urban female."[56] This seems to me an unfortunate way to construct a cultural context for the *propretés des femmes*, since it ties to an urban context texts that circulate, as we have seen, in manuscripts from a wide range of English and French locations, and since it suggests that women were more like what men said they were like than we should like to admit. A more fruitful contextualization, I suggest, might be the growing cultural and specifically textual intimacy between male and female. During the late twelfth and thirteenth centuries, the vernacular became the language of texts shared in those households wealthy enough for written texts to enter at all, and these shared texts increasingly treat secular and affective subject matter. Shared texts breed a more diffuse and more open-ended intimacy than shared sex, as Michel Foucault recognizes in his provocative characterization of the "metamorphosis in literature" consequent upon "Western man" becoming a "confessing animal" at the beginning of the thirteenth century:

> We have passed from a pleasure to be recounted and heard, centering on the heroic or marvelous narration of "trials" of bravery or sainthood, to a literature ordered according to the infinite task of extracting from the depth of oneself, in between the words, a truth which the very form of the confession holds out like a shimmering mirage.[57]

The *propretés des femmes* may be seen as a counter to this, as a way of reasserting distance and difference, evading textual intimacy and the felt need to tell the truth about sexuality.

Evasion of textual intimacy is not necessarily gendered male, although in Harley 2253 it is predominantly male. Is the English lyric "In May hit murgeþ when hit dawes" (no. 44) "secular social satire," or is it sincerely moving, as Dronke implies by his question "Where else does the warning against men who may betray them occur in the medieval lyric?"[58] The poet certainly seems to be speaking very intimately, from personal experience, but this, as we have seen, is how praise poems characteristically represent themselves. I agree with Dronke that there is "considerable originality" in this lyric, but it seems to me that what the poet is doing is not turning inwards towards experience, experiencing Foucault's

---

46–84.

[56] Fiero et al., eds., p. 45.

[57] Michel Foucault, *The History of Sexuality* (vol. 1: *An Introduction* [1976]), trans. Robert Hurley, (London, 1990), p. 59.

[58] Dronke, review, p. 149

"obligation to confess,"[59] but is gender-transforming the warning against marriage characteristic of the *propretés des femmes*, making the same kind of charges against men as *De conjuge non ducenda* makes about women, and making the same kinds of observations about woman's gullibility as that poem does about Gawain's.

The text of *Advice to Women* deliberately misleads us with "ʒef feole false nere" [if many were not fickle] (line 15; fol. 71vb). We assume from the context that *feole* means "many women," but it turns out to be men who are fickle, and women who choose a man too rashly. Gawain's "De lui esposer fust trop somounz" [I was too set upon marrying her] (line 15; fol. 117rb) is transformed into "Heo beoþ to rad vpon huere red" [Women are too intent upon their course of action] when they "fenge fere" [take a companion] (lines 16, 18; fol. 71vb), recalling, perhaps, the first line of the Harley 2253 *Blasme des femmes*, "(Quy femme) prent a compagnie." Whereas the *ABC a femmes* invites women to go to school to see themselves as men see them, *Advice to Women* shows that the lesson and the image may be reversed. Either Other may be Other.

The representation of uninhibited sexuality characteristic of the fabliau may be seen as another stratagem for evading textual intimacy. In the fabliau/interlude[60] *Gilote et Johane* Gilote transposes into her own key an argument from *De conjuge non ducenda*:

Vnqe ne sauoy femme que prist mary
Qe tost ou tart ne se repenty. (lines 61–62; fol. 67vb)

[I never knew a woman who took a husband without repenting sooner or later.]

In *De conjuge non ducenda* the repentance experienced after marriage is used as an argument in favor of having nothing to do with women; here, it is used as an argument in favor of Gilote's determination not to marry but to have as much to do with men sexually as possible. She draws upon the tradition of anti-marriage writings in order to draw a fearful picture of the married woman's wretched lot. Miserable, beaten for no good reason, with too many children, she is in effect a prisoner:

Ie serroi pris de su en ma mesoun,
Desole e batu pur poi d'enchesoun
E auer les enfauntz a trop de foysoun. (lines 57–59)

[I should be taken into the upper regions of my house, abandoned, beaten for trivial reasons, and have a superabundance of children.]

---

[59] Foucault, *History of Sexuality* (vol. 1), p. 60.

[60] On the genre, see Revard, "*Gilote et Johane*," pp. 122–27, and Dove "Study," pp. 168–69.

Johane counters by identifying the praise of women with the praise of virginity and of the Virgin (lines 77–84), and in reply Gilote cites as an exemplum Mary Magdalene,

> La plus orde femme qe vnque fust de cors,
> Pleyne de pecchie dedenz e dehors (lines 130–31; fol. 67*rb)

[the filthiest-bodied woman there ever was, full of sin within and without],

thus identifying the praise of women with the praise of a life of sinful loves followed by a last-minute repentance — as last-minute as possible, in order that God may be given an ideal opportunity to exercise his prerogative of forgiveness: "Vus ne trouerez frere qe vus dirra plus" [You will not find a friar who will say more] (line 146). Johane is converted to Gilote's gospel of promiscuous love, and the rest of the fabliau/interlude is devoted to the overcoming of practical difficulties, in the course of which Gilote assumes the voice of demure daughter and unfaithful pretending-to-be-penitent wife.[61]

"A jolly tale to amuse people," this text calls itself ("vne bourde de reheycer la gent," line 342), placing and dating itself — like a legal instrument — at Winchester in 1301 (lines 344–45).[62] The laughter it offers reassures its readers/hearers, as the thirteenth century becomes the fourteenth, that affective desire can be kept forever at bay. But *propretés des femmes* may also be inscribed within the romance, the predominant secular affective genre — at the climax of the Anglo-Norman poet Thomas's *Tristan*, for instance, where the second Isolt determines to deceive her husband. Throughout the romance, Thomas has employed his courtly scalpel to probe every new and delicate situation as it arises. Here, at the end, without warning, we are wrenched away from a description of Kaherdin's merchant ship tossing on the waves and plunged into *blasme*, in lines which follow on immediately from *Le Blasme de des femmes* in the Cambridge text of that poem:

> Ire de femme fet a douter,
> Mut se deit chescun garder,
> Car la ou plus amé averat
> Ileoc plustost se vengerat.
> Cum de leger vient lur amur
> De plus leger revient lur haur,
> E plus dure lur enemisté
> Qe ne fet lur amisté.

---

[61] There is a fuller description of the text in Dove, "Study," pp. 156–72; the text is printed, pp. 180–87.

[62] Not 1293, as Ker states (*Facsimile*, p. xi); see Revard, "*Gilote et Johane*," pp. 140–41.

L'amur sevent amesurer;
Haur ne sevent atemprer.[63]

[Woman's anger is to be feared; everyone ought to watch out, because where she has loved the most there she will soonest avenge herself. Since their love comes readily, their hate comes even more readily, and their enmity lasts longer than their love does. They know how to moderate their love, but they cannot temper their hatred.]

So much, we might feel, for M. Dominica Legge's suggestion that Thomas's *Tristan* was "too courtly for English taste."[64] Thomas cannot have thought that his audience would regard this passage as "secular social satire," for an amused laugh at this climactic moment would have been disastrous. Negotiation between belief and disbelief, on the other hand, in both male and female readers/hearers ("Surely no lover could be as wickedly vengeful as that? But the *propretés des femmes* tell us that indeed she could"), is exactly what is wanted here.

The *propretés des femmes*, in the late Middle Ages, functions as a marker at the boundaries of textual experiences of desire. About fifty years after Harley 2253 was written, the Gawain of *Sir Gawain and the Green Knight*, knowing himself, at the end of that poem, to have been betrayed by the Lady, reinscribes himself within the *Minnesklaven*, alongside Adam, Samson, and David. He chooses to be remembered as a man who has loved too slavishly rather than as a man who has rejected proffered love and never even known his lady's name. He imagines what would be a utopian kind of loving, for "a leude that couthe," a man who knew how (line 2420). In this kind of loving, "to luf hom wel and leve hem not," loving them dearly and not trusting them at all, the *propretés des femmes* would no longer function as boundary-marker but would lie at the heart of the textual experience of affective desire. That way, however, lies madness; Othello's, for example.

---

[63] CUL Gg.i.1, fol. 627v; compare B. H. Wind, ed., *Les Fragments du Roman de Tristan* (Leiden, 1950), p. 161.

[64] M. Dominica Legge, "The Rise and Fall of Anglo-Norman Literature," *Mosaic* 8/4 (1975): 4.

A Saint "Geynest under Gore":
Marina and the Love Lyrics of the Seventh Quire

Susanna Fein

While there is no evidence that Geoffrey Chaucer had direct knowledge of the manuscript now known as Harley 2253, E. T. Donaldson convincingly demonstrated that the poet knew the idiom of its love lyrics.[1] In one well-known instance of planned layout, the Harley scribe sets the conventions of love-talk directly beside their oppositional counterpart, the amorous language common to lyrics on the Passion. The two poems, matched in meter, appear on fol. 128r, the religious one referring to love of Christ and beginning "Lvtel wot hit any mon / Hou loue hym haueþ ybounde" (no. 92), the secular one beginning "Lutel wot hit any mon / Hou *derne loue* may stonde" (no. 93).[2] The *derne loue* that appears here and in two other Harley love poems is deftly illustrated by Nicholas: "Of deerne love he koude and of solas."[3] The idiom is, of course, particularly strong in The Miller's Tale, where Alisoun (as has often been remarked) seems the very heroine of the wonderful Harley lyric with the exuberant, love-struck refrain:

An hendy hap Ichabbe yhent,
Ichot from heuene it is me sent;

---

[1] E. Talbot Donaldson, "Idiom of Popular Poetry in the Miller's Tale," in *Speaking of Chaucer* (Durham, N.C., 1983), pp. 13–29 (essay first published in 1951).

[2] G. L. Brook, ed., *The Harley Lyrics: The Middle English Lyrics of MS. Harley 2253*, 4th ed. (Manchester, 1968), pp. 70–72; italics added. The numbering of items in the Harley MS follows that found in N. R. Ker, intro., *Facsimile of British Museum MS. Harley 2253*, EETS o.s. 255 (London, 1965), pp. ix–xvi. Evidence from other manuscripts suggests that the precedent lyric is the the secular one, as first observed by Carleton Brown, ed., *English Lyrics of the XIIIth Century* (Oxford, 1932), pp. 235–36; the scholarly discussion is well summarized by Richard Firth Green, "The Two 'Litel Wot Hit Any Mon' Lyrics in Harley 2253," *Mediaeval Studies* 51 (1989): 304–12.

[3] MilT I [A] 3200 (*The Riverside Chaucer*, ed. Larry D. Benson et al. [Boston, 1987], p. 68). For the other references to "derne" acts of love (both in Quire 7), see *Annot and John* (no. 28; fol. 63r–v), line 36, and *A Wayle Whyt ase Whalles Bon* (no. 36; fol. 67r), line 43 (Brook, ed., *Harley Lyrics*, pp. 32, 41, respectively).

From alle wymmen mi loue is lent,
Ant lyht on Alysoun.[4]

There is actually more than such correspondences in diction and topical concern to suggest that Chaucerians and all others interested in Middle English verse ought to take a fresh look at the contents of Harley and the extraordinary compilational product it represents. One would not want to dispute that authorship ranks above compilation on a scale of literary performance, but, even so, one may still recognize how much creative authority is available to an intelligent scribe-compiler.[5] The disposition of items in Harley indicates that, in at least some sections in the book, the compiler allowed for the development of coherently sequenced arguments, accomplished by means of selection and arrangement. As with the secular and religious "Way of Love" poems on fol. 128r, he elsewhere juxtaposed matter to create patterns. The work of Andrew Howell shows that two other poems (*Spring* and *Advice to Women*, nos. 43, 44) — set side by side on fol. 71v — are matched in meter, alliteration, and dialect. The pair becomes, he claims, "an implicit antithetical dialogue, ultimately between the speaker's own love longing and his

---

[4] Lines 9–12 etc.; fol. 63v. *Alysoun* (no. 29; Brook, ed., *Harley Lyrics*, p. 33).

[5] And, conversely, certain poets might be viewed, narrowly, as compilers. I do not wish to engage here the issue of whether Chaucer was *auctor* or *compilator*. Chaucer as the latter has been forwarded by A. J. Minnis, *The Medieval Theory of Authorship: Scholastic Literary Attitudes in the Later Middle Ages* (London, 1984), pp. 190–210. But see, too, the salutory reminder by R. H. Rouse and M. A. Rouse that this term was flexible in medieval usage ("*Ordinatio* and *Compilatio* Revisited," in *Ad Litteram: Authoritative Texts and Their Medieval Readers*, ed. Mark Jordan and Kent Emery, Jr. [Notre Dame, 1992], pp. 113–34). In the study of Harley 2253 the question of compilation (in Malcolm Parkes's sense of "a structured collection" [Rouse and Rouse, p. 116]) enters the debate over whether the MS is best viewed as anthology or miscellany (see Theo Stemmler's essay in this volume). I believe there is enough evidence at local points to attest that someone (presumably the scribe) actively linked certain items to certain other items. At the same time, the MS as a whole does not provide a pattern we can identify as a book unified by a single motive. MS Harley 2253 is best described, then, as a miscellany with some anthologized parts (which are still to be fully identified).

By the term "Harley compiler," I refer to the main scribe of Harley 2253 (the "Harley scribe"), who copied fols. 49–140, parts of MS Royal 12.C.xii and MS Harley 273, and the forty-one deeds and charters listed in Carter Revard's article in this volume. By the use of this term, I suggest that the scribe was responsible for the order and selection of texts found in Harley 2253. This inference cannot, of course, be proven. It is, however, reasonable to assume that the scribe's judgment and taste are displayed in what he chose to copy.

mistrust of women."[6] Analyzing eight poems on four pages (fols. 75r–76v; nos. 49–56), Carter Revard finds them to comprise a sequence that is "planned rather than haphazard." In the compiler's selection of lyric material, Revard detects "a dialectic arrangement that implies [his] ironic awareness of the double view, of parallels between his opposites." Elsewhere, Revard calls this a "principle of selection . . . not mere[ly of] variety but [of] contrariety."[7]

The verifiability of such a principle may raise reasonable doubt among modern readers, who will inevitably wonder about the capacity of a medieval reader to perceive the links without explicit guidance from a compiler, which one might expect to see in the usual manner of incipits, explicits, or marginalia. Do "parallels" and "opposites" exist in the eye of the one looking for them, or can it be demonstrated that the scribe selected specifically for them? How usefully or readily did *mise-en-page* provide an aid by which texts were read? Verbal and metrical links are more readily believable than are thematic repetitions because an identified thematic strand may seem to be entirely reader-based. Theo Stemmler's observation of a reiterated rhyme between the last lines of a macaronic hymn and the opening strains of *King Horn* (nos. 69, 70; fol. 83r) — a thematically weighted repetition of *kynge* and *synge* — is, by this measure, authentically persuasive. Few would deny, moreover, the thematic fit of two Montfortian poems — a celebration and a lament — followed by two lyrics meditating on life as dust (nos. 23, 24, 24a, 24b), a unified foursome bridging two languages (French, English) and two genres (historical poem, religious lyric).[8]

In the seventh quire of Harley 2253 one can similarly detect a compiler's skill at work. Here a particular motif develops within an inventive collage of works. The motif flourishes by means of verbal and topical markers based in the idiom of secular love lyric. The sequence, which spans the length of the quire, includes six of the familiar English love poems, a political poem, a verse tale, a quasi-religious "poet's repentance," a French interlude, and even, perhaps, the beginning of a French prose pilgrimage tract (finished

---

[6] Andrew J. Howell, "Reading the Harley Lyrics: A Master Poet and the Language of Conventions," *ELH* 47 (1980): 639. Given the analogous instance of the two "Litel Wot Hit Any Mon" lyrics on fol. 128r and the plausible hypothesis that English *contrefacta* were composed in the continental fashion (Green, p. 312), Howell's theory that the poems are written by a single poet is unnecessary (p. 635).

[7] Carter Revard, "*Gilote et Johane*: An Interlude in B. L. MS. Harley 2253," *Studies in Philology* 79 (1982): 135, 130, 129.

[8] For Stemmler's observation about *King Horn*, see the 1991 essay reprinted in this volume (p. 120); the effect is similar to that of the "weping and wailing care" linkage of the Clerk's and Merchant's Tales (IV [D] 1212–13; *Riverside Chaucer*, p. 153). On the Montfortian poems, see the essays in this volume by John Scattergood and Michael P. Kuczynski.

in the eighth quire).[9] Taken as a whole, Quire 7 presents a unified inquiry upon a dominant subject. This subject is, not surprisingly, the sexual appeal of women, as viewed (usually) by the male poet. What most thoroughly draws the poems into a coherent sequence is somewhat more specific, however: the mystification of a woman's anatomy with a conspicuous and inquisitive zeroing in on the location of female organs hidden from sight behind clothing.

To see this subject squarely requires that we sweep aside the philological impediments that well-meaning, but over-squeamish editors have put before us. The poems collected by the Harley compiler present, time and again in this sequence, the catalogue of a woman's alluring body parts, a catalogue that works downwards, as the rhetoricians recommended,[10] and then the poets conclude — usually both catalogue and poem — teasingly but unambiguously, with the part that is hidden under "bis" (a kind of linen), or under "gore" (a triangular-shaped cloth or skirt). The editors unanimously want us to believe that the meaning of *geynest under gore* in *Alysoun* is "kindest among women"[11] or, just as weakly, "kindest in a petticoat."[12] The lexicographers of the *Middle English*

---

[9] No. 38; edited with no. 39 in Henri Michelant and Gaston Raynaud, eds., *Itinéraires à Jérusalem et descriptions de la terre sainte* (Geneva, 1882), pp. 229–36. On the quires of Harley 2253, see Appendix.

[10] See, for example, Geoffrey of Vinsauf, *Poetria nova*, trans. Margaret F. Nims (Toronto, 1967), pp. 36–37, lines 563–99. Geoffrey says a writer ought to suggest but not describe directly a woman's private parts, and he models his own advice: "For the other parts I am silent — here the mind's speech is more apt than the tongue's" (lines 594–95).

[11] Brook, ed., *Harley Lyrics*, p. 100 (s.v. *gore*); Robert D. Stevick, ed., *One Hundred Middle English Lyrics*, 2nd ed. (Urbana, 1994), p. 40; and R. T. Davies, ed., *Medieval English Lyrics: A Critical Anthology* (London, 1963), p. 68. These editors interpret *under gore* as a vague generalization that means "alive" or "in the world"; see also John Speirs, *Medieval English Poetry: The Non-Chaucerian Tradition* (New York, 1957), p. 57; Celia Sisam and Kenneth Sisam, eds., *The Oxford Book of Medieval English Verse* (Oxford, 1970), p. 108; Thomas J. Garbáty, ed., *Medieval English Literature* (1984; repr. Prospect Heights, Ill., 1997), p. 646; J. A. Burrow and Thorlac Turville-Petre, eds., *A Book of Middle English* (Oxford, 1992), p. 238; and Thomas G. Duncan, ed., *Medieval English Lyrics 1200–1400* (Harmondsworth, 1995), p. 21. Translators are inclined to bowdlerize the line: see, for example, Jessie L. Weston, trans., *The Chief Middle English Poets: Selected Poems* (1914; repr. New York, 1968), p. 351 ("Fairest maid, in gear so gay"); and Brian Stone, trans., *Medieval English Verse*, 2nd ed. (Harmondsworth, 1971), p. 201 ("Sweetest whom I adore").

[12] Maxwell S. Luria and Richard L. Hoffman, eds., *Middle English Lyrics: Authoritative Texts, Critical and Historical Backgrounds, Perspectives in Six Poems* (New York, 1974), p. 23; Theodore Silverstein, ed., *English Lyrics before 1500* (Evanston, 1971), p. 87; Brown, ed., *Eng. Lyr. XIII*,

A Saint "Geynest under Gore"

Dictionary perpetuate the editors' willful blindspot by repeating these definitions, even beside well-attested, tantalizingly suggestive second meanings — for *gore*, "a triangular piece of land," and for *bis*, "a kind of dark fur."[13] The poet of *The Owl and the Nightingale* leaves no room for doubt that the phrase *stingen under gore* (line 515) means a man's part in sexual intercourse.[14] In fact, the Harley compiler has gathered much of the lexicographi-

---

pp. 260–61 (s.v. *geynest* and *gore*); Charles W. Dunn and Edward T. Byrnes, eds., *Middle English Literature*, 2nd ed. (New York, 1990), p. 209. When editors gloss *geynest* ("most handsome," "loveliest," "kindest") and *gore* ("petticoat," "gown," "clothing") and do not meddle with the preposition *under*, then the phrase at least retains its suggestiveness. Editors rarely explain the line, though. A few frank admissions crop up among critics: Edmund Reiss, *The Art of the Middle English Lyric: Essays in Criticism* (Athens, Ga., 1972), p. 63; Daniel J. Ransom, *Poets at Play: Irony and Parody in the Harley Lyrics* (Norman, Okla., 1985), p. 117n, 132n; Gayle Margherita, *The Romance of Origins: Language and Sexual Difference in Middle English Literature* (Philadelphia, 1994), p. 68.

[13] See *MED gor(e* n.(2), sense 1.(a), and *bis* n.(2), sense (a). *Geynest under gore* is defined "kindest in clothing, kindest in the world"; *brightest under bis* is defined "fairest to behold." For an early citing of these terms as generalizations, see Edwin Guest, *A History of English Rhythms* (1838), 2nd ed., ed. W. W. Skeat (1882; repr. New York, 1968), p. 582n1. On the formulaic quality of the phrases, see J. A. W. Bennett and G. V. Smithers, eds., *Early Middle English Verse and Prose*, 2nd ed. (Oxford, 1968), p. 320.

[14] See J. H. G. Grattan and G. F. H. Sykes, eds., *The Owl and the Nightingale*, EETS e.s. 119 (1935; repr. Bungay, Suffolk, 1959), p. 16. In the Digby 86 version of *Maximian*, an old man complains of his impotence "under gore" (referring to either his own robe or a lady's gown):

Ich mourne and sike sore,

For I ne may be namore

Mon as ich wes þo;

So crafti clerc of lore,

So godlich *ounder gore*,

And al hit is ago. (lines 145–50; Brown, ed., *Eng. Lyr. XIII*, p. 97).

This lyric also appears in Harley 2253 (no. 68; fols. 82ra–83r), but lines 148–50 are altered and the phrase "godlich ounder gore" is absent: "Ys hit no whiþ ȝore / Þat Y bigon to hore / Elde is nou my fo" (lines 124–26; fol. 82rc); the text is printed in Karl Böddeker, ed., *Altenglische Dichtungen des MS. Harl. 2253* (1878; repr. Amsterdam, 1969), p. 249. The birds in *The Thrush and the Nightingale* debate the subject of women at one point by metonymic reference to a pudendum, the thrush calling "hit" the "worste hord [treasure] of pris / þat ihesu makede in parais" and the nightingale defending it as "flour þat lasteþ longe, / And mest I-herd in eueri londe, / And louelich *ounder gore*" (lines 143–44, 148–50; Brown, ed., *Eng. Lyr. XIII*, pp. 105–06); on these lines, see also Daniel J. Ransom, "'Annot and John' and the Ploys of Parody," *Studies in Philology* 75 (1978): 130.

A sly deployment of the convention in a thirteenth-century Franciscan lyric extolling a virgin's espousal to Christ (*Love Rune*) attests that it was both familiar and erotically charged in secular cal evidence in one place, and the cumulative effect is a high-spirited, bawdy, and obsessively sexual motive behind each poem in praise of a woman.

Within the form, there manages to be great variety. In the opening work of Quire 7, *Annot and John* (no. 28; fol. 63r–v), the poet compares the lady to precious stones, flowers, birds, spices, and famous people. His name is John, and he is blissfully successful in wooing his Annot:

> Coynte ase columbine such hire *cunde* ys,
> Glad *vnder gore* in gro ant in gris;
> He is blosme opon bleo, brihtest *vnder bis*.[15]

The explicit reference to her sexual member is phrased so cleverly that modern editors can fudge a more courtly meaning, that is, they may construe *coynte cunde* as "elegant nature,"[16] but the part of Annot being praised is hardly a secret, as Daniel Ransom has pointed out and even Larry Benson has accepted.[17] The motif is repeated with a bit more delicacy in the poem that follows, *Alysoun* (no. 29; fol. 63v), sung by another poet in desperate love longing. He pleads with the one who is "Geynest vnder gore" to respond to his song (lines 37–38). While editors have conspired in modesty, Donaldson blurted out his conviction of lewdness, which he transferred over, as well, to Chaucer's two instances of "under gore" — the hidden site of Alisoun's loins and, comically, of Sir Thopas's amorous hopes:

---

lyric idiom; see the note to line 167 in Susanna Greer Fein, *Moral Love Songs and Laments* (Kalamazoo, Mich., 1998), pp. 53–54. For illustrations of the trope in two fifteenth-century MSS, one English and one French, see V. A. Kolve, "God-Denying Fools and the Medieval 'Religion of Love,'" *Studies in the Age of Chaucer* 19 (1997): 47, 49 (Figs. 23, 24).

[15] Lines 15–17 (in the second of five stanzas); fol. 63r (Brook, ed., *Harley Lyrics*, pp. 31–32).

[16] "Elegant as columbine such is her nature, / Beautiful among women [or delightful in attire] in gray furs, / Of face she's a flower, brightest under linen." See, for example, Luria and Hoffman, eds., *ME Lyrics*, p. 21; Duncan, ed., *Medieval English Lyrics*, p. 11; Garbáty, ed., *Medieval English Literature*, p. 642; and Sisam and Sisam, eds., *Oxford Book*, p. 106. Brown (*Eng. Lyr. XIII*) does not provide a gloss, nor does Thorlac Turville-Petre (ed., *Alliterative Poetry of the Later Middle Ages: An Anthology* [Washington, D.C., 1989], p. 14) or Rolf Kaiser (ed., *Medieval English*, 4th ed. [Berlin, 1961], p. 465).

[17] Ransom, "Annot and John," pp. 128–31; Larry D. Benson, "The 'Queynte' Punnings of Chaucer's Critics," in *Contradictions from "Beowulf" to Chaucer*, ed. Theodore M. Andersson and Stephen A. Barney (Aldershot, 1995), p. 218n4. Explicit words for bodily parts are, of course, natural to the fabliau; the Harley compiler includes, later in the volume, three fabliaux in which a *con*, *cul*, or *vit* is the center of interest (nos. 75a, 84, 87).

An elf-queene shal my lemman be
And sleepe under my gore.[18]

The poem that follows *Alysoun, The Lover's Complaint* (no. 30; fol. 63v), is the lament of an unhappy man whose desire is set upon an aloof lady. He feels himself dying before his time. This inaccessible woman is the means to heavenly pleasure, and the lover is both urgent and blunt about his quest:

Brihtest *vnder bys*;
Heuene Y tolde al his
  Þat o nyht were hire gest.[19]

With no need to cite these familiar lyrics further, one can readily note that more variations of the "under gore" motif occur in the final lines of two more love lyrics found in the quire: *The Fair Maid of Ribblesdale* (no. 34; fol. 66v) and *A Wayle Whyt ase Whalles Bon* (no. 36; fol. 67r). In the former, the poet, after describing the Ribblesdale maid's allurements and clothing, asserts that a night lying beside her requires Christ's favor and bestows a foretaste of heaven (lines 79–84); in the latter, the poet wishes he were a small bird hid "Bituene hire curtel ant hire smok" (line 54).[20]

The love lyrics establish the dominant motive and motif. The other English poems in the sequence offer clear if somewhat less predictable variations. In *Song of the Husbandman* (no. 31; fol. 64r)[21] the conventional phrase surfaces in a wholly different setting. This lyric is a political complaint about taxation so oppressive it will force the speaker out of farming. The document by which the Exchequer called in unpaid bills was sealed in green wax, which the speaker says torments him "vnder gore" (line 55) while the tax collectors hunt him as a hare. Experiencing the unwanted attentions of extortionists and tax agents, the male speaker is rather like the unheard women receiving the attentions of men in the love poems, and the worn idiom by which he chooses to color his complaint underscores his helplessness. Against a panoply of secular love songs, one can hardly avoid hearing in "vs greueþ *vnder gore*" something like "they want to screw us." While the speaker's voice continues to be male, the sense of entitlement forwarded by the many aspirant lovers

---

[18] Thop VII [B²] 787–88, and see Donaldson, "Idiom," pp. 23–24. The other appearance of the word *gore* in Chaucer describes Alisoun (MilT I [A] 3237, *Riverside Chaucer*, pp. 68, 214).

[19] Brook, ed., *Harley Lyrics*, p. 34 (ending of poem), lines 38–40.

[20] Brook, ed., *Harley Lyrics*, pp. 39, 41.

[21] Rossell Hope Robbins, ed., *Historical Poems of the XIVth and XVth Centuries* (New York, 1959), pp. 7–9.

suffers here a reversal. Taxation is an area where one who is engendered male may readily feel the sting of being subject to someone else's unwanted desire.[22]

Another of the English poems, *The Poet's Repentance* (no. 33; fol. 66r), is a *tour de force* of alliterative and stanzaic complexity. It offers a poet's remorse for having slandered women, in a move analogous to Chaucer's prologue to *The Legend of Good Women*. Women, the poet asserts, have not been wicked since the birth of Christ. Ambiguous wordplays build a complex tone that cannot be entirely serious, especially when the poet heaps soaring praise upon a virtuous colleague named Richard and wishes him final happiness in the land of ladies. The poet describes the Incarnation in a way that threatens to deflate sacred decorum, especially amidst the surrounding lyrics, so that sacred mystery becomes also an exposure of the Virgin's anatomy. The reader or listener is asked to imagine Mary's womb "through her seemly side," made transparent both to the Son who enters it and to the visualizing reader:

> In hire lyht on ledeþ lyf,
> Ant shon þourh hire semly syde.
> Þourh hyre side he shon
> Ase sonne doþ þourh þe glas. (lines 19–22)

Even though the trope of light shining through glass is standard for depictions of the Incarnation, the poet's tonal ambiguity set amidst other love verse lends a prurient cast to holy contemplation. Godly penetration thus visualized both exposes a holy, virginal, feminine recess and, simultaneously, absolves womanhood of wickedness:

> Wommon nes wicked non
> Seþþe he ybore was.[23]

Of course, the marvel of women's collective reformation manages to affirm, as well, their unanimous waywardness before the event. By either construction, women are submitted to a view that denies them individuality. Richard's delirious pleasure in a place filled with reformed women ("in londe of leuedis alle") suggests that their now consistent and compliant nature exists solely to serve the lucky man (a poet, of course) able to access their favor through apt and savvy words.

---

[22] An analogous identification between a man's entrapment by a male oppressor and a woman's sexual subjugation occurs in the bawdy marginalia that accompanies Harold's capture in the Bayeux Tapestry, illustrated and discussed by Michael Camille, *Image on the Edge: The Margins of Medieval Art* (Cambridge, Mass., 1992), pp. 126–27.

[23] Brook, ed., *Harley Lyrics*, p. 35, lines 23–24.

A Saint "Geynest under Gore"

In yet another turn of what may be termed the "under gore" topos, *The Meeting in the Wood* (no. 35; fols. 66v–67r) capitalizes on the sartorial element of the motif. This pastourelle fluctuates between two perspectives, the narrator's and the girl's. Spying the maiden in a "fryht," the man judges her to be a prize, glistening as gold, and lovelier than any other clothed creature, "nes ner gome so gladly on gere" (lines 1–4). She at first rejects him, and he then offers to clothe her richly. She responds that it is better to be clad thinly without blame than to be sunk in sin in rich robes (lines 13–16). She wishes for a promise, and he freely, and duplicitously, gives her one. Then she reasons that she may as well embrace a handsome man in fine clothes as be married to a loathsome wretch who beats her (lines 37–40). The poem ends on her rueful thoughts: she is sorry to be a virgin because she is unable to shift her shape (that is, back to being a virgin), and she knows men are false (lines 45–48). The attention that this poet gives to female perspective is of some interest. Here the girl has a thoughtful role in the game of love; she is conscious of the illusions clothes create and of the fixed reality of her own embodied state. Knowing her limited options, she reasons things out and makes a choice. The girl is, like all the other lyric women of Harley Quire 7, inscribed by the text and unable to act as anything other than an object of love or lust, but here at least her thoughts are given voice, and her responses show a male awareness of the lyric heroine's subjugated position.

The French fabliau-interlude *Gilote et Johane* (no. 37; fols. 67va–68va)[24] has a pair of profligate women advising a young wife on how she may take a lover without losing the dower of her old husband. When discovered, she is to stage a scene of sobs and repentance, upon which the priests and friars will enjoin the husband to forgive her. She will cap the scene by reappearing in seductive clothes:

> Vus vendrez deuant ly bien atyre;
> Le cuer li changera si auera piete.
> E vus serrez dame bien recounsile,
> E serrez mestresse si come deuant,
> E serrez riche dame e plus puissant. (lines 300–04; fol. 68rb)

[You will come before him beautifully dressed; his heart will change if he is pious. And you will be fully reconciled as his wife, and be mistress as before, and a rich woman and more powerful.]

---

[24] Achille Jubinal, ed., *Nouveau Recueil de contes, dits, fabliaux et autres pièces inédites des XIIIᵉ, XIVᵉ et XVᵉ siècles* (Paris, 1839, 1842), 2.28–39. I am indebted to Carter Revard for sharing his translation of *Gilote et Johane*.

The foolish husband forgives her and her dower is saved. This comic work gives another refracted look at male desire, through the fantasy of sexually aggressive women. The perspective is richly male, even as it gives voice to female characters. Again there is the subject of clothing: the seductive dress of the wife is irresistible to the old husband, the clothes covering — indeed enhancing and making as bait — the site of lustful fantasies. In many ways, from *Annot and John* to *Gilote et Johane*, the argument comes full circle, sexual pleasure being celebrated with frank speech and zesty license.

There remains, however, one more verse text in Quire 7: *Marina* (no. 32; fols. 64va–65vb) tells the tale of a cross-dressed female monk.[25] Composed in 232 Middle English octosyllabic lines rhymed in couplets, the work occurs in the midst of the sequence just described, tucked between *Song of the Husbandman* and *The Poet's Repentance*. With the exception of the saintly heroine found in this tale, all of the women described in the seventh quire are circumscribed by a man's amorous aspirations. The same can be said of virtually all women in *The Canterbury Tales*, with the plight of Emily establishing the paradigm: a woman must be attached to or defined by her relationship to a man. Even nuns and saints are married to God gendered male. Virginia in The

---

[25] Böddeker, ed., *Altenglische Dichtungen*, pp. 255–63; the text has also been printed in Carl Horstmann, ed., *Sammlung altenglischer Legenden* (Heilbronn, 1878), pp. 171–73. Another ME version of the Marina story survives in the *Northern Homily Cycle* (*IMEV* 89; Carl Horstmann, ed., "Die Evangelien-Geschichten der Homiliensammlung des Ms. Vernon," *Archiv für das Studium der neueren Sprachen und Literaturen* 57 [1876]: 259–61). While each version is independent of the other, both abridge and adapt the story found in the AN *Vitas patrum*, which survives in only two MSS (and not in the Harley version [no. 1]; see n. 38 below); for the AN version, see Léon Clugnet, ed., "Vie de sainte Marine," *Revue de l'Orient Chrétien* 8 (1903): 288–311, and for extracts translated into English, see Brigitte Cazelles, *The Lady as Saint: A Collection of French Hagiographic Romances of the Thirteenth Century* (Philadelphia, 1991), pp. 238–57. The AN tale derives, in turn, from the Latin *Vitae patrum* (J.-P. Migne, ed., *PL* 73:692–96). Analogous medieval lives of St. Marina appear in Jacobus de Voragine, *The Golden Legend: Readings on the Saints*, trans. William Granger Ryan, 2 vols. (Princeton, 1993), 1.324–25; and in Christine de Pizan, *The Book of the City of Ladies*, trans. Earl Jeffrey Richards (New York, 1982), pp. 241–43.

Commentary on St. Marina is not extensive, and the English versions are rarely mentioned. See, for example, John S. Anson, "The Female Transvestite in Early Monasticism: The Origin and Development of a Motif," *Viator* 5 (1974): 1–32; Cazelles, *Lady as Saint*, pp. 63–66, 71, 83–84; Valerie Hotchkiss, *Clothes Make the Man: Female Cross Dressing in Medieval Europe* (New York, 1996), pp. 25–28, 56, 138; F. Nau, "Histoire de Sainte Marine," *Revue de l'Orient Chrétien* 6 (1901): 276–82; Maureen Quilligan, *The Allegory of Female Authority: Christine de Pizan's 'Cité des dames'* (Ithaca, 1991), pp. 228–32; Constance L. Rosenthal, *The 'Vitae Patrum' in Old and Middle English Literature* (Philadelphia, 1936), p. 42; and Edith Wyschogrod, *Saints and Postmodernism: Revisioning Moral Philosophy* (Chicago, 1990), pp. 115–23.

Physician's Tale defines the way that women embody their own danger, possessing what is not their own once a male has noticed, desired, and claimed it. Emily's response to Diana's denial of her first request to remain independent and a virgin resonates with dismay: "What amounteth this, allas?"[26] For all her own deific power, Diana was apprehended by Acteon's transgressive gaze, a deed replicated by the Knight-narrator as he violates the privacy of Emily's prayer in eavesdropping and reporting it to the reader now made voyeur.[27] Emily's request is not to be honored. Women may not be free of men. Instead they must choose from an array of ways in which they will meet their defining fate: to be constructed according to male desire and actualized in acceding to it.

This paradigm also informs the monogendered gaze of Harley Quire 7, so much so that the tale of Saint Marina explicitly puts it to the test. This legend is about a female who evades the desire of men. Clothed as a monk, Marina is the ultimate elusive woman, of whom men fail to write the text. Simultaneously, she is the ultimate female object, her gender known privately by the author, shared privately with the reader, and made the miracle that confirms her sainthood.

The story tells of a newly widowed man of good works who enters a monastery, choosing, as the poet says, Mary for his wife (line 20; fol. 64va). Seven years pass, and the man is always woeful, missing his daughter. The abbot finds out the cause of his distress and compassionately offers to take the child into the monastery. The child in this conversation is referred to in a gender-neutral way — as "child" or "it." But then the abbot asks the crucial question:

"Weþer his hit grom oþer mayde?"
"Sire, a grome," forsoþe he sayde —
He nolde be knowe for no þyng
Þat hit wes a mayde ʒyng. (lines 51–54; fol. 64vb)

The father is obviously trying to protect his daughter in an environment of men. Fetched by her father, Marina is brought to the monastery garbed "ase a mon" (line 64; fol. 64vb). From the point of entry and through her training, the child's gender is labeled "hit," but

---

[26] KnT I [A] 2362 (*Riverside Chaucer*, p. 57).

[27] Much recent criticism has focused on this scene, with a fair amount of debate over whether Chaucer has punned on the word *queynte*. See John V. Fleming, *Classical Imitation and Interpretation in Chaucer's "Troilus"* (Lincoln, 1990), pp. 1–44; A. C. Spearing, *The Medieval Poet as Voyeur: Looking and Listening in Medieval Love-Narratives* (Cambridge, 1993), pp. 166–68; Susan Crane, *Gender and Romance in Chaucer's "Canterbury Tales"* (Princeton, 1994), pp. 177–79; Kolve, "God-Denying Fools," pp. 50–51; and Timothy D. O'Brien, "Fire and Blood: 'Queynte' Imaginings in Diana's Temple," *Chaucer Review* 33 (1998): 157–67.

when "it" becomes a monk, "she" becomes a "he." The father dies. The monk Marinus, beloved by all, is made master of the pantry and must ride outside the monastery to conduct business. The daughter of a dairyman becomes pregnant by a passing knight, and when questioned by her mother, she declares that Marinus raped her. The child is born and delivered (instantly it seems) to Marinus the monk, whose punishment is to be thrown out — with the child — to live at the monastery gates for three years. There he suffers a dire penance, subsisting only on the scraps of anise bread that the monks toss his way. His plight eventually arouses compassion; he is pardoned and restored to the monastery. But the penance has so damaged his constitution that he dies, and in death natural gender is reclaimed:

> Þenne spec a monk to anoþer,
> "Go we whosshen vr dede broþer,
> For þah he habbe don a synne,
> ȝet he is broþer of herynne."
> A nome þe body ant brohte to baþe
> Alas þat he was ded so raþe!
>   "*Hit is a wommon*!" seide þat on.
>   "Þat is soþ, bi Seint Jon!"
> "Iesu shilde vs from pyne,
> For we han lowen on Maryne
> Ant penance duden hire on stronge
> Ant letten hire pyne to longe!"
>   Letten after þe abbot sende
> Ant tolden him þe ord ant end,
> Ant þe covent everuchon
> *Ant shouueden hit wes a womon.*
>   Þe abbot for duel falleþ to grounde,
> Ant þer he liþ a longe stounde. (lines 171–88; fol. 65va)

When the abbot recovers his senses, he thanks God for this miracle and declares to the listening monks and "oþer men mo þer were" (line 192) that Marina is now able to serve them as intercessor:

>   "Nou hit is þus bifalle,
> We moten þenchen among vs alle
> Hire onoure in alle wyse,
> For heo is ded in Godes seruise;
> Ant heo mey to Him biseche
> For ous, þat is oure soule leche." (lines 193–98)

A Saint "Geynest under Gore"

As the legend of a saint, *Marina* offers an odd sort of miracle: one of a single truth, biological and natural, revealed through the mundane action of undressing a corpse in readying it for burial. This moment uncovers the protagonist's holiness, her chosen-ness in God's eyes. The amazement expressed by all — and especially by the abbot's swoon — inscribes this moment as miraculous, when all that has happened is that they have unclothed a body, discovering a "she" where they had presumed to find a "he."

Saint Marina is not like the other cross-dressed female saints in Jacobus de Voragine's *Golden Legend*: Eugenia the educated Roman daughter who becomes a monk to erase gender and status; Theodora the repentant wife; Pelagia the former courtesan; and Margaret who escapes an arranged marriage.[28] Unlike these women, Marina begins monastic life as a pure innocent, virtually genderless. One may assume that she is not even conscious of her own virginity, hence, that she is a true virgin, one not corrupted by even the knowledge of sexual things.[29] But Marina *is* sexual object in spite of her own asexuality. She is made a boy so that she may not tempt the monks, but as a boy she attracts a woman's accusation. Her cross-dressed state maintains, nonetheless, her unspotted record of purity. The unknowing monks did *not* desire her. Her woman's body could *not* have raped the dairyman's daughter. She herself could not have comprehended what actions lay behind the accusation.[30]

By medieval misogynist thinking a woman who maintains her chastity by hiding her gender is already on the way to sainthood. If she endures the penitential vows and existence of a monk, compounded with an imposed penance designed for a man, she is doubly, even triply, proven. What marks her sainthood is not merely that she suffered innocently and grievously, but that she suffered *as a man*, being merely *a woman*. Her

---

[28] Jacobus de Voragine, *Golden Legend*, trans. Ryan, 2.165–67 (Eugenia), 1.365–68 (Theodora), 2.230–32 (Pelagia), 2.232–33 (Margaret).

[29] On the epistemological problem of virginity, see R. Howard Bloch, "The Poetics of Virginity," in *Medieval Misogyny* (Chicago, 1991), pp. 93–112. For other useful discussions of the medieval concept, see Clarissa Atkinson, "'Precious Balm in a Fragile Glass': The Ideology of Virginity in the Later Middle Ages," *Journal of Family History* 8 (1983): 131–43; John Bugge, *Virginitas: An Essay in the History of a Medieval Ideal* (The Hague, 1975); and Jocelyn Wogan-Browne, "The Virgin's Tale," in *Feminist Readings in Middle English Literature: The Wife of Bath and All Her Sect*, ed. Ruth Evans and Lesley Johnson (London, 1994), pp. 165–94.

[30] This fact explains Marinus's seemingly odd acquiescence to the woman's false charges. Aware of primal guilt, he accepts that he has done something he should atone for, although he may little understand the exact nature of the charge. In the *Northern Homily* version Marina (as a girl) associates her situation with Christ's guiltless sacrifice and then "confesses" in an oblique manner: "I may not seyn aȝeyn þis chaunce / þat I nam worþi gret penaunce" (lines 81–82; Horstmann, ed., "Die Evangelien-Geschichten," p. 260).

sainthood is thus figured in terms of a bigendering, which allows Marina to experience God in her lifetime as no man can: "*Þe ioie of hyre ne may mon sugge!*" (line 166; fol. 65rb). Marina comprehends heavenly bliss in a way inaccessible to ordinarily gendered mortals, except by means of her intercession. What mysteries she saw in her penance are translated to the monks, curiously, in terms of *what they see*, that is, her naked female form. Instead of inciting licentious desire, this sight, we are to believe, now stirs male wonder and reverence. The love-poet's equation of female genitalia and heavenly mysteries has been turned on its head by the author of the saint's legend.

The relationship of *Marina* to the surrounding lyrics is intriguing. A more traditional female saint's tale — one of persecution and torture, for instance — would not have had the same effect. This legend of a cross-dressed virgin is predicated upon the covering up of a woman's gender under clothes. That there is a secret under Marinus's robes is, of course, the whole point. Men in the tale are thwarted from their curiosity about female flesh "under gore." These ignorant holy men are also, however, at the climax of the text they could not read, richly rewarded with an ample viewing. Male desire is deflected, refocused, and then abundantly fulfilled. One can hardly avoid the supposition that the compiler chose this tale precisely for titillation of that continuing interest in what women have "under gore," this time the curiosity being the spur of the story rather than the conventional ending of a love poem. And even though Marina escaped the male gaze in life, the suddenly crowded viewing of her in death — by the monks and the "other men mo" (where did *they* come from?) — seems rather to compensate the men for their lost opportunity. Miraculous moment is indelibly marked with prurient response.

And this is not all, for the story has a most interesting denouement. The eventual fate of the dairyman's daughter affirms that this tale of piety is curiously and deliberately blended with salacious wit. The daughter's pregnancy resulted from a pastourelle-like encounter with a roaming knight, so that lurking within the saint's legend is a secondary genre, one marked as secular and overtly sexualized. Quizzed by her mother, the girl names a rapist rather than her consensual lover[31] and thereby hides her own sexuality from her parent — an act that seems to mirror in reverse Marina's father's concealment of his daughter's gender from the monks. Later, when the girl is made aware of the unfortunate

---

[31] A question arises: why does the girl accuse the monk rather than name the real father? While the tale does not provide a direct answer, one reason may be that, with the knight gone and the monk at hand, the monastery can be made to raise the bastard child. Both girl and knight abdicate their guilty parenthood, while Marina/us assumes both maternity and paternity (in devotional terms, she is a blend of the attributes of Mary and Christ). It is assumed, too, that the celibate ideal of the monastic community attracts suspicion; the secular world clearly doubts its veracity, and the monks, too, doubt one of their own, so that the eventual "miracle" of Marinus's exposed womanhood indicts everyone's worldly preoccupation with sexual difference.

monk's female anatomy, she is unable to assimilate her own guilt and thereby loses her mind. The concerned monks pray for aid to Christ in the name of Marina, and the new saint responds — her first postmortem miracle — by restoring the girl's sanity:

> Whil heo þeraboute speke,
> Anon riht hire bondes breke,
> Ant toc to *hire womones cunde,*
> Ant warþ into hire ryhte munde,
> Ant kneulachede ho hade misdon
> To bere þat child hire apon. (lines 215–20; fol. 65vb)

Recovery of her senses returns the girl, simultaneously, to "her woman's nature," with the term for "nature" — *cunde* — relaying the same raw pun found in *Annot and John.* This unsaintly girl is brought to acknowledge her sin *and* her sexuality in a subplot that facetiously mimics Marina's own loss and recuperation of gender, and — as with Marina — she is at that moment surrounded by a host of "caring" monks!

This instance of double-speak — of piety interfaced with profanity — in an apparent saint's legend raises the question of just how a modern reader should gauge the tale's general tone and decorum. The line's surprise value is saved for the end of the tale; it is, in effect, the punch line. The poet builds on the first miracle of a dead virgin female monk, unveiled and gawked at, by staging a second miracle of a sexualized girl acknowledging her true womanly "cunde." Afterwards, the author quickly finishes off the tale with a prayer for Mary's mercy and for Christ's shielding him from "shome" (lines 227–32; fol. 65vb), as if he hopes to protect himself from any repercussions for the offense possibly just committed. In retrospect, the entire tale looks suspiciously profane in motive. The rapturous line about Marina's holy visions, "Þe ioie of hyre ne may mon sugge!" (line 166; fol. 65rb), comes to seem deliciously ambiguous: "no *one* may ever see the heavenly sights *she* saw in her blessed state," or "no *man* ever had the opportunity to *enjoy her,*" with the latter sense about to be comically contradicted when the monks are granted a visual feast. Not only is gender deeply embedded in the line — in the emphatic *hyre* and the shifting *mon* — but pious thoughts based in a celibate, genderless ideal are thoroughly infected by the impure ones held by sexualized, gendered human beings.[32]

Yet to understand the nature of the tale of *Marina,* we ought not for the profane throw out the saintly. In its formal qualities *Marina* is a holy passion in imitation of Christ's life

---

[32] Ambiguity of motive is, it must be noted, a feature of *Marina* throughout. The father's initial desires waver between his wife and Mary (ought his life be secular or holy?), a dilemma resolved "miraculously" (and almost comically, as Michael P. Kuczynski notes in his essay in this volume) by his wife's death.

and suffering. The hero(ine)'s expulsion from the monastery, to "abugge" her "gult ful deore" in perpetual pain and penance outside the gates, occurs at the exact middle of the tale (lines 115–17; fol. 65ra), in likeness to the centered Passion in much contemporary written and visual art. Such a structure suggests less a parody than a devout attempt to locate the comic in what is, in mysterious essence, both without gender and dual-gendered (God as well as Christ embodied male by means of Mary's womanly flesh).[33]

The immediate successor to *Marina* is the tongue-in-cheek *Poet's Repentance*, as if the voice of a new poet has been chastened by the miraculous story of Marina's sainted virginity exposed for men to see.[34] However, this duplicitous lyric does little to prove that a man's avowal to honor all women for the sake of Mary can be free of a sexual motive. It seems instead to confirm the conflicted, comic obsession lurking in the tale. And in the lyric that follows *Repentence* an enraptured love-poet descriptively conjures the wondrous fairy-like maiden of Ribblesdale, with her talismanic powers "under gore."

The playful sequence on desire for what is "under gore" appears to extend, therefore, from *Annot and John* to *Gilote et Johane*. In between these two celebratory end-pieces, passionate exuberance occasionally ebbs enough to allow perception of what it means to be unwitting subject to another's desire. Sometimes even the self-serving goals of the desirer are laid bare. But *Gilote et Johane* ends the sequence on a rollicking, comic note. The quire's final text, on pilgrimage sites, interrupts the sequential obsession with feminine secrets under clothes. Perhaps the compiler sought, by means of this prosaic work, to ease into a calmer topic, transferring, that is, the "geographical" fantasies about the hidden womanly locus — fantasies run riot in the travelling services of Gilote and

---

[33] Sarah Beckwith, discussing a later text (Margery Kempe's book), describes the sacral origin for the kind of dual impulse felt in *Marina*: " . . . if Christ's body is the place where God materializes, if it is the meeting place of finite and infinite, of flesh and spirit, of the material and immaterial, of the sacred and profane in the destabilizing hybridity, the intoxicating boundary-blurring ambiguity of Christ's body, then either pole of that meeting can be stressed at the expense of the other" (*Christ's Body: Identity, Culture and Society in Late Medieval Writings* [London, 1993], p. 25). It must be added that medieval punning frequently works to make evident a correspondence perceived as true between sacred and profane: see Rosemary Woolf, *The English Religious Lyric in the Middle Ages* (Oxford, 1968), p. 85; and the debate on *queynte* (n. 27 above). On the larger issue of profanity embedded in "decorous" medieval texts and our modern inclination to censor, see Sheila Delany's essay, "Anatomy of the Resisting Reader: Some Implications of Resistance to Sexual Wordplay in Medieval Literature," *Exemplaria* 4 (1992): 7–34.

[34] Revard remarks that *The Poet's Repentance* is the palinode of a "converted" antifeminist poet, evoked in part by *Marina*'s "pro-feminist" stance ("*Gilote et Johane*," p. 124n6). Theo Stemmler notes that "in both texts the importance of Mary is emphasized" (see p. 117 in this volume).

Johane — to a more soul-redeeming site: the actual topography of the Holy Land and the location of pilgrimage shrines.

The unified network of texts in Harley's seventh quire is a codicological phenomenon that begs for an explanation. It makes one yearn for more hard evidence as to the manuscript's original purpose and readership. In analyzing here a textual sequence in relation to its quiring, I am hypothesizing that the quires and units of quires in Harley 2253 may give us some information about the compiler's plan for the book, or, at the least, help us to discern his local purposes, unit by unit. Among the fifteen quires, there are seven discernible "independent blocks" (see Appendix), where quire divisions correspond to the beginnings and ends of whole items. Quire 7 (fols. 63–69) does not end cleanly with *Gilote et Johane* or with *Les Pelrinages*. In Ker's codicological groupings (emended slightly as explained in the Appendix), it is part of the fifth block of texts (fols. 63–105), which extends all the way through *King Horn*, the French prose Bible stories, and a Latin listing of the books of the Bible (nos. 70–72). The textual sequences detected by Revard and Howell exist within this block, as does the very intriguing linkage of *King Horn* with the religious lyric that precedes it (fol. 83r), where repetitions of *kynge* and *synge* sound over the generic divide. The "Way of Love" poems appear later, however, in the sixth block, along with all of the fabliaux and much of the French *débat des femmes*, while other texts in this block are concerned (anomalously?) with proverbs, prophecies, and instructions. As with the fifth block, no single subject accounts for all the matter in the sixth one.[35] On the other hand, the fourth block, consisting of just one quire (fols. 53–62), seems to cluster texts that reflect on mortality or life's vanities.

Quiring does not, therefore, provide an absolute means of determining scribal sequencing of matter. The long fifth block, comprised as it is of forty-four items, does not in any plausible sense offer a unified argument upon one subject. Nevertheless, the contents of Quire 7 up to the prose text that fills its last leaves do appear to be more planned than random. The layout of these texts is perhaps a useful consideration. It shows the care that Ker and others have noted is a trait of the scribe: three love lyrics and the political poem fill three pages with a bit of blank space at the end (fols. 63r–64r); *Marina* occupies three pages that end with some blank space (fols. 64v–65v); then four lyrics fill three more pages (fols. 66r–67r). *Gilote et Johane* occupies four pages and runs onto the fifth (fols. 67v–68v[36]). The prose pilgrimage tract uses up the rest of fol. 68v and all of fol. 69r–v. The scribe heads new pages with nos. 28, 31, 32, 33, 34, and 37, so that, in visual

---

[35] Barbara Nolan examines the contents and ordering of the sixth block in her essay in this volume.

[36] There is a misnumbered fol. 67* inserted between fols. 67 and 68.

appearance, nos. 28–30 and nos. 34–36 are copied as two three-lyric units. The first lyric unit opens the quire; then *Husbandman* has its own page and is followed by *Marina* (written, unlike the lyrics, in double columns). After *Marina*, *Repentance* occupies its own page. Then there is the second three-lyric unit and last comes *Gilote et Johane* (written, like *Marina*, in a double-columned format).

We do not know enough about the scribe's exemplars to determine that the compilation found here is his creation and not the result of what he found in a source. But even supposing that he discovered the sequence of Quire 7 (or portions of it) in an exemplar, we would still like to have an explanation for the phenomenon itself: an artful compilation to form a salaciously funny entertainment, one that mixes secular and pious materials and that struck a scribe in western England in about 1340 as worthy of preserving. Unfortunately, we have little means by which to account for it: Was the scribe compiling these texts for his own amusement or were they to provide pleasure for his patron(s)? Were they to be read in private or aloud to a group? Were any of the pieces, such as *Gilote et Johane* with its several dialogues, actually performed? Does the sequence imply that they were to be articulated as a continuous group, or is it merely a clustering of individual texts on a related motif gathered by a connoisseur?

The dialectal evidence may give further clues as to exemplars. Mixed as they are, the dialects point to someone's purposeful collecting efforts. *Annot and John*, *The Lover's Complaint*, and *The Fair Maid of Ribblesdale* have been thought to be by the same poet — Karl Böddeker's proposed (and unprovable) "poet of the Welsh border" who wrote four Harley Lyrics.[37] But *Alysoun* cannot be given a precise dialect, *The Poet's Repentance* is South East or South East Midland, while *The Meeting in the Wood* and *A Wayle Whyt ase Whalles Bon* are both apparently Northern. The latter poems, both in a dialect distant from the scribe's own and suffering some degree of textual corruption, may have come from an exemplar where they were side by side (as in the Harley MS), but if the four "border poet" poems shared an exemplar, then the scribe has separated them in Quire 7 by inserting matter between them, and he has placed the fourth one (a love poem that lacks the "under

---

[37] Böddeker, ed., *Altenglische Dichtungen*, pp. 155–58, and seconded by Brown, ed., *Eng. Lyr. XIII*, pp. xxxviii–xl. The other poem thought to be by this poet is *Blow, Northerne Wynd* (no. 46). G. L. Brook's research into the dialects of the four lyrics determined them to be: nos. 28 and 34 North West Midland; no. 30 indefinite; no. 46 Midland ("The Original Dialects of the Harley Lyrics," *Leeds Studies in English* 2 [1933]: 38–61). For further dialectal work on the exemplars of Harley 2253, see Frances McSparran's essay in this volume. Her work does not particularly support the theory of common authorship; she does, however, identify a sequence of six poems in Quire 7 (nos. 31–36, which includes *Marina*) as likely to have derived — along with no. 40 — from a common exemplar. Interestingly, no. 40 — *Satire on the Consistory Courts*, the complaint of a man hauled into court for seducing a woman — complements well the nature of the sequence in Quire 7.

gore" motif) even further into the manuscript. The dialectal mix as well as the rich metrical variety of the lyrics point to the activity of someone who sought the lyrics' inclusion for their own aesthetic qualities, while the presence of a unified motif suggests some degree of deliberate collection and arrangement.

In our present knowledge of Harley, it is not altogether clear what other local thematic plays and dialectics may be found in the volume. Once we begin to read the book more as it is constituted, that is, as a continuous and multilingual whole, we should be able to comprehend better the compiler's achievement. The first forty-eight folios contain a compendium of stories in Anglo-Norman — the *Vitas patrum*[38] — holy exemplums with sometimes salacious subtexts: how much does this long text prepare for the content of Quire 7 or the *débat des femmes* that surfaces later in the book? Appended to it (and belonging to the same Latin source) is the titillating exemplum of Thaïs, and omitted from it (but belonging to the same source) is the story of Marina, cropping up later in English in Quire 7.[39] Would the compiler have known and used these connections?

There is still a good deal to be learned about the popular insular literature that fed Chaucer's art. To discover more, we will need to examine more closely trilingual books like Harley 2253 for clues we have inadvertently overlooked. Amidst the canon-building efforts of the 1940s and 50s, which were fired up by that period's New Critical fascination with the aesthetics of lyric verse, scholars somehow lost sight of the witty, salacious, and clerkish tale that was put by a compiler right in the midst of the Harley Lyrics. This English tale of Marina amid a batch of delightful love lyrics hints at an interesting native

---

[38] The AN *Vitas patrum* survives in two MSS: Harley 2253, fols. 1ra–22vb, and Paris, BN fr. 24862, fols. 60a–97b. The Harley text has not been printed in its entirety, but Brother Basilides Andrew O'Connor appends the passages unique to Harley to his full edition of the Paris text (*Henri d'Arci's "Vitas Patrum": A Thirteenth-Century Anglo-Norman Rimed Translation of the "Verba seniorum"* [Washington, D.C., 1949], pp. 160–224); see also Paul Meyer, "Notice sur le manuscrit fr. 24862 de la Bibliothèque Nationale contenant divers ouvrages composés ou écrits en Angleterre," *Notices et extraits* 35/1 (1895): 131–68. According to Keith V. Sinclair, the author of the AN *Vitas patrum* was not Henri d'Arci, but instead probably a London priest (maybe an Austin canon) who undertook, ca. 1170–80, to translate the Latin *Vitae patrum* for the edification of Henri d'Arci's "illiterate brethren of the Temple" ("The Translations of the *Vitas patrum, Thaïs, Antichrist*, and *Vision de saint Paul* Made for Anglo-Norman Templars: Some Neglected Literary Considerations," *Speculum* 72 [1997]: 762). For the Latin source text, see Migne, ed., *PL* 73, and for the legend of Thaïs appended to the AN *Vitas patrum*, see R. C. D. Perman, ed., "Henri d'Arci: The Shorter Works," in *Studies in Medieval French Presented to Alfred Ewert in Honour of His Seventieth Birthday* (Oxford, 1961), pp. 279–321; and also Cazelles, *Lady as Saint*, pp. 299–301.

[39] Although these folios are not copied by the Harley scribe, he apparently added titles to each of the items; see Appendix.

culture of learned tale-as-joke-telling, and of clever literary sequences made to provide extended entertaining pastimes, a textual culture probably enjoying — as funny jokes usually do — a certain degree of mobility, from cloister or from university to wealthy private household.[40]

---

[40] I was enriched by opportunities to present portions of this research at different forums: the New Chaucer Society Biennial Meeting, July 1996; the 32nd International Congress on Medieval Studies, May 1997; and the Harvard Medieval Doctoral Conference, October 1998. I am indebted to many who offered smart, provocative comments at those events. Improved (or reproved) by their remarks, I am nonetheless solely responsible for the results. I am particularly grateful to Barbara Nolan and Derek Pearsall for reading and commenting upon this work in a late draft.

APPENDIX. *The contents, quires, and independent blocks of MS Harley 2253*

The following chart is based on the quire divisions provided by N. R. Ker in the facsimile edition. Three scribes are responsible for the texts found in Harley 2253. Items not enclosed in brackets in the chart below were copied by the second scribe (the "Harley scribe"). An earlier scribe wrote the texts on fols. 1–48, and a later one copied the recipes on fol. 52va–b, the end of Quire 5. There are seven independent blocks of matter; Ker notes only six because he omits the division occurring between Quires 2 and 3. The blocks may once have been differently ordered.[41] Wanley (followed by Brook) thought that the two singletons of Quire 4 were originally in Quire 5 with their conjugates (between fols. 52 and 53) cut off. Ker disagrees and finds no evidence of conjugates for fols. 47 and 48.[42] Thus the earlier work of the textura hand does not seem to share any quires with the work of the Harley scribe. According to Ker, however, the titles added to texts on fols. 1–48 are in the hand of the Harley scribe.[43]

INDEPENDENT BLOCK 1 (fols. 1–22)

QUIRE 1, **a**[12] (six bifolia, fols. 1–12)
 [1. Fr verse *Vitas patrum* . . .]

QUIRE 2, **b**[10] (five bifolia, fols. 13–22)
 [. . . Fr verse *Vitas patrum*]

INDEPENDENT BLOCK 2 (fols. 23–48)

QUIRE 3, **c**[12] (six bifolia, fols. 23–34)
 [2. Fr verse *La Passioun Nostre Seignour*]
 [3. Fr prose *Gospel of Nicodemus* . . .]

QUIRE 4, **d**[12+2] (six bifolia + two singletons, fols. 35–48)

---

[41] Ker, *Facsimile*, p. xvi.

[42] See Ker, *Facsimile*, p. xvin1, where he refers to Wanley's notation that, after the recipes on fol. 52v, "two Leaves have been cutt-out; wherein, probably, other like recipes were written" (H. Wanley, D. Casley, et al., *A Catalogue of the Harleian Manuscripts in the British Museum* [1759; rev. and repr. 4 vols., London, 1808–12], p. 586); see also Brook, ed., *Harley Lyrics*, p. 1.

[43] Ker, *Facsimile*, p. ixn4.

[. . . Fr prose *Gospel of Nicodemus*]

[4. Fr prose *De saint Iohan le Ewangel*]

[5. Fr prose *De saint Iohan le Baptist*]

[6. Fr prose *De saint Bartholomeu*]

[7. Fr prose *Passioun saint Piere*]

INDEPENDENT BLOCK 3 (fols. 49–52)

QUIRE 5, e^4 (two bifolia, fols. 49–52)

8. Fr verse *ABC a femmes*

9. Fr verse *De l'Yver et de l'Esté*

[10. Eng prose recipe *Cynople*]

[11. Eng prose recipe *Asure*]

[12. Eng prose recipe *Grass-green*]

[13. Eng prose recipe *Another Green*]

[14. Eng prose recipe *Gaude-green*]

[15. Eng prose recipe *Silverfoil*]

[16. Eng prose recipe *Steel*]

[17. Eng prose recipe *Blankplum*]

INDEPENDENT BLOCK 4 (fols. 53–62)

QUIRE 6, f^{10} (five bifolia, fols. 53–62)

18. Lat prose *Vita sancti Ethelberti*

19. Lat prose prayer *Anima Cristi sanctifica me*

20. Fr verse *Qvant voy la reuenue d'yuer*

21. Eng verse *Harrowing of Hell*

22. Eng verse *Debate between Body and Soul*

23. Eng verse *A Song of Lewes*

24. Fr verse *Lament for Simon de Montfort*

24a. Fr verse *Charnel amour est folie*

24b. Eng verse *Earth upon Earth*

25. Eng verse *The Execution of Sir Simon Fraser*

25a. Eng verse *On the Follies of Fashion*

26. Fr verse *Enseignement sur les amis*

27. Eng verse *The Three Foes of Man*

INDEPENDENT BLOCK 5 (fols. 63–105)

QUIRE 7, **g**[8] (four bifolia, fols. 63–69)

28. Eng verse *Annot and John*
29. Eng verse *Alysoun*
30. Eng verse *The Lover's Complaint*
31. Eng verse *Song of the Husbandman*
32. Eng verse *Marina*
33. Eng verse *The Poet's Repentance*
34. Eng verse *The Fair Maid of Ribblesdale*
35. Eng verse *The Meeting in the Wood*
36. Eng verse *A Wayle Whyt ase Whalles Bon*
37. Fr verse *Gilote et Johane*
38. Fr prose *Les Pelrinages communes que crestiens fount en la seinte terre . . .*

QUIRE 8, **h**[8] (four bifolia, fols. 70–77)

   . . . Fr prose *Les Pelrinages*
39. Fr prose *Les Pardouns de Acres*
40. Eng verse *Satire on the Consistory Courts*
41. Eng verse *The Labourers in the Vineyard*
43. Eng verse *Spring*
44. Eng verse *Advice to Women*
45. Eng verse *An Old Man's Prayer*
46. Eng verse *Blow, Northerne Wynd*
47. Eng verse *The Death of Edward I*
48. Eng verse *The Flemish Insurrection*
49. Fr verse *Les Joies de Notre-Dame*
50. Eng verse *Suete Iesu, King of Blysse*
51. Eng verse *Iesu Crist, Heouene Kyng*
52. Eng verse *A Winter Song*
53. Eng verse *A Spring Song on the Passion*
54. Fr verse *Ferroy chaunsoun que bien deit estre oye*
55. Lat/Fr/Eng verse *Dum ludis floribus*
56. Fr verse *Quant fu en ma iuuente*
57. Fr verse *Marie mere al salueour*
58. Eng verse *Dulcis Iesu memoria . . .*

QUIRE 9, **j**[12] (six bifolia, fols. 78–89)

   . . . Eng verse *Dulcis Iesu memoria*

59. Fr verse *Vne Petite Parole seigneurs escotez*

60. Eng verse *Stond Wel, Moder, vnder Rode*

61. Eng verse *Iesu, for Þi Muchele Miht*

62. Eng verse *I Syke When Y Singe*

63. Eng verse *An Autumn Song*

64. Eng verse *De Clerico et Puella*

65. Eng verse *When þe Nyhtegale Singes*

66. Eng verse *Blessed Be Þou, Leuedy*

67. Eng verse *The Five Joys of the Virgin*

68. Eng verse *Maximian*

69. Eng/Fr verse *A Prayer for Deliverance*

70. Eng verse *King Horn* . . .

QUIRE 10, **k**¹⁰ (five bifolia, fols. 90–99)

  . . . Eng verse *King Horn*

71. Fr prose Old Testament Bible stories . . .

QUIRE 11, **l**⁶ (three bifolia, fols. 100–105)

  . . . Fr prose Old Testament Bible stories

72. Lat prose *Nomina librorum bibliotece*

INDEPENDENT BLOCK 6 (fols. 106–133)

QUIRE 12, **m**⁸ (four bifolia, fols. 106–113)

73. Eng verse *God, Þat Al Þis Myhtes May*

74. Eng verse *Sayings of St. Bernard*

75. Fr verse *Le Jongleur d'Ely et le Roi d'Angleterre*

75a. Fr verse *Les Trois Dames qui troverent un vit*

76. Fr verse *Le Dit des femmes*

77. Fr verse *Le Blasme des femmes*

78. Fr verse Nicholas Bozon, *De la femme et de la pie*

79. Fr verse *Urbain le courtois* . . .

QUIRE 13, **n**⁸ (four bifolia, fols. 114–121)

  . . . Fr verse *Urbain le courtois*

80. Fr verse *Trailbaston*

81. Eng verse *The Man in the Moon*

82. Fr verse *Le Chevalier et la corbaille*

83. Fr verse *De conjuge non ducenda*

84. Fr verse *Le Dit de la gageure*

85. Eng verse *A Bok of Sweuenyng*

86. Fr verse *Ordre de bel ayse . . .*

QUIRE 14, o¹² (six bifolia, fols. 122–133)

    . . . Fr verse *Ordre de bel ayse*

87. Fr verse *Le Chevalier qui fist les cons parler*

88. Eng verse *Satire on the Retinues of the Great*

89. Eng verse *Hending*

90. Fr/Eng prose *The Prophecy of Thomas of Erceldoune*

91. Fr prose *La Distinccioun de la estature Iesu Crist Nostre Seigneur*

92. Eng verse *The Way of Christ's Love*

93. Eng verse *The Way of Woman's Love*

94. Fr prose *Enseignements de saint Louis à son fils*

95. Fr prose extract from Jacques de Vitry, *Historia orientalis*

96. Fr prose *Armes des roys*

97. Lat prose letter on relics at Oviedo

98. Lat prose *Legenda de sancto Etfrido presbitero de Leominstria*

99. Fr/Lat prose prayer for victory

INDEPENDENT BLOCK 7 (fols. 134–140)

QUIRE 15, p⁷ (seven singletons, fols. 134–140)

100. Fr prose occasions for angels

101. Fr prose occasions for psalms

102. Fr verse *Gloria in excelsis Deo*

103. Lat prose prayer *Confiteor tibi Deus omnia peccata mea*

104. Fr prose *Five Joys of Blessed Virgin Mary*

105. Lat prose prayer before confession

106. Fr prose reasons for fasting on Friday

107. Fr prose directions for weekly masses

108. Fr prose seven masses in honor of God and St. Giles

108a. Fr prose prayer to the Three Kings

109. Lat prose extract from John of Wales, *Communeloquium*

109a. Fr prose efficacy of prayers

110. Lat prose occasions for psalms

111. Fr prose occasions for psalms

Layout, Punctuation, and Stanza Patterns in the English Verse

Elizabeth Solopova

The manuscript London, British Library Harley 2253 contains a selection of English verse coming from different sources. Some of the texts are shared with other manuscripts and should have been already in relatively wide circulation at the time Harley 2253 was produced. The collection shows a considerable variety of metrical forms, both accentual and syllabic. Three-, four-, six-, seven-, and eight-stress syllabic lines are all common and appear both separately and in different combinations.[1] There is a number of accentual poems with alliteration and stanzas of different complexity.

The English material is in one main hand and was probably copied over two periods of time with a break in a few years.[2] The compiler of the collection almost certainly had an interest in poetic form and awareness of meter. Thus, since the contents of the book are not arranged according to any apparent plan,[3] the fact that the only three poems in seven-stress verse — *De Clerico et Puella, When þe Nyhtegale Singes*, and *Blessed Be Þou,*

---

[1] Harley 2253, in spite of its metrical diversity, does not contain iambic pentameter verse, which appears to have first been used by Chaucer. Five-stressed lines occur only in two poems, one of which is an imitation of the other. They appear as the third and fourth lines in the stanzas of *The Way of Woman's Love* and *The Way of Christ's Love* (nos. 92, 93; G. L. Brook, ed., *The Harley Lyrics: The Middle English Lyrics of MS. Harley 2253*, 4th ed. [Manchester, 1968], pp. 70–72). Some of these lines are rhythmically irregular. A fairly regular example is line 34 of *The Way of Christ's Love*: "ffor loue of vs his wonges waxeþ þunne" (fol. 128r). Cited numbers for items in the Harley MS are from the list of contents in N. R. Ker, intro., *Facsimile of British Museum MS. Harley 2253*, EETS o.s. 255 (Oxford, 1965), pp. ix–xvi. All citations of Harley texts are transcribed diplomatically from the facsimile.

[2] Margaret Laing, *Catalogue of Sources for a Linguistic Atlas of Early Medieval English* (Bury St. Edmunds, Suffolk, 1993), p. 95; Ker, *Facsimile*, pp. xxi–xxii. According to Ker, Harley 2253 does not look as if it was written over a long period of time, but the last dozen leaves, where the scribe begins to use a horizontal line to bound his writing at the top of the page, may well have been written a few years later than the rest.

[3] Carleton Brown, ed., *English Lyrics of the XIIIth Century* (Oxford, 1932), p. xxxvi.

377

Leuedy (nos. 64–66) — follow one another on fols. 80v–81v may be significant and may mean that metrical considerations played a certain role in the arrangement of items in the collection.[4] The scribe's awareness of meter is demonstrated most clearly in the layout of verse. The layout seems to have been improvised and chosen individually to suit the metrical structure of a particular poem and to reflect its formal features.

The verse texts are written in one, two, or three columns on a folio depending on the length of lines. There is no regular ruling: it changes from section to section.[5] The improvisation rather than planning ahead did not preclude a successful outcome; as was noted by N. R. Ker, "On the whole the scribe was remarkably good at setting out his texts."[6] The manuscript contains some very elaborate verse and displays a highly conscious approach to its layout and punctuation which can almost certainly be attributed to the scribe rather than to his exemplars. This layout is a valuable source of information about the contemporary understanding of metrical form.

One of the most interesting features of the layout of verse in Harley 2253 is the treatment of long and short couplets. As has already been said, the manuscript contains both short syllabic lines of three and four stresses and long syllabic lines of six, seven, and eight stresses. The long lines have caesuras, clearly marked by syntactic breaks, which divide the lines into two equal (as in eight-stress lines), or two unequal hemistiches (as in seven-stress lines). Not infrequently there is a rhyme both at the end of a line and at the caesura, though caesural rhyme is less common in seven-stress poems with their unequal hemistiches. This raises the following question: in cases when caesuras rhyme, how do we know that the line is a single unit, that we are dealing with long six-, seven-, or eight-stress verses and not with short three- and four-stress verses which the scribe wrote two at a line to save space? This question is important for understanding the development of stanza patterns, for editing verse, and for the studies of its compositional arrangement which involve counting lines.

There are two features that distinguish long lines in Harley 2253: they never have leonine rhyme and they are regularly written as long lines in the manuscript. In other words, leonine rhyme, sometimes used in medieval Latin hexameter, where caesuras rhyme with ends of lines, does not appear in verse laid out as long lines in Harley 2253.

---

[4] Brook, ed., *Harley Lyrics*, pp. 62–65.

[5] Compare Ker: "When the scribe had drawn the vertical bounder to define his left-hand margin, his procedure with a verse text was probably *ad hoc*; that is to say he wrote the first two rhyming lines one below the other and according to the amount of space they took up he wrote the rest of the text in one column or two columns or three columns" (*Facsimile*, p. xvii).

[6] Ker, *Facsimile*, p. xviii.

Layout, Punctuation, and Stanza Patterns

Whenever caesural rhyme occurs, caesuras rhyme with themselves and the ends of lines also with themselves, for example:

In afryht as y con fare fremede / yfonde a wel feyr fenge to fere
Heo glystnede ase gold when hit glemede / nes ner gome so gladly on gere /[7]

When þe nyhtegale singes þe wodes waxen grene
Lef 7 gras 7 blosme springes / in aueryl ywene
                 When þe Nyhtegale Singes (lines 1–2; fol. 80v).

At the same time verse laid out in the manuscript as short three- or four-stress lines does not feature alternative rhyme *abab*, but rhymes in couplets *aabb*, or employs the tail-rhyme stanza *aabccb*:

Blessed be þou leuedy ful of heouene blisse
Suete flur of parays moder of mildenesse
Perrey3e iesu þy sone þat he me rede 7 wysse
So my wey forte gon þat he me neuer misse
               Blessed Be Þou, Leuedy (lines 1–4; fol. 81r).

In poems where seven-stress lines appear in combinations with other lines, the alternative rhyme *abab* occurs only in seven-stress lines as caesural and end rhyme, whereas the short lines follow some other pattern. Each stanza of the two closely related lyrics *The Way of Christ's Love* and *The Way of Woman's Love* (nos. 92, 93), for example, starts with two seven-stress lines rhyming both at the end and at the caesura, followed by two shorter lines of five or six stresses and a refrain:

He seh his fader so wonder wroht ⁏ wiþ mon þat wes yfalle
Wiþ herte sor he seide is oht ⁏ whe shulde abuggen alle /
His suete sone to hym gon clepe 7 calle
7 preiede he moste deye for vs alle /
Euer 7 oo [nyht 7 day he haueþ vs in is þohte /
He nul nout leose þat he so deore bohte].[8]

---

[7] *The Meeting in the Wood*, lines 1–4; fol. 66v. Brook, ed., *Harley Lyrics*, pp. 39–40.

[8] *The Way of Christ's Love*, lines 16–22; fol. 128r. *The Way of Christ's Love* and *The Way of Woman's Love* have the same metrical form and numerous verbal parallels. According to Brook (*Harley Lyrics*, pp. 87–88) and Brown *(Eng. Lyr. XIII*, pp. 235–37) the religious lyric is an adaptation of a secular one. According to Betty Hill, however, *The Way of Woman's Love* is a secularization of an earlier religious lyric, probably the one that appears on fol. 2v of London,

Parallel rhyme marks off and ties together the ends of half-lines, as well as the ends of long and short lines. The general pattern of rhyme in each stanza is as follows:

a b
a b two seven-stress lines
c
c   two shorter lines
c
d
d   refrain.

In the manuscript the poem is written in a column with seven-stress lines laid out as long lines.

The poem *Iesu, for Þi Muchele Miht* (no. 61) has the rhyming pattern *ababaabaab* and starts with two seven-stress lines rhyming *abab*, where *a* is a caesural rhyme and *b* is an end rhyme.[9] They are followed by shorter lines in a tail-rhyme stanza *aabaab*, where those rhyming *a* are mainly four-stressed and those rhyming *b* are mainly three-stressed. Seven-stress lines are written as long lines in the manuscript:

> When y þenke on i*e*su ded / min herte ou*e*rwerpes
> mi soule is won so is þe led / for mi fole werkes
> ful wo is þat ilke mon
> þ*at* i*e*su ded ne þenkes on
> what he soffrede so sore
> for my synnes y wil wete
> ant alle ywyle hem for lete /
> nou 7 euermore /. (lines 11–20; fol. 79vb)

The described usage holds true for accentual alliterative verse as well; rhyme *ab* is found only in long lines with rhyming caesuras. Thus it occurs in *The Man in the Moon* (no. 81) and *The Meeting in the Wood* (no. 35) with their long lines, but not in the four-stress lines of *Annot and John* (no. 28):[10]

British Library MS Egerton 613 ("A Note on 'The Way of Christ's Love,' 'The Way of Woman's Love' in B. M. MS. Harley 2253," *Notes and Queries*, n.s. 19 [1972]: 46–47); the Egerton poem is printed by Brown, ed., *Eng. Lyr. XIII*, p. 236.

[9] Brook, ed., *Harley Lyrics*, pp. 57–59.

[10] *The Man in the Moon* and *Annot and John* are printed in Brook, ed., *Harley Lyrics*, pp. 69–70 and pp. 31–32, respectively. The fact that leonine rhyme was used in the Latin hexameter probably

Mon in þe mone stond ⁊ strit ⸴ on is botforke is burþen he bereþ -
hit is muche wonder þat he nadoun slyt ⸴ for doute leste he valle he
shoddreþ and shereþ /

The Man in the Moon (lines 1–4; fol. 114v).

Since alternative rhyme occurs only in verse laid out in long lines and only as caesural and end rhyme, the ends of long lines normally rhyme in couplets, contributing to the status of the couplet as a dominant rhyming pattern. The association of alternative rhyme with long lines rhyming at the caesura was probably linked to the fact that the couplet was regarded as such a fundamental metrical pattern, that a line was not seen as complete unless it was part of a couplet. Parallel rhyme (present also in tail-rhyme stanza) signaled ends of lines as basic metrical units. In tail-rhyme stanza, lines rhyming in couplets served as the core of the metrical pattern, whereas the third and the sixth lines had a subordinate status: they are usually shorter and sometimes have a refrain-like quality in the poems. They were seen as an addition to the core, as the very name "tail-rhyme stanza" suggests.

The scribe of Harley 2253 considered the difference between long and short lines as metrically significant and not just as a matter of convenient layout: he was prepared to sacrifice convenience in order to preserve this distinction and used layout to highlight it. Verse of six, seven, and eight stresses is written as long lines even when the scribe had difficulties fitting it into the writing space. This can be seen in the layout of *An Autumn Song* (no. 63), a poem rhyming *aabaabacac*:

Nou skrnkeþ rose ⁊ lylie flour
þat whilen ber þat suete sauour
in somer þat suete tyde
ne is no quene so stark ne stour
ne no leuedy so bryht in bour
þat ded ne shal by glyde
whose wol fleysh lust for gon / ⁊ heuene blis abyde
on iesu be is þoht anon þat þerled was ys side.[11]

---

means that there it was less likely to break the line into halves and less dangerous for the existence of the line as a unity. The rhyme was less prominent in hexameter since the accentual pattern of two-syllable rhyme was in the majority of cases different: iambic at the caesura and trochaic at the end of a line. Hexameter also was more stable because of a more strictly defined metrical structure than ME long lines.

[11] Lines 1–10; fol. 80ra. Brook, ed., *Harley Lyrics*, pp. 60–62.

Each stanza begins with a tail-rhyme pattern formed by short three- and four-stress lines, and ends with two long seven-stress lines rhyming at the caesuras and at the ends. Since most lines are short, they could have been comfortably placed in the space available on the folio, but the seven-stress lines were too long for this, and the scribe had sometimes to interline their final words when he was running out of space. Thus in the first stanza quoted above the word *abyde* is written above the penultimate line. The scribe preferred to lay the poem out in this cumbersome way rather than break its long lines in halves; his choice was to preserve the contrast between the long and the short lines.

Punctuation employed by the scribe also emphasizes distinction between the long and short lines.[12] *A Spring Song on the Passion* (no. 53) has the rhyming pattern *ababccbddb*.[13] Lines in tail-rhyme stanzas are in trimeter. The first two lines are six-stressed and rhyme *a* at the caesuras and *b* at the ends. The poem is written continuously, as prose, across the page on fol. 76r. The lines are separated from one another by virgules. In six-stress lines, however, the scribe used different punctuation at the ends of lines and at the caesuras; the ends are marked with virgules (/), but the caesuras are marked with *punctus elevati* (؛):[14]

---

[12] The discussion of punctuation is much indebted to Malcolm B. Parkes's description of punctuation in Middle English MSS in *Pause and Effect: An Introduction to the History of Punctuation in the West* (Aldershot, 1993).

[13] Brook, ed., *Harley Lyrics*, pp. 54–55.

[14] There are very few deviations from this practice in the poem. In the second line of the third stanza a *punctus elevatus* at the caesura is preceded by a virgule:

Iesu milde ⁊ softe ؛ ȝef me streynþe

ant myht / Longen sore ant ofte /؛ to louye þe aryht /. (lines 21–24; fol. 76r)
In the fourth stanza caesuras of the long lines are left unpointed:

alas þat y ne couþe

turne to him my þoht / ant cheosen him to lemmon so duere he vs haþ yboht /.
(lines 31–34; fol. 76r)

In two other cases a virgule occurs at the caesura instead of a *punctus elevatus*, e.g.:

When y se blosmes springe / ant here foules song / Asuete louelongynge ؛
myn herte þourh out stong /. (lines 1–4; fol. 76r)
These deviations from the scribe's usual practice are either due to the lack of accuracy and consistency, which is not uncommon in punctuation of casually and even of carefully written texts from any period, or to the influence of syntactic structures in these lines. All punctuation marks had — apart from metrical functions — syntactic and rhetorical functions that could have affected their usage in these cases. Thus, in the last example (lines 1–4), the scribe may have wished to emphasize logical parallels in the first line by using identical punctuation marks after the first and second half-lines.

> When y mi selue stonde ⸲ ⁊ wiþ myn eȝen seo / þur
> led fot ant honde ⸲ wiþ grete nayles þreo /. (lines 11–14; fol. 76r)

In a poem written as prose there is nothing to indicate the different metrical status of lines and half-lines since the ends of both rhyme. Punctuation helps to highlight this difference.

The use of punctuation in poems written as prose in Harley 2253 can be further illustrated by *The Man in the Moon*. This poem is written continuously on fols. 114v–115r because its lines were too long to be fitted in the space marked by the vertical ruling. The caesuras of eight-stress lines are regularly marked with the *punctus elevati* and the ends with virgules.[15]

A similar practice of punctuation is found in poems laid out in columns. Thus *God, Þat Al Þis Myhtes May* (no. 73), a lyric in eight-stress lines written on fol. 106r, has stanzas of four long lines rhyming at the ends and at the caesuras, so that the general rhyming pattern is *abababab*, where *a* is the caesural rhyme and *b* is an end rhyme.[16] The poem is laid out in a column of long lines which are punctuated with *punctus elevati* at the caesuras and with virgules at the ends. In both *The Way of Christ's Love* and *The Way of Woman's Love* copied on fol. 128r, caesuras of seven-stress lines are marked with *punctus elevati*.[17] Punctuation is occasionally used at the ends of lines as well:

> Lvtel wot hit anymon ⸲ hou loue hym haueþ ybounde
> Þat for vs oþe rode ron ⸲ ant bohte vs wiþ is wounde
> Þe loue of him vs haueþ ymaked sounde ⸲
> Ant ycast þe grimly gost to grounde /

---

[15] There are several deviations from this practice. In lines 35–36 the *punctus elevatus* at the caesura is replaced by a virgule:

> Þah ich ȝeȝe vpon
> heþ nulle nout hye / þelostlase ladde con nout o lawe /. (fol. 115r)

In the next line (lines 37–38) the caesura is marked by both a virgule and by a *punctus elevatus*:

> Hupe
> forþ hubert hosede pye /⸲ ichot þart amarscled in to þe
> mawe /. (fol. 115r)

There are three other cases (lines 21–22, 27–28, 31–32) where a virgule and a *punctus elevatus* seem to be superimposed at the caesura and may represent corrections.

[16] Brook, ed., *Harley Lyrics*, pp. 68–69.

[17] An exception to this practice is found in stanza four, where both the virgule and the *punctus elevatus* occur at the caesura:

> He brohte vs alle from þe deþ /⸲ ⁊ dude vs frendes dede
> Suete iesu of naȝareth /⸲ þou do vs heuene mede. (lines 23–26; fol. 128r)

Euer ⁊ oo nyht ⁊ day he haueþ vs in is þohte /
He nul nout leose þat he so deore bohte.

The Way of Christ's Love (lines 1–8; fol. 128r)

A *punctus elevatus* occurs at the end of the third line — this is unusual in Harley 2253 where it is commonly employed to mark midline pauses in verse. From a metrical point of view, punctuation at the ends of lines in verse laid out in columns is redundant, though such punctuation was a common practice in Middle English manuscripts.[18] The scribe's reasons for using punctuation occasionally at the ends of lines could have been syntactic and rhetorical rather than metrical.

The parallel opening stanza of *The Way of Woman's Love* is punctuated in the following way:

Lutel wot hit anymon ⸵ hou derne loue may stonde
Bote hit were a fre wymmon ⸵ þat muche of loue had fonde
Þe loue of hire ne lesteþ no wyht longe
Heo haueþ me plyht ⁊ wyteþ me wyþ wronge
Euer ⁊ oo for my leof icham in grete þohte
Y þenche on hire þat y ne seo nout ofte. (lines 1–8; fol. 128r)

This demonstrates purely metrical punctuation as is commonly used in the Harley MS; the caesuras of long lines are marked with the *punctus elevati*, whereas the ends of lines are left unpointed.

The use of *punctus elevati* to mark midline pauses and of virgules to mark the ends of lines is not entirely regular in Harley 2253, but appears as a sufficiently clear tendency, particularly in poems written as prose. In poems written as verse where there was no real need for consistent metrical punctuation and the stanza patterns were clear from the layout, the scribe's practice was looser. In some poems the *punctus elevatus* was not used at all. Thus in *I Syke When Y Singe* (no. 62) on fol. 80ra virgules are occasionally employed to punctuate both the caesuras and the ends of lines.[19] The same happens in *The Death of Edward I* (no. 47) on fol. 73r, *The Poet's Repentance* (no. 33) on fol. 66r, and *The Meeting in the Wood* (no. 35) on fol. 66v.[20] In poems written as prose the scribe's practice was much more consistent. Thus both *punctus* and virgules are only occasionally used at the ends of lines in poems in three-stress verse: *The Labourers in the Vineyard* (no. 41) on fol.

---

[18] For the tradition of punctuating the ends of lines, see Parkes, *Pause and Effect*, p. 102.

[19] Brook, ed., *Harley Lyrics*, pp. 59–60.

[20] *The Death of Edward I* in Rossell Hope Robbins, ed., *Historical Poems of the XIVth and XVth Centuries* (New York, 1959), pp. 21–24; *The Poet's Repentance* in Brook, ed., *Harley Lyrics*, pp. 35–36.

70vb and *Maximian* (no. 68) on fol. 82ra–c.[21] However, in *The Lover's Complaint* (no. 30) copied continuously as prose on fol. 63v, punctuation is very consistent: lines are regularly separated from one another by virgules.[22]

Punctuation in the Harley MS is closely linked to prosody. In verse it occurs exclusively in the positions of the main metrical pauses: at the caesuras and at the ends of lines. The metrical application of punctuation can be summarized as follows. *Punctus elevatus* very rarely occurs at the ends of lines; its main function is to signal the caesural pause. It is used regularly as midline punctuation mark in poems written as prose; in this way the scribe distinguished between the medial and final metrical breaks. It is often replaced by a virgule in texts written in columns where every verse starts on a new line, and the stanza pattern is obvious from the layout. The virgules or *punctus* are commonly employed to mark the ends of lines.[23] The use of virgules was less dependent on metrical considerations than the use of *punctus elevati;* in texts laid out as verse they occur both at the caesuras and at the ends of lines.

The implications of the metrical and paleographical evidence is that a long line with caesural rhyme is a single unit marked by the choice of the rhyming pattern and by the manuscript presentation. There is evidence that the custom of reserving alternative rhyme for lines rhyming at the caesura, and of laying them out as long lines was widely spread in Middle English manuscripts, though sometimes obscured by the considerations of saving space and by individual scribal policies. Examination of all verse contained in two other large anthologies — Oxford, Bodleian Library MS Digby 86 and Oxford, Jesus College MS 29 (both earlier in date than Harley) — has shown an almost complete consistency with Harley 2253 in this respect.[24] Both Jesus College 29 and Digby 86 share some material with Harley 2253, though the three manuscripts are not directly related.

Jesus College 29 consists of two parts: the first, an incomplete Latin chronicle of the fifteenth century, and the second, a miscellany of English, French, and Latin texts that includes some important Middle English poems.[25] The second part was dated by several

---

[21] *The Labourers in the Vineyard* in Brook, ed., *Harley Lyrics*, pp. 42–43 (no. 10); *Maximian* in Karl Böddeker, ed., *Altenglische Dichtungen des MS. Harl. 2253* (1878; repr. Amsterdam, 1969), pp. 245–53.

[22] Brook, ed., *Harley Lyrics*, p. 34.

[23] On the overlap of functions of virgules and *punctus*, see Parkes, *Pause and Effect*, p. 46.

[24] According to the most recent dating (Laing, *Catalogue*, p. 92), Harley 2253 goes back to the second quarter of the fourteenth century, ca. 1340. On paleographical grounds it was dated by Ker as belonging to the fourth decade of the fourteenth century (*Facsimile*, pp. xxi–xxii).

[25] Betty Hill, "The History of Jesus College, Oxford MS. 29," *Medium Ævum* 32 (1963): 203.

scholars to the second half of the thirteenth century.[26] It is in one hand throughout and was probably written by an amateur scribe.[27] Digby 86 is a commonplace book that dates back to the end of the thirteenth century.[28] About half of the manuscript is in French and a quarter is in Latin. After fol. 119 it contains twenty-two pieces in English. All the English texts are in one hand, which is the main hand of the manuscript.[29]

Exceptions to the practice of reserving alternative rhyme for long lines rhyming at the caesuras are very few in the two manuscripts, particularly in comparison with the number of poems they contain. In Digby 86 they are represented by the English poem *Chauncun del secle* on fols. 163v–164r and the Latin poem *Fides hodie sopitur* on fol. 164v.[30] Both poems are in tetrameter and their rather complex stanzas include verse with alternative rhyme laid out as short lines in the manuscript. Jesus College 29 has only one such exception: the rhyming pattern *abab* is used in *An Orison of Our Lady* laid out in short three- and four-stress lines on fol. 180v.[31] The rhyming patterns of these three poems — *Chauncun del secle*, *ababcccbcb*; *An Orison of Our Lady*, *ababaababa*; *Fides hodie*

---

[26] According to N. R. Ker, the second part of the MS belongs to the second half of the thirteenth century (*The Owl and the Nightingale, Reproduced in Facsimile from the Surviving Manuscripts Jesus College Oxford 29 and British Museum Cotton Caligula A.ix*, EETS o.s. 251 [London, 1963], p. ix). Laing dates it to the last quarter of the thirteenth century (*Catalogue*, p. 145). Hill ascribes it on textual evidence to 1256–1300 ("History," p. 204).

[27] Hill, "History," p. 204.

[28] According to B. D. H. Miller, the MS goes back to the last quarter of the thirteenth century or to 1272–82 ("The Early History of Bodleian MS Digby 86," *Annuale Mediaevale* 4 [1963]: 28–29). This dating is supported by Laing (p. 129). According to Judith Tschann and M. B. Parkes, the collection was copied during the last quarter of the thirteenth and perhaps the earliest years of the fourteenth centuries (*Facsimile of Oxford, Bodleian Library, MS Digby 86*, EETS s.s. 16 [Oxford, 1996], pp. xxxvi–xxxviii).

[29] The MS was described in detail by Miller and more recently by Tschann and Parkes. According to Miller, "The manuscript is in two main hands, *A* and *B*: *A*, a bold, irregular, unprofessional hand of the late thirteenth century, appears on ff. 1–80v, and 97–207v; *B*, a smaller, neater contemporary hand, on ff. 81–96v; the hand changes from *A* to *B*, and back to *A*, within the same work" ("Early History," p. 25).

[30] *Chauncun del secle* in Thomas Wright, ed., *Anecdota literaria: A Collection of Short Poems in English, Latin and French* (London, 1844), p. 92; Brown prints texts from two other MSS (*Eng. Lyr. XIII*, pp. 78–82).

[31] Richard Morris, ed., *An Old English Miscellany*, EETS o.s. 49 (1872; repr. Millwood, N.Y., 1988), pp. 159–62. The references to the folio numbers in Jesus College 29 are in accordance with the foliation adopted by Ker, *Owl and Nightingale*, p. xi, and H. O. Coxe, *Catalogus codicum MSS. qui in collegiis aulisque Oxoniensibus hodie adservantur*, 2 vols. (Oxford, 1852), 2.10–11.

sopitur, abababababbbaab — definitely surpass in metrical complexity all the other poems in these two manuscripts.[32] Examples of verse with alternative rhyme laid out in long lines according to the described practice are, in the Jesus College MS, *The Duty of Christians* in seven-stress verse (fols. 193r–194r), Thomas of Hales's *Love Rune* (fols. 187r–188v), and *The Five Blisses* (fol. 181r–v).[33] Both Jesus College 29 and Digby 86 have a large selection of verse in three- and four-stress lines used both separately and in combination. This verse in couplets and tail-rhyme stanzas is laid out in columns of short lines, and apart from the described exceptions does not feature alternative rhyme.

As for the use of punctuation, in Digby 86 punctuation is scarce. The only mark employed by the scribe is the *punctus* (.). It is used at the ends of the longest lines in the left-hand column of a folio in order to separate them from the text in the right-hand column. Hence, the *punctus* very rarely occurs at the ends of lines in the right-hand column. In the Jesus College MS metrical punctuation is very consistent: the *punctus* is regularly used to mark the ends of lines and the caesuras. At the caesuras *punctus* is sometimes replaced by a *punctus elevatus*.[34] In contrast to the Harley MS, in Jesus College 29 punctuation is not confined to the positions of the main metrical pauses. Apart from indicating metrical division, the *punctus* is used in some poems (for example, *Love Rune* with its didactic rhetoric) to emphasize syntactic and logical structures.

Deviations from the practice of associating alternative rhyme with long lines in Harley 2253 are represented by three poems. Two of them, *King Horn* and *Satire on the Retinues of the Great*, are discussed by Ker, who lists them as cases of exceptional treatment of the texts by the scribe of this manuscript.[35] *King Horn* (no. 70; fols. 83r–92v) is in short, predominantly four-stress couplets but is written in long lines, with two four-stress verses at a line. The lines are separated by virgules. The reason for this treatment could have been the scribe's wish to save space through an economic layout of a long text.

---

[32] The English poems are also characterized by a rather disciplined metrical form. According to Wright, *Chauncun del secle* "possesses considerable elegance for an English composition of this period" (*Anecdota literaria*, p. 126).

[33] *The Duty of Christians* in Morris, ed., *OE Miscellany*, pp. 141–44; Thomas of Hales's *Love Rune* in Susanna Greer Fein, ed., *Moral Love Songs and Laments* (Kalamazoo, Mich., 1998), pp. 32–38; *The Five Blisses* in Brown, ed., *Eng. Lyr. XIII*, pp. 65–67.

[34] For example, on fols. 171v and 179v (*A Moral Ode [Poema Morale]* and *The Woman of Samaria*) in Morris, ed., *OE Miscellany*, pp. 58–71 and 84–86, respectively.

[35] Ker, *Facsimile*, p. xvii. The Harley text of *King Horn* is in J. Rawson Lumby, ed., *King Horn, Floris and Blauncheflur, The Assumption of Our Lady*, 2nd ed. rev. George H. McKnight, EETS o.s. 14 (1901; repr. Bungay, Suffolk, 1962); *Satire on the Retinues of the Great* in Robbins, ed., *Historical Poems*, pp. 27–29.

Satire on the Retinues of the Great (no. 88) occurs on fols. 124va–125r. It is in mono-rhyming quatrains of alliterative accentual lines with four strong stresses per line. The lines have clearly defined caesuras which occasionally feature a rhyme or an assonance. The poem is written in short lines on fol. 124b:

> Of rybaudz y ryme ʹ
> ant rede o my rolle
> of gedelynges gromes ʹ
> of colyn 7 of colle. (lines 1–4; fol. 124va)

It continues in long lines on fol. 125r. Ker explains this as a misunderstanding of the stanza pattern by the scribe, which he corrected as soon as he moved to the next page. Punctuation in the poem seems to support this theory. Long lines on fol. 125r are left with almost no punctuation. In short lines on fol. 124va–b caesuras are marked with *punctus elevati* or sometimes with virgules, or with both *punctus elevati* and virgules; the ends of lines are regularly punctuated with virgules. The use of *punctus elevatus* on fol. 124v can be seen as an attempt to clarify the metrical structure of the poem for the reader; the scribe employed punctuation to distinguish between the ends of lines and the midline breaks, and to show that what appears to be independent lines in the faulty layout on this folio are in fact half-lines, parts of larger metrical units. On fol. 125r where the poem is written in long lines, according to the scribe's usual practice, there was no need for punctuation to clarify the metrical structure.

One other exception is the poem *The Five Joys of the Virgin* (no. 67), which occupies two columns on fol. 81v.[36] Its stanzas consist of three four-stress lines followed by a three-stress and a seven-stress line. The seven-stress line rhymes both at the caesura and at the end. The rhyming pattern of the whole poem is *aaabab*. There is a difference in layout between the left- and the right-hand columns on fol. 81v: in the left-hand column seven-stress lines are written as long lines, whereas in the right-hand column they are broken between two lines, obviously because of the limited space. Seven-stress lines are marked with *punctus elevati* or sometimes virgules at the caesura.

Punctuation in these texts that are laid out in an unconventional way in Harley 2253 is strongly determined by metrical considerations. In the texts where for some reason long verses are broken between two lines, or short verses are written two at a time, the *punctus elevatus* and the virgule tend to be used in their main metrical functions: as midline and end-of-line punctuation marks. In the texts written according to the scribe's "correct" practice, punctuation, although it still occurs only in the positions of the main metrical

---

[36] Brook, ed., *Harley Lyrics*, pp. 65–66.

pauses, is more emancipated from metrical considerations and emphasizes syntactic and rhetorical structures in the texts.

The layout and the presence of alternative rhyme give guidance for distinguishing between the long and the short lines in Harley 2253; layout in long lines and alternative rhyme almost always go together. This usage is more common in early Middle English manuscripts; it loosened in the later period with the spread of more complex stanza forms. In fifteenth-century manuscripts it is less consistent.

In general metrical terms a verse and a hemistich are relative notions. There are no rules in metrical theory that require that they be kept apart or that indicate how to distinguish a single line with a caesura from two separate lines. The caesura is a recurring metrical break at a particular place in a line, determined by the metrical pattern. Its ultimate origin is in the limitations of perception, in our ability to comprehend only a limited sequence of units in a single act of perception. The caesura does not need to coincide with syntactic or logical pauses; its most common indication is a word boundary. The caesura can be strengthened and brought into greater prominence by various means, such as: its coincidence with a syntactic pause; a special form of ending the first hemistich (for example, an obligatory feminine ending); a special form of beginning the second hemistich (for example, an obligatory anacrusis); a consistently used stress before the caesura; or, finally, rhyme. When the caesura is strong, and it is particularly strong when both hemistiches rhyme, the division into lines and hemistiches can be only a matter of convention. In such cases, authorial will expressed in the layout, insofar as it can be determined, becomes decisive.

In early Middle English all lines except for trimeter had a caesura. Even tetrameter and four-stress hemistiches of long lines tended to develop a medial pause. Long lines had a clearly marked caesura that usually coincided with a deep syntactic pause and sometimes had rhyme. A strong caesura tended to set hemistiches apart and was dangerous for the unity of a long line. Long lines with rhyming caesuras were unstable and broke down with the introduction of complex stanzaic patterns, and with the movement of the literary tradition further away from alliterative verse with its culture of long lines with medial pauses.

The Language of the English Poems:
The Harley Scribe and His Exemplars

Frances McSparran

London, British Library MS Harley 2253 is the work of two scribes. The first four quires (fols. 1r–48v) are all in French and in the first hand, and will not be considered further here. The remainder of the manuscript, fols. 49r–140v and 142r, is all the work of the second scribe, with the exception of a run of eight short prose items (nos. 10–17)[1] on the mixing of colors and application of silver leaf for manuscript decoration, which were added by a later hand to blank space at the end of Quire 5, on fol. 52v.[2] This larger section of the manuscript is trilingual; fifty of the texts copied by its scribe are either wholly or partly in Middle English verse. They range in length from the two-line conclusion to a macaronic Latin-French love poem *Dum ludis floribus* (no. 55) to the 1,546 lines of *King Horn* (no. 70), amounting to nearly 5,000 lines of Middle English. The scribe who copied

---

[1] In this essay MS contents will be identified by the numbers assigned to them by N. R. Ker, intro., *Facsimile of British Museum MS. Harley 2253*, EETS o.s. 255 (London, 1965), pp. ix–xvi. Ker retains the numbering supplied by Humfrey Wanley in the Harleian catalogue of 1759, modifying it by intercalating numbers for individual items not noticed by Wanley (thus nos. 24, 24a, 24b, 25, 25a, etc.; H. Wanley, D. Casley, et al., *A Catalogue of the Harleian Manuscripts in the British Museum* [1759; rev. and repr. 4 vols., London, 1808–12], 2.585–91). It should be noted, however, that Wanley mistakenly, though understandably, identified lines 40–60 of no. 40 as no. 42, and that Ker's no. 42 has therefore no referent. It is possible that a similar error made by the scribe himself as he copied nos. 40 and 41 from his exemplar underlies the confusing sequence displayed by these poems on fols. 70v–71r. The facsimile does not reproduce the entire MS, but rather all the leaves copied by the main scribe, thus omitting fols. ir, 1r–48v, 141r–v, and 142v. It includes all the items either wholly or in part in English.

[2] These recipes will not be considered further in this essay. M. L. Samuels describes the dialect of this later scribe as similar to that of the main scribe, but with more southerly features which suggest that the scribe was from nearer Hereford: "The Dialect of the Scribe of the Harley Lyrics," in *Middle English Dialectology*, ed. Margaret Laing (Aberdeen, 1989), p. 262 (this article was originally published in *Poetica [Tokyo]* 19 [1984]: 39–47; all page references to this study refer to the 1989 reprint).

this material in the second quarter of the fourteenth century (the main scribe of Harley) also copied portions of BL MS Harley 273 earlier in the century, and over a period of years copied most of London, BL MS Royal 12.C.xii, a miscellany in Latin, French and English.[3]

The Middle English poems are distributed in clusters among the Latin and French contents of Harley 2253, and one naturally wants to know if the ordering of the texts in the manuscript reflects a deliberate process of arrangement by the scribe, or a more or less accidental sequence of texts, determined perhaps by their groupings in one or more exemplars. Even a superficial examination suggests a rough and ready ordering by subject and type (religious verse, socio-political poems, love lyrics) among groups of texts in one or more of the three languages, and among subgroups within larger units, but striking discontinuities also emerge, and much remains unclear about the process of compilation of the manuscript. Are the discontinuities simply discontinuities, or are they deliberately contrived contrasts in theme and topic? Does the apparent ordering prove that the Harley scribe planned the sequence of texts, or did he merely reproduce groups of texts from his exemplars, whose collocations of texts may in their turn have reflected either design or casual conjunctions of different materials? These problems of origin and transmission, though difficult and perhaps intractable, are of great interest; a number of the religious poems in Harley also occur in manuscripts which are earlier or more or less contemporary with Harley, but the most brilliant and original of the love lyrics and the socio-political-satirical poems are unique copies, making solo appearances in this one manuscript.

It has long been recognized that many of the Harley poems must have been composed outside the West Midlands, since they contain phonological and inflectional features not regularly used in that region. Various studies have attempted to identify the place of origin of individual poems, often with conflicting results.[4] G. L. Brook outlines the limitations of some of these studies as a preliminary to his own study of the original dialects of the Harley lyrics, but he also points out some of the obvious problems involved in an analysis of the dialects of the poems based on rhyme evidence. These caveats still hold. Many of the poems are so short that they offer little evidence of rhymes significant for dialect. It is difficult to estimate how careful a poet will be in his use of rhymes since conflicting

---

[3] See Ker, *Facsimile*, p. xx, and Carter Revard's essay in this volume, "Scribe and Provenance."

[4] Karl Böddeker, ed., *Altenglische Dichtungen des MS. Harl. 2253* (1878; repr. Amsterdam, 1969), *passim*; Mary S. Serjeantson, "The Dialects of the West Midlands in Middle English," *Review of English Studies* 3 (1927): 54–67, 319–31; J. P. Oakden, *Alliterative Poetry in Middle English*, 2 vols. (1930, 1935; repr. Hamden, Conn., 1968), *passim*, especially 1.110–12, 122–24; G. L. Brook, "The Original Dialects of the Harley Lyrics," *Leeds Studies in English* 2 (1933): 38–61.

phonological evidence for the Middle English reflex of an Old English vowel, confirmed by rhyme, may occur in the same poem.[5] Moreover, the same rhymes turn up repeatedly in poem after poem, and one suspects that as poems circulate outside their own area of composition their convenient and ready-made rhymes will be adopted for new poems composed in other areas, even though the rhymes may no longer be exact there. Brook's careful analysis is based on fifteen phonological features and five features of verb inflection, as evidenced by rhyme, augmented by some evidence from within the line. To this he adds some slender evidence from vocabulary, allusions and subject, topographical references, and, finally, the evidence of variant versions.[6] Little advance on his conclusions has been made since then, although in anthologies various scholars have pointed out dialect features and offered useful comments on the possible original dialect of individual poems.[7]

There has been general agreement for many years on the South West Midland dialectal character of the Harley MS, and the manuscript has been variously associated with Leominster and Hereford in Herefordshire, and Ludlow in South Shropshire (see map of South West Midlands below, p. 400).[8] Carter Revard's identification of the scribe's hand

---

[5] Brook, "Original Dialects," p. 40.

[6] Brook's 1933 study of the dialects of the lyrics antedates his edition (originally published in 1948); in it he uses Böddeker's arcane numbering system, which is impenetrable unless one has access to Böddeker's edition. My Appendix lists the English contents keyed to Ker's numbers and to corresponding numbers from five editions: (1) Böddeker; (2) Carleton Brown, ed., *English Lyrics of the XIIIth Century* (Oxford, 1932); (3) Carleton Brown, ed., *Religious Lyrics of the XIVth Century*, 2nd ed. rev. G. V. Smithers (Oxford, 1957); (4) Rossell Hope Robbins, ed., *Historical Poems of the XIVth and XVth Centuries* (New York, 1959); and (5) G. L. Brook, ed., *The Harley Lyrics: The Middle English Lyrics of MS. Harley 2253*, 4th ed. (Manchester, 1968).

[7] See, in particular, J. A. W. Bennett and G. V. Smithers, eds., *Early Middle English Verse and Prose*, 2nd ed. (Oxford, 1968).

[8] The MS itself contains evidence of associations with both Leominster and Hereford. On this, see Ker, *Facsimile*, pp. xxii–xxiii, where he reviews three relevant features: (1) the "Legenda de sancto Etfrido presbitero de Leominstria" (no. 98), preceded and highlighted by a large cross; a binding leaf in the hand of the Harley scribe bearing on one side (2) accounts made at Ardmulghan, County Meath; and on the other side (3) extracts from the ordinal of Hereford Cathedral. The accounts associate the MS with the Mortimer family, who owned Ardmulghan between 1308 and 1330. The editors of the New Palaeographical Society suggest, in a description of fol. 83 of Harley 2253, that Thomas de Charlton, bishop of Hereford (1327–44), who served as Chancellor of Ireland from 1337–40, might be the link that explains the association of the accounts and the ordinal on the one leaf (*Facsimiles of Ancient Manuscripts etc.*, 1st series [London, 1912], facing plate 241), but Ker points out that the account dates are earlier than the period of Charlton's service in Ireland. He

in a series of deeds relating to Ludlow establishes that the Harley scribe worked there for extended periods and provides convincing evidence for the provenance of the manuscript.[9] In 1984, in an important study of the dialect of the scribe, however, M. L. Samuels demonstrated that the scribe's linguistic and orthographic habits show that he must have acquired them in or around Leominster, which lies "twelve miles north of Hereford, nine miles south of Ludlow."[10] Scribes are, of course, mobile, and there is nothing surprising in the notion that a Leominster man might ply his trade in Ludlow or in Hereford, or both. What is remarkable and interesting here is the convergence of linguistic, codicological, and archival scholarship, which together have been able to fine-tune the localization of this manuscript and scribal dialect within such a close range.

The scholars who produced the *Linguistic Atlas of Late Mediaeval English* (*LALME*) and other analytical and theoretical studies of Middle English dialectology and texts have described the different ways in which a scribe can handle and copy exemplars written in dialects other than his own.[11] In 1963 Angus McIntosh described three ways in which a scribe faced with a text in a different dialect might proceed. He may reproduce the forms he finds, effacing himself and his own dialect forms and thus serving merely as an agent of reproduction; he may translate the text into his own dialect; or he may do something in between these two poles of replication and translation, and produce a text that combines forms from the source with those of his own dialect.[12] This third procedure produces a *Mischsprache*, where the finished copy may fall anywhere on the continuum between

---

looks instead for an explanation of the Hereford association to four lines of Latin verse added by the Harley scribe to Royal 12.C.xii, which contain allusions to successive bishops of Hereford Cathedral, and suggests Hereford as the likely place of origin of the MS. The separate investigations of Revard and Samuels render this hypothesis less likely, though some kind of off-and-on relationship between the Harley scribe and a major center of scribal activity like Hereford Cathedral seems very plausible, and Samuels's characterization of the dialect of the later scribe of the paint recipes would accord well with some association of the scribe or the MS with Hereford. See Carter Revard, "Richard Hurd and MS. Harley 2253," *Notes and Queries*, n.s. 26 (1979): 199–202, and "Three More Holographs in the Hand of the Scribe of MS. Harley 2253 in Shrewsbury," *Notes and Queries*, n.s. 28 (1981): 199–200; and Samuels, "Dialect."

[9] See Revard, "Richard Hurd," "Three More Holographs," and the essay in this volume.

[10] Samuels, "Dialect," p. 256.

[11] Angus McIntosh, M. L. Samuels, Michael Benskin, with the assistance of Margaret Laing and Keith Williamson, *A Linguistic Atlas of Late Mediaeval English*, 4 vols. (Aberdeen, 1986), hereafter cited as *LALME*.

[12] Angus McIntosh, "A New Approach to Middle English Dialectology," in *Middle English Dialectology*, ed. Laing, pp. 27–28 (repr. from *English Studies* 44 [1963]: 1–11).

these poles, and indeed may shift its position as the scribe copies, since he may begin with exact copying of an unfamiliar dialect (*literatim* copying), but may move into partial and towards full translation as he becomes more familiar with the forms of his source and confident about their equivalents in his own written dialect. Michael Benskin and Margaret Laing have developed and refined a methodology for dealing with texts written in this fashion, and they have introduced an important distinction between two aspects of a scribe's own practice, namely his active repertoire of written forms — those he would use spontaneously — and his passive repertoire — forms with which he is familiar, but which he is unlikely to use unless they are activated by his encounter with them in the exemplar he copies.[13] The generation of forms from his passive repertoire in this fashion is constrained usage, and this concept will prove important in understanding the practice of the Harley scribe.

In a later essay on the Auchinleck MS copy of *The Four Foes of Mankind*, McIntosh shows how the scribe (the main Auchinleck scribe), who probably came from Middlesex, copied the poem with very minor changes and "transmits the poem in a form which leaves no doubt as to its northern origin," though its language must have seemed somewhat alien to a listener or reader in London at the time. He contrasts this near exact copying with the activity a generation or so earlier of the scribe of Harley 2253, who, when he copied Northern and North Midland poems, "much more thoroughly converts his exemplars into something quite close to his own Herefordshire English" so that "the underlying linguistic characteristics of his originals can only be glimpsed rather dimly and fitfully."[14] Samuels, in his study and localization of the dialect of the scribe of the Harley lyrics, discusses two kinds of scribes: one translates his exemplar into his own dialect and spelling system and is likely to preserve only rhyme-words from the exemplar; the other is not as thorough a translator and may be willing to take over forms from his exemplar "even when not in rhyme." He sees the Harley scribe as the latter kind of copyist, and illustrates some of the variations in spelling forms which result from this.[15]

In my view, the Harley scribe retains a large number of forms from his exemplars which are not part of his own natural practice. The South West Midland character of his language (and probably of the language of his exemplars) is consistent and clear, but in addition to

---

[13] Michael Benskin and Margaret Laing, "Translations and *Mischsprachen* in Middle English Manuscripts," in *So meny people, longages and tonges: Philological Essays in Scots and Mediaeval English Presented to Angus McIntosh*, ed. Michael Benskin and M. L. Samuels (Edinburgh, 1981), pp. 55–106 (later substantially reproduced in *LALME* 1, General Introduction).

[14] Angus McIntosh, "The Middle English Poem 'The Four Foes of Mankind': Some Notes on the Language and the Text," *Neuphilologische Mitteilungen* 79 (1978): 138.

[15] Samuels, "Dialect," p. 256.

his characteristic preferred forms for common lexical and other linguistic items, variants appear which are alternative and well-attested South West Midland forms. Some of these seem to exist in free variation with the dominant preferred form and are likely to be part of the scribe's active repertoire of spellings; others are unevenly dispersed, appearing in some poems but not in others, and it seems probable that his use of them reflects the forms of exemplars from the region, and that they are examples of constrained selection. A smaller component of non-South West Midland forms, including verb inflection (pr. 3 sg. in -*es*, pr. pl. in -(*e*)*s*) and some forms of words, also unevenly distributed among the texts, are relicts and may have survived several layers of copying to appear in his own work. Some of these forms, especially those in rhyme, are probably archetypal; others may have been introduced in the process of transmission into manuscripts which lie behind the Harley copies, and their immediate exemplars. The variation in distributions of forms between one poem and another is, however, hard to demonstrate clearly, because many of the poems are so short that it is difficult to assemble a substantial roster of items which co-occur often in different poems, although different subsets of significant items turn up in individual poems.

Take, for example, the most linguistically eccentric and untypical text in the collection, *The Prophecy of Thomas of Erceldoune* (no. 90), some of whose most interesting features do not recur in the corpus of Harley texts which I have analyzed. It is eighteen lines long, has a repetitive rhetorical structure (a string of sixteen "When . . ." clauses, leading to a two-line conclusion), and has a restricted repertoire of significant features. But it contains an unusually high frequency of untypical forms for these features, both compared to the manuscript as a whole and compared with other individual poems in the manuscript which exhibit one or more of these untypical forms:[16]

(*i*) In the full corpus of texts, the preferred form for 'man' is *mon*: *mon* 54 (*wommon, wymmon, lemmon, anymon,* etc. 24; *monkune, monkunde,* etc. 9); gen. sg. *monnes* 4, *mones* 2; gen. pl. *monne* 1.[17] Forms with -*a*- are much less common: *man* 10; *wymman* 3; *lemman* 1; all but two are in rhyme, and forms with -*a*- must come from the scribe's passive repertoire. This short poem (if poem it is) contains *man* twice in the first line, and the rare form -*mones* in line 2, beside two occurrences of *mon* (lines 2, 6).[18]

---

[16] See further the discussion of relict forms at the conclusion of this essay.

[17] The number following a cited form gives the total number of occurrences in the corpus of forty-three texts. For the contents of the corpus, see n. 28 below.

[18] Forms of *man* (*wymman, lemman*) with -*a*- occur in nos. 21 (2*), 47 (1*), 48 (1*), 61 (1), 64 (2*), 66 (1*), 67 (4*), 90 (2), a total of fourteen occurrences. For *mones*, see no. 40 (1), and

(*ii*) The word *kyrkes* (line 2) is unique in the corpus and highly unusual in a South West Midland text; it is not recorded in any Herefordshire Linguistic Profile by *LALME*, and belongs further north.[19] The form *alde* 'old' (line 8) is the only example of this spelling I have found anywhere in these texts; *burgh* (line 7) is a unique spelling (compare -*bourh* in the same line and in no. 62) and, moreover, contains the only *gh* spelling for the velar fricative I have found anywhere in this corpus of texts. On *ah* 'but' (line 18), at the beginning of a line, see Table 3.

(*iii*) Ppl. forms: *gan* (line 18) occurs in only one other text,[20] beside *gon* 6, *go* 1, -*gonne* 1 elsewhere in the collection. The ppl. form *comen* (line 18) occurs only here; elsewhere we find *come* 10, *ycome* 2.

(*iv*) Pr. 3 sg. forms: *as* 'has' (line 1) does not occur elsewhere in the texts, nor, for that matter, is it recorded in any Herefordshire Linguistic Profile; it is recorded sparsely from the North down into the central Midlands.[21] The invariable form elsewhere in the corpus is *haþ*. There are no occurrences of the scribe's customary -*eþ* for the pr. 3 sg.; the forms are *makes*, *steles*, *prikes*.

(*v*) The eight pr. pl. forms end in -*es* (*kendles*, *werres*, *ledes*) or -*n* (*don*, *flen*), beside the regular scribal preference -*eþ* (*ascenteþ*, *weddeþ*, *drouneþ*).

(*vi*) 'They' appears once only in the text, as *hy* (line 16), a form that occurs only four times elsewhere in the material.

(*vii*) The verb *sellen* 'sell' (line 10) appears with this vowel only once elsewhere (no. 62). This may or may not be significant, for *sulle*, the expected form, is itself rare (4 examples) and confined to one text, no. 31.[22]

(*viii*) The form *whenne* 'when' (line 17) is unique in this corpus.

The *hy* form (*vi*) suggests an exemplar more southerly than Harley, though it may have been an occasional variant in the scribe's own dialect, while most of the forms in (*ii*)–(*v*), especially *kyrkes*, *alde*, and the -*es* pres. pl. endings, point to the North Midlands or further

---

compare *LALME* 4.28, where *mones* is recorded in only two Linguistic Profiles, Wrk LP 4689 and Wor LP 7620.

[19] See *LALME* 2.249–51 (Item Maps, 98 CHURCH [1–6]), for its distribution.

[20] In *Harrowing of Hell* (no. 21) line 72, in rhyme with *ycham*. The ppl. form *ygan* also occurs in rhyme in line 4 of this text.

[21] *LALME* 4.189.

[22] *Sullen* is the invariable form in the 'AB' language of the *Ancrene Wisse*/Katherine Group texts (S. R. T. O. d'Ardenne, ed., *Þe Liflade ant te Passiun of Seint Iuliene*, EETS o.s. 248 [London, 1961], p. 127). See also n. 44 below.

north as the source of the Harley copy.[23] But does "source" here mean that the forms are archetypal, or that they are those of a North Midland or northerly exemplar? None of the other texts displays this density of untypical forms, and some of them, as I have shown, are unique in the corpus. The combination and sequence of forms in this piece suggests that the Harley scribe is fairly close to the pole of *literatim* copying from an exemplar in a dialect from considerably further north of Harley, perhaps Lincolnshire (or possibly from an intervening South West Midland exemplar which likewise retained those more Northern features). How close this exemplar was to the language of the archetype is unclear, but the subject matter and the references to Thomas of Erceldoun, the countess of Dunbar, and the Scottish place-names all suggest a Northern or northerly origin. The Harley scribe, or, conceivably, an intervening copyist, seems to have moved towards translation in the act of copying, since the *man* forms of line 1 are followed in line 2 by *mon*(-), and the pr. pl. forms in *-es* are dropped in favor of *-eþ* towards the end of the piece. These replacements give us some indication of what non-South West Midland forms caused him most orthographic discomfort. Other untypical forms, however, survive right to the end. The form *hy* must be part of the topmost layer of South West Midland features in the piece (e.g., *u* for OE *y*, *-eþ* for pr. pl.), whether attributable to the Harley scribe or his immediate source. I suspect that the Harley scribe is himself the copyist responsible for the partial translation I have described here, and that he added the text as a filler from a source with more Northern features than many of his exemplars. The text is copied on fol. 127rb, the writing is somewhat larger and looser than in the preceding text, with much larger initial letters at the beginning of lines and of many words. It is followed on the verso by another likely filler, a short piece in French, *La Distinccioun de la estature Iesu Crist Nostre Seigneur* (no. 91), leaving half of the second column blank. After a matched pair of poems beginning on the next folio, *The Way of Christ's Love* and *The Way of Woman's Love* (nos. 92, 93),[24] the remaining contents are French and Latin, and, almost without exception, religious or didactic in theme. If this text was something of an impromptu addition, it might explain the high incidence of unusual forms in so short a piece. It is of

---

[23] *LALME* 1.466–67, 500 (Dot Maps 645, 653, 850).

[24] Their proximity in the MS might suggest that nos. 92 and 93 (the pair of poems on divine and secular love) share a common transmission history with no. 90, but if so, they have undergone substantial translation at some stage. A rhyme sequence *deþ: dede* 'deed': *mede: hede: blede* in no. 92 shows that an earlier relict form *ded* 'death' has been purged, and the only other form I have noted that might suggest a link with the relict forms in no. 90 is pr. 3 sg. *haues* in no. 93. Another possible, though I think less likely, explanation for the survival of alien forms in no. 90 could be a conscious decision by the Harley scribe, or a predecessor, to preserve the exotic features as a mark of the "otherness" of this pseudo-prophetic text.

special interest because it suggests the possibility that for some texts with vestigial Northern or North Midland forms, a speedier move to partial translation may have eliminated the more exotic evidence. In that case, this text might be associated with others such as the sequence of poems beginning with no. 60 which is discussed at the end of this essay.

I intend in what follows to examine the distribution of forms in other Harley poems to see what they can tell us about the Harley scribe and the sources and transmission of the Harley poems, but one potential source of difficulty is the problem of distinguishing forms from the exemplars from those of the scribe's own practice. Ideally one would use as a control here an extended sample of the scribe's own spontaneous, unconstrained practice as he writes English (though one wonders if such a thing exists). In any case, failing an author and a holograph, we must use other means. Instead, we must try to distinguish the dominant and consistent complex of dialect forms common to the poems as a whole, from those forms which are occasional, and then further discriminate between the occasional forms which exist in free variation in the scribe's natural and unconditioned practice, from others which are derived from his exemplars. Since, as Samuels points out, this kind of scribe is willing to reproduce forms which are not altogether alien to him when he meets them in an exemplar, even though they are not a natural part of his own written dialect, our best hope for identifying them here is to identify forms restricted to individual poems or groups of poems, or to definable contexts such as rhyme position or the beginning of a line, where a scribe is apt to cling to the forms of his sources. Replacing rhymes which are inexact in the dialect of the copyist calls for an active engagement with the text which many scribes seem to have been unwilling to undertake. And I think that the first word of a line is often exactly reproduced in the process of transmitting brief units of source text to the written page from short-term memory.[25]

A difficulty in attempting to separate out different layers of dialect forms is that while it may be relatively easy to isolate rare forms whose infrequent use shows that they are alien to the scribe (as the discussion above of *The Prophecy of Thomas of Erceldoune* illustrates), it is much harder to winnow out forms with which he may be quite familiar since they occur within the larger geographical area where he functions, though they need not be part of his own local written dialect. In other words, can one with confidence distinguish alternative forms occurring in free variation within the scribe's own usage,

---

[25] My experience as I hunted for and checked forms in the facsimile of Harley 2253 for this study has reinforced my belief in the important function of the first word in a line of verse as a finding tool within a text for scribes to use as their eyes moved back and forth from page of source to page of copy. This encourages a scribe to reproduce the form he finds in his source, even if it is not part of his normal repertoire.

from those constrained forms which are not part of his normal practice, but which are in use in the South West Midlands, including areas close to home? And the difficulty of doing this may be increased by the likelihood that he will be most tolerant of forms circulating closest to him, with his tolerance diminishing as the forms become more remote from his own experience. In the nature of things, in a non-metropolitan and provincial setting like Ludlow or Hereford, the Harley scribe is likely to be most familiar with the scribal practices of the West Midlands and the texts that circulated in that region, especially since a thriving literary culture flourished there, notably in Worcester and Gloucester, in the period before he copied his manuscript. Thirteenth-century manuscripts

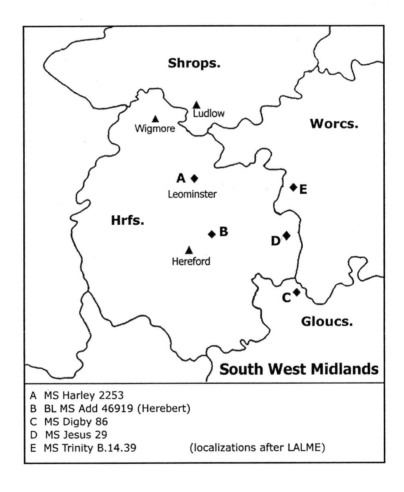

A MS Harley 2253
B BL MS Add 46919 (Herebert)
C MS Digby 86
D MS Jesus 29
E MS Trinity B.14.39   (localizations after LALME)

FIGURE. *Map of South West Midlands.*

whose language belongs to the South West Midlands — like Digby 86, Jesus College 29, Trinity College B.14.39, and Cotton Caligula A.ix — provide models for the kind of religious material he copied, though apparently none was a direct source.[26] The religious and didactic poems copied by the Harley scribe were in circulation in this area, and his exemplars are likely to have been fairly local, so that disentangling personal variants from constrained variants in local use may be difficult if not impossible.

The *LALME* profile of Harley 2253 and the work of Samuels provide the detailed groundwork fundamental to this examination of the language of the poems,[27] but while they naturally present an overall account of the forms, I want to attempt a closer and more detailed account of the prevailing scribal dialect and the significance of the variant forms in individual poems and groups of poems, in the hope that it may help to answer the questions posed above about the process of compilation of the manuscript. In what follows, I hope to discriminate between (1) the dominant and consistently displayed scribal forms and two other categories of forms, (2) occasional forms which for one reason or another seem clearly to belong to the scribe's own practice, as variants he freely uses, and (3) variants which I think are instances of constrained usage or relict forms. Relict forms such as those discussed at the end of this essay are easily assigned to the third category. The more problematic variants mentioned above, chiefly South West Midland forms which are used intermittently, may belong to either (2) or (3), and I have assigned them to one or other category as I think the distribution suggests. They may therefore be discussed in either of the two following sections: "The Language of the Scribe" and "The Scribe and His Exemplars." I have included details of the number of occurrences of relevant forms derived from electronic files and a computer concordance of forty-three of the fifty English texts in the hand of the main scribe.[28]

---

[26] The map shows the *LALME* localizations of the scribal dialects of some of these MSS in relation to Ludlow, Leominster, and Hereford. On the date, language, and contents of these MSS, see Margaret Laing, *Catalogue of Sources for a Linguistic Atlas of Early Medieval English* (Bury St. Edmunds, Suffolk, 1993), p. 34 (Cambridge, Trinity College [hereafter TCC] MS B.14.39); p. 69 (London, BL MS Cotton Caligula A.ix, part I); p. 129 (Oxford, Bodleian Library MS Digby 86); and p. 145 (Oxford, Jesus College MS 29). On the shared contents of Digby 86 and Harley 2253, see Brown, ed., *Eng. Lyr. XIII*, p. xxxvii. [See also Marilyn Corrie's essay in this volume, "Harley 2253, Digby 86, and the Circulation of Literature in Pre-Chaucerian England."]

[27] *LALME* 3.173, LP 9260; Samuels, "Dialect," and M. L. Samuels, "The Dialects of MS Bodley 959," in *Middle English Dialectology*, ed. Laing, pp. 136–49 (originally published in *MS Bodley 959: Genesis-Baruch 3.20 in the Earlier Version of the Wycliffite Bible*, ed. C. Lindberg [Stockholm, 1969], pp. 329–39).

[28] The computer concordance was produced from my files by Marilyn Miller, Review Editor/Systems Analyst of the *Middle English Dictionary* (*MED*), whose generous assistance here,

Frances McSparran

The Language of the Scribe

The language of the Harley scribe consistently displays features characteristic of the South West Midlands, notably *o* before nasals: (-)*mon*(-) 85 beside (-)*man* 14; *moni*(*e* and *mony*(*e* invariably except for *meni* once at the beginning of a line in *Song of the Husbandman* (no. 31); *con* 15 beside *can* once in rhyme (in no. 66); *eo, ue* as reflexes of OE *eo* (beside many forms with *e*): *heo* 21 and *hue* 22 spellings for the pronoun 'they' beside *he* 26; *u* for OE *y*. In inflection, pr. 3 sg. and pr. pl. in -*eþ* occur throughout; exceptions are discussed in the section on "The Scribe and His Exemplars." Present participles end in -*inde* (4) or -*ynde* (4); past participles with a *y*- prefix are common. These features occur throughout and must be the scribe's preferred forms, though they tell us little that would help distinguish this scribe's dialect from that of other South West Midland scribes. What is most distinctive about his written dialect is its combination of conservative South West Midland features, a rather consistent and economical spelling system,[29] some local or personal dialect preferences, all combined with considerable tolerance for forms which do not belong to his own active repertoire.

A distinctive dialect feature of the Harley scribe's language is his use of *feole* 'many' 3, beside *fele* 5. Jeremy Smith points out that forms of OE *fela* with *eo* seem to represent a Mercian tradition, which survives in the 'AB' language of the Corpus text of the *Ancrene Wisse* and Bodley 34.[30] Here the form appears in a fourteenth-century manuscript probably copied at Ludlow, not far from Wigmore Abbey,[31] with which the *Ancrene Wisse* and the Corpus manuscript are associated, and where the 'AB' group may perhaps have been

---

as often before, I gratefully acknowledge. Excluded from the survey, unless otherwise noted, are the following items: nos. 32, 58, 68, 70, 74, 85, 89 (see Appendix for a list of English contents keyed to the Ker numbers). For some forms, however, I have examined some or all of the omitted texts, and I record the results in footnotes as supplementary evidence. The restriction to forty-three texts was not a matter of principle but of availability. I have been assembling SGML-encoded electronic files of the poems for some time, and this is the current state of my collection.

[29] The economy of the spelling system used by the scribe can be illustrated by a very few examples: OE *sc-* at the beginning of words is spelled *sh-* in almost two hundred words while *sch-* is used only once in the corpus. At the beginning of words the palatal fricative /j/ is spelled with *ʒ-* in over one hundred words (*ʒef, ʒeme, ʒer,* etc.), while only three forms with *y-* occur, all in rhyme position, in nos. 21 and 22. Before a consonant the palatal or velar fricative is always spelled *h-*, and never *ʒ-* (*knyht, boht,* etc.).

[30] Jeremy Smith, "Tradition and Innovation in South-West-Midland Middle English," in *Regionalism in Late Medieval Manuscripts and Texts*, ed. Felicity Riddy (Woodbridge, Suffolk, 1991), pp. 58–59.

[31] Samuels, "Dialect," pp. 259–62.

written. The spellings of Harley have much in common, *mutatis mutandis* to allow for the passage of time, with the West Midland dialect represented by 'AB' language. For the thirteenth century *feole* is richly attested, but the form is recessive in the fourteenth century, and *LALME* records it in only five Linguistic Profiles, two from Herefordshire (those for Harley 2253 and Jesus College 29, which also has *veole*), two from Worcestershire, and one from Shropshire.[32] It occurs also, most interestingly, in the *Short Metrical Chronicle* copied by the Harley scribe in Royal 12.C.xii, and must surely belong to the scribe's own repertoire.

The verb 'fetch' occurs five times in the corpus, always with medial -*a*- rather than -*e*-: *vacche* 2 (no. 21), *vachen* 1 (no. 35), and *facche* 2 (no. 48). These forms must represent the scribe's own practice, since for the West Midlands forms with -*a*- are recorded by *LALME* only in a restricted area in Herefordshire, southern Shropshire, and western Worcestershire.[33] I have found similar forms in two other Herefordshire MSS: *vache* in London, British Library Addit. MS 46919, the volume containing the poems of William Herebert, which Samuels places in Hereford;[34] and Royal 12.C.xii once again, where *vacche* occurs in the *Short Metrical Chronicle*, copied by the Harley scribe.

The overall scribal dialect displays many conservative features common in the South West Midlands, including: noun inflection (the survival of OE weak plural endings for nouns, and the extension of the weak plural ending to nouns not historically weak; the retention of OE feminine noun plurals in -*e*); syncopated pr. 3 sg. verb forms and mutation of the stem vowel in *do* and *go*; retention of -*i*- in pr. 1 sg. and pr. pl. of OE class II weak verbs; the frequent marking of case, number, and occasionally gender distinctions for nouns and adjectives;[35] and the use of -*e* as an inflectional marker of weak adjective forms.

In the illustrations of these features which follow, the list of forms is selective, but all occurrences of any quoted form are noted, together with a full count of any alternative

---

[32] A search through all citations in the on-line *Middle English Dictionary* documents numerous thirteenth-century examples, largely, but not exclusively, from the South West Midlands; see *MED* [on-line version], in *Middle English Compendium*, ed. Frances McSparran (Ann Arbor, 1998–), (June 1998 Release); URL http://www.hti.umich.edu/mec/ (accessed Sept. 1998). See also *LALME* 1.524 (Dot Map 986), 4.167.

[33] See *LALME* 4.168-69, which records seven Linguistic Profiles for the area described, besides three from Devon.

[34] Samuels, "Dialect," pp. 258–59.

[35] The preservation of gender distinctions for OE nouns is rare in the corpus, and likely to be constrained usage; I have noticed three survivals of the acc. masc. def. article *þen* before OE masc. nouns in no. 21, and *hue*, the fem. form of the 3 sg. pronoun, is used to refer to *herte*, an OE fem. noun, in no. 47, line 27.

form which occurs, in order to show the relative frequencies of variants. The features discussed here are scattered through the poems and seem to belong to the scribe's normal practice.

(*i*) *Noun inflection*. Weak plural endings are common both for OE weak nouns and for nouns that belonged historically to other OE declensions.

OE weak plural nouns: *doggen* 1; *eren* 1; *eȝenen* 'eyes' 1, *eyȝen* 2, *eȝen* 1, *eye* 1, *heȝe* 1; *feren* 1, *fere* 1; *lomen* 'tools' 1 (beside *lomes* 1).[36]

Nouns from other OE declensions: *blosmen* 1 (both strong and weak forms in OE); *browen* 3 (beside *browes* 2); *deden* 3 (beside *dedes* 1); *doren* 1; *geren* 1; *hennen* 1; *hynen* 1; *honden* 4 (beside *honde* 12); *serewen* 1 (beside *serewes* 2); *siden* 1 (beside *sides* 2); *siþen* 'times' 1 (beside *siþe* 1); *sleuen* 1; *steden* 'steeds' 2 (beside *stedes* 2); *tern* 'tears' 1 (beside *teres* 2); *tren* 'trees' 1; *wounden* 2 (beside *wounde* 5, *woundes* 4).

(*ii*) *Syncopation in verb forms*. Pr. 3 sg. *byd* 'endures' 1; *byhalt* 1, *byholt* 1, *halt* 6 (beside a single pr. 2 sg. *holdest*); *byt* 'commands' 2; *syt* 'sits' 3, *sit* 1 (beside *sitteþ* 1); *slyt* 'falls' 1; *stont* 5, *stond* 2; *strit* 'strides' 1.[37]

TABLE 1 *Adjective inflection*

Singular	Singular (after prep., dem., or poss.)	Plural
foul 1	*foule* 3	*foule* 1
god 5 *good* 2	*gode* 2 *god* 1	*gode* 6
gret 3	*grete* 2 *gret* 2	*grete* 4
mony 12 *moni* 10 'many, many a' with sg. nouns		*monie* 7 *monye* 2
muchel 1	*muchele* 8 *muchel* 2	
smal 5		*smale* 2 *smalle* 1
strong 1		*stronge* 8
wicked 2 *wycked* 2		*wickede* 2

---

[36] *Wonges* 'cheeks,' originally an OE weak neuter noun, appears five times, but strong plural forms of this noun occurred already in OE (A. Campbell, *An Old English Grammar* [Oxford, 1959], ¶ 618).

[37] Forms such as pr. 2 sg. *lis* 'lies' (OE *licgan*) and pr. 3 sg. *seys* 'says' in no. 22, and pr. 2 sg. *sys* 'sees' in no. 28 (all confirmed in rhyme) must predate the Harley scribe, though they may also have been part of his own active repertoire. The pr. 3. sg. form *liþ* 'lies' (OE *licgan*) occurs three times within the line in nos. 31, 47, and 61, and in at least two of the cases is metrically required, so it too may be from either the scribe's active or passive repertoire.

Mutation of the stem vowel is found in pr. 3 sg. of two verbs only: *geþ* 3 beside *goþ* 1; *deþ* 2 beside *doþ* 10.

(*iii*) *Adjective inflection.* -*e* is commonly used with monosyllabic adjectives to mark the dative sg. (or prepositional case), for plurals, and in positions which in OE required weak inflection. Inflection of disyllabic adjectives, including participles, although very frequent, is somewhat less consistent. The evidence in Table 1 suggests that the loss of inflectional -*e* in the singular is in progress, since the scribe is somewhat inconsistent in his practice.

(*iv*) *Weak verbs.* In about half the examples I have found, Class II weak verbs preserve -*i*- in the historically regular positions in the infinitive, the present system (that is, excluding pr. 2 sg. and pr. 3 sg.), and the present participle (Table 2). As one might expect, the loss of -*i*- is more advanced in the infinitive than in the present system. *Make*(-*n* has gone furthest in the elimination of -*i*- throughout. In several

TABLE 2 *Preservation of* -i- *in the infinitive and present system of weak verbs*

infinitive with i/y	infinitive without i/y	present system with i/y	present system without i/y
		pres. subj. *afretye* 1	
		pr. 3 sg. *blykieþ* 1	
	care 3 (2*)	pr. pl. *carieþ* 1	pr. 1 sg. *care* 1*
	clepe 3	pr. 1 sg. *clepie* 1	pr. pl. *clepeþ* 1
cleuyen 1			
		pr. 3 sg. *gladieþ* 2	
		pr. pl. *hatieþ* 1	
heryen 1		pr. 1 sg. *herie* 2	
		pr. pl. *hopieþ* 1	pr. 1 sg. *hope* 1 pr. pl. *hopeþ* 1
to louye 1 *louien* 1	*loue* 2	pr. subj. *louie* 1 pr. subj. *louye* 1	pr. 1 sg. *loue* 3
	make 9 (4*) *maken* 2	pr. 1 sg. *makie* 1 pr. pl. *makyeþ* 1	pr. pl. *makeþ* 7
quakye 1			
þolien 2 *þolie* 1	*þole* 1		pr. 1 sg. *þole* 3
		pr. pl. *hopieþ* 1	pr. 1 sg. *hope* 1 pr. pl. *hopeþ* 1
rotien 1 *rotie* 1	*roten* 1	pr. 3 sg. *rotieþ* 1	
		pr. pl. *wrieþ* 1	

cases the *-i-* has been extended analogically to the pr. 3 sg.[38] The OE Class I weak verb *herian* has *i* or *y* in the historically regular positions, and analogically in the ppl.: pr. 1 sg. *herie* 2; infin. *heryen* 1; ppl. *yheryed* 1, *heried* 1.

(v) *Contracted verb forms.* There are numerous examples of contracted negative forms of *ne* + verb. *Ne* + 'be': *nam* 3, *nis* 13, *nes* 11, *nas* 1, *nere* 5; *ne* + 'will': *nul* 10, *nulle* 3, *nule* 1, *nuly* 1, *nult* 1, *nulleþ* 1, *nolde* 8, *nolden* 5; *ne* + 'have': *nauy* 1, *nast* 1, *naþ* 3, *nabbe* 1; and *ne* + *witen*: *not* 5, *nuste* 1. *LALME* shows that these forms occur primarily in the South Midlands and the South, with heavy concentrations in the South West Midlands.[39] The *nul(l)-* forms are particularly restricted in distribution, occurring almost exclusively in Gloucestershire, Herefordshire, Shropshire, and Worcestershire.[40] Contracted verb + personal pronoun forms are also common: *icham* 16, *ycham* 5 (*1);[41] *ichot* 12 (*7), *ychot* 2; *ichabbe* 2, *ychabbe* *2; *ichaue* 1; *icherde* 1; *ichulle* 6 (*2); *ycholde* 1; *ishal* 1; *hauy* 2. The forms occur all through the texts and presumably are part of the scribe's normal practice.

(vi) *Treatment of consonants.* Occasional spellings reflect the Harley scribe's own dialect. There is some evidence for unvoicing of *d*, usually in final position. The conjunction 'and' is always *ant* when written in full, as it often is, except for one example of *and* (no. 22); elsewhere *t* for *d* is not common; examples include: *sent* 'send' (imper.) 1; *suert* 'sword' 1; *olt* 'old' 1; *þousent* 3; *ascenteþ* 1. Voicing of initial *f* is shown by occasional spellings with *v*: *vader* 1; *vyhte* 1; *vo* 1, *valle* 1; *vacche* 'fetch' 2, *vachen* 1. This is probably a feature of the scribe's own practice, though it occurs in only four texts. Unetymological *h* is added initially by hypercorrection: *hawe* 'fear' 1; *heȝe* 'eyes' 1; *hedy* (OE *eadig* 'blessed') 1; *her* 'ere' 1; *herþe* 'earth' 1; *his* 'is' 1; *hi*, *hy* 'I' 2; and medially in *smhyte* 'smite' 1. The possessive form *is*, *ys* 'his' occurs more commonly than forms with *h* (see Table 3), and presumably indicates reduced stress.[42] Forms with *w* for *wh* include: *wen* 'when' 3 (beside frequent *when*); *wer* 'where' 1 (beside *wher* 9); *wet* 'what' 4 (beside *whet* 19, *what* 4); *wose* 'whoso' 1. Some hypercorrect spellings with *wh* for *w* occur: *whe* 'we' 3; *whrohte* 'worked' 1; *whiþ* 1; *whisseþ* 1; *whene* 'attract' 1.

---

[38] See Campbell ¶ 757, on this levelling in Mercian and Northumbrian in OE.

[39] *LALME* 1.532–33 (Dot Maps 1048, 1049, 1052–55).

[40] *LALME* 4.219.

[41] Numbers in parentheses are subclasses of the overall number of occurrences. When preceded by an asterisk, they occur at the beginning of a line; when followed by an asterisk, they record forms in rhyme position.

[42] On *as* 'has,' see the earlier discussion of *The Prophecy of Thomas of Erceldoune.*

TABLE 3 *Preferred and minority forms for selected items*

	LALME[i]	Preferred forms	Minority forms
SHE	*hue heo (he hy)* ((*ho*))	*heo* 44 (*20)[ii] *he* 26	*hue* 3
THEY	*hue heo he (hy hii hi þey)* ((*hee a*))	*he* 26 *hue* 23[iii] *heo* 21	*hii* 11 *hy* 4 *hee* 3 *hi* 1 *þey* 3 (*2)[iv] *þei* *1
THEIR	*huere hure (here hare ar)*	*huere* 38 *here* 14	*heore* 9 *ar* 3 *hare* 1
HIS	------------------	*is* 58 *ys* 40+ (5*) *his* 30 (10*)	*hys* 6 (1*) *hyse* 2 (1*) *hise* 2
MAN	*mon (monnes)*	*mon* 54	*man* 10 (8*) *-man* 4* *monnes* 4 *mones* 2 *monne* (g.pl.) *1
MUCH	*muche muchele muchel* ((*mykel*))	*muche* 16 *muchel* 7 *muchele* 8[v]	*mukel* 1* *mykel* 1
ARE	*bueþ beþ beoþ aren are* ((*buen buþ*))	*bueþ* 20 *beþ* 17 *aren* 12	*beoþ* 6 *are* 5 *buen* 3 *buþ* 1
WAS	*wes* ((*was wos*))	*wes* 112	*was* 14 *wos* 6 *wees* 1*
THOUGH	*þah* ((*þaþ þou*))	*þah* 27 (*15)	*þou* 1 *þaþ* 1 *alþah* 1
NOT	*nout noht* ((*no noud nouht naht*))	*nout* 35	*noht* 13 (10*) *noþt* 1* *nouht* 2 *noud* 2 *naht* 1
THROUGH	*þourh þurh* ((*þorh þurþ*))	*þourh-* 25 (*13)	*þurh* 6 (*5 1*) *þorh* *1
THERE	*þer- þer* (*þere þare*)	*þer* 38 *þer-* 9	*þare-* 8 (*5) *þar* 1 *þere* 1 *þere-* 1 *þore* 1*
WHEN	*when (wen þo)* ((*þe*))	*when* 81	*þo* *11 *wen* 3 *whenne* 1 *þe* 1
BOTH	*boþe (bo)*	*boþe* 20 (*11, 1*)	*bo* 6 (*1, 4*)

TABLE 3 *Preferred and minority forms for selected items (contd.)*

BUT	*bote*	*bote* 22 (*15)	*ah* *9 *boten* *1
HAVE	*hauen haue habbe* (*han ha*)	*haue-* 61 *habbe-* 22	*han* 10 *ha* 10 *hauy* 'have I' 2
SAY	*suggen sugge* (*segge* *sayen*)	*sugge* 8 (2*)	*sayen* 3 *say* 2* *sai* 1* *segge* 2 *suggen* 1 *seien* 1 *sey* 1* *seyn* 1* *seye* 1*
SIN	*sunne*	*sunne* 18 *synne* 12 (9*)	
THINK	*þenk- y-þenche* *þenche*	*þenk-* 10 *þench-* 5	

[i] The data in LALME are derived from two texts, no. 21, *Harrowing of Hell* and no. 70, *King Horn*; mine are derived from my corpus of 43 of the 50 Middle English texts (see note 28).

[ii] In the remaining texts not covered here, excluding *King Horn*, additional forms of 'she' include: *heo* 20, *hue* 8.

[iii] In the remaining texts not covered here, excluding *King Horn*, additional forms of 'they' include: *hue* 15, *heo* 3, *he* 6. On the significance of the distribution of the various forms for 'they' see Table 5 below and the accompanying discussion.

[iv] *Þey* also occurs once in no. 68, *Maximian*, which is not included in this corpus.

[v] All *muchele* forms are inflected, with *-e*; they all occur after a preposition and, for good measure, most are also preceded by a possessive adjective.

(vii) Preferred and minority forms. As might be expected in such an extensive and varied collection of poems, variant forms appear for many common linguistic items (Table 3). The *LALME* Linguistic Profile of Harley 2253 documents these for its questionnaire, while Samuels's study focuses on key forms that help to localize the scribal dialect most precisely.[43] But the *LALME* profile, naturally enough, shows the relative frequency of forms in the manuscript as a whole rather than item by item, and does not consider forms in rhyme, which are especially relevant to questions of sources. An examination of the actual numbers of occurrences of some *LALME* questionnaire items (and other items) and of their distribution among the individual poems helps to distinguish variants likely to coexist in the scribe's own usage from

---

[43] *LALME* 3.175 (LP 9260); Samuels, "Dialect."

constrained forms, which he is willing to reproduce, but which are derived from his exemplars. By constrained forms, I mean forms that prove to be either restricted to a single poem or a subset of poems, or positionally constrained, occurring either at the beginning or the end of the line and hence likely to be inherited from or influenced by the exemplar. Table 3 includes a selection of items which are sufficiently well attested to exhibit a significant pattern of distribution.[44]

A close look at these forms in context confirms that Samuels's view of the scribe as one who is willing to keep some of the forms of his sources is correct. Some of these forms of common words are demonstrably not part of the scribe's usual repertoire and have been activated by the forms in the exemplars which fell at the beginning or end of a line. The form *þei* 'they' occurs once only in *I Syke When Y Singe* (no. 62) at the beginning of a line; *þey* occurs at the beginning of a line twice in *Harrowing of Hell* (no. 21) and once within the line in *De Clerico et Puella* (no. 64). Although *þ-* forms of the third plural pronoun are attested in Herefordshire,[45] they are exceptional in the scribe's written language, and their appearance three times at the beginning of a line signals reproduction from the exemplar, which for a group of poems including nos. 62 and 64 contained other northerly features.[46] All six uses of the minority variant *þurh* 'through' are likely to be constrained, since they occur either at the beginning or end of a line. The form *þo* 'when' begins the line in all occurrences, while *when* occurs in all contexts; *swo* 'so' occurs three times in rhyme, beside over 150 occurrences of *so*; *meni* 'many' appears once only at the beginning of a line in *Song of the Husbandman* (no. 31); *parfore* *5, *par* *1, all begin the line, beside numerous forms of *þer(-)* in all contexts. Ten of the thirteen occurrences of *noht* 'not' are in rhyme, as are nine of the twelve occurrences of *synne*, which suggests that the forms do not belong to the scribe's spontaneous practice.

He as a variant form of 'she' occurs frequently, but turns out to be heavily concentrated in two poems — *On the Follies of Fashion* (no. 25a) 6 and *Annot and John* (no. 28) 15 — which belong to a group which I think were probably copied from a common source. Eight of the nine occurrences of *heore* 'their' occur in no. 40. Other forms whose frequency of occurrence may seem to suggest they are used spontaneously by the Harley scribe are in

---

[44] I have not included here some evidence for *LALME* questionnaire items which occur very infrequently in the MS, often in very restricted distribution, and whose significance is therefore uncertain. For example, *sulle* 'sell, give' 4 beside *sellen* 1 (no. 90), *selleþ* 1 (no. 62). *Sulle* is the invariable form in 'AB' language (d'Ardenne, *Þe Liflade*, pp. 127, 187), and *sulle* is very likely to be the scribe's own preferred form, but all four examples occur in close proximity in a single poem, *Song of the Husbandman* (no. 31).

[45] Compare *LALME* 2.22 (Item Map 7 THEY [2]).

[46] See further the discussion of relict forms at the conclusion of this essay.

fact restricted to a single text, e.g.: *hii* 'they' 11 (*5) and *hee* 'they' 3 (*2), all in *The Execution of Sir Simon Fraser* (no. 25). I consider all of these to be examples of constrained usage. Beside his usual form for 'but,' the Harley scribe uses *ah* *9, always at the beginning of a line, in nos. 21 (*1), 22 (*1), 40 (*3), 44 (*3), 90 (*1). This form is well attested in earlier South West Midland texts, but must have been obsolescent by the date of the Harley MS, since the last examples recorded by the *MED* are from two manuscripts copied by the Harley scribe, Harley itself, and Royal 12.C.xii. These forms too must be constrained usage here, interesting because they indicate the scribe's conservatism in preserving a form close to obsolescence as he wrote.

Some minority forms in Table 3 are, I believe, variants freely used by the scribe. He alternates *þenk-* and *þench-* forms of 'think'; *þenk-* appears more often, but five of the ten examples are from one poem (no. 61), where the northerly features in his exemplar have influenced his choice of form. He uses the form *ha* 'have' usually as an unstressed auxiliary, but once as an imperative, and in all cases followed by a consonant; before a vowel, forms have [v]. The distribution must reflect his own speech. Similarly, *is/ys* is clearly his preferred form for 'his.' This apparent preservation of spoken variation gives one confidence that the voicing and unvoicing of consonants and other developments listed under (*vi*) above (*olt*, *vader*, *wen*, etc.) are evidence of the Harley scribe's own usage. But other spelling forms are more problematic and will be discussed in the next section.

The Scribe and His Exemplars

(*i*) *Spelling*. Scattered through the manuscript are occasional spellings for *þ*, *ht*, *h* of the kind that are usually attributed to an Anglo-Norman scribe uncertain about the phonetic values represented by these graphs (see Table 4). But such spellings are more likely the product of an English scribe trained to copy Anglo-Norman and Latin texts, as he struggled to develop a writing system for his own written dialect of English after the political and linguistic changes and interruptions which marked the emergence of Middle English. Harley seems a little late for this explanation to apply, though it is true that South West Midland texts are generally conservative, and some similar spellings are found in Herebert's poems in BL Addit. 46919.[47] Spellings like these, however, are common in earlier South West Midland manuscripts such as the late thirteenth-century Digby 86, a

---

[47] On Herebert, who reportedly was buried in Hereford in 1333, see Brown, ed., *Rel. Lyr. XIV*, xiii, pp. 15–29, and *LALME* 3.169 (LP 7410).

Gloucestershire manuscript.[48] Digby 86 shares seven Middle English items with Harley 2253: *Harrowing of Hell* (no. 21), *Debate between Body and Soul* (no. 22), *Suete Iesu, King of Blysse* (no. 50), *Stond Wel, Moder, vnder Rode* (no. 60), *Maximian* (no. 68), *Sayings of St. Bernard* (no. 74), and *Hending* (no. 89). Digby is not thought to be the direct source of any of the Harley copies, but its existence suggests the South West Midland cultural matrix where I believe the immediate exemplars of many of the Harley texts were produced and circulated.

TABLE 4 *Occasional spellings for fricatives*

	-ht for -þ	-þt for -ht	-þt for -þ	-þ for -h, -h for -þ	-th for -ht
no. 21	*wyht** 'with' *gryht** 'peace'				
no. 22					**fyth* 'fight'
no. 25	*oht* 'oath'				
no. 34	*teht* 'teeth'				
no. 41				*doh* (pr. pl.) 'do'	
no. 43				*doh* (pr. pl.) 'do'	
no. 45	*atgoht** 'go away' *cloht** 'clothing' *haht* 'has' *loht** 'displeasing' *wroht** 'angry'				
no. 48		*riþt* 'right'			
no. 50		*wroþt* 'carried out'			
no. 52				*þaþ* 'though'	
no. 62	*siht* 'sees' (?)				
no. 63					*bryth* 'bright'
no. 64		*riþt* 'right'			*brith* 'bright'
no. 81		*hiþte* 'haste' *wyþt* 'creature'	*syþt* 'sees' (?)[i]	*heþ* 'high' *teh* 'teeth'	
no. 90		*noþt** 'not' *riþt* 'right'			
no. 92	*oht** 'oath' *wroht** 'angry'				

[i] It is uncertain if this form, or the *siht* of no. 62, represents *siþ* or *siht*. Campbell ¶ 743 cites Anglian pr. 3 sg. forms without *–h*.

---

[48] *LALME* 3.150 (LP 7790).

The distribution of these forms in the Harley poems is informative, and it suggests (1) that the scribe probably took over many of them from his exemplars, and (2) that they may point to different exemplars for different poems. The forms I have found are distributed as shown in Table 4.[49]

These various spelling forms are not scattered through the poems as one might expect if they were all features of the Harley scribe's indecisions about spelling. Any single poem shows only one type, except for *De Clerico et Puella* (no. 64) and *The Man in the Moon* (no. 81). In *Harrowing of Hell*, *An Old Man's Prayer*, and *The Way of Christ's Love* (nos. 21, 45, 92), the forms occur in close proximity, in rhyme with one another, and must surely reflect the occurrence of the same forms in the exemplar for each poem. The odd pr. pl. form *doh* 'do' in *The Labourers in the Vineyard* (no. 41) is repeated in *Spring* (no. 43), the next English poem in the manuscript. I have found this spelling form elsewhere only in the two late-thirteenth century manuscripts of Layamon's *Brut*.[50] A similar repetition of form occurs in *An Autumn Song* and *De Clerico et Puella* (nos. 63, 64), while the same *-þt* for *-ht* spelling occurs in *The Flemish Insurrection* (no. 48) and in the next English poem, *Suete Iesu, King of Blysse* (no. 50). These various spellings too may well have been activated from the scribe's passive repertoire by their appearance in his exemplars, rather than being variants he might use freely.

(ii) Possessives. The possessive adjective 'my' appears as *mi* 50, *min* 9, *mine* 3, *my* 56, *myn* 47, *myne* 11 in the various texts, and the distribution of most of these forms follows a consistent and predictable pattern, which is clearly that of the Harley scribe: *min/myn* is used before a vowel or *h*, otherwise *mi/my* appears and is invariable; inflected forms of *min/myn* with *-e* are used as a possessive adjective in the conditions described earlier, i.e., following a preposition, and as either a weak or plural form; *min(e/myn(e* is used as a pronoun. The same pattern holds for *þi* 'thy' 57, *þin* 15, *þine* 10, *þy* 29, *þyn* 13, *þyne* 3. But remnants of the earlier system retaining *-n* before consonants occur: *þin riche, þin miltse* 2, with dative, plural, or weak forms sometimes with *-e*, *myne sondes, myne þohtes*, etc. 4, *þine palefreis, of þine childe*, etc. 9, or endingless, *myn bones, myn wonges, myn rouþes*, etc. 12. The inconsistency in the use of inflectional *-e* with these forms contrasts with the regularity of inflection displayed otherwise for the first and second singular possessives. The forms are scattered through the collection, but *Harrowing of Hell* (no. 21) with five examples, and *An Old Man's Prayer* (no. 45) with seven, show higher

---

[49] As elsewhere, an asterisk before a form shows that it occurs in line initial position, after a form shows that it occurs in rhyme position.

[50] BL MS Cotton Caligula A.ix has four examples, and BL MS Cotton Otho C.xiii has two. Laing, *Catalogue*, p. 70, places the language of the Caligula text of Layamon "in NW Worcs.," and *LALME* (1.107) localizes Otho in Somerset.

concentrations than anywhere else, which suggests that such forms may be instances of constrained usage.

(*iii*) *eo/e/ue spellings*. Table 3 gives no indication of how *heo*, *hue*, and *he* are distributed among the individual Middle English poems in the manuscript, but a closer look at the distribution of scribal spellings of OE *eo* in the pronominal forms 'she,' 'they,'

TABLE 5 *Forms showing constrained selection of eo/ue spellings[i]*

GROUP 1 (preference for -ue- spellings)

	SHE	THEY	THEM	THEIR	ARE	All forms of OE *beo-* incl. ARE)	other forms with eo/ue	total eo: ue
no. 21		*he* 3 *þey* *1 *hue* 1 *heo* 1	*hem* 8	*heore* 1	*bueþ* 2 *buen* 1* *be* 1*	*be-* 7 (6*) *bue-* 7 (1*)	*bueten duere* 2 (*1) *hueld* 2 *tuen eorþe heouene* *	9:14
no. 25		*hii* 11 (*4) *hue* 4 *he* 3 *hee* 3 (*1)	*hem* 6	*huere* 4 *here* 4	*beþ* 3 *bueþ* 2 *beoþ* 1	*be-* 11 *bue-* 4 *beo-* 1	*duere* 2 (*1, 1*) *huerte**	1:15
no. 45		*hue* 2 (*1)	*hem* 1			*be-* 1 *bue-* 2	*huerte luef weolewe*	1:6
no. 47	*hue* 1	*hue* 1	*hem* 1		*bueþ* 1 *beoþ* 1	*be* 5 (1*) *bue-* 3		1:5
no. 48		*hue* 12 (*6) *hy* 2 *hi* 1	*hem* 12 *huem* 5	*huere* 18 *here* 1		*beo-* 1 *be-* 3	*drue eorl-* 10	11:36
no. 50						*bue-* 3 *be-* 4	*huerte* 8 *heouene reoweþ*	2:11
no. 73					*bueþ* 4	*bue-* 5 *be-* 3	*luef suen*	0:7
no. 88		*hue* *2	*huem* 5 *hem* 2	*huere* 4 *here* 1	*bueþ* 2 *beþ* 1	*bue-* 2 *be-* 1		0:13

GROUP 2 (preference for -eo- spellings)

	SHE	THEY	THEM	THEIR	ARE	All forms of OE *beo-* incl. ARE)	other forms with eo/ue	total eo: ue
no. 27		*he* 3	*hem* 3		*beþ* 2 *beoþ* 1 *bueþ* 1 *aren* 1	*be-* 7 *bue-* 3 *beo-* 1	*forbeode** *foreode** *leode** *reode** *þeode** *þeo**	7:3
no. 31		*he* 5 (*1)	*hem* 2	*here* 1 *ar* 3 (*1)	*beþ* 3 *buþ* 1 *aren* 1	*be-* 4	*leodes leosen leoseþ leorneþ weole*	5:0

[i] The data, given below under (i), are inconclusive for some texts in the corpus. Under (ii) the figures are given for the seven texts not analyzed for this study. See note 28 and, for all titles, see Appendix.
eo: ue frequencies:
(i) no. 24b 0:0, no. 30 0:2, no. 41 4:4, no. 43 4:4, no. 51 1:1, nos. 52, 55, 61 0:0, no. 69 1:0, no. 90 0:0.
(ii) no. 32 19:3, no. 58 18:2, no. 68 6:7, no. 70 39:119, no. 74 2:31, no. 85 5:22, no. 89 4:18.

'them,' and 'their' shows striking variation in spelling preferences between individual poems and groups of poems. Similar variation extends to forms of 'be' and to the distribution of occasional spellings of other *-eo-* words, which may show *eo*, *e*, or *ue* spellings. All of these are illustrated in Table 5, which shows the range of variation in my corpus.

GROUP 2 (preference for -eo- spellings) TABLE 5 *(contd.)*

	SHE	THEY	THEM	THEIR	ARE	All forms of OE *beo-* incl. ARE)	other forms with eo/ue	total eo:ue
no. 33	*heo* *1	*heo* 3	*hem* 9		*are* 1	*beo-* 1 *be* 2	*feole* 2 (1*) *heouene neode weole luefly*	10:1
no. 34	*heo* 8 (*3) *he* *1				*aren* 4	*beo-* 2 (1*)	*bleo* 2 *(1*) freoly heouene leomeþ leofly neose seo**	18:0
no. 35	*heo* 3 (*2)					*be-* 3	*heowe kneowe reowe weore luef**	7:1
no. 36	*heo* 7 (*1)					*beo* 3 (1*) *be-* 3	*freo* 2* *þreo**	13:0
no. 40	*heo* 2	*heo* 13 (*4) *he* 2	*hem* 6	*heore* 8 (*2, 1*) *huere* 3 *here* 1	*bueþ* 1	*beo-* 2 *bue-* 1	*beodeþ cleopeþ fleo 3eolumon leose weole lued pruest*	31:6
no. 44	*heo* 2 (*1)		*hem* 5	*huere* 2	*beþ* 2 *are* 2 *bueþ* 1 *beoþ* 1	*be-* 2 *bue-* 1 *beo-* 1	*dueres feole freoli freoly* 2 *leor*	8:4
no. 46	*heo* 13 (*7) *hue* 1						*bleo huerte* 2	14:3
no. 53						*beo-* 1*	*cheosen deope feol freo* þreo* seo* duere*	7:1
no. 66					*bueþ* 1 *buen* 1	*be* 2	*deore* 2 *forleose* 2 *feond heouene*	6:2

This table presents important evidence about both the scribe and his sources, since it shows that when it comes to regional spelling forms with which he is familiar, the Harley scribe's practice is heavily conditioned by his exemplars. The primary evidence for this conclusion is the data given above and the material already discussed under Table 3 (which shows his frequent use of forms from his passive repertoire in certain poems and in certain positional contexts). The preservation of non-South West Midland forms in many poems, which will be discussed later, is also relevant here, as an indicator of the scribe's tolerance for forms which are not his own. The commonest South West Midland features of the overall dialect of the manuscript (*-eþ* endings for pr. 3 sg. and pr. pl., *mon*, *moni* forms, *u* for OE *y*, etc.) are ubiquitous in Harley, but they could be expected in any South West Midland manuscript, and may equally well have occurred in his

GROUP 2 (preference for -eo- spellings)   TABLE 5 *(contd.)*

	SHE	THEY	THEM	THEIR	ARE	All forms of OE *beo-* incl. ARE)	other forms with eo/ue	total eo:ue
no. 92							*deore* *deope* *leose* *meoke* *reowen*	5:0
no. 93	*heo* 5 (*2)				*beþ* 2	*be* 3	*gleowes* *heowes leof* *seo luef*	10:1

GROUP 3 (preference for -e- spellings)

	SHE	THEY	THEM	THEIR	ARE	All forms of OE *beo-* incl. ARE)	other forms with eo/ue	total eo:ue
no. 22		*he* 3 *hy* 1 *heo* 1	*hem* 1	*here* 1	*aren* 4 *bueþ* 1 *be* 1	*be-* 8 *bue-* 1	*eoden** *neose** *peose** *bueres*	4:2
no. 23				*here 1* *hare 1*		*be* 4 (*1)	*luef*	0:1
no. 25a	*he* 4 *heo* 1	*he* 3 (*1)	*hem* 3			*be* 3	*duere*	1:1
no. 28	*he* 15 (*8) *heo* 1	*he* 1			*are* 1		*bleo*	2:0
no. 29	*he* 3					*bue-* 1		0:1
no. 60						*be* 6		0:0
no. 62		*þei* *1			*beþ* 2 *beoþ* 1 *are* 1 *aren* 1	*be-* 2 *beo-* 1	*duere*	1:1
no. 63					*beoþ* 1	*be* 5 *beo-* 1	*duere*	2:1
no. 64	*heo** 1 *he* 1	*þey* 1				*be* 4	*luef*	1:1
no. 65						*be* 3		1:0
no. 67	*heo* 2 (*1)	*heo* 1				*be-* 3		3:0

[1] The data, given below under (i), are inconclusive for some texts in the corpus. Under (ii) the figures are given for the seven texts not analyzed for this study. See note 28 and, for all titles, see Appendix.

eo: ue frequencies:

(i) no. 24b 0:0, no. 30 0:2, no. 41 4:4, no. 43 4:4, no. 51 1:1, nos. 52, 55, 61 0:0, no. 69 1:0, no. 90 0:0.

(ii) no. 32 19:3, no. 58 18:2, no. 68 6:7, no. 70 39:119, no. 74 2:31, no. 85 5:22, no. 89 4:18.

415

exemplars. The scribe's fluctuating use of *ue* and *eo* spellings, both of which also belong to the West Midlands, is more distinctive and potentially informative, especially the exceptional use of *hue-* spellings for 'they,' 'them,' and 'their'; *bue-* spellings for 'be' and 'are'; and occasional spellings like *huerte* 'heart,' *luef* 'love,' *duere* 'dear(ly).' As Table 5 shows, the distribution of these spellings must reflect his exemplars rather than his own unconstrained use.[51] The sharply varying ratios of *ue* and *eo* spellings are too extreme to be the result of free variation between alternative pronominal and other forms freely used by the scribe. He is obviously willing to use all three spellings, *eo*, *e*, and *ue*, but his choice between them must have been activated by the forms he found in his exemplars, which means that roughly the same patterns of distribution must have obtained in them.

---

[51] *Hue* as a spelling for 'she' is quite well attested in West Midland texts (*LALME* 2.10–11 (Item Maps 4 SHE [2, 3]), 4.7). As a form of the 3 pers. pl. pronoun, it is a different matter. *LALME* records *hue* 'they,' *huem* 'them' only in Harley, and *huere* 'their' only in two Linguistic Profiles, LP 9260 (Harley 2253) and Wiltshire LP 5331 (4.10, 13, 15). To these examples, thanks to the on-line *MED* (June 1998 Release), I can add occurrences of *hue* 'they' in the TCC B.14.39 MS of the *Proverbs of Alfred*, and others from the alliterative *Alexander* (Fragment A) (Bodl. MS Greaves 60), described as a Gloucestershire MS by R. M. Lumiansky ("5. Legends of Alexander the Great," in *A Manual of the Writings in Middle English 1050–1500*, ed. J. Burke Severs and A. E. Hartung, 10 vols. [New Haven, 1967–99], 1.106 [65]). For the very rare possessive form *huere*, the on-line *MED* also yields *huere* 'their,' cited from a 1448 Worcestershire document; see Bertil Sundby, *Studies in the Middle English Dialect Material of Worcestershire Records* (Bergen, 1964), p. 254: *the heiris of huere towe bodyes*. Margaret Laing, to whom I am indebted for the following information, has found one earlier example of *huere* from the first of two versions of *Poema Morale* in London, BL MS Egerton 613, a mid-thirteenth-century MS, which she places in SW Worcestershire. She has recorded other *-ue-* spellings in this text: *suelf* 'self' 2, *bued* 'is' 1, *bued* 'are' 1, *buen* 'be' (inf.) 1, *bue* (subj.) 1, *bi-fluen* 'flee' (inf.) 1, *duere* 'dear' (adv.) 1, *suelfer* 'silver, 1, *ȝuet* 'yet' 1. Otherwise, she has found few examples of *-ue-* spellings in early ME apart from a few examples distributed among Cambridge, St. John's College MS 15, TCC B.14.39, and Digby 86 (in Digby the *ue* spellings are for OE *y*). For TCC B.14.39 and Digby 86, see the map of the South West Midlands. The localized MSS which display *ue* spellings for OE *eo* (either original, or developed by back mutation or analogically) are thus Harley 2253 itself, Egerton 613, and TCC B.14.29, the latter two localized in Worcestershire, like the later fifteenth-century documentary evidence. The Egerton forms parallel those of Harley closely, and the Worcestershire associations are suggestive, but no more than that, in the absence of more detailed information about the distribution of *ue* spellings. All one can say at present is that one of the Harley scribe's lost exemplars should also be associated with these extant records.

LALME records *bue-* forms for 'are' only from Harley (4.33, compare 3.175, LP 9260); to these may be added numerous *bue-* spellings for infinitive and present forms in BL MS Lansdowne 851, a Chaucer MS.

Thus the spelling variations illustrated here show us that the scribe himself had all three variants within his active repertoire, and that the exemplars for some of his poems showed marked preferences for one or other spelling. It is especially telling that the preference for one or other spelling affects not just a single pronoun here, a word there, which would suggest free variation, but operates rather consistently over all the relevant forms within any given poem, and within certain sequences of poems. As Table 5 shows, examples of two or three of the spelling possibilities may very well occur in any one poem, but a strongly marked preference for one or other spelling for OE *eo* distinguishes many poems and groups of poems from others.

What then does this evidence show? It is inherently unlikely that this finding implies a single exemplar in which the stints of various scribes determined the choice of *eo*, *e*, and *ue* spellings, because the switch from one preferred spelling to the other is determined by individual poem or sequence of poems, and this seems an improbable way for stints to be organized in a single exemplar. It seems much more likely that he used a number of different exemplars, and in some cases copied individual items and in other cases groups of poems from them. Obviously not all texts favoring *ue* (or *eo* or *e*) need come from a single source, but it seems to me probable that some sequences of poems in Harley were copied by the scribe from a single exemplar, perhaps, but not necessarily, *en bloc*. Nor can we safely assume a different exemplar for each of the three groups; several scribes, with different scribal dialects, may have worked on any one of his exemplars, and Harley itself demonstrates that a single manuscript collection in a single hand may contain a mixture of all three types of texts. So it would be foolish at this point to try to specify the number of exemplars used, or the number of scribes who worked on them.

Most of the Middle English poems in Harley conform to one or other of these patterns of variation, but some poems (nos. 24b, 30, 41, 43, 51, 52, 55, 61, 69, 81, 90) cannot readily be fitted into one of the three groups, either for want of data or because the data are ambiguous. The three groups established in Table 5 are preliminary and tentative and may well need modification and further subdividing, but they may serve as a starting point for future analysis of their individual members to see if other evidence supports these rough cuts into groups:

(*a*) The poems in Group 1 are religious, historical, or satirical, and it is worth noting that none of the fourteen unique copies of secular love lyrics in the manuscript belongs here. The three historical poems, *The Execution of Sir Simon Fraser* (no. 25), *The Death of Edward I* (no. 47), and *The Flemish Insurrection* (no. 48), deal respectively with events of 1306, 1307, and 1302, and though nos. 25 and 48 are unique copies, we may assume some textual history for them before they reached the Harley scribe in the second quarter of the fourteenth century. The mixture of forms in *Fraser* must reflect this. The *Satire on the Retinues of the Great* (no. 88), another unique text, occurs in a sequence of texts (nos. 70–89) many of which are French. All the English poems but one in this sequence (nos. 70, 73, 74, 85, 88, 89) are linked by a preference for *ue* spellings, with no. 81, *The Man in the Moon* (itself something of an oddity), the only exception. Nos. 70, 74, 85, and 89 are not included in my corpus, but the note to Table 5 records their strong preference for *ue* spellings over *eo*. This linguistic affinity between members of an otherwise rather motley run of poems invites further investigation to see if they were copied from a common exemplar.

(*b*) Group 2 comprises a mixed bag as to type and subject but is linked by a high incidence of *eo* spellings. It includes satire and complaint, a saint's life, some of the best known secular lyrics, some devotional poems (*A Spring Song on the Passion* [no. 53], *Dulcis Iesu memoria* [no. 58], *Blessed be Þou, Leuedy* [no. 66]), and a pair of poems on divine and secular love (*The Way of Christ's Love* [no. 92] and *The Way of Woman's Love* [no. 93]). Within this larger group, the sequence nos. 31–40 in particular invites closer analysis. All seven Middle English pieces within this sequence (*Song of the Husbandman* [no. 31], *Marina* [no. 32, see note to Table 5], *The Poet's Repentance* [no. 33], *The Fair Maid of Ribblesdale* [no. 34], *The Meeting in the Wood* [no. 35], *A Wayle Whyt ase Whalle Bon* [no. 36], *Satire on the Consistory Courts* [no. 40]) have a high frequency of *eo* spellings, and seem likely candidates for derivation from a common exemplar.

(*c*) The texts in Group 3, which have only thin scatterings of *eo* and *ue* spellings, may come from a number of different sources, but they probably acquired at least their *ue* spellings from either the Harley scribe or South West Midland exemplars used by him. I think *On the Follies of Fashion* (no. 25a), *Annot and John* (no. 28), and *Alysoun* (no. 29) may have been copied from the same exemplar, while the sequence beginning with *Stond Wel, Moder, vnder Rode* (no. 60) and ending with *The Five Joys of the Virgin* (no. 67) is a significant and coherent unit that includes some poems which I think may have travelled together since their composition. The evidence for this will be discussed below.

(*iv*) *Relict forms*. The Harley texts preserve other pointers to the history of their transmission, for the scribe has preserved a fair number of relict forms that contrast markedly with the prevailing South West Midland features of his copies. A number of these are certainly archetypal; others may be. The most distinctive are: (*a*) pr. pl. in -*es*, contrasting with the otherwise regular -*eþ* throughout; (*b*) *ded(e)* spellings for 'death' beside the usual forms *deþ(e)*; (*c*) pr. 3 sg. forms in -*es* or -*s*, in contrast with regular -*eþ* throughout the poems; and (*d*) pr. pl. in *-en*.[52] These last could conceiv-ably be occasional forms of the scribe, but the context of features with which they co-occur suggests they should be associated with an earlier stage of transmission.

(*a*) Pr. pl. forms in *-es* occur in *Satire on the Consistory Courts* (no. 40), *Spring* (no. 43), and *Advice to Women* (no. 44). No. 40 has three, or perhaps four, forms (one in rhyme), no. 43 has one at the beginning of the line, and no. 44 has two in rhyme. Pr. pl. forms in *-es*, *-s* occur also in *When þe Nyhtegale Singes* (no. 65) 2, and *The Prophecy of Thomas of Erceldoune* (no. 90) 3 (discussed above).

(*b*) The forms *ded* (*dede*) 'death' occur once in rhyme in both *Debate between Body and Soul* (no. 22) and *The Execution of Sir Simon Fraser* (no. 25); *ded* (*dede*) next recurs in members of a sequence of poems: *Stond Wel, Moder, vnder Rode* (no. 60) 5 (2*), *Iesu, for Þi Muchele Miht* (no. 61) 4 (3*), and *An Autumn Song* (no. 63) 1.

(*c*) Pr. 3 sg. forms in *-es/-s* occur in *Debate between Body and Soul* (no. 22) 1*, *The Fair Maid of Ribblesdale* (no. 34) 4 (3*), *Spring* (no. 43) 1, *Advice to Women* (no. 44) 1, *Blow, Northerne Wynd* (no. 46) 1, *Iesu, for Þi Muchele Miht* (no. 61) 3 (1*), *An Autumn Song* (no. 63) 2 (1*), *When þe Nyhtegale Singes* (no. 65) 2, *The Prophecy of Thomas of Erceldoune* (no. 90) 3 (discussed above), and *The Way of Woman's Love* (no. 93) 1.

Some of the forms in (*a*) and (*b*) which are in rhyme position can be confirmed as archetypal. The use of pr. pl. endings in *-es* points to the North Midlands or the North, as does *ded*(*e*) 'death' (though the convenience of *ded* as a rhyme word makes one suspect that it may be exported beyond its home turf for use in rhyme). The three features tend to occur in certain poems and runs of poems, namely nos. 22, 40,[53] 43, 44, 46, 60, 61, 63, 64, 65, 90, and this can hardly be coincidence. Associated with these runs of poems are other relict features such as *mukel* in no. 22, pr. 3 sg. *gos* in no. 61, *þei* in no. 62, *þey* in no. 64,[54] *mykel* in no. 64, pret. 2 sg. in *-es* in no. 65. Alongside these relict forms are numerous forms untypical of the scribe's usual practice, such as *man* in rhyme in nos. 47, 48, 61, 64, 66, 67; *synne* (contrasting with the usual form *sunne*) in nos. 22, 40, 61, 62, 63, 66 (9

---

[52] Pr. pl. forms in *-en* occur in nos. 33 (2), 40 (1), 43 (1), 62 (2), 65 (1), 90 (2), 92 (1), a total of ten occurrences. Pr. pl. *aren* occurs in nos. 22 (4), 27 (1), 31 (1), 34 (4), 40 (1), 62 (1), and pr. pl. *han* 'have' occurs in nos. 22 (1), 46 (2), 92 (1). These forms, though not the preferred forms of the Harley scribe, are attested in areas around Hereford.

[53] Codicological evidence further suggests that nos. 40 and 41 were copied as a pair; on this, and on the numbering error which introduced a nonexistent no. 42, see n. 1 above.

[54] The form *þey* also occurs once in *Maximian* (no. 68), which is not included in the corpus.

examples among these poems, 5 in rhyme); *kyn(ne)*, *(-)kynde*, *kyþe* in rhyme in nos. 22, 40, 60, 64, 67; *þynkeþ* in no. 61; *was* (contrasting with the usual form *wes*) in nos. 22, 41, 47, 48, 61, 63, 64, 69.[55] This patterning of relict non-South West Midland features and constrained forms untypical of the scribe's regular practice in nos. 22, 41–48, 60–67 creates suggestive networks of connection within each group, which invite speculation and require further work. The sequences suggest that some poems composed in the same area were transmitted together in groups, along with others which became associated with them by way of theme (consider the theme of Christ's Passion in nos. 60 and 61, and the two Marian lyrics, nos. 66 and 67), while additional members may have been added to groups in transmission through the casual conjunctions of which I spoke at the beginning of this essay. The Harley scribe doubtless made a selection of texts from the exemplars he had access to, but I think it very probable that the sequences outlined above already existed in the sources which lay behind Harley or any immediate South West Midland exemplar.

---

[55] For details of the forms of *man* in the corpus, see n. 18 above.

APPENDIX. *The English contents of MS Harley 2253*

In listing the English contents, the following chart specifies item numbers assigned to individual works in standard editions. (For the five editions, see n. 6.) The chart also supplies the item numbers of the *Facsimile* and the location of each piece by folio and column.

Ker no.	Title and First Line	Brook no.	Brown ed:no.	Robbins no.	Böddeker p. or no.	folio(s)
10–17	*Recipes for Color* "Vor te make Cynople"					52va–b
21	*Harrowing of Hell* "Alle herkneþ to me nou"				p. 270	55va–56vb
22	*Debate between Body and Soul* "In a þestri stude Y stod"				p. 235	57r–58v
23	*A Song of Lewes* "Sitteþ alle stille ant herkneþ to me"		13C:72		P.L. I	58v–59r
24b	*Earth upon Earth* "Erþe toc of erþe erþe wyþ woh"	1	13C:73			59v
25	*The Execution of Sir Simon Fraser* "Lystneþ lordynges a newe song Ichulle bigynne"			4	P.L. VI	59v–61v
25a	*On the Follies of Fashion* "Lord þat lenest vs lyf"		13C:74		P.L. III	61v
27	*The Three Foes of Man* "Middelerd for mon wes mad"	2	13C:75		G.L. I	62v

Ker no.	Title and First Line	Brook no.	Brown ed:no.	Robbins no.	Böddeker p. or no.	folio(s)
28	*Annot and John* "Ichot a burde in a bour ase beryl so bryht"	3	13C:76		W.L. I	63r–v
29	*Alysoun* "Bytuene Mersh ant Aueril"	4	13C:77		W.L. II	63v
30	*The Lover's Complaint* "Wiþ longyng Y am lad"	5	13C:78		W.L. III	63v
31	*Song of the Husbandman* "Ich herde men vpo mold make muche mon"			2	P.L. II	64r
32	*Marina* "Herkeþ hideward ant beoþ stille"				p. 256	64va–65vb
33	*The Poet's Repentance* "Weping haueþ myn wonges wet"	6	13C:79		W.L. IV	66r
34	*The Fair Maid of Ribblesdale* "Mosti ryden by Rybbesdale"	7			W.L. V	66v
35	*The Meeting in the Wood* "In a fryht as Y con fare fremede"	8			W.L. VI	66v–67r
36	*A Wayle Whyt ase Whalles Bon* "A wayle whyt ase whalles bon"	9			W.L. VII	67r

Ker no.	Title and First Line	Brook no.	Brown ed:no.	Robbins no.	Böddeker p. or no.	folio(s)
40	*Satire on the Consistory Courts* "Ne mai no lewed lued libben in londe"			6	P.L. I	70va, 71ra, 71v
41	*The Labourers in the Vineyard* "Of a mon Matheu þohte"	10	13C:80		G.L. II	70vb, 71vb
43	*Spring* "Lenten ys come wiþ loue to toune"	11	13C:81		W.L. VIII	71va
44	*Advice to Women* "In May hit murgeþ when hit dawes"	12	13C:82		W.L. IX	71vb–72ra
45	*An Old Man's Prayer* "Heʒe Louerd, þou here my bone"	13	14C:6		G.L. III	72ra–va
46	*Blow, Northerne Wynd* "Ichot a burde in boure bryht"	14	13C:83		W.L. X	72va–73rb
47	*The Death of Edward I* "Alle þat beoþ of huerte trewe"			5	P.L. VIII	73r–v
48	*The Flemish Insurrection* "Lustneþ lordinges boþe ʒonge ant olde"			3	P.L. V	73v–74v
50	*Suete Iesu, King of Blysse* "Suete Iesu, king of blysse"	15	14C:7		G.L. IV	75rb–va

Ker no.	Title and First Line	Brook no.	Brown ed:no.	Robbins no.	Böddeker p. or no.	folio(s)
51	*Iesu Crist, Heouene Kyng* "Iesu Crist, heouene kyng"	16	14C:8		G.L. V	75va–b
52	*A Winter Song* "Wynter wakeneþ al my care"	17	14C:9		G.L. VI	75vb
53	*A Spring Song on the Passion* "When Y se blosmes springe"	18			G.L. VII	76r
55	*Dum ludis floribus* "Dum ludis floribus velud lacinia"	19				76r
58	*Dulcis Iesu memoria* "Iesu, suete is þe loue of þe"				G.L. VIII	77vb–78va
60	*Stond Wel, Moder, vnder Rode* "Stond wel, moder, vnder rode"	20			G.L. IX	79rb–vb
61	*Iesu, for Þi Muchele Miht* "Iesu, for þi muchele miht"	21	13C:84		G.L. X	79vb
62	*I Syke When Y Singe* "I syke when Y singe"	22			G.L. XI	80ra
63	*An Autumn Song* "Nou skrnkeþ rose ant lylie flour"	23	14C:10		G.L. XII	80rb
64	*De Clerico et Puella* "My deþ Y loue, my lyf Ich hate, for a leuedy shene"	24	13C:85		W.L. XI	80v

Ker no.	Title and First Line	Brook no.	Brown ed:no.	Robbins no.	Böddeker p. or no.	folio(s)
65	*When þe Nyhtegale Singes* "When þe nyhtegale singes þe wodes waxen grene"	25	13C:86		W.L. XII	80v–81r
66	*Blessed Be Þou, Leuedy* "Blessed be þou, leuedy, ful of heouene blisse"	26			G.L. XIII	81r–v
67	*The Five Joys of the Virgin* "Ase Y me rod þis ender day"	27	14C:11		G.L. XIV	81va–b
68	*Maximian* "Herkne to my ron"				p. 245	82ra–83r
69	*A Prayer for Deliverance* "Mayden moder milde"	28	13C:87		G.L. XV	83r
70	*King Horn* "Her bygynneþ þe geste of Kyng Horn"					83r–92v
73	*God, Þat Al Þis Myhtes May* "God, þat al þis myhtes may"	29	13C:88A		G.L. XVI	106r
74	*Sayings of St. Bernard* "Lustneþ alle a lutel þrowe"				G.L. XVII	106ra–107rb
81	*The Man in the Moon* "Mon in þe mone stond ant strit"	30	13C:89		W.L. XIII	114v–115r
85	*A Bok of Sweuenyng* "Her comensez a bok of sweuenyng"					119ra–121ra

Ker no.	Title and First Line	Brook no.	Brown ed:no.	Robbins no.	Böddeker p. or no.	folio(s)
88	*Satire on the Retinues of the Great* "Of rybaudz Y ryme ant rede o my rolle"			7	P.L. VII	124va–125r
89	*Hending* "Mon þat wol of wisdam heren"				p. 287	125ra–127ra
90	*The Prophecy of Thomas of Erceldoune* "La countesse de Donbar demanda a Thomas de Essedoune"			8		127rb–va
92	*The Way of Christ's Love* "Lvtel wot hit any mon / Hou loue hym haueþ ybounde"	31	13C:90		G.L. XVIII	128r
93	*The Way of Woman's Love* "Lutel wot hit any mon / Hou derne loue may stonde"	32	13C:91		W.L. XIV	128r–v

Harley 2253, Digby 86, and the Circulation of Literature in Pre-Chaucerian England

Marilyn Corrie

The uniqueness and the excellence of the English lyric poetry contained in London, British Library MS Harley 2253 have given the manuscript a privileged place amongst both literary historians and connoisseurs of literature from the early Middle English period. As a codicological phenomenon, however, the book is not unique: its inclusion of material in two further languages — French and Latin — alongside its English texts is matched by a number of other codices compiled in England in the thirteenth century or — like Harley 2253 — in the first half of the fourteenth.[1] The manuscript perceived as having the closest correspondences with Harley is Oxford, Bodleian Library MS Digby 86, a trilingual miscellany probably assembled some time between 1271 and 1283, and our sole surviving evidence for the existence of such English poems as *Dame Sirith* and *The Fox and the Wolf*.[2] The similarities between the two manuscripts have been investigated before,

---

[1] Discussions of these multilingual manuscripts include: John Frankis, "The Social Context of Vernacular Writing in Thirteenth-Century England: The Evidence of the Manuscripts," in *Thirteenth-Century England 1 (Proceedings of the Newcastle-upon Tyne Conference, 1985)*, ed. P. R. Coss and S. D. Lloyd (Woodbridge, Suffolk, 1986), pp. 175–84; and Derek Pearsall, *Old English and Middle English Poetry* (London, 1977), pp. 94–101. Pearsall's view that Digby 86 is a "friar's miscellany" has now been superseded.

[2] On the date and importance of Digby 86, see Marilyn Corrie, "The Compilation of Oxford, Bodleian Library, MS Digby 86," *Medium Ævum* 66 (1997): 236–49, at p. 238; compare also my thesis, "A Study of Oxford, Bodleian Library, MS Digby 86: Literature in Late Thirteenth-Century England" (Ph.D. diss., Oxford University, 1995), pp. 1–12. The traditional dating of the MS has been questioned in the recently published Digby facsimile: see Judith Tschann and M. B. Parkes, intro., *Facsimile of Oxford, Bodleian Library, MS Digby 86*, EETS s.s. 16 (Oxford, 1996), pp. xxxvi–xxxviii. My use of the term "miscellany" in this essay to refer to the Digby and Harley MSS contradicts the argument of Theo Stemmler (see his essay in this volume, pp. 111–20) and Carter Revard ("*Gilote et Johane*: An Interlude in B. L. MS. Harley 2253," *Studies in Philology* 79 [1982]: 122–46), that the principles of arrangement evident in Harley 2253 mean that the codex is not a miscellany but an "anthology." While I accept that both Harley and Digby too have been carefully arranged (see below), I would argue that the

most extensively by Carleton Brown in the introduction to his anthology *English Lyrics of the XIIIth Century*, first published in 1932.[3] Yet even this discussion is only partial: it concentrates on the English texts to the virtual exclusion of the French and Latin items present in each manuscript. This essay aims at a more comprehensive overview of the two codices, and notes various similarities and differences between them additional to those described by Brown. It also attempts to discuss the significance of certain key features of the manuscripts, and in particular, the relevance of these to the domains of literary history and modern publishing practice. It argues that the contents of the two collections expose major problems in the work of some of the foremost exponents of these fields, and also that the collections have much to tell us about aspects of the circulation of literature in England in the period in which they were compiled.

Both Harley 2253 and Digby 86 contain an extraordinary range of material. Quite apart from the fact that texts in three different languages are present in each, they both incorporate items radically different from one another in subject matter and in the attitudes which they express. Just as Harley 2253 includes fabliaux which ostensibly revel in bawdiness and sexual abandon along with lyrics in which secular eroticism is abjured, so too Digby 86 mingles the unashamedly profane with the solemnly pious:[4] it also includes fabliauesque tales — the French *Les Quatre Souhés s. Martin* (fol. 113r–v), the English *Dame Sirith* (fols. 165r–168r) — as well as religious narratives, prayers, and a variety of didactic pieces.[5] The generic diversity of the texts in both manuscripts is extreme: each contains saints' lives, *dits*, debate poems, and more, in addition to the kinds of literature already mentioned, and the works possess a variety of forms, verse and prose. But these most obvious similarities between the collections are not their only ones. Despite the fact that each manuscript includes a number of texts which are no longer attested elsewhere, it seems that no item is original to it: the miscellanies are exclusively collections of already existing works.[6] In both, the vast majority of the texts were copied by a single

---

difference between a miscellany and an anthology is not a matter of organization but of *selection* of the contents: those in an anthology are admitted according to restrictive criteria that are not enforced in the compilation of a miscellany.

[3] Carleton Brown, ed., *English Lyrics of the XIIIth Century* (Oxford, 1932), pp. xxxv–xxxvii; compare also M. B. Parkes, "The Literacy of the Laity," in *Literature and Western Civilization [vol 2:] The Mediaeval World*, ed. David Daiches and A. K. Thorlby (London, 1973), pp. 555–77, at pp. 562–63.

[4] Frankis, "Social Context," pp. 182–84.

[5] The contents of Digby 86 are listed in Tschann and Parkes, *Facsimile*, pp. xii–xxxvi.

[6] Brown, ed., *Eng. Lyr. XIII*, pp. xxxiv–xxxv. The texts now preserved uniquely in Digby 86 include the French Arthurian poem *Le Lai du cor* as well as *Dame Sirith* and *The Fox and the Wolf* mentioned above; most Harley lyrics, of course, survive only in that MS.

scribe;[7] this copyist in each case wrote in a cursive hand,[8] producing a manuscript that is far from elegant. Most interestingly, perhaps, the copyists appear to have been working in close proximity to each other, the Digby scribe just south of the Harley one, in Worcestershire.[9] They were not working at exactly the same period, of course — as many as sixty years, possibly even more, may separate the copying of the two collections;[10] otherwise, the general correspondences between the manuscripts are undeniably striking.

There are, nonetheless, several important differences between them. It has long been recognized that the juxtaposition of certain texts in Harley 2253 is not, it would seem, purely accidental: the instance of two contiguous lyrics in the collection, each of which begins with the words "Lutel wot hit any mon," is well known to literary scholars, who have claimed that the divergent ways in which the poems continue — the first a meditation on divine love, the second on secular — invite a reader to reflect on the gulf between the objects of attachment described.[11] More recently, Carter Revard has suggested that other adjacent texts in the manuscript interact in more subtle ways, and this idea has been taken up by Thorlac Turville-Petre, who, in *England the Nation*, describes some of the "parallels and contrasts" existing between sequential items in the miscellany, and compares these to the thematic reverberations that echo through *The Canterbury Tales*.[12] In Digby 86 sporadic, potentially meaningful juxtapositions similar to those identified in Harley 2253 can be perceived. One debate poem in which the merits of chastity and promiscuity are proclaimed by their respective adherents is immediately followed by another that features an exchange of speeches between a body and its damned soul[13] — an item intended to

---

[7] Fols. 81r–96v of Digby 86 are in the hand of a different copyist; on this scribe, see B. D. H. Miller, "The Early History of Bodleian MS Digby 86," *Annuale Mediaevale* 4 (1963): 23–56, at p. 25, and Tschann and Parkes, *Facsimile*, pp. xxxviii–xxxix. N. R. Ker notes those folios of Harley 2253 copied in a hand different from that of the principal scribe (*Facsimile of British Museum MS. Harley 2253*, EETS o.s. 255 [London, 1965], p. ix).

[8] Parkes, "Literacy," pp. 562–63.

[9] Miller, "Early History," pp. 23–56; Tschann and Parkes, *Facsimile*, pp. xi, lvi–lix.

[10] Revard dates the Harley miscellany to "about 1340 " ("*Gilote et Johane*," p. 122); Ker suggests that it may date from some time during "the fourth decade of the fourteenth century" (*Facsimile*, p. xxi).

[11] Pearsall, *OE and ME Poetry*, p. 131.

[12] Revard, "*Gilote et Johane*," pp. 130–39; Thorlac Turville-Petre, *England the Nation: Language, Literature, and National Identity, 1290–1340* (Oxford, 1996), p. 211.

[13] These poems are found on fols. 192v–199v of Digby 86. They are introduced by the rubrics "Ci commence l'estrif de .ii. dames" and "Hic incipit carmen inter corpus et animam," respectively. For the text of the former poem, see Edmund Stengel, ed., *Codicem manu scriptum Digby 86 in Bibliotheca Bodleiana asservatum* (Halle, 1871), pp. 84–93, and Achille Jubinal, ed., *Nouveau*

indicate the relative triviality of the concerns featured in the preceding poem? But Digby 86 displays a further, and a more pervasive, principle of organization in the arrangement of its contents: its compiler seems to have been sensitive to both the form and the language of the texts he collected, and he entered them into distinct sections of the miscellany depending on whether they were in prose, short lines of verse, or longer lines of verse, and also, within the two verse sections, on whether they were in French, English, or Latin.[14] The extended homogeneous sequences of texts which Digby 86 thus contains reveal its compiler to have been a more careful planner than the compiler of Harley 2253 appears to have been — if one who operated on a somewhat unexpected basis.[15]

The Digby miscellany is also much more consistently rubricated than Harley 2253, where very few texts have been given introductory titles.[16] The result is that Digby 86 is a more "user-friendly" manuscript than Harley 2253, with its contents relatively easy to identify and locate. It must have been problematic, by contrast, for even the copyist of the Harley miscellany to find specific items within his collection; for another user, it would have been virtually impossible. This is not to say that the manuscript could not have been used by others: it could have served as a book for perusal, if not one for the rapid consultation or retrieval of material. But the lack of titles does make one question whether the book was produced with other readers primarily in mind: if it was, its copyist seems

---

Recueil de contes, dits, fabliaux et autres pièces inédites des XIIIᵉ, XIVᵉ et XVᵉ siècles, 2 vols. (Paris, 1839, 1842), 2.73–82. For the latter, see: Stengel, pp. 93–101; Karl Reichl, ed., *Religiöse Dichtung im englischen Hochmittelalter: Untersuchung und Edition der Handschrift B. 14. 39 des Trinity College in Cambridge* (Munich, 1973), pp. 339–65; and (for the opening section) John W. Conlee, ed., *Middle English Debate Poetry: A Critical Anthology* (East Lansing, Mich., 1991), pp. 10–17.

Digby 86 and Harley 2253 both seem to display juxtapositions of texts governed by a further principle: Turville-Petre notes that certain contiguous items in Harley share a specific textual reference (*England the Nation*, p. 200), and this is also a feature of Digby 86 (Corrie, "Compilation," p. 240).

[14] Corrie, "Compilation," pp. 237–39.

[15] Theo Stemmler's work on Harley 2253 was brought to my attention only after completion of this essay. In his 1991 article revised and reprinted in this volume, Stemmler argues that Harley displays organizing principles very similar indeed to the ones that I have perceived in Digby 86. The consistency with which these principles have been applied, however, does still seem greater in Digby than in Harley.

[16] See Ker's catalogue of the contents of Harley 2253 for those texts that do have a title in the MS (*Facsimile*, pp. ix–xvi); in most other cases, the beginning of a new text is signaled solely by the presence of a red paragraph mark plus a line of red through the first letter of the work (p. xx).

to have given no more thought to the practicalities of its use than he did to the attractiveness of its appearance.[17]

If, further, there are striking resemblances between the nature of the texts included in the Harley and Digby manuscripts, it should be added that these are not exactly congruent. One of the most conspicuous divergences between the contents is the fact that Digby 86 lacks overtly political material of the kind which, as John Scattergood's essay in this volume shows, forms an important element of Harley 2253. Digby does contain two texts that are complaints against the conditions of contemporary society, but neither of these is concerned — as are many poems in Harley — with circumstances specific to the country in which the manuscript was copied.[18] It is tempting to see this difference between the collections as a reflection of their variant dates: while Digby 86 was compiled during a period of relative stability, in the early years of the reign of Edward I, the Harley scribe was working at a time of great social and political turmoil, with England troubled internally and at war with foreign powers.[19] Yet although some Harley poems such as *Trailbaston* (no. 80) can be associated with events of contemporary significance to the Harley compiler, not all of the political material gathered there is of such obvious

---

[17] Digby 86 also seems to have been copied for its scribe's own use; certainly, the presence, in the margin of the book, of doodles and scribbles in the hand of the principal copyist suggests both that the MS remained in his possession after the main body of texts had been entered and that he had no reservations about defacing the book as he pleased.

[18] The two "political" poems in Digby 86 are the French *Complainte de Jérusalem* (fols. 103v–105r) and a short Latin piece beginning "Fides hodie sopitur, / Uigilatque prauitas" (fol. 164v). Ascribed to the continental writer Huon de Saint-Quentin, the *Complainte* is an attack on ecclesiastical venality and, specifically, papal policy during the disastrous Fifth Crusade (1217–21); for editions of the poem, see Stengel, ed., *Codicem manu scriptum Digby 86*, pp. 106–08, and Arié Serper, ed., *Huon de Saint-Quentin, poète satirique et lyrique: Étude historique et édition de textes* (Madrid, 1983), pp. 87–114. The Latin poem is a lament on the corruption of contemporary society comparable to texts described in Ernst Curtius, *European Literature and the Latin Middle Ages*, trans. W. R. Trask (London, 1953), pp. 94–98; it is printed in Thomas Wright, ed., *Anecdota literaria: A Collection of Short Poems in English, Latin and French* (London, 1844), pp. 92–93.

[19] For outlines of the two periods, see Alan Harding, *England in the Thirteenth Century* (Cambridge, 1993), pp. 294–309; May McKisack, *The Fourteenth Century 1307–1399* (Oxford, 1959), pp. 105–209. The second quarter of the fourteenth century saw much lawlessness in England, some of it a response to the corruption of legal officials in the country: see Barbara A. Hanawalt for a description and an analysis of the period's criminality and its causes (*Crime and Conflict in English Communities, 1300–1348* [Cambridge, Mass., 1979]). The year 1337 also saw the start of the Hundred Years' War, on which see McKisack, pp. 105–51.

relevance. *A Song of Lewes* and the *Lament for Simon de Montfort* (nos. 23, 24), for instance, refer to happenings that occurred around seventy years before the copying of the Harley miscellany, and they appear to have been included because of their historical interest rather than any relevance to current affairs.[20] These two particular poems were already in existence when Digby 86 was copied; their absence from that miscellany is not, therefore, so much the result of a dearth of political literature in the period to which the manuscript belongs, as of either a lack of interest in such texts on the part of the Digby compiler, or a failure in the local availability of such works. To seek to explain the varying proportions of political poems in the two miscellanies exclusively in historical terms is clearly to simplify the complex reasons underlying them: an indeterminable cocktail of competing factors is much more likely to have been responsible.

These divergences between Harley 2253 and Digby 86 have not been registered previously; nor have what are, I would argue, some of the most interesting features shared by the manuscripts. I referred above to the fact that both miscellanies contain French fabliaux, and most of these are fabliaux which appear to have been composed (like the majority of the other surviving examples of the genre in French) on the continent rather than amongst French-speaking milieux in England.[21] Fabliaux are not, however, the only examples of French texts of continental provenance to appear in these English manuscripts: Digby 86 contains the burlesque dream vision *Le Songe d'enfer* by Raoul de Houdenc (fols. 97v–102r), together with *L'Assomption de Nostre Dame* by Herman de Valenciennes (fols. 169r–177r), *La Prière Nostre Dame* by Thibaut d'Amiens (fols. 110r–111r), and *Li Proverbes au vilain* (fols. 143r–149v), a work which is thought to have been composed for Philip of Flanders.[22] Harley 2253 includes Herman de Valenciennes's

---

[20] On the historical background to *Trailbaston*, see Isabel S. T. Aspin, ed. and trans., *Anglo-Norman Political Songs*, ANTS 11 (Oxford, 1953), pp. 67–68. Compare also the Harley *Satire on the Consistory Courts* (discussed by Aspin, pp. 40–51; Rossell Hope Robbins, ed., *Historical Poems of the XIVth and XVth Centuries* [New York, 1959], pp. 24–27). Both *A Song of Lewes* and *Lament for Simon de Montfort* commemorate the events of the Barons' War of 1264–65. On these poems in Harley, see John Scattergood's essay in this volume.

[21] Editors Willem Noomen and Nico van den Boogaard attribute *Les Quatre Souhés s. Martin* in Digby 86 to a continental author (*Nouveau Recueil complet des fabliaux*, 10 vols. [Assen, 1983–98], 4.192). They likewise assign a continental origin to the Harley fabliau *Le Chevalier qui fist les cons parler* (1.51–52), but Harley's *Le Chevalier et la corbaille* is regarded as being "d'origine insulaire" (2.266).

[22] For an edition of *Le Songe d'enfer* and information about its author, see Madelyn Timmel Mihm, ed., *The "Songe d'Enfer" of Raoul de Houdenc* (Tübingen, 1984); compare also the

La Passioun Nostre Seignour (no. 2) — the part of his versified retelling of biblical history to which the account of the Assumption of the Virgin in Digby 86 forms a sequel — plus an extract from Jacques de Vitry's *Historia orientalis* (no. 95) and a copy of the *Enseignements de saint Louis à son fils* (no. 94). The presence of all these texts in the manuscripts is important because it indicates the extent to which continental French literature was circulating in England in the late thirteenth and early fourteenth centuries. It illustrates also the infiltration of such literature into even the provincial environments that seem to have produced both miscellanies. But there is a further reason why the inclusion of these items in the manuscripts is of interest.

Few attempts have been made to survey or assess the corpus of French literature in medieval England. Johan Vising published his slim catalogue of the extant texts, *Anglo-Norman Language and Literature*, in 1923, and his work was supplemented by M. Dominica Legge's discursive treatment of the topic, *Anglo-Norman Literature and Its Background,* forty years later.[23] Legge says nothing about such material of continental origin as is found in Harley 2253 or Digby 86: her subject is solely the French literature that was *composed* in England or was probably composed there, over the three hundred years or so which followed the Norman Conquest. Vising, on the other hand, lists in his manual items such as the fabliaux preserved in Harley 2253,[24] although he does not mention *Les Quatre Souhés s. Martin* found in Digby 86, an omission that shows the

---

discussion in Verena Kundert-Forrer, *Raoul de Houdenc, ein französischer Erzähler des XIII. Jahrhunderts* (Bern, 1960). The texts by Herman de Valenciennes in Digby and Harley have not been published, but for the MS relationships, see Ina Spiele, ed., *Li Romanz de Dieu et de sa mere d'Herman de Valenciennes, chanoine et prêtre (XIIᵉ siècle)* (Leiden, 1975), pp. 144–59; for further discussion, see Jean Bonnard, *Les Traductions de la Bible en vers français au Moyen Âge* (Paris, 1884), pp. 11–41. Thibaut d'Amiens's *Prière Nostre Dame* is printed in Stengel, ed., *Codicem manu scriptum Digby 86*, pp. 30–35, and edited and discussed in Arthur Långfors, "La Prière de Thibaut d'Amiens," in *Studies in Romance Philology and French Literature Presented to John Orr by Pupils, Colleagues and Friends* (Manchester, 1953), pp. 134–57. *Li Proverbes au vilain* is edited by Adolf Tobler, who also associates the "frauns quens" addressed in the text with Philip of Flanders (*"Li Proverbes au vilain": Die Sprichwörter des gemeinen Mannes* [Leipzig, 1895], p. xviii); it is also printed in A. J. V. Le Roux de Lincy, ed., *Le Livre des proverbes français*, 2 vols., 2nd ed. (Paris, 1859), 2.459–70, where the more obscene stanzas are omitted. The work is discussed in Eckhard Rattunde, *"Li Proverbes au vilain": Untersuchungen zur romanischen Spruchdichtung des Mittelalters* (Heidelberg, 1966).

[23] Johan Vising, *Anglo-Norman Language and Literature* (London, 1923); M. Dominica Legge, *Anglo-Norman Literature and Its Background* (Oxford, 1963). See also Legge's *Anglo-Norman in the Cloisters: The Influence of the Orders upon Anglo-Norman Literature* (Edinburgh, 1950).

[24] Vising, *AN Language and Literature*, p. 61.

patchiness of his survey and the need for its revision. The fact that Vising mentions any of the continental French texts circulating in England, though, shows also that his understanding of the word "Anglo-Norman" is radically different from Legge's. He is evidently using it to embrace works that were being copied in the Anglo-Norman dialect rather than just those texts that originated in it. Without explicit recognition of the fact, therefore, these two scholars are actually investigating quite separate aspects of a subject they purport to share, and hence they have created very different impressions of the nature of "Anglo-Norman literature." Legge's book can be seen, furthermore, to be as in-complete as Vising's: since it fails to consider a substantial amount of the French material that was circulating in England in the early medieval period, it gives only a very partial account of the French literary culture of the country at the time.

The picture of this culture as drawn by Legge's study is one dominated by certain genres that are often considered unappealing to modern tastes: religious literature such as saints' lives and sermons, which Anglo-Norman authors seem to have composed with great en-thusiasm. Legge does remark that her corpus does not consist solely of "dreary religious and didactic stuff ground out by a few monks cut off from the world";[25] her evidence for this claim, however, is restricted to a relatively small number of surviving romances and lyrics. An earlier commentator, Ernst Walberg, was even more absolute in his character-ization of Anglo-Norman literature, noting its preponderance of "les œuvres didactiques, religieuses, morales et historiques," and emphasizing "son caractère utilitaire et pieux."[26] The fact that, as Harley 2253 and Digby 86 show, fabliaux were known in England suggests that the French material being read in the country was rather less consistently bleak, and less unremittingly improving, than the works that, according to Walberg and Legge, were being composed there; further scrutiny of the two manuscripts, however, suggests also that even French literature of English origin was not always of the kind that Walberg and Legge describe. Digby 86 contains a substantial number of French works of insular provenance that are anything but solemn and didactic: these include a nonsense poem known as *La Beitournee*; a sequence of occasionally scurrilous stanzas labelled *Ragemon le bon*, which seem to have been intended for use in a fortune-telling game; and a categorically obscene poem to which the scribe has given the demure title *La Vie de vn vallet amerous*.[27] Harley 2253 likewise contains the immoral and entertaining *Gilote et*

---

[25] Legge, *AN Literature*, p. 363.

[26] Ernst Walberg, *Quelques Aspects de la littérature anglo-normande: Leçons faites à l'École des Chartes* (Paris, 1936), pp. 36, 39.

[27] These poems are, respectively, on fols. 111r–112v, 162r–163v, and 114r–116v of Digby 86. *La Beitournee* is printed in Stengel, ed., *Codicem manu scriptum Digby 86*, pp. 118–25; Charity Meier-Ewert, ed., "A Study and a Partial Edition of the Anglo-Norman Verse in the Bodleian Manuscript Digby 86" (Ph.D. diss., Oxford University, 1971), pp. 221–27; and C. L. Kingsford,

Johane (no. 37), which shows the virginal Johane being converted to a life of debauchery through the persuasions of the sexually experienced Gilote.[28] Such texts, although brief, deserve more attention than they have been accorded. They indicate that the better known specimens of Anglo-Norman literature on which Legge and Walberg based their assertions by no means represent the full extent of composition in the Anglo-Norman dialect.

A similar impression of restricted subject matter has been given of the English corpus composed between the Norman Conquest and the middle of the fourteenth century. R. M. Wilson — the only scholar to have written a book-length survey of early Middle English literature — refers to the dominance of pious and didactic works amongst the surviving texts, and, having trawled his way through these, concludes that they offer material that is mostly "of comparatively little interest to the modern reader."[29] The limitations of Wilson's study and its conclusions were forestalled by Carleton Brown, who noted that what survives of early Middle English literature is very probably unrepresentative of what once existed: religious works would simply have had a much greater chance than profane texts of finding their way into the durable medium of manuscript books, since most of these were being produced in this period in England by men of religion, for their own professional use.[30] But there is a second reason why the methodology of Wilson's work is problematic. Both Harley 2253 and Digby 86 show that many of the English texts discussed by Wilson — including the lyric poetry in the former manuscript and *Dame Sirith* and *The Fox and the Wolf* in the latter — were copied and read in the company of works in other languages. To segregate English texts from literature in French and Latin, therefore, is to give a false impression of the autonomy of literature in English in the period. No matter how the English texts of the time can be characterized, any statements about them as a separate linguistic entity give no idea of the range of literature familiar to a sizeable portion of the population of England because many people were competent in

---

ed., *The Song of Lewes* (1890; repr. Brussels, 1963), pp. 154–58. For the text of *Ragemon le bon*, see Meier-Ewert, ed., pp. 238–44; Arthur Långfors, ed., *Un Jeu de société du moyen âge: "Ragemon le bon,"* *inspirateur d'un sermon en vers* (Helsinki, 1920); and Wright, ed., *Anecdota literaria*, pp. 76–81. For *La Vie de vn vallet amerous*, see Stengel, ed., pp. 40–49, and Meier-Ewert, ed., pp. 228–37.

[28] This poem, on fols. 67v–68v of Harley 2253, is printed in Jubinal, *Nouveau Recueil*, 2.28–39, and in Thomas Corbin Kennedy, ed., "Anglo-Norman Poems about Love, Women, and Sex from British Museum MS Harley 2253" (Ph.D. diss., Columbia University, 1973), pp. 146–77. It is discussed in Revard, "*Gilote et Johane*," pp. 122–46, and in Mary Dove's essay in this volume.

[29] R. M. Wilson, *Early Middle English Literature*, 3rd ed. (London, 1968), p. 295.

[30] Brown, ed., *Eng. Lyr. XIII*, p. xxxviii.

two or three languages. Even if English works can be said to have been mainly religious in nature (and the English items for which the Harley and Digby miscellanies are famous show that, as in the case of the Anglo-Norman corpus, a considerable amount of profane material has also survived), the fact that many were used alongside French and Latin texts of a potentially quite different kind means that perceptions such as Wilson's are of restricted value. This is true as well, of course, of the views of scholars such as Legge and Walberg, who have separated Anglo-Norman literature from the trilingual culture in which it was produced, and equally of those who have surveyed the Anglo-Latin corpus in isolation.[31] While it is certainly the case that many people would have read or listened to texts in only one of these languages, the evidence of manuscripts such as Harley 2253 and Digby 86 indicates that at least some people were interested in a linguistically mixed selection of literary material. The separation of literature in one language from that in the two others widely used in England from the mid-eleventh to the mid-fourteenth centuries is a reflection of the monolingual status of modern critics, or the monodisciplinary environments in which they work: it is not an accurate reflection of the multilingual milieu in which the texts were produced and circulated.

Not only has literature from this period been discussed according to the particular language in which it has been written: it has also been published in anthologies and series that associate texts with others written in the same language, instead of preserving the mixed linguistic context in which many are found. The most widely used collection of early Middle English texts, J. A. W. Bennett and G. V. Smithers's *Early Middle English Verse and Prose*, wrenches *Dame Sirith*, *The Fox and the Wolf*, and a selection of the Harley Lyrics out of their medieval trilingual settings, as does Bruce Dickins and R. M. Wilson's anthology *Early Middle English Texts*.[32] Works such as *Le Lai du cor* in Digby 86 are implicitly aligned with other texts in French through publication by the Anglo-Norman Text Society. Anthologies of medieval Latin verse bring together items solely in that language.[33] Some kind of delimitation of the subject matter of an edition or a series

---

[31] On the subject of Anglo-Latin literature, see, in particular, A. G. Rigg, *A History of Anglo-Latin Literature 1066–1422* (Cambridge, 1992).

[32] J. A. W. Bennett and G. V. Smithers, eds., *Early Middle English Verse and Prose*, 2nd ed. (Oxford, 1968); Bruce Dickins and R. M. Wilson, eds., *Early Middle English Texts*, 3rd ed. (London, 1956). Dickins and Wilson's collection also includes *The Thrush and the Nightingale* from Digby 86 (fols. 136v–138r) and *A Song of Lewes* from Harley 2253, as well as an extract from the Harley version of *King Horn*.

[33] For *Le Lai du cor* (fols. 105r–109v), see the edition by C. T. Erickson, ed., *The Anglo-Norman Text of "Le Lai du cor,"* ANTS 24 (Oxford, 1973). For a selection of Latin verse including material found

— as of a discussion — is self-evidently necessary, and the application of linguistic criteria is an obvious means by which to set the bounds. This principle of selection is, however, more problematic for the publication of texts from early medieval England than it is for literature of the country from any subsequent — or even anterior — period.

Most editions also select their texts on the basis of literary interest — that is, because the works are aesthetically pleasing, intriguing, or in some way important on literary historical grounds. Yet here again, Harley 2253 and Digby 86 raise potential objections to the extraction of material according to this rationale. The two manuscripts are known for the literary texts they contain — texts such as those that I have already cited. Less well known, however, is the fact that they comprise as well a diverse assortment of items that can only be described as "practical" in function. Digby 86 includes a vast range of such pieces, many of them copied toward the beginning of the manuscript: there is a compendium of medical lore, in French, derived from the compilation known as the *Lettre d'Hippocrate*, plus various charms, prognosticatory items, material intended for the guidance of someone making confession, and even advice on how to nurture birds of prey and cure them of certain physiological afflictions.[34] Harley 2253 incorporates fewer texts of this kind — it has a more pronounced literary emphasis than does Digby 86, and

---

in English MSS, see F. J. E. Raby, ed., *The Oxford Book of Medieval Latin Verse* (Oxford, 1959).

[34] Much of this material, which is all in French or Latin, is unpublished. For the *Lettre d'Hippocrate* (fols. 8v–15v, 17r–21r), however, see Tony Hunt, ed., *Popular Medicine in Thirteenth-Century England: Introduction and Texts* (Cambridge, 1990), pp. 100–41, and Ö. Södergård, ed., *Une "Lettre d'Hippocrate" d'après un manuscrit inédit* (Stockholm, 1981). Some of the charms are printed in Hunt, ed., pp. 83–89. For prognosticatory items analogous to those in Digby 86 (which include the best days for letting blood, predictions for a year based on the weekday of the previous Christmas, and interpretations of dreams), see, for example: Linne R. Mooney, ed., "Practical Didactic Works in Middle English: Edition and Analysis of the Class of Short Middle English Works Containing Useful Information" (Ph.D. diss., University of Toronto, 1981); Rossell Hope Robbins, ed., *Secular Lyrics of the XIVth and XVth Centuries,* 2nd ed. (Oxford, 1955), pp. 67–70; and Steven R. Fischer, ed., *The Complete Medieval Dreambook: A Multilingual, Alphabetical "Somnia Danielis" Collation* (Bern, 1982). The Digby MS also contains a "lunary" (fols. 41r–46r), which elucidates the significance of each of the thirty days comprising the moon's cycle; compare I. Taavitsainen, *Middle English Lunaries: A Study of the Genre* (Helsinki, 1988). Confessional manuals comparable to the one included in Digby 86 (fols. 1r–8v) are discussed by H. G. Pfander, "Some Medieval Manuscripts of Religious Instruction in England and Observations on Chaucer's Parson's Tale," *Journal of English and Germanic Philology* 35 (1936): 243–58; see also W. F. Bryan and Germaine Dempster, eds., *Sources and Analogues of Chaucer's Canterbury Tales* (New York, 1941), pp. 745–58. A treatise on the rearing of birds similar to the Digby piece (on fols. 49r–62r) is printed by G. Tilander, ed., "Fragment d'un traité de fauconnerie anglo-normand en vers," *Studier i Modern Språkvetenskap* 15 (1943): 26–44.

therefore, despite the fact that it includes some genres absent from the Digby collection, it is overall a less extravagantly heterogeneous manuscript than the earlier miscellany. Nonetheless, it does include a list of the books of the Bible (no. 72), notes of the particular occasions for which certain psalms are apposite (nos. 101, 110, 111), and a description of the curative properties of certain plants (no. 112).[35] Consequently, the isolation by modern editors of these manuscripts' purely literary items results in a further kind of misrepresentation of the context in which the items were both copied and used.

The mingling of the practical with the literary in the Harley and Digby miscellanies is not unique either to them specifically or to the period in which they were compiled: it is a feature also of the many "commonplace books" that survive from the late medieval period and from post-medieval times as well. But it seems more characteristic a feature of the centuries that produced Harley 2253 and Digby 86 in that our only evidence for the existence of many of the texts surviving from England from this era occurs in such "mixed" manuscripts. These perhaps reflect the scarcity and expensiveness of the raw materials of book production at the time: since only the most wealthy would have been able to afford the luxury of having separate volumes for works of different kinds and functions, other compilers must have been forced to include dissimilar texts within a single manuscript. But the mixture of material in Harley 2253 and Digby 86 also suggests a lack of self-consciousness about uniting different kinds of items within the same collection, and even within adjoining pages of that collection.[36] The inclusion of texts is not governed by their conformity to any apparent defining criteria: the compilers' interest in the works and their potential usefulness to them and to any readers whom they envisaged seem to have been the only factors that determined their copying. It is a very different principle of selection from that chosen by compilers of the modern editions in which many of the Harley and Digby texts have appeared.

I have thus far examined the significance of some of the broad correspondences between Harley 2253 and Digby 86, but the two manuscripts in fact have more than just these in common. Brown pointed out that a sizeable number of the actual texts found in Digby 86 appear also in Harley 2253: the dramatic verse retelling of the legend of the Harrowing of Hell; the collection of admonitions and grim observations known as the *Sayings of St.*

---

[35] These texts are copied, respectively, on Harley fols. 105v; 134r, 136v–137r; and 137r. None has been published independently of the facsimile.

[36] The Harley list of the books of the Bible, for example, is followed immediately by two lyrics and then two fabliaux; it should also be noted, however, that the list occurs at the end of a quire.

Bernard; the Passion lyric *Stond Wel, Moder, vnder Rode*; a further lyric, *Suete Iesu, King of Blysse* (which in Digby has been appended to another poem, *The Eleven Pains of Hell*); *Maximian*, which contains the monologue of an old man who regrets the passing of his youth; *Hending*; and the opening section of the body-and-soul dialogue mentioned above.[37] These all are English texts; to them may be added *Le Blasme des femmes*, a French antifeminist poem common to the manuscripts that Brown seems to have missed. This text appears in its entirety in Harley (no. 77) but only in excerpts in Digby, where it follows *Les Quatre Souhés s. Martin* (on fols. 113v–114r), as if to affirm the misogynistic tenor of the fabliau.[38] The fact that Digby contains only an abbreviated version of the poem indicates that the Harley scribe cannot have copied his text from Digby unless he also had a second copy to supply the missing lines: he did not make them up himself, as they are found as well in other surviving copies of the poem that predate Harley.[39] Could the scribe, however, have been using Digby as his source for the other items included in both manuscripts?

Brown dismissed this possibility, and with apparently good reason. Just as the Harley copy of *Le Blasme des femmes* contains sections of text omitted in Digby, so too does the Harley version of the English body-and-soul poem (no. 22): this piece ends with thirty-two lines of exposition not found in Digby, and since, once more, those lines survive in another manuscript anterior to Harley, the Harley scribe must have copied them from a source other than Digby.[40] This is the case as well with *Stond Wel, Moder, vnder Rode* (no. 60), which in Harley contains two stanzas not included in Digby but present in another early fourteenth-century copy of the work.[41]

---

[37] Brown, ed., *Eng. Lyr. XIII*, p. xxxvii.

[38] Corrie, "Compilation," p. 241.

[39] These include the versions in the continental Paris, BN MS fr. 837 (thirteenth century), and the insular Cambridge, University Library MS Gg.i.1 (beginning of the fourteenth century). The complete text of *Le Blasme des femmes* is printed in Gloria K. Fiero, Wendy Pfeffer, and Mathé Allain, eds. and trans., *Three Medieval Views of Women* (New Haven, 1989), pp. 12–16, as well as in Jubinal, ed., *Nouveau Recueil*, 2.330–33, and Thomas Wright and James Orchard Halliwell, eds., *Reliquiae Antiquae*, 2 vols. (London, 1841, 1843), 2.218–23.

[40] The MS of the poem that predates Harley — and also Digby — is Cambridge, Trinity College MS 323, on which see further below. The texts of all three surviving versions of the poem appear in Reichl, ed., *Religiöse Dichtung*, pp. 339–65. Rosemary Woolf discusses the possible reasons for the absence of the Digby poem's final lines (*The English Religious Lyric in the Middle Ages* [Oxford, 1968], p. 97), as does Corrie, "Compilation," pp. 240–41.

[41] Brown, ed., *Eng. Lyr. XIII*, pp. 203–05.

In *The Harrowing of Hell* (no. 21), *Suete Iesu, King of Blysse* (no. 50), and *Hending* (no. 89), however, although Harley again contains either additional or alternative sections of text not found in the Digby copies of each poem, fewer firm conclusions can be reached regarding the source of the variant passages since in each case there is no extant manuscript of a date earlier than Harley that duplicates the reading present there.[42] There is nothing to prove that these items could not have been copied from Digby by the Harley scribe, with the variant passages either added to or rewritten by him. For *Suete Iesu, King of Blysse*, though, this possibility seems unlikely. Brown thought that the Digby version of the poem — which consists of just three stanzas — probably represents the original extent of the text, and the Harley copy — which has a further twelve stanzas — an expansion of it,[43] but Digby 86 contains other examples of works that are much shorter there than in other manuscripts, and it seems justifiable to suspect the Digby scribe of occasionally pruning his texts.[44] If this is what happened with *Suete Iesu, King of Blysse*, then a now lost exemplar prior to the Harley copy must be postulated. And indeed in each of the other texts common to both Harley and Digby — even where such suggestive evidence is not available — a lost exemplar or series of exemplars has been proposed by

---

[42] The opening of *The Harrowing of Hell* is different in Digby 86 (fols. 119r–120v) from that in both Harley 2253 and the one other surviving copy, in the Auchinleck MS (Edinburgh, National Library of Scotland Advocates MS 19.2.1), which is roughly contemporaneous with Harley 2253. See William Henry Hulme's edition for all three texts printed in parallel (*The Middle-English Harrowing of Hell and Gospel of Nicodemus*, EETS e.s. 100 [London, 1907]). The Harley version of *Hending* contains many uniquely attested stanzas: see Hermann Varnhagen, ed., "Zu mittelenglischen Gedichten. XI. Zu den Sprichwörtern Hendings," *Anglia* 4 (1881): 180–200, at pp. 180–81, for a comparison of the Harley and Digby versions, together with the copy in CUL Gg.i.1; see also G. Schleich, ed., "Die Sprichwörter Hendings und die *Prouerbis of Wysdom*," *Anglia* 51 (1927): 220–77. The Harley *Suete Iesu, King of Blysse* is printed in G. L. Brook, ed.,*The Harley Lyrics: The Middle English Lyrics of MS. Harley 2253*, 4th ed. (Manchester, 1968), pp. 51–52; for the shorter Digby text (fol. 134v), see Brown, ed., *Eng. Lyr. XIII*, pp. 91–92.

[43] Brown, ed., *Eng. Lyr. XIII*, pp. 205–06.

[44] A French prayer on fol. 200v, beginning "Beaus sire Ihesu Crist, eiez merci de mai [*sic*]," has either twelve or sixteen stanzas in other MSS, but only three in Digby. Since the poem was copied on the final half-page of a quire, with a new section of texts beginning on the first page of the next quire (Corrie, "Compilation," p. 239), it looks as if it may have been shortened so that it could be fitted into a limited amount of space. The extract from *Le Blasme des femmes* is another example of a text that appears to have been "edited" by the Digby scribe, as is the case of a further passage attached to the end of *Les Quatre Souhés s. Martin*, which is drawn from another antifeminist poem, *Le Chastie-musart* (Corrie, "Compilation," p. 241).

editors seeking to account for divergences between the two versions.[45] Stemmata produced for *Hending* suggest that the Harley and Digby copies actually spring from quite separate textual traditions — that the Harley version is not descended, even ultimately, from its correspondent version in Digby, but from a destroyed progenitor shared by both.[46] All the indications, then, are that the Harley scribe did not know the Digby collection of texts, and that, despite the number of these found in Harley 2253, none was copied either directly or indirectly from Digby 86.

This lack of direct relationship does not mean that the parallels between the contents of the manuscripts are purely coincidental. The fact that the two books were apparently compiled in such very close proximity to each other probably underlies many of their resemblances: they may well represent relics of a localized literary culture that flourished in the South West Midlands of England in the thirteenth and early fourteenth centuries. Harley 2253 and Digby 86 share more constituent items with each other than with any additional surviving manuscript, but, as has been recognized by a number of scholars, they do also have much in common with a series of further late thirteenth-century multilingual miscellanies that were likewise compiled in the South West Midlands.[47] With Cambridge, Trinity College MS 323 (a collection of predominantly English and Latin texts probably assembled by and for a community of friars in the diocese of Worcester in the 1260s[48]), Harley 2253 and Digby 86 both share the English body-and-soul dialogue *In a Þestri Stude* (Digby incipit, "Hon an þester stude I stod," fols. 195v–200r). The Digby and Trinity manuscripts also each hold the long French *Life of St. Nicholas* by Wace (Digby fols. 150r–161r) and another English poem, *Uuen I Þenke on Domesdai* (fols. 197v–198r), which deals with subject matter similar to *In a Þestri Stude*, and which in Digby has been joined to that poem.[49] Another manuscript, Oxford, Jesus College MS 29, appears to have been copied, like Harley 2253, in Herefordshire.[50] It also contains *Uuen I Þenke on*

---

[45] Hulme, ed., *ME Harrowing of Hell*, p. vii; Schleich, ed., "Die Sprichwörter Hendings," pp. 225–47.

[46] Schleich, ed., "Die Sprichwörter Hendings," p. 230. Compare also Schleich's "Zu den Sprichwörtern Hendings," *Anglia* 52 (1928): 350–61, at p. 358.

[47] Frankis, "Social Context," pp. 175–84; Reichl, ed., *Religiöse Dichtung*, pp. 3–92; Turville-Petre, *England the Nation*, p. 182.

[48] Reichl, ed., *Religiöse Dichtung*, pp. 62–67.

[49] For Wace's work, see Einar Ronsjö, ed., *"La Vie de saint Nicolas" par Wace: Poème religieux du XIIe siècle, publié d'après tous les manuscrits* (Lund, 1942); and for *Uuen I Þenke on Domesdai*, see Brown, ed., *Eng. Lyr. XIII*, pp. 42–46 (no. 28a), and Reichl, ed., *Religiöse Dichtung*, pp. 406–36.

[50] Angus McIntosh, M. L. Samuels, and Michael Benskin, with the assistance of Margaret Laing and Keith Williamson, *A Linguistic Atlas of Late Mediaeval English*, 4 vols. (Aberdeen, 1986), 1.199.

Domesdai and three more verse texts found in Digby 86: *The Eleven Pains of Hell*, *The Saws of St. Bede*, and the *Doctrinal sauvage* (another French work of continental origin).[51] The French items that appear in these South West Midland miscellanies are found also in manuscripts copied in other parts of England or on the continent; the English items, by contrast, survive only in the localized miscellanies. While it is always possible that versions of these texts from other areas of the country may once have existed, their preservation uniquely in South West Midland manuscripts seems to suggest that they enjoyed a restricted geographical circulation.[52] Their replication in these manuscripts testifies to the vitality of a tradition of circulating literature in that region, and also to a vital tradition there of collecting English works, together with pieces in other languages, into miscellanies.

No direct connections have been established between any of the copies of texts shared by these manuscripts, however, any more than between those common to the Harley and Digby miscellanies alone. Again, editors of the respective works — English and French — have conjectured that variously complex networks of lost versions separate the copies that survive in the miscellanies. If, further, those texts which are now unique to Harley and Digby are not original to the manuscripts, there must once have been anterior versions of these works also.[53] Although we may retain ample proof of the existence of a literary culture in one small area of England in the pre-Chaucerian period, our knowledge of it — and of the literary culture of early medieval England as a whole — is therefore without

---

[51] For *The Eleven Pains of Hell*, see Carl Horstmann, ed., "Nachträge zu den Legenden," *Archiv für das Studium der neueren Sprachen und Literaturen* 62 (1879): 397–431; Richard Morris, ed., *An Old English Miscellany*, EETS o.s. 49 (1872; repr. Millwood, N.Y., 1988), pp. 147–55; and Joanna I. R. Watson, ed., "An Edition of Certain Lyrics Contained in MS Digby 86" (Ph.D. diss., Oxford University, 1970), pp. 60–80. This poem is also discussed in E. G. Stanley, "Die anglo-normannischen Verse in dem mittelenglischen Gedicht *Die elf Höllenpeinen*," *Archiv für das Studium der neuren Sprachen und Literaturen* 192 (1956): 21–32. For *The Saws of St. Bede*, see Morris, ed.,*OE Miscellany*, pp. 72–83; Carl Horstmann, ed., *Altenglische Legenden: Neue Folge* (Heilbronn, 1881), pp. 505–10; and F. J. Furnivall, ed., *The Minor Poems of the Vernon MS.*, Part 2, EETS o.s. 117 (1901; repr. Millwood, N.Y., 1987), pp. 765–76. For the *Doctrinal sauvage*, see Aimo Sakari, ed., *Doctrinal sauvage* (Jyväskylä, 1967).

[52] This may have been because of the potential barrier to comprehension represented by the dialectal forms used in the English texts or, more probably, because of the physical isolation of the South West Midland area.

[53] The presence of some inexact rhymes in *Dame Sirith* (e.g., lines 25–26, 124–25) suggests that this is indeed the case with this text. Compare also *The Fox and the Wolf*, in which leaps in the narrative seem to indicate the omission of passages: line 65, for example, suggests that the fox has just spoken, but the foregoing passage represents the speech of the cock.

doubt very incomplete, as so much material has clearly been lost. How many more copies of texts than now survive may once have existed? And how many more works for which we now have no evidence at all? The texts contained in Harley 2253 and Digby 86 may once have been very much less unusual than they now appear to be, and the literature of the period may indeed have been of a very different nature from that which the historians of its remains have implied.

Comparison of Harley 2253 and Digby 86 thus invites a reassessment of many of the attitudes that have pervaded scholarship on the literature of pre-Chaucerian England for decades. This period of the country's literature has been persistently ignored by scholars in the latter half of the twentieth century — bypassed by specialists in English, because, I think, of the widespread perception that it produced few texts of any interest, and given scant attention by most scholars of French because of their tendency to concentrate on literature emanating from the continent. Yet study of some of the most remarkable codicological products of the time shows that there remains much to be learned about French literature in this outpost of the French-speaking world, and about the interaction of English literature with it. An adequate appreciation of the literary culture of early medieval England demands of its critics the same multilingual competence as is evident amongst the compilers and hypothetical readers of manuscripts such as Harley 2253 and Digby 86. It demands also an awareness of the circumstances of textual preservation that characterize the surviving works, as well as a consciousness of how fragmentary a part of the original picture these almost certainly are. All this is apparent from an examination of Harley 2253 and its relationship to Digby 86: a relationship of interest not just for the many similarities between the two miscellanies, but for its fundamental significance to the whole study of medieval literature in England up to the middle of the fourteenth century.

Bibliography of Works Cited

Ackerman, Robert W. "The Debate of the Body and Soul and Parochial Christianity." *Speculum* 37 (1962): 541–65.

Alexander of Hales. *Glossa in quatuor libros sententiarum Petri Lombardi.* 4 vols. Florence, 1951–57.

Anson, John S. "The Female Transvestite in Early Monasticism: The Origin and Development of a Motif." *Viator* 5 (1974): 1–32.

Artemidorus. *The Interpretation of Dreams: Oneirocritica by Artemidorus.* Trans. Robert J. White. Noyes Classical Studies. Park Ridge, N.J., 1975.

Aspin, Isabel S. T., ed. and trans. *Anglo-Norman Political Songs.* ANTS 11. Oxford, 1953.

Atkinson, Clarissa. "'Precious Balm in a Fragile Glass': The Ideology of Virginity in the Later Middle Ages." *Journal of Family History* 8 (1983): 131–43.

Atwater, Donald, with Catherine Rachel John. *The Penguin Dictionary of Saints.* 3rd ed. London, 1995.

Aungier, George James, ed. *Croniques de London, depuis l'an 44 Hen. III. jusqu'a l'an 17 Edw. III.* Camden Society 28. 1844; repr. New York, 1968.

Badel, Pierre-Yves. "Le Débat." In *Grundriß der romanischen Literaturen des Mittelalters.* Ed. Hans Robert Jauss, Erich Kohler, and H. U. Gumbrecht. Vol. 8.1: *La Littérature française aux XIVe et XVe siècles (partie historique).* Ed. Daniel Poirion. Heidelberg, 1988. Pp. 95–110.

Baldwin, Frances Elizabeth. *Sumptuary Legislation and Personal Regulation in England.* Baltimore, 1926.

Bibliography of Works Cited

Bannister, A. T., ed. *Registrum Ade de Orleton, episcopi Herefordensis*. Canterbury and York Society 5. 1908.

Barrington, Daines. *Observations on the More Ancient Statutes from Magna Charta to the Twenty-First of James I. Cap. XXVII*. London, 1767.

Bean, J. M. W. *From Lord to Patron: Lordship in Late Medieval England*. Manchester, 1989.

Bec, Pierre. *La Lyrique française au moyen-âge (XIIᵉ–XIIIᵉ siècles): Contributions à une typologie des genres poétiques médiévaux. Études et textes*. 2 vols. Paris, 1977, 1978.

Becker, Franz G., ed. *Pamphilus: Prolegomena zum Pamphilum (de amore) und kritische Textausgabe*. In *Mittellateinisches Jahrbuch*, Beiheft 9. Ratingen, 1972.

Beckwith, Sarah. *Christ's Body: Identity, Culture and Society in Late Medieval Writings*. London, 1993.

Bédier, Joseph. *Les Fabliaux: Études de littérature populaire et d'histoire littéraire du moyen âge*. 6th ed. 1892; Paris, 1964.

Bellamy, John. *Crime and Public Order in England in the Later Middle Ages*. London, 1973.

Bennett, J. A. W., and G. V. Smithers, eds. *Early Middle English Verse and Prose*. 2nd ed. Oxford, 1968.

Bennett, R. F. *The Early Dominicans: Studies in Thirteenth-Century Dominican History*. Cambridge, 1937.

Benskin, Michael, and Margaret Laing. "Translations and *Mischsprachen* in Middle English Manuscripts." In *So meny people, longages and tonges: Philological Essays in Scots and Mediaeval English Presented to Angus McIntosh*. Ed. Michael Benskin and M. L. Samuels. Edinburgh, 1981. Pp. 329–39.

Benson, Larry D. "The 'Queynte' Punnings of Chaucer's Critics." In *Contradictions from "Beowulf" to Chaucer*. Ed. Theodore M. Andersson and Stephen A. Barney. Aldershot, 1995. Pp. 217–42.

Bibliography of Works Cited

Blamires, Alcuin, ed. *Woman Defamed and Woman Defended: An Anthology of Medieval Texts*. Oxford, 1992.

Bloch, R. Howard. *Medieval Misogyny*. Chicago, 1991.

Bloomfield, M. W. "*Piers Plowman* and the Three Grades of Chastity." *Anglia* 76 (1958): 227–45.

Boase, T. S. R. "King Death." In *The Flowering of the Middle Ages*. Ed. Joan Evans. London, 1966. Pp. 203–44.

Böddeker, Karl, ed. *Altenglische Dichtungen des MS. Harl. 2253*. 1878; repr. Amsterdam, 1969.

Bonnard, Jean. *Les Traductions de la Bible en vers français au Moyen Âge*. Paris, 1884.

Bossuat, Robert. *Manuel bibliographique de la littérature française du Moyen Âge*. Melun, 1951.

———, Louis Pichard, and Guy Raynaud de Lage. *Dictionnaire des lettres françaises: Le Moyen Age*. 2nd ed. Rev. Geneviève Hasenohr and Michel Zink. Paris, 1992.

Bossy, Michel-André. *Medieval Debate Poetry: Vernacular Works*. New York, 1987.

———. "Medieval Debates of Body and Soul." *Comparative Literature* 28 (1976): 144–63.

Bramley, H. R., ed. *The Psalter, or Psalms of David and Certain Canticles, with a Translation and Exposition in English by Richard Rolle of Hampole*. Oxford, 1884.

Brewer, D. S. "The Ideal of Feminine Beauty in Medieval Literature, especially 'Harley Lyrics', Chaucer, and Some Elizabethans." *Modern Language Review* 50 (1955): 257–69.

Bromyard, John. *Summa praedicantium*. Venice, 1586.

Bronson, Bertrand H. *Joseph Ritson, Scholar-At-Arms*. 2 vols. Berkeley, 1938.

Brook, G. L., ed. *The Harley Lyrics: The Middle English Lyrics of MS. Harley 2253*. 4th ed. Manchester, 1968.

———. "The Original Dialects of the Harley Lyrics." *Leeds Studies in English* 2 (1933): 38–61.

Brown, Carleton, ed. *English Lyrics of the XIIIth Century*. Oxford, 1932.

———, ed. *Religious Lyrics of the XIVth Century*. Oxford, 1924. 2nd ed. Rev. G. V. Smithers. Oxford, 1957.

Brown, Carleton, and Rossell Hope Robbins. *The Index of Middle English Verse and Prose*. New York, 1943.

Bryan, W. F., and Germaine Dempster, eds. *Sources and Analogues of Chaucer's Canterbury Tales*. New York, 1941.

Bugge, John. *Virginitas: An Essay in the History of a Medieval Ideal*. The Hague, 1975.

Bühler, Carl F. "Two Middle English Texts of the *Somniale Danielis*." *Anglia* 80 (1962): 264–73.

Burrow, J. A., and Thorlac Turville-Petre, eds. *A Book of Middle English*. Oxford, 1992.

Busby, Keith. "Fabliaux and the New Codicology." Forthcoming in a festschrift in honor of Per Nykrog.

Calendar of Close Rolls Preserved in the Public Record Office. London, 1892–1954.

Calendar of Fine Rolls Preserved in the Public Record Office. London, 1911.

Calendar of Inquisitions Miscellaneous (Chancery) Preserved in the Public Record Office. London, 1916.

Calendar of Inquisitions Post Mortem and Other Analogous Documents Preserved in the Public Record Office. London, 1904.

Calendar of Patent Rolls Preserved in the Public Record Office. London, 1891–1916.

Camille, Michael. *Image on the Edge: The Margins of Medieval Art*. Cambridge, Mass., 1992.

Bibliography of Works Cited

Campbell, A. *An Old English Grammar*. Oxford, 1959.

Capes, W. W., ed. *Registrum Thome de Charltone, episcopi Herefordensis*. Canterbury and York Society 9. 1913.

————, ed. *Registrum Ricardi de Swinfield, episcopi Herefordensis*. Canterbury and York Society 6. 1909.

Casieri, Sabino, ed. *Canti e liriche medioevali inglesi dal MS. Harley 2253*. Milan, 1962.

Cazelles, Brigitte. *The Lady as Saint: A Collection of French Hagiographic Romances of the Thirteenth Century*. Philadelphia, 1991.

Cerquiligni, Jacqueline. "Le Clerc et l'écriture: Le *Voir dit* de Guillaume de Machaut et la définition du dit." In *Literatur in der Gesellschaft des Spätmittelalters*. Ed. Hans Ulrich Gumbrecht. Heidelberg, 1980. Pp. 151–68.

Chaucer, Geoffrey. *The Riverside Chaucer*. Ed. Larry D. Benson et al. Boston, 1987.

Chrétien de Troyes. *Lancelot (Le Chevalier de la charette)*. Ed. Mario Roques. Paris, 1958.

Christine de Pizan. *The Book of the City of Ladies*. Trans. Earl Jeffrey Richards. New York, 1982.

Clanchy, M. T. *From Memory to Written Record: England 1066–1307*. 2nd ed. Oxford, 1993.

————. *England and Its Rulers 1066–1272: Foreign Lordship and National Identity*. Glasgow, 1983.

Clugnet, Léon, ed. "Vie de sainte Marine." *Revue de l'Orient Chrétien* 8 (1903): 288–311.

Colledge, Edmund, ed. *The Latin Poems of Richard Ledrede, O.F.M., Bishop of Ossory, 1317–1360*. Toronto, 1974.

Conlee, John W., ed. *Middle English Debate Poetry: A Critical Anthology*. East Lansing, Mich., 1991.

Bibliography of Works Cited

Copeland, Rita. "Introduction: Dissenting Critical Practices." In *Criticism and Dissent in the Middle Ages.* Ed. Rita Copeland. Cambridge, 1996. Pp. 1–23.

Corrie, Marilyn. "The Compilation of Oxford, Bodleian Library, MS Digby 86." *Medium Ævum* 66 (1997): 236–49.

———. "A Study of Oxford, Bodleian Library, MS Digby 86: Literature in Late Thirteenth-Century England." Ph.D. diss. Oxford University, 1995.

Coxe, H. O. *Catalogus codicum MSS. qui in collegiis aulisque Oxoniensibus hodie adservantur.* 2 vols. Oxford, 1852.

Crane, Susan. *Gender and Romance in Chaucer's "Canterbury Tales."* Princeton, 1994.

———. *Insular Romance: Politics, Faith and Culture in Anglo-Norman and Middle English Literature.* Berkeley, 1986.

Cross, F. L., ed. *The Oxford Dictionary of the Christian Church.* London, 1958.

Cross, James E. "'Ubi Sunt' Passages in Old English — Sources and Relationships." *Vetenskaps-Societeten i Lund Årsbok* (1956): 25–44.

Curtius, Ernst. *European Literature and the Latin Middle Ages.* Trans. W. R. Trask. London, 1953.

Danninger, Elisabeth, ed. *Sieben politische Gedichte der Hs. B.L. Harley 2253.* Würzburg, 1980.

d'Ardenne, S. R. T. O., ed. *Þe Liflade ant te Passiun of Seint Iuliene.* EETS o.s. 248. London, 1961.

Davies, R. R. *Lordship and Society in the March of Wales 1282–1400.* Oxford, 1978.

Davies, R. T., ed. *Medieval English Lyrics: A Critical Anthology.* London, 1963.

Davis, Norman, ed. *Paston Letters and Papers of the Fifteenth Century.* 3 vols. Oxford, 1971–76.

Dean, James M., ed. *Medieval English Political Writings.* Kalamazoo, Mich., 1996.

Delaborde, Henri-François, ed. "Le Texte primitif des Enseignements de saint Louis à son fils." *Bibliothèque de l'Ecole des Chartres* 73 (1912): 73–100, 237–62.

Delany, Sheila. "Anatomy of the Resisting Reader: Some Implications of Resistance to Sexual Wordplay in Medieval Literature." *Exemplaria* 4 (1992): 7–34.

Denholm-Young, Neil, ed. and trans. *Vita Edwardi Secundi (The Life of Edward the Second)*. London, 1957.

Denton, Jeffrey Howard. *Robert Winchelsey and the Crown, 1294–1313: A Study in the Defence of Ecclesiastical Liberty*. Cambridge, 1980.

Dickins, Bruce, and R. M. Wilson, eds. *Early Middle English Texts*. 3rd ed. London, 1956.

Dobson, R. B., and J. Taylor, eds. *Rymes of Robyn Hood: An Introduction to the English Outlaw*. London, 1976.

Donaldson, E. Talbot. *Speaking of Chaucer*. Durham, N.C., 1983.

Dove, Mary. "Gawain and the *Blasme des Femmes* Tradition." *Medium Ævum* 41 (1972): 20–26.

———. "A Study of Some of the Lesser-Known Poems of British Museum MS Harley 2253." Ph.D. diss. University of Cambridge, 1970.

Doyle, A. I., intro. *The Vernon Manuscript: A Facsimile of Bodleian Library, Oxford, MS. Eng. Poet. a.1*. Cambridge, 1987.

———. "The Work of a Late Fifteenth-Century Scribe, William Ebesham." *Bulletin of the John Rylands Library* 39 (1956–57): 298–325.

Dronke, Peter. Review of Theo Stemmler, *Die englischen Liebesgedichte des MS. Harley 2253*. *Medium Ævum* 32 (1963): 146–50.

Duffy, Eamon. *The Stripping of the Altars: Traditional Religion in England c. 1400–c. 1580*. New Haven, 1992.

Duncan, Thomas G., ed. *Medieval English Lyrics 1200–1400*. Harmondsworth, 1995.

Dunn, Charles W., and Edward T. Byrnes, eds. *Middle English Literature*. 2nd ed. New York, 1990.

Eames, Elizabeth S. *English Medieval Tiles*. Cambridge, Mass., 1985.

Eliot, George. *Middlemarch: A Study of Provincial Life*. Ed. Margaret Harris and Judith Johnston. London, 1997.

Elliott, Thomas J. "Middle English Complaints against the Times: To Contemn the World or To Reform It?" *Annuale Mediaevale* 14 (1973): 22–34.

Ellis, George, ed. *Specimens of the Early English Poets*. 2nd ed. 3 vols. London, 1801.

Embree, Dan, and Elizabeth Urquhart, eds. *The Simonie: A Parallel-Text Edition*. Middle English Texts 24. Heidelberg, 1991.

England, George, and Alfred W. Pollard, eds. *The Towneley Plays*. EETS e.s. 71. 1897; repr. Millwood, N.Y., 1996.

Erickson, C. T., ed. *The Anglo-Norman Text of "Le Lai du cor."* ANTS 24. Oxford, 1973.

Eyton, Robert William. *Antiquities of Shropshire*. 12 vols. London, 1854–60.

Faulhaber, C. L. "The *Summa dictaminis* of Guido Faba." In *Medieval Eloquence: Studies in the Theory and Practice of Medieval Rhetoric*. Ed. James J. Murphy. Berkeley, 1978. Pp. 85–111.

Faverty, Frederic E. "Legends of Joseph in Old and Middle English." *PMLA* 43 (1928): 79–104.

Feifalik, Julius, ed. *Sitzungsberichte der Kaiserlichen Akademie der Wissenschaften*. Phil.-Hist. Classe 36, II. Vienna, 1861.

Fein, Susanna Greer, "The Harley Lyrics." In *A Manual of the Writings in Middle English 1050–1500*. Ed. Albert E. Hartung. Vol. 11. New Haven, forthcoming.

———, ed. *Moral Love Songs and Laments*. Kalamazoo, Mich., 1998.

Fellows, Jennifer, ed. *Of Love and Chivalry: An Anthology of Middle English Romance.* London, 1993.

Fiero, Gloria K., Wendy Pfeffer, and Mathé Allain, eds. and trans. *Three Medieval Views of Women.* New Haven, 1989.

Firth, J. J. Francis, ed. *Robert of Flamborough's Liber poenitentialis.* Toronto, 1971.

Fischer, Steven R., ed. *The Complete Medieval Dreambook: A Multilingual, Alphabetical "Somnia Danielis" Collation.* Bern, 1982.

————. *The Dream in the Middle High German Epic.* Bern, 1978.

Fitzmaurice, E. B., and A. G. Little. *Materials for the History of the Franciscan Province of Ireland, A.D. 1230–1450.* Manchester, 1920.

Fleming, John V. *Classical Imitation and Interpretation in Chaucer's "Troilus."* Lincoln, 1990.

————. *An Introduction to the Franciscan Literature of the Middle Ages.* Chicago, 1977.

Fletcher, W. G. D. "The Shropshire Lay Subsidy Roll of 1327, Munslow Hundred." *Transactions of the Shropshire Archaeological and Natural History Society*, 2nd. ser., 4 (1892): 287–338.

Ford, Alvin E., ed. *L'Évangile de Nicodème: Les versions courtes en ancien français et en prose.* Geneva, 1973.

Förster, Max, ed. "Beiträge zur mittelalterlichen Volkskunde V." *Archiv für das Studium der neueren Sprachen und Literaturen* 127 (1911): 31–84.

————, ed. "Beiträge zur mittelalterlichen Volkskunde IV." *Archiv für das Studium der neueren Sprachen und Literaturen* 125 (1910): 39–70.

Foucault, Michel. *The History of Sexuality.* Vol. 1: *An Introduction* [1976]. Trans. Robert Hurley. London, 1990.

————. *Discipline and Punish: The Birth of the Prison.* Trans. Alan Sheridan. London, 1977.

Bibliography of Works Cited

Francis, W. Nelson, ed. *The Book of Vices and Virtues, A Fourteenth Century Translation of the "Somme le roi" of Lorens d'Orléans*. EETS o.s. 217. 1942; repr. London, 1968.

Frankis, John. "The Social Context of Vernacular Writing in Thirteenth-Century England: The Evidence of the Manuscripts." In *Thirteenth-Century England 1 (Proceedings of the Newcastle-upon Tyne Conference, 1985)*. Ed. P. R. Coss and S. D. Lloyd. Woodbridge, Suffolk, 1986. Pp. 175–84.

Fryde, E. B. *Peasants and Landlords in Later Medieval England: c. 1380–c. 1585*. New York, 1996.

———. *William de la Pole, Merchant and King's Banker (1366)*. London, 1988.

———. *Studies in Medieval Trade and Finance*. London, 1983.

Furnivall, F. J., ed. *The Minor Poems of the Vernon MS*. Part 2. EETS o.s. 117. 1901; repr. Millwood, N.Y., 1987.

———, ed. *Robert of Brunne's Handlyng Synne*. EETS o.s. 119, 123. 1901, 1903; repr. Millwood, N.Y., 1978.

"G. E. C." *The Complete Peerage of England, Scotland, Ireland, Great Britain, and the United Kingdom*. 2nd ed. 13 vols. London, 1910–59.

Garbáty, Thomas J., ed. *Medieval English Literature*. 1984; repr. Prospect Heights, Ill., 1997.

———. "Studies in the Franciscan 'The Land of Cokaygne' in the Kildare MS." *Franziskanische Studien* 45 (1963): 139–53.

Geoffrey of Vinsauf. *Poetria nova*. Trans. Margaret F. Nims. Toronto, 1967.

Giblin, Rachel G. "Middle English Dreams and Dreams Books." M.A. diss. University of Liverpool, 1971.

Giesebrecht, W. "Die Vaganten oder Goliardi und ihre Lieder." *Allgemeine Monatschrift für Wissenschaft und Literatur*. Braunschweig, 1853.

Bibliography of Works Cited

Göller, Karl Heinz. "The Dream of the Dragon and the Bear." In *The Alliterative Morte Arthure: A Reassessment of the Poem*. Ed. Karl Heinz Göller. Cambridge, 1981. Pp. 130–39.

Gransden, Antonia. *Historical Writing in England II: c. 1307 to the Early Sixteenth Century*. Ithaca, 1982.

Grattan, J. H. G., and G. F. H. Sykes, eds. *The Owl and the Nightingale*. EETS e.s. 119. 1935; repr. Bungay, Suffolk, 1959.

Gray, Douglas. "Medieval English Mystic Lyrics." In *Mysticism and Spirituality in Medieval England*. Ed. William F. Pollard and Robert Boenig. Woodbridge, Suffolk, 1997. Pp. 203–18.

Green, Richard Firth. "John Ball's Letters: Literary History and Historical Literature." In *Chaucer's England: Literature in Historical Context*. Ed. Barbara A. Hanawalt. Minneapolis, 1992. Pp. 176–200.

————. "The Two 'Litel Wot Hit Any Mon' Lyrics in Harley 2253." *Mediaeval Studies* 51 (1989): 304–12.

————. *Poets and Princepleasers: Literature and the English Court in the Late Middle Ages*. Toronto, 1980.

Green, V. H. H. *The Later Plantagenets: A Survey of English History between 1307 and 1485*. London, 1955.

Guest, Edwin. *A History of English Rhythms* (1838). 2nd ed. Ed. W. W. Skeat. 1882; repr. New York, 1968.

Habig, Marion A., ed. *St. Francis of Assisi: Writings and Early Biographies*. Chicago, 1973.

Haines, Roy Martin. *Archbishop John Stratford: Political Revolutionary and Champion of the Liberties of the English Church ca. 1275/80–1348*. Toronto, 1986.

————, ed. *Calendar of the Register of Adam de Orleton, Bishop of Worcester 1327–1333*. London, 1979.

———. *The Church and Politics in Fourteenth-Century England: The Career of Adam Orleton c. 1275–1345*. Cambridge, 1978.

Halliwell, J. O., ed. and trans. *The Harrowing of Hell: A Miracle-Play Written in the Reign of Edward the Second*. London, 1840.

Hamel, Mary, ed. *Morte Arthure: A Critical Edition*. Garland Medieval Texts 9. New York, 1984.

Hanawalt, Barbara A. *The Ties That Bound: Peasant Families in Medieval England*. Oxford, 1986.

———. *Crime and Conflict in English Communities, 1300–1348*. Cambridge, Mass., 1979.

Harding, Alan. *England in the Thirteenth Century*. Cambridge, 1993.

Harriss, G. L. *King, Parliament, and Public Finance in Medieval England to 1369*. Oxford, 1975.

Hartman, Geoffrey H. "Numbers." In *Congregation: Contemporary Writers Read the Jewish Bible*. Ed. David Rosenberg. San Diego, 1987. Pp. 39–49.

Hässler, Herbert. *"The Owl and the Nightingale" und die literarischen Bestrebungen des 12. und 13. Jahrhunderts*. Frankfurt a. M., 1942.

Hathaway, E. J., P. T. Ricketts, C. A. Robson, and A. D. Wilshere, eds. *Fouke le Fitz Waryn*. ANTS 26–28. Oxford, 1975.

Hazlitt, W. Carew, ed., *Remains of the Early Popular Poetry of England*. 4 vols. London, 1864–66.

Hedges, John Kirby. *The History of Wallingford*. 2 vols. London, 1881.

Heffernan, Thomas J. *Sacred Biography: Saints and Their Biographers in the Middle Ages*. New York, 1988.

Heist, W. W. *The Fifteen Signs Before Doomsday*. East Lansing, Mich., 1952.

Bibliography of Works Cited

Heuser, W., ed. *Die Kildare Gedichte: Die altesten mittelenglischen Denkmaler in anglo-irischen Uberlieferung.* 1904; repr. Darmstadt, 1965.

Hilka, Alfons, and Otto Schumann, eds. *Carmina Burana: Die Lieder der Benediktbeurer Handschrift. Zweisprachige Ausgabe.* Trans. Carl Fischer and Hugo Kuhn. Zurich, 1974.

Hill, Betty. "A Note on 'The Way of Christ's Love,' 'The Way of Woman's Love' in B. M. MS. Harley 2253." *Notes and Queries*, n.s. 19 (1972): 46–47.

———. "The History of Jesus College, Oxford MS. 29." *Medium Ævum* 32 (1963): 203–13.

Histoire littéraire de la France. 38 vols. Paris, 1865–1936.

Hog, T., ed. *Annales sex regum Angliae.* London, 1945.

Holthausen, F. "Nachtrag zu Archiv CVIII, 288ff." *Archiv für das Studium der neueren Sprachen und Literaturen* 110 (1903): 102–03.

———, ed. "Die Quelle des mittelenglischen Gedichtes 'Lob der Frauen.'" *Archiv für das Studium der neueren Sprachen und Literaturen* 108 (1902): 288–301.

Horstmann, Carl, ed. *Altenglische Legenden: Neue Folge.* Heilbronn, 1881.

———, ed. "Nachträge zu den Legenden." *Archiv für das Studium der neueren Sprachen und Literaturen* 62 (1879): 397–431.

———, ed. *Sammlung altenglischer Legenden.* Heilbronn, 1878.

———, ed. "Die Evangelien-Geschichten der Homiliensammlung des Ms. Vernon." *Archiv für das Studium der neueren Sprachen und Literaturen* 57 (1876): 241–316.

Hotchkiss, Valerie. *Clothes Make the Man: Female Cross Dressing in Medieval Europe.* New York, 1996.

Howell, Andrew J. "Reading the Harley Lyrics: A Master Poet and the Language of Conventions." *ELH* 47 (1980): 619–45.

Bibliography of Works Cited

Hulme, William Henry, ed. *The Middle-English Harrowing of Hell and Gospel of Nicodemus*. EETS e.s. 100. London, 1907.

Hult, David, ed. *Le Chevalier au lion*. Paris, 1994.

Hunt, Tony, ed. *Popular Medicine in Thirteenth-Century England: Introduction and Texts*. Cambridge, 1990.

Immaculate, Sister Mary. "A Note on 'A Song of the Five Joys.'" *Modern Language Notes* 55 (1940): 249–54.

Jacobus de Voragine. *The Golden Legend: Readings on the Saints*. Trans. William Granger Ryan. 2 vols. Princeton, 1993.

Jacopone da Todi. *Laudi*. Ed. Franca Ageno. Florence, 1953.

James, M. R. "Two Lives of St. Ethelbert, King and Martyr." *English Historical Review* 32 (1917): 214–44.

———. "The Catalogue of the Library of the Augustinian Friars at York, Now First Edited from the MS. at Trinity College, Dublin." In *Fasciculus Ioanni Willis Clark dicatus*. Canterbury, 1909. Pp. 2–96.

———, and E. G. Miller. *The Bohun Manuscripts*. Oxford, 1936.

Jean de Meun. *The Romance of the Rose*. Trans. Charles Dahlberg. Princeton, 1983.

———. *Le Roman de la Rose*. Ed. Félix Lecoy. 3 vols. Paris, 1970–75.

Jeanroy, Alfred, ed. *Les Chansons de Guillaume IX, duc d'Aquitaine (1071–1127)*. 2nd ed. Paris, 1927.

Jeffrey, David L. *The Early English Lyric and Franciscan Spirituality*. Lincoln, 1975.

———, and Brian J. Levy, eds. and trans. *The Anglo-Norman Lyric: An Anthology*. Toronto, 1990.

John of Wales. *Communeloquium (Summa collationum)*. Paris, 1516.

Jones, David J. *La Tenson provençale: Étude d'un genre poétique, suivie d'une édition critique de quatre tensons et d'une liste complète des tensons provençales.* Paris, 1934.

Jonin, Pierre. "Le Songe d'Iseult dans la forêt du Morrois." *Le Moyen Âge* 64 (1958): 103–13.

Jubinal, Achille, ed. *Nouveau Receueil de contes, dits, fabliaux et autres pièces inédites des XIIIᵉ, XIVᵉ et XVᵉ siècles.* 2 vols. Paris, 1839, 1842.

Julian of Norwich. *Showings.* Ed. Edmund Colledge and James Walsh. New York, 1978.

Kail, J., ed. *Twenty-Six Political and Other Poems.* Part 1. EETS o.s. 124. 1904; repr. Millwood, N.Y., 1973.

Kaiser, Rolf, ed. *Medieval English.* 4th ed. Berlin, 1961.

Kane, George. "Some Fourteenth-Century 'Political' Poems." In *Medieval English Religious and Ethical Literature: Essays in Honour of G. H. Russell.* Ed. Gregory Kratzmann and James Simpson. Woodbridge, Suffolk, 1986. Pp. 82–91.

———. *Middle English Literature: A Critical Study of the Romances, the Religious Lyrics, "Piers Plowman."* London, 1951.

———, and E. T. Donaldson, eds. *Piers Plowman: The B Version.* London, 1975.

Keen, Maurice. *The Outlaws of Medieval Legend.* London, 1961.

Keller, Joseph R. "The Triumph of Vice: A Formal Approach to the Medieval Complaint against the Times." *Annuale Mediaevale* 10 (1969): 120–37. Repr. in *Die englische Satire.* Ed. Wolfgang Weiss. Darmstadt, 1982. Pp. 103–23.

Keller, Von Henning, ed. "Die me. Rezepte des Ms. Harley 2253." *Archiv für das Studium der neueren Sprachen und Literaturen* 207 (1970): 94–100.

Kendrick, Laura. "On Reading Medieval Political Verse: Two Partisan Poems from the Reign of Edward II." *Mediaevalia* 5 (1979): 183–204.

Kennedy, Thomas Corbin, ed. "Anglo-Norman Poems about Love, Women, and Sex from British Museum MS Harley 2253." Ph.D. diss. Columbia University, 1973.

459

Ker, N. R., intro. *Facsimile of British Museum MS. Harley 2253.* EETS o.s. 255. London, 1965.

——, intro. *The Owl and the Nightingale, Reproduced in Facsimile from the Surviving Manuscripts Jesus College Oxford 29 and British Museum Cotton Caligula A.ix.* EETS o.s. 251. London, 1963.

Kingsford, C. L., ed. *The Song of Lewes.* 1890; repr. Brussels, 1963.

Knowles, David. *The Monastic Order in England.* Cambridge, 1949.

Kolve, V. A. "God-Denying Fools and the Medieval 'Religion of Love.'" *Studies in the Age of Chaucer* 19 (1997): 3–59.

Kruger, Steven F. *Dreaming in the Middle Ages.* Cambridge, 1992.

Kuczynski, Michael P. "A Fragment of Richard Rolle's *Form of Living* in MS Bodley 554." *Bodleian Library Record* 15 (1994): 20–32.

Kundert-Forrer, Verena. *Raoul de Houdenc, ein französischer Erzähler des XIII. Jahrhunderts.* Bern, 1960.

Laing, Margaret. *Catalogue of Sources for a Linguistic Atlas of Early Medieval English.* Bury St. Edmunds, Suffolk, 1993.

Lampe, David. "Courtly Matters and Courtly Eyes: Two Thirteenth Century Middle English Debate Poems." In *The Thirteenth Century.* Ed. Kathleen Ashley. SUNY Binghamton Center for Medieval and Early Renaissance Studies. *Acta* 3 (1976): 79–93.

Långfors, Arthur. *Les Incipit des poèmes français antérieurs au XVIe siècle: Répertoire bibliographique.* Paris, 1971.

——. "La Prière de Thibaut d'Amiens." In *Studies in Romance Philology and French Literature Presented to John Orr by Pupils, Colleagues and Friends.* Manchester, 1953. Pp. 134–57.

——, ed. *Un Jeu de société du moyen âge: "Ragemon le bon," inspirateur d'un sermon en vers.* Helsinki, 1920.

———, ed. "*Le Dit de Dame Jouenne*: Version inédite du fabliau du *Pré Tondu*." *Romania* 45 (1918–19): 102–07.

Langosch, Karl, ed. and trans. *Weib, Wein und Würfelspiel: Vagantenlieder Lateinisch-/Deutsch*. Frankfurt, 1969.

La Rue, Abbé Gervais de. *Essais historiques sur les bardes, les jongleurs et les trouvères normands et anglo-normands*. 3 vols. Caen, 1834.

LeClerc, Victor. "Fabliaux." In *Histoire littéraire de la France*. 39 vols. Paris, 1895. 23.69–215.

Leclercq, Jean, *The Love of Learning and the Desire for God: A Study of Monastic Culture*. Trans. Catherine Misrahi. New York, 1974.

Legge, M. Dominica. "The Rise and Fall of Anglo-Norman Literature." *Mosaic* 8/4 (1975): 1–6.

———. *Anglo-Norman Literature and Its Background*. Oxford, 1963.

———. *Anglo-Norman in the Cloisters: The Influence of the Orders upon Anglo-Norman Literature*. Edinburgh, 1950.

Le Goff, Jacques. *The Birth of Purgatory*. Trans. Arthur Goldhammer. Chicago, 1984.

Le Roux de Lincy, A. J. V., ed. *Le Livre des proverbes français*. 2 vols. 2nd ed. Paris, 1859.

LeStrange, Hamon. *LeStrange Records: A Chronicle of the Early LeStranges of Norfolk and the March of Wales A.D. 1100–1310*. London, 1916.

Lewis, N. B. "The Organization of Indentured Retinues in Fourteenth-Century England." In *Essays in Medieval History*. Ed. R. W. Southern. London, 1968. Pp. 200–12.

———. "The Recruitment and Organization of a Contract Army, May to November 1337." *Bulletin of the Institute for Historical Research* 37 (1964): 1–19.

Linnow, W., ed. *Þe Desputisoun bitwen þe Bodi and þe Soule*. Erlangen, 1889.

Bibliography of Works Cited

Little, Andrew G. *The Grey Friars in Oxford*. Oxford, 1892.

Lloyd, T. H. *The English Wool Trade in the Middle Ages*. Cambridge, 1977.

Lockhart, J. J. C., trans. "The King and the Minstrel of Ely." In *The Keepsake*. Ed. Frederic Mansel Reynolds. London, 1829. Pp. 354–59.

Luard, Henry Richards, ed. *Flores historiarum*. 3 vols. Rolls Series 95. 1890; repr. Wiesbaden, 1965.

Lumby, J. Rawson, ed. *King Horn, Floris and Blauncheflur, The Assumption of Our Lady*. 2nd ed. Rev. George H. McKnight. EETS o.s. 14. 1901; repr. Bungay, Suffolk, 1962.

Lumiansky, R. M. "5. Legends of Alexander the Great." In *A Manual of the Writings in Middle English 1050–1500*. Ed. J. Burke Severs and A. E. Hartung. 10 vols. New Haven, 1967–99. 1.104–13, 268–73.

Luria, Maxwell S., and Richard L. Hoffman, eds. *Middle English Lyrics: Authoritative Texts, Critical and Historical Backgrounds, Perspectives in Six Poems*. New York, 1974.

Lynch, K. F. "The Doctrine of Alexander Hales on the Nature of Sacramental Grace." *Franciscan Studies* 19 (1959): 354–64.

Macray, W. D., ed. *Chronicon abbatiae de Evesham, ad annum 1418*. Rolls Series 29. London, 1863.

Maddicott, J. R. *Simon de Montfort*. Cambridge, 1994.

———. "Poems of Social Protest in Early Fourteenth-Century England." In *England in the Fourteenth Century: Proceedings of the 1985 Harlaxton Symposium*. Ed. W. M. Ormrod. Woodbridge, Suffolk, 1986. Pp. 130–44.

———. *Law and Lordship: Royal Justices as Retainers in Thirteenth- and Fourteenth-Century England*. Past and Present Society Supplement 4. Oxford, 1978.

———. *The English Peasantry and the Demands of the Crown, 1294–1341*. Past and Present Society Supplement 1. Oxford, 1975.

————. *Thomas of Lancaster 1307–1322: A Study in the Reign of Edward II*. Oxford, 1970.

Margherita, Gayle. *The Romance of Origins: Language and Sexual Difference in Middle English Literature*. Philadelphia, 1994.

Marie de France. *Die Fabeln der Marie de France*. Ed. Karl Warnke. Halle, 1898.

Martin, Lawrence T., ed. *Somniale Danielis: An Edition of a Medieval Latin Dream Interpretation Handbook*. Frankfurt, 1981.

————. "The Earliest Versions of the Latin *Somniale Danielis*." *Manuscripta* 23 (1979): 131–41.

Matsuda, Takami. *Death and Purgatory in Middle English Didactic Poetry*. Woodbridge, Suffolk, 1997.

Matzke, John E., ed. *Les Oeuvres de Simund de Freine*. Paris, 1909.

Maurer, Friedrich. "Der Topos von der *Minnesklaven*." *Deutsche Viertejahrsschrift für Literaturwissenschaft und Geistesgeschichte* 27 (1953): 182–206.

McIntire, Sandra. *The Doctrine of Compunction in Medieval England: Holy Tears*. Lewiston, N.Y., 1990.

McIntosh, Angus. "The Middle English Poem 'The Four Foes of Mankind': Some Notes on the Language and the Text." *Neuphilologische Mitteilungen* 79 (1978): 138.

————. "A New Approach to Middle English Dialectology." In *Middle English Dialectology*. Ed. Margaret Laing. Aberdeen, 1989. Pp. 22–31.

McIntosh, Angus, M. L. Samuels, Michael Benskin, with the assistance of Margaret Laing and Keith Williamson. *A Linguistic Atlas of Late Mediaeval English*. 4 vols. Aberdeen, 1986.

McKisack, May. *The Fourteenth Century 1307–1399*. Oxford, 1959.

McSparran, Frances, ed. *Middle English Compendium*. Ann Arbor, 1998– (June 1998 Release). URL http://www.hti.umich.edu/mec/.

Meier-Ewert, Charity, ed. "A Study and a Partial Edition of the Anglo-Norman Verse in the Bodleian Manuscript Digby 86." Ph.D. diss. Oxford University, 1971.

Menner, R. J. "The Man in the Moon and Hedging." *Journal of English and Germanic Philology* 48 (1949): 1–14.

Méon, M. *Nouveau Receuil de fabliaux et contes inédits*. 2 vols. Paris, 1823.

Meyer, Paul. "Notice du MS Bodley 57." *Romania* 35 (1906): 570–82.

―――. "Notice sur le manuscrit fr. 24862 de la Bibliothèque Nationale contenant divers ouvrages composés ou écrits en Angleterre." *Notices et extraits* 35/1 (1895): 131–68.

―――. Review of S. Berger, *La Bible française au Moyen Âge*, and Jean Bonnard, *Les Traductions de la Bible en vers français au Moyen Âge. Romania* 17 (1885): 140.

―――. "Notice et extraits du MS. 8336 de la Bibliothèque de Sir Thomas Phillips à Cheltenham." *Romania* 13 (1884): 497–541.

―――. "Notice du ms. Douce 210 de la Bibliothèque Bodleienne à Oxford." *Bulletin de la Société des anciens textes français* 6 (1880): 46–84.

Michel, Francisque, ed. *La Riote du monde*. Paris, 1834.

Michelant, Henri, and Gaston Raynaud, eds. *Itinéraires à Jérusalem et descriptions de la terre sainte*. Geneva, 1882.

Middle English Dictionary. Ann Arbor, 1930–.

Migne, J.-P., ed. *Patrologiae cursos completus . . . series latina*. Paris, 1844–64.

Mihm, Madelyn Timmel, ed. *The "Songe d'Enfer" of Raoul de Houdenc*. Tübingen, 1984.

Miller, B. D. H. "The Early History of Bodleian MS Digby 86." *Annuale Mediaevale* 4 (1963): 23–56.

Minnis, A. J. *The Medieval Theory of Authorship: Scholastic Literary Attitudes in the Later Middle Ages*. London, 1984.

Mirk, John. *Instructions for Parish Priests*. Ed. E. Peacock and F. J. Furnivall. EETS o.s. 31. 1868; repr. New York, 1969.

Mitchell, Sydney Knox. *Taxation in Medieval England*. Ed. Sidney Painter. New Haven, 1951.

Moffatt, Douglas, ed. and trans. *The Old English "Soul and Body."* Wolfeboro, N.H., 1990.

————, ed. *The Soul's Address to the Body: The Worcester Fragments*. East Lansing, Mich., 1987.

Montaiglon, Anatole de, ed. *Recueil de poesies françoises des XVe et XVIe siècles, morales, facétieuses, historiques*. 13 vols. Paris, 1855–78.

————, and Gaston Raynaud, eds. *Recueil général et complet des fabliaux des XIIIe et XIVe siècles*. 6 vols. 1872–90; repr. New York, 1964.

Montgomery, Edward D., Jr., ed. *Le Chastoiement d'un pere à son fils: A Critical Edition*. Chapel Hill, 1971.

Mooney, Linne R., ed. "Practical Didactic Works in Middle English: Edition and Analysis of the Class of Short Middle English Works Containing Useful Information." Ph.D. diss. University of Toronto, 1981.

Moor, Charles. *Knights of Edward I*. Harleian Society 80–84. London, 1929–32.

Moore, Arthur K. *The Secular Lyric in Middle English*. Lexington, 1951.

Morey, James H. "Peter Comestor, Biblical Paraphrase, and the Medieval Popular Bible." *Speculum* 68 (1993): 6–35.

Morris, Richard, ed. *Cursor Mundi*. 7 vols. EETS o.s. 57, 59, 62, 66, 68, 99, 101. 1874–93; repr. Oxford, 1961–66.

————, ed. *An Old English Miscellany*. EETS o.s. 49. 1872; repr. Millwood, N.Y., 1988.

Murphy, James J., ed. *Medieval Eloquence: Studies in the Theory and Practice of Medieval Rhetoric*. Berkeley, 1978.

————. *Rhetoric in the Middle Ages: A History of Rhetorical Theory from Saint Augustine to the Renaissance*. Berkeley, 1974.

Myers, A. R., ed. *The Household of Edward IV: The Black Book and the Ordinance of 1478*. Manchester, 1959.

Napier, Arthur S., ed. *Iacob and Iosep, a Middle English Poem of the Thirteenth Century*. Oxford, 1916.

Nau, F. "Histoire de Sainte Marine." *Revue de l'Orient Chrétien* 6 (1901): 276–82.

Nelson, Venetia, ed. *A Myrour to Lewde Men and Wymmen: A Prose Version of the "Speculum vitae."* Middle English Texts 14. Heidelberg, 1981.

New Catholic Encyclopedia. New York, 1967.

New Palaeographical Society. *Facsimiles of Ancient Manuscripts etc.* 1st series. London, 1912.

Newhauser, Richard. *The Treatise on Vices and Virtues in Latin and the Vernacular*. Turnhout, 1993.

Newton, Stella Mary. *Fashion in the Age of the Black Prince: A Study of the Years 1340–1365*. Woodbridge, Suffolk, 1980.

Nichols, Stephen G., and Siegfried Wenzel, eds. *The Whole Book: Cultural Perspectives on the Medieval Miscellany*. Ann Arbor, 1996.

Nicholson, Ranald. *Edward III and the Scots 1327–1335*. Oxford, 1965.

Nicolas, Harris. "A Memoir of the Author." In *The Letters of Joseph Ritson*. Ed. Joseph Frank. London, 1833. Pp. i–lxxxi.

Nolan, Barbara. "Promiscuous Fictions: Medieval Bawdy Tales and Their Textual Liaisons." In *The Body and the Soul in Medieval Literature*. Ed. P. Boitani and A. Torti. Woodbridge, Suffolk, 1999. Pp. 79–105.

————. "Turning Over the Leaves of Medieval Fabliau-Anthologies: The Case of Bibliothèque Nationale MS. Français 2173." *Medieval Perspectives* 8 (1998): 1–31.

Noomen, Willem, and Nico van den Boogaard, eds. *Nouveau Recueil complet des fabliaux.* 10 vols. Assen, 1983–98.

Nykrog, Per. *Les Fabliaux.* 2nd ed. Geneva, 1973.

Oakden, J. P. *Alliterative Poetry in Middle English.* 2 vols. 1930, 1935; repr. Hamden, Conn., 1968.

O'Brien, Timothy D. "Fire and Blood: 'Queynte' Imaginings in Diana's Temple." *Chaucer Review* 33 (1998): 157–67.

O'Connor, Brother Basilides Andrew, ed. *Henry D'Arci's "Vitas Patrum": A Thirteenth-Century Anglo-Norman Rimed Translation of the "Verba seniorum."* Washington, D.C., 1949.

Owst, G. R. *Literature and Pulpit in Medieval England.* 2nd ed. New York, 1961.

Paden, William D., ed. and trans. *The Medieval Pastourelle.* 2 vols. New York, 1987.

Palgrave, Sir Francis. *Cy ensuyt une chanson moult pitoyable des grievouses oppressions* . . . London, 1818.

Pantin, W. A. *The English Church in the Fourteenth Century.* Cambridge, 1955.

Paris, Gaston. "Le Cycle de la *Gageure.*" *Romania* 32 (1903): 481–551.

Parkes, Malcolm B. *Pause and Effect: An Introduction to the History of Punctuation in the West.* Aldershot, 1993.

———. "The Influence of the Concepts of *Ordinatio* and *Compilatio* on the Development of the Book." In *Medieval Learning and Literature: Essays Presented to R. W. Hunt.* Ed. J. J. G. Alexander and M. T. Gibson. Oxford, 1975. Pp. 115–41.

———. "The Literacy of the Laity." In *Literature and Western Civilization [vol. 2:] The Mediaeval World.* Ed. David Daiches and A. K. Thorlby. London, 1973. Pp. 555–77.

———. *English Cursive Book Hands 1250–1500.* 1969; repr. Berkeley, 1979.

Bibliography of Works Cited

Parry, J. H., ed. *Registrum Ludowici de Charltone, episcopi Herefordensis.* Canterbury and York Society 14. 1913.

Parsons, H. Rosamond, ed. "Anglo-Norman Books of Courtesy and Nurture." *PMLA* 44 (1929): 383–455.

Patterson, Lee. *Negotiating the Past: The Historical Understanding of Medieval Literature.* Madison, 1987.

Pearcy, Roy J. "A Fabliau Crux: *Les Coup le roi.*" *French Studies Bulletin* 54 (1995): 1–4.

Pearsall, Derek. "The Timelessness of *The Simonie.*" In *Individuality and Achievement in Middle English Poetry.* Ed. O. S. Pickering. Woodbridge, Suffolk, 1997. Pp. 59–72.

———. "The Origins of the Alliterative Revival." In *The Alliterative Tradition in the Fourteenth Century.* Ed. Bernard S. Levy and Paul E. Szarmach. Kent, Ohio, 1981. Pp. 1–24.

———. *Old English and Middle English Poetry.* London, 1977.

Peck, Russell A., ed. *Heroic Women from the Old Testament in Middle English Verse.* Kalamazoo, Mich., 1991.

———. "Public Dreams and Private Myths: Perspectives in Middle English Literature." *PMLA* 90 (1975): 461–68.

Percy, Thomas, ed. *Reliques of Ancient English Poetry.* 3 vols. London, 1765.

Perman, R. C. D., ed. "Henri d'Arci: The Shorter Works." In *Studies in Medieval French Presented to Alfred Ewert in Honour of His Seventieth Birthday.* Oxford, 1961. Pp. 279–321.

Peter, John. *Complaint and Satire in Early English Literature.* Oxford, 1956.

Pfander, H. G. "Some Medieval Manuscripts of Religious Instruction in England and Observations on Chaucer's Parson's Tale." *Journal of English and Germanic Philology* 35 (1936): 243–58.

Phillips, Helen, and Nick Havely, eds. *Chaucer's Dream Poetry.* London, 1997.

Bibliography of Works Cited

Phillips, J. R. S. "Edward II and the Prophets." In *England in the Fourteenth Century: Proceedings of the 1985 Harlaxton Symposium*. Ed. W. M. Ormrod. Woodbridge, Suffolk, 1986. Pp. 189–201.

Pickford, C. E. "A Fifteenth-Century Copyist and His Patron." In *A Medieval Miscellany, Presented to Eugene Vinaver*. Ed. F. Whitehead, A. H. Diverres, and F. E. Sutcliffe. Manchester, 1965. Pp. 245–62.

Pope, M. K. *From Latin to Modern French with Especial Consideration of Anglo-Norman*. Manchester, 1934.

Pugh, Ralph B., ed. *Calendar of London Trailbaston Trials under Commissions of 1305 and 1306*. London, 1975.

Quilligan, Maureen. *The Allegory of Female Authority: Christine de Pizan's 'Cité des dames.'* Ithaca, 1991.

Raby, F. J. E., ed. *The Oxford Book of Medieval Latin Verse*. Oxford, 1959.

———. *A History of Secular Latin Poetry in the Middle Ages*. 2nd ed. 2 vols. Oxford, 1957.

Ransom, Daniel J. *Poets at Play: Irony and Parody in the Harley Lyrics*. Norman, Okla., 1985.

———. "'Annot and John' and the Ploys of Parody." *Studies in Philology* 75 (1978): 121–41.

Rattunde, Eckhard. *"Li Proverbes au vilain": Untersuchungen zur romanischen Spruchdichtung des Mittelalters*. Heidelberg, 1966.

Reed, Thomas L., Jr. *Middle English Debate Poetry and the Aesthetics of Irresolution*. Columbia, Mo., 1990.

Rees, William, ed. *Calendar of Ancient Petitions Relating to Wales*. Lampeter, 1975.

Reichl, Karl. "Popular Poetry and Courtly Lyric: The Middle English Pastourelle." *REAL: The Yearbook of Research in English and American Literature* 5 (1987): 33–61.

————, ed. *Religiöse Dichtung im englischen Hochmittelalter: Untersuchung und Edition der Handschrift B. 14. 39 des Trinity College in Cambridge*. Munich, 1973.

Reinsch, Robert. "Mitteilungen aus einer französiscen Handscrift des Lambeth Palace zu London." *Archiv für das Studium der neueren Sprachen und Literaturen* 63 (1880): 51–96.

Reiss, Edmund. *The Art of the Middle English Lyric: Essays in Criticism*. Athens, Ga., 1972.

Revard, Carter. "'Annote and Johon,' Harley 2253, and *The Book of Secrets*," *English Language Notes* 36 (1999): 5–19.

————. "The Outlaw's Song of Trailbaston." In *Medieval Outlaws: Ten Tales in Modern English*. Ed. Thomas H. Ohlgren. Stroud, Gloucestershire, 1998. Pp. 99–105, 302–04, 329–31.

————. "*Gilote et Johane*: An Interlude in B. L. MS. Harley 2253." *Studies in Philology* 79 (1982): 122–46.

————. "The Scribe of MS. Harley 2253." *Notes and Queries*, n.s. 29 (1982): 62–63.

————. "Three More Holographs in the Hand of the Scribe of MS. Harley 2253 in Shrewsbury." *Notes and Queries*, n.s. 28 (1981): 199–200.

————. "Richard Hurd and MS. Harley 2253." *Notes and Queries*, n.s. 26 (1979): 199–202.

————. "The Lecher, the Legal Eagle, and the Papelard Priest: Middle English Confessional Satires in MS. Harley 2253 and Elsewhere." In *His Firm Estate: Essays for F. J. Eikenberry*. Ed. D. E. Hayden. Tulsa, Okla., 1967.

————. "The Medieval Growl: Some Aspects of Middle English Satire." Ph.D. diss. Yale University, 1958.

Richardson, H. G. "Letters of the Oxford *Dictatores*." In H. E. Salter, W. A. Pantin, and H. G. Richardson, eds. *Formularies Which Bear on the History of Oxford 1204–1420*. Oxford Historical Society, n.s. 5. Oxford, 1942. Pp. 329–450.

————. "Business Training in Medieval Oxford." *American Historical Review* 46 (1941): 259–80.

————. "An Oxford Teacher of the Fifteenth Century." *Bulletin of the John Rylands Library* 23 (1939): 436–57.

Rigg, A. G. *A History of Anglo-Latin Literature 1066–1422.* Cambridge, 1992.

————, ed. *Gawain on Marriage: The Textual Tradition of the "De Coniuge Non Ducenda" with Critical Edition and Translation.* Toronto, 1986.

————. *A Glastonbury Miscellany of the Fifteenth Century: A Descriptive Index of Trinity College, Cambridge, MS. O.9.38.* London, 1968.

Ritson, Joseph, ed. *Ancient Songs and Ballads, from the Reign of King Henry the Second to the Revolution.* 2 vols. London, 1829.

————, ed. *Ancient Songs, from the Reign of King Henry the Second to the Revolution.* London, 1790.

———— (published anonymously). *Observations on the Three First Volumes of the History of English Poetry, in a Familiar Letter to the Author.* London, 1782.

Robbins, Rossell Hope. "Dissent in Middle English Literature: The Spirit of (Thirteen) Seventy-Six." *Medievalia et Humanistica,* n.s. 9 (1979): 25–51.

————. "Poems Dealing with Contemporary Conditions." In *A Manual of the Writings in Middle English 1050–1500.* Ed. J. Burke Severs and Albert E. Hartung. 10 vols. New Haven, 1967–99. 5.1385–1536, 1633–1725.

————. "Middle English Poems of Protest." *Anglia* 78 (1960): 193–203.

————, ed. *Historical Poems of the XIVth and XVth Centuries.* New York, 1959.

————, ed. *Secular Lyrics of the XIVth and XVth Centuries.* Oxford, 1952. 2nd ed. Oxford, 1955

————, and John L. Cutler. *Supplement to the Index of Middle English Verse.* Lexington, 1965.

Bibliography of Works Cited

Ronsjö, Einar, ed. *"La Vie de saint Nicolas" par Wace: Poème religieux du XIIe siècle, publié d'après tous les manuscrits*. Lund, 1942.

Rosenthal, Constance L. *The 'Vitae Patrum' in Old and Middle English Literature*. Philadelphia, 1936.

Ross, Charles. *Edward IV*. Berkeley, 1974.

Rossi, Luciano. "A propos de l'histoire de quelques recueils de fabliaux: Le Code de Berne." *Le Moyen Français* 13 (1985): 58–94.

Rothwell, Harry, ed. *English Historical Documents [vol. 4:] 1189–1327*. London, 1975.

Rothwell, William. "From Latin to Modern French: Fifty Years On." *Bulletin of the John Rylands University Library of Manchester* 68 (1985): 192.

Rotuli Scotiae. 2 vols. London, 1814, 1819.

Rouse, E. Clive. *Medieval Wallpaintings*. 4th ed. Princes Risborough, 1990.

Rouse, R. H., and M. A. Rouse. "*Ordinatio* and *Compilatio* Revisited." In *Ad Litteram: Authoritative Texts and Their Medieval Readers*. Ed. Mark Jordan and Kent Emery, Jr. Notre Dame, 1992. Pp. 113–34.

Russell, Delbert W., ed. *Légendier apostolique anglo-normand: Édition critique, introduction et notes*. Montreal, 1989.

Rychner, Jean. "Deux Copistes au travail: Pour une étude textuelle globale du manuscrit 354 de la Bibliothèque de la Bourgeoisie de Berne." In *Medieval French Textual Studies in Memory of T. B. W. Reid*. Ed. Ian Short. London, 1984. Pp. 187–218.

———, ed. *Contribution à l'étude des fabliaux: Variantes, remaniements, dégradations*. 2 vols. Geneva, 1960.

Sakari, Aimo, ed. *Doctrinal sauvage*. Jyväskylä, 1967.

Salter, Elizabeth. *England and International: Studies in the Literature, Art and Patronage of Medieval England*. Ed. Derek Pearsall and Nicolette Zeeman. Cambridge, 1988.

Bibliography of Works Cited

Samuels, M. L. "The Dialect of the Scribe of the Harley Lyrics." In *Middle English Dialectology*. Ed. Margaret Laing. Aberdeen, 1989. Pp. 256–63.

―――. "The Dialects of MS Bodley 959." In *Middle English Dialectology*. Ed. Margaret Laing. Aberdeen, 1989. Pp. 136–49.

Sandison, Helen Estabrook. *The "Chanson d'aventure" in Middle English*. Bryn Mawr, 1913.

Scattergood, V. J(ohn). "*An Old Man's Prayer* and Bastard Feudalism." In *Expedition nach der Wahrheit: Poems, Essays, and Papers in Honour of Theo Stemmler*. Ed. Stefan Horlacher and Marion Islinger. Heidelberg, 1996. Pp. 119–30.

―――. *Reading the Past: Essays on Medieval and Renaissance Literature*. Dublin, 1996.

―――. "Skelton and the Elegy." *Proceedings of the Royal Irish Academy* 84, C 10 (1984): 333–47.

―――. *Politics and Poetry in the Fifteenth Century*. London, 1971.

Schleich, G. "Zu den Sprichwörter Hendings." *Anglia* 52 (1928): 350–61.

―――, ed. "Die Sprichwörter Hendings und die *Prouerbis of Wysdom*." *Anglia* 51 (1927): 220–77.

Scofield, C. L. *Life and Reign of Edward the Fourth, King of England and France and Lord of Ireland*. 2 vols. New York, 1923.

Serjeantson, Mary S. "The Dialects of the West Midlands in Middle English." *Review of English Studies* 3 (1927): 54–67, 319–31.

Serper, Arié, ed. *Huon de Saint-Quentin, poète satirique et lyrique: Étude historique et édition de textes*. Madrid, 1983.

Shirt, David J. "Chrétien de Troyes et une coutume anglaise." *Romania* 94 (1973): 178–95.

Short, Ian. "Bilingualism in Anglo-Norman England." *Romance Philology* 33 (1980): 467–79.

Bibliography of Works Cited

Silverstein, Theodore, ed. *English Lyrics before 1500*. Evanston, 1971.

Sinclair, Keith V. "The Translations of the *Vitas patrum, Thaïs, Antichrist*, and *Vision de saint Paul* Made for Anglo-Norman Templars: Some Neglected Literary Considerations." *Speculum* 72 (1997): 741–62.

————. *French Devotional Texts of the Middle Ages: A Bibliographic Manuscript Guide* and *First Supplement*. Westport, Conn., 1979, 1982. *Second Supplement*. New York, 1988.

Sisam, Celia, and Kenneth Sisam, eds. *The Oxford Book of Medieval English Verse*. Oxford, 1970.

Skeat, W. W. "Elegy on the Death of King Edward I from a New MS." *Modern Language Review* 7 (1912): 149–50.

Smeets, J. R. "Les Traductions-adaptations versifiées de la Bible en ancien français." In *Les Genres littéraires dans les sources théologiques et philosophiques médiévales*. Publications de l'institute d'Études Médiévales. Louvain-La-Neuve, 1982. Pp. 249–58.

Smith, Jeremy. "Tradition and Innovation in South-West-Midland Middle English." In *Regionalism in Late Medieval Manuscripts and Texts*. Ed. Felicity Riddy. Woodbridge, Suffolk, 1991. Pp. 53–65.

Smith, L. T., and P. Meyer, eds. *Les Contes moralisés de Nicole Bozon*. Paris, 1889.

Södergård, Östen, ed. *Une "Lettre d'Hippocrate" d'après un manuscrit inédit*. Stockholm, 1981.

————, ed. *La Vie d'Edouard le Confesseur: Poème anglo-normand du XIIe siècle*. Uppsala, 1948.

Southern, R. W. *Saint Anselm and His Biographer: A Study of Monastic Life and Thought, 1059–c. 1130*. Cambridge, 1963.

Southward, Elaine C. "Arthur's Dream." *Speculum* 18 (1943): 247–51.

Sparrow, Rev. W. C. "The Palmers' Gild of Ludlow." *Transactions of the Shropshire Archaeological and Natural History Society* 1 (1878): 333–94.

Bibliography of Works Cited

Spearing, A. C. *The Medieval Poet as Voyeur: Looking and Listening in Medieval Love-Narratives*. Cambridge, 1993.

———. *Medieval Dream Poetry*. Cambridge, 1976.

Speckenbach, Klaus. "Die Deutschen Traumbücher des Mittelalters" and "Die Deutsche *Somniale Danielis*—Rezeption." In *Traüme und Kraüter: Studien zur Petroneller "Circa instans"-Handschrift und zu den Deutschen Traumbücher des Mittelalters*. Ed. Nigel F. Palmer and Klaus Speckenbach. Cologne, 1990. Pp. 123–27, 128–49.

Speirs, John. *Medieval English Poetry: The Non-Chaucerian Tradition*. New York, 1957.

Spiele, Ina, ed. *Li Romanz de Dieu et de sa mere d'Herman de Valenciennes, chanoine et prêtre (XIIe siècle)*. Leiden, 1975.

Stanley, E. G, ed. *The Owl and the Nightingale*. London, 1960.

———. "Die anglo-normannischen Verse in dem mittelenglischen Gedicht *Die elf Höllenpeinen*." *Archiv für das Studium der neuren Sprachen und Literaturen* 192 (1956): 21–32.

The Statutes of the Realm. 11 vols. 1810–28; repr. London, 1963.

Stemmler, Theo, ed. *Die englischen Liebesgedichte des MS. Harley 2253*. Bonn, 1962.

———. "Zur Datierung des MS. Harley 2253." *Anglia* 80 (1962): 111–18.

Stengel, Edmund, ed. "Desputeison de l'ame et du corps, ein anglo-normannisches Gedicht." *Zeitschrift für romanische Philologie* 4 (1880): 74–80.

———, ed. *Codicem manu scriptum Digby 86 in Bibliotheca Bodleiana asservatum*. Halle, 1871.

Stevenson, J., ed. *Chronicle of Melrose*. Edinburgh, 1935.

Stevick, Robert D., ed. *One Hundred Middle English Lyrics*. 2nd ed. Urbana, 1994.

Stone, Brian, trans. *Medieval English Verse*. 2nd ed. Harmondsworth, 1971.

Bibliography of Works Cited

Strohm, Paul. *Hochon's Arrow: The Social Imagination of Fourteenth-Century Texts.* Princeton, 1992.

Strutt, J. *Horda Angel-Cynnan.* London, 1776.

Studer, P., ed. *Le Mystère d'Adam.* Manchester, 1918.

Sundby, Bertil. *Studies in the Middle English Dialect Material of Worcestershire Records.* Bergen, 1964.

Swanson, Jenny. *John of Wales: A Study of the Works and Ideas of a Thirteenth-Century Friar.* Cambridge, 1989.

Taavitsainen, I. *Middle English Lunaries: A Study of the Genre.* Helsinki, 1988.

Taylor, John. *The Universal History of Ranulf Higden.* Oxford, 1966.

Thompson, John J. *The "Cursor Mundi": Poem, Texts and Contexts.* Medium Ævum Monographs New Series 19. Oxford, 1998.

———. "The Governance of the English Tongue: The *Cursor Mundi* and Its French Tradition." In *Individuality and Achievement in Middle English Poetry.* Ed. O. S. Pickering. Woodbridge, Suffolk, 1997. Pp. 19–37.

———. "The *Cursor Mundi*, the 'Inglis tong,' and 'Romance.'" In *Readings in Medieval English Romance.* Ed. Carol M. Meale. Woodbridge, Suffolk, 1994. Pp. 99–120.

Thorndike, Lynn. *A History of Magic and Experimental Science.* 8 vols. New York, 1923–58.

Thrupp, Sylvia. *The Merchant Class of Medieval London.* Ann Arbor, 1948.

Tilander, G. ed. "Fragment d'un traité de fauconnerie anglo-normand en vers." *Studier i Modern Språkvetenskap* 15 (1943): 26–44.

Tobler, Adolf, ed. *"Li Proverbes au vilain": Die Sprichwörter des gemeinen Mannes.* Leipzig, 1895.

Bibliography of Works Cited

Tolkien, J. R. R., and E. V. Gordon, eds. *Sir Gawain and the Green Knight*. 2nd ed. Rev. Norman Davis. Oxford, 1967.

Trachsler, Richard. "Le Recueil Paris, BN ms fr. 12603." *Cultura Neolatina* 54 (1994): 189–211.

Transactions of the Shropshire Archaeological and Natural History Society, 2nd ser., 4 (1892): 301.

Tschann, Judith, and M. B. Parkes, intro. *Facsimile of Oxford, Bodleian Library, MS Digby 86*. EETS s.s. 16. Oxford, 1996.

Turville-Petre, Gabriel. "An Icelandic Version of the *Somniale Danielis*." In *Nordica et Anglica: Studies in Honor of Stefan Einarsson*. Ed. Allan H. Orrick. The Hague, 1968. Pp. 19–36.

———. "Dream Symbols in Old Icelandic Literature." In *Festschrift Walter Baetke*. Ed. Kurt Rudolph. Weimar, 1966. Pp. 343–54.

———. "Dreams in Icelandic Tradition." *Folklore* 69 (1958): 93–111.

Turville-Petre, Thorlac. "English Quaint and Strange in 'Ne mai no lewed lued.'" In *Individuality and Achievement in Middle English Poetry*. Ed. O. S. Pickering. Woodbridge, Suffolk, 1997. Pp. 73–83.

———. *England the Nation: Language, Literature, and National Identity, 1290–1340*. Oxford, 1996.

———, ed. *Alliterative Poetry of the Later Middle Ages: An Anthology*. Washington, D.C., 1989.

Ulrich, J., ed. "*La Riote du monde*." *Zeitschrift für romanische Philologie* 8 (1884): 275–89.

Utley, Francis Lee. "VII. Dialogues, Debates, and Catechisms." In *A Manual of the Writings in Middle English 1050–1500*. Ed. J. Burke Severs and Albert E. Hartung. 10 vols. New Haven, 1967–99. 3.669–745, 829–902.

———. *The Crooked Rib*. Columbus, Ohio, 1944.

van den Boogaard, Nico. "Le Fabliau anglo-normand." In *Proceedings [of the] Third International Beast Epic, Fable, and Fabliau Colloquium* (1979). Ed. Jan Goossens and Timothy Sodmann. Vienna, 1981. Pp. 66–77.

Varnhagen, Hermann. "Das altfranzösische Gedicht 'Un samedi par nuit.'" In *Þe Desputisoun bitwen þe Bodi and þe Soule*. Ed. W. Linnow. Erlangen, 1889. Pp. 113–96.

———, ed. "Zu mittelenglischen Gedichten. XI. Zu den Sprichwörtern Hendings." *Anglia* 4 (1881): 180–200.

Vising, Johan. *Anglo-Norman Language and Literature*. London, 1923.

Waddell, Helen. *The Wandering Scholars*. London, 1927.

Walberg, Ernst. *Quelques Aspects de la littérature anglo-normande: Leçons faites à l'École des Chartes*. Paris, 1936.

Walsingham, Thomas. *Historia Anglicana*. Ed. H. T. Riley. 2 vols. Rolls Series 28. London, 1863, 1864.

Walther, Hans. *Das Streitgedicht in der lateinischen Literatur des Mittelalters*. Quellen und Untersuchungen 5.2. Munich, 1920. 2nd ed. Rev. Paul Gerhard Schmidt. Hildesheim, 1984.

———. *Initia carminum ac versuum Medii Aevi posterioris Latinorum: Alphabetisches Verzeichnis der Versanfänge mittellateinischer Dichtungen*. 2nd ed. Göttingen, 1969.

Wanley, Humfrey. *The Diary of Humfrey Wanley 1715–1726*. Ed. C. E. Wright and Ruth C. Wright. 2 vols. London, 1966.

———, D. Casley, et al. *A Catalogue of the Harleian Manuscripts in the British Museum*. 1759; rev. and repr. 4 vols. London, 1808–12.

Ward, Sister Benedicta, trans. *The Prayers and Meditations of St. Anselm*. Harmondsworth, 1973.

Warton, Thomas. *The History of English Poetry from the Eleventh to the Seventeenth Century*. 4 vols. 1774–81. 2nd. ed. 1824; repr. New York, 1968.

Bibliography of Works Cited

Watson, Joanna I. R., ed. "An Edition of Certain Lyrics Contained in MS Digby 86." Ph.D. diss. Oxford University, 1970.

Wenzel, Siegfried. *Preachers, Poets, and the Early English Lyric*. Princeton, 1986.

Weston, Jessie L., trans. *The Chief Middle English Poets: Selected Poems*. 1914; repr. New York, 1968.

Whitaker, Thomas Dunham. *A History of the Original Parish of Whalley and the Honour of Clitheroe . . .* 3rd ed. London, 1801.

Whiting, B. J., and H. W. Whiting. *Proverbs, Sentences, and Proverbial Phrases from English Writings Mainly before 1500*. Cambridge, Mass., 1968.

Wilkinson, Bertie. "The Protest of the Earls of Arundel and Surrey in the Crisis of 1341." *English Historical Review* 46 (1931): 177–93.

Willard, James Field. *Parliamentary Taxes on Personal Property, 1290 to 1334: A Study in Medieval Financial Administration*. Cambridge, Mass., 1934.

Wilshere, A. D. "The Anglo-Norman Bible Stories in MS Harley 2253." *Forum for Modern Language Studies* 24 (1988): 78–89.

Wilson, R. M. *Early Middle English Literature*. 3rd ed. London, 1968.

Wind, B. H., ed. *Les Fragments du Roman de Tristan*. Leiden, 1950.

Wogan-Browne, Jocelyn. "The Virgin's Tale." In *Feminist Readings in Middle English Literature: The Wife of Bath and All Her Sect*. Ed. Ruth Evans and Lesley Johnson. London, 1994. Pp. 165–94.

Wood, A. C., ed., *Registrum Simonis de Langham, Cantuariensis Archiepiscopi*. Canterbury and York Society 53 (1956).

Woolf, Rosemary. "The Theme of Christ the Lover-Knight in Medieval English Literature." In *Art and Doctrine: Essays on Medieval Literature*. Ed. Heather O'Donoghue. London, 1986. Pp. 99–117.

————. "The Construction of *In a fryht as y con fare fremede.*" *Medium Ævum* 38 (1969): 55–59.

————. *The English Religious Lyric in the Middle Ages*. Oxford, 1968.

Wright, C. E. *Fontes Harleiani: A Study of the Sources of the Harleian Collection of Manuscripts*. London, 1972.

Wright, Thomas, ed. *Anecdota literaria: A Collection of Short Poems in English, Latin and French*. London, 1844.

————, ed. *Specimens of Lyric Poetry, Composed in England in the Reign of Edward the First*. Percy Society 4. 1842; repr. New York, 1965.

————, ed. *The Latin Poems Commonly Attributed to Walter Mapes*. Camden Society 16. 1841; repr. New York, 1968.

————, ed. *Political Songs of England, from the Reign of John to That of Edward II*. 1839; repr. with an Intro. by Peter Coss, Cambridge, 1996.

————, and James Orchard Halliwell, eds. *Reliquiae Antiquae*. 2 vols. London, 1841, 1843.

Wulff, August. *Die frauenfeindlichen Dichtungen in den romanischen Literaturen des Mittelalters bis zum Ende des XIII. Jahrhunderts*. Halle a. S., 1914.

Wyschogrod, Edith. *Saints and Postmodernism: Revisioning Moral Philosophy*. Chicago, 1990.

Zink, Michel. *La Pastourelle: Poésie et folklore au moyen âge*. Paris, 1972.

Index of Items in MS Harley 2253

481

Index of Manuscripts

General Index

A number followed by "n" indicates that the subject occurs in one or more notes on that page. All works found in the Harley MS are indicated by title and item number. For the contents of Harley in sequence, see the **Index of Items in MS Harley 2253** (p. 481). For citations of manuscripts other than Harley 2253, see the **Index of Manuscripts** (p. 485).

Aaron 128, 129, 284, 287

ABC a femmes (no. 8) 9, 12, 18n, 115, 155–56, 331–32, 334–36, 343n, 347, 372

Abelard, Peter 229

Abraham 134

Ace, Thomas 25, 84, 86

Ace family 23

Ackerman, Robert W. 227n, 253n, 254

Acts of Pilate see Gospel of Nicodemus

Adam 68, 70, 134, 143, 248, 294n, 337n, 338, 349

Adam Davy *see* Davy

Advice to Women (no. 44) 3n, 17, 117, 336, 346–47, 352–53, 373, 414, 419–20, 423

Against the King's Taxes (no. 114) 18, 23, 24n, 28–29, 62–64, 74, 80, 114, 163–69, 209, 268, 376

Ageno, Franca 267n

Ajax 229

Alberbury 77, 108

Alcuin 219

Alexander, J. J. G. 291n

Alexander see alliterative *Alexander*

Alexander of Hales 265, 266n

Alexandria 131

Alfonsi *see* Peter Alfonsi

Alice de Lacy, countess of Lincoln 69n

Allain, Mathé 335n, 346, 439n

alliteration 73, 206, 207, 377, 380, 388, 389

alliterative *Alexander* (Fragment A) 416n

alliterative *Morte Arthure* 248, 252

Als I Lay in a Winteris Nyt 227n, 254

Altercatio Phyllidis et Florae 229, 236–37

Altercatio Yemis et Estatis 223, 225n

Alysoun (no. 29) 3, 4n, 5, 14, 17, 73, 116, 329, 351–52, 354, 356–57, 368, 373, 415, 418, 422

Ami et Amile 71, 73

Amiens 298

Ancrene Wisse 23, 397n, 402

Andersson, Theodore M. 356n

Andrew, Laurens 225n

Anglo-Saxon literature 242, 253

Anima Cristi sanctifica me (no. 19) 114n, 140, 147, 150, 372

Annot and John (no. 28) 14, 16, 116, 351n, 356, 360, 365, 366, 367–68, 373, 380–81, 404n, 409, 415, 418, 422

Annunciation 145, 157

Another Green (no. 13) 18, 114n, 372, 391, 421

Anselm of Canterbury, St. 12, 126, 146, 152n, 270

Extract from questions to the dying (no. 113) 18n, 126, 146, 270, 376

489

Blamires, Alcuin 229n

Blankplum (no. 17) 18, 114n, 372, 391, 421

Le Blasmes des femmes (no. 77) 119, 296n, 310, 318, 320, 322, 330n, 335–36, 337–49, 374, 418, 439, 440n

Blessed Be Þou, Leuedy (no. 66) 7n, 16, 117–19, 157, 262, 374, 377–78, 379, 396n, 402, 414, 418–20, 425

Bloch, R. Howard 363n

Bloomfield, M. W. 336n

Blow, Northerne Wynd (no. 46) 3, 17, 18, 117, 191–92, 368n, 373, 414, 419–20, 423

Boase, T. S. R. 255n

bob-lines 331–32

Böddeker, Karl 6–7, 111, 126, 227n, 233n, 235n, 236, 332n, 333n, 355n, 360n, 368, 385n, 392n, 393n, 421–26

Bodleian Library *see* Index of Manuscripts

Bodley manuscripts *see* Index of Manuscripts

body/soul debates 227–29, 241, 246, 252–59, 429, 439, 441 *see also Debate between Body and Soul*

Boenig, Robert 152n

Boethius 345n

Bohun family 12, 268–70

Boitani, P. 294n

A Bok of Sweuenyng (no. 85) 9, 12, 70–71, 73, 119–20, 241–49, 259, 375, 402n, 413, 418, 425

Bonaventure, St. 269

Boniface VIII 171, 174

Bonnard, Jean 128n, 129n, 433n

La Bonté des femmes 295n

Book of Vices and Virtues 215

Boroughbridge 87–89

Bossuat, Robert 220n, 226n, 227n

Bossy, Michel-André 220n, 221n, 222n, 227n, 239n

Bowyer, Jonah 1

Bozon, Nicholas 12, 226–27, 230, 339n, 263, 270n

  La Bonté des femmes 344n

  De la femme et de la pie (no. 78) 119, 226, 230, 263, 296n, 310, 330n, 335, 339, 340, 345, 374, 418

Bramley, H. R. 131n

Brewer, D. S. 191n

Breydel, John 28, 172–73

Bridgnorth 29, 87

British Library *see* Index of Manuscripts

British Museum 2

Bromyard, John 213

Bronson, Bertrand B. 3n

Brook, G. L. 4–7, 10, 16–17, 112, 125, 126, 143, 150–51, 158, 159n, 189n, 191n, 192n, 205n, 207n, 233n, 235n, 236n, 261, 262n, 264, 265n, 266n, 267n, 297n, 331n, 351n, 352n, 354n, 356n, 357n, 358n, 368n, 371, 377n, 378n, 379n, 380n, 381n, 382n, 383n, 384n, 385n, 388n, 392, 393, 421–26, 440n

Brown, Carleton 5n, 6–7, 16, 111–12, 155, 156n, 158, 235n, 236n, 351n, 354n, 355n, 356n, 368n, 377n, 379n, 380n, 386n, 387n, 393n, 401n, 410n, 421–26, 428, 435, 438–40, 441n

Brown, T. J. 21n

Bruce, Robert 176

Bruges 171–74

Bryan, W. F. 437n

Buckinghamshire 83

Bugge, John 363n

Bühler, Carl F. 242n, 244n, 245n

Burford 22

Burghersh 77